Praise for *The 1998 Nunav...*

D0444613

"The 400-page travel guide, by 45 most[...] covers everything..." — ...ean's

"The Nunavut Handbook — an invaluable, locally produced guide..."
— The Sunday Times

"Written by (over) 40 talented writers who know this part of the world like the back of their hand..." **— The Toronto Sun**

"If you do consider visiting Nunavut, you would be wise to read The Nunavut Handbook *first."* **— The Toronto Star**

"...a must-have for anyone traveling into the region as well as for those interested in learning about Canada's newest territory." **— Editor's Reference Choice**

"...this massively detailed travel guide...has everything a visitor could ever want to know about this extraordinary land..." **— Essentially America**

"An amazingly complete and handy directory and guidebook for the venturesome, or for those who simply want to visit one of Earth's few remaining pristine wildernesses." **— The Globe and Mail**

"Written for the backpacker as well as the luxury-cruise set, (The Nunavut Handbook) will give you a leg up on dog-sled expeditions, polar travel, Inuit culture and the spectacular mountainous parks." **— The Vancouver Province**

Praise for *The 1998 Nunavut Handbook* web site

"Bigger, better and completely up-dated...a nicely packaged guide to...one of the last great untouched wilderness areas on our quickly shrinking planet."
— USA Today

"The website alone is a great resource, both for travel information and historical accounts of life in the Arctic." **— The Globe and Mail**

"Arctic travel has stepped into the 21st Century with a new website, home to The Nunavut Handbook." — **Canadian Geographic**

"The Nunavut Handbook — *Discover the people and wildlife of Canada's Eastern Arctic, one of the last untouched wilderness areas.*"
— **The Eisenhower National Clearinghouse for Mathematics and Science Education**

"*If the Northern Lights beckon you, start your travels…with the on-line version of the book,* The Nunavut Handbook." — **Computerworld**

"*…up-to-date, clear and realistic…an excellent handbook for anyone contemplating travel in that all-day, all-night world.*" — **Explore Magazine**

"*The new site features in-depth content (and) numerous enhancements which include phototours, virtual reality images, audio files…*"
— **Travel Courier (National Edition)**

Praise for *The Baffin Handbook*
(predecessor to *The 1998 Nunavut Handbook*)

"*…an excellent new travel guide to the eastern Arctic.*"
— **The New York Times**

"*Don't go north without* The Baffin Handbook…*packed with information essential to planning any trip in the region.*"
— **The Globe and Mail**

"*Written by local residents or experienced Arctic hands… the first ever tourist guide to Canada's Eastern Arctic.*"
— **Canadian Geographic**

"*Precisely the kind of information first-time travelers to Baffin and environs need…*" — **Yukon News**

"*The Baffin Handbook is an indispensable guide.*"
— **Winnipeg Free Press**

THE
Nunavut
HANDBOOK

Travelling in Canada's Arctic

MANAGING EDITOR
Marion Soublière

COVER PHOTOGRAPH
Nick Newbery
Mike Beedell (inset and back cover photo)

EDITORIAL ADVISORY BOARD
Peter Ernerk
Millie Kuliktana
Paul Landry
John MacDonald

Printed and bound in Canada.

Canadian Cataloguing in Publication Data

Main entry under title:
    The Nunavut handbook

ISBN 1-55036-587-8

    1. Nunavut (N.W.T.) — Guidebooks. I. Soublière, Marion
    II. Title: Nunavut handbook.

FC4195.N8A3 1998   917.19′2043   C98-900349-3
F1060.4.N55 1998

Published by Nortext Multimedia Inc., Box 8, Iqaluit NT X0A 0H0, Canada

For ordering information:
Nortext Multimedia Inc.
Box 8
Iqaluit NT X0A 0H0
Canada
Tel.: 1-800-263-1452 (in North America)
      1-613-727-5466 (outside North America)
Fax: 1-613-727-6910
E-mail: ingam@nortext.com
Web site: www.arctic-travel.com

Cover photo of young Inuk boy was shot in Pangnirtung.
Inset and back cover photo: Some of Nunavut's magnificent icebergs.
Photos without credits in this book appear courtesy of Nunavut Tourism.

FOREWORD

Arctic fever (ärk'tik fē'vər): a state of constant restlessness, distraction and longing suffered by certain individuals in non-circumpolar regions of the world. Symptoms include impatience with the confines of urban life, muggy temperatures, the pretensions of pop culture, and manicured lawns. Shortness of breath and palpitations may occur when conversation shifts to life north of the 60th parallel. The prognosis? Not good. Arctic fever is an affliction of the heart and soul for which there is no known cure.

Except to go there.

Fortunately, the Internet has become a balm, for web sites and e-mail seem to lessen the distance. "I often look at the Arctic map and wonder and wonder and wonder," wrote Toronto's Julian Moss on a visit to *The Nunavut Handbook*'s companion web site at **www.arctic-travel.com**. "You have opened my eyes as wide as the tundra." Added a wistful Ann Blodgett of Bowmanville, Ontario: "I would love to see an iceberg, plus seeing the daylight at midnight."

"I spent the months of August and September '97 camping and photographing the land and wildlife of Ellesmere Island," Peter Robinson of Vegreville, Alberta told us. "It is truly a land of miracles and I am definitely going to return!!!!"

Of course, it's not only the lure of the land but the genuine warmth and abiding realness of the people that draw travellers back. And although *Nunavummiut* are few in number, their spirit is as large as the land they have fought so hard to call their own.

On April 1, 1999, the world will pay tribute to the Inuit of Canada's central and eastern Arctic as history unfolds and Nunavut forever alters the map of Canada, officially and legally becoming this country's third territory.

That means there's even more for the Nunavut novice to explore. This updated edition of *The Nunavut Handbook* includes photos, maps, and new chapters on the territory's fledgling government, the economy, key organizations in Nunavut, interesting gateways to the territory, plus more about Inuit society — an aspect of the book that truly struck a chord with readers last year — and more things to do while here.

I owe many people in Nunavut, and elsewhere, a debt of gratitude for their help in making this edition a reality: the talented team of more than 50 largely Nunavut-based writers, my invaluable editorial advisory board members and editorial staff, and the tireless production, marketing and sales crew at Nortext.

Many others generously helped as we fact-checked information. Special thanks go to Eric Doig, Marion Glawson, Rick Hamburg and Dave Monteith of the GNWT's Department of Resources, Wildlife and Education; Dyan Gray and Cheri Kemp-Kinnear of Nunavut Tourism; Richard Cherepak and Marc Ledwidge of Parks Canada; Sonja Maviglia of First Air; and the Iqaluit and Rankin Inlet offices of Qamutik Travel, and Top of the World Travel.

Getting reader feedback and suggestions after our inaugural edition of *The Nunavut Handbook* came out in 1998 made all the hard work worthwhile. Again, I encourage readers to fax or e-mail me their comments, criticisms, or suggestions for ways to improve this travel guidebook.

In return, we promise to let you know if ever a cure is found for Arctic fever.

Marion Soublière, Managing Editor

Fax: 1-613-727-6910
E-mail: marions@nortext.com

Facts About Nunavut

Population (1996 Census of Canada):	24,730 (number of Inuit: 20,480)
Population of western NWT (1996 Census of Canada):	39,672
Birthrate in 1996 (Statistics Canada):	Nunavut 2.9%
	Canada 1.2%
Population under 25 years of age	Nunavut 56%
(1996 Census of Canada):	Canada 34%
Languages spoken:	Inuktitut (various dialects), English
Official languages of government of Nunavut:	Inuktitut, English, French
Size of territory:	1.994 million square kilometres
Size of Inuit-owned lands:	355,842 square kilometres
Size of Canada:	9.98 million square kilometres
Size of Sweden:	440,964 square kilometres
Distance of Grise Fiord,	
Nunavut's northernmost community, to Toronto:	3,647 kilometres
Territorial status:	Begins April 1, 1999
Capital:	Iqaluit
Population of Iqaluit (1996 Census of Canada):	4,220
Iqaluit's mean temperature in January:	–29.7° C
Iqaluit's mean temperature in July:	11.4° C

INTRODUCTION

Arctic Canada has been home to Inuit and earlier inhabitants for thousands of years. Throughout history, Inuit and their predecessors travelled in step with the seasons, inland across barren tundra and back to the coastline. They hunted the wildlife that would nourish their families: caribou, seal, fish, walrus, whales.

Our traditional lifestyle is here to stay, even if we spend as much time surfing the Internet as checking the fishing nets, or any other land-based analogy that comes to mind. We can thank the very modern Nunavut Land Claims Agreement for that. It protects and enshrines Inuit traditional values and culture. While a new public government readies itself for the territory of Nunavut in 1999 and Inuit rise to the educational challenges forced by the managerial needs of the new government — in all this busyness, we remember where we came from.

I saw a television documentary some years ago about the Alaska land claims settlement act and the Inuit desire to continue to harvest bowhead whales. In one part, the documentary showed senators or congressmen questioning some Alaskan Inuit about their land claim settlement. The line of questioning went something like this:

"Do you live in wooden houses?" they asked.

"Yes," replied the Inuit.

"Do you drive cars and trucks?"

"Yes."

"You're not real Eskimos anymore, are you?"

Here in Canada, we have had the same problem with some people who thought that just because we no longer live in igloos or travel only by dogteams, that we are no longer "real Inuit." We live in wooden houses, drive Jeep Cherokees, and fly in jumbo jets all over the world. But we are still Inuit. It is our spirit, our inner being, that makes us Inuit.

I predict that sometime within the next hundred years — perhaps 50 years from now — an Inuk will be elected prime minister of Canada. That prime minister will live at 24 Sussex, fly in jets, and hobnob with world leaders. But that prime minister will still be an Inuk.

I also predict that in the next thousand years, Inuit will become world leaders, starship captains, and travel to the far corners of our galaxy. But they will still be Inuit.

Sometimes it's hard to believe the future. It's such a contrast to the cultural upheaval of the past 35 years or so. Government policies that took nomadic hunters and their families away from the land and forced them into communities, that took the families' children away from their parents and punished them for speaking their mother tongue while attending residential schools — these colonial scars still hurt many Inuit. And their children, whose parents trade away childhood memories for drugs and booze. Time is a slow healer, but endless years spent surviving in an arctic environment have taught Inuit to be patient.

The years ahead are exciting for all northerners living in the central and eastern Arctic, but especially for Inuit. The trip into the future is a return to the best of the traditional past.

John Amagoalik

Map of Nunavut

Arctic Ocean

Beaufort Sea

Axe
Heib
Is

HIGH ARCTIC

North
Magnetic Pole
★
Bathurst
Island

Melville Island

Cornwalli
Island

Resolute ●

P a r r y

Yukon
Territory

Somer
Islan

Prince
of Wales
Island

● Holman

Victoria Island

Boothia
Peninsu

Cambridge
Bay ●

King
William
Island

● Ta

Kugluktuk Coronation
Gulf

Queen Maud
Gulf

● Gjoa

Umingmaktok ●

●Bathurst Inlet

Coppermine
River

Back River

Northwest
Territories

Thelon Ri
● Bake

Yellowknife ●

Rankin In

British
Columbia

Kazan
River

Arvi
●

Alberta

Saskatchewan

Manitoba

Chur
●

Scale

| 0 | 100 | 200 | 300 | 400 | 500 | 600 | 700 | 800 | 900 | 1000 |

Kilometres

FOR PARKS AND PROTECTED AREAS, PLEASE SEE DETAILED MAPS ON THE FOLLOWING PAGES.

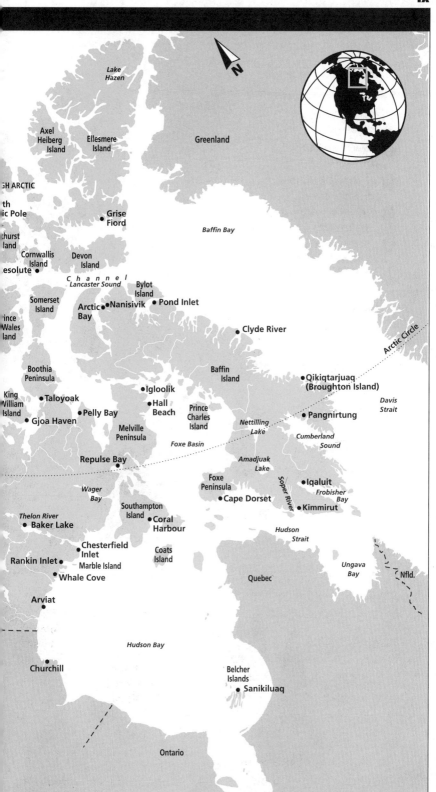

High Arctic and North Baffin Island

Parks and Protected Areas

1. Ellesmere Island National Park
2. Nirjutiqavvik National Wildlife Area
3. Polar Bear Pass National Wildlife Area
4. Prince Leopold Migratory Bird Sanctuary
5. Seymour Island Migratory Bird Sanctuary
6. Sirmilik National Park (including Bylot Island Migratory Bird Sanctuary)

Arctic Ocean

Axel Heiberg Island

Bathurst Island

Cornwallis Island

Resolute ● ●Beeche

P a r r y

Somerset Island

Prince of Wales Island

Victoria Island

Boothia Peninsula

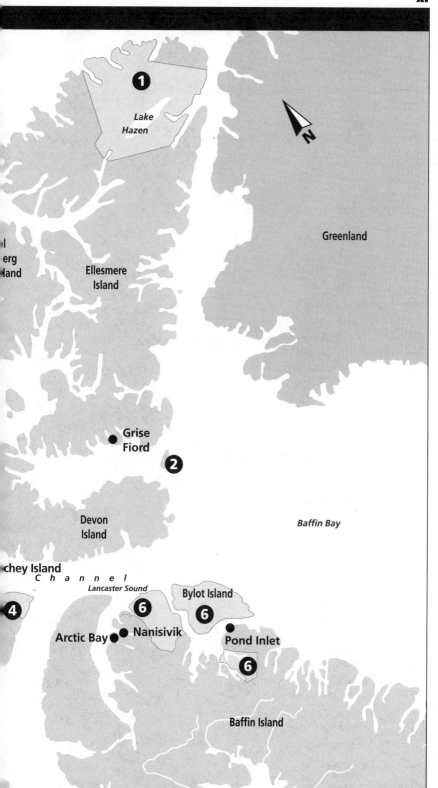

Arctic Coast, King William Island, Boothia Peninsula, Melville

Holman

Victoria Island

Cambridge Bay

Kugluktuk
1

Coronation Gulf

Queen Maud Gulf

Coppermine River

Umingmaktok

Arctic Circle

Bathurst Inlet

7

Back River

8

Parks and Protected Areas

1 Bloody Falls Territorial Historic Park

2 East Bay Migratory Bird Sanctuary

3 Harry Gibbons Migratory Bird Sanctuary

4 Ijiraliq (Meliadine) River Territorial Historic Park

5 McConnell River Migratory Bird Sanctuary

6 Northwest Passage Territorial Historic Park

7 Queen Maud Migratory Bird Sanctuary

8 Thelon Wildlife Sanctuary

* Canadian Heritage River

Kazan River *

Peninsula Area and West Coast/Hudson Bay

Somerset Island

Prince of Wales Island

Arctic Bay

● Nanisivik

● Pond Inlet

Baffin Island

Boothia Peninsula

● Igloolik

● Hall Beach

● Taloyoak

King William Island

● Pelly Bay

6 ● Gjoa Haven

Melville Peninsula

Foxe Basin

Repulse Bay ●

Wager Bay

Southampton Island

2

Thelon River *

● Baker Lake

Coral Harbour ●

3

Chesterfield Inlet ●

4

Rankin Inlet ●

Marble Island

Coats Island

● Whale Cove

Arviat ●

5

Hudson Bay

North, Central and South Baffin Island, Southampton Island and

Lancaster Sound

Bylot Island

Arctic Bay ● Nanisivik

Pond Inlet ●

Baffin Island

● Igloolik

● Hall Beach

Prince Charles Island

● Pelly Bay

Melville Peninsula

Foxe Basin

3

Repulse Bay ●

Arctic Circle

Foxe Peninsula

Cape Dorset

7 **2**

Wager Bay

Southampton Island

Coral Harbour ●

Chesterfield Inlet ●

Coats Island

● Rankin Inlet
Marble Island

● Whale Cove

Belcher Islands

Clyde River

Parks and Protected Areas

1. Auyuittuq National Park
2. Cape Dorset Migratory Bird Sanctuary
3. Dewey Soper Migratory Bird Sanctuary
4. Igaliqtuuq (Isabella Bay) Biosphere Reserve and National Wildlife Area (still to be finalized)
5. Katannilik Territorial Park Reserve
6. Kekerten Territorial Historic Park
7. Mallikjuaq Territorial Historic Park
8. Qaummaarviit Territorial Historic Park
9. Sylvia Grinnell Territorial Park

* Canadian Heritage River

Isabella Bay

Qikiqtarjuaq (Broughton Island)

Pangnirtung

Nettilling Lake

Cumberland Sound

Amadjuak Lake

Iqaluit

Frobisher Bay

Soper River

Kimmirut

Hudson Strait

Hudson Bay

Belcher Islands

Quebec

Sanikiluaq

Ungava Bay

Nfld.

Table of Contents

Land and Wildlife

Activities

Destinations

Gateways to Nunavut

West Coast/Hudson Bay

Southampton Island

Melville Peninsula Area

Planning Ahead

1. TRAVEL INFORMATION AND TOURS

by Carol Rigby, with contributions from Jennifer Bernius

Everyone's first trip to Nunavut is memorable, in one way or another. Take, as an example, the experience of two of the contributors to this guidebook.

In January 1986, they moved north to Frobisher Bay (now called Iqaluit), before the advent of daily jet service between Iqaluit and Ottawa. So they flew in a Hawker-Siddeley 748, eight hours of turboprops rumbling through the icy air with a refuelling stop in what is now called Kuujjuaq.

He was looking forward to research work with a local Inuit organization. She was wondering what her life would be like as an at-home mother with a three-year-old and a five-month-old.

True to form, the flight itself was eventful. Shortly after takeoff, the flight attendant announced that the ovens recently installed in the plane didn't work, so there would be no hot meals. Everyone snacked on unheated portions of their meals and cold pizza left over from somewhere. The five-month-old didn't mind, since he had Mum. Nor did the three-year-old, who was sick with some bug and running a fever by mid-flight. Mother did not take this to be an auspicious start to a new life in the North!

Yet, later in the flight, the feverish child lulled to sleep by the roar of the turboprops, a spectacular display of northern lights appeared, covering the entire sky. Those green and purple lights seemed to be a sign of greeting.

Today, more than a decade later, those children have grown up in Nunavut and consider it their home. They have welcomed many visitors to the homes in which they have lived. Other travellers will tell other tales, but almost everyone will have something to relate about a trip that proves unique, whether it is about adventures on the land, about the hospitality of the people they meet, or about the sheer beauty of the landscape. Welcome to Nunavut.

Watching Nunavut Grow

One thing is certain over the next few years in Canada's Arctic, and that is that change will be constant. For some time now, residents have been calling the central and eastern Arctic "Nunavut" (pronounced "noo-na-voot"). It's a word that means "our land" in the language of its aboriginal people, the Inuit, who make up the majority of Nunavut's residents at 85 per cent of the population. This name has now been applied to Canada's newest territory, which officially comes into existence April 1, 1999. The creation of Nunavut — comprising more than half the existing Northwest Territories — is a unique political achievement in Canada.

Dividing the old Northwest Territories, however, means there will be an initial establishment phase that may involve carrying over legislation of the government of the Northwest Territories (GNWT) or buying back GNWT services, in some areas of government. That is partly why readers will see references to GNWT regulations throughout this edition. It's not confirmed yet, either, whether "Northwest Territories" will remain the name of the western portion of the territory.

At the time of writing, the exact form of many relevant government regulations isn't yet in place for Nunavut. As *The Nunavut Handbook* is updated, watch for changes that reflect the rapid evolution of Canada's newest territory.

How to Hire an Outfitter or Tour Operator

To choose wisely among an ever-growing number of tour operators and outfitters for your trip to Nunavut, you'll need to understand the kinds of service they offer. Some definitions might help you here.

Tour operators, based in the North or South, generally offer packages that include any or all of the following: transportation to and within Nunavut, accommodation, meals, and excursions. They may refer you to an outfitter who will organize tours for you and supply you with the equipment and guidance you need for your stay in the region.

Outfitters are individuals or companies, based in the North or South, that provide varying levels of service. This service may include tours, guides, transportation, accommodation, clothing and equipment. Some locally based outfitters provide only basic services, such as transportation to or from a park. Others offer complete packages: dogsledding tours, for example, or fishing trips to local outpost camps with meals included.

Guides usually work for tour operators or outfitters, and guides must be licensed as well. They accompany you on your travels in the North, and may offer naturalist, cultural or historical interpretation.

Currently, all tour operators, outfitters and guides operating in Nunavut must be licensed under the Northwest Territories' *Travel and Tourism Act*, and carry liability insurance. It's not known yet whether this will change after April 1, 1999.

Before you pay a deposit to a tour operator or outfitter, however, check that they're indeed licensed. If they assure you they are, but have no proof, verify with one of the **government tourism licensing officers** listed in the directory at the end of this section. All outfitters and tour operators named in *The Nunavut Handbook* were licensed at the time of writing. However, individuals should verify they are still licensed before booking a trip.

Responsibility for licensing tour operators, outfitters and guides will go to the new Nunavut government's **Department of Sustainable Development** once the Northwest Territories divides on April 1, 1999. In fact, Sustainable Development takes over everything handled by the GNWT's **Department of Resources, Wildlife and Economic Development** (RWED). Where there are references to RWED in this guidebook, be sure to contact the Department of Sustainable Development instead come April 1999.

At present, should you hire a licensed outfitter who's later unable to deliver the tour you agreed upon, the government, under the NWT Tourism Deposit Assurance Program, will reimburse you for your deposit. (Licensed tourism businesses have the right to display the seal of this Tourism Deposit Assurance Program in their brochures and advertising.)

Although government tourism licensing officers can't promote one operator over another, they're satisfied that all are safety-minded and generally provide excellent service. You can obtain lists of licensed outfitters and tour operators by contacting these government officials. Each officer's jurisdiction covers one of the administrative regions within the central and eastern Arctic — the Baffin Region, the Kivalliq (formerly called the Keewatin) Region or the Kitikmeot Region.

The new government of Nunavut plans to carry on with these jurisdictions, and travellers will find that people throughout Nunavut widely refer to them in conversation, although at least one organization, **Nunavut Tourism**, pegs communities more closely to geographic features, where possible. In 1969, the fledgling GNWT took a cue from the federal government and decided to carry on with administrative regions in order to manage the North's huge land mass. The Keewatin and Baffin regions were set up first. Years later, so was the Kitikmeot. For the purposes of this travel guidebook, the references to Nunavut's three regions have been retained in the chapters to follow, although our maps at the front of this book and index of destinations group communities according to common geographic denominators. Here's how both systems mesh:

The Kivalliq Region includes the communities of Rankin Inlet, Arviat, Whale Cove, Chesterfield Inlet and Baker Lake (roughly along the west coast of Hudson Bay, except for inland Baker Lake). The Kivalliq also includes Coral Harbour (on Southampton Island) and Repulse Bay (in the Melville Peninsula area). According to the 1996 Census of Canada, the Kivalliq's population was 6,868. The time zone here is Central Time.

The Kitikmeot Region includes Pelly Bay, located on Simpson Peninsula just west of the Melville Peninsula. Taloyoak (on Boothia Peninsula), Gjoa Haven (on King William Island), and Umingmaktok, Bathurst Inlet, Kugluktuk and Cambridge Bay, all along the Arctic coast, account for the remainder of the Kitikmeot communities. The Kitikmeot's population stood at 4,644 in the 1996 Census. The time zone here is Mountain Time.

The Baffin Region includes Arctic Bay, Nanisivik, Pond Inlet and Clyde River on North Baffin Island; Pangnirtung and Broughton Island on Central Baffin Island; and Iqaluit, Kimmirut and Cape Dorset on South Baffin Island. The High Arctic is home to two settlements, Grise Fiord and Resolute. So is the Melville Peninsula area: Igloolik and Hall Beach. And far to the south, on the Belcher Islands in Hudson Bay, is Sanikiluaq. The Baffin's combined population tallied 13,218 in the 1996 Census. The time zone here is Eastern Time (except for Resolute, which uses Central Time).

A common thread running through communities in Nunavut these days is the growing interest in tourism and the growing numbers of guides, outfitters and tour operators. Most are members of Nunavut Tourism, an organization formed in 1995 to represent tourism operators in Nunavut. Nunavut Tourism will provide you with listings for all their member tour operators and outfitters, as well as up-to-date information packages for all areas of Nunavut.

Still, to find the outfitter or guide who will best meet your needs, do your research. If you plan to view bowhead whales, don't go with an outfitter to a location where there are no whales! Always make sure your tour guide or outfitter is familiar with local conditions. Your safety and comfort depend on it. Ask how long an operator has been in business. How many clients do they work with each year? Ask for references, and the telephone numbers of past clients. Talk to anyone who has travelled to Nunavut as well. Word of mouth may be your most reliable source.

Ask lots of questions. Be sure that what you're paying for is what you really want. Outfitters provide varying levels of service. One may only transport you to a park, for example. Another may transport you to the park and interpret for you while you're there. A third may offer you transportation, interpretation, necessary clothing and a lunch.

How about equipment? Will the operator supply you with tents and fishing rods? Northern clothing and emergency gear for poor weather?

Communicate your needs. Inuit outfitters won't necessarily tell you everything they offer if you don't ask questions, because they may assume you already know. So ask, for example: "When and where will I be going? What will I do while I'm there? Where will I stay? What exactly am I paying for?"

It's imperative to inquire about provisions for your safety. Adventure travel in the North is exciting, but can turn life-threatening if you don't have the right safety equipment, the right training to pull yourself out of a dire situation, or a properly trained guide or outfitter to watch out for you. If you're travelling on open water, a licensed guide or outfitter must provide you with a survival suit — a flotation device that covers you from head to toe. Find out, as well, the kind of communications equipment they carry and whether they have a first-aid kit and training.

And, of course, be sure that a prospective outfitter speaks your language! A telephone conversation with him or her should clarify that. Some outfitters speak little English and rely instead on a son or daughter to interpret for them.

Outfitters usually operate between March and September only, since Nunavut's peak travel season is summer. You can still contact them in the off months to do advance planning.

A final thought: If you're already visiting a northern community and feel like taking a tour of the tundra, say, or a fishing trip, check in with the hamlet office or Hunters and Trappers Organization (HTO). They'll gladly refer you to a local licensed guide or outfitter. Staff at the HTOs are highly skilled on the land and water, and they too may provide an outing for you. However, not all HTOs in Nunavut are licensed tourism operators. Make sure you check with the individual HTO. A renewable resource officer in each community can also assist you, as can a local visitors centre, if available.

Outfitter Charges

Many visitors are startled by the high cost of outfitter services. If you use the services of a reputable outfitter, you won't be gouged, but it's still wise to compare prices. In some communities, such as Pangnirtung, outfitters have formed associations that calculate typical costs for specific trips and then set standard fares. It's a good idea to compare prices with those in communities where no "set prices" exist.

Remember, however, that in many cases, rates that are high by southern standards are fair in the North, giving outfitters a reasonable economic return for their labor and investment. If you find a cut-rate bargain, be warned that you may get cut-rate service. If you run into bad weather or other hazardous conditions, your life can literally depend on the skill of your outfitter, so don't skimp on outfitter costs.

While the outfitters, guides and tour operators providing services in Nunavut change frequently, you will find among them many operators who have been in business for years and have a wealth of experience.

Package Tours

Generally, southern tour operators offer more complete packages, though they may be less flexible in their options. If you want maximum flexibility or have unusual requirements — a scientific field party, for example — you're best to book with a local outfitter. But if you prefer a more conventional package tour, you'll likely find what you're looking for with a southern tour operator. Although many tourists like to organize their own trips, package tours are often the wise choice when travelling in Nunavut, especially the first time. Many smaller communities are unaccustomed to travellers and may lack facilities to support visitors who are on their own. A reliable tour operator with a proven track record, however, would give you a range of options that would be hard for you to organize.

If you're visiting Nunavut with a package tour, most of your itinerary will have been planned in advance. Contact your tour operator if you have questions about what the tour includes. If you're planning your own trip, it's essential to collect as much material as you can. Contact Nunavut Tourism for up-to-date information on packages, outfitters and other options. Read Chapter 15 in this guidebook to find out about periodicals, books and Internet resources on Nunavut.

If you plan to hike, camp, or travel extensively on the land, remember that by southern standards, most of Nunavut is a wilderness. Northern solitude may bring considerable risk, so be prepared and healthy if you plan to move off the beaten track. Read "Adventure Travel," Chapter 11, if you're planning such a trip. Nunavut Tourism can put you in touch with knowledgeable local contacts who can advise you about travelling in their area. You can also speak to elders, who have years of wisdom, by approaching a community elders' society or an office of a regional Inuit birthright association for a referral.

Northern travel agencies can be very helpful in planning trips to and within Nunavut. As a rule, these agencies are more familiar with flight schedules, accommodations and other arrangements than are southern agents, particularly if you choose not to go with a package tour operator.

Visitor Information Centres

Several communities and parks have **visitor information centres** that help orient you to a local area. These are listed in the "Planning Ahead" directory, as well as in the community chapter directories. In smaller communities, visitor information centres are usually located in or with libraries, museums or other institutions. Check the community chapters for exact locations.

Where no visitor centre or library exists, the best place to find information is from a lodge, hotel, or government liaison officer.

Maps

If you're planning an adventure trip with canoeing or extensive hiking, you'll want to order maps well in advance of your trip. This way, you'll be assured of having the maps, and they'll help you in planning. You can't count on obtaining maps once you're in Nunavut because supplies are quickly exhausted in busy summer months. Contact Nunavut Tourism for suggestions on maps that are appropriate for your trip. Staff will give you addresses of map outlets elsewhere in Canada. A 1:50,000 scale map is usually the scale required to give you sufficient detail. If you're planning to stray from the more frequently used routes, be forewarned that many areas of Nunavut haven't yet been mapped to this level of detail. For lists of available maps, check out **Geomatics Canada**'s web site, or contact **Federal Maps** in Ottawa. For boaters, hydrographic charts are available from **Canadian Hydrographic Services**; they can also get information about river flow rates, drops, etc., from the **Water Survey of Canada**.

When planning a trip involving extensive adventure travel such as hiking, canoeing or kayaking, you might consider purchasing a global positioning system (GPS). This hand-held receiver — ranging in price from around $150 to $300 — uses satellite information to identify your current location and to allow you to follow the route you have planned. Learn to use it before you arrive in Nunavut. A GPS won't replace your maps, but it will tell you where you are on the map and the distance you have travelled. In an emergency, you can then indicate your exact location if you radio for help.

2. ENTERING CANADA
by Carol Rigby

All visitors from outside Canada, except those from the United States, Greenland, and St. Pierre and Miquelon, must present a valid passport to enter the country.

Visitors from approximately 130 countries require a Canadian visitor's visa as well as a passport.

In some cases, visitors may also require papers certifying that they've had a recent medical examination or inoculations. Be sure to inquire at the Canadian Embassy, High Commission, or Consulate serving your country to determine what papers are required to enter Canada.

Visitors to Canada normally may stay up to six months. All visitors must be able to satisfy an immigration officer that they are genuine visitors, they they have enough funds for their stay in Canada, that they intend to, and are able to, voluntarily leave Canada at the end of their stay, that they are not criminals, and that they do not pose a health or security risk to Canada. Foreign visitors are not allowed to work or attend an educational institution in Canada, and are not eligible for Canadian government social assistance programs.

Sport hunters should check in advance with the Royal Canadian Mounted Police (RCMP) to determine any restrictions on the importation of firearms. Recently revised gun control legislation affects how guns are handled at entry points. See the directory at the end of this section for contact information on the **Canadian Firearms Centre**, which answers questions about the new gun legislation.

Nunavut is an excellent place for travelling with children, as they are widely accepted at almost all functions. Be aware, however, that as a result of worldwide cases of abduction and missing children, travellers with children come under heightened scrutiny. To avoid unpleasant grilling by **Customs Border Services** officers, follow these tips recommended by Our Missing Children, a program jointly run by the RCMP, Revenue Canada Customs, Citizenship and Immigration Canada, and the Department of Foreign Affairs and International Trade.

- Always carry proper identification for yourself and your child or children.
- If you have legal custody of the child or children, have copies of relevant legal documents, such as custody rights.
- If you are not the legal guardian of the child or children, carry a letter of permission or authorization for you to have custody when entering Canada. A letter would also facilitate entry for any one parent travelling with their child or children. If possible, this permission should contain contact telephone numbers for the legal guardian or parent.
- If you're travelling as part of a caravan, be sure you're in the same vehicle as your child or children when you arrive at the border.
- Have your children memorize your home and office telephone numbers and teach them how to reach you in an emergency situation.

For more information, contact the national office of **Our Missing Children**. The program asks that if you're travelling with children, be patient if you encounter more questions than usual at Customs Border Services. The process is intended to prevent child abductions and runaways.

Non-residents of Canada are entitled to a Goods and Services Tax (GST) refund on goods and accommodation, as long as they stay less than one month at that accommodation. Visitors can also claim half of tax paid on tour packages. In Nunavut, the GST is seven per cent. When entering Canada, ask Customs Border Services officials for the necessary literature and forms, so you'll know which receipts to keep to claim a refund upon departure.

Restrictions exist on what you can bring into and take out of Canada, Nunavut and the Northwest Territories — such as alcohol. You should also consult with the Customs Border Services office at your point of entry and departure to determine restrictions that apply to goods you're bringing in or taking out of the country. Some items considered souvenirs within Canada, such as jewelry made from walrus ivory, might be affected by restrictions under the Convention on International Trade in Endangered Species. Contact Customs Border Services offices for information. It's best to know before you arrive what you can and can't remove from the country.

3. ALCOHOL, TOBACCO AND DRUG RESTRICTIONS

by Carol Rigby

In the Northwest Territories (NWT), regulations on importing and consuming alcohol differ greatly from those in Southern Canada.

It is expected that, at least initially, existing legislation will be enforced for Nunavut as well. Any references to NWT legislation should be assumed to be valid for Nunavut; if you have any questions, contact the **NWT Liquor Commission** office in Iqaluit or the local detachment of the RCMP for the places you are visiting. The rules are complex, vary from community to community, and any community can change its status by plebiscite.

Alcohol can't be sold or given away by individuals visiting Nunavut. It is also illegal to trade alcohol for carvings or anything else. All of these are considered bootlegging and constitute a serious offence in Nunavut.

A permit is required to bring into Nunavut more than the following amount of alcohol (per visit):

- 1,140 ml of spirits or wine
- 12 355-ml beers.

Permits can be obtained from the NWT Liquor Commission office in Iqaluit. A fee applies, determined by the amount of alcohol being imported. Visitors are not allowed to import home-made wine or beer.

In Nunavut, each community has one of three policies on alcohol, confirmed by community plebiscite. These are "prohibition," "restricted," and "unrestricted." Individuals can be charged under the *NWT Liquor Act* for breaching these policies. If found guilty, a fine or imprisonment will result.

Prohibition, or "dry," communities do not allow any alcohol to be imported or made within a certain radius. You may not bring alcohol into these settlements except if you are in transit and it then must stay on the plane. Any liquor in transit must be sealed during the time you are travelling through the prohibited area. Prohibition communities include:

- Kimmirut
- Pangnirtung
- Sanikiluaq
- Arviat
- Coral Harbour
- Whale Cove.
- Gjoa Haven
- Pelly Bay

Restricted communities regulate the use of alcohol. For the majority of them, permission is required from the community's Alcohol Education Committee to bring alcohol into town.

Orders are usually approved, except in cases where the applicant has demonstrated he or she cannot drink responsibly. If you intend to bring alcohol into a community so restricted, you must contact the Alcohol Education Committee or other licensing body in advance (see telephone numbers in community chapters in the "Destinations" section). The following communities fall into this category:

- Arctic Bay
- Broughton Island
- Cape Dorset
- Clyde River
- Hall Beach
- Igloolik
- Pond Inlet
- Repulse Bay
- Resolute.

In a few communities that are called "restricted," the restrictions are of a slightly different nature. These include:

- Rankin Inlet
- Iqaluit
- Cambridge Bay.

Rankin Inlet has licensed establishments in its hotels, but liquor consumption there is restricted to hotel guests. If you are not staying at the hotels, you cannot walk in and obtain a drink. In Cambridge Bay, the restriction applies to individuals. If you are found to have misused liquor, your eligibility to place orders for it may be withdrawn. Otherwise it is unrestricted. In Iqaluit, restaurants serve alcohol as they do in Southern Canada, and there are bars and lounges in hotels, and a number of private clubs. However, there is no local liquor or beer store. As is also the case for Rankin Inlet and Cambridge Bay, alcohol for personal consumption may be ordered from Yellowknife or brought in from Southern Canada under an import permit. There is a Liquor Warehouse in Iqaluit, but it is only to supply the requirements of licensed establishments, special occasion permit holders, and mail orders from other communities. The restrictions on importing liquor still apply.

Unrestricted communities are governed only by the provisions of the *NWT Liquor Act*; they have no additional rules on consuming alcohol. Unrestricted communities include:

- Baker Lake
- Bathurst Inlet
- Umingmaktok
- Chesterfield Inlet
- Kugluktuk
- Grise Fiord.
- Nanisivik
- Taloyoak

If you know you will be travelling to open or controlled communities and wish to take alcohol with you, you may place an order with the Iqaluit Liquor Warehouse. This will save you the cost and trouble of importing the alcohol into Nunavut. The liquor will be sent collect to the community via air freight (you must pay freight charges upon receipt). If you are travelling through a controlled community, the Alcohol Education Committee must approve your order ahead of time.

If you are visiting Iqaluit, you will not be able to purchase alcohol through the warehouse. By having it flown in from Yellowknife, you will save the cost and trouble of importing it into Nunavut. Please note that both the Iqaluit and Yellowknife Liquor Warehouses only accept cash, not credit or debit cards. There is a bank machine in the Yellowknife liquor store, however.

The rules are complicated, so it is always worthwhile to consult the NWT Liquor Commission/Iqaluit Liquor Warehouse for up-to-date information if you want to bring alcohol into Nunavut.

Tobacco

There are also restrictions on the amount of tobacco you can bring into Nunavut. Until March 31, 1999, contact the GNWT's **Department of Finance** to determine how much you can bring in, or to obtain a tobacco import permit. Legislation affecting Nunavut as of April 1, 1999, was not confirmed at press time, so contact the GNWT Department of Finance for more information at that point. Tobacco use is widespread in the North so cigarettes are usually available in most stores, but they bear the same inflated price as most other northern commodities. Because of the heavy impact of tobacco use on the health of the local population, there is an ongoing debate with regard to regulating smoking in public places, so smokers should inquire if smoking is permitted in any public building. There is a bylaw in Iqaluit against smoking while in a taxi, as well.

Illegal Drugs

As in most countries, the possession or sale of opiates, narcotics and hallucinogens is illegal in Canada. Possession of illegal drugs is a serious offence, carrying a maximum penalty of seven years of imprisonment. Possession includes having a small quantity intended for personal use. People from outside Canada who use non-medical steroids should also be aware that these are illegal in Canada.

Drug trafficking is the giving, selling, administering, transferring, transporting, sending, delivering or receiving, or offering to do any of those things, of any narcotic, opiate or hallucinogen.

Even though drug trafficking is an indictable offence — carrying a maximum penalty of life imprisonment in some cases — it is still a problem within Nunavut. The regional centres of Iqaluit, Rankin Inlet and Cambridge Bay, as major transportation hubs with direct connections to southern sources, are at the centre of much of this illegal activity. A common technique among traffickers is to ask someone travelling to one of the smaller communities to carry a package containing illegal drugs to a friend there. If the package is inspected by the RCMP and found to contain illegal substances, the carrier can be convicted of drug trafficking.

Never carry packages or parcels for someone you do not know well without verifying the contents, and avoid leaving your baggage unattended at any airport. You and your luggage may be searched by the RCMP if they have reasonable grounds to suspect you are carrying illegal substances (which in prohibited communities includes any form of alcohol). This does not mean that visitors are generally searched. The RCMP must have prior information about you that gives them grounds for suspicion. Respect community standards, and you should encounter no difficulties whatsoever.

4. HEALTH CARE AND MEDICAL INSURANCE

by Carol Rigby

Almost every Nunavut community has some form of health facility. Iqaluit has a hospital, while other communities have a health centre staffed by nurses equipped to treat minor emergencies and illnesses.

There are plans for a new hospital in Iqaluit and improved and expanded facilities in Rankin Inlet and Cambridge Bay, although it will be some time before these are completed.

Nurses are on duty at health centres during regular business hours weekdays and on call for emergencies 24 hours a day. Patients requiring more serious medical attention are flown either to a regional centre or to a larger community outside Nunavut.

To learn more about what to expect in the event of medical emergencies while hiking and camping, please be sure to read the section on search and rescue in Chapter 11, "Adventure Travel."

Regional Centres

The **Baffin Regional Hospital** in Iqaluit, open 24 hours a day, handles most local health-care needs and also serves patients brought in from smaller Baffin communities. For more specialized treatment, patients are flown to Ottawa. Iqaluit also has a **dental clinic** and an **optical outlet**. The dental clinic is equipped to handle most dental emergencies. The optical outlet can make minor repairs to glasses and dispense new ones, provided you have a prescription and the time to wait for them, which may take two weeks or more. If the dispensing optician is visiting another Baffin community, the outlet may be closed.

Rankin Inlet has a health centre and a birthing centre, but no complete hospital facility as yet. In serious medical emergencies, patients are normally flown to a hospital facility in Churchill, Manitoba or directly to a hospital in that province's capital, Winnipeg. Rankin Inlet also has a **dental clinic**, but no optical outlet.

Serious cases that can't be treated at the **Cambridge Bay Health Centre** are flown to the Stanton Regional Hospital in Yellowknife. Cambridge Bay also has a **dental office**.

Communities Outside the Regional Centres

If medical needs can't be met by the local health centre in the small Baffin communities, patients are flown to the hospital in Iqaluit. In the Kivalliq Region, patients are flown either to Churchill or Winnipeg. Kitikmeot patients are flown directly to Yellowknife. Doctors and dentists visit smaller communities periodically, but it's unlikely they would be present for emergencies. A few communities, such as Kugluktuk, Baker Lake and Gjoa Haven, have their own dental clinics.

Health Insurance

Visitors, students, and transient and temporary workers from elsewhere in Canada aren't eligible to enrol in the **NWT Health Care Plan** (which is expected to be carried over for Nunavut, at least initially). Their provincial or Yukon health plan will cover most medical costs incurred in Nunavut. But if they've been billed personally for health services, they should keep their documentation and seek reimbursement from their provincial or Yukon health care plan within six months. Visitors not covered by the NWT Health Care Plan must pay up front for services.

The NWT Health Care Plan doesn't cover non-residents for ground or air ambulance (medevac) services. Ambulance services used while in Nunavut will be billed at their full cost. Travel on scheduled flights for medical services will also be charged to non-residents, even if ordered by a physician. In an emergency, the NWT plan will cover the bill, but the costs will be charged back to the patient or the patient's insurance plan. Air ambulance services are extremely expensive, running to thousands of dollars. Some non-residents may have full or partial coverage under private, employer or government health insurance plans. Check your coverage before you leave home and purchase supplemental coverage where necessary.

Medication and Vaccinations

Visitors who require regular medication should carry enough with them to last the length of their stay, plus an allowance for unexpected delays. Community health nurses recommend a month's supply for a two-week visit. Medication should be carried on your person, not packed in luggage. There are two pharmacies in Nunavut, one in Iqaluit and one in Rankin Inlet. Pharmacies nearest to Kitikmeot communities are in Yellowknife. Health centres in the communities carry basic drugs, but they can't be counted on to have specialized medication.

Generally, visitors to the North don't require immunizations other than those needed to get into Canada from other countries. **Parks Canada** recommends, however, that visitors to Ellesmere Island National Park obtain precautionary vaccinations against rabies and tetanus before coming to the park, due to its extreme isolation. If you are planning any kind of isolated adventure trip, this is probably a wise precaution to take. It's also a good idea to make sure all your normal immunizations are up-to-date before coming north.

5. TIME AND COSTS
by Carol Rigby

When planning a northern itinerary, consider two things above all else: time and cost.

As most travel in Nunavut is by air, it's expensive and living costs are high. Allow yourself more time and money for almost every part of a trip here than you would when visiting less remote areas.

Flights can easily be delayed by bad weather, particularly in the small communities where air operations run under visual flight rules. Allow yourself ample time — preferably a whole day — to make connections between communities. A missed flight in some places can mean a wait of two or three days, depending on flight schedules. Three extra days of hotel and meal expenses could cost you another $500 or more. Budget for the unexpected.

Activities that take you outside the communities, such as hiking or canoeing, require a few extra days built in to cover the possibility of bad weather. Remember that life proceeds at a slower pace in the North. Don't expect everything to move quickly or on a precise schedule. If you bring a relaxed and flexible attitude, you'll have the time of your life.

Transportation and General Costs

Due to the great distance of Nunavut from major commercial centres, the cost of living here is high. Remoteness is part of the appeal of the North, but it does mean that nearly everything is more expensive than in Southern Canada. Food, fuel and consumer goods from Southern Canada are generally shipped in by sealift or barge. A sealift is cheaper but must be planned carefully to coincide with a short period in the summer when shipping lanes are ice-free. Waiting for an annual sealift means goods have to be purchased long before they're used in the North, adding to the expense. The further north you go, the more you can expect to pay for most items, especially food. The climate also plays a role in raising prices. Everything from building costs to utility charges are higher because of the cold.

One way to save money is by camping and cooking for yourself, rather than staying in hotels or lodges. Expect cool, wet weather, though, and be prepared to really "rough it." There are no campgrounds with showers and electrical hookups here!

6. ACCOMMODATION
by Carol Rigby

M ost Nunavut communities have at least one hotel or lodge, although neither Nanisivik nor Umingmaktok has one.

Accommodation can range from the relatively sophisticated hotels of larger communities, with their conference facilities and restaurants, to more modest lodges in smaller communities, often operated by community co-operatives. Bed and breakfast establishments, called "tourist homes" in Nunavut, are becoming more widely available. You'll find these in Iqaluit and in a few other communities. Camping is the most economical way to go, but educate yourself beforehand so that you are safe while out on the land.

If you plan to stay in hotels and lodges during your visit, be prepared to pay high prices — often between $150 to $200 per person per night — for modest accommodation. Many community hotels or lodges include meals with the price of a room. (Details on individual hotels and tourist homes are listed within the community profiles in the "Destinations" section.) In most communities, space is booked by the bed, not by the room. Hotels can become suddenly busy when bad weather grounds an airline flight and passengers need a place for the night. So if you're travelling alone and space is limited, you'll have to share a room. In some cases, that may mean sleeping in a bunk room with several other people. Guests of the opposite sex, however, aren't expected to double up.

Sharing your room with a stranger also brings up the issue of the security of your valuables — although in smaller communities, where one is more likely to end up having to bunk in with a stranger, people are more offended by the implication of dishonesty. Some hotels have locked storage space for valuables; others don't. If security is a concern, the best advice is to keep your wallet with you at all times, and try not to bring anything too valuable on your trip north.

Most accommodation is *not* luxurious — but it's clean and comfortable, and the local artwork on the walls might make southern luxury hotel owners envious! Generally, decor in northern hotels is slightly worn or shabby.

www.nunatour.nt.ca

The adventure starts here

Celebrate the new territory and let Nunavut Tourism help you make the most of an exotic Arctic adventure.

Before you head north, take a virtual trip to Nunavut. Visit the Nunavut Tourism web site and discover all that awaits you. Our site is filled with information: outfitters, lodgings, special sites, activities, tours, attractions, and much more. Contact us, before you leave, and make the most of your trip to Nunavut.

Nunavut TOURISM
ᓄᓇᕗᑦ ᑐᖅᖦᑐᓕᕆᔨᒃᑯᑦ

Calm Air
Canadian Partner

Scheduled and Charter Air Service

For reservations or information see your travel agent or call
1-800-839-2256
Charter or Cargo Information **1-888-225-6247**
Visit us on the internet: http://www.calmair.com

Hotel rooms often have TV sets but may not always have phones. Fax service may be available at the front desk. Conventional plumbing is usually available, but water use is restricted in some communities at certain times of the year, or because it's delivered by truck. This may mean that showers have to be brief or taken every other day. You might also encounter shared bathrooms. And be aware that it's difficult to find smoke-free accommodation.

Some hotels have curfews, although your room key will usually get you in the front door. Check at the hotel's front desk if there isn't anything posted on this.

Visitors are encouraged to book well in advance. In summer particularly, accommodation fills up with workers who are in town for the short summer construction period. Several Nunavut communities are experiencing construction booms due to the new infrastructure required for government offices and housing, which means space will be at a premium.

Tourist Homes and Home Stays

A few communities offer licensed tourist homes, the equivalent of bed and breakfasts. A bona fide tourist home must meet specific criteria established through legislation to ensure guests of a certain standard of service. Since proprietors must own their tourist home, most of these lodgings aren't operated by Inuit, if you are specifically interested in staying with an Inuit family.

A stay in a tourist home in a small community will give you the feeling of what it's like to live in the North. Bed and breakfasts in Iqaluit, on the other hand, are more like small inns. You'll be certain to get a bed, washroom facilities and breakfast if you stay in one of these establishments. You will want to check out restaurants or lodge dining rooms for your other meals, or ask the tourist home proprietors whether they will prepare meals for you or allow you to use facilities to prepare your own meals.

Tourist homes are marginally less expensive than hotels or lodges. When you factor in the costs of meals, though, there isn't a significant difference. The main advantage to a tourist home is its personal service and low level of noise and activity. A hotel full of construction workers isn't always quiet!

If you really wish to billet with a local family in a community instead of a licensed tourist home, then investigate a "home stay." Check with the local hamlet office for information on residents who accommodate this type of request. Hamlets decide who may carry on such a business. Home stays aren't licensed by the GNWT, however. If you do choose this option, you're on your own, so *caveat emptor*.

Be sure to clearly determine the following before agreeing to a home stay: What am I paying for? A bed? A bed and a room? How many people live in the house? (Housing conditions in the North are notoriously crowded.) Is there plumbing? (Many homes in the smallest communities still use "honey buckets.") Are any meals provided? Can facilities be used for cooking if no meals are provided? Have you provided this service to others before? Inuit families are extremely hospitable and helpful, but northern living conditions are different, and can often be a shock to people raised in urban settings.

7. MONEY

by Carol Rigby

There are very few bank branches in Nunavut, although the increasing presence of debit card facilities in stores allows visitors to withdraw funds from their own accounts, provided the stores have enough cash on hand.

The phenomenon of cash shortages in the smaller communities often takes visitors by surprise. If the community is isolated by weather, for example, cash flow can be severely hampered. You should therefore ensure that you have adequate cash on hand to cover any immediate needs.

You should also conduct significant banking transactions in Nunavut's largest communities — Iqaluit, Rankin Inlet or Cambridge Bay — before travelling to the smaller communities. If you're coming from outside Canada, it's best to exchange your currency before you arrive in Nunavut.

In Iqaluit, the **Royal Bank of Canada** and the **Bank of Montreal** have branches conveniently located across the street from each other. These are the only banks on Baffin Island. In Rankin Inlet, you'll find branches of the **Canadian Imperial Bank of Commerce** (CIBC) and the **Royal Bank**. Cambridge Bay has a branch of the **Royal Bank**.

Iqaluit also has three automated teller machines: one in the Bank of Montreal, one in the Royal Bank, plus a Royal Bank machine in the Brown building/highrise complex. The Royal Bank also has automated teller machines in Rankin Inlet and Cambridge Bay. Whale Cove has an automated teller machine in its Co-op store.

In other communities, the local Northern store or Co-operative usually cashes recognized traveller's cheques in Canadian funds. But because cash shortages often occur in the communities, it's a good idea to carry Canadian money. The currency used here is the Canadian dollar. Money consists of notes — $5, $10, $20, $50, $100 — and coins — 1¢, 5¢, 10¢, 25¢, $1, $2.

Credit and Debit Cards

Many retailers and hotels in Iqaluit, Cambridge Bay and Rankin Inlet accept credit cards, as do most hotels in smaller communities, but not all stores in small communities accept credit cards. Credit and debit card information for hotels and stores is listed in the directories of community chapters in this book. Generally, outfitters accept only cash or occasionally traveller's cheques, but always ask.

Interac, the Canadian debit card system, is in place at all Northern and Co-op stores in Nunavut now, and funds can be withdrawn from your own account if cash flow permits. Some places accept personal cheques if you have proper identification. Smaller communities don't usually accept them, so don't count on using them. Traveller's cheques are more useful.

Sunday shopping is permitted in the Northwest Territories, although the practice may differ from community to community. In Nunavut's smaller communities, stores will sometimes close during the lunch hour.

8. FOOD
by Carol Rigby

Many Nunavut restaurants offer delicious, well-prepared "country foods," the name for the kind of foods traditionally eaten by Inuit.

Arctic char, a fish with a taste that lies between salmon and trout, is one of the most popular. Scallops gathered from Cumberland Sound are sometimes available at restaurants and retail outlets in Iqaluit and other northern communities. Greenland shrimp is also a local favorite. Turbot from Pangnirtung may be available in season, in the Baffin. Caribou is a northern staple. It is very nutritious and low in fat, so it's a good choice for the diet-conscious, and widely available. Muskox, largely available in the Kitikmeot, is very much like well-marbled beef and well worth trying.

Many restaurants offer some kind of "northern" appetizers or combination entrées on their menus. These may include *maktaaq*, the outer layer of skin from whales (beluga and narwhal), served raw. An Inuit delicacy, this food is very warming due to its high caloric content. But for the novice, unless you like whale-flavored chewing gum, it's best not to chew it much. A common method of eating *maktaaq* is to cut it in small bits and swallow whole.

For the more adventurous palate, community feasts offer traditional fare such as raw and boiled caribou, seal and raw frozen char. Everyone is welcome at community feasts, but for those who have always lived an urban lifestyle, be prepared to experience culture shock: you will see whole seals laid out on the floor, being butchered and consumed raw as Inuit have done for centuries. Local shellfish such as mussels in Rankin Inlet and clams from Frobisher Bay near Iqaluit are also popular fare in some communities. But these are almost never available on a commercial basis — you will have to be lucky enough to have someone invite you to join them.

Because of the short growing season, the traditional Inuit diet was heavily based on the results of the hunt, by land or sea. There are a few edible greens and berries gathered from the land in the summer, such as the tart lemony mountain sorrel, arctic blueberries and cranberries, and crowberries (often called "blackberries" by the Inuit due to their glossy dark color, but not the same as blackberries in Southern Canada). None of these are available commercially. In many parts of Nunavut the vegetation is very fragile, so visitors are asked not to pick berries on their own. It's best to do so only if you are out with an Inuit outfitter or local family who knows the traditional berry-picking spots.

Hotel and Lodge Food in the Smaller Communities

Oddly, in the smaller communities you are likely to find less traditional food on hotel or lodge menus, and more standard North American fare, most of it not enhanced by the distance it has travelled before being prepared. Many lodges cater primarily to construction workers, so their food is usually hearty and plentiful, but uninspired. It is also expensive due to the high costs of importation. In many small communities there are no restaurant facilities outside the lodge. Check individual community listings for the food outlets available.

Campers and other visitors planning to prepare their own meals should come well supplied with food, particularly if specialized products like dehydrated camping food are required. Vegetarians should also bring their own meat-substitute products, as these are not widely available, and fruits and vegetables are expensive.

The availability of fresh food like dairy products or fruits and vegetables is a function of flight schedules and weather delays. Although supplies are reliable in the communities with daily airline service, it is not uncommon for fresh milk, eggs or bread to be completely unavailable in a small community. Be prepared to pay up to $2 for a single apple or orange in the more remote villages, and more than $5 for a litre of milk. If you are coming to visit friends or family in Nunavut, among the best gifts you can bring are supplies of fresh fruit, vegetables and dairy products. These should be carried in hand luggage to protect them from freezing.

Exporting Food

Many "country foods" can be easily transported, so you may want to share the taste of northern food with friends and family back home. Frozen food is almost always available at retail outlets, and can usually be obtained through local hunters and trappers organizations as well. In some communities there are local businesses that specialize in providing country food. For example, you can take home vacuum-packed frozen locally smoked char from Iqaluit Enterprises, whole char from Pangnirtung Fisheries, vacuum-packed muskox chops or jerky from Kitikmeot Foods in Cambridge Bay, or caribou jerky from Keewatin Meat and Fish in Rankin Inlet. Some plants supply retail outlets as opposed to selling directly.

If you receive a gift of fish or any portion of a marine mammal (like *maktaaq*) from a beneficiary of the Nunavut Land Claims Agreement, that person must also write you a note saying he or she is giving you such gifts. Otherwise, the activity is illegal. As for wild game, visitors must pick up an export permit from the local office of the Department of Sustainable Development (or until April 1999, GNWT's Department of Resources, Wildlife and Economic Development) in order to take home any part of a wild animal, such as meat, bone or fur, that has not been manufactured into something else. Processed meats, for example, don't apply. Export permits are free. For information about export amounts, restrictions and importing challenges, contact the appropriate government office before you head to Nunavut if you think you'll be bringing food back with you.

When carrying food in your luggage aboard an airline from the North, you may be asked to sign a waiver saying that if it spoils it is not insured by the airline. If you prefer, you can ship food home by cargo fridge/freezer. Check with your airline. However, unless you have extended travel plans with layovers in warm areas, food will usually stay quite well frozen if wrapped in several layers of newspaper, since the cargo hold is not heated while in the air.

9. COMMUNICATIONS

by Carol Rigby

Nunavut is linked to the rest of the world by satellite, telephone, television and radio.

Many individuals and businesses in the North use facsimile machines, computer modems and the Internet to communicate with other regions of Canada and abroad. Northerners have made a virtue of necessity by using sophisticated modern technology to link communities separated by long distances.

Telephones

Telephone service exists in every community, although in Bathurst Inlet and Umingmaktok it is restricted to satellite telephone service. Pay phones aren't widely available, except in some hotels, airport terminals and a few stores in larger communities. Visitors who aren't staying at a hotel or lodge with telephone service can usually get permission to use a phone in any building that serves the public. It's a good idea to have a calling card number to which you can charge long-distance calls. As telephone service is by satellite, you may hear the echo effect of "satellite bounce" during your phone calls, or a delay during conversations. All calls made to numbers outside the community of origin must include the area code in the number dialed, even if the number being called is within the same area code. Nunavut's area code is 867.

Television

The Canadian Broadcasting Corporation (CBC) North transmits television to Iqaluit and other communities. The Inuit Broadcasting Corporation (IBC) develops programming in Inuktitut (the language of the Inuit), including news and entertainment. Television Northern Canada (TVNC) is devoted to programming by and for northerners and native people. Cable satellite TV is widely available, offering a range of commercial programming from across North America.

Radio

The radio is the lifeline of small communities, broadcasting personal messages and community news. It also helps save lives. High frequency (HF) radio is the main communications tool for emergencies and other situations. The radiotelephone — invariably the Spillsbury SBX-11 — is used by all HTOs in monitoring land travellers and families living on the land. See Chapter 11, "Adventure Travel," for more information about HF radio procedures. However, portable satellite (MSAT) phones are increasingly being used, and even though they still carry a hefty price tag of $2,000 to $3,000, their prices are falling. Satellite phones are lighter to carry than HF radios and may be less susceptible to interference from weather, although it depends on the condition of the satellite, and whether local obstacles such as mountains interfere with satellite waves.

The CBC, the only local station that's easily receivable in every Nunavut community, broadcasts on the FM band in all communities except Iqaluit, where it is on the AM band. Some communities also have a non-commercial community station, such as CFRT in Iqaluit — the only francophone station in Nunavut. Shortwave radio enthusiasts can receive many stations from around the world. Batteries aren't always available in local stores, so bring an adequate supply. An alternative is to get a small solar-powered charger and two sets of rechargeable batteries. This system works well during the long periods of daylight in summer.

Mail

All correspondence must be picked up at the post office. Mail is flown into the communities, so service can be delayed by bad weather or missed planes, particularly in the smaller communities. If you expect to be in Nunavut long enough to receive mail, have it addressed to you care of "General Delivery" in a community convenient to you. Mail should be marked "Hold for Pickup" and carry a note with a forwarding address in case it isn't picked up by a specified date. Ask post offices about their hours of operation because they're highly variable, especially outside Iqaluit, Rankin Inlet and Cambridge Bay. Don't be surprised to find the post office closed while the postmaster is taking a coffee break!

Newspapers and Magazines

Not so long ago, northerners regarded it as a great treat to get their hands on a daily newspaper. Now, in communities serviced by daily flights, it's easy to obtain copies of several Canadian dailies, including *The Globe and Mail*, and a wide variety of magazines. Check at local retail outlets. In smaller communities, don't count on finding a daily paper, though you'll likely find copies of northern weekly papers such as *Nunatsiaq News*, *News/North* or *Kivalliq News*.

E-mail and the Internet

Nunavut is wired! Despite complications caused by slow line speeds and satellite bounce, local Internet servers in Cambridge Bay, Rankin Inlet and Iqaluit have Nunavut plugged in and loving it — there's a very high rate of Internet users among residents. There are major programs under way to improve the infrastructure of Nunavut's telecommunications network, with high-speed lines to all communities, so the state of any telephone-based communication is likely to evolve rapidly over the next year or two. The Internet is also a high priority on Nunavut schools' curricula. Many schools already have Internet access, and several have their own web sites.

You may be able to find public access to the Internet in some of the larger communities, thanks to the federally funded Community Access Program (CAP). However, these programs are run by volunteers for a limited number of hours each week. In Rankin Inlet, the community access site is at Leo Ussak School. Check with the public library for more information about the community access site, if school staff can't be reached. In Iqaluit, there is a CAP site at the Nunatta Campus building of Nunavut Arctic College, and there will be another at the public library after the autumn of 1998.

Check with libraries or information centres in other Nunavut communities as more community access sites spring up. If you're travelling with a computer (on business, for example), and have your own Internet server and account, you can access it through the phone lines in the major centres. Connections may be trickier in smaller communities that haven't yet upgraded their phone lines.

10. NATURALIST AND CULTURAL TOURS
by Jennifer Bernius

As time luxuriously stretches ahead of you in Nunavut, you may prefer to chart your own agenda and explore this wilderness on your own terms.

But you may also want to take advantage of the rich bounty of naturalist and cultural tours available in many Nunavut communities. If that's the case, do your homework and book the tour you want before arriving in Nunavut.

A naturalist or cultural tour led by a trained interpretive guide will deepen your understanding and appreciation of Nunavut. A well-informed guide could take you to interesting places that might either be inaccessible, or hazardous if you travelled there on your own: to muskoxen on the shores of the Kazan and Thelon rivers, for example; or to seals and narwhals at the floe edge along Baffin Island; or to an Inuit outpost camp. A guide also interprets landmarks that otherwise might escape you, such as archeological sites.

The kind of tours you'll discover throughout Nunavut are as varied as the new territory's communities. A visitors centre, for example, may organize an afternoon stroll through a community, with stops at local points of interest.

An HTO or outfitter may arrange a day's trek on the tundra in hopes of viewing migrating caribou. Or they could take you on the trip of a lifetime: a 10-day, guided, customized journey by dogteam or snowmobile to an Inuit outpost camp where you can photograph whales and polar bears at the floe edge and stay in an igloo and heated cabin.

Nunavut Tourism has published a vacation planner called *The Arctic Traveller*, and it contains a directory of outfitters plus a brief description of their offerings. You'll find excursions to suit a broad range of interests: tours that appeal to adventurers, to history buffs, rockhounds, photographers, lovers of wildlife, wildflowers, Inuit art, legends and other cultural lore.

Some tours begin and end in a community, allowing you the freedom to explore the North your way. Others are packaged tours originating in southern Canadian cities. They include transportation, accommodation, meals, excursions, interpretation, equipment and clothing.

Several factors will influence your choice of tour. For a start, what interests you? Do you want to see wildlife? Marine mammals, inland grazing animals, migratory birds? If you love history, what cultures and periods fascinate you? Ancient Thule? Modern Inuit? European whalers and explorers? Hudson Bay traders? What regions attract you: the mountains and fiords of Baffin's spectacular Auyuittuq National Park? The rugged marsh country of the Hudson Bay lowlands? The richly varied terrain of the Arctic Islands? The magnificent Bloody Falls of the Coppermine River in the Kitikmeot Region? You'll find tours geared to many interests and regions. Some expose you to several aspects of northern life at once, combining ecotourism with an interpretation of Inuit culture and lifestyle as well as an account of prehistoric or modern historical sites.

Time and money? Depending on how many people are in your group, a day of hiking with a guide around a settlement or out on the land could cost you about $70 to $150. For a tour by dogteam, snowmobile or all-terrain vehicle, or a cruise along a river or coastline by motorboat, increase that amount significantly. A typical three-day guided tour of the tundra, with two nights spent in a community hotel and another night in a tent, could amount to about $1,000. (That includes tent and all other equipment except sleeping bags.)

Add more days and you'll have to add a lot more dollars: that 10-day "total immersion" experience of an Inuit outpost camp at the mouth of a south Baffin fiord, which includes transportation by snowmobile or dogteam, meals (a combination of "country food" and southern fare, plus drinking water from 1,000-year-old icebergs), traditional Inuit clothing (caribou parkas), and accommodation (tents, cabins, igloo and a night in a hotel) will run up to $2,300. That doesn't include air transportation into Nunavut.

If you prefer greater comfort, however, your choice may be to take scenic and historical tours of the tundra from an ecotourism lodge. A week in one such establishment in Bathurst Inlet in the Kitikmeot Region, including room, meals, tours and airfare from Yellowknife, comes to about $3,400. This former Hudson's Bay Co. trading post and Oblate mission has been converted into a retreat for naturalists. Some of the lodge's guided tours include outings to the central barren lands to view muskoxen, caribou, nesting birds and wildflowers. There are also visits to ancient Inuit stone houses and caches, as well as an excursion to a camp site used during Sir John Franklin's expedition through the Northwest Passage.

Choosing when to go on a tour, of course, will have to take into consideration prevailing weather conditions. An outfitter in the Coral Harbour area of Hudson Bay, for instance, will take you by boat to the vast walrus colonies of Bencas and Walrus islands, and to the thousands of thick-billed murres that nest along the cliffs of Coats Island. But the business operates only from the end of July through August. By early September, storms begin. The weather can be unpredictable even sooner. (So travel schedules may be unpleasantly affected.)

On the other hand, another outfitter in an inland Baffin region is open for business from March through to the end of August, with an array of tours and vehicles to get you to the best spots at just the "right" times. From July to August, you could travel by boat from Iqaluit to see huge popula-tions of migratory birds — loons, geese, ducks, terns, owls — that nest along the shorelines of southern Baffin. Or, if you prefer to travel by snowmobile over land or ice, you could be escorted to the home turf of caribou, fox, seals and the occasional polar bear anytime between March and May. In summer, you could fly by Twin Otter over that same terrain to view the wildlife.

Most tour operators and outfitters are flexible and informal in their approach to business. While they may offer pre-packaged tours for individuals and groups, they'll also customize a tour for you. Are you backpacking with friends and want to go sightseeing? No problem. Nunavut Tourism, the local hamlet office, or local HTO will refer you to a licensed local outfitter who will arrange a tour of your choice. Are you a naturalist who also loves Inuit art and culture? Visit Cape Dorset, Inuit art capital of the world. An outfitter there will guide you through the world-famous studios of the West Baffin Eskimo Co-operative where you'll meet renowned printmakers, sculptors and needleworkers. Tours are timed to fit your schedule: they could be a one-hour town walkabout, or they may be intensive week-long archeological and naturalist excursions to Foxe Peninsula. (These would show you, for example, the sites of ancient Thule dwellings and the largest collection of *inuksuit* — rock cairns in the shape of humans — in the world. The Co-operative or the community development office in Cape Dorset can arrange a tour.)

Generally, naturalist and cultural tours are less physically demanding than adventure excursions. Many educational tour operators create a relaxed, unhurried atmosphere so that visitors appreciate the serenity and purity of a northern environment. Still, you'd be wise to ask an operator how much physical activity, such as hiking, will be required in a tour. Some educational adventures are planned specifically for older adults. In the summer, at Nunavut Arctic College in Iqaluit, **Elderhostel Canada** offers a week-long program of discussions and activities on Inuit language and culture, the political development of Nunavut, and the flora and fauna of the Baffin Region.

As for accommodation, a wide variety of options exists. If you're the hardy sort, you might feel at home sleeping overnight in an igloo or camping on the tundra in a prospector's tent supplied by your outfitter. As mentioned earlier, some operators combine several forms of accommodation in one tour: on a five-day outing on the land, as an example, you might camp for three days and stay in a community hotel for the other two. Some outfitters encourage you to stay with local Inuit families to truly experience northern life. At the other end of the spectrum, you may prefer the comfort of an ecotourism lodge.

Be sure to check with outfitters about clothing and equipment for your tour. Many operators provide tents and other camping gear, as well as wilderness clothing. Ask them for a list of what they provide, and what other items you should bring.

11. ADVENTURE TRAVEL

by Carol and Bruce Rigby

When travelling in Nunavut, take great care to protect yourself from natural hazards and to minimize disturbance to the very fragile arctic environment.

Don't underestimate the challenges of travelling on the land or sea. It's important to be self-sufficient. Natural hazards, from extreme weather to polar bears, can test your physical endurance, wilderness experience, and equipment to their limits. (Even for day trips, precautions should be taken. Please read the chapters on camping and hiking for more information.)

Because of greatly reduced hours of daylight in all areas and extreme cold almost everywhere, it's very uncommon for visitors to travel on the land in winter in most of Nunavut. Only those with specialized skills and equipment should attempt such travel.

A little more than 350,000 square kilometres of Nunavut's almost two million square kilometres became Inuit-owned lands under the Nunavut Land Claims Agreement. Although their boundaries are not physically marked, these lands are private property and certain access restrictions apply (see sidebar on page 26).

Clothing and Equipment

Careful thought should be given to the clothing brought for trips "out on the land," where one is at the mercy of the weather (see also Chapter 13, "Clothing and Personal Effects," for general advice for all visitors). Summer weather in the Arctic can be very pleasant, but can change rapidly and dangerously. Freezing temperatures and snow are possible even in midsummer. Hypothermia — the inability of the body to maintain its vital core temperature — is insidious, painless and lethal. Be prepared.

In the Kivalliq and Kitikmeot regions, temperatures can get quite hot for about three weeks starting in mid-July. As a rule, however, dress for spring or fall temperatures, with long sleeves and full trousers. If you're going out on the land, avoid wearing blue jeans; an unexpected dunk in a river will have you freezing in your jeans in no time. We speak from experience! Even if you're just taking a short hike out of town, dress warmly. T-shirts and shorts may be fine on warmer days, but be prepared for cold weather.

Layered clothing is essential. Dress in layers that can be easily added or removed as required. This will keep you comfortably warm whether you are active or resting. Avoid getting sweaty, since drying can be difficult and damp garments don't provide warmth when it may be needed most. It's easy to become chilled when physical exercise stops. Synthetic pile or wool garments are excellent as they stay warm even when damp. On active days, avoid cotton clothes (including sweatshirts and sweatpants), which can get damp and cold.

For any trip longer than a day hike, a sweater and long johns or other warm undergarments will guard against hypothermia should the weather turn foul. Polypropylene or pile undergarments are a good investment because they "wick" moisture away from the skin while keeping you warm. At least one complete change of clothes is necessary, should you get wet.

A good set of rain gear, including pants, is also necessary. You'll want a suit that keeps you dry in cold, driving rain. Windproof jackets and pants, preferably made from Gore-Tex or an equivalent "breathable" fabric, are also essential, not only to keep you warm, but to allow moisture out. Winds can be constant in many areas and very chilling if not counteracted.

Even for a summer trip, bring windproof mitts or gloves, a warm knitted hat or tuque, and a scarf, balaclava, or neck gaiter to protect your face. You'll also need a peaked cap or hat with a brim to keep the sun away from your eyes, neck and ears. Sturdy, well broken-in hiking boots will keep your feet comfortable most of the time, although running shoes are fine for wearing around camp. A walking pole, or two poles used in tandem, will help you over rough terrain. If you plan to cross any rivers during your trip, neoprene booties are highly recommended. If you do have to cross a river and don't have neoprene booties, remove your hiking boots and wear your sneakers, which will dry out faster if they're of lighter construction than your hiking boots. Any water you cross will be icy and can cause foot or leg cramps. Pile or wool socks are good for hiking as they'll stay warm even when slightly damp. Pile can be wrung out and will dry quickly.

Good quality sunglasses with ultraviolet filters are a must. Though expensive, prescription sunglasses for those who require corrective lenses are much more effective than the clip-on type. If you wear contact lenses, give careful thought whether or not to use them out on the land. Summer weather conditions often mean a lot of wind-blown grit in the air, and winter conditions are dry and very cold. Proper hygiene and maintenance of contacts can be difficult. If you do decide to wear them, be sure to bring all the necessary solutions, as you may not be able to resupply, and in winter travel, keep them inside your coat to keep from freezing. Carry a backup pair of eyeglasses.

If you'd like to take in some skiing while in Nunavut, please read Chapter 50, "Skiing," for important information about clothing and equipment. This information is largely relevant to other types of arctic spring trips on the land, too, such as a dogsledding expedition.

Dressing for Boat Trips

When you travel by boat with an outfitter, be sure to dress very warmly. The air may seem relatively mild in summer, but the water is icy cold. (Sea water is 4° C at best, and glacier runoff is even colder.) Pay special attention to your feet, as they will be in contact with the hull, which is usually close to freezing. Those who spend lots of time on the water favor either heavily insulated rubber boots, or regular rubber boots worn a size or two larger, with duffel cloth socks and layers of wool or pile socks inside. These will keep your feet warm and dry. Be sure to have a warm hat, gloves or mitts, and wear windproof clothing.

Licensed outfitters who run boat tours are required by the GNWT to supply full flotation suits for everyone aboard the boat. Wear them — these suits have saved lives. Life-jackets are inadequate for arctic waters; normally,

ACCESS RESTRICTIONS

A little more than 350,000 square kilometres of Nunavut's almost two million square kilometres became Inuit-owned lands under the Nunavut Land Claims Agreement. Although their boundaries are not physically marked, these lands are private property and certain access restrictions apply.

If you're travelling with a licensed guide or outfitter, it is that person's responsibility to make the necessary arrangements to cross Inuit-owned lands. If travelling on your own (or conducting research or any commercial endeavor), first check a map to see whether your route takes you over Inuit-owned land. Maps are available from Nunavut Tunngavik Incorporated, the organization set up to see Nunavut's land claims agreement carried out.

If your travels take you over Inuit-owned lands, contact the appropriate Inuit Land Administration Office for restrictions on the area. For recreational purposes, individuals are allowed access to a strip along a shoreline of any navigable body of water within Inuit-owned lands, extending either 30.5 metres (100 feet) into the water or 30.5 metres (100 feet) onto the land. However, there are also cases where Inuit have exclusive possession of land, such as Marble Island in the Kivalliq Region, which removes public right to use that land.

Visitors can obtain guidelines to access restrictions from one of the three land administration offices. To obtain clearance to travel on Inuit-owned lands, fax your itinerary, a map and the number of people in your party to the land administration office closest to the area where you'll be journeying. Allow two weeks for approval to be processed.

Inuit Land Administration Offices

Baffin Region:
Tel.: (867) 979-5391. Fax: (867) 979-3238
E-mail: taudla@nunanet.com

Kivalliq Region:
Tel.: (867) 645-2810. Fax: (867) 645-3855
E-mail: tsandy@arctic.ca

Kitikmeot Region:
Tel.: (867) 982-3310. Fax: (867) 982-3311
E-mail: jkaniak@polarnet.ca or wynetsm@polarnet.ca

Maps

Maps are available from the regional land administration offices, as well as NTI. There is a nominal fee for maps.

Nunavut Tunngavik Incorporated (NTI)
P.O. Box 1041, Cambridge Bay NT,
X0E 0C0 Canada
Tel.: (867) 983-2517. Fax: (867) 983-2723.
E-mail: ntilands@polarnet.ca

the life expectancy of someone wearing a life-jacket in arctic waters is about 20 minutes. Don't take any unnecessary risks while in a boat. That's where accidents tend to happen.

Water

Flowing water outside the communities is generally safe to drink. There have been no recorded cases of giardia infestation, for example. As when camping anywhere, always draw water from running sources rather than from stagnant ponds or pools, but a special consideration in the North is to avoid consuming too much water from silt-laden glacial streams, which can cause digestive upset. Let water from a glacial stream settle before using it. Otherwise, water treatment is required only for peace of mind, or for people with very sensitive digestion. Be sure to carry plenty of water with you to avoid dehydration — especially problematic in cold conditions. Adopting the Inuit tradition of frequent tea breaks, or drinking some other warm beverage, is recommended.

Search and Rescue

Don't take any unnecessary risks when travelling on the land or water in Nunavut. Be sure to plan your routes carefully. Carry adequate maps and, if possible, a GPS receiver. A search and rescue evacuation may be difficult or impossible under certain weather conditions and could be very costly. While magnetic compass readings are far less precise here (and useless near the North Magnetic Pole), you can calculate the magnetic declination to get back on course with maps or computer software. The **Geological Survey of Canada** offers help on its web site. Despite its failings, a magnetic compass eventually indicates directions; a GPS receiver won't.

Ground search and rescue operations in the Baffin Region are co-ordinated out of Iqaluit by the RCMP Emergency Measures Organization, in conjunction with local community authorities, the Department of Sustainable Development (or until April 1, 1999, GNWT's Department of Resources, Wildlife and Economic Development), Parks Canada, and others. When regional emergency measures offices send an alert for missing boats, marine searches are made by the Canadian Coast Guard. Searches for downed aircraft are co-ordinated by the federal Department of National Defence through a rescue centre in Halifax, Nova Scotia or Edmonton, Alberta.

In the Kivalliq Region, the RCMP is responsible for co-ordinating ground search and rescue. The RCMP works with communities and the Emergency Measures Organization to conduct searches. Neither the Canadian Coast Guard nor the Department of National Defence has offices in the Kivalliq. When an alert is sent for a missing vessel, the RCMP joins forces with Iqaluit's Canadian Coast Guard office. The RCMP may also conduct initial search efforts for downed civilian aircraft; Canadian Forces takes command when military co-ordination is established.

In all Kitikmeot communities, local groups of highly trained Rangers — civilian members of the Department of National Defence — work in search and rescue efforts, and RCMP detachments become involved when their services are called upon. The Kitikmeot deals with the Emergency Measures Organization in Yellowknife. The Canadian Coast Guard heads marine searches for missing boats on the Arctic Ocean while National Defence is involved in the hunt for downed aircraft.

Those who plan climbing, skiing, glacier travel, or advanced mountaineering trips in national and territorial parks should know that the rescue capability of the parks is restricted to basic evacuation only. The parks' warden service is geared towards resource conservation, not rescue operations, and recent budget cuts have limited the number and availability of park staff. High-angle technical mountain rescue services are not provided by any agency in Nunavut. Visitors planning on doing mountaineering, glacier travel, climbing or other hazardous activities must realize that the responsibility for their safety lies solely with themselves. Search and rescue must be discussed with park staff before you set off on any expedition. During registration on entering a park, staff will provide specific information about their rescue capabilities and your responsibilities.

Registration, Orientation and Emergency Supplies

For public safety reasons, registration and orientation are mandatory before entering a national park, or Katannilik Territorial Park Reserve. (Registration is not mandatory for territorial historic parks, but visitors are strongly encouraged to register with the RCMP. See below.) Wardens and their staff will bring you up-to-date on the condition of local routes and will advise you of any specific hazards. You might also contact them prior to your arrival to help you select routes suitable for your skill level.

When travelling elsewhere on land or water, it's imperative that a responsible person be aware of your intended route and date of return. If you're planning to go out on the land or sea, you should register with the RCMP. While this is not mandatory, police and other experienced northerners agree that adventure travellers would be extremely foolish *not* to register with the RCMP. A second choice is to register with the local search and rescue group. You can get in touch with them through the hamlet office.

Be sure to supply yourself adequately for your trip. In Ellesmere Island National Park, emergency supplies are kept at the Tanquary Fiord and Lake Hazen warden stations, as well as several other locations. Otherwise, emergency supplies aren't generally available for those out on the land.

Emergency Radios and Personal Locator Beacons

In Nunavut, HF radio is the main means of communication for both emergency and other purposes, although portable satellite (MSAT) telephones are becoming a more affordable option (see Chapter 9, "Communications"). The most common HF radio is the Spillsbury SBX-11, known to some as a radiotelephone. These radios can have up to four frequencies or channels, two of which are usually assigned to the HTOs in the communities. These frequencies are common across Nunavut. Individual agencies such as Parks Canada, **Nunavut Research Institute**, Polar Continental Shelf Project and others all have their own frequencies. Channel 5031, an open frequency used across Nunavut, is constantly monitored by Inuit hunters. Don't hesitate to break into the conversation to broadcast your message. When available, HF radios may be rented or borrowed from outfitters or community organizations such as HTOs. The problem with bringing your own HF radio is that the manufacturer must install the correct crystal for the channel in question, as well as an intact wire dipole antenna tuned for frequency.

Within Auyuittuq National Park, HF radios are stationed in each of the emergency shelters. Sometimes the batteries need to be warmed up first. Cover them under your jacket, if that's the case. In Ellesmere Island National Park and Katannilik Territorial Park Reserve, it's recommended that each group rent and carry an HF radio as part of its communal gear. Radio "blackouts" — intense solar disturbances that prevent radio reception — are a serious communications problem in the Arctic. In some cases, radio communication is impossible for hours or even days. When an emergency coincides with a radio blackout, you're on your own.

Personal locator beacons are also commonly used and available for sale, rent or loan. When triggered, these beacons emit a radio distress signal to a satellite, which then transmits to emergency measures organizations. The beacons are to be used only in an emergency. Once triggered, they can't be turned off. When one of these signals is received, the receiving agency assumes that immediate rescue or evacuation is required. If a beacon is triggered by mistake, you may bear the cost of the emergency response. These beacons are particularly recommended for those travelling in extremely remote areas, in the off-season, or in areas where dangers (such as large numbers of polar bears) are known to be present.

Wildlife and Plants

Polar bears can be encountered throughout Nunavut, including at all parks. As they're marine mammals, they spend most of the year roaming the sea ice. In summer, they travel along the shoreline and occasionally venture great distances inland. Visitors aren't allowed to carry firearms, even for personal protection, within national parks. Several spray deterrents have been developed, but they have yet to be proven effective against polar bears. To avoid polar bears — and barren-ground grizzly bears on mainland Nunavut — choose routes that don't pass through their habitat. Also be scrupulous in your management of food and waste. The pamphlet, *Safety in Bear Country*, is available from the Department of Sustainable Development (or until April 1, 1999, GNWT's Department of Resources, Wildlife and Economic Development), Nunavut Tourism offices and visitor centres, and some community visitor information centres.

It can be dangerous to approach too closely to muskoxen, particularly if they're lone bulls. Be extra careful. In Ellesmere Island National Park, muskoxen, when threatened, have been known to charge and gore people.

Rabies is present throughout Nunavut, especially in the fox population, and it has been found in arctic wolves as well. Wolves and foxes are very curious and may come right up to you. Avoid contact with all wildlife. Feeding wildlife is prohibited in parks and isn't wise in any case. Feeding also results in the "habituation" of wildlife. Once accustomed to human food, many species quickly become troublesome and can cause extensive damage to personal equipment and food stores.

Respect the need of the region's wildlife for undisturbed territory. When approaching wildlife to take a photograph or a closer look, stay downwind. Respect their need for distance, and don't make sudden move-ments. Never chase or harass animals. Respect for them is especially critical in calving, nesting and feeding areas, or when they are already stressed.

Travel quietly. You'll be more aware of your environment, and wildlife will be less disturbed. In fact, you'll increase your chances of observing wildlife. If you're travelling in a park, learn as much as you can about those species that are easily disturbed. Inquire about places and times when disturbance is most likely so you can avoid travelling there during critical periods.

There are a few edible plants in Nunavut, notably several varieties of berries and others such as mountain sorrel. No known poisonous plants exist in the area. Don't eat any edible plants, however, unless you find yourself in an emergency. Much of Nunavut's vegetation is sparse, and some species, such as arctic blueberry in Ellesmere Island National Park, are rare, existing here only marginally at the most northern extent of their range. If a local outfitter takes you to a traditional berry-picking spot, though, it's usually okay to sample a few.

Natural Objects, Artifacts, Archeological Sites and Cairns

Allow others a sense of discovery by leaving rocks, plants and other natural objects, such as muskoxen skulls and caribou antlers, as you found them. Not only does collecting degrade the experience for others, but you may be breaking laws protecting archeological artifacts. See precautions for rockhounds in Chapter 54, "Rock Collecting."

If you use rocks to secure your tent, return them to their original location before you leave. Don't camp on any archeological site, and don't remove rocks from any archeological feature (such as a cairn, tent ring, food cache, burial or fox trap) or from any source that looks like an archeological site. Partially buried symmetrical arrangements of stone may be all you see on the ground surface in the area of a prehistoric site. Some of the most ancient archeological remains, such as the older Paleoeskimo sites in Ellesmere Island National Park, may be almost indiscernible to the untrained eye. These rare sites, however, are important cultural resources containing invaluable information about life in the area 4,000 years ago! Please don't touch any of these. The exact arrangement and location of bones, artifacts and structural remains are crucial in determining what occurred at the site. Moreover, archeological sites in Nunavut are protected by law, and the unauthorized disturbance or removal of artifacts or other cultural specimens from any site is prohibited. Human burials and their associated grave offerings, as well as sacred and spiritual sites, are of special significance. Visitors should not disturb graves under any circumstances.

In some Nunavut parks, you can visit prehistoric sites that have been excavated. Check with the park staff. If you find an archeological or historical artifact, do not touch it or remove it. Instead, photograph it if possible, mark its location on your map and report it to staff when you leave the park. If you find what appears to be an undiscovered site outside a park, you're encouraged to report it to the **Inuit Heritage Trust** in Iqaluit, or to the Nunavut government's **Department of Culture, Language, Elders and Youth**.

Don't build cairns or other markers, or leave messages in the soil. These signs may be confusing to others and they detract from other visitors' sense of discovery and feeling of wilderness. Don't disturb or destroy any cairns that you find, because some are of great historical importance.

Glaciers

Glaciers abound in the Baffin Region. All members of groups planning glacier travel, such as ski-mountaineering, must be well versed in the techniques of such travel. When travelling on a glacier, ski-mountaineering groups should be properly roped together at all times. This means while in camp, as well. Even among experienced glacier travellers, deaths have occurred when someone has stepped outside the camp and fallen unroped into a crevasse. All team members must be capable of crevasse rescue techniques such as the Z-pulley and drop-loop systems. Harnesses, crampons, ice axes, carabiners, pulleys, ice screws, prusiks, jumar ascenders, and ropes that are nine millimetres in diameter or thicker are among the recommended equipment for hiking parties planning to cross glacier tongues along their routes. (Look for the UIAA stamp of approval on ropes and other climbing gear that the international mountaineering association deems acceptable.) Hikers must know how to use all equipment.

If planning extended trips onto an ice cap, you should wear plastic double mountaineering boots and carry an HF radio. If you're travelling within a park, before you set out, discuss with park staff possible drop-off and pickup points and escape routes. (If travelling outside a park, discuss this with another responsible person.) Don't be lulled into a false sense of security by the deceptively flat terrain of ice caps. They can harbor enormous hidden crevasses.

Avalanches and Rock Falls

It's essential that all members of parties travelling in areas where an avalanche may occur be well versed in avalanche avoidance and self-rescue techniques. Each party member should carry a dual frequency (227.5 kHz and 457 kHz) avalanche beacon that is switched on and set always to transmit (for example, Pieps DF, Ortovox FZ, Avalrt). They should also carry an avalanche probe, as well as a shovel. Practise self-rescue techniques beforehand. A pre-trip battery check is also recommended.

In many areas of Nunavut, rock falls are a serious hazard. Prolonged periods of rain greatly increase the frequency of rock falls. There's also an increased hazard of falling rock during periods of daily freezing and melting. Take particular care in selecting routes along steep slopes. Camp sites should be set up in protected areas away from the immediate base of mountains or cliffs. A growth of lichen on rock surfaces is a good sign of a protected area. Avoid areas of bare, clean rock.

Crossing Streams, Rivers and Lake Ice

Many streams and rivers in Nunavut are glacier-fed. Even with continuous daylight, their depth and speed change throughout the day. The ice-cold water is frequently opaque from glacial silt, and currents can be deceptively strong. If in doubt about your ability to ford a stream, wait until late at night or early morning to cross, as water levels are usually lower at these times. Unfasten your waist belt and loosen the shoulder straps on your pack. A hiking staff used as a third leg adds stability in stream crossings. Groups may wish to use buddy techniques, such as chains, wedges, or the people pivot, with arms linked and with the strongest members upstream. Wet suit, "reef boots" or windsurfing-type neoprene boots and pants are recommended to aid in fording the extremely cold glacier-fed rivers and streams, notably in Auyuittuq and Ellesmere Island national parks. Once committed to the crossing, you should be resolute and unfaltering, with eyes fixed on a point on the opposite side to prevent visual disorientation by moving water on all sides.

In a few lakes in Nunavut, ice lasts late into the summer. Although this persistent ice sometimes looks like a tempting shortcut compared with more gruelling land routes, lake ice, particularly if there are shore leads, should be considered unsafe and avoided from around June 1.

Although the sea ice almost always breaks up around communities in the summer, year-round sea ice does occasionally occur. "Ice pans" floating in and out on the tides are common during the summer. Never attempt to walk on an ice pan, as it can carry you out to sea. Even worse is to be stuck on one with a polar bear. It has happened!

Tides

Tides in parts of Nunavut are among the highest in the world. They ebb and flow very quickly and can be dangerous when exploring tidal flats. To be stranded by the tide is not an adventure you want to experience! Tides have a considerable effect on boat travel. It's difficult to get in and out of Auyuittuq National Park at low tide, for example, because of the long, shallow flats that develop. Canadian Hydrographic Services has tide and current tables for various areas of Nunavut. It's also a good idea to consult the **Department of Fisheries and Oceans** before scheduling any boat trips. Tides vary by about an hour a day, so a high tide that comes at noon one day will arrive several hours later at the end of the week.

12. WEATHER
by Carol Rigby

Nunavut is a huge territory, and the weather can vary widely.

As a rule, in July and August, inland areas are warmer than coastal ones, while western regions are definitely warmer than the Baffin Region.

Summer highs can differ widely. The warmest day on record in Iqaluit was a balmy 24.4° C, whereas Baker Lake once experienced a torrid 33.6° C day in July. (The highest temperature recorded in the Arctic was 43° C in Kugluktuk. But this is the exception, not the rule!) If the temperature is right, visitors can even swim at some sandy beaches in Nunavut — there are several in Rankin Inlet and one in Kugluktuk. Broughton Island, on the other hand, has never seen a day warmer than 19° C.

Spring temperatures are more consistent throughout Nunavut, with average daytime highs between –20° C and –10° C. Cool days are tempered by lots of sunshine. From late March to the end of May, sun reflected off snow and ice can cause severe sunburn.

Daylight

In winter, visitors should be prepared for cold temperatures and short days. On the shortest days of winter in Iqaluit, the sun rises and sets within four hours. The further north you go, the shorter the winter days get. Communities north of the Arctic Circle don't see the sun at all for stretches at a time, although the sky may lighten a bit at midday. Conversely, at the summer solstice, the sun shines for up to 21 hours a day in Iqaluit and many Kivalliq communities. The further north you go above the Arctic Circle, the more days you'll experience 24-hour daylight. Unsuspecting visitors, wishing to sleep in the open under the stars at night, have been known to wake up with lovely sunburns!

Winter Cold

Low humidity reduces the impact of the cold, making a –20° C day feel more like –5° C in Southern Canada. Winds, however, can cause frostbite, so it's wise to have a parka with a ruff around its hood for wintertime visits. January, February and March are the coldest months, with an average high in Iqaluit of –22° C and a low of –30° C. The record low was –46° C. Cambridge Bay is even colder: January averages are –30° C for high and –37° C for low. But the coldest day on record anywhere in Nunavut was in Pelly Bay where the temperature, combined with the windchill, reached –92° C!

Precipitation

As most of the Arctic is a polar desert, long stretches of almost cloudless days without precipitation are common. Total annual precipitation in Iqaluit, converted to a water equivalent, is 43 centimetres. (Ottawa gets more than twice this amount in an average year, and despite its much shorter winter, gets about the same amount of snow.) However, throughout most of Nunavut, cool temperatures mean that snow cover generally doesn't finish melting until June. On most of the land, the only months without snow are June, July and August. Sea ice doesn't finish melting until later. Most rain falls just after the sea ice breaks up, usually between mid-July and the end of August.

Winds

The wind always seems to blow in the Arctic! In all regions of Nunavut, many communities have steady average winds of 15–20 km/h almost daily. Some communities are notorious for occasional extreme winds. In Pangnirtung, for example, many of the older houses have cables fastening their roofs to the ground to protect them against gusts of more than 100 km/h. Precipitation tends to fall sideways, as it's almost always accompanied by winds of 30–60 km/h. If you plan to spend extended time out on the land or water, you must consider the wind as a factor — it will magnify any chilling effects of the weather. The windchill factor is often more significant than the actual air temperature.

Weather Delays

Blizzards are most common during autumn — especially in October and November — and early spring, February through April. Travel to the smaller communities can be severely affected at these times, because pilots must rely on good visibility to approach airstrips that don't have instrument landing systems. In the summer, weather delays can also be caused by strong winds, unpredictable cloud cover, and along a coastline, fog. Build time into your schedule to allow for the possibility of being "weathered in" or "weathered out" of a community by poor visibility or strong winds. If outdoor activities such as hiking or boating are on your agenda, make allowances in your plans for days when you'll choose to stay put, rather than travel in terrible, hypothermia-inducing weather.

Length of Midnight Sun and Arctic Night in Select Nunavut Communities		
Community	24 Hours of Sunshine	24 Hours of Darkness
Grise Fiord	April 22 to August 20	October 31 to February 11
Resolute	April 29 to August 13	November 6 to February 5
Nanisivik	May 6 to August 6	November 11 to January 30
Arctic Bay	May 6 to August 6	November 11 to January 30
Pond Inlet	May 5 to August 7	November 12 to January 29
Clyde River	May 13 to August 9	November 22 to January 20
Broughton Island	May 29 to July 15	December 16 to December 26
Pangnirtung	June 8 to July 4	no 24-hour darkness
Repulse Bay	June 4 to July 9	no 24-hour darkness
Hall Beach	May 21 to July 22	December 2 to January 10
Igloolik	May 18 to July 26	November 26 to January 15
Pelly Bay	May 21 to July 22	December 4 to January 7
Taloyoak	May 17 to July 27	November 25 to January 16
Gjoa Haven	May 22 to July 21	December 3 to January 9
Cambridge Bay	May 20 to July 23	November 30 to January 11
Kugluktuk	May 27 to July 17	December 10 to January 2

SOURCE: ENVIRONMENT CANADA

The limits of 24-hour sunlight and 24-hour darkness are not coincident, but extend approximately 50 nautical miles north and south of the Arctic Circle. This is due to a combination of effects: the "radius" of the solar disk accounts for approximately one-third of the shift, while the effects of refraction for the other two-thirds. Along the Arctic Circle, half the solar disk remains visible on the northern horizon at sunset on the longest day, and half the solar disk appears on the southern horizon during the shortest day.

13. CLOTHING AND PERSONAL EFFECTS
by Carol Rigby

Your choice of clothing and personal effects can make or break your arctic holiday.

If you're properly dressed and equipped, you'll find few obstacles to enjoying yourself. But if you're ill-equipped, you may be miserable. The clothing and equipment you need when visiting the North depends on when you're coming and what you're planning to do. A trip involving hiking, camping or some other outdoor summer activity will have different requirements than a dogsledding trip.

In most of Nunavut, summer weather is equivalent to cool spring or fall conditions in most of Southern Canada, the northern United States, or Europe. However, the climate can vary dramatically from one region to another. Coastal sections of the Kivalliq and Baffin regions occasionally experience days that are warm enough for short sleeves and pants. The air is usually chilly, though, and nights can be downright cold. Kugluktuk in the Kitikmeot, on the other hand, can have hot spells of up to 30° C; in this case, it's worthwhile bringing along a swimsuit.

Expect conditions near the water to be cold all summer, with warmer weather possible in the interior. T-shirts may be comfortable on many days and come in handy as undershirts in cooler weather. Judge your need for shorts by your tolerance for cool temperatures and insect bites.

Check on the weather for the region you're planning to visit. If you love swimming, bring a bathing suit. Some communities have swimming pools, and you might join the few hardy souls who take dips in nearly freezing waters. For example, the Duval River in Pangnirtung has a swimming hole of sorts, where brave teens like to go. It's not for the faint-hearted or easily chilled!

For summer travel to the communities, you'll want a good breathable set of rain gear, top and bottom. Don't bother to bring an umbrella, though, because it will just blow inside out and won't protect you against the rain, which often blows sideways in the Arctic! Make sure your jacket has a good hood that's sewn in or zipped on rather than snapped on.

Arctic dress is casual. Usually only elderly Inuit ladies wear skirts, and then with trousers underneath. Nearly everyone wears pants, sweatsuits or tights, usually with T-shirts, casual shirts and sweaters. Footgear should be low-heeled and sturdy, as most roads are gravel and have no sidewalks. Footwear with ankle support is excellent for walking on the tundra; heavy leather hiking boots are necessary only if you plan to walk extensively on the land. Rubber boots with heavy felt or duffel liners and/or heavy wool socks are crucial for those planning fishing or sightseeing trips on freighter canoes. Even if you plan to stay within a community, be sure to bring warm wool or pile sweaters for cool summer days and nights.

If you plan to visit a community in winter, it's essential to bring a warm coat or parka with a good hood and a face-protecting ruff. Warm, low-heeled boots, a scarf, a close-fitting knitted hat, and windproof mitts are other essentials. Long underwear, turtlenecks, sweaters and warm trousers are all necessary if you plan to go outside. If you like to walk even in winter, windproof outer pants or pile-lined wind pants are indispensable. You can expect central heating in virtually all buildings. If you can rent well-fitting caribou clothing for a winter trip outside the communities, great. Otherwise, conventional gear for extremely cold weather is a must. Goggles are also great for winter snowmobile trips.

You should also bring good sunglasses with UV (ultraviolet) filters, unless you're visiting above the Arctic Circle at Christmas, when the sun doesn't rise. The sun is up at least 20 hours a day in the summer; in the spring, reflection off the snow can be intense. Anyone without sunglasses who is out on the land in the spring risks snow-blindness. A cap with a brim is essential in spring and summer, as well. Baseball caps are a sure bet for visitors who like to trade!

Spring sunburns from forehead to neck are very common in the Arctic, so bring a good sunblock. (An "arctic tan" is very brown face and hands, and pale skin everywhere else.) Since the climate is dry, it's also a good idea to bring moisturizing lotion and lip salve. Make sure you bring all the personal toiletries you'll need, especially if you plan to travel beyond the larger communities of Iqaluit, Rankin Inlet or Cambridge Bay.

Most hotels and lodges have outlets for razors and hair dryers that operate on the standard 120-volt North American system.

14. INSECTS
by Carol Rigby

Parts of Canada's North are infested with insects for several weeks in the summer — somewhere between July and August — although the problem varies from one area to another.

Mosquitoes can be especially annoying, but they are a necessary nuisance within the Arctic's ecosystems, since they are breakfast, lunch and dinner for many of Nunavut's birds, and also help in the pollination of beautiful arctic flowers. Other than mosquitoes, blackflies, wasps and bumblebees, there are no biting insects in the North. Nor are there any snakes in the North.

The Kivalliq Region has many shallow tundra lakes and is ideal for breeding mosquitoes. Blackflies are found inland during the last two weeks of August (Baker Lake is the Kivalliq's only inland community). Visitors will also encounter lots of blackflies and mosquitoes along the rivers and lakes in the Kitikmeot Region, and wasps and bumblebees around Kugluktuk. However, the more mountainous terrain and almost constant winds of the Baffin Region mean that fewer insects breed there.

If you plan to be outdoors for long in the Baffin, be sure to use a good insect repellent in case the wind drops or you find yourself hiking through a sheltered valley or along a pond or river bed where mosquitoes breed. When they do come, they can be thick. Generally, however, a bug hat or jacket shouldn't be necessary unless you're extremely sensitive to bites. You're more likely to encounter great numbers of mosquitoes in communities surrounded by flat terrain. There are no blackflies in most of the Baffin.

In the Kivalliq, good bug protection is essential. One of the new light-weight, all-in-one bug jackets with hood and face mask is ideal. The visitors centres sell these for around $70.

People have been known to tape shut sleeves and pant cuffs to keep bugs out of clothes. If you're camping, good screening on your tent is also essential. And carry lots of repellent!

Here are a few other tips from officials in Nunavut's tourism industry.
- Wear light-colored clothing. Insects are not as attracted to these as they are to dark clothing. Teal and green are the worst colors to wear.
- Forget the hype about Avon's Skin-So-Soft(tm) moisturizing lotion — despite its reputation for doubling as an insect repellent, it doesn't work very long in the Arctic.

- Use a repellent containing the chemical DEET, a deterrent to bugs. According to the Drug Information Centre with the Faculty of Pharmacy, University of Toronto, 30 per cent DEET is acceptable for adults and 10 per cent DEET for children under five. High concentrations of DEET have proven toxic to some people. Its effect varies on individuals; generally, the younger you are and fairer your skin, the greater the toxic effect.
- Try bug hats, an inexpensive alternative. They come in several styles, from the hoop kind to caps with netting inside.
- Check the netting and door zippers on your tent before bringing it north. Buy a tent first-aid kit with netting patches for repairs.
- If you are allergic to bees, bring appropriate medication with you. There are very few pharmacies in Nunavut.
- When bugs are bad, do as the caribou do and head for the high ridges where the wind will blow bugs away! Or take up the Inuit practice of burning moss to smoke away mosquitoes.

15. PERIODICALS, BOOKS AND INTERNET RESOURCES

by Carol Rigby and Marion Soublière, with contributions from Dave Sutherland

Periodicals

When planning a trip to Nunavut, you may want to check out the following periodicals.

Above and Beyond
Tel.: (867) 873-2299. Fax: (867) 873-2295
E-mail: abeyond@internorth.com
First Air's in-flight magazine carries general interest articles on life in the North.

Inuit Art Quarterly
Tel.: (613) 224-8189. Fax: (613) 224-2907
E-mail: iaf@inuitart.org
Web site: www.inuitart.org
Published by the Inuit Art Foundation, this magazine is for the serious art enthusiast.

Inuktitut
Tel.: (613) 238-8181. Fax: (613) 234-1991
E-mail: itc@magi.com
A quarterly published by the Inuit Tapirisat of Canada, *Inuktitut* is a cultural magazine featuring articles on traditional ways of life, and current issues of interest to Inuit. It is published in English and Inuktitut.

Nunatsiaq News
Tel.: (867) 979-5357. Fax: (867) 979-4763
E-mail: nunat@nunanet.com
Web site: www.nunatsiaq.com
An Iqaluit-based weekly newspaper that focuses on current political events.

The Arctic Traveller: Nunavut vacation planner
Tel.: 1-800-491-7910 or (867) 979-6551. Fax: (867) 979-1261
E-mail: nunatour@nunanet.com
Web site: www.nunatour.nt.ca
A useful publication for planning your visit; contains listings of outfitters,
trip packages, etc. Published by Nunavut Tourism, it's one of the best print
sources of current tourism information.

Up Here: Life in Canada's North
Tel.: (867) 920-4652. Fax: (867) 873-2844
E-mail: outcrop@internorth.com
Another general interest magazine focusing on the North.

Books

Once in Nunavut, you may find it worthwhile to visit a local branch of the
public library system. There are libraries in Iqaluit, Rankin Inlet, Arviat,
Baker Lake, Igloolik, Iqaluit, Kugluktuk, Nanisivik, Pangnirtung and Pond
Inlet. Collections are small, except in Iqaluit and Rankin Inlet, which house
regional collections. However, even the small libraries contain northern
materials and, often, items of local interest. Many are located in visitor
centre/museum complexes or in local schools. Hours are limited but should
be clearly posted. Visitors are welcome to use materials in the libraries, but
may not borrow materials unless they are staying long enough to warrant
a temporary membership. The Iqaluit Centennial Library houses the
Thomas Manning collection of polar books, which contains many rare items
and would be of interest to antiquarians, book lovers, and scientists. The
library of the Nunatta Campus of Nunavut Arctic College is the home of the
Pilot and Hochelaga historical collections; these too can be viewed by visitors.

Before coming to Nunavut, though, you might find the following
books enlightening. Most are currently in print, though some older titles
might only be available from a library. Many stores in the North carry some
books of local interest, but the only wide selection is in the bookstore
section of Arctic Ventures in Iqaluit.

Items in this listing that might not have received widespread publicity
outside the Arctic have been annotated briefly.

Anthropology and General Interest

Alexander, Bryan and Cherry. *The Vanishing Arctic.* Fitzhenry and Whiteside,
1997; Facts on File, 1997.

⚲ Boas, Franz. *The Central Eskimo.* University of Nebraska Press, 1964.

Boult, David (editor). *The Inuit Way.* Ottawa: Inuit Women's Association of
Canada, 1991. A booklet published by Pauktuutit, the Inuit Women's
Association, with the express intent of explaining traditional Inuit
attitudes and the social values of Inuit today to a non-Inuit audience.

Brody, Hugh. *Living Arctic: Hunters of the Canadian North.* Douglas &
MacIntyre, 1987. Also *The People's Land: Eskimos and Whites in the Eastern
Arctic.* Penguin, 1975.

Bruemmer, Fred. *Seasons of the Eskimo: A Vanishing Way of Life.* McClelland &
Stewart, 1971. Available in French as *Les Saisons de l'Esqimau: un mode de*

vie qui disparait. Cercle du livre de France, 1994. Also *The Arctic.* Optimum Publishing International, 1982; and *The Arctic World.* Key Porter, 1985.

Hall, Ed (editor). *A Way of Life.* Yellowknife: Government of the Northwest Territories (Department of Renewable Resources), 1986. Describes traditional tools and techniques that have helped aboriginal peoples of the Northwest Territories cope with life. One fascinating chapter describes the making of sealskin *kamiit* (boots).

Hancock, Lyn. *Nunavut.* Lerner Publications, 1995.

Jenness, Diamond. *The Life of the Copper Eskimos.* S.A. Acland, Printer to the King, 1922.

Kusugak, Michael and Robert Munsch. *A Promise is A Promise.* Annick Press, 1988. This children's book, beautifully illustrated by Vladyana Krykorka, is a tale of the *Qallupilluit,* imaginary creatures living underwater who snatch children straying too close to cracks in the ice. Kusugak and Krykorka have collaborated on a number of other titles for children: *Baseball Bats for Christmas, My Arctic 1 2 3, Hide and Sneak, Northern Lights: the Soccer Trails,* all illuminating some aspect of Inuit childhood.

Lopez, Barry. *Arctic Dreams: Imagination and Desire in a Northern Landscape.* Charles Scribner's Sons, 1986.

MacDonald, John. *The Arctic Sky: Inuit astronomy, star lore and legend.* Toronto and Iqaluit: Royal Ontario Museum and Nunavut Research Institute, 1998.

Pitseolak, Peter and Dorothy Harley Eber. *People from our side: a life story with photographs and oral biography.* McGill-Queen's University Press, 1993 (reprint edition). Pitseolak, born in 1902, is considered Baffin's first Inuk photographer. His account of changes brought to the nomadic lifestyle of the Inuit by fur traders, government schools, and missionaries is filled with photos from the 1940s on, capturing a historic time of transition.

Steltzer, Ulli. *Inuit. The North in Transition.* Douglas & McIntyre, 1982.

Wilkinson, Douglas. *The Arctic Coast.* (The Illustrated Natural History of Canada series.) Jack McClelland, 1975. An excellent overview of the physical geography and ecology of the Arctic coastline.

Arts, Crafts, Inuit Writing

Gedalof, Robin (editor). *Paper Stays Put: A Collection of Inuit Writing.* Hurtig, 1980. An anthology of essays, stories and legends by Inuit authors.

Houston, James, *Confessions of an Igloo Dweller.* McClelland & Stewart, 1996.

Ipellie, Alootook. *Arctic Dreams and Nightmares.* Penticton, BC: Theytus Books, 1993. Twenty short stories accompanied by drawings and an introductory essay, all by Ipellie, who has a distinctive artistic style and writing voice.

Larmour, W.T. *Inunnit: The Art of the Canadian Eskimo.* Ottawa: Government of Canada (Department of Indian Affairs and Northern Development), 1967. Available in French as *Inunnit: L'art des Esquimaux du Canada.*

Markoosie. *Markoosie: Harpoon of the hunter.* McGill-Queen's University Press, 1970. This powerful novella, the first work of Inuit fiction to be published in English, tells the story of a young man who reaches manhood during the hunt for a wounded polar bear, and his long journey home alone. Also available in Inuktitut.

Métayer, Maurice (editor and translator). *Tales from the Igloo.* Hurtig, 1972. Traditional Inuit tales illustrated by Holman artist Agnes Nanogak. Followed by *More Tales from the Igloo* by Agnes Nanogak. Hurtig, 1986.

National Museum of Man. *The Inuit Print: A Travelling Exhibition of the National Museum of Man.* National Museum of Man, Ottawa, 1977.

Oakes, Jill E. and Rick Riewe. *Our Boots: An Inuit Women's Art.* Douglas & McIntyre, 1995.

Petrone, Penny (editor). *Northern voices: Inuit writing in English.* University of Toronto Press, 1988. A wide-ranging anthology with selections from different Inuit culture groups (such as Copper Inuit, Iglulik Inuit).

Roch, Ernst and Patrick Furneaux. *Arts of the Eskimo: Prints.* Signum Press (in association with Oxford University Press), 1974.

Seidelman, Harold and James Turner. *The Inuit Imagination: Arctic Myth and Sculpture.* Douglas & McIntyre, 1993; Thames and Hudson, 1994.

Strickler, Eva and Anaoyok Alookee. *Inuit Dolls: Reminders of a Heritage.* Canadian Stage and Arts Publications Limited, 1988.

Swinton, George. *Sculpture of the Inuit,* revised edition. McClelland & Stewart, 1992. This classic survey of the field has been republished in an updated edition (former title was *Sculpture of the Eskimo*); the older edition may still also be available.

Flora and Fauna

Most libraries carry copies of such standard reference works as A.W.F. Banfield's *The Mammals of Canada* (also available in French as *Les mammifères du Canada*), Adrian Forsyth's *Mammals of the Canadian Wild*, William E. Godfrey's *Birds of Canada* (also available in French as *Les oiseaux du Canada*), and, of course, Roger Tory Peterson's *A Field Guide to the Birds East of the Rockies.* The following titles focus more specifically on arctic flora and fauna:

Bruemmer, Fred. *Arctic Animals: A Celebration of Survival.* McClelland & Stewart, 1986.

Chung, In-Cho. *Eastern North America as Seen by a Botanist: Pictorial I (The Arctic Region).* Daytona Beach, Florida: Samhwa Printing Co., 1989. An excellent pictorial survey of the grasses and wildflowers of the region. Makes it easy to identify specific plants.

Graves, Jonquil and Ed Hall. *Arctic Animals.* Yellowknife: Government of the Northwest Territories (Department of Renewable Resources), 1985. Illustrated by well-known Inuit artist Germaine Arnaktauyok, this is a concise but thorough survey of animal species found in the Canadian Arctic. It covers virtually all wildlife a visitor is likely to encounter on a trip to Nunavut, along with the Inuktitut name or names for each species.

Mech, L. David. *The Arctic wolf: Living with the Pack.* Key Porter, 1988; Voyageur Press, 1988.

Pielou, E.C. *A Naturalist's Guide to the Arctic.* The University of Chicago Press, 1994. A well-written, non-technical overview of arctic animals, birds, fishes, plants and insects, illustrated by hand drawings.

Stirling, Ian. *Polar Bears.* Fitzhenry & Whiteside, 1988; University of Michigan Press, 1988. By one of the world's foremost polar bear biologists, this also contains many amazing photographs collected during Stirling's years of studying the beautiful and dangerous animal known to the Inuit as *nanuq*.

History

Alia, Valerie. *Names, Numbers and Northern Policy: Inuit, Project Surname and the Politics of Identity.* Halifax: Fernwood, 1994. A look at the federal government program that changed Inuit history by assigning family names to Inuit.

✗ Berton, Pierre. *The Arctic Grail: The Quest for the Northwest Passage and the North Pole, 1818-1909.* McClelland & Stewart, 1988; Viking, 1988.

Copeland, A. Dudley. *Coplalook: Chief Trader, Hudson's Bay Company 1923-39.* Winnipeg: Watson & Dwyer, 1989. Copeland's autobiography describes his various postings in the Arctic in the '20s and '30s. A firsthand view of the early interactions between the Hudson's Bay Co. and the Inuit.

Crowe, Keith J. *A History of the Original People of Northern Canada.* McGill-Queen's University Press, 1991, revised edition. An alternative view of the history of the North, focusing on its indigenous peoples. This edition includes discussion of land claims and current issues in the relationship between native peoples and the federal and territorial governments.

Eber, Dorothy Harley. *When the Whalers Were Up North: Inuit Memories from the Eastern Arctic.* McGill-Queen's University Press, 1989.

Francis, Daniel. *Discovery of the North: the exploration of Canada's Arctic.* Hurtig, 1986.

Grant, Shelagh D. *Sovereignty or security: Government Policy in the North, 1936-1950.* University of British Columbia Press, 1988.

✗ McGhee, Robert. *Canadian Arctic Prehistory.* Van Nostrand Reinhold, 1978. A classic on Inuit prehistory and the archeological record. Also available in French as *La préhistoire de l'Arctique canadien.* Fides, 1984. Also *Ancient People of the Arctic.* University of British Columbia Press with the Canadian Museum of Civilization, 1996.

Schledermann, Peter. *Crossroads to Greenland: 3,000 Years of Prehistory in the Eastern High Arctic.* The Arctic Institute of North America, 1990. An archeology text with a high level of technical content, this book is of interest for the controversy it's stirred up regarding the migration and settlement patterns of the ancestors of today's Inuit.

Life With the Inuit/Eskimos

Another sub-genre of arctic writing is the group of books written by explorers, scientists, bureaucrats and just plain folks describing their time spent living among the Inuit (once known by outsiders as Eskimos). Many of these, especially the older titles, are available in different editions and are most likely to be found at a library.

✗ Freuchen, Peter. *Peter Freuchen's Book of the Eskimos.* Several editions published. Dates from the early part of the century.

Georgia. *Georgia: An Arctic Diary.* Hurtig, 1982.

Rowley, Graham S. *Cold Comfort: My Love Affair with the Arctic.* McGill-Queen's University Press, 1996.

Stefansson, Vilhjalmur. *My life with the Eskimo.* Various editions. A classic.
Wilkinson, Douglas. *Land of the Long Day.* Clarke, Irwin, 1966.

Inuit columnists and writers such as John Amagoalik, Peter Ernerk,
Rachel Qitsualik and Mark Kalluak also convey the Inuit perspective
first-hand in northern newspapers.

And, of course, if one is interested in adventure travel, there are
innumerable accounts of people's trips and explorations, from Sir John
Franklin and Sir Charles Francis Hall to modern-day explorers like Will
Steger and Paul Schurke, Mike Beedell and Ed Struzik, and many others.
Chances are if someone has done a trip to the North Pole, they've written
a book about it!

Internet Resources

The Internet, far more than just a plaything for inhabitants of remote
Northern Canada, is already a vital resource tool for school and government-
driven networks, and it will play a key role in the Nunavut government. By
relaying information digitally for everything from medical services to
business conferences, Nunavut could recoup enormous costs that, until
now, have been poured into expensive and necessary air travel.

Each of Nunavut's regions has an Internet service provider and
more communities continue to go on line. Usenet discussion groups like
rec.travel.usa-canada, **rec.backcountry**, **soc.culture.native** or **can.politics** are
good places to get feedback on other adventure travel experiences in the
Arctic, learn what's new in the Inuit art world, or sense the political
momentum as the world watches Nunavut prepare to take its place on the
international stage.

Here are some web sites that virtual and real travellers to the Arctic
may want to check out.

Travel

Airlines serving Nunavut
See the "Getting Around" directory in this book.

Canadian Tourism Information Network   **xinfo.ic.gc.ca/Tourism/index-e.html**

Geomatics Canada   **Maps.NRCan.gc.ca/cmo/dealers.html**
For topographic maps, aeronautical charts or National Atlas of Canada publications.

Infonorth.org   **www.infonorth.org**
Extensive community profiles backed by socio-economic statistics, daily weather forecasts,
detailed descriptions of community airfields and more.

NWT Explorers' Guide   **www.nwttravel.nt.ca/**
Travel info geared mainly to the western Arctic.

NWT Yellow Pages   **www.ssimicro.com/yellowpages**

Natural Resources Canada   **GeoNames.NRCan.gc.ca**
Plug in an official geographical name, get its latitude and longitude, see what else is within
a 20-kilometre radius, or calculate distances between any two points in Nunavut or the
rest of Canada.

✓ **nunavut.com**   **www.nunavut.com**

An evolving news and information service for Nunavut, in English and Inuktitut.

✓ **The Nunavut Handbook**   **www.arctic-travel.com**

Photo tours, audio clips of Inuktitut phrases, an updated calendar of events, answers to questions from travellers and more.

Nunavut Parks   **www.nunavutparks.com**

The goods on territorial and national parks (including proposed parks) in Nunavut, as well as heritage rivers.

Nunavut Tourism   **www.nunatour.nt.ca**

Features a searchable services database so arctic travellers can get a head start on the planning process.

Parks Canada   **parkscanada.pch.gc.ca/**

Also check out their web site on new northern parks at **www.newparksnorth.org/index.htm.**

Water Survey of Canada   **www.ec.gc.ca/envhome.html**

For river flow rates, drops and other technical information for canoeists and kayakers.

✓ **Weather**

Environment Canada carries forecasts for a few Nunavut communities at **www.tor.ec.gc.ca/forecasts/index.html**. The InfoNorth web site updates weather conditions daily in its community profiles section (**www.infonorth.org**).

Internet Service Providers

Links River	**www.denendeh.com/linksriver/**
Nunanet Worldwide Communications	**apa.nunanet.com/**
PolarNet	**www.polarnet.ca**
Sakku Arctic Technologies	**www.arctic.ca/**

Discussion Groups/ListServs

Arctic Forum	**borealis.lib.uconn.edu/HyperNews/get/arcticforum.html**
Forum sur *Le toit du monde* In French.	**www.autochtones.com/cgi-bin/ hypernews/get/nunavut.html**
News/North Discussion Board	**www.ssimicro.com/ssipages/ ssi-bin/forum/forum?nnsl**
Nunatsiaq News Talk Back	**www.nunatsiaq.com/cgi-bin/web.pl**
nunavut.com	**www.nunavut.com**
Nunavut Political Discussion	**www.findmail.com/list/nunavut-p/**
Political Discussion Forum	**www.nunanet.com/politics/**

Government and Politics

Department of Indian Affairs and Northern Development	**www.inac.gc.ca/index_e.html**
Ed Picco, MLA	**www.nunanet.com/~epicco/**

Picco is the member of the legislative assembly for Iqaluit in the government of the Northwest Territories (effective until division of NWT).

Government of the Northwest Territories   www.gov.nt.ca/

Nunavut institutions of public government and other agencies
See the "Nunavut Takes Control" directory in this book.

Office of the Interim Commissioner of Nunavut   www.icon.gov.nu.ca/
Learn about the mandate and responsibilities of the office setting up the new government of Nunavut, as well as who's working for the Nunavut government, who's hiring, and what's the latest progress report.

Inuit Organizations

Nunavut land claims and Inuit organizations
See the "Nunavut Takes Control" directory in this book.

Art, Culture, and Recreation

✓ **Canadian Museum**   www.civilization.ca/cmc/cmceng/welcmeng.html
of Civilization
Watch for Nunavut exhibits and celebrations coming up at the museum in 1999.

Great Northern Arts Festival   www.greatart.nt.ca/index.html

The Hudson's Bay Co. Archives   www.gov.mb.ca/chc/archives/hbca/index.html
A valuable source of historical information about Canada's North.

Inuit Artists' Shop   www.inuitart.org/artshop.htm

Inuit Broadcasting Corporation   www.tvnc.ca/Members/ibc.html

✓ **Polar Pilots**   www.nunanet.com/~tbert/polar_pilots.html

Prince of Wales Northern Heritage Centre   pwnhc.learnnet.nt.ca/

Education

Joamie Elementary School   www.nunanet.com/~joamie

Leo Ussak Elementary School   www.arctic.ca/LUS

Nakasuk Elementary School   www.nunanet.com/~nakasuk/

The Northern Learning Network   www.learnnet.nt.ca

✓ **Nunavut Arctic College**   www.nunanet.com/~nachq

Selected Bibliography on Nunavut   www.nunanet.com/~jhicks/nunabib.htm
An excellent research tool.

Media

L'Aquilon   users.internorth.com/~aquilon/index.html
A French-language weekly covering the western Northwest Territories and Nunavut.

Le toit du monde   www.nunanet.com/~mensuel/index.html
A French-language online magazine about Canada's North.

CBC North   www.cbcnorth.cbc.ca/
Hear Real Audio radio broadcasts.

News/North   www.nnsl.com
With contributions from *Kivalliq News*, this site covers Nunavut and the western Northwest Territories.

Nunatsiaq News   www.nunatsiaq.com
Nunavut's leading newspaper publishes in English and Inuktitut.

Science and the Arctic

Arctic Circle   **borealis.lib.uconn.edu/arcticcircle/**

Arctic Council   **www.nrc.ca/arctic/index.html**
An intergovernmental forum addressing the concerns and challenges common to arctic peoples.

Arctic Perspectives   **www.arcticpersp.org**

Beverly and Qamanirjuaq Caribou Management Board   **www.arctic-caribou.com**
A good primer on subsistence hunting in Northern Canada.

Canadian Arctic Resources Committee   **www.carc.org**
A 5,000-member "citizen's organization" dedicated to bridging the gap between Southern and Northern Canada.

Nunavut Research Institute   **kinguk.nunanet.com/research/index.html**
Promotes the use of traditional knowledge, science, research and technology as ways to help Nunavut flourish.

References to more books and Internet resources can be found on *The Nunavut Handbook* web site at **www.arctic-travel.com**.

PLANNING AHEAD: DIRECTORY

Government Departments and Services

Customs Border Services
Automated Customs Information System (ACIS): 1-800-461-9999 (within Canada).
Contact offices at port of entry, Customs Border Services:
Ottawa (613) 993-0534
Montreal (514) 283-9900
Toronto (416) 973-8022
Vancouver (604) 666-0545
Iqaluit (867) 979-6714
Yellowknife (867) 920-2446
Winnipeg (204) 983-6004
Calgary (403) 292-8750
Edmonton (403) 495-3400
Quebec City (418) 648-4445

Department of Culture, Language, Elders and Youth, Government of Nunavut
Tel.: (867) 979-4720
Fax: (867) 979-5240

Department of Finance, Government of the NWT
Tel.: 1-800-661-0820
Tel.: (867) 920-3470
Fax: (867) 873-0325

Department of Fisheries and Oceans, Government of Canada
Winnipeg:
Tel.: (204) 983-5108
Fax: (204) 984-2401

Iqaluit:
Tel.: (867) 979-8000
Fax: (867) 979-8039

Rankin Inlet:
Tel.: (867) 645-2871
Fax: (867) 645-2880
E-mail: info@www.ncr.dfo.ca
Web site: www.ncr.dfo.ca

Department of Resources, Wildlife and Economic Development, Government of the NWT
In Nunavut, replaced by Department of Sustainable Development as of April/99.
Tel.: (867) 979-5011
Fax: (867) 979-6791

Department of Sustainable Development, Government of Nunavut

Assumes responsibilities, in April/99, previously handled by the GNWT's Department of Resources, Wildlife and Economic Development.
Tel.: (867) 979-5134
Fax: (867) 979-5920

Geological Survey of Canada

For calculating magnetic declination.
Web site: www.geolab.nrcan.gc.ca

Government of Nunavut Departments

For a complete list, see the directory at the end of the "Nunavut Takes Control" section.

Inuit Heritage Trust, Inc.

Tel.: (867) 979-0731
Fax: (867) 979-0269
E-mail: heritage@nunanet.com

Nunavut Research Institute

Tel.: (867) 979-6734
Fax: (867) 979-4681
E-mail: exdir@nunanet.com
Web site: nunanet.com/~research

Parks Canada

P.O. Box 353, Pangnirtung NT,
X0A 0R0 Canada
Tel.: (867) 473-8828
Fax: (867) 473-8612
E-mail: nunavut_info@pch.gc.ca

Government Tourism Licensing Officers

Baffin Region

Tel.: (867) 979-5070
Fax: (867) 979-6026

Kitikmeot Region

Tel.: (867) 982-7240
Fax: (867) 982-3701

Kivalliq Region

Tel.: (867) 645-5067
Fax: (867) 645-2346
E-mail: ron_roach@gov.nt.ca

Health-Care Services

Baffin Optical

Tel.: (867) 979-4300

Baffin Regional Hospital

In Iqaluit.
Tel.: (867) 979-7300
To order an ambulance, call 979-4422.

Cambridge Bay Dental Office

Tel.: (867) 983-2285
Fax: (867) 983-2168

Cambridge Bay Health Centre

Tel.: (867) 983-2531
Fax: (867) 983-2262

Iqaluit Dental Clinic

Tel.: (867) 979-4437
Fax: (867) 979-1365

NWT Health Care Plan

Health Services Administration
Bag 003, Rankin Inlet NT,
X0C 0G0 Canada
Tel.: 1-800-661-0833 or (867) 645-5002
Fax: (867) 645-2997

Rankin Inlet Dental Clinic

Tel.: (867) 645-2776
Fax: (867) 645-2750

Rankin Inlet Health Centre

Tel.: (867) 645-2816
Fax: (867) 645-2688

Maps

Canadian Hydrographic Services

For tide and current tables.
P.O. Box 6000,
9860 W. Saanich Rd., Sidney BC,
V8L 4B2 Canada
Tel.: (250) 363-6358
Fax: (250) 363-6841

Federal Maps

Tel.: 1-888-545-8111 or (613) 723-6366
Fax: (613) 723-6995
E-mail: fedmaps@fedmaps.com
Web site: www.fedmaps.com

Geomatics Canada

Tel.: (613) 992-8118
Fax: (613) 947-2410
Web site: Maps.NRCan.gc.ca/cmo/
dealers.html

Water Survey of Canada

For river flow rates, drops, etc.
Yellowknife office:
Tel.: (867) 669-4749
Fax: (867) 873-6776
E-mail: randy.wedel@ec.gc.ca
Web site: www.watersurvey.sk.ca/
index.html

Special Services

Bank of Montreal
Iqaluit:
Tel.: (867) 979-2901
Fax: (867) 979-2906

Canadian Firearms Centre
Tel.: 1-800-731-4000
Fax: (613) 941-1991
E-mail: canadian.firearms@
      justice.X400.gc.ca
Web site: www.cfc-ccaf.gc.ca

Canadian Imperial
Bank of Commerce
Rankin Inlet:
Tel.: (867) 645-2863
Fax: (867) 645-2573

NWT Liquor Commission/Iqaluit
Liquor Warehouse
Tel.: (867) 979-5918
Fax: (867) 979-5836

Our Missing Children
Tel.: (613) 993-1525
Fax: (613) 993-5430

Royal Bank of Canada
Cambridge Bay:
Tel.: (867) 983-2007
Fax: (867) 983-2754

Iqaluit:
Tel.: (867) 979-5344
Fax: (867) 979-4845

Rankin Inlet:
Tel.: (867) 645-3260
Fax: (867) 645-3261

Travel Agencies, Organizations and Programs

Eetuk Outfitting and
Equipment Rentals
P.O. Box 1090, Iqaluit NT,
X0A 0H0 Canada
Tel.: (867) 979-1984
Fax: (867) 979-1994

Elderhostel Canada
Tel.: (613) 530-2222
Fax: (613) 530-2096
Web site: www.elderhostel.org

NorthWinds Arctic Adventures
P.O. Box 820, Iqaluit NT,
X0A 0H0 Canada
Tel.: (867) 979-0551
Fax: (867) 979-0573
E-mail: plandry@nunanet.com
Web site: www.northwinds-arctic.com

Nunavut Tourism
P.O. Box 1450, Iqaluit NT,
X0A 0H0 Canada
Tel.: 1-800-491-7910 (for Canada and
the United States)
Tel.: (867) 979-6551
Fax: (867) 979-1261
E-mail: nunatour@nunanet.com
Web site: www.nunatour.nt.ca

Qamutik Travel
Iqaluit office:
P.O. Box 417, Iqaluit NT,
X0A 0H0 Canada
Tel.: 1-800-642-8597 (only for callers
from Canada's 867 area code)
Tel.: (867) 979-0707
Fax: (867) 979-1265

Rankin Inlet office:
P.O. Box 190, Rankin Inlet NT,
X0C 0G0 Canada
Tel.: 1-800-642-8619 (only for callers
from Canada's 867 area code)
Tel.: (867) 645-2932
Fax: (867) 645-2113

Top of the World Travel
Enokhok Centre, Cambridge Bay NT,
X0E 0C0 Canada
Tel.: (867) 983-2031
Fax: (867) 983-2340

YFB Corporate Travel
P.O. Box 2229, Iqaluit NT,
X0A 0H0 Canada
Tel.: 1-800-661-0898 (from anywhere
in Canada)
Tel.: (867) 979-8686
Fax: (867) 979-8687

Visitor Information Centres

Akumalik Visitors Centre, Baker Lake
Tel.: (867) 793-2456
Fax: (867) 793-2175 or (867) 979-2509

Angmarlik Interpretive Centre, Pangnirtung
Tel.: (867) 473-8737
Fax: (867) 473-8685

Arctic Coast Visitors Centre, Cambridge Bay
Tel.: (867) 983-2224
Fax: (867) 983-2302

Clyde River Visitors Centre, Clyde River
Tel.: (867) 924-6034
Fax: (867) 924-6362

The Katannilik Park Centre, Kimmirut
Tel.: (867) 939-2084
Fax: (867) 939-2406
E-mail: rjaffray@nunanet.com

Keewatin Regional Visitors Centre
Visitor information provided by
Nunavut Tourism, Rankin Inlet.
Tel.: (867) 645-3838
Fax: (867) 645-3904
E-mail: silatour@arctic.ca

Kugluktuk Heritage Centre, Kugluktuk
Tel.: (867) 982-3232
Fax: (867) 982-3229

Mallikjuaq Historic Park Visitors Centre, Cape Dorset
Tel.: (867) 897-8996
Fax: (867) 897-8475

Margaret Aniksak Visitors Centre, Arviat
Tel.: (867) 857-2841
Fax: (867) 857-2519

Nattinnak Centre, Pond Inlet
Tel.: (867) 899-8225
Fax: (867) 899-8175

Parks Canada Interpretive Centre, Pangnirtung
Tel.: (867) 473-8828
Fax: (867) 473-8612
E-mail: nunavut_info@pch.gc.ca

Unikkaarvik Visitors Centre, Iqaluit
Tel.: (867) 979-4636
Fax: (867) 979-1261
E-mail: nunatour@nunanet.com

Getting Around

16. FLYING TO NUNAVUT AND ITS COMMUNITIES

by Carol Rigby, with contributions from Jennifer Bernius

Most people visiting Nunavut arrive by air. There are no road links from the South and, with the exception of a 21-kilometre stretch between Arctic Bay and Nanisivik, no roads between communities.

Although cruises are sometimes available, there's no ferry or scheduled passenger ship service. Nunavut isn't linked either internally or to the South by rail.

In Nunavut, Iqaluit is the "gateway" city to the Baffin Region, while Rankin Inlet is the gateway to the Kivalliq. There are direct flights from Yellowknife (the capital of the Northwest Territories in the western Arctic) to five of the Kitikmeot's seven communities. There is no scheduled service to either Umingmaktok or Bathurst Inlet.

Greenland, a country that shares with Nunavut the same arctic climate and Inuit culture, is a gateway from Europe. **First Air** flies once a week between Kangerlussuaq, Greenland and Iqaluit in the winter, and twice weekly in the summer.

The Iqaluit Airport, a modern international facility, is the transportation hub of the Baffin Region. It serves as an entry point to Canada for flights from Greenland, and receives corporate traffic from jets looking for Customs clearance at a quieter official Canadian point of entry. One airline, First Air, offers direct jet service to Iqaluit from Montreal or Ottawa in Southern Canada. The flight generally takes from three to six hours, depending on whether a stop is made in Kuujjuaq (a community in northern Quebec). Schedules, departure points and the frequency of flights can change considerably from season to season, and this contributor's experience has been that southern travel agents aren't always aware of northern connections. Check with **Nunavut Tourism** or a northern travel agency if you're making travel arrangements yourself. If you're travelling with a tour, your best airline connections should be arranged with the tour company.

From Eastern Canada, flights to Iqaluit originate in Montreal and Ottawa. Connections can be made from any major city in Canada. Contact a travel agent or First Air for up-to-date schedules and fares. From the Kivalliq, Kitikmeot and Western Canada, connections can be made to Iqaluit through Yellowknife and Rankin Inlet. Contact a travel agent, **Canadian North** or First Air for up-to-date schedules and fares.

Air Inuit flies to Sanikiluaq from Montreal with connecting flights in the northern Quebec community of Kuujjuarapik.

Travellers to the Kivalliq usually arrive at Rankin Inlet via Winnipeg or Yellowknife. Its airport accommodates jet aircraft and has a new terminal. If you're coming from the east, the routing to Rankin Inlet is through Iqaluit. From the west, the routing is through Yellowknife. There are also flights to Rankin Inlet from Winnipeg, Thompson and Churchill, Manitoba.

Rankin Inlet is served by First Air, Canadian North, **Calm Air** and **Skyward Aviation**.

You can reach Cambridge Bay from Yellowknife if coming from Western Canada, or from Iqaluit if coming from Eastern Canada. If your point of origin is due south, a connection to Edmonton and the Edmonton-Yellowknife flight is probably the least complicated option. Within Nunavut you can reach Cambridge Bay from Rankin Inlet via Yellowknife or Iqaluit. Another option for larger groups is to charter a flight directly from Iqaluit or Rankin Inlet to Cambridge Bay. If a group is large enough, a charter can be economical. Yellowknife also has direct flights to Taloyoak, Pelly Bay, Gjoa Haven and Kugluktuk. There is daily service with First Air; Cambridge Bay is also served by Canadian North.

Getting to the Communities

Regular scheduled air services link most Nunavut communities. Many flights to the smaller communities operate two or three times a week. Some of the medium-sized communities have daily service, although not by jet aircraft. If you can't find a scheduled flight to your destination, a charter service can probably get you there (see the directory at the end of this section).

Canadian Airlines flies to Resolute from Edmonton through Yellowknife and Cambridge Bay.

First Air serves Broughton Island, Cape Dorset, Clyde River, Coral Harbour, Hall Beach, Igloolik, Kimmirut, Pangnirtung, Pond Inlet, Resolute, Nanisivik, Rankin Inlet, Kugluktuk, Pelly Bay, Taloyoak, Gjoa Haven and Cambridge Bay. **Kenn Borek Air** also serves Pangnirtung and Cape Dorset.

In the High Arctic, Kenn Borek Air offers scheduled air service from Resolute to Grise Fiord, Arctic Bay, Nanisivik and Pond Inlet. Calm Air has scheduled flights from Rankin Inlet to Repulse Bay, Arviat, Whale Cove, Chesterfield Inlet, Baker Lake and Coral Harbour. Skyward serves Arviat, Whale Cove, Chesterfield Inlet and Baker Lake from Rankin Inlet.

Whatever airline you use, it's best to make arrangements in advance through a travel agent. They'll design a package to fit your needs and will make reservations for you at no charge. Flights within Nunavut are frequently delayed by bad weather, particularly in the small communities where air operations run under visual flight rules. There are also instances when aircraft are taken off scheduled service to fly as air ambulances. Be sure to check with your air carrier for up-to-date information before each flight.

Charter Services

Charter aircraft are the usual way to reach destinations in Nunavut not serviced by scheduled airline flights. They're also the only way to reach many fishing camps and parks.

If you're taking a package tour, the charter cost will probably be included, but check to be sure. If you're planning a trip on your own, you or your travel agent will have to make charter aircraft arrangements.

Recreational Flying

Many private pilots dream of flying in the Arctic, enjoying the long days that lend themselves to flying at all hours. This is feasible, provided you are an experienced pilot, thoroughly prepared and well equipped with navigation and communication aids. Nunavut communities are separated by long distances with few distinguishing landmarks, and the region is considered an area of compass unreliability. GPS (satellite navigation systems) are highly recommended. To help plan your flight, find people with experience flying in arctic conditions, either at the commercial air carriers or with recreational flying associations or clubs, like Iqaluit's **Polar Pilots**. A flight service specialist with any Canadian flight service station can also provide you with references.

If entering Canada by air in the North, contact **CANPASS** (see phone number in the "Getting Around" directory) no later than one hour and no sooner than 72 hours prior to departing from a foreign country. For more information, consult the *Canada Flight Supplement* from **Transport Canada**.

Although Iqaluit, Rankin Inlet, Cambridge Bay, Kugluktuk, Nanisivik and Resolute have the facilities to support jet aircraft, most community airfields are gravel, operate on visual flight rules, and may not have the type of fuel required by your aircraft. Again, the *Canada Flight Supplement* has more information. (Polar Pilots in Iqaluit has a small hangar with cold parking sometimes used by visiting flyers.) Contact an airline carrier to see if they can ship a supply of fuel to your landing point ahead of time.

Flying conditions are often very chilly, so take precautions. Private pilots are, in many ways, going out "on the land" and should read Chapter 11, "Adventure Travel," for general safety advice and access restrictions to Inuit-owned land. Check the aviation web sites listed in the directory at the end of this section for more information.

Airports, Security, Baggage

Airport facilities at many of the smaller communities are limited to a ticket counter, a baggage office, a small waiting area and washrooms. As the result of a building program launched by the government of the Northwest Territories, several communities boast new airport buildings that are slightly larger and well laid out, although still modest in size. Iqaluit, Rankin Inlet and Cambridge Bay have more complete facilities.

In the small communities, standby passengers have lower priority than cargo, especially if they arrive at the last minute, so plan to get to the airport early if you don't have a seat reserved. In Iqaluit, a security check is performed on passengers heading south or to Greenland. The RCMP in other communities will check your baggage if they have reason to believe you're bringing in an illegal substance such as drugs or, in some communities, alcohol.

It's illegal to carry hazardous goods in your luggage. If in doubt, check with the airline. The following items are restricted at all times: matches, lighters, flammable liquids or gases, fireworks, signal flares, bleaches, drain cleaners, aerosols, mercury and solvents. If you require camp stove fuel, buy it at your destination.

Cargo and luggage space may be unheated. In the winter and early spring, your luggage may get very cold, so don't pack anything that will be damaged by freezing. Small items that should be kept from freezing can be carried in the cabin of the aircraft. It's also advisable to use soft-sided luggage of reinforced fabric, rather than vinyl or plastic luggage, which is likely to crack in freezing temperatures. Luggage isn't at the mercy of automated baggage machines, but it can get thrown around a bit when transferred from trucks to luggage holds. Experienced northern travellers like duffel bags and frameless backpacks.

17. SPECIAL NEEDS, AND TRAVELLING WITH CHILDREN
by Carol Rigby

People with special needs or those travelling with children may wonder if travelling in Nunavut is for them, since weather conditions can be unpredictable, health facilities are modest, specialized drugs or equipment may not be available, and wheelchair access has only been enforced as part of the building code in the last few years.

The answer is yes — but special needs travellers should prepare well in advance if they intend to visit Nunavut. The warmth of the welcome and the openness of society to people of all ages and levels of ability should help to offset these drawbacks. There is a long-standing tradition in the North of including people with special needs in the daily lives and activities of the communities, and you will find children present at virtually all public events and gatherings.

Elderly or disabled people should make advance arrangements if they intend to travel to any communities outside Iqaluit, Rankin Inlet or Cambridge Bay. Making travel plans through a tour operator who is aware of any special needs may be the best approach. The **Elderhostel** program frequently offers Nunavut destinations, and these trips are usually fully booked. (Elderhostel is a non-profit organization that provides cultural learning experiences by grouping travellers over 55 with their peers.) Special arrangements are made to accommodate the needs of those on Elderhostel trips.

In Iqaluit, Rankin Inlet and Cambridge Bay, most buildings constructed within the past few years are wheelchair accessible. In Iqaluit, **R. L. Hanson Construction Ltd.** has a Handi-Van that can be hired for transport around town or to and from the airport. Mobility and accessibility may be more of a problem in the smaller communities.

The principal air carriers will also provide facilities and services both on and off the ground for passengers with special requirements. When booking, inform reservations agents of any special needs the traveller may have. Requirements can include special meals, wheelchairs, oxygen, and so on.

Travel with children is not especially difficult. People generally welcome children and are responsive to them. Parents should check ahead if they are worried about supplies for special needs and should carry a back-up supply of items like formula and baby food or any special medications. Items such as diapers and formula are expensive and often in short supply, as there are many babies in all Nunavut communities.

When travelling on the land with kids, apply common-sense rules and monitor the children closely. They may be too young to tell you that something is wrong. Dress them in layers, keep them dry, change wet diapers as soon as possible, take frequent breaks for warm drinks, and have them wear good quality sunglasses and sunscreen. Bring warm wraps, like caribou skins, blankets or sleeping bags, for kids to sit on or under. Keep them moving, watch for frostbite if it's really cold or windy, and at the first sign of hypothermia, take immediate action by wrapping the child inside a blanket or sleeping bag next to another warm body. Make sure footwear and clothing are not too tight because that will cut off circulation. If the expedition involves going near any body of water, bring a spare change of clothing. And bring lots of high-energy snacks (the highlight of many a child's field trip!).

18. VEHICLES
by Carol Rigby

Don't plan to drive much while you're in Nunavut. Unlike the western Arctic, Nunavut is no place to tour by car.

In the Baffin Region, the only road connecting two communities is a 21-kilometre section linking Arctic Bay and Nanisivik. Most Kitikmeot communities are scattered over islands and archipelagos. There are no direct land connections between the Kivalliq and Southern Canada, either. In some areas of the Kitikmeot, around communities such as Cambridge Bay, there's a network of roadways or tracks. People drive out of town along these roads to cottages and camps in outlying areas. Some communities have roads around town leading to local features of interest. Although there are a few stretches of pavement in towns like Iqaluit and Rankin Inlet, most roads are unpaved. To pave over permafrost is expensive and difficult.

Taxis

Many Nunavut communities offer taxi service. Taxis usually charge a flat rate per head, so more than one group can use the cab at the same time. Think of Nunavut taxis as stop-at-your-door buses. Don't be surprised if the driver pulls up at other destinations to pick up or drop off passengers before getting to your stop. Don't pass up a taxi just because you see a passenger inside. There may be only one or two taxis in town, so hop in, if there's room.

Snowmobiles and All-Terrain Vehicles (ATVs)

All Nunavut communities are small enough for you to explore easily on foot. Most local people walk around town and use snowmobiles or ATVs to go longer distances or to carry loads. Contact your travel agent or an outfitter if you'd like an excursion on the land by ATV or snowmobile. These vehicles should only be driven by experienced operators, however. ATVs are also hard on the environment. When travelling by snowmobile, never travel alone. If your machine breaks down, a second can take you back home. It's also wise to carry a spare motor belt, spark plugs, extra gas, food, camp stove, tarp or tent, and even a sleeping bag for a winter day trip. Always tell someone where you're going and how long you expect to be gone. For more important safety information, read "Adventure Travel," Chapter 11.

Nunavut Tourism can give you an up-to-date list of firms that rent ATVs and snowmobiles. Several companies operate in Iqaluit and Rankin Inlet, and a few in other communities, such as Resolute.

Drivers of ATVs are required by territorial law to wear helmets. In Nunavut, individual communities decide whether a helmet, driver's licence, insurance and the like are required for snowmobile drivers. Most communities don't require that helmets be worn, although Baker Lake, Gjoa Haven and Cape Dorset do. Check with the hamlet for its policy.

Car, Truck and Bus Rentals

In most communities in Nunavut, it's possible to rent an assortment of vehicles, and community chapters in the "Destinations" section of this book often list such companies in the "Services" section of their directory. Traffic in Nunavut's capital, in fact, has recently grown to the point where a couple of four-way stop signs were actually needed in the town. If you think you need a vehicle to drive around Iqaluit, R. L. Hanson Construction Ltd. and **Norwheels Enterprises** rent cars and vans, while **Toonoonik Hotel** rents trucks and vans. Rentals are about $80 per day. You can also rent a bus, with a driver, from R. L. Hanson in Iqaluit.

To rent a vehicle in Nunavut, you should have a Canadian provincial/territorial or an international driver's licence, which means first having a valid driver's licence from your home jurisdiction. Motor vehicles are driven on the right side of the road in Canada.

GETTING AROUND: DIRECTORY

Airlines Serving Nunavut

Adlair Aviation 83 Ltd.
Charter service.
Cambridge Bay office:
P.O. Box 111, Cambridge Bay NT,
X0E 0C0 Canada
Tel.: (867) 983-2569
Fax: (867) 983-2847

Yellowknife office:
P.O. Box 2946, Yellowknife NT,
X1A 2R3 Canada
Tel.: (867) 873-5161
Fax: (867) 873-8475

Flies charters anywhere in Nunavut but best known in the Kitikmeot. Operates Lear 258, King Air 100, Twin Otter and Beaver planes.

Air Inuit
Scheduled and charter services.
547 Meloche, Dorval QC,
H9P 2W2 Canada
Tel.: 1-800-361-5933 or (514) 636-9445
Fax: (514) 636-8916

Flies charters to Nunavut from La Grande Rivière, Povungnituk and Kuujjuaq with a Twin Otter and HS748. Flies into northern Quebec from Montreal with a Dash 8.

Air Nunavut
Charter service.
P.O. Box 1239, Iqaluit NT,
X0A 0H0 Canada
Tel.: (867) 979-4018
Fax: (867) 979-4318

Charter flights cover Nunavut, western Northwest Territories, northern Quebec and Greenland. Operates twin-engine Super King Air 200 and Piper Navajo airplanes.

Air Tindi
Charter service.
P.O. Box 1693, Yellowknife NT,
X1A 2P3 Canada
Tel.: (867) 669-8200
Fax: (867) 669-8210
E-mail: airtindi@ssimicro.com
Web site: www.ssimicro.com/~airtindi/

Flies charters anywhere in Nunavut with Husky, Cessna 185, Caravan, Beaver, Turbo Otter, Twin Otter, King Air 200, King Air 90 and Dash 7.

Aklak Air
Charter service.
General Delivery, Cambridge Bay NT,
X0E 0C0 Canada
Tel.: (867) 983-2415
Fax: (867) 983-2538
E-mail: aklakair@inuvialuit.com

Flies charters throughout Nunavut using Twin Otter aircraft.

Arctic Sunwest
Charter service.
P.O. Box 1807, Yellowknife NT,
X1A 2P4 Canada
Tel.: (867) 873-4464
Fax: (867) 873-9334

Flies charters anywhere in Nunavut with Beaver, Cessna 185 and Navajo Chieftain aircraft.

Calm Air
Scheduled and charter services.
Thompson office:
90 Thompson Dr., Thompson MB,
R8N 1Y8 Canada
Tel.: 1-800-839-2256 (from Nunavut only) or (204) 778-6471
Fax: (204) 778-6954
E-mail: calmair@gatewest.net
Web site: www.calmair.com

Rankin Inlet office:
P.O. Box 309, Rankin Inlet NT,
X0C 0G0 Canada
Tel.: (867) 645-2900
Fax: (867) 645-2191

Flies charters anywhere in Nunavut with three Saab 340Bplus, five HS748s, two Twin Otters and one Navajo Chieftain.

Canadian North
Scheduled service.
Tel.: (867) 669-4000
Fax: (867) 669-4040

First Air

Scheduled and charter services.
Head office:
3257 Carp Rd., Carp ON,
X0A 1L0 Canada

For charter information.
Iqaluit office:
P.O. Box 477, Iqaluit NT,
X0A 0H0 Canada
Tel.: (867) 979-5841
Fax: (867) 979-0746

Ottawa office:
Tel.: (613) 839-3340
Fax: (613) 839-5690
E-mail: reservat@firstair.ca
Web site: www.firstair.ca

Resolute office:
P.O. Box 150, Resolute NT,
X0A 0V0 Canada
Tel.: (867) 252-3981
Fax: (867) 252-3794

Yellowknife office:
P.O. Box 100, Yellowknife NT,
X1A 2N1 Canada
Tel.: (867) 669-6600
Fax: (867) 669-6603

Their charters, based in Yellowknife,
Resolute, Iqaluit and Ottawa, fly any-
where in Nunavut using Twin Otter,
King Air, Beaver, 727, 737, Gulf Stream,
Beech 99, Hercules Freighter, and
Hawker Siddeley 748 aircraft.

Keewatin Air

Charter service.
Head office:
15-20 Hangar Line Rd., Winnipeg MB,
R3J 3Y8 Canada
Tel.: (204) 888-0100
Fax: (204) 888-3300

Rankin Inlet office:
P.O. Box 38, Rankin Inlet NT,
X0C 0G0 Canada
Tel.: (867) 645-2992
Fax: (867) 645-2330

Churchill office:
P.O. Box 126, Churchill MB,
R0B 0E0 Canada
Tel.: (204) 675-2086
Fax: (204) 675-2250

Their charters fly anywhere in Nunavut
with twin-engine Merlins and King Air
B200 pressurized turbine aircraft, and
from Winnipeg, with LearJet 35A.

Kenn Borek Air

Scheduled and charter services.
Iqaluit office:
P.O. Box 1741, Iqaluit NT,
X0A 0H0 Canada
Tel.: (867) 979-0040
Fax: (867) 979-0132

Resolute office:
P.O. Box 210, Resolute NT,
X0A 0V0 Canada
Tel.: (867) 252-3845
Fax: (867) 252-3777

Flies charters anywhere in Nunavut
with a Twin Otter; operates a DC3, King
Air 300, King Air C90 and Beech 99 to
communities with airstrips.

NWT Air

See First Air (NWT Air was recently
purchased by First Air).

Skyward Aviation Ltd.

Scheduled and charter services.
P.O. Box 562, Rankin Inlet NT,
X0C 0G0 Canada
Tel.: 1-800-476-1873 or (867) 645-3200
Fax: (867) 645-3208
E-mail: skyward@arctic.ca

Based in Rankin Inlet, their charters
fly anywhere in Nunavut with a wide
range of single and multi-engine
aircraft.

Recreational Flying

CANPASS
Tel.: 1-888-226-7277

**Canadian Owners and
Pilots Association**
Web site: www.copanational.org/

Flight Service Stations
Iqaluit:
Tel.: (867) 979-5865
Fax: (867) 979-2945

Site Manager:
Tel.: (867) 979-5247
Fax: (867) 979-4205

For information on flight service
stations in other Nunavut communities:
Tel.: 1-800-667-4636

Infonorth.org
Check community profiles for detailed
descriptions of runways, airport
facilities, etc. in Nunavut.
Web site: www.infonorth.org/

Nav Canada
For weather briefings and other info.
Web site: www.navcanada.ca/

Polar Pilots
Web site: www.nunanet.com/~tbert/
polar_pilots.html

Transport Canada
Tel.: (613) 990-2309
Fax: (613) 954-4731
Web site: www.tc.gc.ca/aviation/

Also see www.tc.gc.ca/PacificRegion/
services/aviation for its "Frequently
Asked Questions" section.

Travel Agencies

**See the directory at the end of the
"Planning Ahead" section.**

Travel Programs and Services

Elderhostel Canada
4 Cataraqui St., Kingston ON,
K7K 1Z7 Canada
Tel.: (613) 530-2222
Fax: (613) 530-2096
E-mail: ecmail@elderhostel.org
Web site: www.elderhostel.org/

Nunavut Tourism
P.O. Box 1450, Iqaluit NT,
X0A 0H0 Canada
Tel.: 1-800-491-7910
(for Canada and the United States)
Tel.: (867) 979-6551
Fax: (867) 979-1261
E-mail: nunatour@nunanet.com
Web site: www.nunatour.nt.ca

Vehicle Rentals

Norwheels Enterprises
Tel.: (867) 979-0000 or (867) 979-6631
Fax: (867) 979-5804

R. L. Hanson Construction Ltd.
Tel.: (867) 979-6004
Fax: (867) 979-4873
E-mail: rlhanson@nunanet.com

Toonoonik Hotel
Tel.: (867) 979-6733
Fax: (867) 979-4210

The People

19. ARCHEOLOGY
by Sue Rowley

The cold, dry arctic climate of Nunavut often makes it a difficult place to live.

In fact, the Arctic was the last habitable region in the world to be occupied by people. However, this environment also makes Nunavut an archeologist's dream. Unlike most areas, where the remains of human occupation (sites) are quickly covered by vegetation and soil, in Nunavut they are often visible right on the surface. Also, because of the cold, dry climate, tools of antler, ivory and bone can be remarkably well preserved.

As you explore, please remember that these sites and artifacts are part of Nunavut's cultural heritage. They are fragile and irreplaceable. Nothing must be moved. Under the Nunavut Land Claims Agreement, every archeological artifact is owned jointly by the Inuit Heritage Trust (for the people of Nunavut) and by the government of Canada (for the people of Canada). It is illegal to buy, sell or remove archeological artifacts. For information about reporting undiscovered archeological sites, please see Chapter 11, "Adventure Travel."

Research indicates Nunavut has been occupied continuously for more than 4,000 years (small pockets of the Kivalliq Region were occupied sporadically by Indian groups beginning 8,000 years ago). Archeologists divide Nunavut's inhabitants into two distinct but physically related groups: the Paleoeskimo people from at least 4,000 to 700 years ago; and the Neoeskimo people who entered Nunavut some 1,000 years ago.

The Paleoeskimo People

The Paleoeskimos emigrated from the west (Alaska) in small groups consisting of only a few families. Archeologists separate these original migrants into two groups: Pre-Dorset (in southern Nunavut) and Independence I (in northern Nunavut).

Pre-Dorset/Independence I people probably lived year-round in skin tents. Single-walled in summer, in winter the walls were most likely doubled. A layer of heather or willow may have been placed between the skin layers and an exterior layer of snow added for extra insulation. Fires provided heat and soapstone oil lamps gave light.

These people wore skin clothing and made tools from bones, antlers, ivory, skins and rocks. They travelled mostly by foot, although they did have a few dogs and a small single-person boat similar to a *qajaq* (kayak). All animals except the massive bowhead whales were hunted.

Through time, the Paleoeskimo people adapted to minor fluctuations in climate, ice conditions, and resource availability. Then, around 2,700 years ago, the Nunavut climate became significantly cooler and the Paleoeskimo lifestyle underwent a period of rapid transition. The changes that occurred were so dramatic, archeologists refer to these people by a different name: the Dorset culture.

At the beginning of the Dorset period, several useful items of technology mysteriously disappeared, including the bow and arrow and the bowdrill. Dogs also disappeared.

New tools appeared, hunting techniques were modified and dwelling forms changed. Archeologists suggest that snowhouses were first built by the Dorset people, as the earliest known snow knives are found in sites from this time period. The Dorset people also had a rich artistic tradition, carving miniature artistic masterpieces from ivory and antler for ceremonial and decorative use.

Despite the lack of dogs and little evidence they used large boats, the Dorset people travelled and traded materials over long distances. Copper from the Kugluktuk area and meteoric iron from northern Greenland have been recovered from Late Dorset sites in eastern Nunavut.

The Neoeskimos

About 1,000 years ago, life again changed dramatically in Nunavut, this time when the climate grew warmer and a new group of people emigrated from northern Alaska. These people were bowhead whale hunters. They had large *umiat* (skin-covered boats capable of carrying several families) and *qamutiit* (sleds) pulled by dogteams. They could cover distances at speeds unimaginable to Dorset people. Archeologists refer to these migrants as the Thule, the first of two Neoeskimo subgroups. The second subgroup is referred to as the Historic Inuit.

There is little archeological evidence of contact between the Dorset people and the Thule people. However, Inuit oral history identifies the *Tuniit* or *Tunirjuat* as the people who occupied Nunavut before their own ancestors, the Thule, arrived. The *Tuniit* were regarded as a peaceful and shy people distrustful of the new arrivals. Although there were intermarriages between the two groups, there were also fights, and the *Tuniit* removed themselves from areas occupied by the Thule. Sightings of the *Tuniit* became rarer and eventually they disappeared.

The Thule migrants brought a highly structured society with them based on the leadership of the whaleboat captain. With time, their dependence on bowheads decreased. They adapted to regional variations in resource availability and modified their social organization accordingly. Some moved into the interior of the Kivalliq Region, becoming largely dependent on caribou. Others lived on the coast, hunting mostly marine mammals.

The Neoeskimo lifestyle was forever altered by the arrival of European explorers, traders, and whalers. The Historic Inuit period began with the voyages of Martin Frobisher to Baffin Island in the 1570s. Sporadic contact after this time period had little impact on Inuit culture. Then, in the 1820s, Europeans and Americans began whaling in eastern Nunavut. This whaling depleted bowhead stocks, concentrated Inuit into areas around whalers, and introduced both devastating diseases and new materials to Inuit society. This is the beginning of the modern period, a time marked by many rapid changes in material culture, religion, and social organization.

Archeological Sites

Nunavut is rife with evidence of human occupation, although many of these structures are difficult to date. Some of the most common features are *inuksuit* (rock cairns). These had many functions. The one on the horizon may be a route marker between two camping spots. Another by the side of the lake indicates where to find fish. A lone, long rock marks a nearby food cache. A row of *inuksuit* was used for driving caribou towards a river crossing or towards a group of hiding hunters.

Look closely at that pile of rocks at your feet. Is there a black stain on the rocks? Is there lichen growing on them? Are animal bones visible? If so, then this pile of rocks may be an old cache where hunters stored food.

On high ground you may come across rock graves. The deceased's belongings were often placed on or nearby the grave. Resist the temptation to touch these objects. Please treat graves with special respect.

You may also notice small rock boxes, *pullatit*, that were used to trap foxes. The fox entered the trap to retrieve the bait and a rock or piece of ice dropped, blocking the entrance. Strange rock formations that look like stone igloos are *ullisautit*, tower fox traps. Bait was placed atop the trap and the fox would fall inside. Very large tower traps were even used for hunting polar bears.

Camp Sites

Camp sites are the places where people lived. By careful observation you can begin to determine both the time period and the season of occupation. In addition to the remains of homes, you may also see caches, outdoor fire-places, box traps and *inuksuit*. Boys sat in rock outlines of *qajait* (kayaks) pretending to paddle and hunt. Girls built models of snowhouses and tents out of rocks to play house. There are many other interesting features to discover.

Both summer and winter Paleoeskimo camp sites consist of tent rings. The earliest Paleoeskimo dwellings were oval. Later Dorset dwellings vary in outline, but were frequently oval or rectangular. Oftentimes, all that remains of a Paleoeskimo dwelling are a few rocks, a small vegetated patch, or a slight depression along a beach ridge.

In contrast, Neoeskimo camp sites are more varied. Camps occupied in summer contain circular and oval tent rings. These are often bisected by a line of rocks separating the living area from the sleeping area.

Late fall/winter camps were often large. Today these sites are characterized by areas of lush vegetation and what appear at first to be large mounds. These mounds are actually semi-subterranean houses, constructed of whalebones, rocks and sod. Inside are sleeping platforms elevated for warmth. A layer of gravel, and then a mattress of heather, willow, or moss topped by heavy skins were placed on these platforms to provide insulation from both cold and rising damp. People slept on these beds in caribou-skin sleeping bags. Soapstone lamps provided heat and light. When occupied, these houses were roofed with a skin cover supported by whalebone rafters. Sometimes heather or willow was sandwiched between two skin covers as insulation. The roof was held in place with rocks, sod and snow.

In winter and early spring, many Thule and Historic Inuit lived in snowhouses. Most were built on the sea ice, but some were constructed on land, and these can sometimes be identified. Snowhouse dwellers often threw the remains of their meals and the burnt blubber from their lamps just outside the door. This detritus left a semicircle of bones and blubber-blackened ground — all that is left of the long since melted snowhouse.

20. HISTORY
by Kenn Harper

In 1999, Canada's newest territory becomes a reality. Yet it already has a history, rich and colorful.

It is the history of the Inuit who originally inhabited this land, by turns rich and sparse, and of the *qallunaat* who arrived in their changing quests — for a sea route westward, for whales, for furs and other natural resources, and finally, to stay. It is a history of culture contact and cultural conflict. It is the history of the three regions of Nunavut.

Baffin Region

Historians identify the Baffin coast with Helluland of the Norse sagas, and there may have been sporadic contacts between Norse and Inuit. But the recorded history of Baffin Island began in 1576 when Martin Frobisher, on an expedition in search of a Northwest Passage, discovered what he thought was gold in the bay that bears his name. The ore was worthless and Frobisher's encounters with the Inuit were not friendly. He seized four Inuit in 1576 and 1577 and took them to England where they quickly died. In 1585, John Davis, also in search of the Northwest Passage, explored Cumberland Sound; unlike Frobisher, his relations with Inuit were cordial.

Henry Hudson, in 1610, followed the south coast of Baffin Island into Hudson Bay, and five years later, William Baffin and Robert Bylot mapped that coast. But Baffin Island itself was, at best, only a landmark and, at worst, an obstacle in the path of those searching for a Northwest Passage. Its coastline remained largely unexplored.

In 1616, Baffin and Bylot sailed north as far as Smith Sound and discovered the entrances to Lancaster and Jones sounds. Returning south, they mapped a good deal of the Baffin coast, but after this voyage, northern Baffin Island was ignored for two centuries.

In the early 19th century, the search for a Northwest Passage came in vogue again. John Ross entered Lancaster Sound in 1818 and concluded erroneously that it was a bay rather than a strait. The next year his second in command, Lieutenant William Edward Parry, travelled through Lancaster Sound; the following summer he discovered the entrances to Admiralty and Navy Board inlets. In 1821, under Admiralty orders, Parry passed two winters exploring and mapping the Igloolik area, and established good relations with the Inuit.

In 1845, John Franklin, commanding a large expedition in search of the passage, sailed through Lancaster Sound and into oblivion. His failure to return ushered in a new era in Arctic exploration, that of the Franklin searches. It lasted until 1880 but, again, explorers generally considered Baffin Island an obstacle. One notable exception was Charles Francis Hall, who explored Frobisher Bay from 1860 to 1862. Hall was one of the first to use Inuit clothing and travel methods. His Inuit friends, Tookoolito and her husband Ebierbing, accompanied him as interpreters and assistants for over a decade.

While the Franklin searches were under way, the last migration of Inuit from Canada to Greenland was also taking place. The shaman Qillaq (known later in Greenland as Qitdlarssuaq) led a group of Inuit from the Pond Inlet area to northwestern Greenland in the 1850s and 1860s, in search of new land and perhaps to avoid retribution for murders he had committed. Descendants of this group live there today.

British whalers reached northern Baffin Island by 1817, in their hunt for the bowhead whale, prized for its oil and baleen, which was used in corset stays, buggy whips, and other products requiring elasticity and flexibility. In 1840, William Penny, a whaling master from Peterhead, Scotland, with the help of a young Inuk, Eenoolooapik, rediscovered the entrance to Cumberland Sound, lost since Davis last entered it over two centuries earlier; it proved to be rich in bowhead whales. Its rediscovery marked a turning point in Baffin Island whaling. Whalers began wintering in Cumberland Sound in the 1850s to get an early start on whaling the following spring. American and Scottish companies established shore stations at Kekerten Island on the north shore of the sound and at Blacklead Island on its southern coast. The Americans sold their stations to the Scots in 1894, the same year that Reverend Edmund Peck established an Anglican mission at Blacklead. The mission remained open until 1926, by which time whaling had ended. A shore whaling station was also established by Scots at Albert Harbour near Pond Inlet in 1903. Everywhere, whaling had a profound impact on Inuit; it changed settlement patterns and provided Inuit with metal, tools, guns and whaleboats.

By the turn of the century, bowhead whale stocks were severely depleted and whaling had evolved into what was known as free trading. Small trading companies, all British, bartered with Inuit from shore stations or ships that called in summer. From 1900 until 1913, a Dundee company also operated a mica mine near Lake Harbour (now Kimmirut). In 1912, three expeditions, two Canadian and one from Newfoundland (then not part of Canada), visited Pond Inlet in search of gold. Each party subsequently returned to open a trading post. The Sabellum Company operated sporadically in southern Baffin from 1911 until 1926, using native traders and a small ship that arrived from Scotland in the summers. The only white employee of the company, Hector Pitchforth, died in 1924 at his lonely post near Clyde River.

Scientific research played a major role in Baffin history. In 1882–83, a German meteorological expedition overwintered at Sermilik Bay in Cumberland Sound as part of the International Polar Year. The following year, the pioneer geographer and ethnographer, Franz Boas, passed one winter in the sound; the extensive report that he published, *The Central Eskimo*, was the first major ethnographic study of Canadian Inuit. In 1909, Bernhard Hantzsch, an ornithologist, travelled with Inuit to Foxe Basin, where he died in 1911, probably of trichinosis. The geologist, prospector and filmmaker, Robert Flaherty, overwintered at Amadjuak Bay in 1913–14. (His film, *Nanook of the North*, made in northern Quebec, is an ethnographic classic.) Between 1921 and 1924, Knud Rasmussen and his Fifth Thule Expedition conducted ethnographic research in the Igloolik area, and Peter Freuchen and Therkel Mathiassen explored much of northern Baffin Island, Freuchen accompanied by the Greenlander Nasaitdlorssuarssuk and the Baffinlander Mala. Inland southern Baffin Island was explored and mapped by Burwash, Soper, Weeks and Haycock in the 1920s. Between 1936 and 1940, the British-Canadian Arctic Expedition completed most of the geographical investigation of Foxe Basin.

The Arctic Islands had been transferred from Britain to Canada in 1880, but it was not until 1897, when William Wakeham erected a cairn at Kekerten, that Canada took any active interest in exerting its sovereignty. In 1903, an official expedition under A. P. Low visited the High Arctic and Cumberland Sound. Between 1906 and 1911, the Canadian government dispatched Joseph Bernier on three official voyages to the High Arctic, to show the flag and collect Customs duties from whalers.

Canada became increasingly concerned over the activities of foreigners in the High Arctic — the Norwegian Sverdrup from 1898 to 1902, Robert Peary on his many attempts on the North Pole, Donald MacMillan's Crocker Land Expedition, and Rasmussen's interest in the Arctic Islands. Its response to these perceived threats was to establish Royal Canadian Mounted Police posts in the High Arctic. Pond Inlet was opened in 1921, and Craig Harbour on Ellesmere Island the following year. Dundas Harbour opened in 1924, Bache Peninsula in 1926, and Lake Harbour in 1927.

The Hudson's Bay Co. established its first post on Baffin Island at Lake Harbour in 1911. Cape Dorset was opened in 1913, Pangnirtung and Pond Inlet in 1921, Clyde River two years later and Arctic Bay in 1926. The Bay provided a more reliable supply of goods to hunters than had the earlier free traders, whom they displaced. The Bay trade was for fox pelts, later shifting to sealskins. In recent years, since the decline in the sealskin market, the trading posts have been transformed into modern department stores.

The Second World War and the Cold War that followed it forcibly opened the Canadian Arctic. The United States Air Force built an airfield at Frobisher Bay (now Iqaluit) during the war to handle aircraft transporting war materials to Europe. In 1955, construction began on the Distant Early Warning (DEW) Line, a joint project of Canada and the United States to create an early-warning radar chain across the Arctic to warn of any Soviet incursions. With this, Iqaluit became the supply and administrative centre for the Baffin Region. A weather station was established at Resolute in 1947, and in the early 1950s, Inuit were relocated from northern Quebec to Resolute and Grise Fiord. In the late 1950s and the 1960s, federal schools were built in most communities. A mammoth housing program was undertaken in the mid-1960s, and Inuit in general abandoned traditional camp life as a permanent lifestyle.

Keewatin Region

In 1610, in search of a Northwest Passage, Henry Hudson explored what others had thought was a gulf between Baffin Island and Labrador. Following its shores, Hudson reached the great inland sea that bears his name. Other explorers followed, and the Hudson's Bay Co. established a fur trading post at Churchill in 1717 to open trade with Indians farther west. Inevitably, this led to contact with Inuit in the Keewatin.

In 1719, James Knight's expedition in search of the elusive Northwest Passage disappeared north of Churchill. Nothing was known of its fate for almost 50 years, until the remains of a house and two ships were found at Marble Island, near Rankin Inlet. The crew had perished of scurvy and starvation, despite the efforts of local Inuit to keep them alive.

As in Baffin, so in Keewatin, the whaling industry had a major impact on the lives of Inuit in the mid-19th century, attracting many to live near the whaling stations, providing trade goods which made life easier, but also introducing diseases to which the Inuit had no immunity. The first whalers to visit Hudson Bay wintered at Depot Island in 1860, losing many men to scurvy, but securing a fortune in baleen. In the remainder of that decade, over 40 American whaling voyages went to the Keewatin coast. The three most popular wintering sites for whalers were Repulse Bay, Depot Island and Cape Fullerton, and Marble Island, a place of legendary importance to the Inuit; when they visit they crawl the first few feet onto the island out of respect for an old woman whose spirit is said to reside there.

After 1870, the industry declined rapidly. As elsewhere, the whalers diversified into trading for "scraps" — whaler jargon for furs, skins, and ivory — and even mining. Scholars estimate that there were 146 whaling voyages to Hudson Bay between 1860 and 1915; 105 of these voyages overwintered, trading with and employing Inuit. Between 1899 and 1903, a Dundee firm operated a shore station on Southampton Island, manned by three Scots and Inuit relocated from Baffin Island. In 1903, the company sent its vessel, the *Ernest William*, to Repulse Bay, where it acted as a floating station until 1910. The decline of whaling quickened after the turn of the century; the last whaler into Hudson Bay, the *A. T. Gifford*, burned and was lost with its entire crew in 1915.

The most famous American whaling captain in Hudson Bay was George Comer, who made six whaling and trading voyages there. Aside from running profitable trips, Comer was an untrained scientist who, under the tutelage of the anthropologist Boas, made important contributions in anthropology, natural history, cartography and exploration.

While whaling activities dominated the Keewatin coast, other forces were at work in the interior. In 1893, Joseph and James Tyrrell, employed by the Geological Survey of Canada to survey the Keewatin interior, travelled from Lake Athabasca to the Dubawnt River, and from there to Chesterfield Inlet and along the coast to Churchill. The following year, Joseph Tyrrell explored and mapped more of the southern interior of the Keewatin.

In 1899, the naturalist David Hanbury travelled from Churchill north to Chesterfield Inlet and via Baker Lake to Great Slave Lake, making important contributions in geology, anthropology and natural history. The following year, James W. Tyrrell explored some of the same area. In 1901, Hanbury made an epic journey, from Great Slave Lake to Chesterfield Inlet and Marble Island, returning to Baker Lake to winter with Inuit. The next spring, he travelled to the mouth of the Coppermine River, where he sought information from the Inuit on copper deposits. He made contributions in geology, natural history, meteorology and anthropology.

In 1903, the Canadian government, concerned about Canadian sovereignty and the unchecked activities of whalers in Hudson Bay, established the first Arctic detachment of the Royal Canadian Mounted

Police at Fullerton Harbour, north of Chesterfield Inlet, intending to gradually enforce Canadian laws and exert "supervision and control."

In the forested areas to the south, the Hudson's Bay Co. faced increased competition from rival traders. So, after 1912, the company made a concerted effort to move north and promote white fox trapping among the Inuit. They opened a post at Chesterfield Inlet in 1912 and an inland post at Ennadai shortly thereafter. In 1916, a post was opened on the south side of Baker Lake and another one at Repulse Bay, at Arviat (then known as Eskimo Point) in 1921, and at Southampton Island in 1924.

Father Arsène Turquetil, an Oblate priest, established a Roman Catholic mission at Chesterfield Inlet in 1912. From there, Catholicism spread to Eskimo Point, Southampton Island, Baker Lake, and even to Baffin Island. The RCMP relocated its Fullerton post to Chesterfield Inlet in 1922. A doctor was resident there by 1929, and the Oblates built a hospital and established a Grey Nuns convent in 1931 and an old folk's home in 1938. In 1951, they built the first school in the eastern Arctic; from 1954 until 1969, they also operated a large residential school. In 1970, the present government of the Northwest Territories assumed responsibility for education; by that time most communities had their own schools. That, combined with the rise in importance of Rankin Inlet, contributed to the decline of Chesterfield Inlet.

The Anglican Church also established missions in the region. Luke Kidlapik, a catechist from Blacklead Island, started a mission at Coral Harbour, and Donald Marsh established one at Eskimo Point in 1926, two years after the Roman Catholics had established there. Both churches were established in Baker Lake in 1927.

Knud Rasmussen's Fifth Thule Expedition, in the region in the early 1920s, was of profound importance to our understanding of traditional Inuit culture. Pioneering studies in ethnology, archeology, linguistics, botany and zoology were conducted in the Keewatin and other regions. Rasmussen's and Kaj Birket-Smith's monographs on the culture of the Caribou Eskimos are classics of modern anthropology.

In 1955, a nickel mine was developed at Rankin Inlet, an area previously of little importance and never a major site of Inuit occupancy. North Rankin Nickel Mines operated until 1962 and became a major employer of Inuit, resulting in the most major population shift since the whaling days. In 1958, at the height of the mining operation, the federal government established a settlement at Itivia, half a mile from the mine, as a rehabilitation project for Inuit from the interior, whose living conditions had deteriorated with major shifts in caribou migration patterns. In the 1970s, the government of the Northwest Territories moved its administration offices out of Churchill and made Rankin Inlet the administrative centre of the Keewatin Region, a role it holds to this day.

Kitikmeot Region

In 1770 and 1771, Samuel Hearne, with a Chipewyan guide, Matonabbee, travelled overland from Churchill to the Coppermine River, becoming the first white man to reach the Arctic Ocean. To his horror, his Indian companions massacred a group of Inuit, their traditional enemy, near the mouth of the Coppermine River at the site known since as Bloody Falls. Hearne's amazing trek proved that no Northwest Passage would be found from the low latitudes of Hudson Bay.

The Arctic coast was mapped between 1819 and 1846. Franklin mapped 900 kilometres of coastline east from the Coppermine River to Coronation Gulf; in 1826, Dr. John Richardson mapped from the Mackenzie River to the mouth of the Coppermine. The British government's objectives were to promote geographical exploration, scientific research, and to confirm its territorial claims. Mapping was continued by George Back in 1834, by Thomas Simpson and Peter Warren Dease from 1836 to 1839, and finally by Dr. John Rae in 1845–46.

Important sea expeditions were also carried out. In 1819, Parry sailed through Lancaster Sound to Melville Island where he wintered. Ten years later Captain John Ross, in the *Victory,* became icebound in Prince Regent Inlet and remained there for three years. He and his crew got on well with local Inuit who hunted with them, supplied them with food and taught them Inuit travel techniques.

In 1846, the ships of the Franklin Expedition got caught in the ice northwest of King William Island. The crews abandoned the ships after 18 months and made a futile effort to reach the South; all 105 men died of starvation and scurvy. Beginning in 1847, numerous search expeditions visited the Arctic, producing a wealth of information on the area. In 1854, John Rae, having heard Inuit tell stories of the expedition's fate, took the news back to England. Countless books have been written on the Franklin story and the subsequent searches, and the fate of Franklin has passed into northern mythology.

In 1903, the Norwegian, Roald Amundsen, seeking to locate the North Magnetic Pole, passed two winters on King William Island in the harbor that he named Gjoa Haven after his vessel. The *Gjoa* reached Nome, Alaska, in 1906, becoming the first ship to complete the Northwest Passage.

The westernmost reaches of Nunavut were the last to be explored by non-Inuit. Whalers based at Herschel Island gradually extended their whaling grounds east, and one, a Dane named Christian Klengenberg, passed the winter of 1905–6 trading off Victoria Island. Between 1908 and 1912, Vilhjalmur Stefansson, intrigued by Klengenberg's stories of fair-complexioned Inuit on Victoria Island (later sensationalized by newspapers as the "Blond Eskimos"), explored in the area. In 1913–18, Stefansson returned to Coronation Gulf and Victoria Island with a large multi-disciplinary scientific party on the Canadian Arctic Expedition. A New Zealand-born anthropologist, Diamond Jenness, accompanied this expedition and in 1922 produced a classic of northern ethnographic literature, *The Life of the Copper Eskimos,* which many scholars considered the best description of a single Inuit group.

Independent fur traders wasted no time in establishing posts in the central Arctic. Christian Klengenberg established a post near the mouth of the Coppermine River in 1916 and, in 1919, another one on Victoria Island. In 1920, he wintered his schooner at Bathurst Inlet. His descendants today live in Kugluktuk (Coppermine) and Holman Island. Other traders gradually moved into the area overland from Great Bear Lake, and were soon followed by geologists and trappers.

In November of 1913, two Oblate priests, Jean-Baptiste Rouvière and Guillaume LeRoux, were murdered by Inuit near Coppermine. The crime, caused by misunderstanding on the part of the Inuit and insensitivity on the part of the priests, was investigated and two Inuit were taken to Edmonton in 1917 for trial. They were sentenced to life imprisonment at Fort Resolution, but were released in 1919. An inevitable result of this case was the establishment of new police posts and the undertaking of regular patrols in the region.

The Hudson's Bay Co. opened a post at Bernard Harbour in 1916, Cambridge Bay in 1921, and King William Island in 1923. The Coppermine post was established in 1927 and Bathurst Inlet in 1934. The latter closed in 1964 and the buildings are now a naturalist's tourist lodge. Pelly Bay is the only place in the region where the Hudson's Bay Co. never established a post. In 1935, Father Pierre Henry built a famous stone church there. The community remained very isolated until 1961, when a school was built.

As elsewhere, missionaries arrived at about the same time as the traders. An Anglican mission was established in Coppermine in 1928, and both Anglicans and Roman Catholics built churches in Cambridge Bay in the 1920s.

Knud Rasmussen of the Fifth Thule Expedition travelled through the area in 1923 and 1924 with his Greenlandic assistants, Miteq and Arnarulunnguaq. Rasmussen produced detailed ethnographic monographs on the *Netsilik* and Copper Eskimos.

Spence Bay (now Taloyoak) has a curious history. In 1934, the Hudson's Bay Co. moved Inuit from Cape Dorset, Pangnirtung and Pond Inlet to Dundas Harbour on Devon Island to trap foxes. Two years later, the post was abandoned and the Inuit were moved to Arctic Bay, and from there to Fort Ross. That post proved difficult to resupply because of ice conditions, and in 1947 it closed. Most of the Inuit relocated to Spence Bay.

As elsewhere in the Arctic, Inuit largely abandoned camp life and moved into communities in the 1960s in conjunction with government housing programs and the construction of schools. In 1981, the territorial government designated Cambridge Bay as the regional administrative centre, and the community has grown steadily since.

Toward Nunavut

In this decade, the Nunavut land claim has been settled and the *Nunavut Act*, proclaiming the advent of the new territory of Nunavut, passed. Inuit are a majority in their homeland. Today Inuit and *qallunaat* approach the millennium determined to create a vibrant new territory, aware of both its past and the promise of its future.

21. INUIT CULTURE

An age-old hunting and trapping lifestyle has created a culture among Inuit that is largely shared throughout the central and eastern Arctic, although regional differences sometimes exist. Here, three Inuit writers who hail from different corners of Nunavut describe their culture.

The Baffin Region
by Ann Meekitjuk Hanson

Inuit "culture" and Inuit "ways" are difficult to distinguish because we don't have different words for them in our language. We use the word *iliqqusiq* to mean "ways and habits." *Iliqqusiq* includes all aspects of the Inuit way of life: survival skills, games, clothing, arts, medicine, the language, weather, the land, the sea, the way people are brought up — in short, life itself. In English, when I see the word "culture," I think of piano, ballet, opera, dance, poetry, theatre and anything that involves entertainment. I use the word *isumainaqijjutiit* to describe this kind of "culture" because it means "things to make us relax when chores have been completed." I use the word *suiilaqijutiit* to describe culture in the sense of "making fun."

Cultural Change

Cultures change with the times and Inuit culture is no exception. My grandmother, Koovianatukulook, and grandfather, Makivik, grew up in southern Baffin Island. In their time they enjoyed strength games, wrestling contests, throat singing, drum dances, storytelling, and even learning Scottish dances. In the winter, the games and celebrations took place in a *qaggiq* (a giant snowhouse); in summer, they were held outdoors. The songs were created specially for different occasions and were verbally "copyrighted"; no one was allowed to use them unless they were properly introduced and rightfully credited to their creator. The songs could be about anything: hunting experiences, humorous times, starvation, children, poems, mythical beings, or predictions of the future.

Pauta Saila, a well-known artist, statesman and elder from Cape Dorset, once shared the following prediction song created by a shaman named Atsiluaq. According to Pauta, Atsiluaq was alive "when the world was new." Atsiluaq, along with Enusiarajuk (another famous Inuk), were young men several generations before the *qallunaat* ("white people") came to the North. At a huge gathering in a *qaggiq*, Atsiluaq took the drum and began to sway back and forth, beating the circular instrument with a thick, rounded baton. He closed his eyes and continued to beat the drum to and fro. His feet firmly on the hardened snow floor, he was getting used to the rhythm. Finally, he was attuned to the movements of the drum and baton as if they were no longer controlled by him. He began his new song:

Atsiluaq
Angakunirataugajappuq
   Hoooo… Hoooo… Hoooo… Hoooo… Hoooo…

Kananiilak, kingaaluni
Saangani kanani
Takujauppat
Qallunaattaapik
Aupaluttaapik
Atsiluarli
Angakunirataugajappuq
   Hoooo... Hoooo... Hoooo... Hoooo... Hoooo...

When he finished the song, there was silence in the crowded dome; the people were in absolute disbelief. By this time Atsiluaq was steaming and bare from the waist up. There was a new word in the song that the people had not heard before; it was *qallunaat*. When he sensed the people's disbelief, he sang the song again and again:

Atsiluaq, this man
He would be called a great shaman
   Hoooo... Hoooo... Hoooo... Hoooo... Hoooo...
There, over there
The high mountain
In the front, over there
You will see
A lovely cloth
A lovely red shade
Atsiluaq, this man
He would be called a great shaman
   Hoooo... Hoooo... Hoooo... Hoooo... Hoooo...

Atsiluaq was one of the last well-known shamans who saw into the future. He saw this lovely red cloth fluttering in the wind. He was telling his people that the *qallunaat* were coming and they will fly a flag that contains red shades. The Hudson's Bay Co. flag and the Canadian flag both contain red colors. Atsiluaq was right. Today, with proper credit to Atsiluaq, people sing the song that predicted the coming of the lovely red cloth!

In my mother and father Josie and Meekitjuk's time, there were hardly any celebrations or rituals because the Inuit way of life was entering a new era. My mother and father were learning the new dances and music that came from Scotland. The Scottish and American whalers introduced a new type of culture that would live side by side with our Inuit ways. My mother and many others learned to play lively tunes on the "squeeze-box" (accordion). They also learned dances that involved many people, unlike the Inuit drum dance, which is done by one person in the middle.

Our leaders created new steps according to the music. One dance practised today imitates harp seals. It is a wonderful dance to see because it is so much like the way the harp seals actually move. Some of the dances have been named after their creators. Each community has a favorite dance. A dance can last at least an hour and an evening of dancing can extend well into the early morning hours. The squeeze-box musicians are revered for their talent, endurance, and their ability to play without repeating a tune all night. In some communities our young people are trained to dance for audiences. They wear traditional costumes as part of their performance, and as a symbol of their pride.

Storytelling is a most important element in our culture because it saves and enriches our language. The stories are often accompanied by a song that describes events and helps explain the purpose of the story. The story of Kaujajuk, an orphan boy who was badly mistreated, is a good example. Kaujajuk slept among the dogs on the porch to keep warm.

He sang this song as he nestled by his dogs and looked at the moon:

Moon, up there
My brotherlike, up there
You give me a little bit of warmth,
The window has become bright,
Moon up there, you are the only source of light,
I am trying to dry my clothes,
It is unlikely, it is hopeless, it will not...

The moon was like a brother to Kaujajuk. He gained his strength from it. A man from the moon came down and made Kaujajuk very strong. The man whipped him until he grew and grew. Although the song sounds bleak and hopeless, Kaujajuk becomes a very strong and powerful man. There was one woman in the village who showed a little bit of kindness and he saves her to be his wife. This is just a synopsis of the legend; the full story of Kaujajuk is very long with a lot of adventure, and mythical beings, and more songs. We have kept these kinds of stories alive by encouraging our elders to keep telling them. They are told on the radio and television, in schools, and lately our writers have been documenting them in their books.

Baffin Island is brimming with talented people who keep our culture alive by singing, carving, drawing, writing, producing radio and television programs, and by just being here.

Cultural events have been making a strong comeback recently. They help us mark important occasions with prominence and they satisfy our need for relevance in our homeland.

Food

Food is the connector to everything that surrounds our culture. Each celebration includes a huge feast. We believe food tastes better when it is shared with family, relatives, and many other people. In my grandfather Makivik's time, all types of food were cached on the land, ready for a celebration. Back then there were many ways to prepare the foods, including different types of sauces and dips. I know of three sauces that are very good: *aalu*, *misiraq*, and *nirukkaq*.

Aalu is made from choice parts of caribou or seal. Here is the recipe. Make sure the meat is very lean and clean. Cut it up in tiny pieces and put it in a bowl. Add a few drops of melted fat. Then add a few drops of blood. Add *uruniq* (ptarmigan intestine) to taste. Stir everything very friskily with your fingers until the volume doubles and the mixture turns fluffy. This is one of the most popular dips for all kinds of meat.

Misiraq is another dip that is made all over the North today. It is made from blubber. Cut up pieces of seal blubber, whale, or *ujjuk* (square flipper seal), making sure not to include any meat. Put the blubber in a safe container with a perforated top — for example, an old coffee tin container. Don't use plastic bags or containers with airtight lids. Store it in a cool place where it can be slowly aged away from heat. When it ages properly the liquid ends up clear, like a fine white wine. The aroma is delicious and never bitter. (If it smells bad, throw it out! The offensive smell means it hasn't aged properly.) All kinds of meats can be dipped in *misiraq*.

The third dip is called *nirukkaq*. It requires special care. *Nirukkaq* is the contents of caribou stomach. Here is my Uncle Annowalk's recipe. The hunter, when butchering the caribou, carefully removes the stomach contents and puts them into a container. The contents are frozen until ready to be used. When the time comes, the contents are thawed and a process called *siingijaijuq* is begun. This involves cleaning the contents very carefully with kneading motions. Undesirables like pieces of grass, leaves, lichen or lumps are removed. When smooth, it is ready. Caribou meat is used for dipping.

Our food is much more than just frozen or raw meats and sauces. We also enjoy different types of dried fish and meats, such as caribou. A traditional caribou stew made on the land using blackberry bush also makes a delicious meal that has a woody taste and a very refreshing smell. We have also developed recipes for caribou and fish dishes prepared the "new" way with spices.

When we feast on a seal we follow the traditions of our ancestors. One particular feast is called *alupajaq*. The men are around the seal, and two or three of them cut up the animal in a particular way. The women are grouped together in another area several feet away. The men's conversation is audible to the women. They tell hunting stories, pleasant stories. The women are talking about the seal, how nice it is to be so blessed with plenty.

The meat is then passed from the men to the women. The choice parts of the seal are for the women only. The first parts to come are the upper flippers. Two women are responsible for cutting up pieces for everyone. It is considered rude to leave anyone out. Next, the heart is cut up in small slivers and passed around, followed by the liver. The upper spine is then passed to the women while the men take the lower half. The ribs are cut into equal parts, with the women taking the front ribs and the men eating from the back ribs.

Guests are careful not to eat up every part of the seal. They must leave some for their kind hosts, unless they are urged to take some home. Some guests leave as soon as they have eaten, even before washing up. They feel they must not take up too much space and overstay their welcome. Appreciation is expressed more than once before leaving. The remaining guests help clean up everything.

Stories and pleasantries are exchanged. There is much laughter. This kind of feast rotates throughout the community, with each home taking a turn. In a community feast where everyone gathers in a public place, all food is donated by families that have something to give. In bigger communities, much of the food is provided by designated hunters.

Feasts are very special because we believe sharing food is an important part of our culture and is an important link with our heritage. We believe food makes friends out of strangers. When we eat together, we feel more harmonious. And food doubles its volume when it is shared.

Staying With an Inuit Family

When we have a guest in our home it is a great honor because it means we are accepted as we are. We feel needed and humble that our home is good enough for other people. This includes parents, relatives, friends, visitors, or anyone who needs a place to rest. There are just a few guidelines you should know before staying with an Inuit family because sometimes we take it for granted people already know what to expect.

First of all, you are very welcome even if no one tells you so. You must feel at home at all times. Do not knock at the door before entering. Make normal noise. We don't like it when people try to be too quiet; it seems like they are sneaking behind our back.

In earlier times we never needed to lock any doors or secure any personal belongings because everything was shared. Our elders told us stealing was a very bad thing to do. As children, we were told that if we took something we were not supposed to have when no one was at home, a big hand would appear and grab us. Communities had different superstitions to discourage stealing. Today, it is still like that in some communities. When we enter a house where no one is home, we simply make tea and wait. This is considered one of the ways to become part of the family. The host feels esteemed and valued for her or his generosity. In bigger communities, locking doors has become a new custom, but this doesn't mean you are not welcome when your hosts are not at home.

It is important to take part in the household. This does not mean you have to do chores or take over. When guests are willing to try our country food, the host feels pride. At first, the host might be shy to offer any country food for fear of rejection. Sometimes we think our food will not be accepted by our guests because it has blood in it or it does not look clean enough. When we are feasting on a seal, caribou, ptarmigan or any other country food, we hate to be stared at and we don't like it when people take pictures of us eating. We would rather have you eat with us, or try a small piece and swallow fast. Please don't express any "yucks" or other words of ridicule. When our guests take interest in our food fare, we feel we are sharing our culture. If you don't like the meat raw, just ask your host to cook it for you.

Your hosts may take you for a trip on the land in any season. Do what they do and say; they know best. When we are getting ready to go on the land, it is often hot and it is very tempting to leave dressed as we are, but we know it will be a lot colder out there on the sea or land. Help with the grub, camping equipment, and children as much as possible. Everyone is expected to help as much as they can, no matter how big or little. Your hosts are doing their best to make you feel welcome and important.

There are three age groups of hosts that you will probably meet. First, there are the more mature Inuit who speak only Inuktitut. They were born on the land and lived the "real" nomadic Inuit way of life that existed before today's community-based wage economy. We look to them as experts on hunting, weather, directions, astronomy, plants, beliefs, ethics and anything else that has to do with the Inuit world. Please respect them as we do.

Then there is the 35 to 45 age group, the first bilingual generation. These people were born when transitions to a new wage economy were taking place. People in this group know both the Inuit and white worlds and are comfortable with both. The memories of those who grew up on the land are held dearly because this generation is the link between life on the land and life in a settlement. They are called the "in the middle" crowd.

Thirdly, there are the younger people who are in their 20s and early 30s. Most of them were born in a hospital. They are modern in just about everything they do, yet the elders have taught them ancient values such as respect for the land, the sea, the animals, and the weather. They have been taught to be good to other people, to share what they can, and to expect less.

Our young people, who have been in school most of their lives, have spent much less time on the land and sea than their parents and grand-parents had by their age. To save our language, they had to be taught Inuktitut in school. They have gone through a lot of public scrutiny because they have been told over and over that they are our future and that they must carry on our "Inukness." This has been discussed on radio and television, in newspapers, and even in land claim negotiations. Sometimes this age group has heard unpleasant comments such as: our young people are not Inuk enough anymore, they are forgetting our language, they don't know the land well enough, or they are breaking the law too often. But in reality we know that our young people are still as Inuk as we are. They can be your most interesting hosts because they have gone through a lot of history in a short time and still maintain their Inukness.

No matter what age they are, Inuit hosts are family-oriented. We like to show our family and relatives to our visitors. If you stay with a family, there might be grandparents, aunts, uncles, cousins, and adopted children in the household. Some older children and young people might be sent to stay with other relatives to make room for you. This is very normal and readily accepted because a guest is so important and everything must be done to make him or her feel at home. No one feels rejected or unwanted. The guest need not feel that she or he is separating the family.

We welcome visitors in our homes for several reasons: you are visiting because you are interested, you are sharing our lives, you are receiving knowledge and spreading knowledge, you are gathering memorable times, and above all, we enjoy your company.

Most of all, be yourself. You do not need to lower or heighten your normal standards. Your Inuit hosts are being themselves. Talk in a normal voice. Some people talk louder to us and use "pigeon English." This is so embarrassing to us. We are not hard of hearing. We want to be treated as equal human beings. It has been our experience that some visitors expect us to be historic pieces. They expect us to always be smiling. Their roman-tic notion is that we still live in snowhouses and have been frozen in time. Some people have been disappointed to see the modern side of our life. But we are still Inuit — in our hearts, minds, body and soul. Enjoy your visit!

The Kivalliq Region
by Peter Ernerk

For beginners, let's get one thing clear! Although myth has it that there are 100 ways of saying the word "snow" in Inuktitut, there is in fact only one word for it: *aput.* But just as the English language has different terms for different conditions of snow (for example, powdery snow, packing snow, slush, sleet), Inuktitut has different terms for different conditions of snow, too.

When men and women kiss each other, Inuit do not consider it "rubbing noses"; it is a kiss, filled with compassion, love, caring, and romance. It is called *kunik* in the Inuktitut language. And Inuit have always called themselves

Inuit — the people. The name "Eskimo," a Cree Indian word that means "eaters of raw meat," is a derogatory term that is no longer used in Nunavut.

Malinnga (follow me), I have some spiritual thoughts that I want to share with you. It's about Inuit language and culture, but let me say it my way! You know that the land and snow speak to us often, especially when there are lots of caribou footprints on the snow, or on the sandy lakeshores and on the soft moss in summer.

Inuit always had unwritten social laws that were extremely important to daily life. Most of them still apply today. The Inuit identity is that of kindness, compassion, giving, caring, helping, concern for others rather than oneself, laughing and joking, discipline, endurance, common sense, and most of all, responsibility.

Inuit culture and language are inseparable. The Inuit culture is oral and it's been passed on since time immemorial. We Inuit have one language with regional dialectical differences. We live in complete harmony with our environment and take our land and sea for granted. Nature is there for us, and we will leave the environment in good condition for our children. What's there is for us to take but we never abuse the animals and we treat them with great respect! The environment has a language of its own. Every notable landscape, lake and river has a name. We name them for the way they are shaped; for example, *Iviangirnalik* (like a breast), *Kuugjuaq* (big river) and *Inuksulik* (having *inuksuit*, the Inuit rock cairns shaped like humans).

We are subsistence hunters and gatherers, and thus have survived for many thousands of years. We hunt to live and clothe ourselves, we gather vegetation, such as berries and seaweed, to supplement our diet during spring and summer. We share what we have with our fellow Inuit, and through sharing we survive.

While growing up in the Kivalliq Region in the *Naujaat*-Repulse Bay area, we lived in *Nattiligaarjuk* (the lake that has seals) most of the time. We used to travel by dogteam to *Naujaat* for Christmas and Easter to participate in festive celebrations or to trade our carvings and fox furs. In the spring, when the days got longer, we would travel for many miles, then stop for tea and frozen caribou meat or fish. My father, who lived the Stone Age life, would look at the next hilltop, so far away on the horizon that it looked bluish. In Inuktitut he would say, "Far away! It's not moving, it will be reached." We did indeed reach the hill, but very slowly. From that I took our Inuit culture to mean patience!

Inuit life is a seasonal cycle. We look back to the past to plan our future. We vision seasons. Let me begin with the main fall activities. Fall meant moving inland as far as possible in an attempt to reach caribou country. If it was several nights' sleep, it didn't matter — just as long as there was enough caribou for us to catch so that we had food for the winter and good clothing for the entire family.

Caribou hunting was not an easy task, but not impossible. On some days it was easy to spot an animal, and that was good. But most other times we had to walk for many, many miles before we spotted one or saw a track or two of a caribou. As custom would have it, my father at times used to carefully cut around a caribou footprint with his pocket knife and place it backwards in the same spot. "Let the caribou return!" he would exclaim. This type of spiritual expression was used only as a last resort.

When we did catch caribou, we cached the meat and preserved it for the winter. The fishing season was also good during the ice freeze, especially in October. We would fish for arctic char through the ice by making holes. After eating caribou meat all summer, it was also a welcome change to start eating fish.

December, January and February meant winter. There was hardly any hunting or fishing, except for occasional caribou hunts. Being inside a small *iglu* for an extended period of time was lonesome and frustrating. Nevertheless, people played games and sang traditional Inuit songs. Inuit songs were composed by hunters telling their experiences, mostly of hardships. Traditional Inuit songs were both powerful and entertaining. The drum dancer would also beat his/her drum to accompany a traditional song. On the other hand, spiritual or shaman's songs were sung only at rituals. They were set aside for special purposes, the same way as Christians do.

With the arrival of longer days in March and April, in spring, it became necessary to hunt seals through seal holes on the ice. This was very difficult work as we had to wait for seals to come up. The other hunters had their dogs sniffing for the holes through the thick snow. Seal holes are normally on the east side of ice ridges because of the prevailing westerly winds.

When the hunter caught a seal, it meant that we would have fresh meat for ourselves and our dogs, a welcome event. It also meant that we would have light from the oil fat of a seal for our *qulliq* (a soapstone oil lamp in the shape of a half-moon, its carved-out hollow contains the fat and wick). I remember, when my father or brother-in-law would bring home a seal, it was my mother's responsibility to butcher the animal. Before she skinned the seal, however, she would put out a small piece of freshwater ice — a message to all the other seals swimming under the ice that they would not be thirsty. Inuit respected all animals and cruelty was not accepted.

After a bit of a breather for about a month, we began hunting seals again. When all the snow had melted on the ice we looked for young mature seals, called *nattiaviniit*. The Hudson's Bay Co. clerks used to call them "silver jars." We traded these seals mostly for their coats, and this allowed us to obtain economic gains. It must be remembered that all animals we hunted were used for food for humans, for clothing, and for dog food.

We welcomed June and July, summer, with great excitement! This was and still is because the snow had melted. The month of June is *manniit* (egg) month and people are out gathering eggs, and the lakes and rivers are opening up. Arctic char swim downstream and people catch fish once again. Migratory birds such as geese and ducks arrive. For most, it's a welcome change to the diet. Inuit also carefully cut up caribou meat for drying. Arctic char, painstakingly filleted and hung to dry, provides the stomach with variety.

You know, Inuit are extremely terrified of bugs. It's guaranteed that bugs arrive each spring and summer. They usually come in great numbers. Most children are terrified of bugs, especially *iguttat* — bumblebees. They seem to want to stick around unless a person runs away from them.

Inuit named their people after various parts of the body, or animals. Sometimes *iguttaq* (a bumblebee) is used as a proper name of a person, such as the case with my older sister. There is some spiritual connection to this particular incident. In 1982, when my uncle (my father's younger brother) and his wife were out fishing in June on the ice, an *iguttaq* flew around them persistently most of the day. I was vacationing in Quebec at the time and on that particular day an *iguttaq* was flying around me, also persistently. I didn't think much of it, but a day or so later I learned that my sister had died. Our daughter's name is Iguttaq, named after my sister.

After fishing at a stone weir in mid to late August and catching lots of arctic char, we have enough fish for the winter. It is time to move inland again to hunt caribou. At this time there is good fat on the caribou. Inuit are great ones for wanting fat from caribou. No wonder; fat has many uses. To begin with, it is a good supplement to the meat that we eat. During the time that I was living a primitive and nomadic life with my parents, when we would move inland and catch caribou with lots of fat, we used the fat as candles. First we would chew the fat well to get rid of all the blood and moisture. Then we would find a piece of material from a flour bag, normally, and use that as a wick. It would light our tent brightly when days got dark. We also used to mix the fat with berries we had picked (we called this concoction "mixed"), and that tasted good!

This was also the time of year when the hair on the caribou skin was good for clothing, not too thin and not too thick. In the old days, Inuit used to catch as many caribou as we could. Whether we saw a herd of five or 30, we used to try and shoot them all. Food was always so scarce in those days that we had to have enough for our family and dogs. In order to preserve the meat, we would cache it in late summer and pick it up in the winter.

Even though all-terrain vehicles and snowmobiles have taken over as our means of transportation, we still follow the same seasons.

A new season is coming. Consider coming with me to experience the Inuit language and culture. You never know, it may speak to you in its own words. *Tukisiviitt?* (Do you understand?)

The Kitikmeot Region
by Joe Otokiak

Like other regions of the circumpolar world, Inuit culture in the Kitikmeot Region has gone through a cultural shock over a very short period of time. Its culture comprises bits of the western Arctic flavor from Holman (which won't become part of Nunavut) and Kugluktuk; Cambridge Bay, Umingmaktok and Bathurst Inlet in the central region; and Gjoa Haven, Taloyoak and Pelly Bay in the east. In the Kitikmeot, there may be slight variations in style and time in all aspects of Inuit life — physical, mental and spiritual.

About 40 to 50 years took Inuit from a nomadic way of life to more permanent settings, as small communities evolved with the coming of other cultures into the Arctic. Much of Inuit life flowed in sync with the seasons, harvesting game and necessities to ensure survival for the future. Families travelling with others made the pursuit of game safer, and the chances of success more attainable. Over the generations, knowledge of what game was accessible during a specific time of the year was passed on among Inuit. The pursuit of game during the various seasons is still followed to some extent today in less vigorous ways.

Preserving
a rich and
vibrant culture

ᕿᑭᖅᑕᓂ ᐃᓄᐃᑦ ᑲᑐᔾᔨᖃᑎᒌᖏᑦ
QIKIQTANI INUIT ASSOCIATION

The Inuit of the Baffin Region have a fascinating culture that stretches back thousands of years. We invite you to experience our land, meet our people, and share in our traditions. The Qikiqtani Inuit Association is responsible for preserving the culture of the Baffin Inuit. By safeguarding, administering and advancing our language, culture, and self-sufficiency, we are ensuring the survival of a historic people for today and for generations to come.

For further information, please contact:
Qikiqtani Inuit Association, P.O. Box 219, Iqaluit, NT X0A 0H0
Tel: (867) 979-5391 • Fax: (867) 979-3238
Toll-free: 1 800 667-2742
Or visit our web site at: www.nunanet.com/~lands

THE 1999 NUNAVUT TRADE SHOW

A Celebration of Opportunity

Plan to attend the 8th Annual 1999 Nunavut Trade Show. Happening just weeks before Nunavut becomes a new territory, this will definitely be our most exciting and popular business trade show ever.

NUNAVUT TRADE SHOW

Where Business Meets in Nunavut

Hosted by the Baffin Regional Chamber of Commerce (BRCC), the Nunavut Trade Show offers unlimited opportunities for new contacts and contracts. Celebrate Canada's new territory with us; book now to secure your space at the 1999 Nunavut Trade Show.

For more information contact:
Trade Show Co-ordinator
1999 Nunavut Trade Show
P.O. Box 59, Iqaluit, NT X0A 0H0
Tel: (867) 979-4653
Fax: (867) 979-2929
E-mail: brcc@nunanet.com
(Visa accepted)

BRCC supports and encourages the development of new and existing industries and businesses within the trade and service area of the Baffin Region.

BRCC
Baffin Regional Chamber of Commerce

In earlier times, during the winter months, Inuit travelled to areas where caribou was plentiful, and to coastal areas for seal.

In the spring, Inuit headed for the rivers along the coast where they'd fish for arctic char and hunt migrating birds. Fish were caught by jigging through the ice along the edge of lakes and coastal waters; as the ice melted, natural holes were used. Seals could be caught as they gathered to feed on the fish coming down the river. Birds were snared as they nested — much like snaring rabbits. The bird would get caught around the neck as it attempted to fly when scared off the nest.

When spring harvesting was done, Inuit would travel inland to caribou crossings and hunt them by kayak and bow and arrow. Caribou could be herded to an area where the men readied themselves to pursue them with kayaks. The places were carefully chosen and surveyed to ensure a good hunt. Another tactic used involved *inukhuit* (spelled elsewhere in Nunavut as *inuksuit*). *Inukhuit* were raised to help guide the animals along a route to men behind blinds, waiting with bow and arrow.

When fall approached, Inuit returned to the coast to do more fishing and caribou hunting.

Early winter was spent mostly seal hunting. Seal blubber was used to provide heat and cooking fuel for the *qulliq*. There were also caches of seal blubber in skin sacks which could be used in times of hardship.

All members of the Inuit family, with the exception of babies, had a part in carrying out responsibilities, whether large or small, in day-to-day life.

Elders were revered for the wisdom they gained over the years; their word was the unwritten law.

The young were taught at an early age to listen and obey those older than them because they knew better. Inuit children were taught to treat others in a way that they themselves would like to be treated, with respect. They were told never to talk back to an older person who may be correcting them out of concern for their own good and safety. Sometimes this was not adhered to, and the child learned by her or his mistake. Children were seldom hit when being corrected; rather, they were spoken to with love and assurance that this was done in their best interest.

Every human being was treated as an equal, regardless of his or her physical condition. Necessities of life were shared with those less fortunate to ensure survival. Inuit cared for each other and family ties were strong. If a difficult situation occurred, both the immediate and extended family would support each other and help in any way they could to bring about a solution. Inuit in smaller communities tended to have stronger family and community ties than those in larger settings.

The spirit of the Inuit was always that of contentment, even through hardship. It's reflected in the saying *"Ajurnarmat"* (which means "it can't be helped"). Inuit were quick to accept natural occurrences in life and move on. They had a great respect for their fellow man, the environment, and every living creature used for their survival. One would dare not say "I'm going to catch that game," even if it seemed certain that the chances of catching the game were high. The only comment was *"Angunahuarniaqara"* (pronounced "ah-guu-na-hwak-nia-kah-gah," this means "I'll try and catch it"). Successful hunters were not boastful or proud;

simply grateful and very fortunate. Inuit would not allow wounded animals to suffer unnecessarily. They were pursued, caught, and killed as quickly as possible.

Inuit believed that people's spirits lived on after death. As Inuit passed away, newborn babies were named after them by their close relatives and were treated as if the deceased person's spirit occupied the child. Children named after respected elders, in particular, were raised with great care, love, and gentleness.

The environment was respected and kept in its natural state as much as possible for others to use. Disposed material, not eaten by scavengers, soon disintegrates back into the ground with the help of the elements. Inuit were very much aware of weather conditions and could forecast the following day's weather.

Most food did not require extensive preparation. It was eaten raw, frozen, dried, boiled to make broth, and aged while sitting in caches and in the animal's own fat. Boiled caribou was often accompanied by *qajuq* (pronounced "ka-yok," this is the animal's blood stirred into the broth after the meat has been taken out to form a thick soup). It warmed those who ate it.

Food left to age in caches is an acquired taste for those not accustomed to such food. Inuit savor these delicacies, especially elders. One such delicacy is seal flippers aged in seal blubber. When the fur can easily be removed, this is the time to enjoy them. Food was covered with a certain moss and cooked on flat rocks in an open fire in the summer. Hot stones were placed inside caribou stomachs filled with blood to make instant pudding. Dried food was usually eaten with different animal fats, solid or liquid. Various parts of game were eaten raw as they were being prepared for future use. Country food is still the main diet of Inuit today. It's more nutritious and less expensive than store-bought food.

Many Inuit traditions continue to be practised, utilizing both past and present techniques, but there needs to be more of it as Inuit move toward their new role in the government of Nunavut. Inuit survived by their wits for thousands of years and will continue to do so with the wisdom of elders helping to build a strong foundation for future generations.

This glimpse into Inuit culture in the Kitikmeot Region is a very small piece of the iceberg, so to say. As the "people from the other side" will tell you, welcome to *Kiilinirmiut* country.

22. INUIT SPIRITUALITY
by Peter Ernerk

My close friend once said to me that because of Christianity and my Christian upbringing, he could not make me the way he was — an *angatkuq* (shaman).

The Roman Catholic and Anglican churches would make every effort to destroy what we believed in. And they did!

You know, I have been disappointed ever since.

Many people, mostly non-Inuit, pronounce the word "shamanism" with ease. For me, the mere mention of it in English is sensitive because Inuit shamanism is spiritual. It's not just any spirits, either. Individual shamans have their own selected spirits. I believe I have my father, Angutitaq, for my spirit helper.

Shamanism is the original religion of Inuit. It was our way of life for many, many years before Roman Catholic and Anglican missionaries arrived on the heels of European traders to forcibly replace shamanism with their religion. I remember Father Henry calling shamanism an "act of the devil." He would put down our religion, and tell us that Roman Catholicism had more power than shamanism.

Western society believes that every Inuk is spiritual. This is not so. In order to understand and appreciate the world of spirituality and shamanism, Inuit themselves must understand the religious belief. Without understanding, it has no meaning! For most of my life, I pretended to understand Christianity only for wanting to be a good Roman Catholic and wanting to impress others that I was a good Roman Catholic.

A friend of mine from Repulse Bay who died a few years ago used to try very hard to believe in and pray in Christianity. He never once saw or dreamt of angelic figures, he said, but he had seen spirits of Inuit figures. I believe it depends on where one comes from — not on the beliefs that have been imposed upon them by someone else.

The Structure of Traditional Inuit Society

Shamanism is common to perhaps all hunting cultures around the world. It embodies the people's attachment to the land and environment.

In traditional Inuit society, the shaman was seen as a doctor-advisor-healer. The shaman was not the camp leader, though. That honor went to the oldest person in the group, an experienced hunter and trapper. Inuit camps did not have chiefs, as did First Nations (Indians).

The role of teacher was upheld by mothers and fathers. It was very important for parents to teach their children the qualities of discipline and endurance, in order to survive the bitter arctic climate. What if the children were to become separated from the rest of the camp, for example, drifting on ice that had broken off from the mainland? They would need to know how to be resourceful in order to beat the odds and survive.

The Skills of the Shaman

Inuit camps sometimes had more than one shaman, and they could be either men or women. But that doesn't mean anyone could be an *angatkuq*. No, that person had to have the ability to vision, to see spirits. Shamans were born, not made.

As with Christianity and other religions, shamanism was never meant as an instant remedy for all problems. Inuit didn't use shamanism every time they got into trouble. Shamanism was respected, and used only as a last resort.

Inuit shamans had spirits known as *tuunngait*. My friend, for example, had his mother as his most powerful spirit. With the help of his mother he used to heal and sometimes cure the sick in our family. I, for one, still believe that with the combined powers of the *angatkuq* and the Roman

Catholic priest in Repulse Bay, I was saved from certain death. I was perhaps three or four years old when I became very sick. A local Roman Catholic priest provided me with a powerful medicine to try to heal my sickness. On the other hand, through his mother spirit, my friend identified the cause of my sickness. Several times, members of my family were healed through the helping spirits of my friend.

In the spirit world, the expression of the good, the bad and the ugly played a major role. In other words, there were good and bad spirits. Bad spirits of other shamans were sometimes sent to curse a family member. My friend had *ijiraq*, a good spirit, for his other *tuunngaq* (one spirit). *Ijiraq* is a caribou-like spirit whose literal translation is "one that hides." When there were no more caribou around, my friend used to identify the whereabouts of the animals through his *ijiraq* spirit.

There were two ways of performing rituals. The first could be done in one of three ways: by lifting a rock, by lifting someone's head, or by having the troubled person lift his or her own leg. In all three cases, the heaviness of the thing being lifted indicated whether a good or bad spirit was present.

Take, for example, the rock-lifting ritual. A small rock would be placed on top of a caribou skin, skin side up. A shaman would tie a sealskin rope around it, then start to lift it slowly. Eventually it would become heavier and heavier, an indication that an *apiqsaq* (*apiqhaq* in *Nattilik* dialect) is beginning to grab it from down below. Then, one or two members of the family would start to ask questions. *Apiqsaq*, "the one asked," is a spirit who communicates directly with the shaman. I remember, in addition to being quite scared, either my father or the shaman starting to ask questions: "*Unnirniaqqutit* (you will identify), *Kiglurittuq* (is this the bad one?) *Ilurramutittuq* (is this the good spirit?)" A light lift indicated a yes. When the rock was too heavy for the shaman to lift, it signalled a no.

Shamans had their own language. Here are some important questions asked: *Tau?* (alive-human?), *tauviniq?* (the dead one?), *kumaruaq?* (caribou?), *quattiaq?* (child?), *punnguq?* (dog?). When the problem was identified, it was told loudly to get out of the area, far away. When that happened, the patient began to heal. Or through consulting an *ijiraq*, hard-to-find caribou were discovered nearby a day or two later.

Another way of performing rituals was through the songs of *sakauhiit* — spiritual songs. The shaman would sing the song of *alianait, alianait* (joy, joy, joy). The *pisiit/pihiit* are traditional songs that begin with the words *ajaijaa, aijaijaa…*

When performing either of these two rituals, the room in the *iglu* or tent would be darkened. When there was 24-hour daylight, we of course could not do anything about this. But when it was done in an *iglu* or a tent, the *qulliq* (oil lamp) was only slightly lit, so as to make the room much darker.

Through the songs of *alianait, alianait,* the *angatkuq* identified bad spirits and where they were located, as well as who was causing sickness, bad weather or scarceness of animals. Years ago my father said that *tupilait*, the worst of the bad spirits, would be caught by the shaman outside the *iglu*, I believe, in the dark most times. My friend used to say that once you catch a *tupilak*, your hands and part of your arm would have a lot of blood on them, and only with urine could you wash off the blood of the *tupilak*. Some people who have been to Greenland might have seen ivory carvings of *tupilait*.

Praying to the Same Spirits

Today, the worship of shamanism in Nunavut is still secret, not openly practised as it is in other circumpolar countries such as Russia. But it is being discussed by curious young Inuit who have heard shamanism was a good way to heal. They see it as a positive thing. It may not be visible on the surface, but shamanism is being practised by some. You practise shamanism within your own self.

I believe in my spirits who help me in life, whether I am in danger on the land or seeking and finding animals. One of those spirits that I believe in is my father. Even though my father died in 1971, I believe that he sometimes hunts animals through me. I also believe that he speaks the thoughts of goodness through me. Among some tribes of Inuit and especially among *Nattilikmiut*, where my father comes from, we believe in the existence of *Naarjuk*. This supreme being, equivalent to the Christian God, made the earth and water. Someone else, according to our beliefs, made arctic char fish. I don't fear *Naarjuk*. I am told that he exists somewhere in the universe, he is the boss of *sila*, the sky, looking after all our relations who have passed away.

On the other hand, *Nuliajuk* is a spirit from the sea, the boss of all sea animals, especially seals. She is half woman and half fish, with a fin. Europeans refer to her as "Sea Goddess." In my time, when seal hunters were not catching any seals, my father would say it is because we made *Nuliajuk* angry. And then it became necessary for the shaman to find out why *Nuliajuk* was angry. Only then was it possible to catch seals again. Many Inuit are named after spirits such as *Nuliajuk*. Many of our traditional names are spiritual.

The missionaries and the churches, as well as the governments, have put down and belittled Inuit spirituality since coming here a bit over 50 years ago. Instead of looking at it as evil, society must look at it as a positive answer to our social problems. All denominations should make mention of Inuit spirituality now and then, when delivering sermons in the churches. I think we are really praying for answers from the same Almighty, *Nunaliuqti* — the earthmaker. Don't you think so?

23. LANGUAGE

by Ann Meekitjuk Hanson, with contributions from Joe Otokiak

Inuktitut, the language of the Inuit, is alive and growing. It is widely used throughout the North, and Inuit from across the Arctic can understand one another.

Dialects and accents vary from region to region, but Inuktitut is a single language.

One of the first things a newcomer might notice is that a single word may be spelled many different ways. A white person is *qallunaaq, kabloona* — words that are spelled differently but sound roughly the same. The differences have come about because of our language's oral history. When a writing system was introduced for the first time more than 100 years ago, the words were written phonetically, and those phonetic versions varied from region to region. Today, Inuktitut is written in syllabics in the Baffin and Kivalliq regions, and in the eastern part of the Kitikmeot Region. In the western part of the Kitikmeot, it's written in roman orthography. Since the mid-1970s, Inuit have made efforts to standardize Inuktitut so that the language becomes consistent throughout the circumpolar world. The "new orthography," the result of the standardization process, is gradually being used more, but the move to standardize Inuktitut is still ongoing.

In the Kitikmeot, the name given to the language of Inuit is "Inuinnaqtun." Some phrases used in the Baffin and Kivalliq regions of Nunavut are fairly similar in sound and are recognizable to people living in western Nunavut. There are some similarities among words spoken in Gjoa Haven, Taloyoak and Pelly Bay and those spoken in the Baffin and Kivalliq regions, but the language structures are quite different.

A large portion of the population in the far western reaches of Nunavut speak English and are attempting to strengthen their Inuinnaqtun in all areas, from schools to workplaces. As you move eastward, the Inuit language becomes more commonly used by Inuit. One difference visitors will notice in western Nunavut is that where Inuit from the eastern part of Nunavut use the "s" and "sh" sound, it is usually an "h" sound in the west. "Siksik," the ground squirrel, becomes "hikhik" in the western part of the Kitikmeot.

When she was a little girl, my great-grandmother Kalajuk's Inuktitut was pure, without a trace of any other tongue. Her language evolved out of nature and daily living. This was in the middle 1800s.

When the whalers came, they brought with them many things that would alter this way of life, including a new language. Words like tea, sugar, flour, waistcoat and paper became everyday Inuktitut words, but their pronunciation was distinctly Inuk: "tea" became *tii,* "sugar" was pronounced *sukaq, palaugaaq* meant "flour," "waistcoat" became *uasikuaq,* and "paper" was pronounced *paipaaq.*

When the clergy came, more new words and phrases were added to our language. The people were taught a new way to communicate, called syllabics, which was the first "written Inuktitut." The syllabics system was developed by Rev. James Evans for the Cree and was introduced to the Inuit by Anglican missionary Edmund Peck. Its symbols are fashioned after secretarial shorthand. My great-grandmother learned to read and write syllabics, but she had to do it mostly from memory because there was no paper!

When the Hudson's Bay Co. came, more terms and phrases were invented, all in Inuktitut. At the same time, my people were teaching the ministers and clerks Inuktitut, which secured our language. When the RCMP came, they too brought new words and expressions that broadened our language. They also had to learn Inuktitut.

I was born in 1946, at a time when my parents still depended on the land and sea for survival. Like generations before them, they were saving the language by oral traditions. I was brought up completely in Inuktitut, but my parents used items for which no real Inuktitut word existed, like primus stoves, cups, teakettles, spoons, beads, plastic combs, rifles, tobacco, squeeze-boxes, and a few other things. Words for all of these items were invented in our language.

I was 11 years old when I started formal classroom instruction. I learned by translating everything into Inuktitut. When I could not translate what I learned, it was very hard to understand. For example, when I learned about cows, horses and pigs, I couldn't understand why they didn't run away from the people. All the animals I had ever seen always ran away from people. The teacher did not explain that these were domesticated animals. A word quickly came to mind: *nujuattaittut*, which means "animals that do not run away." After that, new things were easier to understand, but I had to form my own language to help me learn.

In 1964, I graduated from a secretarial school in Toronto. At the time I was one of very few fully bilingual Inuit. My services as an interpreter were in great demand by government departments. By this time all school-age children were receiving formal education in English only.

In 1965, I became aware that I did not know enough of my own culture — I mean the legends, songs, dances, myths, beliefs and histories of my people. I was working at the CBC at the time and my cousin Jonah Kelly and I started to tape the stories of our elders and air them on the radio. This was a new way to preserve both Inuktitut and our legends for all time. I like to think that we helped save a huge chunk of our language by taping the words of our people.

We have a huge language to keep alive. I say this because Inuktitut has the ability to grow without limit because it is a very descriptive language.

It is a good feeling to be able to carry on a conversation in Inuktitut without using a single word of English or any other language. That is why most imported items and concepts are given descriptive names and terms. I believe this method has enriched our language and made it grow.

The word *asujutilli* has been used in recent times as a greeting. Inuit traditionally didn't say anything when they greeted each other, preferring to communicate with a warm smile and a handshake. Conversation would begin after proper introductions, but words or expressions like "hello" or "how are you?" were historically uncommon in Inuktitut.

Asujutilli cannot be translated into a single English word; its closest meaning is something like: "it is truly you" or "you are truly you."

To say "I am from," first name your country or city and end it with -*miungujunga*. For example: England-*miungujunga* or Toronto-*miungujunga*.

I want to learn to speak Inuktitut: *Inuktitut Uqariurumavunga*.

Uvanga means "me," so to say "my name is," first say *uvanga* then say your name. For example: *Uvanga* Ann or *Uvanga* Peter. To say the same thing in the western part of Nunavut, you would say -*ngujunga* after the name: Ann-*ngujunga*.

In order to learn useful Inuit phrases that might come in handy when travelling in the North, you should start by practising common Inuktitut sounds, like those listed in the sidebar on the following page.

COMMON INUKTITUT SOUNDS
by assorted writers

i	(ee)	**u**	(oo)	**a**	(ah)	**li**	(lee)	**lu**	(loo)	**la**	(lah)
pi	(pee)	**pu**	(poo)	**pa**	(pah)	**ji**	(yee)	**ju**	(yoo)	**ja**	(yah)
ti	(tee)	**tu**	(too)	**ta**	(tah)	**vi**	(vee)	**vu**	(voo)	**va**	(vah)
ki	(kee)	**ku**	(koo)	**ka**	(kah)	**ri**	(ree)	**ru**	(roo)	**ra**	(rah)
gi	(ghee)	**gu**	(ghoo)	**ga**	(ghah)	Guttural 'k':					
mi	(mee)	**mu**	(moo)	**ma**	(mah)	**qi**	(khi)	**qu**	(khoo)	**qa**	(khah)
ni	(nee)	**nu**	(noo)	**na**	(nah)	Nasal 'g':					
si	(see)	**su**	(soo)	**sa**	(sah)	**ngi**	(ngee)	**ngu**	(ngoo)	**nga**	(ngah)

PRONUNCIATION OF CONSONANTS:

The 'r' in Inuktitut is similar to the French 'r.' The sound is made in your throat and not in your mouth. It is called a guttural 'r.' The 'q' sound is the most difficult consonant for non-Inuktitut speakers to pronounce. It is a 'k' pronounced in your throat (a guttural 'k'). To adapt to making sounds in your throat, think of what you do when you gargle water. Now think of refining that gargling noise to an 'r' or a 'k.' When first learning Inuktitut, if the 'q' sound is too difficult to produce, try substituting it with a guttural 'h' (an 'h' produced in your throat). The 'ng' sound in Inuktitut is the same as the 'ng' in 'singing.' However, the 'ng' sound is placed differently in Inuktitut words. Be careful not to pronounce it just as an 'n.'

Some other consonants differ from English pronunciation. The 'p' is softer in Inuktitut. Some say it sounds a little like a 'b,' but it is somewhere in between 'p' and 'b' (closer to a 'p'). Similarly, the 't' is softer as well. It leans towards a 'd' sound (but is still a 't').

The 'g' in Inuktitut is much softer than the English 'g.' Instead of making a hard 'g' sound, keep the sound open, as in 'ghee' (omit the 'guh' sound in 'g'). Where there is a double consonant, always hold the consonant sound longer than normal when pronouncing the word.

USEFUL PHRASES (where letters are underlined, emphasize that syllable):

English	Inuktitut	Pronunciation
How are you?	Qanuippit?	"Khah-nweep-<u>peet</u>?"
I am fine	Qanuinngittunga	"Khah-nwee-<u>nngit</u>-toonga"
What is your name?	Kinauvit?	"Kee-<u>nah-oo</u>-veet?"
Thank you	Qujannamiik	"Khoo-yannah-<u>meek</u>"
You are welcome	Ilaali	"E-<u>laah</u>-li"
That's all	Taima	"<u>Tie</u>-ma"
I am hungry	Kaaktunga	"<u>Kaak</u>-toonga"
I am cold	Qiuliqtunga	"<u>Khiu</u>-lirk-toonga"
It is cold (weather)	Ikkiirnaqtuq	"Ek-<u>keer</u>-nak-tokh"
Help!	Ikajunnga!	"Eekah-yoo-<u>nnga</u>!"
Did you make this?	Una sanajait?	"Oo-na sana-<u>yait</u>?"
How much is it?	Qatsituqqa?	"Khat-see-tok-<u>khaw</u>?"
How many?	Qatsiit?	"Khat-<u>seet</u>?"
Yes	Ii	"Ee"
No	Aakka or aagaa	"<u>Ah</u>-ka" or "<u>Ah</u>-ga"
Maybe	Immaqqaa	"<u>Eem</u>-mak-haw"
I have to use the washroom	Quisuktunga	"Khwee-suk-toonga"
What is it?	Una suna?	"Oo-na soo-na?"
Goodbye (to an individual)	Tavvauvutit	"Tub-<u>vow</u>-voo-teet"
Goodbye to you all	Tavvauvusi	"Tub-<u>vow</u>-voo-see"

24. LIFE IN NUNAVUT TODAY

by Ann Meekitjuk Hanson

Two days out of Iqaluit, the land looked like a black thread stretching out on the sea as we children scanned the horizon, urged by the adults to be the first to see shiny objects twinkling up to the skies.

To an 11-year-old, there was no name for these objects, yet they held a future that would alter my life forever.

In the summer of 1957, we were travelling from Kimmirut to Iqaluit in a whaling boat that held three families and several dogs. My Uncle Annowalk wanted to be closer to his wife and my mother who were in a Hamilton, Ontario, sanatorium with tuberculosis. In 1957, Iqaluit had airplanes once in a while. In Kimmirut we had air drops at Christmas. My uncle thought he might get a letter and that his letters might get to his wife. My uncle was looking for better ways to communicate, taking advantage of technology available at the time.

While we waited for my aunt and mother to come home from a place I did not know, I attended school for the first time. It was exciting, enticing and wondrous to learn another language! It was even more exciting to convert that new knowledge into my learned ways, for if I could not translate or interpret the newly gained knowledge, it was harder to learn and believe.

I remember families moving in from Pangnirtung and Cape Dorset. They came by dogteams in winter and by boats in summer. We were meeting relatives we had never met. When we were not blood relatives, we found a way to be related, by marriage or extended families.

In Kimmirut we had lived in small groups with one leader. In Iqaluit, there were many people with not one leader, but many! There were government administrators, the Hudson's Bay Co. manager, teachers, social workers, church ministers, Inuit leaders and doctors. Who were we to follow?

With many people in a whirl of new activities, employment, education, meetings, parties and travelling, it was easy to go unnoticed and stray away from generations-old traditions. We were learning English in school by day and hanging out in coffee shops, dance halls, stores, pool halls, theatres, or visiting teachers at night. We talked about Elvis Presley, Bob Hope, Johnny Cash, Paul Anka, Sal Maneo, Audie Murphy. All this was painful for our elders because we were not speaking our language.

The traditional language in hunting terms, garment making, food, family terms, weather, land and seascapes, animals, shelter making, crafts making, was not being used anymore. Storytelling, drum dancing, singing old songs and poems were no longer practised. They were not forgotten but put aside while we were busy learning new things.

In the early 1970s, I became aware I did not know enough about my language, culture, survival skills, garments, food and family anymore. I learned, too, that I was not the only one.

Many young Inuit who'd gone away to residential schools had a difficult time readjusting to the Inuit way of life with their families. Children as young as five years old were taken from their families. They went to Chesterfield Inlet and later to Churchill and Yellowknife. Once they entered school, they were not allowed to speak Inuktitut. They were punished if they uttered one word of Inuktitut. I once had a wallet thrown at me. It missed my face by a few inches! Children did not come home until the next summer. I was away for over three years without ever coming home. Grandparents, parents, older siblings and aunts and uncles were strangers when we came home. We were strange to them, too, because we dressed differently, had haircuts, squeaky clean shirts and hair, a different language and altered manners. From that time on, we, without knowing it, were in mourning for the loss of language, culture, skills and spirituality that is connected to nature. We turned to alcohol, drugs, substance abuse and self-destruction.

To learn and regain our language, culture, skills and arts, we formed education committees, alcohol and drug education groups, hunters and trappers organizations, social committees and other self-help groups that would help us to retrieve what we nearly lost. Today we may not use the traditional terms our fathers used when hunting, navigating, or creating new tools, but we have created new terms for the technology that is available to us. Our language is flourishing because we create names for computers, fax, satellite, telephone, television, HIV, primus stove, jet, hockey, Internet, religion, and other things. Our young people are taught in Inuktitut in our schools.

When we lived in our *ukkialivik* — a place to spend late autumn together with several families, usually relatives — activities were predictable and controllable. Social order was manageable. Everyone had a chore to do according to their talents. My mother knew how to manage the social order, deliver her neighbor's baby, clothe her family, care for the sick and tend the dying. My father hunted for his family and the village. Women and young people hunted the smaller game — ptarmigan, rabbit — fished, picked berries, and gathered berry bushes for insulation and bedding.

The children, the young people, and especially the orphaned were lectured on values, families, futures, beliefs, and generalities for a good life at every opportunity. We had to listen without ever talking back or arguing. We were yelled at, insulted or drilled purposely to strengthen our minds. This was our preparation for life.

Values were simple to follow: no telling lies, no stealing, be honest, be generous, be helpful in every way, be kind, think of others before oneself. All these we acknowledged by saying "yes, I understand," or nodding our heads.

All relatives from both sides have terms to distinguish which side they come from. For example, the grandmother from father's side is called *Anna*. The grandmother from the mother's side is *Anaanatsiaq*. By this term we understand right away which grandmother. Great-grandparents are called *illupiruq*. Aunts from mother's side are called *aja* and uncles *anga*. All their children have terms also, and in this way we know how we are related. There are terms for in-laws, their family members, all their children. All namesakes are treated with special respect and extra love.

Families, in the Inuit world, mean not only continuation of the blood line, but survival. Couples who cannot have babies are given babies so they will survive. The baby given away at birth is fully aware of his or her natural parents, siblings, aunts and uncles from the beginning. The child grows up with dual families.

As a young girl, suicide was unheard of with our youth. We were lectured that life is precious and a wonderful gift. We have to protect it and enjoy it. We only knew that elders, when they wanted the village to have enough to eat for survival, committed suicide with full blessing from families. Today, we are told suicide is the highest among our young people. I believe this is true. I have lost relatives. My friends have lost their children in their teens and early twenties. We cry and mourn together, not understanding why it happens. We have theories, maybe's, what if's, and guesses. To prevent further suicides, individuals and community groups have created workshops, crisis lines, healing groups and recreational activities. The young people have started to talk about responsibilities among themselves. They have created a board run by the youth, and take part in political talks with governments and Inuit organizations.

When I was growing up, marriage was scary and painful for some women. When a girl child was born, she would be promised to a boy child, agreed by the families. When the young girl matured, a menstrual flow was an indication of maturity and her ability to have children. Then the young man took the girl, whether she was willing or not. She often struggled and cried. She was very frightened. If they had to travel, she was tied up and held by men. She would struggle and cry until she got used to her new husband. I saw my aunts and their friends crying for help and wrestling with the men they were to spend the rest of their lives with. I am told by my women friends that a kind, considerate man did not force his new wife to have sex with him. He waited until she was tamed! Some women were not so fortunate; they were raped! Today, those who married the old way are still together and manage to find humor in how they got to be together. Some say they cannot imagine life without each other. Rough beginnings and yet destined to sail along into new horizons today.

One of my great-aunts talked about the elders of her time. She said her family had to obey the wishes of their elders. Once, they were travelling inland hunting for caribou, and were walking on their way back home, each carrying their load, including the dogs. The elder called for a family meeting. After talking about how grateful she was for everything, she said she wanted to be left alone to die. The family did everything to discourage the elder, but the elder said she wanted the family and the village to survive. The elder wanted the people to have more to eat, more skins for clothing, and to travel with ease. The family had to listen to the elder. The family left and never looked back.

We respect elders not because they are old and feeble, but because age is part of life. My friend Leah Nutara, who died at the age of 107 on Feb. 14, l990, often talked about her mother lecturing her to respect and help the elders. There was one elder in the village Leah visited every day. She fetched her water from the river, gave her the cup of water by her side, emptied her urine pots, tidied her tent. When Leah finished, the elder would say "You will live a long life." Leah believed she lived for so long because she listened to her mother.

From snowhouses to modern housing — people from the South are often amazed how we have coped with the changes. It is not so hard, really.

I have some friends from Perth, Ontario, who went to a little red schoolhouse, rode in horse and buggy, fetched water from the river, and churned butter. No one has a monopoly on material items that make us more comfortable or make living easier. No one has a monopoly on wanting to be more educated or using science to our advantage.

In the past, classroom education was foreign to our parents, aunts and uncles, and the people before them, because there were no schools. They were educated on the land about the plants, seas, weather, animals, histories of people, biographies, song creation, natural laws, beliefs and endless ways of survival.

In the late 1950s and early '60s, formal classroom education was introduced and it was accepted as one of those "have to's" that crept into our lives without our involvement. Our parents understood it was important because they were told it was.

Even though formal education is relatively new, we are now starting to really understand why education is important. It is no longer just a word. Our relatives are on education committees and boards; our nieces, nephews, and grandparents are writing books in Inuktitut. Our grandmothers and grandfathers are coming into our schools to tell stories, sing songs; our sons and daughters have become teachers and principals.

We know it takes educated people to run governments, to doctor and to nurse sick people, to determine what is right or wrong in the court of law, to pursue sciences for better living, to stay healthy and well, to preserve nature so humans may survive, to preserve histories for generations to enjoy.

When our elders talked about the future many years ago, they said "you will live like the *qallunaat*." It was hard to believe because we knew of no life other than the one we had. Since we were taught not to talk back or ask too many questions, we just wondered how that would be. The elders said that a shaman had a vision long before that there were ships from the South and passed on the knowledge. We are the living proof today of that prediction.

We are nomads. We chase opportunity in order to survive. In the days before metal technology, we made tools to make hunting easier, shelter for comfort, arts for pleasure, wordsmithing by memory for stimulation and continuation of a language. All these have survived in spite of another dominant language imposed upon us without ever asking for it. Through our kindness and instinctively welcoming attitude, we nearly lost all. But we took action when everything was on the verge of becoming a memory.

We are still nomads, chasing opportunity by negotiating our way with words. We cope with changes by taking full advantage of a situation, by being completely involved in decision-making. We are no longer the subjects only, but contribute to making life in the North a living memory, mingling traditions with high technology!

I was not the first to see the shiny object on the horizon on Frobisher Bay that day in 1957, but my questions were answered before reaching the shores of Iqaluit. The shiny objects, part of the Distant Early Warning (DEW) Line radar system, were *naalagutiit* — listening devices from faraway places. A new word was added to my vocabulary.

25. ECONOMY
by Colleen Dupuis

I remember once sitting down for dinner with a Hall Beach hunter in his 40s who proudly explained to me that he had never had a job.

He supported his nine children through hunting a variety of marine mammals and caribou, and acting as a fishing guide, when he had the opportunity, for the little cash he needed. Some of his children are now in college and he continues to support them this way.

While Canada ranks as one of the world's most industrialized nations, there are still places in Nunavut where people live off the land by hunting and fishing for food. What cash they need comes from social assistance, carving, or some guiding for tourists. In fact, not more than 35 years ago, parts of Nunavut existed solely as a subsistence economy.

This meant that the local Inuit traded furs, usually fox or seal, with the Hudson's Bay Co. store for items like sugar, bullets and flour. It was a hard life, but one that brought a great deal of self-respect and pride. The traditional way of life is very important to Inuit. According to the GNWT's Department of Resources, Wildlife and Economic Development, the annual economic value of subsistence harvesting in Nunavut, in terms of replacing country food with store-bought meat, is between $30 million and $50 million. (This estimate, extrapolated from a Baffin Region economic baseline study done in 1984, assumes all edible portions of the harvest are consumed.)

A limited wage economy exists in Nunavut today, but there is a difference in the way residents participate. According to a 1994 Labour Force Survey conducted by the GNWT, 60 per cent of Nunavut's adult Inuit population is in the labor force. Although 28 per cent of that group is unemployed, it should be recognized that most Inuit do not register with Employment Canada, and will take jobs in their communities when they are available. Ninety-one per cent of Nunavut's small non-aboriginal population is in the labor force; that group has a four per cent unemployment rate. Average annual income figures for Nunavut are misleading because they do not take into account the hidden benefits from subsistence hunting and the carving industry. Nunavut's new government plans to support the traditional Inuit lifestyle through job sharing and flexible work hours to accommodate subsistence hunting and fishing.

Beset by relatively few salaried jobs, Nunavut's economy faces the challenge of a low education level and a high proportion of young people (56 per cent of Nunavut's population was under 25 years of age, compared to a Canadian level of 34 per cent, according to the 1996 Census of Canada). It's expected that the Nunavut government will rely on federal transfer payments for at least 90 per cent of its revenue in the territory's initial years.

Government is a mainstay of the wage economy. Government, minerals and furs have traditionally propelled the economy here, with the public sector today accounting for close to 39 per cent of all employment. The services that government employees will need to do their jobs, and the spinoffs from the wages they will earn, will continue to drive the economy for some time. Many of Nunavut's small businesses and retail outlets have been established to support government needs, or those of public servants.

After the demise of the whaling industry in the late 1800s, fox and seal pelts lured trading companies north — notably the Hudson's Bay Co. There was such a demand for the luxurious white arctic fox pelts that quality and supply tapered off in the 1930s.

Sealing was a major industry in Nunavut until a public outcry against it occurred in the 1970s. A ban on the import of marine mammal products into Europe and the United States, coupled with lobbying efforts by animal rights groups, resulted in losses of hundreds of jobs and approximately $2 million coming into Nunavut each year. Much of the current poverty in the territory can be directly linked to this single issue. Its toll on the traditional Inuit way of life was even more devastating, leading to myriad social problems, including suicide.

Over the past few years, there has been an increased interest in Nunavut seal fur products, although vocal anti-sealing groups continue to impede market growth. As with all resource use in Nunavut, all parts of the seal are used, not just its pelt. Furs are being promoted as a byproduct of subsistence hunting. Three collections have been designed by southern designers and shown in Southern Canada and abroad to rave reviews.

Mining currently contributes 500 jobs to Nunavut's wage economy, but more than 85 per cent of these jobs are filled by non-residents. Still, many hopes are staked on the future of mining in Nunavut. The geology of the area is rich in base metals such as lead and zinc, and gold, with the potential for diamonds also found. North Rankin Nickel Mines outside Rankin Inlet was a major factor in that community's development in the 1950s. However, at the moment, low prices have put new mineral development in several parts of Nunavut on hold.

The Polaris Mine on Little Cornwallis Island in north Baffin, in production for 16 years, produced more than 1.02 million tonnes of lead, zinc and silver in 1996. Polaris's 219 jobs are 85 per cent filled by staff from the South, and Polaris is virtually a stand-alone community. The Nanisivik Mine produced 150,000 tonnes of concentrate in 1996. At the time of writing, operations at the Lupin Mine in the Kitikmeot Region were suspended due to low gold prices.

Tourism and construction have the potential to create a more diversified economy here. Nunavut's tourism industry contributes $30 million annually to the economy, but high transportation costs remain a hindrance to the sector's full development. With the creation of Nunavut in 1999, 18,000 pleasure and business travellers are expected to visit. The range of travel products offered, combined with an increased interest in Canada, and Nunavut's unique position as one of the world's last unspoiled wilderness areas, are assets in expansion of the territory's tourism sector.

Construction has been growing over the past few years. A more self-reliant construction industry is developing, thanks in part to Article 24 of the Nunavut Land Claims Agreement, which helps Inuit-owned businesses in Nunavut benefit from federal and territorial contracts. That means fewer southern workers are coming north and more of the revenue from the numerous capital projects needed in Nunavut is staying at home. Many of these projects have a built-in training component, again a stipulation of the land claim agreement, so more Nunavut residents will become skilled tradespeople. Apprenticeship programs are being set up to train Nunavut employees working in the new territory.

Several fishing and meat processing plants operate in Nunavut. A larger share of the fish quota in Nunavut would enable growth both in fishing and processing the catch.

If Nunavut has an underground economy, it is the arts and crafts sector. Official estimates put the arts and crafts industry here at more than $20 million per year, with more than 2,500 people deriving all or part of their income from this industry. The real number is much higher when independent artisans who sell directly to the public are included.

Nunavut has travelled a great distance in the last 35 years, but its wage economy still has a long way to go. As the world around us changes, and the education level of *Nunavummiut* rises, the potential for Nunavut will grow. One can only hope the traditional values will remain.

26. DOING BUSINESS IN NUNAVUT
by Tracy Wallace

For the southern businessperson, doing business in Nunavut can be a unique, enlightening, and profitable experience.

But reaping the rewards of doing business here means understanding that things are sometimes done differently in a land where polar bears outnumber conference rooms and sealskin vests are more fashionable than Hugo Boss.

At the very least, southern businesspeople should begin a dialogue with their northern partners long before they arrive in Nunavut. These interactions will help southerners get a feel for the unique business environment into which they are venturing. Many individuals have said they would have saved a considerable amount of time and effort had they been aware of these differences beforehand.

The Business Environment

Two protectionist policies help northern and Inuit-owned businesses battle an exorbitant cost of living, lack of skilled labor, and other business obstacles: the government of the Northwest Territories' Business Incentive Policy, and Article 24 of the Nunavut Land Claims Agreement. Businesspeople coming to the North must understand how dramatically these policies tilt the economic playing field. A free market environment does not yet reign here. (At the time of writing, however, it was not confirmed if the Business Incentive Policy would be adopted by the new government of Nunavut, or if a similar policy would be put in place.)

Traditionally, the GNWT has played a very significant role in the economy of the territory. While many programs are being privatized, government — and that includes the new Nunavut government — will continue to remain the single largest employer in many communities.

The GNWT's reach extends into the private sector as well. Its Business Incentive Policy favors qualified northern businesses vying for government contracts. So businesses receiving territorial grants are strongly encouraged to use northern contractors, suppliers and manufacturers whenever possible. This policy is beneficial for the northern economy, but there are disadvantages. Orders sometimes take exceedingly long to process; goods and services can bear inflated northern price tags.

You'll also find that Nunavut is not short on bureaucracy. In fact, there seems to be a board, department or agency for virtually everything. Often, these groups need to approve major business deals, which can also slow transactions to a snail's pace.

For a hunting society that maintained a subsistence lifestyle throughout its history, the addition of a wage economy is still relatively new to Inuit in Nunavut. Article 24 of the Nunavut Land Claims Agreement aims to see Inuit-owned businesses in Nunavut benefit from federal and territorial contracts. Businesses must be at least 51 per cent Inuit-owned. The clause is meant to give fledgling Inuit-owned enterprises a leg up as business opportunities boom and construction of Nunavut's government infrastructure snowballs. It's also meant to benefit the people who, at 85 per cent, make up the majority of Nunavut's population.

Shoulds and Should Nots

Many businesspeople tend to live in a cultural vacuum, thinking that business is business, no matter where on Earth you go. This kind of attitude won't win you any friends in Nunavut, though, where your interests will be much better served if you take some time to learn about the people and the land with which you are interacting.

Check your "yesterday is too late" attitude at the door. Things in the North take time, and you must respect this above everything else. In addition to the various bureaucratic obstacles mentioned earlier, you'll find that northern businesspeople just don't have the same frenzied attitude as many southerners. The river runs the show, as they say; northerners understand that blizzards don't care about the importance of your deal. Remember: very rarely do things run like clockwork here. (Don't forget, too, that you will be dealing with three different time zones in one territory.) Accept this, and you'll save yourself a lot of stress. Remember, too, that with the exception of the construction and tourism sectors, the North virtually shuts down in the summer. Your business partners will likely be more interested in fishing, hunting, or camping on the land than dealing with you.

You'll also find in Nunavut that sometimes business deals are still sealed with a handshake as opposed to legal paperwork.

English is not the first language of Nunavut, so provide translation services for all meetings and correspondence. Most Inuit businesspeople speak English, but unilingual elders are often asked for their opinions in these matters. Inuktitut will be an official language of the new Nunavut government; failure to recognize the importance of Inuktitut, whether in written correspondence or verbal transactions, could spell business failure. The larger communities should have seasoned translators for hire; you may have to ask around in the smaller hamlets.

If your business takes you to Nunavut's smaller settlements, you must recognize the importance of the community and try to get involved. In the past, too many businesspeople have come to Nunavut with one thing in mind: make as much money as possible, then leave. This attitude has grown tiresome. Don't be a hermit. Start networking by contacting the hamlet office before you arrive. Once there, become a participant in the community, and you will be that much closer to gaining your business partners' respect and admiration. It'll also help you understand why things grind to a stand-still when there's a big sale at the Northern store or Co-op. Also respect community bylaws, especially those prohibiting alcohol consumption.

Business Facilities

Business facilities in Nunavut run the gamut from cutting-edge technologies, such as videoconferences and Internet access, to hotels with a single rotary phone. Call beforehand to find out what they have or don't have. Some communities have more than one hotel, so you may have options.

Meeting facilities are generally restricted to the larger communities of Iqaluit, Rankin Inlet and Cambridge Bay, although hotels in smaller communities — such as Gjoa Haven's new Amundsen Hotel or Baker Lake's Iglu Hotel — sometimes have facilities that belie their size.

The Astro Hill Complex in Iqaluit contains, for example, an elegant conference room for up to 30 participants and a theatre that seats 130; the Siniktarvik Hotel in Rankin Inlet has a translation booth in one of its board-rooms and the usual overhead projector, screens, televisions and video cassette recorder required for presentations. Arctic Islands Lodge also has audiovisual equipment, plus Internet access.

Such facilities are the exception rather than the rule. You may also find yourself conducting a conference in the community gym, provided it's not being used for a square dance.

Telecommunications are slowly becoming a greater reality throughout the territory. You may be able to save yourself the exorbitant airfare by conducting a meeting via teleconference or videoconferencing, available in the regional centres. In addition, more people are getting on line, but it seems to take forever to get the necessary equipment and expertise.

Bed and breakfast establishments are slowly becoming more common-place in communities. Since these establishments are usually run out of a home, they won't have sophisticated business facilities. Your hosts may, however, offer some insight into the community and its people — knowledge that might ultimately foster your business dealings more than any fax machine could.

For a complete list of Nunavut's accommodation and business facilities, contact **Nunavut Tourism**.

Business Networks

Today, more business decisions in Nunavut are being made at the community level, so more initiative is being focused on job creation through the private sector and self-employment.

Nunavut has three regional chambers of commerce, and they make up the newly established **Nunavut Chamber of Commerce**, whose offices rotate among the regional offices on an annual basis. For business projects with Nunavut-wide implications, as well as regional endeavors, get in touch with the regional Chamber of Commerce.

Each of Nunavut's three regional Inuit birthright associations has an economic development arm interested in sound investments and joint venture prospects that promise good returns on the financial interests they are safeguarding for area Inuit. Business projects have ranged from mining, surveying, shrimp fishing, construction and heavy equipment sales, to electronic technology. For more information, contact the **Qikiqtaaluk Corporation** in Iqaluit, **Sakku Investments Corporation** in Rankin Inlet, or the **Kitikmeot Corporation** in Cambridge Bay. There is also a Nunavut-wide Inuit development corporation — **Nunasi Corporation**.

Kivalliq Partners in Development, based in Rankin Inlet, is a partnership between Sakku Investments Corporation, the **Keewatin Business Development Centre**, and the GNWT's Department of **Resources, Wildlife and Economic Development** (the government of Nunavut's **Department of Sustainable Development**, come April 1999). Contact Kivalliq Partners in Development for information on business and development opportunities.

A chart describing Nunavut's business, training, land claim and other organizations is available free from the Iqaluit, Rankin Inlet and Cambridge Bay offices of **Nunavut Tunngavik Incorporated**.

Finally, the biggest networking event of the year is the **Nunavut Trade Show**, usually held in early March in Iqaluit but slated for mid-February in 1999. The 1998 edition drew close to 3,000 visitors.

THE PEOPLE: DIRECTORY

Baffin Business Development Centre
Tel.: (867) 979-1303 or 1-800-263-2232
Fax: (867) 979-1508
E-mail: bbdc@nunanet.com

**Department of Sustainable
Development,
Government of Nunavut**
Tel.: (867) 979-5134
Fax: (867) 979-5920

Iqaluit Chamber of Commerce
Tel.: (867) 979-4095
Fax: (867) 979-2929

Iqaluit Trade and Promotion Office
Tel.: (867) 979-3156
Fax: (867) 979-2929

Kakivak Association
Tel.: (867) 979-0911
Fax: (867) 979-3707
E-mail: p.angnakak@nunanet.com

**Keewatin Business
Development Centre**
Tel.: (867) 645-2126
Fax: (867) 645-2567

Kitikmeot Corporation
Tel.: (867) 983-2200
Fax: (867) 983-2995
E-mail: dgeneral@polarnet.ca

**Kitikmeot Economic
Development Commission**
Tel.: (867) 983-2458
Fax: (867) 983-2075
E-mail: kpeterson@polarnet.ca

Kivalliq Partners in Development
Tel.: (867) 645-2124
Fax: (867) 645-2170
E-mail: brianz@arctic.ca
Web site: www.arctic.ca/kpd/

Nunasi Corporation
Tel.: (867) 920-4587
Fax: (867) 920-4592
E-mail: nunasi@internorth.com
Web site: www.nunasi.com/

Nunavut Chamber of Commerce
Baffin Regional Chamber of Commerce:
Tel.: (867) 979-4653
Fax: (867) 979-2929
E-mail: brcc@nunanet.com
Web site: nunanet.com/~brcc/

Keewatin Chamber of Commerce:
Tel.: (867) 793-2311
Fax: (867) 793-2310

Kitikmeot Chamber of Commerce:
Tel.: (867) 982-3232
Fax: (867) 982-3229

Nunavut Construction Corporation
Tel.: (867) 979-2600
Fax: (867) 979-2601
E-mail: patricka@nunanet.com

Nunavut Tourism
Tel.: 1-800-491-7910 (for Canada and
the United States)
Tel.: (867) 979-6551
Fax: (867) 979-1261
E-mail: nunatour@nunanet.com
Web site: www.nunatour.nt.ca

Nunavut Trade Show
Tel.: (867) 979-4563
Fax: (867) 979-2929
E-mail: brcc@nunanet.com
Web site: nunanet.com/~brcc/

Nunavut Tunngavik Incorporated
Department of Business Development:
Tel.: (867) 645-5400 or 1-888-236-5400
Fax: (867) 645-3451
E-mail: ntiecdev@nunanet.com
Web site: www.tunngavik.com

Iqaluit office:
Tel.: (867) 979-3232
Fax: (867) 979-3240

Cambridge Bay office:
Tel.: (867) 983-2517
Fax: (867) 983-2723

Qikiqtaaluk Corporation
Tel.: (867) 979-4047 or (867) 979-8400
Fax: (867) 979-8433
E-mail: QC@nunanet.com
Web site: www.qikiqtaalukcorp.nu.ca

**Resources, Wildlife and Economic
Development, GNWT**
Tel.: (867) 979-5071
Fax: (867) 979-6026
Web site: www.gov.nt.ca/RWED

Sakku Investments Corporation
Tel.: (867) 645-2805 or (867) 645-2742
Fax: (867) 645-2063
E-mail: rdewar@arctic.ca

Nunavut Takes Control

27. THE NUNAVUT LAND CLAIM

by John Amagoalik

When the $1.1 billion Nunavut Land Claims Settlement was proclaimed at a special ceremony in Kugluktuk on July 9, 1993, it was the culmination of two decades of hard work and negotiations that, in the end, gave birth to the most comprehensive settlement ever reached between a state and an aboriginal group anywhere in the world.

None of this would have transpired had Inuit not become politically organized. The roots of Inuit political organization go back to the late 1960s and early '70s, and the struggle for control of natural resources.

Inuit had just experienced the boom and bust of the '60s' High Arctic oil exploration. (By 1980, more than $800 million had been invested in oil and gas exploration in the Arctic Archipelago over 21 years of exploration activity. Only a few land-based sedimentary basins across the country produce oil or gas now. Today, Canada's greatest potential for future sources of hydrocarbons lies offshore in the Arctic and off the East Coast.)

In Canada, managing oil and gas development north of 60 N latitude is a federal government responsibility. The period of intense exploration in the 1960s made Inuit realize just how little control they had over their traditional lands. They discovered that governments and big business could do just about whatever they wanted in the homeland of Inuit. This was like a wake-up call for Inuit leaders.

Discovery of Oil in Arctic Alaska

The large oil discovery on the Alaskan North Slope and the Beaufort Sea in 1976 promised more exploration activity in the Canadian Arctic. There were proposals for tanker routes, pipelines, flying tankers, and giant submarines to transport the expected oil bonanza. Inuit in Alaska, the Northwest Territories, Labrador and Quebec started to express serious concerns about all these proposed mega-projects.

The oil was found, but by then, the energy crisis that began in the early 1970s was over and oil prices dropped. This made it economically unfeasible to transport the oil out of the Arctic. The question of who owned the land and its resources was also a key factor in creating uncertainty in the oil business.

Spurred on by the discovery of oil and the building of a pipeline from the North Slope to southern Alaska, the federal government of the United States and the state government of Alaska signed the first modern treaty with the aboriginal peoples of that state. Negotiating modern treaties was suddenly seen as a real possibility in Northern Canada.

The Calder Case

British Columbia's landmark Calder Case in 1973 introduced the terms "land claims" and "aboriginal rights" into the everyday language of Canadians. The case, brought to court by Chief Calder of the Nishga Indians of northwestern British Columbia, reviewed the existence of "aboriginal title" claimed over lands historically occupied by the Nishga. In a split decision, the Supreme Court of British Columbia acknowledged the existence of aboriginal rights in Canada. The government of Canada, which had dismissed any suggestions of land and other rights of aboriginal peoples, suddenly found themselves having to take the issue much more seriously. It forced a reluctant government to the negotiating table.

A New Generation of Inuit Leaders

Around all these events, a generation of better educated and less timid young Inuit activists was emerging. They started networking among themselves. They travelled to all parts of the Inuit homeland within Canada — the Northwest Territories, Quebec, Labrador — to talk about Inuit rights and to provide forums to debate the issues of the day.

They organized, raised funds, and started research into land claims. Inuit political organizations were born. The Committee for the Original Peoples Entitlement (COPE) in the Beaufort Region, the Inuit Tapirisat of Canada, and the Northern Quebec Inuit Association were the first ones to be established. The first few steps towards Nunavut had been taken.

After its formation in 1971, the Inuit Tapirisat of Canada had the responsibility to pursue and negotiate land claims for the Inuit of Canada. One of the options debated at the time was to negotiate one claim for all Inuit living in Labrador, Quebec, and the Northwest Territories. But it quickly became apparent that this would not be possible. Bringing all the parties, the provincial governments, the territorial government, the federal government, and the Inuit from the three different jurisdictions, to the same table to negotiate one claim, was just too difficult. It was decided that regional negotiations were the way to go.

The James Bay and Northern Quebec Settlement

When the provincial government of Quebec decided to forge ahead with the James Bay hydroelectric project in 1971, it forced the Cree of James Bay and the Inuit of Nunavik (northern Quebec) to go to court to stop the project until aboriginal claims were settled in the area. They were successful in getting a temporary injunction, which forced the provincial government to the negotiating table. Two years later, the first modern land treaty in Canada, involving the province of Quebec, the federal government, the James Bay Cree, and the Inuit of Nunavik, was signed. The terms of that modern treaty became the starting point for all succeeding negotiations.

The Inuvialuit Settlement

Under pressure from oil exploration in the Beaufort Sea and an expected oil pipeline down the Mackenzie Valley, the Inuvialuit (Inuit) of the western Arctic felt it necessary to break away from the Nunavut land claim negotiations and settle quickly. The Inuit of Nunavut reluctantly gave them their blessing to pursue their own settlement.

The Inuvialuit settlement, which included some Dene tribes in the Mackenzie Delta, was modelled very much on the James Bay settlement. It was signed in June 1984.

The Nunavut Claim

No longer under pressure from oil or hydro development, the Inuit of Nunavut were now able to take the proper time to negotiate a comprehensive agreement. Negotiations had been off and on several times since 1974. By 1982, the Tungavik Federation of Nunavut (TFN) was incorporated to pursue land claims negotiations on behalf of the Inuit of Nunavut, taking the mandate from the Inuit Tapirisat of Canada. TFN, in turn, was succeeded by Nunavut Tunngavik Incorporated in April 1993.

Thirteen years of intense and detailed negotiations followed. One reason why negotiations were so slow was because the federal government had no real land claims policy. This was a totally new area for them and they found themselves having to create new policy as they went along. They had never discussed such things as offshore rights, sharing of royalties, or self-governing institutions with real legal powers. The Nunavut Inuit claims negotiations are largely responsible for the much broader and liberal land claims policy that Canada now has, as opposed to the very narrow definition of aboriginal rights that existed in the 1970s. The nationally televised First Ministers Conferences on Aboriginal Rights of the early 1980s — even though they failed to reach agreement on the definition and broadness of aboriginal rights — did much to educate Canadians about aboriginal issues. This increased support from the general public for aboriginal rights, and, as a result, the federal government became more willing to discuss broader issues.

Finally, an agreement-in-principle was reached in 1990. Two more years of negotiations followed until a final agreement was signed in September of 1992. It was ratified by 84.7 per cent of Inuit beneficiaries in a plebiscite two months later.

The Nunavut treaty is seen around the world as an important benchmark in aboriginal matters. This modern, comprehensive accord is structured to guarantee Inuit majority control over their future, giving them, for example:

- title to Inuit-owned lands measuring 355,842 square kilometres, of which 35,257 square kilometres include mineral rights
- capital transfer payments of $1.1 billion, payable over 14 years, beginning in 1993
- a share of federal government royalties from oil, gas and mineral development on Crown lands
- the right to harvest wildlife on lands and waters throughout the Nunavut Settlement Area
- the right of first refusal on sport and commercial development of renewable resources in Nunavut
- a wildlife management board that is devising a wildlife management system to serve and promote the long-term economic, social and cultural interests of Inuit harvesters
- procurement preference policies that ensure federal and territorial government contracts awarded for Nunavut-destined projects will see increased participation of Inuit firms (providing training and education where needed). Also, the labor force hired must reflect the proportion of Inuit in Nunavut
- Inuit Impact and Benefits Agreements (IIBAs), negotiated in advance of major development projects (such as mining development) that could have a detrimental impact *or* provide benefits to Inuit.

The Nunavut Land Claims Agreement, having literally changed the map of Canada, is now profoundly changing the course of life for Inuit in Nunavut.

28. THE NEW TERRITORY OF NUNAVUT

by John Amagoalik

From the time land claims negotiations started between Inuit and the federal government, the idea of creating a new territory was always part of the proposal.

The Inuit of Nunavut were determined not just to settle their land claim, but to create a new political entity for themselves.

The federal government, on the other hand, informed the Inuit that political issues could not be discussed at the land claims negotiating table. The creation of a new territory, they insisted, had to be pursued through other forums. The Inuit reluctantly agreed, but told the government that a final agreement would not be signed unless it included a commitment to create a new territory. The two parties agreed to disagree on this point, but still began serious negotiations on a land claim settlement.

The idea to split the Northwest Territories into two new territories was first introduced as a bill in the federal House of Commons in 1963. Some eastern Arctic residents appeared before a House of Commons committee to oppose the bill because the population had not been properly consulted. As a result, the bill never got second reading and died on the order paper.

The federal government wanted the issue examined further, and created the Carrothers Commission to study political development in the North and to report back to Parliament. In 1966, after holding hearings in northern communities, the three-member commission recommended that the issue of dividing the Northwest Territories be further examined in 10 years.

It was almost a decade later when the Inuit started to force the issue of division onto the agenda of the Northwest Territories legislative assembly. The assembly was very hostile to the idea and wanted, instead, to devolve more power to the territorial government from the federal government. The Inuit opposed this devolution of powers, insisting that the issue of division be resolved first.

The territorial government finally agreed to put the question of division to the residents of the Northwest Territories in a plebiscite in April 1982. The Inuit leadership campaigned hard for division and the voter turnout in Nunavut's communities was very high. The campaign against division was much less committed and the voter turnout in western Northwest Territories was low. In Nunavut's communities, the yes vote for division was around 90 per cent. The overall result of the plebiscite was 56.5 per cent for division. Nunavut had cleared its first major hurdle.

Years of sometimes acrimonious negotiations on the boundary followed. Finally, in 1992, all interested parties had agreed on a line on the map. This was again put to voters in a Northwest Territories-wide plebiscite to ratify the negotiated boundary between Nunavut and the remainder of the Northwest Territories. Again, there was a high voter turnout in the east and a lower turnout in the west. The boundary was ratified and Nunavut cleared its second major hurdle.

By this time, the negotiations on a final land claims agreement were reaching the home stretch. Most of the major issues had been resolved — except for the territory of Nunavut. In a meeting between the Inuit leadership and Indian and Northern Affairs Minister Tom Siddon in September 1992, the federal government made a last attempt to exclude Nunavut from the final agreement. The Inuit stood their ground and informed the minister that they were prepared to delay the signing of a final agreement until after an expected federal election and a new government. They also informed the minister that they could not recommend ratification by the Inuit of a final agreement that did not include Nunavut. After some phone calls, the minister informed the Inuit leaders that the government would include a provision in the final agreement, committing the government of Canada to create Nunavut.

The final agreement was ratified by the Inuit and the *Nunavut Act* passed by Parliament in June 1993.

What Nunavut Will Be

On April 1, 1999, Nunavut becomes the first territory to enter the federation of Canada since Newfoundland joined in 1949. Nunavut, subject to the Canadian Constitution and the *Canadian Charter of Rights and Freedoms*, will be a public government with all of its citizens having the same rights. But because the population will be about 85 per cent Inuit, it will reflect that reality.

Since 1997, the task of putting Nunavut's new government in place has been overseen by federally appointed Interim Commissioner Jack Anawak. The model of government he has been instructed to implement is the result of studies made by the Nunavut Implementation Commission (NIC), a public body whose primary role has been to advise how the government of Nunavut should be designed. NIC released a comprehensive set of recommendations in its 1995 report *Footprints in New Snow*, and later, *Footprints 2*.

In 1997, Nunavut voters were asked to consider an NIC recommendation that Nunavut's legislative assembly be made up of two-member constituencies, with each constituency represented by a man and a woman. Voters rejected the proposal, which would have made Nunavut's legislature the first in the world to have guaranteed equal participation of both sexes. The gender parity idea, a controversial one that had its opponents, was seen as a way to help Nunavut regain the badly needed balance between men and women, once such an important part of Inuit culture.

Nonetheless, the Nunavut electorate will vote in 19 legislative assembly members to represent Nunavut on Feb. 15, 1999, enabling the new territory to begin the work of governing soon after its inauguration.

29. THE NUNAVUT GOVERNMENT

by Randy Ames

Nunavut refers to both a territory and a government.

The Nunavut territory will be carved out of the existing Northwest Territories, just as the territory of Yukon and provinces of Manitoba, Saskatchewan, Alberta, as well as parts of northern Quebec and northern Ontario, were carved out in the past. Its area will correspond roughly to the area of Inuit traditional and contemporary use, and will also include the northern portions of the High Arctic Islands, plus those islands of Ungava Bay, Hudson Bay and James Bay that do not belong to adjacent coastal provinces. Responsibility for the territory's operation and administration will be that of the new Nunavut government.

Nunavut will have a public government — one that respects and reflects Canada's political traditions and institutions, and one that remains firmly entrenched within the bonds of Confederation. The rights and responsibilities of all its residents will be subject to the *Canadian Charter of Rights and Freedoms*. The administration of the Nunavut government, which was still in the process of being set up at the time of writing, was to be implemented according to recommendations contained in *Footprints 2*. This report was prepared by the Nunavut Implementation Commission, an agency created under federal statute to advise on the design of the new government of Nunavut. *Footprints 2* was accepted by all three parties to the *Nunavut Act* — the government of Canada, the government of the Northwest Territories, and Nunavut Tunngavik Incorporated.

A Territory vs. a Province

The Nunavut government will have powers and responsibilities similar to those of the current government of the Northwest Territories (GNWT) and those of the provinces. But a province is different than a territory. A province exists in its own right, a direct creature of the *Constitution Acts, 1867–1982*.

A territory, on the other hand, is a creation of federal legislation, the current effect of which is threefold. One: unlike the provinces of Canada, which own provincial lands in the Crown in right of the province, Crown lands in the territories are retained by the federal government in the Crown in right of Canada. Two: federal Parliament may intrude into provincial-type affairs, such as school curriculum or the organization of municipalities, in the case of a territory. And three: territorial governments are not included in the constitutional amending formula. Nunavut, though, will be represented by its own federal member of Parliament and will have its own senator.

The genesis of Canada's newest territory can be traced to a seminal document entitled *The Nunavut Proposal*. In 1976, the Inuit of the Northwest Territories, represented by the Inuit Tapirisat of Canada (ITC), submitted this proposal to the government of Canada for the settlement of their land claim and the creation of Nunavut. Even though Inuit leaders negotiated only territorial status for Nunavut at its outset, they may one day press for provincial status, as articulated in an ITC discussion paper approved at its 1979 annual general meeting, entitled *Political Development in Nunavut*. This document advocated the creation of a Nunavut territory within 10 years, with the attainment of provincehood within the following five years.

Territorial Symbols, and Official Languages

Until it modifies itself, the Nunavut government will initially be similar to that of the existing GNWT. Existing GNWT legislation will be "grand-fathered" over to the Nunavut government and will remain in effect until amended by the Nunavut legislative assembly. Nunavut will have its own flag and coat of arms, as well as other symbols that distinguish it as a government and territory in its own right.

Inuktitut, which includes Inuinnaqtun (the dialect spoken in the communities of Cambridge Bay, Kugluktuk, Umingmaktok and Bathurst Inlet of the Kitikmeot Region), will be an official language of the Nunavut territorial government, along with English and French. Nunavut leaders are also confident that Inuktitut will form the day-to-day working language of the Nunavut government and society. A federally appointed commissioner for Nunavut will have powers and responsibilities similar to those of the current commissioner of the NWT and the lieutenant-governors of the provinces. There will be two levels of government in Nunavut: territorial and municipal.

The seat of government will be in Iqaluit, its location decided in a 1995 Nunavut-wide plebiscite between Nunavut's two largest communities, Iqaluit and Rankin Inlet. Political authority at the territorial level will be concentrated in the legislative assembly, while hamlet councils will be responsible for municipal affairs. Nunavut leaders place considerable importance on the devolution of greater responsibility to municipal governments over time. The present division of Nunavut into three regions (Baffin, Kivalliq and Kitikmeot) will be maintained for administrative purposes.

Elections and the Legislative Assembly

The Nunavut **legislative assembly** will consist of 19 members elected every four years by popular vote. Anyone living in Nunavut who meets electoral residency requirements — Inuk and non-Inuk alike — may run as a candidate for the Nunavut legislative assembly. There are no political parties in Nunavut at the territorial level of politics. Like the current NWT legislative assembly, the Nunavut legislative assembly will operate on the basis of consensus politics — that is, decisions of the legislative assembly will be based on the consensus of the majority of its members, rather than on political party lines. The GNWT has prided itself on consensus-style government, based on the aboriginal tradition of decision-making by consensus. Political parties do exist in Nunavut for the purposes of supporting candidates running in federal elections, however.

The operation of the legislative assembly will be overseen by a speaker elected by all members of the legislative assembly (MLAs) in a secret ballot. The government will be headed by a premier, also elected by secret vote of all the MLAs. The executive (cabinet), too, will be chosen by all the MLAs

GOVERNMENT OF NUNAVUT

- Legislative Assembly
- Department of Executive and Intergovernmental Affairs
- Department of Finance and Administration
- Department of Personnel
- Department of Justice
- Department of Public Works, Telecommunications and Technical Services
- Department of Sustainable Development
- Department of Health and Social Services
- Department of Education
- Department of Culture, Language, Elders and Youth
- Department of Community Government, Housing and Transportation

Boards, Commissions, Corporations and Agencies

- Nunavut Boards of Education
- Nunavut Arctic College
- Nunavut Boards of Health
- Nunavut Business Credit Corporation
- Nunavut Development Corporation
- Nunavut Legal Services Board
- Nunavut Liquor Commission
- Nunavut Liquor Licencing Board
- Sport Nunavut
- Power Corporation
- Workers' Compensation Board

through secret ballot, and it will operate on the principle of cabinet solidarity. Although voting for the various positions is by way of secret ballot, the process will be open to public scrutiny, as will the regular sittings of the assembly. The Nunavut government will have 10 departments, with ministers responsible for their operations. MLAs without ministerial portfolios will perform the role of the opposition.

The first election will be held Feb. 15, 1999, with the first sitting of the legislative assembly beginning in early April, 1999. If the Nunavut legislative assembly follows current NWT legislative assembly practices, it will sit at least twice a calendar year, and often more frequently.

A Decentralized Government

About 700 new headquarters positions will be required to run the new Nunavut government. It will be a decentralized government, however, with new headquarters responsibilities in Iqaluit and 10 other communities — Igloolik, Rankin Inlet, Cambridge Bay, Cape Dorset, Arviat, Gjoa Haven, Kugluktuk, Pangnirtung, Baker Lake and Pond Inlet. The functions of the core machinery of government (the **Department of Executive and Intergovernmental Affairs**, the **Department of Finance and Administration**, the **Department of Personnel**, the **Department of Justice**, and the legislative assembly), along with the ministerial, policy and planning, financial and administration, and personnel-related functions of the Nunavut government's other departments, will be located in Iqaluit. The balance of headquarters functions, along with autonomous and semi-autonomous boards, commissions, corporations and agencies, will be based in the other 10 communities.

By structuring the government headquarters in this manner, Nunavut leaders hope to devolve some headquarter decision-making authority to the three regions and extend new employment opportunities to as many communities as possible without compromising the government's effectiveness. They also hope to minimize impacts associated with moving too many new people into a single community.

In keeping with the objective of spreading out new employment opportunities, Nunavut leaders decided that the community chosen as the capital should not be a regional centre for government administration as well. Iqaluit, Rankin Inlet and Cambridge Bay are now the communities where most of the regionally based senior government administrators are located.

Since Iqaluit will be Nunavut's capital, its regional government positions will be transferred to Igloolik. Rankin Inlet and Cambridge Bay will continue to function as regional government centres in the Kivalliq and Kitikmeot regions respectively.

Running an effective decentralized government for a population sprinkled over such a large, high-cost area as Nunavut will depend on a modern telecommunications infrastructure capable of supporting a government information technology network. Recent and continuing advances in the information technology field will make it more cost-effective for the government to move information rather than people. Moving people in Nunavut is tremendously expensive. An advanced telecommunications infrastructure will allow individuals in Nunavut communities to both access the Internet, and to receive Nunavut government programs and services from a distance. Once the infrastructure is in place, the government can establish a network of community access centres for people without computers and Internet access.

Effect of Land Claim on Nunavut Government

The Nunavut government, albeit a public government, will be affected by certain provisions of the Nunavut Land Claims Agreement (NLCA). One requirement is the employment of Inuit in the public service in proportion to their number in Nunavut society. As an initial target for April 1, 1999, Nunavut planners set a 50 per cent Inuit hire goal across all categories of government employment. This target will be gradually raised to as high as 85 per cent to reflect the Inuit proportion of the population in Nunavut.

The Nunavut government will also gain some decision-making capacity in areas of jurisdiction that the federal government normally reserves for itself in Canada's territories. The NLCA requires the appointment of Inuit and Nunavut government representatives along with federal government representatives to positions on institutions of public administration established under the NLCA. Inuit appointees and Nunavut government representatives (many of whom may also be Inuit) will sit as equals with federal officials on such bodies as the Nunavut Wildlife Management Board, Nunavut Planning Commission, Nunavut Impact Review Board and the Nunavut Water Board.

The Nunavut government, along with Inuit appointees, will have a voice in matters of federal jurisdiction, such as the management of wildlife species under federal jurisdiction; the disposition of rights in lands, waters and mineral resources on Crown lands; the approval of official land use plans; and the approval of project development certificates for projects on Crown lands. Also, because the land and resource management provisions of the NLCA apply to marine areas, the Nunavut government will have a role in decisions affecting the use and control over offshore areas and resources — something it might otherwise lack.

Financing

The Nunavut government will largely depend on the government of Canada for its operational costs and the cost of providing public services. Under a recently negotiated five-year formula financing agreement, commencing April 1, 1999, the Nunavut government will receive an unconditional grant from the government of Canada of about $600 million each year over a five-year period. This grant will account for approximately 95 per cent of Nunavut government revenues, the balance of which will be raised by the Nunavut government through taxation (for example, personal, corporate, fuel, and property) and through the sales of goods and services.

The Nunavut government will be implemented over three to four years, beginning with a small core government of roughly 150 to 225 new headquarters public servants by April 1, 1999. The Nunavut government will remain dependent on the current GNWT for the delivery of programs and services it cannot immediately provide for itself. As it gradually fills the roughly 700 staff positions, and expands its program and service delivery capacity, the role of the GNWT will be simultaneously phased out. The 700 new positions will add to the approximately 2,000 regional, community and facility positions that exist today in the Nunavut region of the NWT, and the almost 1,000 municipal positions indirectly funded by the GNWT.

30. NUNAVUT ORGANIZATIONS

by Terry Rudden

Visitors frequently comment that Nunavut boasts an astonishing abundance of three things: beautiful land, friendly people and...acronyms.

The creation of a new territory and implementation of the largest land claim in history have meant a bewildering proliferation of organizations. Even lifelong northerners get lost in the maze. But don't worry...what follows will enable you to survive a late-night discussion with even the most seasoned Nunatics.

A couple of easy acronyms will get you started. Slide them into your conversation and impress your hosts.

Designated Inuit Organization (DIO): an organization controlled by Inuit, implementing one or more sections of the Nunavut Land Claims Agreement (NLCA).

Institution of Public Government (IPG): an agency jointly governed by Inuit, federal representatives, and the government of the Northwest

Territories (after March 31, 1999, it will be the government of Nunavut instead).

Got it? Good. We'll begin the tour with a look at the major Inuit organizations.

Nunavut Tunngavik Incorporated (NTI)

The Nunavut Land Claims Agreement is a contract between the government and Inuit, giving Inuit rights and obligations associated with management of land, water and wildlife. **Nunavut Tunngavik Incorporated** (NTI) oversees the implementation of Inuit responsibilities — and ensures that governments live up to theirs!

It's a big job. NTI administers more than 35,000 square kilometres of subsurface land, creates and monitors numerous DIOs, and represents Inuit in the creation of the Nunavut government. NTI also provides a pension for elders, a program to support Inuit hunters, scholarships, and a fund to promote the development of Inuit-owned businesses.

Want more information about the claim? Ask NTI.

Regional Inuit Associations (RIAs)

While NTI represents all Inuit of Nunavut, each of Nunavut's three regions has its own Inuit association. The **Qikiqtani Inuit Association**, **Kivalliq Inuit Association** and **Kitikmeot Inuit Association** are partners with NTI in implementing the claim and managing Inuit-owned land. They control surface rights to approximately 350,000 square kilometres, slightly less than the size of Newfoundland.

The RIAs' mandates go beyond land management and claims implementation. They promote social and business development in their regions; they're also the focal points of regional political activity, particularly in health, education, and economic development.

Each RIA has created a private-sector ("birthright") corporation to support the development of Inuit businesses (see Chapter 26, "Doing Business in Nunavut").

Nunavut Trust

Who pays for all this? The land claim included a $1.1-billion settlement that funds operation of claims-related organizations. **Nunavut Trust** manages the purse strings and invests the money on behalf of Inuit. An advisory committee of leading financial and investment experts provides recommendations. Final decisions, however, are made by an appointed Inuit board of trustees.

Nunavut Implementation Training Committee (NITC)

Nunavut means the creation of almost 1,000 DIO and government jobs — an important source of work in a region with one of Canada's highest levels of unemployment. But Alaska and other claims regions have proven that without adequate training, most of these jobs — certainly the best ones — go to outsiders.

The **Nunavut Implementation Training Committee** (NITC) was created to ensure that Inuit are trained to take on these positions. NITC provides training funds to DIOs, offers an Inuit scholarship, and supports special, fast-track training for Inuit managers and executives.

ᓄᐊᕗᑦ ᑲᒥᓯᓇᒍᓚᒃᑐᑉ ᑦᑕᐅᐱᕌᑦ

TATJA KAMISINAGOLAKTOP TITIGAKVIA
OFFICE OF THE INTERIM COMMISSIONER OF NUNAVUT
BUREAU DU COMMISSAIRE INTÉRIMAIRE DU NUNAVUT

Vision for Nunavut
ᑐᖖᒐᖅᑕᖒᑦ ᓴᖅᑭᑕᐅᒍᒪᖕᑦ

For information, contact:

IQALUIT
P.O. Box 1750
Iqaluit, NT X0A 0H0
Tel: (867) 979-5822
Fax: (867) 979-5833

www.icon.gov.nu.ca

OTTAWA
307-350 Sparks Street
Ottawa, ON K1R 7S8
Tel: (613) 233-1818
Fax: (613) 233-1175

In preparation for Nunavut, we are guided by a vision of a government that:

- Places people first;
- Represents and is accountable and fair to all its residents;
- Is a servant of the people of Nunavut;
- Seeks direction from the people;
- Is shaped by and belongs to the people of Nunavut;
- Offers programs and services in an integrated and holistic manner;
- Promotes harmony amongst people;
- Places ownership of well-being into the hands of individuals, families, and communities;
- Conducts itself with integrity and openness;
- Encourages excellence and welcomes creativity; and
- Incorporates the best of Inuit and contemporary government systems.

ᐸᖅᓇ�dᑦᓴᐊᓗᓂ ᓄᐊᕗᑦ, ᕐᔅᐤᒃᑯᑦᓂᖃᕐᑦᓕᐊᓗᑦᑦ ᒪᑐᖕᓚᖒᓄᖒᑦ ᓂᕿᓕᐊᑦ ᐃᓚᐊᒪᖕᑦᕐᐊᖅᒪᖒᑦ:

- ᕐᔅᑕᐊᑐᕐᕿᐊᕐᓂᖖᑦ ᐃᓄᑐᐅᓐᑦ ᓄᐊᕐᑕᐊᖖᑦ;
- ᒃᐱᓗᖅᑐᐊᓗ ᐊᑦᓗ ᒃᐱᒡᔅᖕᒃᑦᑎᕌᕐᐹᓴᑦᓗ ᐃᓄᐊᖖᑦ ᐊᑦᓗ ᐊᕐᓯᐃᑐᑦᑐᓚᖒ ᓄᐊᕐᑕᐊᖖᑦ;
- ᓕᐊᕐᓯᖖᑦᓇᑐᖒᖖᑦ ᓄᐊᕐᑕᐊᖖᑦ;
- ᐱᓂᖅᓗᑐᖖᑦ ᑐᕐᒃᐊᒃᑐᐊᕐᓂᖖᑦ ᐃᓇᖕᐊᕐᓂᑦ;
- ᐊᖅᐱᐅᖅᑕᐊᖖᑕᐅᑐᐊᓗ ᐊᑦᓗ ᐊᖖᒃᓯᐅᕐᑦᕐᑦᐊᓗᓂᐊ ᐃᓄᐊᖕᐃᒪᐊᑦ ᓄᐊᕐᑦ;
- ᐸᑦᓕᖅᑦᒃᖕᑦᑎᕌᑐᖖᑦ ᐸᓕᓐᑦᐊᖖᑦᓄᖒᑦ ᐊᕐᑦᓗ ᓕᐊᕐᓯᖒᖅᓯᐅᑦᐱᑐᖒᖖᑦ ᐊᖖᒃᓚᒃᓄᖒᑦ ᐊᖖᑦᓗ ᐃᓄᐊᑦᔅᓗᖒᖖᑦ;
- ᐃᓄᒃᐅᓐᑦᑦᕐᔅᔪᐊᓗᖕᑦᑦᑐᕐᕐᔅᖒᐊᕐᖖᑦᐊᑦ;
- ᕿᐃᓄᐊᓐᒃᑕᐅᑦᓗᐊᖖᑦᒃᑦᐊᓗ ᐊᖖᑦᓕᖕᖒ ᓕᐊᑐᕐᐊᖅᖒᐊᖖᑦᑐᖒᕐᑦᐅᕐᑦ ᐃᓄᐊᐃᑦ, ᒃᑦᑎᖖᒃᓚᒃᔅᕐᓄᑦᑦ, ᐊᖖᑦᓗ ᓄᐊᒃᔅᕐᑦ;
- ᐊᐱᑦᓄᖒᖖᓚᖅᓄᖒᑦ ᕐᔅᓄᖅᐅᕐᖖᖕ ᐊᖖᑦᓗ ᓗᒐᐊᔅᓕᖅᓗᐅᕐᑦᖒᖖᑦᐅᕐᑦ;
- ᑲᒃᔅᐱᖅᓚᐊᐃᐊᑐᖖᑦ ᐃᓄᐊᐤᑕᕐᔅᐆᔅᓱᖒᐊᕐᑎᖒᕐᖒᕐᑕᐅᕌᕐᖖᒃ ᐊᖖᑦᓗ ᑐᓇᒃᖒᓚᑦᓄᖒᕐᓚᒃ ᑲᐅᐊᑐᕐᑕᐅᑦᖒᕐᔅᕐᔪᕌᐊᖖᒃᑦᐊᕐᕐᑦ ᐊᖖᑦᓗᐊ;
- ᑲᓇᑕᓚᖒᕐᑦ ᐸᑦᓄᐊᖒᑦᑦ ᐊᓄᐊᐤᑦ ᐃᓕᖒᖕᑐᖒᓚᑦᑦ ᐊᖖᑦᓗ ᓚᖖᐊᑐᖕᒃ ᓄᐊᕌᖕᑦᓄᖒᑦ ᐊᖖᑦᑕᐅᐊᑕᑦᑦ.

NUNAVUT TUNNGAVIK

Our land.
Our culture.
Our identity.

Nunavut Tunngavik Incorporated (NTI) ensures that Inuit interests are protected and encouraged under the Nunavut Land Claims Agreement. Our goal is to give the Inuit of Nunavut further control of their destiny and promote Inuit language and values in a way that reflects Nunavut's cultural diversity.

By advancing the business interests of Inuit in Nunavut, NTI helps promote Inuit economic self-sufficiency and prosperity through strategic partnering and responsible management of Inuit-owned land.

For more information, visit our web site at: www.tunngavik.com

Ottawa
130 Albert Street
Suite 1510
Ottawa, Ontario
K1P 5G4
Tel: (613) 238-1096
Fax: (613) 238-4131

Iqaluit
Parnaivik Building
P.O. Box 638
Iqaluit, NT
X0A 0H0
Tel: (867) 979-3232
Fax: (867) 979-3240

Cambridge Bay
P.O. Box 1041
Cambridge Bay, NT
X0E 0C0
Tel: (867) 983-2517
Fax: (867) 983-2723

Rankin Inlet
Sakku Building
Box 280
Rankin Inlet, NT
X0C 0G0
Tel: (867) 645-5400
Fax: (867) 645-3451

NUNAVUT TUNNGAVIK INCORPORATED

Safeguarding the rights and benefits of the Inuit of Nunav

Regional Wildlife Organizations (RWOs), Hunters and Trappers Organizations (HTOs)

Hunting is the heart of Inuit culture. Ensuring the protection and responsible management of wildlife was a key reason for the claim. Harvesting in Nunavut is managed regionally by three organizations: the **Keewatin Wildlife Federation**, **Qikiqtaaluk Wildlife Board**, and **Kitikmeot Hunters and Trappers Organization**. The RWOs combine traditional and scientific knowledge to set regional hunting policies, ensuring long-term sustainability of wildlife populations.

RWOs represent the 27 community-based Hunters and Trappers Organizations (HTOs) in their regions. These associations of local hunters appoint members to the RWOs, administer programs for hunters' support, and provide grass-roots policy direction to the RWOs.

Nunavut Social Development Council (NSDC)

Social policy affecting Inuit was historically handed down from Ottawa and Yellowknife. Now the **Nunavut Social Development Council** (NSDC) provides an Inuit perspective to government when laws and programs affecting Inuit are being developed. NSDC is working with RIAs, NTI and the OIC on long-term strategies to incorporate traditional knowledge into Nunavut policy-making.

Inuit Heritage Trust (IHT)

The **Inuit Heritage Trust** (IHT) plays an important role in the management and protection of Nunavut's heritage resources. The Trust reviews applications to conduct archeological research, consults with government and Inuit organizations on the loan and use of archeological, ethnographic and archival collections, and assists government in the development of heritage policy and legislation.

One of IHT's most interesting tasks is its involvement in Nunavut's gradual transition to traditional Inuktitut placenames, a project that will guarantee a new look for maps, resource material — and this handbook!

Inuit Broadcasting Corporation (IBC)

He's not quite Kermit, but the Nunavut Puppet To Know is definitely Johnny the Lemming, small, fuzzy star of *Takuginai*, one of several award-winning programs produced by the **Inuit Broadcasting Corporation** (IBC). IBC operates five northern studios, broadcasting five hours weekly of Inuktitut news, current affairs, children's and youth shows, and cultural and entertainment programming.

Congratulations! You've made it through the labyrinth of Inuit organizations. Now brace yourself for...the IPGs.

While these organizations are distinct and independent of each other, their common goal is the protection of Inuit rights relating to land and wildlife. Together, they form an integrated lands and resource management system.

Nunavut Wildlife Management Board (NWMB)

While the RWOs and HTOs oversee harvesting at the regional and local levels, the **Nunavut Wildlife Management Board** (NWMB) develops wildlife management and regulates access to wildlife throughout the entire Nunavut Settlement Area (the area defined in Section 3.1.1 of the Nunavut Land Claims Agreement). The NWMB spearheads a management system that supports and complements Inuit harvesting rights while ensuring the long-term health of wildlife. It also co-ordinates its activities with the RWOs and HTOs.

The NWMB promotes informed policy development and decision-making in wildlife management by funding scientific and traditional knowledge research through its Research Trust Fund (for government agencies) and Wildlife Research Fund (for non-governmental organizations).

Current projects include a five-year study on populations of wildlife species harvested by Inuit, and research on Inuit knowledge of the bowhead whale.

Nunavut Water Board (NWB)

You guessed it...the **Nunavut Water Board** (NWB) regulates the use and management of inland fresh water. They safeguard the quality, quantity and flow of water in lakes, rivers, streams and wetlands. While their policies won't affect most visitors, corporate consumers of water — hamlets, prospecting and mining companies, and fishing, hunting and tourism operators — must obtain licences for water use.

Nunavut Planning Commission (NPC)

Inuit are attempting to balance two distinct needs: the preservation and protection of land and wildlife for future generations, and the creation of revenue through sustainable development of Nunavut's rich resources. The **Nunavut Planning Commission** (NPC) is developing plans to protect that delicate balance.

The NPC works with Nunavut residents, governments, Inuit organizations, industry and others to establish land-use planning goals and design comprehensive regional land-use plans to guide resource use and development. Combining Inuit knowledge with digital mapping technology, NPC's planning will give Inuit control over activities on settlement lands, and a voice in the development of Crown lands.

Nunavut Impact Review Board (NIRB)

To develop a project in Nunavut, certain authorization is required for the use of land, water and the marine environment. But before an agency can authorize this kind of use in the Nunavut Settlement Area, the **Nunavut Impact Review Board** (NIRB) may have to assess the ecosystemic and socio-economic impacts of the project proposal to see whether the project should go ahead, and if so, under what conditions. NIRB uses traditional knowledge and scientific methods in making these assessments.

Nunavut Surface Rights Tribunal (NSRT)

If an RIA and a developer can't agree on terms of access, the issue may be referred to the **Nunavut Surface Rights Tribunal** (NSRT), which can issue entry orders permitting developers to enter and use Inuit land, subject to the payment of a fee. Fees vary depending on the market value of the land, the impact of land use on hunting, the land's cultural significance, and other considerations.

The next two public agencies evolved out of the *Nunavut Act*, the federal legislation responsible for the creation of the territory of Nunavut.

Nunavut Implementation Commission (NIC)

Since 1993, a small team of planners has been working on the challenge of a lifetime...the design of a new government, from scratch.

The **Nunavut Implementation Commission** (NIC) was established to prepare recommendations for the federal government, the GNWT and NTI on governance structures reflecting Nunavut's special character and needs. Under the direction of Chief Commissioner John Amagoalik, NIC grappled with issues ranging from the choice of a territorial capital to the size of Nunavut's legislature. Their recommendations, published as *Footprints in New Snow* and *Footprints 2*, are essential reading for anyone interested in Nunavut politics.

Nunavut's government will have powers similar to those of existing territorial governments, with an elected legislative assembly, a cabinet and a territorial court. There will, however, be important differences. Many departments will be headquartered in smaller settlements, bringing government closer to the communities. Moreover, an official working language of the new government will be Inuktitut.

Office of the Interim Commissioner (OIC)

In April 1997, Jack Anawak, previously member of Parliament for the federal riding that represents Nunavut, was appointed Interim Commissioner. His task...to create a working Nunavut government by April 1, 1999. Ten new deputy ministers and their staff are designing new departments, negotiating funding formulas, preparing staffing and training plans...rather like competing in a dogteam race while simultaneously building the *qamutik*.

OTHER INUIT ORGANIZATIONS

Although most Canadian Inuit live in Nunavut, there are significant Inuit populations in northern Quebec, Labrador and the western Arctic. Many Inuit concerns aren't confined by territorial and provincial boundaries. That's why national Inuit organizations, as well as international Inuit organizations, are an important part of Nunavut's political and social environment.

Inuit Tapirisat of Canada (ITC)

The **Inuit Tapirisat of Canada** (ITC) represents the 41,000 Inuit of the Northwest Territories, northern Quebec and Labrador, providing a voice on national concerns.

Since its creation in 1971, ITC has launched many of the organizations and leaders that shape the current political landscape. The Nunavut Land Claims Agreement, the creation of a Nunavut territory, and the IBC all began as ITC initiatives.

Much of ITC's work in the early '90s focused on the constitutional relationship between Inuit and Canada. Today, ITC promotes Inuit positions on a wide range of political, economic, social and environmental issues.

Inuit Circumpolar Conference (ICC)

Created in 1977, the **Inuit Circumpolar Conference** (ICC) is a non-government organization representing the 135,000 Inuit of Canada, Alaska, Greenland and Chukotka (Russia). ICC works to strengthen unity among Inuit, promoting sustainable development and Inuit rights and interests internationally.

Initially focused on environmental and political concerns, ICC has recently begun to promote Inuit participation in economic development and joint ventures across the circumpolar region, and with indigenous peoples internationally.

Pauktuutit

Pauktuutit works to raise awareness of the social, cultural and economic needs of Inuit women, and to encourage their participation in community, regional and national concerns. Pauktuutit is recognized for its ground-breaking work on such culturally sensitive issues as family violence, youth suicide, and substance abuse. A current priority is development of a strategy to address the growing threat of HIV/AIDS among Inuit.

NUNAVUT TAKES CONTROL: DIRECTORY

Department of Community Government, Housing and Transportation
Government of Nunavut
Brown Building
Bag 800, Iqaluit NT,
X0A 0H0 Canada
Tel.: (867) 979-4690
Fax: (867) 979-5220

Department of Culture, Language, Elders and Youth
Government of Nunavut
Brown Building
Bag 800, Iqaluit NT,
X0A 0H0 Canada
Tel.: (867) 979-4720
Fax: (867) 979-5240

Department of Education
Government of Nunavut
Brown Building
Bag 800, Iqaluit NT,
X0A 0H0 Canada
Tel.: (867) 979-4720
Fax: (867) 979-5240

Department of Executive and Intergovernmental Affairs
Government of Nunavut
Grinnell Place
Bag 800, Iqaluit NT,
X0A 0H0 Canada
Tel.: (867) 979-4802
Fax: (867) 979-4774

Department of Finance and Administration
Government of Nunavut
Building 1079
Bag 800, Iqaluit NT,
X0A 0H0 Canada
Tel.: (867) 979-4730
Fax: (867) 979-5250

Department of Health and Social Services
Government of Nunavut
Brown Building
Bag 800, Iqaluit NT,
X0A 0H0 Canada
Tel.: (867) 979-6020
Fax: (867) 979-5250

Department of Justice
Government of Nunavut
Court House
Bag 800, Iqaluit NT,
X0A 0H0 Canada
Tel.: (867) 979-6000
Fax: (867) 979-5977

Department of Personnel
Government of Nunavut
Building 1079
Bag 800, Iqaluit NT,
X0A 0H0 Canada
Tel.: (867) 979-4642
Fax: (867) 979-4755

Department of Public Works, Telecommunications and Technical Services
Government of Nunavut
Brown Building
Bag 800, Iqaluit NT,
X0A 0H0 Canada
Tel.: (867) 979-4720
Fax: (867) 979-5240

Department of Sustainable Development
Government of Nunavut
Brown Building
Bag 800, Iqaluit NT,
X0A 0H0 Canada
Tel.: (867) 979-5134
Fax: (867) 979-5920

Inuit Broadcasting Corporation
Suite 703,
251 Laurier Ave. W., Ottawa ON,
K1P 5J6 Canada
Tel.: (613) 235-1892
Fax: (613) 230-8824

Production Centre:
P.O. Box 700, Iqaluit NT,
X0A 0H0 Canada
Tel.: (867) 979-6231
Fax: (867) 979-5853
E-mail: ibc@nunanet.com
Web site: www.tvnc.ca/Members/
ibc.html or www.icsl.ca

Inuit Circumpolar Conference
Suite 504,
170 Laurier Ave W., Ottawa ON,
K1P 5V5 Canada
Tel.: (613) 563-2642
Fax: (613) 565-3089
E-mail: tuktu@magi.com
Web site: www.inusiaat.com

Inuit Heritage Trust
P.O. Box 2080, Iqaluit NT,
X0A 0H0 Canada
Tel.: (867) 979-0731
Fax: (867) 979-0269
E-mail: heritage@nunanet.com

Inuit Tapirisat of Canada
Suite 510,
170 Laurier Ave W., Ottawa ON,
K1P 5V5 Canada
Tel.: (613) 238-8181
Fax: (613) 234-1991
E-mail: itc@magi.com
Web site: interimpact.com/itc/index.html

Keewatin Wildlife Federation
P.O. Box 229, Arviat NT,
X0C 0E0 Canada
Tel.: (867) 857-2695
Fax: (867) 857-2990
E-mail: kwfjan@nunanet.com

Kitikmeot Hunters and Trappers Organization
P.O. Box 309, Kugluktuk NT,
X0E 0E0 Canada
Tel.: (867) 982-4207
Fax: (867) 982-4047
E-mail: khtaedi@nunanet.com

Kitikmeot Inuit Association
P.O. Box 18, Cambridge Bay NT,
X0E 0C0 Canada
Tel.: (867) 983-2458
Fax: (867) 983-2701
E-mail: basler@polarnet.ca

Kivalliq Inuit Association
P.O. Box 340, Rankin Inlet NT,
X0C 0G0 Canada
Tel.: (867) 645-2800
Fax: (867) 645-2348
E-mail: quasa@arctic.ca

Legislative Assembly
(Temporary contact information
until April 1999.)
Building 917
Bag 800, Iqaluit NT,
X0A 0H0 Canada
Tel.: (867) 979-6770
Fax: (867) 979-6811

Nunavut Impact Review Board
P.O. Box 2379, Cambridge Bay NT,
X0E 0C0 Canada
Tel.: (867) 983-2593
Fax: (867) 983-2594
E-mail: nirb@polarnet.ca
Web site: ipg.nunavut.ca/nirbpg.htm

Nunavut Implementation Commission
P.O. Box 1109, Iqaluit NT,
X0A 0H0 Canada
Tel.: (867) 979-4199
Fax: (867) 979-6862
E-mail: sawa@nunanet.com
Web site: www.nunanet.com/~nic

Nunavut Implementation Training Committee
P.O. Box 469, Rankin Inlet NT,
X0C 0G0 Canada
Tel.: (867) 645-5441
Fax: (867) 645-3878
E-mail: nitckut@arctic.ca

Nunavut Planning Commission
Bag 12, Taloyoak NT,
X0E 1B0 Canada
Tel.: (867) 561-6896
Fax: (867) 561-6897
E-mail: npc@npc.nunavut.ca
Web site: www.npc.nunavut.ca

Nunavut Social Development Council
P.O. Box 300, Igloolik NT,
X0A 0L0 Canada
Tel.: (867) 934-8065
Fax: (867) 934-8073
E-mail: nsdcig@nunanet.com

Nunavut Surface Rights Tribunal
P.O. Box 1019, Iqaluit NT,
X0A 0H0 Canada
Tel.: (867) 979-1555
Fax: (867) 979-1528
E-mail: nsrt@nunanet.com

Nunavut Trust
Suite 1415,
50 O'Connor St., Ottawa ON,
K1P 6L2 Canada
Tel.: (613) 238-8089
Fax: (613) 238-1299
E-mail: acampbell@istar.com

Nunavut Tunngavik Incorporated
Rankin Inlet office:
P.O. Box 280, Rankin Inlet NT,
X0C 0G0 Canada

Tel.: (867) 645-5400 or 1-888-236-5400
Fax: (867) 645-3451 or 645-3452

Cambridge Bay office:
P.O. Box 1041, Cambridge Bay NT,
X0E 0C0 Canada
Tel.: (867) 983-2517
Fax: (867) 983-2723

Iqaluit office:
P.O. Box 638, Iqaluit NT,
X0A 0H0 Canada
Tel.: (867) 979-3232
Fax: (867) 979-3240

Ottawa office:
Suite 1108,
130 Albert St., Ottawa ON,
K1P 5G4 Canada
Tel.: (613) 238-1096 or 1-800-465-3232
Fax: (613) 238-4131

E-mail for all: nticom@nunanet.com
Web site for all: www.tunngavik.com

Nunavut Water Board
P.O. Box 119, Gjoa Haven NT,
X0E 1J0 Canada
Tel.: (867) 360-6338
Fax: (867) 360-6369
E-mail: nwb@netcom.ca
Web site: ipg.nunavut.ca/nwb

Nunavut Wildlife Management Board
P.O. Box 1379, Iqaluit NT,
X0A 0H0 Canada
Tel.: (867) 979-6962
Fax: (867) 979-7785
E-mail: jnoble@nunanet.com
Web site: www.nunanet.com/~nwmb/

Office of the Interim Commissioner
P.O. Box 1750, Iqaluit NT,
X0A 0H0 Canada
Tel.: (867) 979-5822
Fax: (867) 979-5833
E-mail: earreak@nunanet.com
Web site: www.icon.gov.nu.ca/

Pauktuutit
192 Bank St., Ottawa ON,
K2P 1W8 Canada
Tel.: (613) 238-3977
Fax: (613) 238-1787
E-mail: pauktuut@comnet.ca

Qikiqtaaluk Wildlife Board
P.O. Box 478, Iqaluit NT,
X0A 0H0 Canada
Tel.: (867) 979-1560
Fax: (867) 979-1491

Qikiqtani Inuit Association
P.O. Box 219, Iqaluit NT,
X0A 0H0 Canada
Tel.: (867) 979-5391
Fax: (867) 979-3238
Web site: www.qikiqtani.nu.ca

Art, Music and Recreation

31. INUIT ART AND FINE CRAFTS

by Dave Sutherland

Nunavut's flourishing artistic output is a unique phenomenon, especially given the harsh environment, limited resources, and large volume of work of very high quality that issues from a relatively small population.

Yet it is the harshness of the environment and the limited resources that have contributed to the phenomenon.

Inuit are extremely resourceful and, because of this, they have survived. Men developed a high degree of technical skill and ingenuity to fashion the tools necessary for survival. Women developed a high degree of technical skill to provide the clothing essential to survival. Along with the development of technical skill comes an intimate understanding of, and sensitivity to, the available materials. Also, people from a hunting culture develop strong powers of observation and a strong visual memory, valuable assets for any artist. Excavations have revealed ancient figurative carvings believed to have been talismans. In the historic period, artistic work presents the artist's world — the people and the animals that inhabit it. Sometimes mythical figures are depicted, or creatures from the artist's imagination. More recently, social issues have become the theme of some artists' work. Self-expression, the common motivation of southern artists, is not considered appropriate by the older generation of Inuit artists, but is appearing occasionally in the work of young artists.

There is ample evidence that Inuit carved figurative objects long before contact with Europeans, and certainly women were fashioning garments for their families in those times. During early contact with Europeans, Inuit men created objects to exchange for goods brought by the new strangers, and Inuit women crafted clothing for them. This continued into the 20th century. However, the present phenomenon began with the visit of a young art school graduate, James A. Houston, to the Canadian Arctic in 1948. Houston was able to impress the Canadian government with the income earning potential of the small sculptures that he brought back from his arctic trip. The Hudson's Bay Co. and the government provided support, and the first exhibition of Inuit work was presented by the Canadian Guild of Crafts in Montreal.

If one is unfamiliar with Inuit art, or has only seen the little carved objects in souvenir shops and airport boutiques, a great surprise lies in store. Not only are there beautiful sculptures from miniature to monumental size, but also fine art prints, fabric art, jewelry, ceramics, and exquisite fur products. There is also great stylistic variety from community to community, and from artist to artist.

While the care of Inuit art follows the common-sense guidelines that go hand in hand with fine art, visitors planning to buy untanned fur products to take home should be aware these require special care. Products made of traditionally dressed fur or traditionally tanned hide should be stored in a cool, dry place, preferably in sealed paper bags (not plastic). If you suspect that they have become a home for moths, put them in the freezer for 24 hours.

LAND, SPIRITUALITY, AND MYTHOLOGY IN INUIT ART

by Alootook Ipellie

Inuit culture, like aboriginal cultures from other parts of the world, has a long history of relating to and living off the land's natural resources — the flora and fauna indigenous to the circumpolar Arctic.

It is this long and often intimate relationship with the land that has inspired its craftsmen and artists from ancient to modern times. As evidenced by findings from known archeological excavations, the Dorset and Thule cultures — forebears to the modern Inuit — were expert carvers and craftsmen who designed their own tools and weapons to make survival possible in such a harsh climate.

Many of their tools and weapons were decorated with images of animals that served as spirit helpers, aiding practising shamans in their search for game when famine and starvation invaded their camps. These intricate carvings were often done individually or in clusters on a piece of stone, driftwood, antler, bone or ivory. Some of these spiritual aids would end up on a shaman's clothing or became part of his amulet, which would be strung around his waist or around one or both shoulders with sealskin rope. On occasion, certain shamans would use waterfowl feathers, or skin or fur from different animals, as charms to help evoke animal spirits.

Ancient Inuit had no means to write their people's history, and relied instead on an oral tradition to pass on the stories, legends and mythical tales to each succeeding generation over thousands of years. These same stories often end up depicted in various Inuit art mediums, interpreted in different ways by artists or carvers in each Nunavut community.

One reason so many Inuit become such good artists or carvers is that they come from a very visual culture. Their very livelihood depended solely on dealing with the landscape every day during hunting or gathering expeditions. They were always visualizing animals in their thoughts as they searched the land, waters and skies for game. It is not surprising, then, that their visual talents and imaginations were and are so easily manifested in their art.

Inuit children growing up on the land were exposed to the elements daily while being taught by their elders how to live off the land. They were learning a lifestyle from experts who knew the behavior of all seasons; experts who knew how to hunt each species in a particular way, with certain hunting tools and weapons. When the time came for them to become hunters and gatherers, they had to know how to make and use these same tools and weapons just like their elders.

The Inuit storytelling tradition was passed on to children the same way. That experience of living on the land, together with the knowledge of ancient stories and legends, result in the high standards one sees in Inuit art today.

Inuit have always respected the land. That high regard is still evident in the numerous themes they draw upon, whether these are realistic depictions of everyday life on the land, spiritual images of animals, or mythological interpretations of legends of long ago.

Sculpture

The most common carving material is stone. One regularly hears it referred to as "soapstone." Soapstone or steatite was used for early carvings as it is soft and easily worked. However, because it breaks easily, it is not a good carving material. Most artists now work in serpentine, a stone similar in chemical composition but harder. Argillite, quartzite, and marble are also used.

Most stone is obtained from quarry sites near each community, so it's generally possible to identify the community of origin by the appearance of the stone. For example, Kimmirut quarries an even-textured grey-green stone and a brighter green stone that has the appearance of green marble. Cape Dorset uses similar stone quarried in the same area. Pangnirtung stone and that of many other communities is black. A smooth grey argillite is used by the artists of Sanikiluaq. Repulse Bay has a dark green stone. Arviat stone is very coarse grey that no doubt has influenced the type of work from that community. It does not lend itself to detailed work. Baker Lake stone is similar but darker in tone. There are, of course, exceptions to the rule. If a community finds its local stone difficult to get at, it may take stone from another area. Occasionally, stone has been imported from the South. In communities where stone is scarce, caribou antler, whalebone and ivory have been put to good use.

The quality of the carving material imposes some similarity in the style of work from each community, and no doubt the stronger artists influence others, as happens in every creative community. But within each community, very individualistic styles exist and, with familiarity, one can begin to pick out the work of individual artists. In the whole of Nunavut, there is great variety from artist to artist.

Prints

It is important to first distinguish between commercially lithographed prints produced in editions of hundreds, and fine art prints produced by hand in a studio, usually in editions of 50 and often printed by the artist. It is the latter for which Nunavut artists have become famous.

Printmaking began in Cape Dorset. James Houston was inspired to try printmaking when an Inuk artist, Osuitok, commented that Inuit could do it. The result is that Cape Dorset artists have produced annual editions highly prized by collectors for more than 35 years. Beautiful prints are also produced by artists in Pangnirtung.

Frequently, the drawings are done by older artists and given to others to print. In a number of cases the artist is the printmaker. In some communities (Cape Dorset, for example), the printmaker controls the final image. In other communities, the printmaker tries to produce a print that is as close to the original drawing as possible. A variety of processes are used: stone cuts (the image is cut in a stone block and the paper laid on the inked block), stencils, and lithography. In all cases, the finest quality paper and inks are used to ensure stability of the images.

Fabric Arts

Although many women work in stone, an attempt was made by the federal government to find activities in the art and fine craft field that would be more in keeping with women's traditional skills. A weaving project started in 1969 in Pangnirtung produces beautiful tapestries using European tapestry techniques. The designs are taken from drawings by elders and transformed by highly skilled weavers.

In Baker Lake, women began making garments for sale in the early '60s — winter parkas and vests cut from the heavy wool blanket called "duffel," originally imported from England by the Hudson's Bay Co. The garments were appliquéd and embroidered. The garment industry was not an easy one to master because of constant style changes and the remoteness of northern communities from fashion centres. It was found, however, that the skills used to decorate parkas could be put to use making beautiful cloth pictures. Baker Lake's appliquéd and richly embroidered wall hangings have been featured in public and private art gallery exhibitions in Canada and the United States.

There is evidence that Inuit women made dolls from the earliest times. The women of today have almost raised doll-making to an art form. Each community has women who make dolls on a casual basis. Some years ago, the women of Taloyoak organized production of what was referred to as the "packing dolls" — animal figures wearing an *amauti* or baby-packing parka containing a miniature of the mother animal. The women, who have achieved a reputation for exquisite workmanship, are now inventing variations on the theme under the name "Taluq," using new synthetic fabrics that are washable.

Another artisan who does similar work is Martina Anoee of Arviat. She makes very fine dolls from seal fur and hide, the faces of which are reminiscent of apple dolls.

Jewelry

The early inhabitants of the Arctic worked in ivory and bone. Their work was small in size, as necessitated by their nomadic lifestyle. It is natural, then, that people today readily take to the production of jewelry. Even before a jewelry workshop was established in Iqaluit in the late '60s, much was produced on an individual basis from local materials.

At the workshop, artists have been trained in the use of fine metals, predominantly silver. They also use local materials such as ivory, caribou antler and colored stones. Some artists have carried silversmithing into the realm of metal sculpture. Artist Looty Pijamini of Grise Fiord uses skills learned at the jewelry workshop to produce sculpture in silver.

Ceramics

In the 1960s and early '70s, artists in Rankin Inlet were encouraged to try working with clay. While the results achieved critical success, the project was not successful economically. Recently, a private gallery in Rankin has encouraged artists to return to the medium, inspiring younger people to try their hand. The new work shows a definite link with the past, but artists are also experimenting with new themes and techniques. A few pieces have been cast in bronze.

Prices

Should one wish to purchase objects to take home, a great range in size, quality and price can be found. The following is a rough guide.

Sculpture: small pieces can be found for $100. The prices rise with size and quality to monumental pieces of several thousand dollars.

Prints range in price from $100 to $800. The prices are set when the prints go to market and are the same at all galleries throughout the country.

Fabric Arts: Pangnirtung tapestries range in price from $450 to $5,000. Embroidered wall hangings can be had for $100 to $400 for those considered fine crafts. Those categorized as fine art are from $600 up to several thousand dollars. Dolls range from $150 to $400.

Jewelry: while it is possible to find small items for less than $50, most jewelry is in the $50 to $200 range.

Ceramic pieces are in the $250 to $400 range. Those cast in bronze range from $1,500 to $2,500.

For restrictions on exporting Inuit art objects from Canada, see Chapter 2, "Entering Canada."

32. INUIT MUSIC

by David Serkoak, with contributions from Ann Meekitjuk Hanson and Peter Ernerk

For centuries, music has been an important part of daily life in Nunavut. From traditional forms such as drum dancing and throat singing to contemporary stars such as Susan Aglukark and the singing duo Tudjaat, music has helped define Inuit culture through rapidly changing times.

Of all forms of traditional Inuit music, none was more popular than drum dancing, which played a part in almost every gathering, whether it be a celebration of birth, a marriage, the changing of the seasons, a successful hunt, a first kill, a greeting for visitors, or to honor someone who had died. In these instances, news of a special event would be spread by word of mouth; many people would travel long distances to attend. Some dances took place with just a few participants; others might fill the huge *qaggiq*, a special snowhouse where people gathered to socialize.

Drum dancing was enjoyed by people of all ages. In the traditional dance, singers — usually women — sat in a circle. Sometimes a man would volunteer to be the first dancer; at other times a group of men sitting behind the singers would coax someone to start. If no one came forward, the women would start singing, usually a personal song (*pisiit*) of a man in attendance, who would then be obligated to dance. Except for occasional tea breaks, drum dances continued unabated long into the night. Women and children usually participated in the drumming toward the end of the dance.

While drum dancing is not as important to Inuit life as it once was, it is still practised in communities such as Arviat, Baker Lake, Rankin Inlet, Repulse Bay, Gjoa Haven, Kugluktuk, Cambridge Bay, Pelly Bay, Taloyoak and Igloolik. Unfortunately, drum dancing is generally no longer practised for traditional reasons; in most places it is done for tourists. It is sometimes performed at symbolic celebrations, such as opening ceremonies for conferences and festivals, at graduations, and in movie productions. I grew up with the sound of the drum beating in my ears. It was always exciting to have other adults and children visit our home for a drum dance. When the children were invited to participate, we would say the drum was too heavy. My mother never accepted that excuse. She would hold one side of the drum for me and I would dance, my friends chuckling all the while.

Today, I enjoy drum dancing with my youngest daughter, Karla. My parents believed drum dancing enhanced your life, and it brings me joy to watch my daughter drum dancing beside me. The late Donald Suluk, a respected elder from Arviat, once said: "When I was a child I didn't know the meaning of the songs. I thought at the time they were just for fun and that they belonged to the shamans. Now I know they are not only for shamans, they are for the world to enjoy."

In the past, singing was also a very important part of Inuit culture. Almost every adult had their own personal song, of which there were many types: songs of contest, songs of satire, and occasionally, humorous songs with obscene lyrics. There were songs about hardship, happiness, loneliness, love, and hatred. There were also songs of legends that have been a part of Inuit music for centuries. Some songs were rivalry songs, where two "enemies" would insult each other through lyrics. One such song might go like this:

"*Aijaa, una-ija-ija*, how I think the little old squaw is foolish! Oh, how old squaw is foolish, *ija-ija-ja-ji-ja-jaa*!

Aijaa, why I think it is foolish that old squaw is moving on to the other side of the world, how I feel it is foolish."

Every song was a story in itself, a life experience of the composer. Some songs, however, had no ownership. These were sung to Inuit transients who attended a dance while passing through a camp, and were sometimes even sung to non-Inuit. Personal songs could also be given to another person. A song owner might give his song to show appreciation for help given in time of need, or to someone bearing the same name as himself.

Throat singing is a well-known form of Inuit music that is usually performed by two women. The singers stand face to face; it helps if one singer is taller than the other. Each singer repeats a different sound in a fast rhythm. The low-pitched sound that is the trademark of throat singing represents sounds made by different birds and animals. Sometimes, throat singing can be a contest to see who can sing the longest. Some women are able to throat sing by themselves, using a large bowl or kettle held near the singer's mouth to give resonance. This method is common in the Arviat area.

If you would like to try throat singing, here are the basics. Try to make a sound deep in your throat without making noise from your mouth. Make the sound as you exhale, then inhale quickly without making a sound. Repeat this, remembering to make sounds only when you exhale. The sounds can be long or short.

European music first came to the Inuit from whalers and traders of the Hudson's Bay Co. in the form of songs and instruments, especially the mouth organ, button accordion, fiddle, and jew's-harp. With the arrival of radio, country-and-western and bluegrass music also came to Nunavut. Many Inuit sent to southern hospitals also heard new tunes that they brought back to Nunavut.

Most of today's famous Inuit musicians are self-taught, and continue to be largely influenced by country-and-western music. Gospel music is another very popular style of singing. Inuit musicians, especially pioneers like Charlie Panigoniak, Simon Sigjariaq, Mary Atuat Thompson, Peter and Susan Aningmiuq, William Tagoona, Colin Adjun and Itulu Itidlui are very popular with the general public here. Many combine aspects of traditional Inuit music with modern instruments.

Many Inuit musicians first became well known across the North after being heard on CBC North radio. Today, the annual True North Concert and media coverage of regional music festivals bring these performers to an even wider audience.

Today's social gatherings and community celebrations are often highlighted by square dances (see Chapter 55, "Dances"). Bands play time-worn tunes from across the Atlantic that were introduced to the North long ago by homesick whalers and traders. Each region has a distinct style of square dancing.

33. TRADITIONAL INUIT GAMES
by Simeonie Kunnuk

Tavvauvugut **means "Here we are!" It is good to be here and alive! Life. What is it that makes Inuit life bearable in the Arctic where extremes persist in a variety of forms?**

First, there are the three months of winter darkness accompanied by freezing temperatures averaging –30° C during the coldest months. Next, there are nine months of snow, beginning in autumn and lasting through to spring.

For Inuit who have learned to embrace their arctic homeland completely, this is where games play a very important aspect in adapting to the severe environment. Both men and women compete in tests of strength — as a diversion during the long months and as a means of staying physically fit. The traveller to Nunavut has the opportunity to witness the wonders and excitement of an Inuk sharing in friendly competitions and battles of abilities and skills to which the human body can acquire greatly unexpected potential.

To thrive and succeed rather than just survive — that is what makes living not only bearable, but also satisfactory and enjoyable!

Interactive Arm Strength

One of the most popular Inuit games is the *aqsaaraq* (the hand-pull). It is also one of the simplest tests of physical strength. A short thong of about five centimetres is tied to a handlebar at either end of the thong. Two individuals each grasp a handlebar with both hands. One person locks into position by placing an elbow firmly to the body, or by leveraging the elbow against the knee, depending on whether the competition is done standing up or sitting down. The other player is invited to pull after being informed that the lock is fully secure. Testing each other for the first one or two attempts, one player may bluff and let the other pull his or her own locked position. Then one will take the initiative to actually prevent the other from pulling one's locked position. This they will do until one concedes to the winner gracefully, while the winner thanks the opponent for being allowed to win for that particular competition. It is a game of strategy as well as skill, for it is commonly known that strength varies for different reasons. Sometimes players prefer not to reveal all their talents at once, lulling opponents into false confidence.

Arm pulling has two variations. In *basic upper-arm competition*, two opponents sit down and face each other, each with a foot placed on the other's bent knee. The individuals lock one set of forearms together and, upon a signal, pull at the same time until one straightens his or her arm in concession to the winner. In *combined upper-body-and-arm competition*, competitors lock either their right or left arms at the elbow for greater strength, and bring their bodies closer by lacing legs together. If right arms are locked, for example, each competitor grips his opponent's right leg using his left hand. This creates leverage when pulling. The upper body and especially the back is used when pulling until, once again, the loser is pulled up by the winner who has leaned as far back as possible.

High Kicks

High kicks are the most spectacular games. There are three types: the two-foot and one-foot high kicks, and the Alaskan high kick. The two-foot high kick and the one-foot high kick are attention-getters because they demand a high level of impressive activity that suggests poetry in motion. Both involve jumping up, kicking a suspended object, and landing in a style unique to that game. The suspended object, often a rolled-up piece of sealskin, is tied to a string and hoisted gradually higher as competitors take turns trying to kick it until only one player remains eligible. Three attempts per turn are allowed.

Two-foot high kick: both feet are kept together throughout the jump, the kick, and the landing. The record kick for this game is more than eight feet in height.

One-foot high kick: the contestant jumps with both feet, kicks the suspended object with one foot, then lands with the same foot while keeping the other foot off the floor. The record held in this event is more than nine feet.

Alaskan high kick: this involves single-hand-and-foot balance on the floor while the other hand holds the contra-lateral foot (contra-lateral refers to a diagonal motion; the right hand would grasp the left foot, for example). The contestant supports his or her body using only the contra-lateral hand and foot. A suspended object is the target of the kick. Using his foot, the contestant kicks up toward the target while balancing on the one hand. Executing this movement calls for practice because it requires wrist strength as well as body co-ordination in extending the leg toward the suspended object. The landing is tricky, too, because the same contra-lateral hand-foot balance must be regained after kicking the target.

One-hand reach: this is difficult to execute. Balancing on two hands in the beginning, the individual reaches up with one hand toward the suspended target without letting any part of the body touch the floor. One needs to have good balance in addition to strong arms and wrists in order to complete this very challenging event.

These are the most impressive Inuit games, and they are commonly known throughout the circumpolar Inuit community. However, there are many other intricate Inuit games that defy explanation in one short chapter. Among them are the airplane/bird flight, seal-hop, *aattaujaq* (teams try to keep possession of ball), *amaruujaq* (wolf tag), *aqsaq* (soccer, in which teams assume names of birds), *tigluuti* (shoulder-hitting or temple-hitting), lip-pulling, head-pull, muskox fight, leg wrestle, and a variety of Inuit gymnastics performed on a rope suspended horizontally above the ground. Some of these games are part of the annual Northern Games or the biennial Arctic Winter Games.

Most games were relevant to survival tactics, and tested one's ability, too. In the days of survival, strong arms and hands were required to harpoon walruses, whales and polar bears and then hold on to the powerful, struggling animal. Strong and agile legs ensured one could jump over bears, outrun wolves or catch caribou. There are many stories that have turned into legends about one Inuk or another capable of incredible athletic feats, kept hidden until it became absolutely necessary to use them.

These abilities probably exist still today. Who knows? Mysteries abound forever. *Taima* ("that is all").

Land and Wildlife

34. PHYSICAL GEOGRAPHY

by Olav Loken

Nunavut is a large territory covering some two million square kilometres. This is about one-fifth of Canada, or an area close to half of Europe, excluding Russia.

The distance from Nunavut's western boundary to Cape Dyer on the east coast of Baffin Island is approximately 2,400 kilometres; in the other direction, it is about 2,700 kilometres from the Manitoba border to the northern tip of Ellesmere Island. (For comparison, the distance from Toronto to Calgary is about 2,700 kilometres. In Europe, the distance between London and Istanbul is slightly more than 2,400 kilometres.) The territory also includes Sanikiluaq and other islands in Hudson Bay and James Bay, hundreds of kilometres south of the main part of Nunavut. This chapter gives a general overview of the physical geography of this large area; see the chapters in "Destinations" for details on specific areas, as well as the maps at the beginning of this book.

Approximately 45 per cent of the land area of Nunavut lies on the northern part of Canada's mainland. The rest is distributed throughout a large archipelago of hundreds of islands, including Baffin Island (Canada's largest), as well as Ellesmere, Axel Heiberg and Devon islands. Twelve of the 20 largest islands in Canada lie entirely within Nunavut. The Parry Channel, running from Lancaster Sound off Baffin Bay in the east to the Arctic Ocean in the west, separates the Queen Elizabeth Islands to the north from the rest of the territory.

Climate

Nunavut covers the northernmost and coldest parts of Canada. January mean surface temperatures range from around –20° C at the southern tip of Baffin Island, which is influenced by the Labrador Sea to the southeast, to less than –37° C around Lake Hazen on northern Ellesmere Island. As would be expected, the lowest winter temperatures occur in the northernmost part of the territory, but temperatures almost as low (below –35° C) are experienced in an area west of Wager Bay, almost 2,000 kilometres farther south. This is due to its continental location far from the major oceans.

July mean temperatures range from above 10° C in the southern part of the mainland to less than 2° C in the north. The maritime influence keeps the coastal areas relatively warm during the winter, but cool in the summer when the land is generally warmer than the sea. During the summer, inland locations, such as the Tanquary Fiord-Lake Hazen area on Ellesmere Island, often enjoy temperatures well above the regional averages. Due to the low mean temperatures, there is continuous permafrost throughout the territory; only a rather shallow surface layer (15 to 150 centimetres) thaws every summer and refreezes during the following winter.

Annual precipitation ranges from more than 600 millimetres in an area on southern Baffin Island to less than 100 millimetres in the northern part; the area around Eureka on Ellesmere Island is the driest part of Nunavut.

Precipitation levels are generally low, and only a small part of the territory receives more than 300 millimetres per year. The highest precipitation occurs in the highlands along the eastern seaboard from southern Baffin Island to Ellesmere Island, due to a combination of topography and the maritime influence of the Labrador Sea and Baffin Bay. While the north-western part of the archipelago is close to the Arctic Ocean, the continuous ice cover reduces evaporation and limits the maritime influence of this water body. This part of Nunavut receives less precipitation than parts of the Sahara Desert, and can be described as a polar desert.

Geology and Landforms

The southern part of the territory — the mainland and Baffin Island — is part of the Canadian Shield, consisting of rocks typically more than a billion years old. This rock formation extends to parts of Ellesmere Island. Younger, sedimentary rocks in largely horizontal layers cover the northern part of the Shield on Nunavut's western islands and along the Parry Channel, as well as smaller isolated areas further south, such as the islands in Foxe Basin and parts of Southampton Island. Except for their southern and eastern parts, the Queen Elizabeth Islands consist of still younger, and in part heavily folded, formations.

The highest mountains in Nunavut are found along the eastern part of the territory, where the land has risen in relatively recent geological time. A highland with many peaks reaching 1,500 metres to 2,000 metres above sea level extends from south of Cape Dyer on Baffin Island to Ellesmere Island. Northern Ellesmere is even higher and contains Nunavut's highest mountain: Mount Barbeau (2,616 metres). The mountains on Axel Heiberg Island reach about 2,200 metres above sea level. From the eastern Baffin highland, the Shield slopes gradually southwestwards to Foxe Basin and re-emerges on the west side of Hudson Bay, rising towards the west. The Boothia Peninsula, at the northern extreme of the mainland, reaches altitudes of about 600 metres, and this higher ground extends southward, although most of the mainland is less than 300 metres above sea level. Farther north, along Barrow Strait, typical altitudes are between 400 to 500 metres above sea level, but the islands to the west of the Boothia Peninsula (such as Prince of Wales Island and the eastern part of Victoria Island) are mostly less than 150 metres above sea level. The islands to the west of Axel Heiberg Island are very low, and the land rarely rises to more than 150 metres above sea level.

Most of Nunavut's landforms are shaped by ice sheets and glaciers. The Laurentide Ice Sheet extended north from its centre near Hudson Bay to the north side of Parry Channel, while the highlands of Ellesmere, Axel Heiberg and Devon islands supported separate ice centres with ice flowing in all directions, coalescing in many places. Except for Bathurst Island and Cornwallis Island, the low northwestern islands were not ice-covered during the Wisconsin glaciation, some 18,000 years ago. However, previous ice sheets reached the Arctic Ocean coast. The spectacular valley and fiord landscape of parts of the archipelago was shaped during the glacial periods. On Baffin Island, the Laurentide ice spilled over the height of land and out toward Baffin Bay, carving out deep valleys and fiords, some reaching depths of more than 900 metres. The fiords are often separated by alpine landscapes, making this a favored area for climbers.

The ice sheets left large deposits of till (an unsorted mixture of clay, gravel and boulders), especially along the old ice margins, such as the distinct moraine features along eastern Baffin Island, and on the islands south of the Parry Channel, such as on Victoria Island. The last remnant of the Laurentide Ice Sheet is believed to have melted down over the Shield area to the west of Hudson Bay, leaving large till deposits, often in the forms of drumlins. The area also has many eskers, long sinuous ridges of sand and gravel.

The earth's crust was depressed under the weight of the ice sheet, and when it melted, extensive low-lying areas were inundated by the sea. The land has since risen, and marine deposits and old shoreline features can be found at altitudes of more than 200 metres above sea level. In fact, the phenomenon continues and in some areas of Nunavut, such as the area surrounding Igloolik, the land is rising at a rate of about 0.6 metres per century.

Present Ice Caps and Glaciers

At present, ice caps and glaciers cover some 150,000 square kilometres of Nunavut; more than half of this is on Ellesmere Island, where ice covers an area larger than the province of New Brunswick. Several outlet glaciers on Ellesmere, Devon and Bylot islands reach tidewater and calve off icebergs. Along the north coast, the ice streams form small ice shelves.

Baffin Island has mostly mountain glaciers, some reaching tidewater, but there are also two ice caps — the Penny and the Barnes. The former rests on the top of the high mountain region of Auyuittuq National Park on the Cumberland Peninsula, with ice tongues flowing in several directions. The latter lies west of Clyde River like an elongated loaf of bread on the sloping surface of the Shield, well to the west of the height of land. It has been suggested it is a remnant of the Laurentide Ice Sheet.

Hydrology and Lakes

The major rivers in Nunavut are on the mainland. The Back and the Coppermine flow toward the Arctic coast, while to the east, the Thelon, Kazan and Dubawnt rivers flow to Hudson Bay. These rivers have generally gentle profiles. The irregular land surface and low relief provide for numerous lakes, particularly in the southern Kivalliq Region. The largest lake on the mainland is Dubawnt Lake.

On the islands, the distance to the sea is short and so are the rivers. The longest river and major watersheds are found on the west side of Baffin Island. Nettilling Lake, the largest lake in Nunavut, and Amadjuak Lake lie on southern Baffin. There are numerous lakes in the Shield area on Baffin Island. The eastern part of Victoria Island and the adjacent islands also have a large number of mainly small lakes.

Lakes are much less common on the Queen Elizabeth Islands, and many of those that do exist are glacier-dammed. The 72-kilometre-long and almost 10-kilometre-wide Lake Hazen on Ellesmere Island is the largest in the area.

All lakes and rivers freeze over during the winter, but are generally ice-free during the summer, except for some in the Far North that may retain their ice cover. Runoff peaks during the spring snowmelt, except where glacier meltwater contributes significantly to the discharge. Permafrost prevents infiltration of water into the ground and this contributes to rapid runoff.

The Offshore Area

The Nunavut archipelago separates the more than 3,500-metre-deep Arctic Ocean to the northwest from the 2,100-metre-deep Baffin Bay to the southeast. The channels in the archipelago are shallow by comparison, rarely reaching more than 500 metres and then only in areas where they have been over-deepened by glaciers. The channels along the Arctic coast are very shallow. Only in Nares Strait between Ellesmere and Greenland does the sill depth between the two major water bodies exceed 200 metres. Water flows through the archipelago and into Baffin Bay, but only the relatively fresh and cold surface waters can pass through the shallow channels.

Sea Ice

The Arctic Ocean is perpetually ice-covered, and a persistent current feature, the Beaufort Gyre, sweeps the sea ice southwestward along the northwest coast of Nunavut. Old (multi-year) ice from the Arctic Ocean penetrates into the Parry Channel and other channels opening toward the northwest. During the winter, sea ice forms in all the channels. Near shore and in the narrower channels, the ice is landfast; in other areas it shifts back and forth with the winds and tides. The sea ice facilitates travelling with dogteams and snowmobiles and, during the winter and early spring, the area is more like a continuous land mass than an archipelago.

Even during the winter, some small areas have regularly no, or very thin, ice covers. They are known as polynyas and are important for wildlife. The largest and best known polynya is the North Water at the north end of Baffin Bay. A combination of winds and upwelling ocean currents keeps the area relatively ice-free.

In the spring, the North Water expands as the temperature rises, causing the northern part of Baffin Bay to become ice-free before the more southern parts. As open water expands south and west into Lancaster Sound, migration routes for whales and marine mammals are opened, the marine biota — plants and animals — flourishes, and the sound becomes the feeding ground for millions of seabirds nesting in the adjacent cliffs. Sea ice distribution during the summer depends on weather conditions and varies from year to year; usually minimum ice cover occurs in September. By then, Baffin Bay, Jones Sound, the eastern part of Parry Channel, and the channels along the mainland are normally free of ice, but extensive ice cover persists among the Queen Elizabeth Islands.

Icebergs are numerous in the coastal waters along the Baffin Bay coast. Some of them have calved off glaciers on Ellesmere and Devon islands, but the majority — including all the largest ones — stem from tidewater glaciers on Greenland. After breaking off from the glaciers, the icebergs drift north with the West Greenland current and, as it turns at the head of the Bay, flow south along the Canadian side. Some eventually reach the Grand Banks off Newfoundland, more than 3,500 kilometres to the south.

35. FLORA

by Judy Farrow

For the flora of Nunavut, life is a precarious phenomenon. Winter wraps the land in an icy headlock for months on end, finally yielding to a spring where −30° C temperatures are not uncommon.

Summer, consisting of the months of July and August, is brief. Temperatures can still dip well below freezing, and dry winds often cause significant damage to plants. Arctic soils, which are usually acidic and low in nitrogen, are inhospitable hosts. Plants must eke out an existence in a few meagre centimetres of earth, their roots confined by unwieldy bedrock or permafrost that is never far from the surface. These rather uncivil factors combine to produce plants that are small, prostrate, and always straddling the tenuous line between wakefulness and dormancy.

Arctic plants endure these conditions through a series of adaptations. Most tundra plants are perennials, which helps ensure their long-term survival. So while even the hardiest species in more temperate latitudes easily succumb to freak frosts or storms, the flora of Nunavut can be completely frozen one minute and thawed the next as if nothing had happened. This physiological mystery still baffles scientists: arctic plants freeze with impunity!

Plants here also protect themselves against the elements by crowding together and creating small microclimates. Temperatures in these microclimates are significantly higher than that of the surrounding air, thereby promoting photosynthesis and metabolism that may otherwise be impossible. This is why you'll find Nunavut's plant life nestled in sheltered rock crevices or hugging the contours of the ground. Indeed, soil is rarely visible on the tundra because it is covered by a perpetual layer of mosses and lichens, through which other herbaceous and shrubby plants grow.

Botanists say that since arctic conditions have only existed for a few million years (a mere blink of an eye on the evolutionary time scale), there are no true arctic plant species; arctic conditions have not existed long enough for unique arctic species to have evolved. So you might be surprised at the number of plants you recognize: dandelions, chamomile daisies (look for them on the beach in Pond Inlet), harebells, and buttercups, to name a few. And while harsh arctic conditions can only support a relatively small number of species, all major categories of plants are represented in Nunavut. About 200 species of flowering plants are found above the tree line, and an even greater number of lichens and mosses.

On the Tundra Meadow

Even before the snow disappears, fluffy willow catkins have emerged, taking full advantage of Nunavut's abbreviated growing season. The hairs of the pussy willows are transparent, conducting sunlight down the hair shaft to the catkin body, warming it several degrees above air temperature. This warmth is then trapped by the insulating effect of the tiny hairs, allowing the willows to get a head start on summer. Similar devices are employed by other arctic plants.

As the snow melts, vibrant blooms of purple saxifrage begin to appear. Yellow cinquefoils peek out from between protective leaves at ground level; a delicate perfume carried on a cool breeze sends you combing the tundra for its source, Lapland rosebay.

Delicate white bells dress up the otherwise untidy-looking arctic heather, which was traditionally collected in great quantities by Inuit for use in sleeping mattresses in summer tents. The plant was also an important source of fuel, as a high resin content in the stems and leaves makes this shrubby material burn readily to produce a very hot flame. Arctic heather is still widely used as fuel by families spending time on the land in summer: two rocks and a pile of arctic heather will bring a teakettle to boil in no time. Look around for some Labrador tea to add to the kettle and treat yourself to a refreshing and soothing drink. Labrador tea features prominently in traditional Inuit medicine, and was often used as a calming agent for people undergoing potentially painful procedures.

While searching, observant visitors might notice that the pale cream flowers of the ubiquitous mountain avens always point toward the sun. The Inuit call this flower *malikkat* ("the follower") because it chases the sun across the sky. The cup-shaped dish formed by the petals acts as a solar collector, concentrating the sun's rays in the centre of the flower and directing heat to its reproductive structures, thus speeding seed production. Insects often use these flowers to warm themselves before flying off in the cool arctic air. In its fruiting stage, mountain avens develop long, fluffy plumes. Long ago, these spiralling plumes prompted a caribou hunt among Inuit, who knew the animals would soon start growing their winter coats, which were more difficult to sew into clothing than their summer coats.

The curious round leaves of wintergreen are tough and often have a slight reddish-brown tinge that enables them to absorb more heat from sunlight and photosynthesize even when the surrounding air temperature is cool. As the name of the plant suggests, the leaves maintain their color in winter, frozen and dormant. If conditions are right, moss campion grows in a perfectly round clump, which soon becomes covered with tiny pink flowers. Underneath these clumps is a substantial tap root, once eaten by Inuit in times of starvation.

In wetter areas of the tundra and lakeshores you'll find arctic cotton, a type of sedge whose flower heads develop beautiful white, silky plumes. Inuit once collected these cotton heads and used them with dried moss to make wicks for traditional seal-oil lamps known as *qulliq*. An 11-kilogram sack of cotton heads would supply one *qulliq* for a year. The silky cotton from willow catkins was also used.

With a protective helmet and a protruding lower lip, louseworts are curious plants, their tiny flowers somewhat reminiscent of garden snapdragons. They produce a good supply of nectar at the base of the flower tube and are frequently visited by large arctic bees. The plant's delicate leaves are often mistaken for small ferns, hence its other common name, the fernweed.

The Arctic even has its own version of fireweed, a prostrate variety that can turn whole hillsides or valleys bright pink. The young shoots also make a tasty salad. Prickly saxifrages are straggly plants with three-pronged leaves bearing sharp spikes. The plant's pretty white flowers form a bunch at the top of a flowering stem that grows a few centimetres above ground level. The plant makes a good strong tea that was once used by Inuit for upset stomachs and general aches and pains; the flowers may also be eaten.

If you happen across a patch of especially green, luxuriant growth during your wanderings across the tundra meadow, you can be sure you've come to an animal den, old human camp site, dump site, or bird roost. The arctic terrestrial environment is generally lacking in nitrogen, and plants take full advantage of nitrogen-rich areas such as these. Bladder campions, mountain sorrel, mouse-ear chickweed, and stitchwort are often found in these locations.

Black, plump crowberries are a favorite of the Inuit, but their many seeds give them a gritty taste. Blueberries are small, but sweet. Bright red cranberries are great for cooking, although they taste like sour apples when eaten raw. In late summer, the foliage of alpine bearberry turns a brilliant scarlet, coloring entire hillsides. The berries become almost black when ripe. Despite their delicious appearance, though, the taste is very disappointing.

Lichens, while seemingly unspectacular, are nonetheless vital elements of the arctic environment. Lichens are not single plants, but rather, a symbiotic association of algae and fungi cells living together. The ubiquitous map lichen is named for its map-like growth pattern on rock faces. The rock tripe lichen that speckles tundra rocks saved many explorers from starvation. Caribou moss, which is actually a lichen, is a winter staple for caribou.

You are encouraged to enjoy the arctic flora, but treat it with the respect and tenderness it deserves. An eminent arctic botanist once reported that the woody stem of Lapland rosebay, which was no thicker than a man's thumb, showed no less than 400 annual rings!

36. LAND MAMMALS

by Marian and Mike Ferguson

The land mammals of Nunavut — models of adaptive perfection — have helped sustain Arctic inhabitants for more than 4,000 years by providing raw materials for tools, food, clothing and shelter.

Each species is uniquely adapted to survive Nunavut's harsh, unstable terrestrial ecosystems and temperature extremes. These mammals are subjected to wider temperature extremes than their arctic marine counterparts.

Since the abbreviated arctic summer provides resident populations little opportunity to recover from harsh winters, the diversity of species in Nunavut is low compared with warmer parts of the world. Nevertheless, the adaptive success of these few species is witnessed in the massive numbers their populations sometimes reach, and the proven ability of remnant populations to recover after decades at low numbers. In turn, the peoples who have lived in the Arctic have proven *their* ability to adapt, prospering despite dependence on such wildly fluctuating environments and resources.

With some planning and luck, visitors to Nunavut will have an opportunity to observe many of these unique species in their natural habitats. The sheer expanse of the territory makes it unlikely that you could view all species during one visit, but residents can advise you where, when and how to see wildlife of greatest interest to you. Although not all populations are migratory, most exhibit seasonal behaviors that make them difficult to observe at some times.

If seeing terrestrial wildlife is an important part of your visit, plan on using an experienced guide to maximize viewing opportunities. A variety of tours, lasting from a day to over a week, are available through outfitters or booking agents in most communities (see the individual community chapters in the "Destinations" section). Information can also be obtained from the Renewable Resources Officer (contact the government of Nunavut's **Department of Sustainable Development**, or until April 1999, the GNWT's Department of **Resources, Wildlife and Economic Development**) and the HTO in each community. Information on national parks is available from park staff.

Caribou

When Europeans arrived in North America, they encountered a species known to them as reindeer. American Indians called these animals caribou. In Nunavut, the caribou is known as *tuktu*.

More than 750,000 caribou — in two distinct ecological situations — live in Nunavut. On the mainland, caribou live on the tundra from spring to late summer, then migrate south into the vast boreal forest for the winter. Caribou that remain on the tundra throughout the year are, for the most part, restricted to relatively small islands. These animals are usually seen in smaller groups than the migratory caribou that winter among the southern trees. Nevertheless, caribou wintering on the tundra migrate between seasonal habitats within Nunavut. Most migrate over shorter distances than mainland caribou, but some on Baffin Island travel several hundred kilometres each spring.

Caribou can be seen near several communities in winter and spring. In summer and fall, bulls may be seen along the coast, but cows are usually farther inland near their June calving areas.

The caribou has always been the most important land mammal to the Inuit; until very recently, the lives of Inuit were inextricably linked to these great wanderers. In times of scarcity, the Inuit not only risked starvation, but faced winters of perpetual cold without the unsurpassed insulation of caribou-skin clothing. The unique structure of the caribou's hollow hair makes its fur extremely warm, yet easily worn. A hunter's caribou clothing needs to be replaced every few years because it will not retain its warmth.

In Nunavut, biologists have traditionally recognized three subspecies of caribou. Barren-ground caribou is the most common, occupying the mainland and some southern Arctic islands. Although caribou on Baffin Island are officially barren-ground caribou, Inuit recognize several distinct characteristics between Baffin and mainland animals. Some scientific data suggests that there may be a genetic basis for these distinctions.

More recent DNA genetics tests suggest that barren-ground, Baffin and the diminutive Peary caribou may all be one subspecies. Nevertheless, Peary caribou on the Queen Elizabeth Islands, which are north of Parry Channel, are recognized as "endangered" by the Committee on the Status of Endangered Wildlife in Canada. Peary caribou are naturally rare because the sparse vegetation in the High Arctic is usually buried beneath snow and ice for up to 10 months each year.

Many caribou on the mid-Arctic islands west of Baffin Island appear similar to Peary caribou, while others look more like barren-ground caribou.

A third subspecies, reindeer originally descended from Siberian stock, was introduced to the Belcher Islands in eastern Hudson Bay in 1978, about 100 years after native caribou had disappeared. Concerned that unrestricted growth of this free-ranging population could lead to overgrazing and potential future extinction, Inuit of Sanikiluaq have successfully stabilized their numbers at 600 to 800 animals. There are concerns that some woodland caribou from Quebec have migrated across 100 kilometres of sea ice, and some of the reindeer have joined them on their return to Quebec.

Caribou bulls average 100 to 150 kilograms, while cows reach 75 to 100 kilograms. The types of caribou differ in size, color and behavior. Peary caribou are the smallest. During summer, Peary and Baffin caribou are not known to form dense groups numbering in the thousands, as do the barren-ground caribou on the mainland, perhaps because they do not have to endure thick clouds of mosquitoes and other insects. Reindeer are typically seen in large, dense groups, even during winter.

Muskoxen

Should you be lucky enough to see the trademark shaggy coat of the muskox (*umingmak*), you may feel like you've been transported back in time. Indeed, it's easy to imagine continental ice sheets covering much of North America — as they did some 18,000 years ago — when in the company of the "bearded one."

Unlike caribou, which prefer slow-growing lichens, muskoxen depend largely on grasses and sedges that recover relatively quickly from heavy grazing. In the summer, these herbivores may be seen in river valleys, along lake shores and near damp meadows. If grasses and sedges become unavailable in winter, muskoxen move onto ridges and hilltops to feed on willows and other plants. They are often seen in groups of 10 to 20, depending on season and location. When threatened, muskoxen form defensive circles with adults facing outwards and calves in the centre. This behavior, while effective against four-legged predators, makes muskoxen easy prey for human hunters.

Large numbers of muskoxen roamed the tundra of Nunavut before the arrival of European and Canadian traders. The subsequent market for meat and hides reduced their populations to dangerously low numbers until Canada protected them in 1917. Since then, muskoxen have recovered and recolonized most of their historic range so that closely regulated harvesting can be sustained. Today, Nunavut holds most of Canada's muskoxen, with about 60,000 animals. The species occupies much of Nunavut, except for the eastern mainland and Baffin Island.

Inuit do not usually prefer muskoxen over caribou, although the meat can be delicious and the skins produce warm sleeping robes. Beginning in May, muskoxen shed large quantities of their underfur (*qiviut*), which can be spun into a luxurious wool. Bulls weigh about 350 kilograms, some 50 kilograms heavier than cows. Muskoxen mate in the summer; bulls can become unpredictable during this period. Do not approach muskoxen too closely, especially if you're not accompanied by an experienced guide. They can be aggressive.

Barren-Ground Grizzlies

The barren-ground grizzly is found on the mainland of Nunavut and is more common in the Kitikmeot Region than in the Kivalliq Region.

The barren-ground grizzly bear (*atsaq*) is smaller than its cousins elsewhere in North America; males weigh up to 215 kilograms, while females weigh up to 108 kilograms. Their hair, ranging from black to blond, is often flecked, or "grizzled," with white or grey. These bears exist on the margins of their range. Normally, grizzlies kill or scavenge animals, especially ungulates such as caribou, ground squirrels and insects, as well as garbage. (To read about polar bears, see Chapter 37, "Marine Mammals.")

Wolves and Wolverines

Two types of wolves (*amaqqut*; the singular is *amaruq*) are found in Nunavut. Tundra wolves on the mainland are often brown or grey and weigh 30 to 40 kilograms, while arctic wolves on the islands are usually smaller and white. Wolves on the mainland and Baffin Island prey mostly on caribou, while arctic wolves on the smaller Arctic islands hunt mainly muskoxen and arctic hares.

On Ellesmere Island, some wolves take the often abundant muskoxen almost exclusively, while other packs may concentrate on the large herds of arctic hares. Peary caribou are taken, but their mobility and small, scattered groups probably do not allow wolves to depend on them. Wolves will also eat lemmings, birds, fish, foxes and garbage. Wolf packs tend to be small and widely scattered. Wolves are usually found wherever there is suitable prey, but these quick and secretive animals are never easy to spot. In winter and spring, your guide may show you fresh tracks. With some luck you may even see the wolves that made them. In summer, wolves are often at inland denning sites raising pups or hunting. You will need considerable perseverance, patience and luck to see signs of wolves once the snow melts.

Being a mammal of the boreal forest, the wolverine (*qavvik*), the largest of weasels, is most common on the mainland of Nunavut, and is rarely seen on the Arctic islands. The stocky body, short, powerful legs and large feet give the wolverine the appearance of a small bear. Its dark brown fur is streaked with two tan stripes running the length of the body. Wolverine fur is used for trimming parka hoods because frost slips off hairs easily. Weight ranges from about 14 to 28 kilograms; females are smaller than males.

Foxes, Weasels, Lemmings and Hares

These smaller animals are relatively abundant throughout Nunavut, and can be seen near most communities. In 1919, red foxes crossed Hudson Strait from Quebec to Baffin Island, and reached the Queen Elizabeth Islands by 1962. The red fox (*tiriganniarjuaq*) goes through phases of colors, including silver, black, brown and red. On average, they have litters of four to eight pups. The arctic fox (*tiriganiaq*) is white during winter, but changes to largely dark brown in summer. Arctic foxes usually bear only four to six young. As with the red fox, litter size increases significantly in years when lemmings are numerous.

Foxes travel extensively in search of food — they can be found almost anywhere. Although it's hard to predict if you will see any, foxes are curious and may approach your camp. However, a fox that approaches too closely and appears overly friendly could have rabies; play it safe and scare it away. The young become independent in September so you might see them in their quest for food. Foxes eat lemmings, hares, ptarmigan, bird eggs, decaying flesh from carcasses, and garbage.

The least weasel, or ermine (*tiriaq*), is probably the most commonly seen mammalian predator of the arctic tundra. The weasel lives wherever it can form a den to raise young and store prey in times of abundance. They den among rock piles, loose earth and both Thule and modern-day houses. When lemmings are abundant, so are weasels. You may see them flashing behind a building, across a street or even between your feet. In summer, these long, sleek animals are brown, but in winter they don an all-white coat, ending in a long, black-tipped tail. Although they depend mainly on lemmings, these small but fierce predators will tackle prey up to the size of arctic hares. They are usually no problem to larger animals, although they will defend themselves if cornered.

On a warm spring day, have you caught a glimpse of a dark fur ball skittering across the snow that magically vanishes? It was probably a lemming (*avinngaq*) out for its first above-snow adventure in many months. For smaller predators like the weasel, fox and snowy owl, lemmings are the life-blood of the arctic tundra. Snowy owls often produce young only when lemmings are in abundance. Lemmings are mainly seen in summer but are active throughout the winter, living in nests made of grass and burrowing through snowy tunnels along the ground. Lemming numbers usually go through a four-year cycle, but some peaks may bring greater abundance than others and some areas may experience peaks sooner than elsewhere. Nunavut is home to two species: the brown (*kajuqtaq*) and collared (*amirta* or *qilangmiutaq*) lemming. The brown lemming prefers wetter areas, while the collared lemming is usually seen in rocky terrain. The collared lemming turns white in winter, and is the only one to occupy the High Arctic islands.

The arctic hare (*ukaliq*) is widely distributed across Nunavut. They live among rocks on rough hillsides and mountains, where they have ready shelter from foxes, gyrfalcons and other predators. Hares eat grasses, sedges, willows and other plants. Across most of their range, they are seen in small family units, but on the Queen Elizabeth Islands you may encounter herds of 100 or more. From a distance, these groups look like white clouds flowing across the summer tundra. In southern parts of their range, they may moult to grey or brown in summer.

37. MARINE MAMMALS

by Mike Vlessides

Traditionally, few cultures in the world were more dependent on the creatures of the sea than the Inuit.

Indeed, in a land where resources were often scarce, the fertile waters of Nunavut and its vast populations of marine mammals provided the raw materials that helped Inuit society thrive in one of the world's harshest climates. Even today, as massive material changes continue to reshape Inuit society, the people of Nunavut use marine mammals as important sources of food, clothing, and increasingly, revenue.

Seals

While Canadian seas are home to nine species of seals, three of the most bountiful in the Arctic are the ringed, harp, and bearded seal.

Other marine mammals may garner more attention than the demure ringed seal, but few play as integral a role in Inuit society. For nearly four millennia, Inuit have relied extensively on *natsiq*, the smallest and most common marine mammal in the territory.

Traditionally, the ringed seal (which gets its name from the irregular, light-colored rings with dark centres that characterize adults) was the main staple of the Inuit diet; its skin was used as clothing, its blubber fuelled the soapstone lamps that provided both light and warmth, and its intestines, a delicacy to Inuit, were even used as containers and igloo windows. The skin also furnished harnesses for huskies, and soles for *kamiit* (boots). While the animal is no longer used to this extent, the ringed seal is still an important food source for the people of Nunavut, who also use the skin for boots and mitts, and less frequently, parkas, pants, and even artwork.

The ringed seal's importance in Inuit culture is largely the result of logistics. In addition to being the only seal that spends the entire year in the Arctic, ringed seal populations also number well into the millions. In spring, seals haul themselves through cracks and breathing holes in the ice to bask in the warmth of the sun. Often you'll spot several of them sleeping together, though you may find it difficult to get very close to them. They are fitful sleepers, rising every few minutes to scan the horizon for potential danger.

You'll find ringed seals far more daring in their aquatic element, however, often popping their inquisitive heads out of the water to observe passing boats. Still, they are somewhat difficult to spot in ice-free waters. The ringed seal is ubiquitous in Nunavut, populating arctic and subarctic waters. A few venture as far south as the Gulf of St. Lawrence.

Slightly larger than ringed seals, harp seals are distinguished by the black, harp-shaped saddle on their backs. Harp seals have never been as vital to Inuit as ringed seals, probably because they stay farther from shore. About 500,000 of them summer in Nunavut, migrating north when the sea ice finally yields in spring. They return south to warmer waters with the coming of autumn.

Inuit call the harp seal *qairulik*. This species of seal has a penchant for porpoising and frolicking in arctic waters. They are found mostly in the eastern part of the territory, ranging throughout Foxe Basin, northern and eastern Hudson Bay, Hudson and Davis straits, and the northern parts of Baffin Bay.

The *ugjuk*, or "square flipper," as the bearded seal is sometimes called, is unique among Nunavut's seals in that it is a bottom feeder, eating crustaceans, mollusks, worms, hermit crabs, and clams. Despite the energy the animal expends to attain its food, the bearded seal nonetheless grows to great proportions, maxing out at 350 kilograms.

Unlike more gregarious harp and ringed seals, bearded seals are usually found in pairs or small groups instead of large herds. These dark grey creatures spend most of their time on fields of drifting ice, diving 50 to 200 metres for food below. As their English name suggests, bearded seals are distinguished by the long, drooping whiskers around their mouths.

Despite their great girth, bearded seals are the most cautious of all Nunavut's seals. On the ice, they will head for safer pastures underwater long before humans get very close. In the water they are slightly braver. Often they'll allow your boat to get within several dozen metres; especially brazen individuals may even circle your vessel for a closer look before disappearing with a splash.

Bearded seals can be found throughout Nunavut, especially in shallow waters.

Walruses

Relaxed yet irksome, graceful yet clumsy, gentle yet ferocious, the walrus (*aiviq*) is a paradoxical animal that defies categorization. They can often be found packed like sardines on ice floes, but that doesn't stop one from occasionally rising up and jabbing his or her neighbor with a pair of ivory tusks. On land, these massive mammals (adult males can reach 3.5 metres and 1,400 kilograms) move with the grace of three-legged elephants, but in the water they are masterful swimmers.

Walruses dine extensively on clams, using their sensitive whiskers to detect the unfortunate mollusks on the sea floor. An adult walrus eats as many as 3,000 clams each day, although they also eat other bottom-dwelling creatures such as fish, crabs, worms and snails. Because they rarely dive deeper than 75 metres, walruses stay close to shallow waters.

The walrus's most distinguishing feature is its tremendous overbite. Both male and female walruses are blessed with these dentures. Despite their Latin name, *odobenidae* ("those that walk with their teeth"), walruses don't actually use their tusks for walking. Neither are the tusks used to dig up food. The tusks, serving as a symbol of dominance or social rank, are also used to help animals haul themselves from the water.

Walruses are restricted to Hudson Bay, the waters around Baffin Island, and the High Arctic.

Whales

Glorious to behold, belugas, narwhals, and bowheads are the three true arctic whales, although others are occasionally spotted here in summer. Of the three arctic whales, belugas are the most numerous and widely distributed. More than 60,000, and perhaps as many as 100,000, live in arctic and subarctic waters.

The snow-white beluga (*qinalugaq* or *qilalugaq*) stands out conspicuously in dark waters. Congregating in large numbers in the same areas every summer, these small-toothed whales are also the most gregarious and most vocal of the arctic whales, spending hours rollicking in shallow waters, chirping, trilling, and clicking to one another in apparent delight. Early whalers actually dubbed them "sea canaries."

Belugas, which reach about four to five metres in length, are found throughout Nunavut. They winter in areas of open water or shifting ice, where they have access to air, moving northward with spring.

The narwhal (*tuugaalik* or *allanguaq*), the mysterious unicorn of the sea, also boasts significant Nunavut populations, though its range is more restricted than the beluga. The majority winter in northern Davis Strait and southern Baffin Bay. Toward the end of June they head for the fertile waters of Lancaster Sound and the deep bays and fiords of northern Baffin Island and beyond. A distinct population spends the winter in Hudson Strait, moving into northwestern Hudson Bay in spring.

Narwhals average four metres in length and weigh nearly two tonnes. Yet it is not this mottled whale's girth that gives the creature its reputation, but its unforgettable ivory tusk that twists from its upper jaw like the overgrown tooth it really is. Hundreds of years ago, reports of the existence of unicorns were fostered by serendipitous discoveries of narwhal tusks by imaginative European whalers.

The large majority of tusked narwhals are males, although females occasionally grow them as well. The purpose of this appendage is still unknown, although different theories have been championed for centuries. Most often, the tusk is used in displays of aggressive behavior; scientists believe they may be used to determine social rank, much like the tusk of the walrus.

The bowhead whale (*arviq*) is the giant of the arctic whales, reaching 18 metres in length and 100 tonnes. These gentle behemoths were hunted to near extinction in the 1800s and early 1900s; to this day their populations in the eastern Arctic remain dangerously low, thus their endangered status. There were once more than 11,000 bowheads in these waters; today, most biologists agree there are no more than 1,000. Nonetheless, the recently settled Nunavut Land Claims Agreement paved the way for the legal harvest of a bowhead for the first time in a generation; in August 1996, a group of hunters representing a cross-section of Nunavut took part in this historic hunt. A second bowhead was harvested in 1998.

Although not considered true arctic whales because they do not winter in the Arctic, killer whales are often associated with Nunavut because of their summer migrations. These carnivores are very deserving of their rather intimidating name, preying on fish, seals, and even small whales. It is believed that one of the reasons Nunavut's bowhead whales have not rebounded is because killer whales are preying on bowhead calves.

Killer whales tend to follow seal and whale populations north when the ice begins to break. They are found in Foxe Basin, Hudson Bay, Hudson and Davis straits, Lancaster and Eclipse sounds, and Admiralty Inlet.

Other whales visiting Nunavut's waters in summer are blue whales and sperm whales. Blue whales, the world's largest living mammals, can reach lengths in excess of 30 metres and weights of 100 tonnes. These endangered creatures sometimes venture into Davis Strait, the northernmost limit of their range in Canadian waters. Sperm whales, the largest of all toothed whales, are also occasional summer visitors to Davis Strait. Only bull sperm whales travel to arctic waters, however.

Polar Bears

More than any other creature, the world's largest land carnivore has come to symbolize the wild, rugged character of Nunavut. What may seem puzzling, however, is why the polar bear (*nanuq*) is considered a marine mammal at all. The reason is simple: polar bears, which are extraordinarily adapted for frigid arctic waters and are excellent swimmers, spend most of their lives on the sea ice and in the water. These abilities and adaptations allow the polar bear to successfully hunt and kill the staple of its diet, the ringed seal, which it hunts at breathing holes, at the floe edge, along cracks in the ice, and at polynyas.

The polar bears of Nunavut tend to be solitary creatures, generally travelling alone in winter. If you see more than one bear together, it is probably a mother and her cub or cubs. Cubs stay with their mothers for the first two or three years of life.

When the seemingly impenetrable shell of ice finally breaks up across Nunavut, polar bears are forced to concentrate somewhat in fiords and bays, where ice usually lasts longer. When this ice finally melts, the bears have few dietary options other than vegetation, small animals, and dead material that has been washed ashore. Occasionally, hungry bears wander into communities, drawn by the scents emanating from town dumps.

Polar bears are found throughout Nunavut, but they are especially common throughout Barrow Strait and Lancaster Sound, along the east and southeast coasts of Baffin Island, and north throughout Jones Sound.

38. BIRDS AND BIRDING
by Robin Johnstone

The drama from this distance is a faint blur of activity, but my binoculars convey a dramatic tale.

A horned lark is in the lead, streaking over the land, trying to gain some distance and some cover. Close behind, a female peregrine falcon, hungry after her long migration from coastal Brazil, matches every move of the fleeing appetizer. The distance between does not seem to close though, and the chances of escape begin to look good. Then, a sudden blur across my view, so fast my brain barely registers it. It is the tiercel, the female peregrine's mate. The hapless lark has been ambushed. Distracted by the peregrine in pursuit, the lark does not see its partner gaining height above it. The small male peregrine misses the lark in its first steep dive or stoop, but turns up, up, and completely over in a large loop that points him straight back down at his lunch. The second stoop is deadly accurate this time, and a cloud of lark feathers are left floating on the breeze. The dead lark is deftly passed in mid-air to his mate, and the pair returns triumphantly to their nesting cliff. One more meal in a summer of hunting to provide for a growing family.

– An excerpt from my field diary:
Rankin Inlet, Nunavut, Canada. May 27, 1995.

Birding opportunities in Nunavut are extensive and exciting, whether you are an expert birder hoping to add rare arctic species to your life list of birds, or someone who simply delights in watching birds going about their business. The Arctic is characterized by having few bird species, relative to temperate or tropical ecosystems. For instance, only two dozen or so species breed on Ellesmere Island, with another 10 to 20 species sighted. The lack of species number is made up for by the exotic nature of some of the species and the awe-inspiring sight of incredible numbers of others found in the large breeding colonies. Not all places harbor incredible densities of birds, but a long walk on the tundra may be very rewarding.

Being the world's largest land carnivore, the polar bear (nanuq) commands respect, even from its cubs

The caribou crosses rivers and other obstacles that lie in its path during annual migrations. Tuktu *remains a key source of food and clothing for Inuit. Inset: A muskox* (umingmak) *grazes near the Kazan River in the Kivalliq Region*

Colorful arctic flowers triumph over chilly temperatures and a meagre soil base by crowding together to boost the heat in small microclimates

Camping and travelling on the land calls for careful preparation, including registering your agenda with the RCMP. Still, camping is one of the best ways to experience the Arctic

Inuksuit, *markers built to resemble humans, dot the tundra. This* inuksuk *overlooks Nunavut's second largest community, Rankin Inlet*

Drum dances marked important occasions in Inuit society; today, led by performers like this Pelly Bay drum-dancing troupe, "they are for the world to enjoy"

A siksik (ground squirrel) maintains a wary lookout for predators like the barren-ground grizzly bear. Siksiit make their home on Nunavut's mainland

A ringed seal near Pond Inlet; natsiq *lives in arctic waters year round.*
*Inset: Walruses (*aiviit*) can put away close to 3,000 clams each day*

One of the biggest thrills of any birder is to witness the gyrfalcon, the largest of all falcons, in its white color phase, as seen here near Wager Bay

Although husky dogs (qimmiit) have been replaced by snow machines as the main mode of transportation in everyday life, exhilarating dogsledding excursions are still widely available to visitors throughout Nunavut

A practised hand is required to construct a cosy iglu. *While snowhouses are rarely spotted these days in the wake of permanent housing, several communities and outfitters in Nunavut make spending the night in an* iglu *a real possibility*

Photo by Bill Belsey

Roger Hitkolok of Kugluktuk displays one of his soapstone sculptures. In Nunavut, where many subsistence hunters supplement their income by carving, almost every community boasts its own distinctive style of this art form

Tours or outfitters rarely cater specifically to birders in Nunavut; however, they provide excellent access to superb birding, as many destinations in Nunavut provide ideal opportunities for viewing birds, as well as other wildlife. For instance, a canoe trip down the Thelon River through the Thelon Wildlife Sanctuary is a wilderness adventure that also includes excellent birding opportunities. Tree-nesting gyrfalcons, short-eared owls, snowy owls, rough-legged hawks, golden eagles and many other species may be seen.

Interpretive and birding skills among outfitters vary greatly. Novice through to expert birders will benefit from the world-class interpretive program at the long-running **Bathurst Inlet Lodge**, which sets an extremely high standard for the industry.

The best time for birding in Nunavut is mid- to late May through August. There are excellent opportunities for birding throughout Nunavut in spring as the land begins to peek from beneath its heavy burden of snow and migrant species return in large numbers. By mid-August, many birds have finished breeding and dispersed from their colonies or nest sites. Storms can be very disruptive to any tour in August, especially when boat transportation is involved. Constant darkness and bitter cold leave Nunavut almost devoid of bird life in winter, except for the hardiest of species — common ravens, gyrfalcon, ptarmigan.

A birding trip by snowmobile and *qamutiik* (wooden sled) in late May or June can be very rewarding, and is recommended for anyone of a mildly adventurous nature. At this time birds tend to concentrate on patches of land free of snow, or areas of open water. On land, you may be entertained by sandhill cranes doing their graceful, though somewhat awkward, courtship displays. Magnificent flights of geese and tundra swans may be seen, and stunning aerial dogfights of peregrine falcons staking a territory and a mate may be observed from a safe distance. Long-tailed ducks (formerly known as oldsquaw), common and king eider ducks, black guillemots and many other seabirds may easily be found at leads — patches of open water — in the sea ice, or at the floe edge throughout Nunavut. Local outfitters can best advise when to visit their community to coincide with spring thaw and the appearance of leads. Dark sunglasses and sunscreen with an SPF 30 minimum are necessary at this time.

The following is a selection of highlighted species that characterize the Arctic, and some good places at which to observe them, in my opinion. Many excellent birding opportunities and exciting sightings may be gained by the self-reliant birder, though, at destinations that don't specify birding opportunities or interpretive programs.

Gyrfalcon, the largest of all falcons, rank highly on the wish list of keen birders, and seeing an individual of the white color phase is one of the biggest thrills any naturalist, amateur or professional, can experience. They prey mainly on ptarmigan and, if their food supply is good, they may remain in the North through winter. They are not common birds, but close proximity and relatively high densities may provide viewing opportunities at **Sila Lodge**, Wager Bay, and also at Repulse Bay.

Ptarmigan are one of the true arctic species, adapted for year-round life in this harsh environment. Dense feathers on the top and bottom of their feet and long claws equip ptarmigan with an effective pair of winter boots that protect them from the bitter cold, and crampons for traction on ice. Rock ptarmigan are found throughout Nunavut, and willow ptarmigan are found through much of Nunavut except eastern Baffin Island. They may be difficult to find close to communities because they are a country food item.

The snowy owl is a magnificent sight on the open tundra. Blatantly obvious perched upon the tundra, a snowy owl appears so white it is almost luminescent. Snowy owls are active during the day and may be seen throughout Nunavut when populations of lemmings peak. As lemming populations may vary among areas, check with local outfitters or the wildlife officers at the community Department of Sustainable Development office (or until April 1999, the Resources, Wildlife and Economic Development office) as to whether they have been recently seen in the area you plan to visit.

Tundra peregrine falcons can be seen at many places across Nunavut. Peregrine falcon hot spots include Wager Bay, Bathurst Inlet, Rankin Inlet and Repulse Bay. They also breed close to Coral Harbour. Surrounding Rankin Inlet is one of the densest and most easily accessible populations of peregrine falcons in the world. They are often seen at the airport, or you can take a taxi ride to the Ijiraliq (Meliadine) River Territorial Historic Park to observe a nearby nest. Peregrines may be observed hunting over colonies of black guillemots, flying almost at ground level over the tundra searching for fledgling passerines, and even lemmings — a prey item unusual for this species. The Rankin Inlet peregrine population has been studied for the last 15 years, and visiting biologists will happily answer any questions you may have. Unfortunately, the future of this program is uncertain, so check with the local Department of Sustainable Development (or RWED) office for their activities. Your visit may coincide with one of their public slide presentations.

Keen birders seeking to lengthen their life list of birds may choose to visit Nunavut for a sighting of the ivory gull. Rarely venturing out of the Arctic, it is common in the eastern High Arctic. It spends the winter along the floe edge between Greenland and Canada and may be seen along the floe edge at Pond Inlet, especially during migration in late May/early June and later in October, as well as during the summer months in open coastal waters adjacent to colonies further inland. Occasional sightings are also made of the Ross's gull by lucky birders in the Baffin Region, although it seldom breeds in the Canadian Arctic. They have also been spotted on the Boothia Peninsula, Igloolik, Cornwallis Island, and McConnell River, so wherever you are, keep your head up, and your binoculars handy.

Parasitic jaeger and long-tailed jaeger nest on the arctic tundra throughout Nunavut. A third species, the Pomarine jaeger, is limited to parts of the Kitikmeot, southern Baffin Island, and southern Southampton Island. Described as "dashing pirates" for their habit of robbing other birds of food, jaegers also prey on lemmings, the eggs and young of nesting song-birds and shorebirds. All three species may be seen around Kugluktuk, Cambridge Bay, Bathurst Inlet and Umingmaktok.

Few places in the world can match the sheer scale of seabird colonies in the Arctic. An incredible place to observe seabirds is the Prince Leopold Migratory Bird Sanctuary, which is accessible from Resolute. The steep cliffs of this small island are home to almost 375,000 seabirds, including thick-billed murres, northern fulmars, black-legged kittiwakes and black guillemots. Other places to enjoy the spectacle of such dense concentrations of seabirds are Bylot Island Migratory Bird Sanctuary, accessible from Pond Inlet, and the Nirjutiqavvik National Wildlife Area on Coburg Island, accessible from Grise Fiord.

Few groups of birds herald the arrival of the warm months in Nunavut like waterbirds. Early June, when bodies of open water are limited, is one of the best times to observe them. Flocks of common eider and the gaudy king eiders are often seen skimming low over the sea ice and at meltwater ponds or leads. They are relatively numerous near Igloolik and Cape Dorset, but may be seen from many coastal communities along the ice edge during migration. Males gather on the sea from early July before departing for the South. Rafts of females and young persist in northern regions through September and into November in southeastern Baffin Island. Long-tailed duck (oldsquaw) and northern pintail are probably the most common ducks throughout the region, but surf scoter and common scoter may be seen. The red-throated loon breeds throughout Nunavut, while Pacific loons may be seen on tundra ponds throughout most of Nunavut, except for the High Arctic and northern Baffin Island. The yellow-billed loon breeds on tundra lakes and rivers throughout the Kitikmeot Region, northern parts of the Kivalliq Region and Baker Lake. It is replaced by the common loon in the southern Baffin and southern Kivalliq regions.

Many North American birders will be familiar with the species of geese that are found in Nunavut. A visit to Nunavut will give the opportunity, however, to see these species on their breeding grounds. Some 450,000 lesser snow geese, particularly those of the blue color phase, 50,000 Canada geese, and 1,600 Brant can be seen on the vast sedge lowlands and tidal flats of the Dewey Soper Migratory Bird Sanctuary. This is an excellent birding area and has been recognized by the United Nations Educational, Scientific and Cultural Organization (UNESCO) as "a wetland of international importance." Sabine's gulls and red phalaropes also nest here. Presently, the only way to get there is by air charter from Iqaluit. More easily accessible, and for less money, is the McConnell River Migratory Bird Sanctuary, just south of Arviat, where 300,000 lesser snow geese and Ross' geese nest. Northern pintail, black duck, common goldeneye, lesser scaup, and green-winged teal may also be seen here, and perhaps a short-eared owl. Harry Gibbons Migratory Bird Sanctuary on Southampton Island, accessible from Coral Harbour, is rich with waterfowl, nesting black-bellied plovers, and Brant. Brant may also be seen at Katannilik Territorial Park Reserve, near Kimmirut.

Shorebirds form one of the principal groups of arctic avifauna, with a variety of species nesting in Nunavut, including black-bellied, semi-palmated, and lesser golden plovers; ruddy turnstones; dunlin, pectoral, Baird's, semi-palmated, and white-rumped sandpipers and two species of phalaropes — both red and red-necked. Arviat and Coral Harbour are prime locations for excellent views of shorebirds.

Responsible Birding and Photography of Birds

"Leave only footprints, and take only photographs" is a good adage for any ecotourist. For those wishing to observe or photograph nesting birds in any environment, however, a more stringent code of ethics and behavior is necessary. Nesting birds in the Arctic, like anywhere else, can be very sensitive to disturbances. Keeping an adult off the nest for a prolonged period may attract the unwelcome attention of predators, or result in the nest being abandoned, the lethal cooling of eggs, or death of nestlings due to exposure. For many species, the only indication of a nearby nest may be the raucous or seemingly bizarre behavior of the adult in attendance. Walk away and let the adult return to the daily grind of raising a family in a harsh environment. For some raptor species, this may entail walking even up to a couple of kilometres away from the nesting cliff. An undisturbed adult may treat the patient observer to intimate portraits of family life.

Equipment

The amount and expense of gear actually necessary for an enjoyable birding trip to Nunavut is pretty minimal. Bring your own binoculars to Nunavut as availability and selection are likely to be limited. Most birders will find the *Field Guide to the Birds of North America* — Second Edition, National Geographic Society, a useful reference in the field. Check on the Internet or at your local specialist birding store for this book and other specialist guides. Stout, waterproof footwear is necessary for hikes across the sometimes soggy tundra.

Don't leave home without a plentiful supply of mosquito repellent. In my experience, I've found repellents containing less than 95 per cent DEET are almost worthless for protection. However, according to the Drug Information Centre with the Faculty of Pharmacy, University of Toronto, 30 per cent DEET is acceptable for adults and 10 per cent DEET for children under five. High concentrations of DEET have proven toxic to some people. Its effect varies with individuals.

Unfortunately, DEET is as repellent to humans as it is to bugs! Make sure you don't get any on your fingers or in your eyes. DEET may also melt many plastics and rubbers, so take care with your cameras and binoculars! For more tips on battling bugs in the Arctic, read Chapter 14, "Insects."

LAND AND WILDLIFE: DIRECTORY

Bathurst Inlet Lodge
P.O. Box 820, Yellowknife NT,
X1A 2N6 Canada
Tel.: (867) 873-2595 or (867) 920-4330
Fax: (867) 920-4263
E-mail: bathurst@internorth.com
Web site: www.virtualnorth.com/
bathurst/

**Department of Sustainable Development,
Government of Nunavut**
Tel.: (867) 979-5134
Fax: (867) 979-5920

Nunavut Tourism
P.O. Box 1450, Iqaluit NT,
X0A 0H0 Canada
Tel.: 1-800-491-7910 (for Canada and
the United States)

Tel.: (867) 979-6551
Fax: (867) 979-1261
E-mail: nunatour@nunanet.com
Web site: www.nunatour.nt.ca

Resources, Wildlife and Economic Development
Tel.: (867) 979-5011
Fax: (867) 979-6791

Sila Lodge/Frontiers North Inc.
173 Ragsdill Rd., Winnipeg MB,
R2G 4C6 Canada
Attention: Lynda Gunter
Tel.: 1-800-663-9832 or (204) 949-2050
Fax: (204) 663-6375
E-mail: frontiers_north@mb.sympatico.ca

Activities

39. HUNTING AND FISHING
by Jerome Knap

Big-game hunting is a major component of Nunavut's tourism industry, with good reason.

Nunavut also boasts some of the world's premier big-game animals. In addition to majestic polar bears, elusive barren-ground grizzlies and seemingly prehistoric muskoxen, hunters can set their sights on caribou, wolves, wolverines and, for the first time since the 1950s, walruses.

Nunavut Tourism has published the comprehensive *Nunavut Sport Hunting Guide*, which lists all hunting operators in Nunavut. When booking a hunting or fishing trip, make sure the outfitter is licensed, bonded, and has liability insurance. Any operator should also be able to provide references of past clients.

Polar Bears

The ice bear is arguably the planet's top big-game trophy. With 50 per cent of the world's population of polar bears, Nunavut is the premier place to hunt them. But venturing out in search of *nanuq* is not for the faint of heart. By international agreement, these hunts must be conducted by traditional methods, utilizing dogteams. Each community in Nunavut controls an annual quota for polar bears through the community Hunters and Trappers Organizations, usually referred to as HTOs. Sometimes, HTOs also act as outfitters by hiring guides and organizing hunts.

Until very recently, polar bear trophies could not be imported into the United States (U.S.) according to the *U.S. Marine Mammal Protection Act.* This act has recently been amended, however, and American hunters are now permitted to take back trophies from approved polar bear populations in Canada. American hunters are advised to check with the Office of Management Authority, **U.S. Fish and Wildlife Service**, to make sure that the bears in the area they are planning to hunt in have been approved for importation into the United States, and also to obtain information on the procedure for importation of the skin and skull.

Muskoxen

With the exception of Baffin Island, muskoxen are found across Nunavut. The largest populations are found on Victoria Island, where there is an estimated population of 45,000. As with polar bears, all hunting and outfitting for muskoxen is subject to annual quotas, as allocated and organized through community HTOs.

In the Baffin Region, muskox hunting is restricted to the High Arctic: southern Ellesmere Island, Devon Island, Bathurst Island, and northern Prince of Wales Island. Hunts in these areas can be organized from Grise Fiord and Resolute. High Arctic muskoxen are generally smaller than those found farther south.

In the Kitikmeot Region, muskox hunting can be arranged from most communities. Hunting takes place along both the Coronation and Queen

Maud gulfs, Victoria Island, King William Island, Boothia Peninsula, and southern Prince of Wales Island. The world's largest trophies are taken from mainland quotas in the Coronation Gulf and Queen Maud Gulf areas. In many communities, it is possible to take advantage of combination hunts, both for caribou and muskoxen, and to hunt opportunistically for wolves and wolverines.

Caribou

Nunavut has three races, or subspecies, of caribou, and a hybrid between the barren-ground and Peary caribou. Members of the smallest race, Peary caribou are near white and found most commonly on the High Arctic islands, although they can also be found on northwest Victoria Island and the northern portions of Prince of Wales Island, Somerset Island, and the Boothia Peninsula. Recent, drastic winter starvation has reduced some Arctic islands caribou herds by as much as 80 per cent. Peary caribou are currently under intensive management scrutiny. Subsistence hunting has been voluntarily restricted, and sport hunting within the animal's range has been banned. The reindeer on the Belcher Islands are the private property of the people of Sanikiluaq and are hunted only by the people of Belcher Islands.

Larger and more numerous barren-ground caribou are found on the Nunavut mainland and Baffin Island. These caribou form the large, well-known migrating herds, and include the Bathurst, Bluenose, Beverly, and Qamanirjuaq herds. Caribou can also be found on Southampton Island. In total, these herds now comprise more than 1.2 million animals in populations that are either stable or increasing. Trophy hunting is done by intercepting the caribou during their autumn migration. Hunts can be arranged from many communities.

The intergrade or hybrid caribou found on southern Victoria Island and King William Island are classified as Arctic islands caribou by the Safari Club International. Quotas are available in Cambridge Bay and Kugluktuk. The status of these animals is currently under investigation. Limited non-resident hunting takes place on Victoria Island.

Barren-Ground Grizzlies

Extirpated over much of its range during the height of the fur trade, this relatively small but aggressive grizzly has made an amazing comeback in recent years.

Commercial quotas for sport hunts are only available in the Kivalliq and Kitikmeot regions. The most consistent hunts take place around the communities of Kugluktuk, Umingmaktok, and Bathurst Inlet, where close to 10 bears are taken annually. Hunts are conducted almost exclusively in early May, when bears come out of hibernation and there is still enough snow on the ground for tracking.

Wolves and Wolverines

Wolves are common in Nunavut, and can be separated into two types. On the mainland, wolves move seasonally with caribou, their main prey. In the High Arctic, wolves are more resident and tied to locally available prey species. Wolves are highly prized for their pelts, which are commonly used to trim traditional parkas. Wolf hunting is available upon request with some outfitters, and can be done opportunistically along with a grizzly or muskox spring hunt.

The wolverine is prized everywhere in Nunavut as a source of superior parka trim and hood trim. Densities of these terrestrial scavengers are highest within the ranges of the major caribou herds. Most of the annual wolverine catch occurs in the western Kitikmeot Region.

Marine Mammals

Until 1994, only aboriginal hunters or hunters who had aboriginal dependants could hunt walrus in Nunavut. Now a very limited — and somewhat experimental — hunting season has been opened for non-resident hunters. Special quotas have been established to benefit communities with walrus populations. Non-resident hunters take the tusks; the walrus meat stays in the village. Igloolik and Coral Harbour are currently operating walrus hunts.

The only other marine mammals for which licences are available are ringed and harp seals.

Licences and Export Permits

Visitors wishing to hunt in Nunavut are required to use licensed outfitters; hunting licence and tag must be purchased before embarking on the hunt. Hunting licences are processed and issued by the nearest office of the **Department of Sustainable Development** (or until April 1999, GNWT's **Resources, Wildlife and Economic Development**).

All big-game animals except walrus are subject to trophy fees paid to the government of the Northwest Territories. This trophy fee must be paid prior to the export permit being issued.

At the time of writing, it is required to have a Northwest Territories Export Permit to export all wildlife parts from Nunavut, including wildlife hunted. Permits can be obtained in all hamlets from local wildlife officers or other government personnel. No territorial permit is required to export fish or items manufactured from wildlife parts. Exporting marine mammal parts requires a separate Marine Mammal Transportation Licence. For details on export permits, licence fees, trophy fees, and hunting seasons, contact the Department of Sustainable Development (RWED, before April/99).

Exporting certain wildlife products (polar bears, grizzlies, wolves, and walruses) from Canada requires an international export document called CITES (Convention on International Trade in Endangered Species). The regional offices of the Department of Resources, Wildlife and Economic Development in Iqaluit, Arviat, and Kugluktuk can issue CITES documents in Nunavut. (Check with the Department of Sustainable Development if inquiring after March 31, 1999.)

Before coming to Nunavut, hunters must learn the import regulations of their home countries. You may want to defer this responsibility to a Customs broker familiar with these requirements.

Fishing

From huge lake trout lurking in the deep, cold lakes of the Kivalliq Region and the Arctic coast, to battling arctic char cruising the pools and estuaries of arctic rivers, Nunavut is home to some of the world's best fishing.

Many Nunavut outfitters and tour operators specialize in fishing trips. Unless you are an experienced northern traveller, it's probably wise to start out with a package trip that provides a local guide. Some packages also provide visits to Inuit outpost camps. There are a few fishing lodges in Nunavut, though not as many as in the western Northwest Territories.

Most arctic fishing is done with lures. Dedicated fly fishermen, however, will enjoy the thrill of arctic char and grayling. Due to the slow rate of growth of arctic fish, catch-and-release fishing is encouraged for sport fishermen, although you are certainly allowed to keep and eat your catch, within limits. There is usually no difficulty in taking some of your catch home if it can be frozen.

Of all the game fish found in Nunavut, none is as sought after as the legendary arctic char, considered by many fishermen to be one of the top game fish in the world. There are, however, only a few established char fishing camps in Nunavut, and only three lodges offer char fishing. Community outfitters and guides will be well versed in the best local char fishing spots.

Baffin Region

On Baffin Island, all the rivers in Steensby Inlet — including the Erickson, Nina Bang, Rowley, and Isortoq — have excellent char runs, but only the Rowley has an airstrip suitable for a Twin Otter. This is also true of the rivers on the isolated west side of Baffin Island, where only the Koukdjuak, flowing from huge Nettilling Lake, is accessible by landings.

In north Baffin, the Robertson River, which flows into Milne Inlet near Pond Inlet, is excellent for char fishing but requires an expensive air charter. Two other outstanding char rivers in north Baffin are the Jungersen and Moffat, which offer superb fishing in late August and early September.

Several river estuaries on Cumberland Sound offer excellent char fishing in early and midsummer, although stocks here have decreased somewhat in recent years due to commercial fishing in the area. There is also char fishing in the Tongait River, whose stunning scenery will appeal to all anglers. Clearwater Fiord is another popular char fishing spot in the sound.

Not all of the best char fishing in the Baffin Region is confined to Baffin Island itself, however. Near the community of Hall Beach, huge char inhabit the waters of Hall Lake (as do superb lake trout); on Melville Peninsula there is also a usable gravel airstrip at the southwest end of the lake. The rivers that empty into Hall Lake offer exciting char runs, too.

The most unique fishing spot in Nunavut has to be Lake Hazen, the most northerly lake in North America, located in Ellesmere Island National Park. Char here are surprisingly abundant, though smaller than their southern brethren. The problem is that, in some years, the ice on the lake never melts completely. Nearby Ruggles River offers an excellent char run as well.

Kitikmeot Region

Two fishing lodges in the Kitikmeot currently specialize in char fishing: **Plummer's Arctic Lodge** at Tree River in the Coronation Gulf, and the **High Arctic Lodge** on Victoria Island, at Surrey Lake. The Tree River once yielded a world-record char of 32.4 pounds and a fly-fishing record char of

21.6 pounds. Tree River is extensively managed and only 700 char can be landed and kept each year. High Arctic Lodge offers excellent wildlife viewing opportunities in addition to outstanding char fishing.

There are also many char runs available to those willing to charter planes or boats to remote locations. The Bathurst Inlet area offers more than five char runs and boasts some of the most stunning scenery in the entire region. These runs include the Nauyak, Ekalulia, Hiukitak, Burnside, Western, and Hood rivers.

From Cambridge Bay, char runs can be accessed at Ferguson Lake and Char Lake on Victoria Island. Char runs in the Queen Maud Gulf area (the Perry and Ellice rivers) are also accessible from here. Adlair Aviation of Cambridge Bay can arrange day trips to these locations.

What may be perhaps the world's largest char run takes place every year on the Coppermine River, where char can be taken in spawning grounds some 300 kilometres inland from the river mouth. This is one of the few places in Nunavut that char can be taken in sight of trees. Subsistence use of this river is high, though, limiting sport-fishing opportunities. The community of Kugluktuk stages an annual fishing derby that is gaining popularity among visitors.

Several char runs occur in the Chantry Inlet area, south of Gjoa Haven. Smaller runs are also accessible on King William Island. Taloyoak boasts fine runs on the Netsilik, Lord Lindsay, and Garry rivers.

Arctic char taken near Pelly Bay are renowned for their taste and distinctive deep crimson flesh, indicative of a diet high in crustaceans. These fish are often the preference of Kitikmeot residents.

The major sport fish of the Kitikmeot Region is the lake trout, found in every significant lake system in the region. These fish can be taken at almost any time of year, either by jigging through the ice, trolling on large lakes, or casting from shore.

Northeast of Taloyoak, fishermen have the privilege of fishing the most northerly lake trout in continental North America in Lord Lindsay Lake. The lake trout in those far northern lakes grow very slowly, but it is still possible to catch a 10-pound fish with almost tiring rapidity.

Taloyoak and Cambridge Bay are the gateways to the most accessible large lakes in the region. Near Taloyoak, lakes such as the Hansteen, Jekyll, Angmaluktuk, Ishluktuk, Lady Melville, and Netsilik offer excellent trout fishing. Legend says that trout have swamped kayaks in some of these lakes, pulling down hapless paddlers. This, of course, is a bit of a fish story, but huge 60-pound lunkers have been caught here on rod and reel. Out of Cambridge Bay, Kitiga and Ferguson lakes offer excellent trout fishing.

In Kugluktuk, try for lake trout in Emagyok and Imik lakes, both within 60 kilometres of town.

Lake whitefish are also common, and easily caught with a slower, deeper retrieve. Grayling are generally confined to the western portion of the region, and can be caught in most moving freshwater streams and rivers.

Kivalliq Region

Like other Nunavut communities, those in the Kivalliq Region all have access to char rivers. Of course, some have more than others, and the abundance of char varies with the season. There are some exemplary fishing spots, however.

Duke of York Bay on Southampton Inlet boasts a number of char rivers. Char spend much of the short arctic summer in the bay and can be caught by simply casting from rocky points. The problem here is access; it's a day's travel from Repulse Bay through a strait that frequently remains clogged with ice throughout the summer. Closer to Coral Harbour, Sixteen-Mile Brook and Rocky Brook offer excellent char runs.

Most of the rivers that flow into the west shore of Hudson Bay boast arctic char. The Maguse River and Maguse Lake near Arviat are particularly good spots, as is Sandy Point, which is also accessible from Whale Cove. In Rankin Inlet, try the Dianne River and Corbet Inlet.

Chesterfield Inlet is also an outstanding place for char fishing. In fact, the fish run from Chesterfield Inlet to Baker Lake and on into the Thelon River system as far as Shultz Lake.

The major sport fish of the Kivalliq Region is the lake trout. Lakes in the southern part of the region also have huge northern pike; many streams are filled with arctic grayling.

The biggest lake in the region is Dubawnt Lake. Trout as big as 40 pounds lurk here; grayling fishing is outstanding. East and south of the lake are several lodges with excellent fishing. This may well be the best lake trout water in Nunavut. If interested, fishermen can also fly to the Kazan River for lake trout, grayling and northern pike.

Shultz Lake, in the Thelon River system, also has lake trout and arctic grayling.

Anglers planning a fishing trip to Nunavut must keep in mind that many of the lakes and rivers are very remote and difficult to access. Some are so remote that even local Inuit don't fish in them. Many of the rivers and lakes have absolutely no infrastructure, such as accommodation or boats. If you go in, you must fly them in with you. If you are using the services of an outfitter, you must make certain that your outfitter has all of the necessary camping equipment and a boat suitable for fishing.

Fishing Regulations

If you are between the ages of 16 and 65 and plan on fishing in Nunavut, you must first buy a sport fishing licence, which is readily available in most communities from the local office of the Department of Sustainable Development (or RWED, until April 1999). You will receive a copy of the *Northwest Territories Sport Fishing Guide* when you get your licence, or get one in advance from Nunavut Tourism.

As the guide notes, "Sport fishing in the Nunavut Settlement Area may be subject to terms and conditions in accordance with the Nunavut Land Claims Agreement." Your tour operator should be aware of these access restrictions. If you're out fishing on your own, contact the Inuit Land Administration Office responsible for the region you intend to visit in advance of your trip. The sidebar on access restrictions in Chapter 11, "Adventure Travel," provides more details.

Sport fishing is only allowed in national parks with a National Park Fishing Permit.

40. PHOTOGRAPHY

by Mike Beedell

Photography in the North can be one of the most exhilarating and rewarding experiences imaginable.

It's complicated by enormous seasonal variations in light and temperature. Severe cold and long winter nights evolve into the perpetual daylight of spring and summer, with a quality of light unsurpassed on Earth. This wide range of conditions creates special challenges; to make the most of your photographic journey, it's essential that you be prepared.

Cold

Most photographic equipment today is battery-operated. Be sure to take plenty of extras, especially if you'll be travelling in cold weather. I suggest you take three complete sets of rechargeable batteries and a few lightweight chargers. This way you'll be saving the environment and money, as well. You'll find some good small solar-powered chargers for AA batteries on the market. Remember that batteries lose power quickly in the cold, so try to keep a spare set warm in your pocket. Don't throw away cold batteries; they may work again once they're warmed up. Some northern photographers recommend that in cold weather you keep your camera inside your coat or parka, taking it out only to compose and shoot. This usually keeps the camera warm enough to function well all day without a battery charge. This approach can cause condensation to form on lenses and film, however, especially if you're sweating.

Manual cameras are best for extremely cold temperatures of –20° C and lower. If you have your gear under your coat, keep it in a zip-lock plastic bag to minimize the effect of moisture from your body. Then when you move from a cold to a warm environment, always put your equipment in a sealed plastic bag filled with cold air and allow your gear to warm up slowly. This will minimize condensation on your camera bodies and lenses. (Nothing is more annoying than that moment when you reach for a lens to capture a magnificent polar bear prowling along the pressure-ice, only to find that a frostsicle has formed inside your lens!) As film becomes very brittle when temperatures drop below –25° C, always try to keep some rolls warm inside your coat. Wind your film slowly so it doesn't shatter or cause static to build up. If you wear lightweight polypropylene or silk gloves inside your mitts, these will help you to change film or lenses and perform intricate zooms with your video camera in the cold.

An extension wire that clips on to your video or still camera is another handy item to carry; it allows you to keep your camera batteries on your body to avoid power drain from the cold. A good photography store should have one that's appropriate for your needs. A hand-warmer that runs on solid fuel or lighter fluid is also beneficial. You can even strap one to your motor-drive or video to keep it going in the cold!

Light

Illumination can be very intense during spring and summer days in the North. You may find that you take your best pictures on early spring mornings, late evenings, or during long luminous nights when the sun never sets. In winter and spring, much of this intensity comes from reflections off snow and ice, which are difficult for light meters to measure accurately. If your camera has a standard built-in meter, your exposures will usually be inaccurate and render your subject in underexposed greyish tones. To capture the beauty of a landscape and the whiteness and brilliance of snow, you'll have to increase exposure by 1.5 to 2 stops. If you're not sure what your meter tells you, then "bracket" your shots by overexposing and underexposing what your meter tells you is correct so you cover a number of exposures.

Generally, the light at midday is too harsh and intense for good photography. Morning and evening light is softer, gentler, and more pleasing. The low slanting light of an arctic night has a magical quality. Side-lighting, with the low sun either on your left or right, rather than directly behind you, accentuates contours and texture in snow, giving form and relief to a landscape. Back-lit pictures can also be dramatic. When you shoot directly into the sun just as it's rising above the horizon, however, you should, once again, bracket your exposures. To improve your imagery, study the angle of light and remember these light-awareness rules:

- front-lighting enhances light and color
- side-lighting enhances texture and form
- back-lighting enhances mood and silhouettes.

Nature and Photo Tours

Nunavut is a stunning photographic showcase of the arctic world. You can explore the northern landscape for years, yet still not fully capture the extraordinary variety of its natural and cultural life. You'll be awestruck when you photograph your first titanic-sized iceberg glistening in the midnight sun. Or when you focus on a swift narwhal, its ivory tusk piercing mirror-calm waters. Or when you zoom in on a polar bear as it moves ghost-like over pack ice in search of seal. If wildlife isn't your passion, then the magnificent tundra and Nunavut's hardy Inuit and other northerners will keep you enthralled. There never seems to be enough film!

Until recently, travel to many northern sites was difficult, even impossible, unless you had a lot of time, money and northern contacts. Today, photo tours can offer you wonderful experiences that suit your budget and time frame. Whether you're an eager beginner, advanced amateur or seasoned professional, photography is now within reach of everyone who can afford it. Photo tour accommodation can be arranged at base camps, in the homes of Inuit, or at local hotels within most communities.

In spring and summer, your best times for shooting are during sunlit nights between 8 p.m. and 3 a.m. Shadows are long at this time of day, and color and texture are defined unlike anywhere else on the planet. A quality photo tour will recognize that your schedule will be upset and will allow you time to explore and photograph late at "night" and sleep during late morning or early afternoon. When booking a photo tour, ask how flexible the schedule will be. Many Inuit families and guides also like to travel during the luminous nights of summer.

Your stay at a base camp will help you to get good photographic results at a relaxed pace. Once your comfortable tents are set up in a wilderness area, you can venture out on your own or shoot with the group. On some tours, photo workshops are offered. You get to set the pace. You may have access to an Inuit freighter canoe, a small inflatable boat like a Zodiac, or a larger boat for travel on water. Or you may hike on the tundra, where you can photograph ancient Inuit sites, peregrine falcons and other wildlife, and dazzling displays of tiny wildflowers and colorful lichen.

Back at the base camp, your day winds down over a hot meal with new friends who share your interest in photography and adventure travel. Be aware, though, that group tours require compromise on your part; they offer you less privacy than you'd have travelling on your own or with a few friends. If this is a problem, you'll find that many tour companies arrange customized trips for individuals or private groups.

Point-to-point photo tours (unlike those where you stay in one community or base camp) offer the most variety; accommodation is in northern hotels or camping out on the land with Inuit families. During your tour, you may travel extensively to wildlife and cultural "hot spots." Expect to see everything from congregations of beluga whales to cliffside colonies of seabirds; from community festivals to intriguing historical sites. Serious shutterbugs may find such a tour a whirlwind, especially considering the leisurely pace of community life and the unpredictability of arctic weather.

A home stay with an Inuit family can be culturally and photographically rewarding. Before booking with a tour company, confirm with them that the family is comfortable with you documenting their daily life. If they are, you can ask permission to photograph them flensing sealskins, for example, or worshipping at a local church. The instant results provided by a Polaroid or video camera can help ease any discomfort, by enabling you to share the experience with your hosts. Be sure to respect the family's privacy. Remember, too, to follow through with your promise to send copies of photos to them after you return. That way, the experience will be happily remembered by everyone.

Find out, as well, how long the tour operator has been in business. Keep in mind, however, that experience doesn't necessarily equal excellence. Ask the company to give you phone numbers of previous clients who might tell you what they think of the operator. **Nunavut Tourism** will give you the names of licensed photo tour operators, although they won't recommend one over another. Obtain the name of the tour leader, and ask about his or her arctic expertise. Don't forget that an "expert" or "famous photographer" doesn't necessarily make a good leader. Such a leader may have poor social skills — and a penchant for too much single-malt whisky! The best leaders have a loyal clientele who return as much for them as for their tours. Beware the "famous photographer as guide" approach, a hook that's used on many photo tours. Be sure the person is a good teacher and pleasant travelling companion, not some pompous egotist whom you'll be stuck with for a week!

You should also ask the company for the number of participants on your tour, their ages, and their photographic experience. The operator should provide you with a list of suggested equipment to bring. As well, ask whether they will assist in transporting your gear; some companies will, others won't. They should describe the kind of terrain you'll be travelling and the level of physical fitness required to make the trip. Most photo tours involve light to moderate physical activity; some can accommodate the physically handicapped. In the event of bad weather, companies don't offer refunds because such conditions are a fact of life in the Arctic. Be patient — your safety is of foremost concern.

If you don't want to book with a photo tour company, but prefer to create your own customized trip, contact Nunavut Tourism for a list of licensed outfitters. These outfitters know the land and wildlife intimately, and should offer you a safe and fulfilling journey.

With planning and patience, you'll capture images to treasure for the rest of your life. Remember, however, that northern weather can change in an instant. Whether it is deadly or simply dramatic may depend on your attitude and level of preparedness.

Photographic Equipment and Supplies

Before you leave for the North, be sure you have enough film for your entire trip; you may have difficulty finding a particular film outside major centres. Take a camera, or cameras, that you're familiar with. A northern journey, where you're surrounded by unparalleled photographic opportunities, is no time to learn what your camera can or cannot do!

In Nunavut, summer travel in an open boat is usually a marvellous, safe way to see the territory. Boating has its hazards, however: you and your equipment can get very wet. A spray of salt water across your camera can damage it forever. If you're paddling a wild river — actually, if you're any-where near water — a waterproof camera case, such as the Pelican Box, is excellent for carrying lenses. It can be a heavy, awkward load, though, to carry on long hikes. A cheaper, more versatile way to keep your gear dry is a waterproof bag that you can tuck inside your backpack. If you're not on a tight budget, I'd take both. The following is a list of equipment I carry on northern photographic trips:

- Lowe-Pro camera backpack
- waterproof Pelican Box
- sturdy, light tripod
- extra batteries
- camera bodies — one electronic, one manual
- video camera and monopod or shoulder-pod
- 20 millimetre lens 2.8, 28-75 zoom, 80-200 2.8, 100 macro, 300 millimetre, 500 millimetre
- flash with extension cable and reflective material for floral work (aluminum foil)
- filters — polarizer, warming filters, ultraviolet, skylight
- light meter
- cable release, lens tissue and fluid

- small umbrella, or heavy gauge plastic bag for shooting during rough weather
- duct tape, jeweller's screwdriver, leatherman tool.

Film

If you're a keen photographer, I'd take a minimum of five rolls a day. If you're a pro, go for 10 rolls a day. For slides, I recommend Fujichrome 50 Velvia and Provia 100, Kodachrome 64 and 200, Fujichrome 400, and Kodak Elite 400. For prints, choose similar ASA ratings. Black and white film is also very rewarding. Remember to take videotapes and extra nicad batteries, as well.

Light at high latitudes, and altitudes, tends to be bluish, especially on overcast days. An ultraviolet or skylight filter will eliminate some of the excess blue without you having to change your exposure. A filter will also protect your lens. A warming filter will balance out the cool tones of a bluish cast.

These suggestions should help you to appreciate and capture the exquisite beauty and clarity of the northern light and landscape. If you have patience and a keen eye, you'll return from your travels with photos that reveal the majesty of this extraordinary land.

41. CAMPING

by Carol and Bruce Rigby

Campers in Nunavut must be thoroughly self-sufficient. There are few specially designated camping spots and, for the most part, when camping you're generally on your own.

A few communities have a designated campground with outhouses and perhaps running water, but these are the exception rather than the norm. Chapters in the "Destinations" section indicate whether a community has a campground. But there are no trailer parks, electrical hookups, and the like. If you go camping, you must be prepared to "rough it." For important information about weather, search and rescue measures, proper clothing, water outside the communities, protecting yourself from natural hazards, minimizing damage to the fragile arctic environment and other travel advice, please read Chapter 11, "Adventure Travel," as well.

Most communities have a spot where they prefer campers to pitch their tents. This preference is usually based on protecting the hamlet's water supply, so inquire at the hamlet office before setting up in any community.

Under the Nunavut Land Claims Agreement, a portion of Nunavut's almost two million square kilometres became Inuit-owned land. Although their boundaries are not physically marked, these lands are private property and certain access restrictions apply.

Aside from these lands, campers are free to pitch a tent almost anywhere on the open tundra, but it's important to remember that the land you are camping on is probably part of the traditional territory of an Inuit family. Though you are welcome to use it, treat it with respect. When outside parks, existing camp sites on the tundra are probably the best places to set camp. Most camp sites exist for reasons of shelter, availability of drinking water, depth of water for boats, shoreline conditions for those travelling by boat, lookout points for wild game or marine mammals, or because they are sacred places.

If you can't find an existing camp site, choose sites in durable locations that will show no trace of being used. A durable site is especially important if you plan to use the site as a base camp or if you are travelling in a large group. Avoid vegetated sites or soil types that are sensitive to disturbance. Wearing "soft" shoes around camp is not only a great relief after a day spent in heavy hiking boots, but they also minimize your impact on the ground around your camp site. Avoid camping near sensitive wildlife areas such as grass-sedge meadows. Do not dig trenches around tents or build windbreaks from rocks. Always leave camp sites as clean or cleaner than you found them.

Most parks indicate preferred camping areas. Within Auyuittuq National Park, the areas near and around the warden stations and emergency shelters provide good camp sites. Around the Tanquary Fiord and Lake Hazen warden stations in Ellesmere Island National Park, camping is only permitted in designated areas to avoid expanding disturbance beyond sites that already show the heavy impact of visitors.

Camping Stoves, Tents and Sleeping Bags

Campers should bring their own gear with them to Nunavut even if they are booking through an outfitter (unless the outfitter says otherwise). General camping gear and supplies are sold in Nunavut's larger settlements and some other communities, but specialized backpacking or technical gear may not be widely available. Camping equipment, like everything else, is much more expensive in the Arctic than in other areas.

Nunavut is above the tree line, so a camp stove is required. Camp stove fuel must be purchased in the nearest community because it is illegal to pack it in luggage carried aboard aircraft. Camp stoves should be capable of burning either naphtha (white gas) or kerosene, which are generally available in small communities. There are few places where propane can be purchased in a convenient form for camping (Rankin Inlet and Iqaluit are two exceptions), and often there are local bylaws governing the safe storage of propane. A naphtha stove is highly recommended because kerosene supplies frequently run low in small communities in late summer before the year's supply arrives by sealift.

Your camping stove must be capable of operating reliably in high winds. You should also test and practise using it before you arrive — there's nothing worse than trying to figure out how to use a new piece of equipment when your hands are freezing, the wind is howling and you're famished!

Lightweight tents designed for backpacking trips must be able to withstand high winds. Wind speeds in Auyuittuq National Park, for example, easily reach 100 kilometres per hour, and there are no trees to offer windbreaks. Low-profile shapes are recommended.

Don't skimp on your tent. If caught in a heavy storm, your survival may depend upon it.

Sturdy white canvas tents may be provided by an outfitter, but these are most frequently used as cook tents or mess tents. You are still well advised to have a small dome tent for your sleeping quarters. Fire-rated tents are important because accidents do happen when cooking in tents.

Unless you're an experienced cold-weather camper and know your tolerance for cold precisely, bring a warm sleeping bag. Even in mid-summer, the nights can be very chilly, and rapidly changing weather means hypothermia is always a risk when camping for extended periods. Your sleeping bag should be rated to at least –15° C. Anyone planning a spring skiing trip in Nunavut should prepare as they would for a midwinter camping trip in more southern climates. A bag rated to –35° C is recommended.

You will be much warmer and more comfortable if you bring a sleeping pad to insulate you from the ground. Closed-cell foam or Thermarest™ pads are effective, though air mattresses are not good (they're inclined to deflate, especially in cold temperatures). A bivy sack can also provide you with an extra layer of insulation. If you're going anywhere near the water, bring a waterproof covering (even a securely fastened garbage bag!) for your sleeping bag. A wet sleeping bag is useless.

Food

Be generous in estimating food requirements. Nunavut's generally cool environment and rugged terrain place heavy demands on the body's energy reserves, especially when backpacking or doing other activities out on the land.

Campers or others planning to prepare their own meals should come well supplied with food, particularly if specialized products like dehydrated camping food are required, since they may not be widely available. Stores in larger communities offer a reasonable selection of food, and prices are competitive once you factor in shipping costs.

On the other hand, selection in the smaller communities can be extremely limited, especially during the peak visitor season in July and August, which is usually before the annual resupply by ship.

Water

As when camping anywhere, always draw water from running sources rather than from stagnant ponds or pools. A special consideration in the North is to avoid consuming too much water from silt-laden glacial streams, which can cause digestive upset. Let water from a glacial stream settle before using it. Be sure to carry plenty of water to avoid dehydration — especially problematic in cold conditions. Frequent breaks for warm drinks, such as the traditional Inuit tea break, are recommended.

Litter

Pick up and pack out all of your litter. Smokers, that includes your cigarette butts. You can help by picking up any litter left by others. Report any large accumulations of litter, or large items such as empty fuel drums, to local authorities. You can minimize litter and food scraps with careful planning and preparation. Food can be packaged in plastic bags instead of cans, bottles, or tin foil. Carefully measured meals help minimize leftovers and reduce both waste and weight.

If you burn garbage to reduce its volume, use an existing charred area or make the fire on rock or sand. Fire can easily be hidden in moss, and although there's no risk of forest fires, tundra fires have been known to happen — they spread insidiously and are very hard to put out. Take special care to ensure that any fires you light are completely extinguished before you break camp.

Human Waste

In low-use areas away from toilet facilities, feces should be left on the surface, well away from trails, camp sites, and all bodies of fresh water. Choose a dry, open exposure away from travel routes. Leaving feces exposed on the surface will maximize their exposure to the light and air and accelerate their decomposition. If you are travelling with a large group, particularly if you are using a base camp, it is advisable to dig a shallow communal latrine (15 centimetres) in dry soil at least 50 metres away from traffic routes, camp sites, and bodies of fresh water. Make sure the latrine is properly covered after use to hide its presence from those that follow and to discourage animals from digging it up.

If travelling along a body of salt water, it is acceptable to deposit your feces in a shallow pit below the tidal high-water mark.

Minimize the use of toilet paper. Burn it as completely as possible. Sanitary napkins or tampons should be packed out with other garbage, unless you are travelling in an area where encounters with bears are possible. In that case, they should be burned in a hot fire by soaking them in naphtha. Sanitary supplies should never be buried.

While camping in any national or territorial park at identified sites, such as the Sylvia Grinnell campground outside Iqaluit or the warden or emergency shelters in the national parks, use the toilet facilities provided and adhere to the instructions for their use.

Waste Water

Use soap sparingly — even the preferable biodegradable types. Leftover soap should not be dumped in lakes or streams. Take sponge or "bird" baths using a pot of water. Do this well away from bodies of water. This allows the biodegradable soap to filter through the soil and break down before reaching any body of water. Clothes can be cleaned by rinsing them thoroughly. Soap is not necessary and can cause skin irritation if not thoroughly rinsed out.

Waste water from washing dishes and excess cooking water should be poured into a shallow pit away from camp sites and bodies of water. Pick up food scraps and pack them out with other litter. If travelling in bear country, though, smelly garbage should be burned and any odorless residue packed out.

42. HIKING
by Carol and Bruce Rigby

You are probably well aware of the adage "take only pictures, leave only footprints."

In the Arctic, where the land itself is very sensitive to disturbance, we request that you "take only pictures, and leave as few footprints as possible."

By hiking amid Nunavut's wild beauty, however, you'll also be taking home some indelible memories.

Before arriving in Nunavut, check to see whether your planned hiking trail takes you across Inuit-owned land. Under the Nunavut Land Claims Agreement, a portion of Nunavut's almost two million square kilometres became Inuit-owned land. Although their boundaries are not physically marked, these lands are private property and certain access restrictions apply.

For important information about this and stream and river crossings, rockfalls, safeguarding archeological finds, search and rescue measures, proper clothing, and other travel advice, please read Chapter 11, "Adventure Travel." The chart close to the beginning of the "Destinations" section also points out hiking trails around Nunavut.

Some communities have marked hiking trails in their vicinities. Often there are brochures available locally or from **Nunavut Tourism** to indicate where these are. Within Auyuittuq National Park, most of the hiking trails are marked with *inuksuit*. But in other parks, such as Ellesmere Island National Park, Katannilik Territorial Park Reserve and Sylvia Grinnell Territorial Park, there are no trail-marking systems (other than suggested routes marked on the park's photo-mosaic trail maps).

As you hike along, stay on the marked trails. Where these do not exist, plan your route ahead to include durable terrain that can withstand high traffic. Resistant routes include gravel stream bottoms and bedrock. Other hard, stable, plant-free surfaces and snow patches will provide paths with minimal environmental damage.

Avoid soft soil and vegetated areas, particularly grass-sedge meadows. Their drainage patterns can be disrupted by trails running through them. These grass-sedge meadows are critical feeding habitat for wildlife. If you remove or disturb vegetation, soils will be exposed to the elements, disturbing the critical balance of frozen and unfrozen ground, and resulting in erosion damage.

Parks Canada studies also show that low-lying wet areas and wind-deposited dunes are particularly delicate.

In steep terrain, it is least damaging to ascend or descend on rock outcrops or snow. On soil-covered surfaces, it is less damaging to ascend than to descend steep slopes. If slopes are so steep that it's necessary to dig your toes and heels into the soil to get a grip, you should use another route if possible.

If you come to an area in a park where the shape of the land forces you to hike over steep terrain in a place where marked trails do not exist, look for game trails such as those left by muskoxen or caribou. These usually provide the safest and best passage. Keep in mind, however, that most arctic wildlife are far more agile and capable climbers than the average hiker. When descending loose scree, move slowly and cautiously. Rapid descents can cause large quantities of scree to slide, leaving obvious scars and altering erosion patterns. They can also result in sprained ankles or worse.

43. BOATING AND CANOEING
by Carol and Bruce Rigby

Boating is a popular way to see Nunavut in summer, once the ice has broken up by mid-July.

A variety of vessels ply northern coasts and some rivers. However, boating in the region does require skills and preparation unique to the arctic environment. (Be sure to read Chapter 11, "Adventure Travel," for important information about clothing, safety, and search and rescue measures. Also be aware that there are access restrictions to Inuit-owned lands.) Many experienced outfitters and tour operators offer boating packages. If this is your first boating trip in the Arctic, you're wise to sign up with a group package.

Outfitters must provide boat passengers with flotation suits. If boating on your own, be sure to rent a suit. Life-jackets are just not good enough for frigid arctic waters.

Motorized freighter canoes and Lake Winnipeg boats, used by most outfitters, are common in Nunavut. These are six to seven metres long with large outboard motors, and are usually used to transport visitors to parks and other sites of interest. Because of the dangerous conditions that prevail in the North, though, when you rent any kind of motorboat here, you'll also have to hire a guide. If you think the additional cost is unnecessary, you'll probably change your mind once you experience the challenges of extreme tides, winds and rocky seacoasts. Even seasoned northern travellers won't set out on the water without a good local pilot.

Canoeing
The Kivalliq and Kitikmeot regions offer excellent canoeing opportunities on such rivers as the Back, the Coppermine, the Thelon, the Dubawnt and the Kazan. The Kazan and the Thelon are part of Canada's Heritage Rivers System. The Back, Dubawnt and Thelon flow through parts of the Thelon Wildlife Sanctuary. Canoeing is an ideal way to experience the sanctuary's majestic landscape and wildlife.

Canoeing these rivers shouldn't be undertaken lightly. As all rivers are far removed from most Kivalliq communities, safety should be your first priority when planning a canoe trip. While not hard and fast rules, consider the following as guidelines: go in a group of at least six canoeists, and use three canoes at least five metres long. This will give you a margin of safety, should damage occur to any one of the canoes. Spray decks for canoes are recommended, as the water will be cold and there may be patches of white water. Weather may cause delays, so allow yourself plenty of time and calculate supplies accordingly. (One estimate is that 20 kilometres per day is a reasonable average distance to travel.)

Also be sure to carry a second set of maps, as they'll be essential to your safety. If you can obtain a global positioning system, you'll find it a valuable piece of equipment, because it will help you locate your position and destination through the use of satellite information. Before heading out, be sure to leave your itinerary with a responsible body, such as the RCMP or the local search and rescue group, in the nearest community. That way, if you're delayed, they'll know when and where to look for you.

In the Baffin Region, canoes are used on only one river — the Soper, also part of Canada's Heritage Rivers System. Other Baffin rivers, where mountainous terrain has given birth to some of the wildest rapids in North America, are sometimes used by kayakers.

Rafting

Rafting has been tried on three rivers: the Sylvia Grinnell, outside Iqaluit; the Soper, near Kimmirut; and the McKeand, which drains from the Hall Peninsula into Cumberland Sound. Iqaluit's one experienced rafting operator runs tours primarily on the Soper. The Sylvia Grinnell provides some white water during late spring/early summer runoff. For most of the summer, though, that river is a float trip. The Soper River, too, isn't a demanding whitewater trip. Take suitable precautions, however, as the water will be cold.

Sailing

During the whaling era, Inuit used to sail extensively, but once motorboats became available, sailing fell out of favor. Although there are still a few dedicated sailors today, sailing small boats is uncommon in Nunavut because of the danger of hypothermia. Sailboats and sailboards aren't available for rent.

44. KAYAKING
by Renee Wissink, with contributions from Carol Rigby

Aside from a dogsled trip, what could be a more natural way to travel in Nunavut than by kayak?

After all, the kayak (*qajaq*) was an Inuit invention, a mode of transport for which these Arctic inhabitants are famous. Apart from the *umiaq,* a much larger open boat used to transport whole families and their possessions, the kayak was the main method of water transport, be it for hunting caribou on inland lakes, or hunting whales, walrus and seals on the sea. While styles of kayaks varied from region to region within Nunavut, they were generally a broader, more robust craft with a large cockpit — quite different from the stereotypical sleek, fast kayak of West Greenlandic design that most people assume all Inuit used.

Traditional kayaks were usually made from a driftwood frame and covered with sealskins. Hunters would generally wear a sealskin *annuraaq* that doubled as a cockpit cover. (This men's jacket, in addition to having drawstrings at the hood and wrists, also cinched at the waist, where the drawstring attached to the kayak cockpit.) Hunters also had to juggle an assortment of weapons and implements (harpoons, floats, lines, toggles, plugs) in order to hunt.

Imagine the bravery required to paddle this frail craft, armed only with a harpoon, in quest of a 750-kilogram bull walrus, or even a bowhead whale! Many hunters were lost in the hunt or blown out to sea.

The advent of the kayaking tourism industry in Nunavut has brought the modern kayak back to its homeland. Kayaking venues are endless. But only experienced kayakers should try kayaking in the North. Be aware, too, that there are access restrictions to Inuit-owned lands in Nunavut. To learn more about this, as well as safe travel advice, read Chapter 11, "Adventure Travel."

For the river runner looking for the adrenaline high of white water, short, fast rivers like Baffin Island's Sylvia Grinnell River outside Iqaluit, or the Soper River near Kimmirut, are ideal. Outfitters and packages are available for both. **Nunavut Tourism** can provide names of outfitters and put you in touch with experienced northern kayakers.

Baffin Island can also provide a number of first descents for the real adventurer. In 1984, for instance, a small group from the Iqaluit Kayaking Club did the first descent of the McKeand River on south Baffin Island.

The river kayaker should not overlook the Kivalliq and Kitikmeot regions since their rivers, including the Thelon and Coppermine, accommodate most of the classic river trips that canoeists have been paddling for years. For the sea kayaker, Nunavut, with its thousands of kilometres of marine coastline, is a paddler's dream. To explore its myriad bays, fiords and inlets would take several lifetimes. Access to Nunavut's marine environment is excellent since almost all communities are located on the coast.

Kayaking in Nunavut has its special problems: cold water, unpredictable weather, sea ice, walruses, polar bears, and large tides are a few of them. Frobisher Bay, for example, has a tidal range in the 12- to 15-metre range, the third largest in Canada. Paddlers must come fully prepared in accordance with the difficulty of the trip they choose. In addition to the standard gear, a good wetsuit or dry suit is a must, because life-jackets alone are inadequate. Remember to take along two paddles in case you lose one of them. The ability to self-rescue — including being able to Eskimo roll — is also essential. Take the time to learn about local knowledge of prevailing winds, tides and currents. Get in touch with the local HTO. You could also contact **Canadian Hydrographic Services** for tide and current tables.

If you're looking for a safe, all-inclusive recreational trip, travel with one of the growing number of licensed tour operators offering kayak tours. Communities such as Pond Inlet offer pre-organized tours that save you the headache and expense of transporting boats and gear up north. Hire an outfitter to take you and your kayak to magnificent paddling areas like the territorial historic parks or the Bylot Island bird sanctuary near Pond Inlet.

If travelling on a self-guided tour, make sure your equipment and training are up to the task. Assume everything will take longer than on a southern trip and have contingency and emergency plans in place. River runners in the Arctic add one level to the whitewater classification because of the cold water. A rapid that would be Class 3 in the South is rated as Class 4 in Nunavut. Carry an HF radio and/or a global positioning system, and know how to use them. But above all, respect the land and water, and have fun.

45. CRUISES
by Mike Vlessides

The stark reality of a trip to Nunavut is that you are likely to suffer some sort of inconvenience during your visit.

The sheer size and remoteness of the place are enough to throw a monkey wrench into the best-laid plans. Add midsummer blizzards, shared accommodation and once-weekly fresh foods, and it's easy to understand why vacations here are rarely steeped in luxury. Unless, of course, you take to the water.

Every summer since 1987, ice-breaking and ice-strengthened ships have been plying the seas between Siberia and Greenland, offering passengers a kinder, gentler northern experience. These ships offer a broad range of services, from basic accommodation and meals to amenities more typically associated with world-class hotels than the Arctic. But this kind of luxury does not come cheaply.

Cost

Cruise prices are as varied as Nunavut itself. The least expensive begin at about $2,500, which will get you airfare from Ottawa and as many as 12 days at sea. You can expect clean, comfortable accommodation — similar to that of a three-star hotel — and simple yet hearty buffet-style meals. Just don't hold your breath waiting for someone in a tuxedo to offer you a piece of baked alaska.

The more luxurious end of the spectrum carries a much weightier price tag. For more than $20,000, you can enjoy several weeks cruising the Arctic with European chefs whipping up international cuisine, fluted crystal glasses bubbling with champagne, saunas and indoor swimming pools. The newest and most luxurious vessel now visiting the area is the *MS Hanseatic,* currently owned by Radisson Seven Seas Cruises. And while the *Hanseatic* may be long on luxury, it is still not immune to the vagaries of arctic travel. In the summer of 1996, the ship ran aground in shallow waters near Gjoa Haven, spurring a well-publicized removal of its passengers.

The average naturalist cruise (a cruise that showcases the destination's wildlife and environment) takes from 10 to 14 days and costs about $11,000.

Itineraries

Itineraries tend to change from year to year, so check with the tour company before setting your heart on one particular route. There seem to be more ships in Nunavut every year, though, so the chances of finding one that offers what you want are always increasing. An especially popular route over the past decade has been the Northwest Passage cruise, which often begins in Russia and travels across the top of Alaska and Canada, usually terminating at the High Arctic community of Resolute, near the North Magnetic Pole. The problem with ending in Resolute, however, is that you never get to Baffin Island, which boasts some of the most spectacular scenery in Nunavut. Other popular routes travel between Canada and Greenland.

A Day in the Life

Once you get past the niceties of the vessel itself, most arctic cruises offer a similar combination of activities. These are all-inclusive affairs, so you won't have to worry about making separate arrangements with guides in individual communities. While on the boat you can look forward to interpretive slide shows on arctic natural history from experts in the field, entertaining stories from seasoned northern travellers, and the discerning eye of at least one staff naturalist who's always on the lookout for birds and marine mammals.

Wildlife and bird spotting is not limited to the ship itself, however. Most are usually equipped with smaller and far more agile, sturdy inflatable boats — such as Zodiacs — that are used to visit less-accessible areas where mammals roam and birds nest. These boats are also often used for trips to shore, whether to visit a community, an archeological site, a place of historical importance, or a simple day hike across the tundra. The bigger and more expensive icebreakers also make shore excursions via helicopter.

Community visits not only give you a chance to purchase art from local craftspeople, but also to get a more intimate feel for the people of Nunavut and their unique way of life, an experience most definitely absent on board the ship. Most shore visits are prefaced with an informative seminar; staff or local guides will also provide information and answer questions at the site itself. Sometimes, cruise lines will also book special guest speakers in different communities.

Many tours will also give passengers an opportunity to stretch their legs with a variety of tundra hikes, ranging from short interpretive trips to more vigorous undertakings, such as climbing small mountains. Several tour companies also have arrangements with remote lodges and camps, where there is typically an abundance of a particular bird or mammal.

When booking your trip, always inquire about trip leaders. Don't be impressed solely by a recognizable name. Make sure that the person you're relying on has ample arctic experience, especially with people. There's nothing worse than pulling into a community and finding that your trip leader has an unfavorable reputation there. Travelling with a leader who speaks Inuktitut is always a plus.

Protocol

Some years ago, residents of Broughton Island were shocked when a score of passengers from a cruise ship descended on their Baffin Island community and blatantly walked into homes, took snapshot after snapshot and left with little more than a "thank you." Apparently, the unwitting passengers had been told by their guides that the community was a sort of "living museum," and visitors were free to come and go as they pleased before shoving off for the next port of call.

The resulting din raised by residents was so loud that the now-defunct Baffin Region Tourism Association stepped in and drafted protocol guidelines for all cruise ships entering Nunavut. Cruise ships visiting Nunavut are still required to send copies of their itineraries to government tourism licensing officers who, in turn, advise communities of the ship's impending arrival. Individual communities will then inform the cruise director how passengers should conduct themselves while in the community. Ask your cruise director for a copy of these dos and don'ts.

If they are unavailable, rely on your common sense. Don't barge into someone's home unless invited, and don't stick a zoom lens in someone's face without first asking their permission.

Since you'll be entering the community by boat, there's a chance you may come across townspeople on hunting trips. These encounters, while an excellent opportunity to witness Inuit hunters in action, can also be quite gory, and therefore upsetting to the unprepared visitor. Inuit have been relying on marine mammals as a natural resource for countless years; be careful to respect this cultural difference.

Finding the Right Ship

There are only so many ice-breaking and ice-strengthened vessels floating around out there, so your choices are finite. And while there seem to be more companies operating in Nunavut every year, spaces do fill up quickly. Plan at least six months in advance — longer for novel trips that rewrite the record books. For example, a first-ever circumnavigation of Baffin Island that took place in the summer of 1997 was booked up more than a year in advance.

As with any trip, it's never a bad idea to consult a travel agent. Just don't be surprised if the person on the other side of the desk looks at you bug-eyed when you tell them you want to take a trip through the Northwest Passage. These trips are surely not mainstream, and many travel agents will have no idea what you're talking about. Any travel agent worth their salt should be able to dig up the necessary data, however.

If you find yourself on the receiving end of a travel agent's blank stare, don't despair. In an age where worlds of information are just a mouse click away, there's always the Internet. You'll find that most arctic cruise lines have their own web site, replete with itineraries, amenities, costs and dates. And since most arctic cruises have a naturalist bent, you should find these companies advertising in nature-related magazines and periodicals. **Nunavut Tourism** will also field questions on arctic cruises.

46. WHALE WATCHING
by Mike Vlessides

The boat slips quietly through the molten-crystal waters of the frigid arctic sea. It seems as if I've been staring across this vast expanse for hours, with nary a whale in sight.

Perhaps, I begin to think, there's something wrong with me. An Inuk shipmate senses my edginess. "Just listen for the blow," he keeps telling me. "Listen for the blow."

Listen for the blow. Although I've never seen a whale in Nunavut, I know well what he's describing. The "blow" occurs when the whale surfaces to exhale through its blowhole, sending a pillar of mist metres into the air. I relax a bit. I know that when the whale does blow, it will not take me by surprise.

I should have known better. The whales I'd seen in the past were breathtaking, regal creatures, but pedestrian compared to the leviathan we now seek: the bowhead, which maxes out at some 18 metres and 100 tonnes. For when the bowhead finally blows, it is like nothing I've ever heard. The hiss of an angry polar bear. The bellow of a distant foghorn. And a V-shaped tower of mist lingering in the air long after the whale has descended into its watery domain. For a brief moment, I am in the company of kings.

Although a relatively recent phenomenon, whale-watching trips in Nunavut are becoming increasingly popular both with tourists and outfitters. In fact, would-be whale watchers can book trips from many Nunavut communities, especially those conveniently located near prime whale habitats. As with any organized trip, though, you'll find that service varies widely between outfitters. Do your homework and you'll be amply rewarded.

The Hot Spots

Every spring and summer, the three arctic whales — ghostly snow-white belugas, unicorn-like narwhals and massive bowheads — migrate north along common avenues. Their destinations, however, are quite different. Narwhals head for deep fiords, bowheads for areas rich with plankton, and belugas for shallow river mouths.

In Nunavut, the best place to spot whales is around the Baffin Region. The coast of Baffin Island, with its countless inlets, fiords and bays, is bountiful whale habitat. Most communities in the Kivalliq Region sit on the shores of mammoth Hudson Bay, a good whale habitat, but you may have to travel further afield to find them in any concentrations. The Kitikmeot Region is not known for its whale populations, although residents say there is great excitement when a whale is spotted.

The Baffin Region

Most communities here are in whale country. There are, however, a few spots that warrant particular attention because of nearby concentrations at certain times of year. Lancaster Sound, the long finger of water that separates Baffin Island from Devon Island, is not only one of the best whale-watching spots in Nunavut, it is also one of the most fertile wildlife regions in the entire Arctic. Every spring and summer, these waters play host to thousands of whales, seals, and walruses, as well as countless birds. The waterways around Lancaster Sound, especially Admiralty Inlet and Eclipse Sound, are also prime whale habitats. The four closest communities are Pond Inlet, Arctic Bay, Nanisivik and Resolute. Nanisivik is a mining town with no outfitters. Resolute, at the west end of Lancaster Sound, doesn't have as great a view of the whales. Pond Inlet and Arctic Bay, where outfitters are keenly in touch with whale watching, are your best bets.

One of the most amazing spring whale phenomena occurs near the communities of Pond Inlet and Arctic Bay, where whales awaiting breakup congregate at the floe edge, in leads (wide cracks in the ice), or in polynyas (areas of water that remain ice-free throughout the year). While there are never any guarantees when it comes to viewing wildlife, the odds of seeing whales here are better, since they tend to return to the same spots every year.

Isabella Bay has long been known to residents of nearby Clyde River as bowhead country. In August and September, dozens of bowheads use these shallow waters to splash, court, and mate. In fact, a protected area, the Igaliqtuuq (Isabella Bay) Biosphere Reserve and National Wildlife Area, is in the process of being set up. But the issue of tourism has still to be finalized. Access to the bay is also difficult. However, the local HTO had agreed a few select groups of tourists could enter the Isabella Bay area in late summer with a licensed outfitter, provided a cautious approach into the bay was taken.

Cunningham Inlet, on Somerset Island, is one of the best beluga habitats in all of Nunavut. Every summer, especially in July/August, hundreds of whales fill the inlet and the warm, shallow waters of a local river estuary. Visitors who have watched whales here say it is one of the most amazing sights in the natural world.

Other spots of note are: Cumberland Sound (bowhead, beluga, narwhal); Foxe Basin, especially around Igloolik (bowhead); and Sanikiluaq (beluga). Cumberland Sound and Igloolik/Foxe Basin are good for whales in either spring or summer; Sanikiluaq in summer.

The Kivalliq Region

With the exception of Baker Lake, every Kivalliq community is either on or close to Hudson Bay, where thousands of whales summer. The biggest problem is that, unlike the Baffin Region, there are relatively few places in the Kivalliq where you are guaranteed seeing large concentrations of whales. On the other hand, belugas often congregate in river estuaries by the hundreds along the east coast of the bay in northern Quebec (known as Nunavik) and to the south near Churchill, Manitoba — a point of interest to cruise-bound visitors to Nunavut whose journeys take them to other waters as well. Coral Harbour is known for large populations of belugas, as is Arviat; Repulse Bay is good for all three arctic whales in summer.

The Kitikmeot Region

As noted before, the Kitikmeot is not as good as its sister regions. Nonetheless, small populations of whales do inhabit the waters of the Arctic coast, and there's always the odd chance you'll see one if out on a boat. But unless you have an indeterminate amount of time to dedicate to whale watching, your best bet is to go elsewhere.

What to Expect

As with any kind of wildlife excursion, there are vast differences in outfitters' service and prices. At a minimum, though, you want to make sure your outfitter is safe, especially when heading out to sea with them, and currently licensed. If you are even the least bit skeptical, politely take your leave.

Your licensed guide or outfitter will provide a survival (flotation) suit for boat travel. These overall-type units not only keep you afloat, but preserve precious body heat in case of an accident.

Whale-watching trips also vary in their length. Some outfitters will take you out for an afternoon only, others overnight. Prices are quite variable, depending on travel distances and extras offered by your outfitter; expect to pay anywhere from $75 per person for a half-day trip to around $300 per person for a full day (prices based on group rates). Also remember there's no guarantee you'll actually see anything, so don't think about trying to get your money back if you come home disappointed.

You'll enjoy your trip immensely if you take warm, waterproof clothing — more than you think necessary. Chances are, they will be necessary. You should also bring a pair of binoculars, a camera and/or video camera (both with a powerful telephoto lens), seasickness pills if travelling on water, insulated rubber boots, and some extra food, in case your taste differs from your guide's.

In addition to community-based outfitters, some of the larger non-Nunavut-based tour companies, also organize spring and summer whale-watching excursions. Often, whale watching is a component of a larger eco-package, but companies sometimes offer whale-watching tours only. Amenities range from kayaks and tents to the luxury of a refurbished icebreaker. A few of the many companies offering these trips include: **Marine Expeditions**, **Adventure Canada**, **Arctic Marine Wildlife Tours**, and **Canadian River Expeditions**. See Chapter 45, "Cruises," for more information on extended boat trips through and around Nunavut.

When to Go

Most visitors to Nunavut come in the summer: July and August. At this time of year you can watch whales from the deck of a boat or the relative comfort of a land-based observation site. Nevertheless, it is possible to see these marvellous creatures in other seasons as well, especially spring. At this time of year, your mode of travel will be in a *qamutik*, pulled behind a snowmobile.

One last note: Inuit have hunted and eaten whales for many, many years. If you would rather avoid witnessing a whale hunt, express this clearly to your guide, especially if your destination is the floe edge, a lead, or polynya.

47. DOGSLEDDING

by Peter Ernerk

Thirty years ago, in *Naujaat*-Repulse Bay, the Roman Catholic mission told us three people had drowned in a lake where they were doing spring char fishing.

Later we heard that the victims' *qimmiit* (husky dogs) had walked to a neighboring outpost camp, and that is how members of the other camp knew immediately that something had gone wrong.

Qimmiit, huskies, Eskimo dogs, or *canis familiaris borealis* are all names for these Inuit workhorses. For more than 2,000 years they pulled *qamutiit* (wooden sleds) and provided companionship, helped communicate messages, and guided explorers across the Arctic. As far back as I can remember, my father, Athanasie Angutitaq, held these *qimmiit* in high regard. While snowmobiles have replaced dogsled teams in many parts of Nunavut today, the importance of these dogs remains visible. Nostalgic reminders of an earlier lifestyle, they are used for transportation, tourism, and in annual dog races such as Nunavut 200.

Huskies are built to live and work in the North. Their warm coats do not require protection even in the coldest winters; they think nothing of the meanest blizzards. The fish they eat gives them beautiful fur coats, while walrus and seal give them strength to pull heavy loads. In the past we fed our dogs mostly arctic char, caribou meat, and sometimes seal meat in Nattiligaarjuk ("a lake that has few seals"). Huskies are adaptable. They can continue to work even if they go without food for several days. I remember in olden days, when we were running low on food, sometimes we did not feed them for a week at a time, and yet they pulled the heavy *qamutiit*. No mercy!

In Nattiligaarjuk my family and I would fish at *saputit,* a stone weir, a dam built across the river to trap fish. After spearing fish with the leister (a two-pronged spear used by Inuit) in cold waters, my father and I used to cuddle under the warm caribou blankets with his dog Nakataq, especially in the evenings. Nakataq was the boss of our dogs. He became our *tasikuaq,* the sniffer of seal holes in the winter, and *isuraqtujuq* — the lead dog. During the years that I spent in *Naujaat,* we depended upon Nakataq for being a good leader.

Years ago, when we travelled inland from the coast in search of caribou, we would walk for many miles. Adults, both men and women, would carry a lot of belongings such as bedding, skin blankets, and a few extra clothes. Our dogs carried the rest of the load, including wooden sticks needed to set up the tent. While caribou hunting, we also depended upon our dogs to sniff the caribou tracks, especially when we were travelling downside of the wind. If conditions were right, our dogs would smell the scent and begin to run towards the herd. Soon, we would see caribou.

Going back to the coastal regions was more difficult as both people and dogs carried caribou meat from the land. *Tunnuq* (caribou fat) was particularly heavy to carry, but in the end we all managed.

In March, when the days were getting longer, we would go out to the sea to hunt seals through their breathing holes. The holes were covered with snow but we used the huskies to sniff out the seal holes. Depending where the wind was coming from, we would walk beside the ridges of snow. Breathing holes were normally on the east side of ice ridges; westerly winds would build up thick snowdrifts here, giving seals, especially their young pups, more protection. Once the dogs smelled a seal hole, they would run until they located the hole. Then we poked through the thick snow until the seal hole was revealed. My father would prepare to wait at the seal hole, while my sister, brother-in-law and I continued to look for other holes. While hunting for seals in the winter, dogs were also used to chase polar bears in case they came to the area. While the huskies fought the bear, it was easier for the hunter to kill the animal by harpooning it. Living in coastal areas can be dangerous at times. I remember two occasions when a polar bear came to our camp. And polar bears are dangerous! Our husky dogs barked and helped to keep the polar bear away from our tent. This gave my father time to load his rifle and kill the polar bear. When danger came, *qimmiit* alerted members of the camp by barking at dangerous animals.

Some lead dogs were trained to find their way home in the middle of a blizzard. I remember once when my brother-in-law and I were returning home to Nattiligaarjuk from a caribou hunt. The wind picked up and started to blow snow in every direction. Soon we could not see much ahead of us. After travelling a bit longer, we decided to camp for the night and tied up the dogs, so they wouldn't walk away. The next morning, after the blizzard had cleared up, we discovered to our great surprise that we were only about two miles away from home!

In the 1960s, huskies were declining so much that some people became concerned about their complete disappearance. Part of this concern was due to the high cost of snowmobiles (in Repulse Bay, for example, a snow machine was worth about $700) and a drop in demand for furs, one of the few sources of cash for hunters and trappers.

But between 1973 and 1974, Yellowknife's Bill Carpenter, who Inuit call *Qimmiliriji* — "a dog man" — established the Eskimo Dog Research Foundation and breeding kennels, developing a love for the kindly Eskimo husky. Because the Royal Canadian Mounted Police had introduced other types of sled dogs to many Arctic communities, and because snowmobiles and pet dogs were becoming more common, too, the husky was no longer pure. Carpenter managed to find some huskies that he felt were pure, and began a breeding program. With help from the Canada Council, companies and all levels of government, he raised several thousand dogs and established a registered line of the Canadian Eskimo Dog. Often, for the price of transporting animals to their communities or outpost camps, he would donate surplus dogs to Inuit team owners. Carpenter has continued this tireless work over the years.

The community of Igloolik can also take credit for the continued existence of these beautiful *qimmiit*. In years past, Igloolik supplied other communities in Nunavut with these dogs. And in Iglulik Isuma Productions' documentary film *Nunavut,* which depicts Inuit life in the 1940s, real *qimmiit* are used to transport the actors. In many communities, these dogs are back in a big way, but as a slightly different breed, smaller in size. They require doghouses, some even insulated, and nutritional southern dog food. What's more, they have shorter fur. However, one elder in Rankin Inlet still operates his dogs the way he did years ago, feeding them country food — uncooked, of course. Seventy-one-year-old dog musher Robert Tatty won the $l0,000 first prize during the 1996 Nunavut 200 dog race from Arviat to Rankin Inlet, and finished first again in 1997.

Tourists can go dogsledding, too. Prices range up to about $300 for a full-day outing. Dress warmly because weather conditions up here can get cold and wicked without warning. Also, while it's fine to photograph *qimmiit* from a distance, don't try to pat them as you would pets. These are working animals, and can be aggressive. If you follow this advice, however, you'll find dogsledding to be a lot of fun. Guaranteed!

48. FLOE EDGE TOURS
by Andrew Taqtu and Jennifer Bernius

In choice spots around Nunavut each spring, a fascinating world unfolds at the floe edge — the place where open water joins landfast ice, where still waters meet waters propelled by currents.

Surrounded by a landscape of colossal icebergs and glacial valleys, waters come alive with migrating marine mammals and birds that have started their annual trek north in March. With luck, you may see bowhead whales, walruses, harp seals, bearded seals, narwhals, beluga whales, seagulls, white-fronted geese, thick-billed murres, black guillemots, ivory gulls, pintail ducks, and polar bears.

Camped in their backyard, visitors might see belugas and narwhals just 20 metres away. An underwater view is even more intimate, although diving is still in its infancy in Nunavut's tourism industry (see Chapter 53, "Diving," for more information). Film crews shooting underwater footage have been able to get within about five metres of these magical creatures. On land, you may find yourself about 15 metres from a polar bear, if it's not running away. And that's probably the direction you'll hope it will take. Polar bears are dangerous. Your only security is your guide, armed with a rifle, who acts as a bear monitor while you drink in the panorama.

You can also inspect archeological camp sites while out on the land, or lie in wait for a seal at its breathing hole. (If the seal hasn't appeared after 20 minutes, that means it's getting some fresh air at another breathing hole!)

Tours often set out from Pond Inlet and Resolute, with the intended destination being Lancaster Sound and its environs. It has some of the richest concentrations of wildlife anywhere in the North because of migration routes that open up for whales and marine mammals, thanks to its early ice-free conditions made possible by winds and upwelling ocean currents. Around southern Baffin Island, Cape Dorset has tours to the nearby floe edge.

How to be a well-outfitted Arctic traveller...

Arctic waters are fascinating, but they are also frigid. If you're planning to explore Arctic waters, there are a couple of things **you** should do to make sure you're on friendly and safe terms with our beautiful but challenging Arctic environment. First make sure your guide is licensed and also properly equipped with signalling devices, radios and first-aid equipment to handle any possible emergency. Second, as a well-outfitted Arctic traveller, **you** should make sure you have a floater suit for yourself and everybody else to wear in the boat. Once your personal safety is dealt with, then you can focus on having a great time!

Northwest Territories Canada

Department of Resources, Wildlife and Economic Development

The best time of year to head out is between April and mid-July when the weather, though still chilly at night, is not so cold that people unaccustomed to an arctic climate won't enjoy it. Bring warm clothing, as well as sunglasses and sun lotion to survive spring's intense sunshine. Waterproof boots should also have warm insulation. Rainy weather clothing is also recommended for nasty wet weather that can pop up between May and July. Many outfitters will supply you with survival suits and winter boots anyway.

An experienced guide will tell you that even for first-time visitors, there's nothing to worry about at the floe edge as long as you're careful. Be on the alert when close to current-filled water. Don't travel on newly formed ice. Stay away from the rim of the floe edge. People have been known to fall into the water after treading too close to the edge on unstable ice that hangs above the water; they don't realize water has worn it away. Also be on the lookout when a northwest wind is blowing, something that can happen any time of year when the moon is full. The wind whips up waters, and, as a result, waves chip away at the floe edge.

Tours

Floe edge tours generally run between seven and nine days, and can range from about $2,000 to $4,000, depending on the length and degree of "luxury" factored into the package. On many tours, travellers get to the floe edge via a *qamutiik* pulled by a snowmobile, or in some cases, dogteam. Crossing frozen ocean and tundra through scenery of breathtaking beauty, this four- to six-hour trip can be a highlight in itself. Depending on ice conditions, the going is rough in places, smooth in others. There are breaks for lunch and tea, and opportunities to photograph a playful seal or two and enjoy the awesome silence.

One outfitter offering two nine-day tours in June flies groups of up to 20 by chartered Twin Otter from Resolute to a base camp at Cape Crawford on Lancaster Sound. Travellers take daily outings from this fixed camp by snowmobile or dogteam to points of interest, including the spectacular bird sanctuary of Prince Leopold Island. Proposed as a United Nations World Heritage Site, the island is a nesting place for thousands of murres, kittiwakes, ivory gulls, gyrfalcons and jaegars.

Travellers sleep in a spacious, heated, doubled-walled canvas tent with two or three others and dine in a cook-tent on standard southern fare with some "country food." The bill here covers the flight to and from Resolute to the base camp, plus travel to the floe edge, and a hotel room in Arctic Bay on the last night before flying home. Also included in the price tag are tenting gear, meals and flotation (survival) suits. Guides are skilled Inuit hunters who may speak only Inuktitut. They're accompanied by younger Inuit who translate for them.

The floe edge experience from Pond Inlet — usually a mid-May to June trip by snowmobile and *qamutiik* — is likely to transport you to the extraordinary wildlife sanctuary of Bylot Island in Eclipse Sound, adjacent to Lancaster Sound and part of the new Sirmilik National Park. A photographer's dream, the island is renowned for the multitudes of marine and land mammals that migrate here each summer. Its cliffs are also summer home to some 52 species of birds. With its varied landscapes, including sandy beaches and towering mountains, the island itself is fascinating. Near the edge of the island are hoodoos, strangely contoured sandstone formations carved by wind and weather into columns that rise up to 23 metres. You'll also have the opportunity to stand on Sermilik Glacier and drink glacial water — the purest in the world! On Ikpiarjuk Glacier, on Baffin Island, you can visit an exquisite ice cave.

Travellers stay in expedition-style tents (two people per tent) at the floe edge. Your guides will move your camp to maximize wildlife viewing opportunities. Southern and northern food is eaten in a heated communal tent. All trips include transportation to and from the floe edge and tenting gear — warm sleeping bag, survival suit, winter boots, all meals while out on the land, and the services of guides.

One final word of advice from an experienced guide: if the ice you're standing on happens to break away, stay on the ice floe till the wind takes you back to landfast ice. This is why hunters with floe edge experience make sure their boat is nearby at the floe edge.

Better yet, stay away from ice that's likely to break away! Even if the weather is calm, remember that cracks in ice can be caused by water currents eroding the ice from below.

49. MOUNTAIN CLIMBING
by Beverly Illauq

Mountain climbing is elevating Nunavut to new heights.

For years, climbers have been flocking to two of the most striking, uninterrupted cliff faces on Earth. The 1,000-metre overhanging west face of Mount Thor and the 800-metre west face of Mount Asgard, located in **Auyuittuq National Park** near Pangnirtung, have attracted attention ever since their "discovery" by climbers. The upper face of Mount Thor has an average angle of 105 degrees, and the view of the towers of Asgard from the west are awe-inspiring. Big wall Grade VI aid routes have been established on both of these peaks, as well as on other walls in Auyuittuq National Park.

There is also almost limitless potential for new free-climbing Grade IV to V routes on the peaks accessed by the Weasel Valley. The quality of the granite is variable, ranging from the flawless to decaying crumbling rock. Many of the peaks in Auyuittuq National Park have been climbed over the last few decades, with new routes established virtually every year. Some noteworthy ones that have been scaled include Breidablik, Friga, Odin, Bilbo Tirokwa, Adluk, Tyr, plus many that are still unnamed.

The driest months for climbing in Auyuittuq appear to be late April to mid-June, but temperatures seldom rise above freezing before mid-May. However, 24-hour daylight and sun-warmed elements can make up for the arctic climate. Summer temperatures are milder, but wet conditions are not uncommon.

Recently, other parts of Nunavut have started to earn mountaineering acclaim, too. In 1995 and 1996, European, Japanese and American teams made major big wall climbs in the area of Sam Ford Fiord, close to Clyde River on north Baffin Island. In 1996, the American-Canadian Hollinger/Synott/Chapman team summitted the difficult north face of Polar Sun Spire, which they established as one of the three highest sheer walls in the world at 1,338 metres.

Other fiords near Clyde River have been assessed for mountaineering and climbing potential. Although these areas remain virtually untouched, the number of walls and mountains of good quality rock and grade within a 160-kilometre radius of Clyde River is said to be limitless. Clyde Inlet, Scott Inlet and Sam Ford Fiord are the closest big wall areas to Clyde River. All of the mountains in these areas are accessible by snowmobile and *qamutik* during the snowmobile season, and by boat in summer. The sea ice provides a platform for access to the walls. (Climbers should first acquaint themselves with the rigors of Nunavut's unique environment by reading Chapter 11, "Adventure Travel." As when doing any activity on Nunavut's land or waterways, check first to see if there are any access restrictions to the area you plan to visit.)

While the use of helicopters is possible, seldom can they be booked very far in advance. What's more, the use of helicopters or airplanes to bring gear or climbers into Auyuittuq National Park is no longer permitted.

The most dependable method for getting "gear to the wall" is to send it north six or eight months in advance and make arrangements for an outfitter to haul it in during the winter and spring. This requires more advance planning, but the result is fewer disappointments when climbing season arrives.

The best time to climb in the Sam Ford Fiord/Clyde River area is May and June, even though ice conditions vary greatly during this period. Only by May is the weather warm enough to allow even uncomfortable climbing, and if climbers want to avoid being stranded for the six-week breakup period, they must be picked up by their outfitter by June 30. It can take from 10 to 36 hours by snowmobile and *qamutik* to reach your climbing destination, depending on the distance from the community and ice conditions.

In July and August, climbers must contend with tremendous winds and difficult water conditions. Access to climbing areas would be unpredictable, and the logistics of scaling walls rising directly from the sea very challenging. For this reason, summer climbs are usually not attempted.

Because of the harsh climate and the area's remoteness, it is essential to hire licensed guides for consultation about local conditions, for support throughout an expedition if needed, and for taxi services between the community and the climbing areas. Be advised, though, that there are no mountain-climbing guides in Clyde River and there is no means of rescue. Inuit guides, however, can provide invaluable ground and sea support.

50. SKIING

by Terry Pearce, with contributions from Carol Rigby

Springtime skiing in Nunavut is one of the best-kept secrets in Canada. There are open and often spectacular views wherever you go, and you don't have to climb 300 metres or so to reach the tree line.

This, combined with about 18 hours of sunshine or more, depending where you are in Nunavut, create near perfect cross-country skiing. Exotic, too.

In a two-hour circuit outside Nunavut's capital, Iqaluit, you can ski in the company of caribou, sometimes hundreds of them, grazing in herds in the hills and valleys that surround the town.

In other locations you may be lucky enough to see muskoxen, white wolves, arctic hares or flocks of migrating birds. Some communities have parks or park reserves nearby, and it is usually not difficult to hire a local guide to take you and your gear by snowmobile to the starting point of your trip. Bring your own equipment. Ski rentals are not common, even for guided packages.

Another unique experience in Nunavut is skate skiing on the frozen ocean. In late spring, the sea ice is an average of 160 centimetres thick along all coastlines, bays and fiords. When the snow has melted from the surface, usually in May, it is possible to skate ski on the ice for miles in any direction to visit islands and other places along the coast. It's a real blast!

At present, Nunavut has no downhill ski resorts (although tour operator **Arctic Odysseys** of Seattle, Washington, started Twin Otter-based skiing in the mountains of Auyuittuq National Park and Cumberland Peninsula in 1996). The short ski season and limited traffic is compounded by the drawback of hard, ridged, wind-sculpted snow that can lead to loss of control when skiers encounter a chance soft patch.

Self-Guided Skiing

Any community in Nunavut can provide accommodation and serve as a good base for one-day or multi-day ski trips. Once outside a community, be aware that there are access restrictions to Inuit-owned lands.

For the confident and physically fit, the 97-kilometre Akshayuk Pass can be the trip of a lifetime. Located in Baffin Island's Auyuittuq National Park, this awesome mountain valley runs north/south of the western edge of the Penny Ice Cap. Glaciers from the ice cap pour down into the pass, adding to the spectacular scenery. Glaciers in the vicinity of Summit Lake (the halfway point in the pass) can be accessed without too much difficulty. Excellent ski touring possibilities are unlimited on these glaciers.

But experience in glacier travel, with all appropriate safety and rescue equipment, is essential. Whether it's for a few hours or days, any wilderness activity is conducted at your own risk.

Guided Skiing

Currently, only a few licensed outfitters in Nunavut cater to cross-country skiers. **NorthWinds Arctic Adventures** in Iqaluit provides guided ski trips (dogteam-supported, and no heavy pack to carry!) to a number of destinations, including the Katannilik Territorial Park Reserve trail, where river valleys and the low mountains of the Meta Incognita Peninsula are traversed to reach the small community of Kimmirut. Another journey cuts across the land and sea ice to a cabin one day's travel from town. Or try the Akshayuk Pass, or even a trip to the North Magnetic Pole or geographic North Pole.

Equipment

You'll need:

- warm, lightweight clothing with the ability to wick moisture away from your body

- windproof outer jacket with hood, and windproof pants
- a balaclava and warm headgear (an insulating headband enables you to release heat from your head while keeping your ears warm and wind-free during periods of physical exertion)
- several pairs of windproof mitts. Glove liners are handy for doing up bindings and tying knots without having to expose your hands to the wind, but gloves alone are not recommended because they won't keep your hands as warm as mitts
- steel edge skis
- heavy-duty, double ski boots or single boots with good insulated boot gaiters
- skins for use on glaciers.

In fact, bring all the equipment and clothing you would take on a backcountry, above-tree-line trip in the Canadian Rockies.

If you're doing a multi-day ski trip, remember that while daytime temperatures out on the snow can be very pleasant with the longer days and reflected sunlight, nighttime temperatures can easily dip below –20° C and wind-chills can make it seem even colder.

Bring a warm three-quarter length parka — not to wear when physically active, but as protection in case of a spring blizzard or for evenings sitting around camp. Ideally, the parka should have some kind of ruff around the face as protection against the wind (northerners wear fur around their faces for a very good reason).

In springtime, you'll need warm, well-insulated footgear with lots of room to layer on extra socks. A pair of down booties for wearing in the tent or when your feet get chilly is also a good idea.

51. ASTRONOMY

by John MacDonald

To those who care to look up, the skies above the Arctic offer unique rewards.

Summer's midnight sun aside, the full wonder of the arctic sky is best seen during the dark months of winter when the dominant moon brilliantly illuminates the snow-clad landscape and the stars and planets glimmer eerily through animated curtains of lilac-colored northern lights. For winter travellers to Nunavut, the arctic sky could well be the highlight of their visit.

Due to the proximity of the polar regions to the Earth's axis, as one journeys into the higher latitudes, the visible portion of the celestial sphere decreases, while its various luminaries — the sun, moon, stars and planets — appear to take on increasingly eccentric itineraries. Throughout spring and summer at the latitude of north Baffin Island, the sun never sets, the stars are masked, and the moon, if it can be seen at all, hangs pale and ineffective in the light-flooded sky. In winter, things are reversed and the sun retreats to the south, leaving the celestial stage to the moon, stars and planets.

If you are familiar with southern skies, you will notice immediately that the stars and constellations, particularly above northern Nunavut, appear in unfamiliar positions. Orion will be lower, the Big Dipper unexpectedly higher, and Sirius, if it appears, will be seen only briefly, progressing slowly along the southern horizon, emitting its brilliant display of prismatic colors rarely seen in more southerly latitudes.

Tilting your head awkwardly backwards you'll be able to spot the North Star seemingly directly above you, its altitude above the horizon equalling the latitude of your position. In early spring and fall, twilight lingers interminably, seamlessly joining today's sunset with tomorrow's dawn. And, in some years, the midwinter moon (depending on the position of the plane of its orbit around the sun), will circle the sky for days on end without setting — winter's spectacular equivalent of summer's midnight sun.

A quest of many winter visitors to the Arctic is the unforgettable sight of the aurora borealis, the northern lights. These are caused by the glow of molecular gases in the atmosphere, activated by charged particles from the sun. The aurora normally occurs in a broad 500- to 1,000-kilometre-wide belt known as the "auroral oval," which is centred on the North Magnetic Pole. Rarely as colorful as auroral displays occurring along the 60th parallel, the northern lights seen across Nunavut are no less awe-inspiring infused with their subtle, shifting greenish hues. According to Inuit tradition, whistling at the northern lights makes them come nearer. Beware!

Over countless generations, Inuit developed an astronomy well suited to a number of their practical needs, including time-reckoning and the prediction of the sun's return after the winter's dark period, an event heralded by the sighting of the stars Altair and Tarazed in December's morning sky.

Stars were also used for navigation, particularly when hunting on the moving ice floe, where they provided the only points of known reference. The moon provided their calendar, 13 lunations accounting for the seasonal year. Each moon was usually named for some significant event in the natural world coinciding with its appearance. In the Igloolik area, for example, the "moon of returning sun" corresponded to a period beginning approximately in mid-January. June was called the "egg moon" when migratory birds, particularly eider ducks, started nesting. Between mid-October and mid-November, the period when the sea ice freezes over, the moon was known as *Tusaqtuut* — "hearing" — because travel by dogteam was now possible and one could "hear" news from neighboring camps.

The arctic sky was an important focus for Inuit spiritual belief and mythology. Stars, in some areas, were said to be the spirits of the dead, particularly of those who in life had broken taboos. People who died through loss of blood went to the northern lights where, for eternity, they played an endless game of football using a walrus head as the ball. The occasional reddish tinge of the aurora symbolizes the manner of their death.

A widespread myth accounts for the sun and the moon. Abbreviated, the story tells of a sister's discovery of her brother's incest and their subsequent flight to the sky in shame, each carrying torches of flaming moss. She, with her bright flame, became the sun, while her brother, whose torch was soon reduced to smoldering embers, became the moon. The celestial pursuit continues. The sister-sun, however, still aggrieved at her brother-moon's treachery, alternates between feelings of pity and revenge, sometimes feeding him, sometimes not. Thus the moon is forever doomed to a cycle of feast and famine, waxing or waning each month in response to his sister's disposition.

Other myths imaginatively account for particular groupings of stars, as well as for a number of other celestial and atmospheric phenomena, including eclipses, meteor showers, sundogs and rainbows. During your visit, talk with an elder about these. Your appreciation of the arctic sky will be greatly enriched and you'll discover the remarkable talent Inuit have for observation, imagination and inventiveness.

Some Inuit Star and Constellation Names:

Altair and Tarazed	Aagjuuk (no known meaning)
The Big Dipper (Ursa Major)	Tukturjuit ("caribou")
Pollux, Castor, Capella and Menkalinan	Quturjuuk ("collar bones")
Aldebaran	Nanurjuk ("polar bear")
The Pleiades	Sakiattiak ("the breast bone")
Sirius	Singuuriq ("the flickering one")
Orion's "belt" stars	Ullaktut ("the runners")
Three stars in the constellation Cassiopeia	Pituaq ("the lamp stand")
The North Star	Nuutuittuq ("does not move")
Betelgeuse and Bellatrix	Akuttujuuk ("far apart")

52. EVENTS AND FESTIVALS
by Jennifer Bernius

There are so many reasons to celebrate in Nunavut, and never more so than in 1999! April 1, 1999, marks the official launch of Nunavut as a territory.

Although plans for festivities were still sketchy at the time of writing, the Nunavut Implementation Commission (NIC) — the group that has helped draft Nunavut's new government — is organizing ceremonies in Iqaluit to honor Nunavut's creation. The first elected members of the new legislative assembly will also be sworn in on that date. Every northern community will celebrate the occasion in its own special way. And in Hull, Quebec, just across the river from the Canadian capital of Ottawa, the Canadian Museum of Civilization will focus on Nunavut in 1999 in exhibits showcasing Inuit sculpture and prints, northern photography, and a display on the history of Baffin Island entitled *Meta Incognita*. CBC TV News will carry live coverage of events in Iqaluit and Ottawa.

Check the NIC's web site at www.nunanet.com/~nic for celebration updates, or contact Bert Rose (tel.: 867-979-4199 or fax: 867-979-6862). **Nunavut Tourism** can also provide information (tel.: 867-979-6551 or 1-800-491-7910; fax: 867-979-1261; e-mail: nunatour@nunanet.com; web site: www.nunatour.nt.ca). For details on community celebrations, contact the recreation co-ordinators in hamlet offices (see community chapters in this book, or browse the "Recreation" section of the web site www.nunavut.com).

The people of Nunavut will still hold regular community festivals toasting the return of sunlight and warmer days, as well as festivities for customary holidays. Most settlements stage fun-filled events on Canada Day, July 1, and Nunavut Day, July 9. Activities vary but usually include races, contests, parades, traditional and modern games, dances and community feasts.

At Christmas, week-long festivities transform virtually every community. Carolling, school pageants, traditional games and races, and church services are some of the ways northerners honor this special time.

Easter celebrations might include dogteam and snowmobile races, and indoor and outdoor games. Feel free to join the events and to attend any church service. During the Victoria Day weekend in May, most communities sponsor fishing derbies.

For information on these and other events, call the hamlet office (ask for the recreation co-ordinator) of the community you intend to visit. Be sure to verify the dates of these festivities, as they can change due to bad weather.

Here is a sampling of some other annual celebrations that *Nunavummiut* (people of Nunavut) look forward to.

ARVIAT

Phone the hamlet recreation co-ordinator at (867) 857-2880 or fax (867) 857-2519 for more details.

Inummarit Music Festival (September): This three-day annual event in Canadian singer Susan Aglukark's home town is not to be missed. It's a celebration of traditional and contemporary Inuit music, and features talents from across Nunavut performing in Inuktitut and English.

BAKER LAKE

Phone the hamlet recreation co-ordinator at (867) 793-2874 or fax (867) 793-2509 for more details.

Hamlet Days (Mid-May): Celebrate the anniversary of Baker Lake's hamlet status and the arrival of spring with dogteam races, a children's carnival, elders' tea and bannock, and a contest to judge the best traditional outfit.

CAMBRIDGE BAY

Phone the hamlet recreation co-ordinator at (867) 983-2337 or fax (867) 983-2193 for more details.

Omingmak Frolics (May long weekend): This 10-day celebration of spring offers a treat for everyone: snowmobile races, ice sculpting, arctic games, kids' games, bike racing, parade, King and Queen, plus Prince and Princess contests.

Music Festival (Mid-July): This jamboree brings together artists from across Nunavut performing traditional and contemporary music.

GJOA HAVEN

Phone the hamlet recreation co-ordinator at (867) 360-7151 or fax (867) 360-7009 for more details.

Qavvarrvik Carnival (May): This long weekend of traditional events includes *iglu*-building contests, dogteam races, cod fishing and family games.

Summer Sun Golf Classic (Mid-August): This 18-hole tournament features an all-natural golf course on the tundra.

IGLOOLIK

Return of the Sun (Mid-January): This traditional celebration, organized by the Igloolik Inullariit Elders Society, is full of Inuit symbolism and ritual, and is usually accompanied by traditional games and a fashion show of traditional dress. For more information, contact Leah Otak at the Igloolik Inullariit Elders Society at (867) 934-8836 or fax (867) 934-8792.

IQALUIT

Nunavut Trade Show (Mid-February): This is Nunavut's premier business event, and is pivotal for those who need to network. The 1998 edition drew several thousand visitors, with close to 100 exhibitors. For more information, contact the Baffin Regional Chamber of Commerce at (867) 979-4653 or fax (867) 979-2929. E-mail: brcc@nunanet.com or check their web site for an overview of last year's trade show (www.nunanet.com/~brcc).

Nunavut Mining Symposium (Mid-February): Sponsored by Canadian mining companies and the GNWT Department of Resources, Wildlife and Economic Development, this major event features discussions on trends in the mining industry, workshops and networking sessions. For more information, contact the Baffin Regional Chamber of Commerce as above.

Annual Arctic Foods Celebration (Mid-February): Coinciding with the Nunavut Trade Show, this event offers a selection of northern foods prepared in traditional ways. For more information, contact Colleen Dupuis at (867) 979-4653 or fax (867) 979-0048. E-mail: cdupuis@nunanet.com.

Toonik Tyme (Mid-April): Nunavut's biggest spring festival. For more information, contact Dave St. Louis at the Iqaluit recreation department, tel.: (867) 979-5617 or fax: (867) 979-3712.

KUGLUKTUK

Contact the hamlet recreation co-ordinator at (867) 982-4471 or fax (867) 982-3060 for more details.

Nattik Frolics (April): Traditional games, snowmobile races, seal hunt, King and Queen contest, square dances, community feast.

Kitikmeot Summer Games (July): Join competitors in duck-plucking, seal-skinning, tea-boiling, bannock-making, fish-filleting. Cheer the athletes as they compete in the high kick, one-arm reach and other traditional games.

Coronation Gulf Annual Golf Tournament (July): Enjoy a weekend of golfing at one of Canada's most northerly 18-hole golf courses.

Iqalukpik Fishing Derby (August): Lots of prizes, lots of categories and one main quest — to land an arctic char.

NANISIVIK

Midnight Sun Marathon (July 1st long weekend): This marathon, celebrating the longest day of the year, is organized by Nanisivik Mines and attracts runners from as far away as Europe and Australia. They compete in 10-, 32-, 42- and 84-kilometre races between Arctic Bay and Nanisivik along Nunavut's only stretch of road linking two communities. Due to limited hotel space, the marathon is open to only 125 runners. For more information, contact Nanisivik Mines, (867) 436-7502 or fax (867) 436-7435.

PANGNIRTUNG

Phone the hamlet recreation co-ordinator at (867) 473-8953 or fax (867) 473-8832 for details.

Summer Music Festival (Early August): Join artists from across Nunavut as they play traditional and modern Inuit music.

RANKIN INLET

Phone Rick Denison, Hamlet of Rankin Inlet, (867) 645-2895 or fax (867) 645-2146 for details.

Nunavut 200 Dogteam Race (April): Competitors in this exciting annual event race the 200 kilometres along the sea ice from Rankin Inlet to Arviat.

Pakallak Time (April): Rankin's ode to spring. This annual event usually includes dogteam and snowmobile races, indoor and outdoor games, a fashion show and square dances.

UMINGMAKTOK

Phone the Arctic Coast Visitors Centre at (867) 983-2224 or fax (867) 983-2302 for more details. Or e-mail Peter Kapolak, president of the Umingmaktok Hunters and Trappers Organization, at peterk@polarnet.ca.

Kalvik Frolics (Easter weekend): Each year, the highlight of this very traditional festival is the search for a beautiful wolverine pelt.

53. DIVING

by Brad Heath

Arctic diving is emerging in Nunavut as a way to give explorers an opportunity to venture into one of the last unexplored frontiers on the planet — yet it's a world fraught with dangers. Only a handful of Nunavut companies offer arctic diving expeditions at this point.

The attractions of diving here are many: exploring in pristine waters beneath almost three metres of ice or from the floe edge, discovering abundant marine life, exploring newfound shipwrecks and searching for elusive wrecks that haunt historians. There are three types of diving: ice diving, open-water diving, and diving with whales (the last of which requires local expertise).

Yet the dangers of arctic diving are significant, and divers ignore them at their own peril. Drifting icebergs, frigid water temperatures, strong tides, reduced visibility where salt and fresh waters meet, and long distances from recompression chambers are just some of the sport's obstacles.

Anyone considering plunging into arctic waters should be an advanced **Professional Association of Diving Instructors** (PADI) diver with about 50 dives. Diving in Nunavut requires expertise and experience in cold-water diving. It's also critical that divers be accompanied by a PADI dive master, established and experienced in cold-water diving in Nunavut. Using the "buddy" system is critical. Divers must wear drysuits (although divers in the Kivalliq Region have reported using wetsuits in the summer with good success), and three-fingered mitts (not five-fingered gloves). They must also use an arctic regulator, and in the case of open-water diving and diving with whales, a good float and a reliable boat.

Ice diving, in which a hole is cut in the ice to allow the diver access to the water, requires a safety line. Divers should avoid ice floes because they are too dangerous.

For all types of diving, prior arrangements must be made for getting tanks filled. If heading out without a licensed outfitter, register your plans with the local RCMP by filling out a wilderness travel registration form.

While ice diving usually refers to freshwater lake diving, in Nunavut the term refers to a marine environment. Ice diving in salt water is a unique type of diving that can only be done in a few places. Diving through sea ice means extreme cold-water diving with an overhead environment. The experience is made special because of the abundance of marine life, with potential for very good visibility up to roughly 100 metres.

Open-water diving is considered cold-water diving. It offers more flexibility and can be done from the shore or a boat.

Divers who've experienced the Arctic say they're drawn by the allure of the unknown; the opportunity to explore where possibly no human has gone before. Perhaps a diver will discover an unknown and as-of-yet unnamed fish? Or perhaps the final resting place of Franklin's lost ships?

Phenomenal underwater photography also attracts divers, although divers must be careful when near marine mammals. Some species, like walrus, should be avoided. Although divers won't find the bright hues of tropical fish here, they will encounter the unexpectedly vivid colors of soft coral, sea anemone and giant kelp beds.

Divers will enjoy extreme visibility in salt water, likened by one diver to diving in crystal-clear gin or vodka! The exception is in areas where large freshwater rivers empty into the ocean and produce milky waters.

Little equals the wonder of diving under sea ice in spring in Nunavut. Visibility under the ice is enhanced by the long hours of sunlight under the midnight sun. The ice protects divers from storms, but these dives must be done under controlled conditions using a safety line and a heated tent covering the dive hole. Dives should never be made when the ice begins to break up.

Experienced arctic divers highly recommend diving in sheltered bays and inlets such as those near Pond Inlet. This beautiful area is probably one of the world's premier spots for marine life. Baffin Island is generally a prime venue, especially near Pond Inlet and Pangnirtung. Cape Dorset is attracting divers to the recently discovered wreck of the *Nascopie*, which went down in 1947 but is amazingly well preserved (even some books have survived). Far to the north, other popular diving destinations include Grise Fiord and Resolute.

Sheltered areas along Hudson Bay, near Rankin Inlet, Whale Cove or Coats Island, for example, also come highly recommended. Cambridge Bay in the Kitikmeot Region offers excellent diving near the shipwreck of the *Maud*. A more isolated area is Creswell Bay on Somerset Island where whales, such as beluga, congregate in the spring.

54. ROCK COLLECTING

by Carol Rigby

Some people seem born to collect rocks — and Nunavut offers plenty of scope for that activity!

Much of the territory belongs to the Canadian Shield, with rocks dating back a billion years. Mineral exploration has uncovered zinc, silver, lead, copper, nickel, gold and gemstones. So evolving into a rock lover is natural. As toddlers, budding rockhounds bring home heart-shaped chunks of granite from the rock-strewn beach. As schoolchildren, they offer their precious collections to visiting geology professors who inspect their findings rock by rock, discussing the provenance and characteristics of each. Rock collecting is a great hobby in a place where the bare bones of the land are clear for all to see.

The visiting rockhound's main challenge is to not be mistaken for a scientific researcher or a prospector. Both professionals are frequent visitors to Nunavut. The rock formations that fascinate the amateur collector bear valuable geologic and climatic information for the scientist, and the possibility of exploitation by the prospector. Because of its harsh climate, Nunavut has few other non-renewable natural resources. Mineral resources offer the potential for employment and commercial development. Likewise, the undisturbed nature of much of the landscape provides ideal conditions for scientific study. Scientific research and prospecting are carefully regulated, licensed and monitored.

For rockhounds the world over, access to land in order to obtain mineral samples is a sensitive issue. In Nunavut, it is even more so because of access restrictions on Inuit-owned lands, Crown lands and national parks in the Nunavut Settlement Area (the area defined by the Nunavut Land Claims Agreement). There is also the real possibility of disturbing archeological sites. Much evidence of occupation of these sites lies in the arrangement of stones; many early tools are chipped rocks. And because the Inuit were nomadic, such sites are fairly widespread. Many sites also have natural or scientific significance. In areas where glaciation has occurred, for example, erratics are fairly common: rocks that were carried along by the glaciers and deposited far from their place of origin, often perched in the most unlikely and fascinating positions. But if an erratic is disturbed, its geologic significance is totally lost. Likewise, substantial and often unique fossil deposits can be severely disturbed by visitors removing samples.

If you intend to collect rocks in Nunavut, it is imperative that you do so with sensitivity and awareness. Do your homework before you arrive. Study the geology of the Arctic, making sure you can recognize an erratic when you encounter it! You should also read up on the archeology of Inuit sites (see Chapter 19, "Archeology") so that you lessen your chances of disturbing one. It's best to restrict collecting to sites where disturbance is natural or obvious, such as tidal flats or quarries. Take care to avoid areas of recent rockfalls. As tempting as they might be, they're also highly unstable and dangerous. Check with the local visitors centre or hamlet office to determine where it is permissible to pick up rocks. Verify any restrictions on access to Inuit land where you plan to go. It is illegal to collect rocks in national parks.

Be sure to carry a camera so that you can record interesting formations or samples that shouldn't be moved.

In the Northwest Territories and Nunavut, there are no rock collectors clubs or amateur rock and mineral associations. In the Baffin Region, however, the **Qikiqtaaluk Corporation** (an Inuit birthright organization) sponsors the "Great Baffin Rock and Mineral Collecting Contest" every year in an effort to support economic development. While the contest is only open to Baffin residents, the corporation would make a good contact regarding the types of rocks and minerals to be found, and could advise where collecting may or may not be appropriate. The **Department of Sustainable Development** (or until April 1999, GNWT's **Resources, Wildlife and Economic Development**) is another good source. For information on scientific aspects of geologic research in Nunavut, contact the **Nunavut Research Institute**.

In addition to the normal safety precautions the responsible rockhound should take — bringing safety goggles and first-aid equipment, for example — it is important to follow the advice provided in Chapter 11, "Adventure Travel." Visitors planning to do rock collecting in the Nunavut Settlement Area outside municipal boundaries should contact the **Nunavut Impact Review Board** to see if their proposed activities require screening.

55. DANCES

by Mike Vlessides

It's your first trip to a Nunavut community, and you're wondering "What, exactly, do people do for fun around here?"

Then you hear something coming from the community hall. You meander over and are met with something you never thought you'd see this close to the North Pole... a square dance.

Although schedules differ from community to community, Inuit dances usually concur with a special event such as Nunavut Day, Canada Day, and especially the period between Christmas and New Year's Day. Some communities even host dances when special guests visit. If you catch word that a dance will be happening on a certain night, there's a good chance there will be a feast earlier that day. Ask around; you might experience a Nunavut double treat.

At the dance, you'll be surprised to find that the music doesn't sound very "country" at all. That's because most of what's being played is of Scottish origin, introduced to Inuit by 19th-century whalers. And while each region has its own distinct style, most of the dances are variations of Scottish country dances. The music is traditionally supplied by a local on the "squeeze-box," or accordion, who is often accompanied by a guitarist, drummer, and sometimes, a bass player. In the Kitikmeot Region, you will often find a fiddler plays, too.

The serious dancing begins somewhere around 11 p.m. and can go into the wee hours of the morning, especially around Christmas. In other places, dances begin at around 8 p.m. and end near midnight. As adults slowly arrive and spend time visiting with one another, children rule the roost. They race willy-nilly throughout the hall, narrowly avoiding high-speed collisions with one another. Then, as the dancing begins, the children slowly disperse. It's not as if they've gone to bed, though; they've just found somewhere else to play.

Inuit dances are affairs of endurance, and after a few minutes of jigging and twirling you're guaranteed to be bathed in sweat. In fact, the community hall will become so muggy that someone will prop open the back door. In the middle of winter this causes a ghostly phenomenon: –40° C air rushes into the building, condenses as soon as it comes inside, and creates an eerie fog effect near the door.

In the Kitikmeot Region, dances are directed by a caller, similar to typical western square dances. But in other parts of Nunavut, Inuit "square" dances do not offer the luxury of a caller, so there's nobody actually telling you what to do. Your safest bet is to watch intently for a dance or two, then join when the next one begins. Don't hold out for too many dances, though; at some of these gatherings, a single dance can last as long as two hours!

Unfortunately, no two dances are alike. So while you may think you've mastered the footwork of one, you're probably going to be clueless during the next number. Don't fret! The dancers in your vicinity will either tell you what to do as the dance progresses, or for those that don't speak English, simply push you in the right direction.

So how do you join in? Again, the sheer size of Nunavut dictates broad differences in style between towns. Most likely, though, a group of men or women will begin to congregate in the middle of the room. If you're of the same gender, simply go up and join. If you happen to be in one of the more accomplished square-dancing communities and you've exceeded the expected number of participants for the upcoming dance, you will politely be asked to wait until the next number. In other places, the dance is only limited by the number of willing participants, and you'll be more than welcome. If you're not of the same gender as the group gathering in the centre, you'll have to wait and hope to be chosen as somebody's partner, or just walk up to a member of the opposite sex who's partnerless.

Rest assured that you will make a spectacle of yourself, what with spinning the wrong way and grabbing someone's left arm when you were supposed to grab their right. But don't think your lack of prowess has caused your partner to quickly abandon you when the dance ends. Square dances in Nunavut are not typically followed by the handshakes or small talk that accompany southern versions. When the dance is over, it's over.

Bring a good sense of humor, and you'll find these dances a great way to have fun in a small northern community.

ACTIVITIES: DIRECTORY

All Activities

Nunavut Tourism
P.O. Box 1450, Iqaluit NT,
X0A 0H0 Canada
Tel.: 1-800-491-7910 (for Canada and
the United States)
Tel.: (867) 979-6551
Fax: (867) 979-1261
E-mail: nunatour@nunanet.com
Web site: www.nunatour.nt.ca

Boating/Canoeing/ Kayaking

Canadian Hydrographic Services
Arctic volume of tide and current tables
is $6.50. Payment required in advance.
VISA, MasterCard.
Department of Fisheries and Oceans
(Hydrographic Chart Distribution Office)
1675 Russell Rd.,
P.O. Box 8080, Ottawa ON,
K1G 3H6 Canada
Tel.: (613) 998-4931
Fax: (613) 998-1217
E-mail: chs_sales@chshq.dfo.ca

Maps
See map sources in "Planning Ahead"
directory.

Cruises

Cruise web sites:

www.cybercruises.com
Going by the name of *Tutto Crociere —
the Cyberspace Cruise Magazine*, this site
has loads of links to other cruise sites,
cruise lines, cruise travel agencies, plus
tidbits of cruise news in a "Seen and
Heard" corner.

www.travelpage.com
Includes extensive profiles of all kinds
of cruise lines.

Diving

Arctic Divers Ltd.
Commercial divers, based in Yellowknife.
Tel.: (867) 873-2824
Fax: (867) 920-7657

Nunavut Underwater Marine Explorers Society
Tel.: (867) 897-8851
Fax: (867) 897-8410
E-mail: tmperry@juno.com

Professional Association of Diving Instructors (PADI) Canada
Tel.: 1-800-565-8130 or (604) 273-0277
Fax: (604) 273-0299
Web site: www.padi.com

Tukturjuk Outfitting
In Iqaluit.
Tel.: (867) 979-2289
E-mail: glenwill@nunanet.com

Hunting and Fishing

Department of Sustainable Development, Government of Nunavut
Tel.: (867) 979-5134
Fax: (867) 979-5920

High Arctic Lodge
On Victoria Island.
P.O. Box 280, Penticton BC,
V2A 6K4 Canada
Tel.: (250) 493-3300
Fax: (250) 493-3900
E-mail: higharctic@vip.net
Web site: www.higharctic.com

Plummer's Arctic Lodge
At Tree River in the Coronation Gulf.
Tel.: (204) 774-5775
Fax: (204) 783-2320

Resources, Wildlife and Economic Development, GNWT
Arviat office:
Tel.: (867) 857-2941
Fax: (867) 857-2499

Iqaluit office:
Tel.: (867) 979-5011
Fax: (867) 979-6791

Kugluktuk office:
Tel.: (867) 982-7240
Fax: (867) 982-3701

U.S. Fish and Wildlife Service
Office of Management Authority
Room 420
44401 North Fairfax Dr., Arlington VA,
22203 U.S.A.
Tel.: (703) 358-2104
Fax: (703) 358-2281
E-mail: R9IA_OMA@mail.fws.gov
Web site: www.fws.gov/r9dia/

Mountain Climbing

Auyuittuq National Park
P.O. Box 353, Pangnirtung NT,
X0A 0R0 Canada
Tel.: (867) 473-8828
Fax: (867) 473-8612
E-mail: nunavut_info@pch.gc.ca

Qullikkut Guides and Outfitters
For an information package on climbing
in the Clyde River area, or a videotape
of the 1996 ascent of Polar Sun Spire by
the Hollinger/Synott/Chapman team.
Tel.: (867) 924-6268
Fax: (867) 924-6362
E-mail: qullikkut@arctic.ca

Rock Collecting

**Department of Sustainable
Development**
(See listing under "Hunting and
Fishing.")

Nunavut Impact Review Board
Tel.: (867) 983-2593
Fax: (867) 983-2594
E-mail: nirb@polarnet.ca
Web site: ipg.nunavut.ca/nirbpg.htm

Nunavut Research Institute
Tel.: (867) 979-4115
Fax: (867) 979-4681
E-mail: exdir@nunanet.com
Web site: nunanet.com/~research/

Qikiqtaaluk Corporation
Tel.: (867) 979-4047
Fax: (867) 979-8433
E-mail: qc@nunanet.com
Web site: natsiq.nunanet.com/~qc/

**Resources, Wildlife and
Economic Development**
(See listing under "Hunting and
Fishing.")

Rock collecting web sites:

Cyberwall
www.nb.net/~downs/downsrm.htm

**Canadian Directory of Rock and
Mineral Associations**
pangea.usask.ca/~dfs846/rmac/

The Canadian Rockhound
Internet magazine.
pangea.usask.ca/~dfs846/rockhound/
home.html

Skiing

Arctic Odysseys
Tel.: (206) 325-1977
Fax: (206) 726-8488
E-mail: arctic4u@aol.com
Web site: miraclemile.com/arctic/

NorthWinds Arctic Adventures
Tel.: (867) 979-0551
Fax: (867) 979-0573
E-mail: plandry@nunanet.com
Web site: www.northwinds-arctic.com

Whale Watching

Adventure Canada
Tel.: 1-800-363-7566 or (905) 271-4000
Fax: (905) 271-5595

Arctic Marine Wildlife Tours
Tel.: (506) 459-7325
Fax: (506) 453-3589

Canadian River Expeditions
Tel.: (604) 938-6651 or 1-800-898-7238
Fax: (604) 938-6621
E-mail: canriver@direct.ca
Web site: www.whistler.net/resort/
          canriver/index.htm

Marine Expeditions
Tel.: (416) 964-9069 or 1-800-263-9147
Fax: (416) 964-2366
E-mail: marine_expeditions@
          sympatico.ca

Destinations

Some gateways to Nunavut are far more than just checkpoints on the trek to Canada's central and eastern Arctic. They share a cultural or political history with the new territory, and so, may offer up more insight. Here are three gateways worth exploring: Nuuk, Greenland; Yellowknife, Northwest Territories; and Churchill, Manitoba.

56. NUUK
by James Demcheson

Since my second visit to Nuuk, I've come to regard it, as well as the rest of Greenland, as my second home.

Population:	13,478 Source: Municipality of Nuuk, August 1998
Telephone Area Code:	299
Time Zone:	-3 GMT
Postal Code:	DK 3900
En Route to Nunavut:	By air:
	• Copenhagen-Nuuk
	Passengers continue from Nuuk to Kangerlussuaq by Greenlandair, then travel on to Iqaluit by First Air
	By sea:
	• Cruise ship routes around Nunavut and the Arctic may also include Nuuk
Banks:	Groenlandsbanken and Spar Bank Vest. Greenland's currency is the Danish Kroner
Taxis:	Yes! Be ready to cruise in style in Audi and Mercedes-Benz taxis

Although there's a Danish flavor about this colorful northern capital city, it is also unmistakably *Kalaallit* (Kah-laah-sthleet), native Greenlandic. Canadian Inuit and the aboriginal peoples of *Kalaallit, Nunaat* (Greenland), have spiritual and cultural traditions in common and speak a language that's very similar. Many *Kalaallit* in Nuuk still live as their ancestors did from hunting, trapping and fishing, their main source of income.

Nuuk is the centre of Greenland's Home Rule government, which has complete authority over internal affairs. While the Greenland experience could be a model for the new territory of Nunavut, the consensus style of governing that Nunavut is adopting may be of special interest to Greenland's leaders.

History
The forebears of contemporary Greenlanders, the Thule, inhabited the island for some 1,000 years, hunting seals and whales from their kayaks. In the 10th century, the Norse chieftain Eric the Red explored the land, discovering patches of green along coastal fiords of this otherwise ice-capped land. To lure farmers of the Viking culture from Iceland, he called it Greenland. In 1728,

the Norwegian priest Hans Egede established a Lutheran mission on the west coast, converting *Kalaallit* to Christianity. The Danish system of government administration was adopted. In 1979, Home Rule was established, giving Greenland self-government while remaining part of Denmark.

Nuuk: Its Land and Wildlife

In the Greenlandic language, *Kalaallisut*, Nuuk means "peninsula" and refers to its spectacular location on a headland at the outlet of the Godthåb Fiord next to an immense system of fiords and islands. Like all of Greenland, the city lies above the tree line. Its climate is subarctic, with average temperatures of 7° C in July and –8° C in January. While the Irmingerstream gulf stream keeps offshore waters around Nuuk ice-free, the city's location on the coast ensures plenty of snow in winter. Colossal icebergs drift by offshore, castaways of giant glaciers. In summer, valleys and meadows of the south coast are lushly carpeted with a forest-like brush, as well as birches, willows, ferns and other flora. Sea water abounds with a variety of sea mammals and fish, including seals, whales, salmon, halibut and cod. Whale-watching tours are popular.

Tours

Across from the Hotel Hans Egede, you'll find the Greenland Parliament. At the south end of town on one of many harbors is the Greenland National Museum. Close to the Teachers College is the statue of Hans Egede, a key figure in Greenland's history. And at the new Greenland Cultural Centre, the Katuaq, art exhibitions, folk dances and concerts are held; the Centre also includes a cinema. For information on tours in and around Nuuk, contact **Greenland Tourism** or **Nuuk Tourism**.

Shopping

A mini-mall behind the Hotel Hans Egede sells a variety of high-quality goods. Check out the craft shops, too, where you'll find Greenlandic beadwork, *tupillat* (figures carved in wood, antler or ivory), soapstone carvings, and graphic art. At the sewing shop, Kittat, you can order purses and *kamiit* made of embroidered skin. For Danish pastry, try the great bakeries in town.

Events

All year round, the Katuaq is Nuuk's cultural hot spot. In March, the Snow Sculpture Festival is held in the city's centre. June 21 is Greenland's National Day, when people celebrate in traditional music and dance. In July, the 10.5-kilometre marathon takes off in and around Nuuk. And in August, great music happens at the Nuuk Festival.

Accommodation and Dining

In the centre of town is the modern **Hotel Hans Egede** with its 110 rooms. Prices are $245 Cdn per person per night and $300 for double occupancy, including breakfast. A special conference rate of $200 per person per day includes all meals and the use of conference facilities. The hotel has a restaurant serving international, Danish and Greenlandic food, a bar, jacuzzi and sun bed. All rooms have bathrooms, TV and telephone. No airport pickup.

Near the harbor is the 30-room renovated **Seaman's Home**, which describes itself as a non-alcoholic Christian hotel with a homey atmosphere. Prices are $132 Cdn for a single room with bath and $191 for a double with bath. This includes breakfast only. The hotel also serves lunch and dinner. No airport pickup. There is also a youth hostel and several bed and breakfasts in town.

Restaurants in town include dining rooms at the Hotel Hans Egede and the Hotel Godthåb, the Café Rudolph, Tulles Rock Café and Crazy Daisy's. Whether you fancy country food, such as reindeer, muskox or salmon, or European-style dishes, you'll find something to satisfy you. For more information, contact Nuuk Tourism.

Entertainment and Recreation

For the sports-minded, there are several fitness and sports clubs in Nuuk. In summer, soccer matches are held, the passion of many Greenlanders. Five kilometres from town on top of Lille Malene Mountain are ski lifts and a skiing/snowboarding resort. A number of bars and dance clubs will take care of your nightlife.

Services

The **Arctic Umiaq Line A/S** will transport you by ship to other communities along the west coast of Greenland. Or with **Greenlandair** you can charter a helicopter to fly you from Nuuk to Sisimiut and other destinations in Greenland.

DIRECTORY

Accommodation

Hotel Hans Egede
(Aqqusinersuaq 1-5)
P.O. Box 289
DK 3900 Nuuk
Tel.: +299 32 42 22
Fax: +299 32 44 87
E-mail: hhe@greennet.gl
Web site: www.greenland-guide.dk/hhe

Seaman's Home
(Marinevej 13)
P.O. Box 1021
DK 3900 Nuuk
Tel.: +299 32 10 29
Fax: +299 32 21 04

Services

Arctic Umiaq Line A/S
P.O. Box 608
DK 3900 Nuuk
Tel.: +299 32 52 11
Fax: +299 32 32 11
E-mail: kniship@greennet.gl

Greenland Tourism A/S
(Hans Egedesvej 29)
P.O. Box 1552
DK 3900 Nuuk
Tel.: +299 22 88 8
Fax: +299 22 87 7
E-mail: tourism@greennet.gl
or nuuktour@greennet.gl

Greenlandair Inc.
P.O. Box 1012
DK 3900 Nuuk
Tel.: +299 32 88 88
Fax: +299 32 72 88
E-mail: glsales@greennet.gl
Web site: www.greenland-guide.dk

Municipal Office
Nuup Kommunea
P.O. Box 1005
DK 3900 Nuuk
Tel.: +299 23 37 7
Fax: +299 29 18 7
E-mail: nuuk@nuukom.ki.gl
Web site: www.nuuk.gl

Tikilluarit A/S — Nuuk Tourism
For information on stores and businesses in Nuuk.
P.O. Box 199
DK 3900 Nuuk
Tel.: +299 22 7 00
Fax: +299 22 7 10
E-mail: nuuktour@greennet.gl

57. YELLOWKNIFE

by Mike Vlessides

I t's been more than seven years since I first set eyes on Yellowknife's compact skyline, but the experience lingers in my memory with surprising clarity.

Population:	18,124 Source: 1996 Census of Canada
Telephone Area Code:	867
Time Zone:	Mountain Time
Postal Code:	Numerous
En Route to Nunavut:	Flight routes:
	• Edmonton-Yellowknife
	Edmonton to Yellowknife (992 kilometres north) is via Canadian Airlines or First Air. Flights to Cambridge Bay, Kugluktuk, Taloyoak, Pelly Bay and Gjoa Haven are from Yellowknife, Which is also a gateway to Rankin Inlet and the Kivalliq Region from Western Canada. The Edmonton-Yellowknife-Cambridge Bay flight also goes to Resolute in the Baffin Region
Banks:	All major Canadian banks have branches here
Taxis:	Yes

I was travelling with a group of friends on a monumental midwinter road trip from Toronto to what I then thought was the most northerly place on the planet. The final hours of our trek were spent on the lonely, snow-glowing roads that characterize this part of the world.

Then, emerging quite unexpectedly in the early morning glow, was something I never expected to see this far north. A skyline against a backdrop of white heralded our arrival to Yellowknife. I was immediately taken with the place.

Since that day, my outlook on Yellowknife has matured. It is *not*, I now know, the most northerly place in the world. In fact, Yellowknife is a bit of a paradox by northern standards. Most residents consider themselves hardy frontier types, ever ready to weave tales of bravery in the face of winter's bite. For many of the people who reside in smaller communities throughout the Arctic, however, Yellowknife is not really the North at all.

History

For all its foibles, Yellowknife *is* an interesting place to spend a couple of days, and boasts a colorful history. The first aboriginals to the area were Dene peoples from the northernmost of the prairie Chipewyan tribes. The city owes its name to a small tribe — the Yellowknives — that was known for using tools made of copper.

Yellowknife's contemporary history is rooted largely in gold, which was discovered here in the 1930s. From that point the town grew into the administrative centre for the North; Yellowknife was declared capital of the Northwest Territories in 1967. The discovery of diamonds in 1991 at nearby

Lac de Gras, and the recent completion of Canada's first diamond mine, promise to continue Yellowknife's mining tradition well into the next century.

Yellowknife: Its Land and Wildlife

Though it's rare you'll see much wildlife in Yellowknife proper, it doesn't take much to leave the city behind. The most numerous of the big mammals in the area is the caribou. The land around Yellowknife is also summer home to more than 120 known species of birds.

The topography of the area is characterized by flat, boggy areas of muskeg, intermittent outcrops of low rock, and sparse forests of stunted sub-arctic trees. Countless small lakes and ponds make the region a mosquito's dream.

Tours

The **Prince of Wales Northern Heritage Centre** is a museum located directly across from the Explorer Hotel in downtown Yellowknife. Flanking the museum are the **NWT Legislature**, an equally impressive structure built in the early 1990s, and the **Northern Frontier Regional Visitors Centre**.

The most popular getaway route from the city is the Ingraham (pronounced "Ing-rum") Trail, a partially paved road that ends abruptly after some 70 kilometres. Along the road is a host of campgrounds, picnic areas, and popular starting points for various backcountry experiences. In the city, the Frame Lake Trail is an interesting walk.

Shopping

Herein lies what may well be Yellowknife's greatest contribution to the arctic world. Most northerners see Yellowknife as a place to pick up necessary items hard to come by in smaller communities. Wal-Mart, Canadian Tire and Saan stores all hold court here.

There are also many places to buy native arts and crafts, but prices can be quite a bit higher than in other places. Then again, you'd be hard-pressed to find shops anywhere else in the North that carry such a handsome array of handiwork.

Events

One of Yellowknife's most popular festivals is Caribou Carnival, held on frozen Frame Lake every March. Caribou Carnival includes a Canadian championship dogteam race, live entertainment, ice-sculpting exhibitions, frontier-type contests, and food kiosks galore.

On June 21, the longest day of the year, comes Raven Mad Daze, a streetside fête that lasts long into the night. Local merchants sell their wares at bargain basement prices alongside omnipresent food kiosks.

Over the years, Folk on the Rocks has become known as a first-class folk festival. Held on the shores of Long Lake in July, this concert features performances by northern and southern musicians alike.

Accommodation

Yellowknife offers the widest range of accommodation of any destination in the North. Most prominent is the **Explorer Hotel**, which sits high atop a hill overlooking Frame Lake. There are also several motels, two apartment/suite housing units, and a few bed and breakfasts. Expect to pay anywhere from $65 to $175 per night.

Dining

Dining is Yellowknife's next great contribution to northern life. The city has a bevy of eateries with a wide range of quality, price and fare — from pizza to muskox.

Located in Yellowknife's Old Town section is **The Wildcat Cafe**, the city's most popular eating establishment with visitors. Small, dark, and infinitely cosy, the one-room log cabin offers a combination cultural/dining experience. Here you're as likely to share a table with a fellow tourist as with a local gold prospector ready to share geological tales of riches and woes.

Another Old Town favorite is **Bullock's**, a delightful restaurant that oozes small-town charm. There's always some sort of freshly baked bread product cooling on the counter, a wonderful accompaniment to their famous fish and chips. And how can you not love a place that sells *boutine*, a uniquely northern combination of *poutine* and caribou?

Entertainment and Recreation

With a movie theatre, a few local theatre groups, a bowling alley, a swimming pool, two ice arenas, curling, a tennis club, a nine-hole golf course, and (hold your breath) karaoke, what isn't there to do in Yellowknife?

The city also has a wide array of dance and music clubs. The most famous night spot in the city, for better or worse, is **The Gold Range**, a rough-and-tumble bar in the heart of downtown.

Services

Stanton Regional Hospital, the largest health-care facility in the Northwest Territories, handles all routine care, as well as most emergency situations. Yellowknife also has a number of private medical and dental offices.

DIRECTORY

Accommodation and Dining

Bullock's Bistro
4 Lessard Dr., Latham Island,
Old Town, Yellowknife NT
X1A 2G5 Canada
Tel.: (867) 873-3474

The Executive
4920-54 Ave, Yellowknife NT,
X1A 2P5 Canada
Tel.: (867) 920-3999
Fax: (867) 920-4716
E-mail: tcent8@internorth.com

Explorer Hotel
P.S. 7000,
4825-49 Ave., Yellowknife NT,
X1A 2R3 Canada
Tel.: 1-800-661-0892 or (867) 873-3531
Fax: (867) 873-2789

The Wildcat Cafe
Open mid-May to September.
P.O. Box 763,
3904 Wiley Rd., Yellowknife NT,
X1A 2N6 Canada
Tel.: (867) 873-8850

Entertainment and Recreation

The Gold Range
5010-50th St., Yellowknife NT,
X1A 2N5 Canada
Tel.: (867) 873-4567

Prince of Wales Northern Heritage Centre
P.O. Box 1320, Yellowknife NT,
X1A 2L9 Canada
Tel.: (867) 873-7551
Fax: (867) 873-0205
Web site: pwnhc.learnnet.nt.ca/

Services

Stanton Regional Hospital
419 Byrne Rd., Yellowknife NT,
X1A 2N3 Canada
Tel.: (867) 920-4111

Weather Information
Tel.: (867) 873-4027 (weather office) or
873-2734 (24-hour weather line)
Web site weather forecast:
www.tor.ec.gc.ca/forecasts/index.html
(check under Regional Weather
Summaries) or www.infonorth.org

Shopping

Arctic Art Gallery
4801 Franklin Ave., Yellowknife NT,
X1A 2N7 Canada
Tel.: (867) 873-5666 or 1-800-661-0799
Fax: (867) 873-9155
E-mail: gallery@arcticartgallery.com
Web site: www.arcticartgallery.com

Aurora Gallery
Centre Square Mall
P.O. Box 1826, Yellowknife NT,
X1A 2P4 Canada
Tel.: (867) 873-4256
Fax: (867) 873-3939

Northern Images
4801 Franklin Ave., Yellowknife NT,
X1A 2N7 Canada
Tel.: (867) 873-5944
Fax: (867) 873-9224
E-mail: norimage@ssimicro.com
Web site: www.ssimicro.com/~norimage

Visitor Services

NWT Arctic Tourism
P.O. Box 610, Yellowknife NT,
X1A 2N5 Canada
Tel.: 1-800-661-0788 or (867) 873-7200
Fax: (867) 873-4059
E-mail: nwtat@nwttravel.nt.ca
Web site: www.nwttravel.nt.ca

NWT Legislative Assembly
For tours:
P.O. Box 1320, Yellowknife NT,
X1A 2L9 Canada
Tel.: (867) 669-2200

Northern Frontier Regional
Visitors Centre
#4–4807 49th St., Yellowknife NT,
X1A 3T5 Canada
Tel.: (867) 873-4262
Fax: (867) 873-3654
E-mail: nfra@internorth.com
Web site: www.northernfrontier.com

58. CHURCHILL

by Shirley Tagalik

Churchill, Manitoba, situated where the great Churchill River spills into the vast expanse of Hudson Bay, lies along a major migration route for multitudes of birds and other wildlife.

Population:	1,060 Source: 1996 Census of Canada
Telephone Area Code:	204
Time Zone:	Central Time
Postal Code:	R0B 0E0
En Route to Nunavut:	By air:
	• Winnipeg-Churchill
	Winnipeg to Churchill (1,000 kilometres northeast) is via Canadian
	Airlines, Calm Air or Skyward Aviation; flights continue to Rankin Inlet.
	Calm Air and Skyward also fly between Thompson, Manitoba and
	Churchill, continuing on to Rankin Inlet
	By rail:
	• Winnipeg, The Pas, Thompson or Gillam, Manitoba to Churchill by
	Via Rail Canada
	By sea:
	Cruise ship routes around Nunavut and the Arctic may also include Churchill
Banks:	Royal Bank
Taxis:	Yes

With a history linked to Nunavut's Kivalliq Region, Canada's only subarctic seaport is also the only community so close to tundra that can be accessed by rail.

History

Remains of Pre-Dorset, Dorset, Thule, Inuit, Chipewyan and Cree camp sites around the tundra reveal the area's occupation over the centuries. A Hudson's Bay Co. post erected in 1685 was later replaced by the massive Fort Prince of Wales on the west side of the Churchill River estuary in the early 1700s. The fort still stands as evidence of French-English rivalry for control of the New World and of the lucrative fur trade. Across the river from the fort is Cape Mercy, where a gun battery, built in 1746, points its cannons protectively out to Hudson Bay. Further upriver, at Sloop Cove, the names of the explorer Samuel Hearne and other former Hudson's Bay Co. employees may be seen carved into the rocks along the shore.

In 1930, the Canadian National Railway linked Churchill to Winnipeg with 1,920 kilometres of rail so that prairie grain could be shipped to Europe. Today, both the rail line and the grain-handling facility are privately operated by the Hudson Bay Rail and Port Corporation.

During the Second World War, the American and Canadian military recognized Churchill's strategic importance as the northernmost town near Hudson Bay with rail links from the south for supplies and equipment. In 1942, a large airbase was built here and expanded after the War. In 1980, the base was closed, but the airport and rocket ranges are still in use.

From 1965–1975, Akudlik, a "suburb" outside Churchill, was Keewatin regional headquarters of the government of the Northwest Territories. The site was dismantled after headquarters were later moved to Rankin Inlet.

Churchill: Its Land and Wildlife

Churchill is in taiga country — halfway between tundra and forest. More than 400 species of plants burst to life during the short, intense growing season. Some 200 species of birds, including the rare Ross's Gull, migrate to the area in spring, attracting avid birdwatchers from around the world.

Churchill is renowned as the polar bear capital of the world. During October and November, these majestic animals gather along the shore near town waiting for freezeup so they can venture onto the ice to hunt seals. In and around Wapusk National Park, southeast of Churchill on the Hudson Bay coast, females build their dens for winter.

After spring breakup, migrating beluga whales arrive to feed in the Churchill River estuary and to birth their young. In July and August, you can watch these musical "sea canaries" from a tour boat on the river.

Tours

Among an array of tours and outfitting services, Adventure Walking Tours offers outings that last from an hour to a day. Arctic Nature Tours couples interpretive nature tours with historic and archeological excursions. Tundra Domes and White Whale Lodge allow you to watch the spectacular aurora borealis from the comfort of heated observation facilities. Sea North Tours will take you on a tour of the Churchill River to watch belugas that congregate there each year. Churchill Wilderness Encounters offers bird tour packages in June. Tundra Buggy Tours and Great White Bear Tours take you out to watch polar bears roaming along the shores of Hudson Bay. Epic Sled Dog Adventures and other companies offer dogsled rides. Bus tours of the town and surrounding area can be arranged through North Star Tours and other companies.

Visits to the **Parks Canada Visitor Reception Centre** and the **Eskimo Museum** prepare you for your travels to Nunavut. The **Churchill Northern Studies Centre** offers courses in arctic ecology, survival, photography, ornithology, geology and meteorology. Tours at the Boreal Gardens demonstrate the profusion of produce that can be grown during endless northern summers.

Shopping

Native crafts and souvenirs are available in many local shops, including the **Arctic Trading Company**, **Tundra Buggy Gift Shop**, **Bear Country Inn**, **Polar Inn Gift Shop**, **Northern Images**, **Great White Bear Tours Gift Shop**, **Eskimo Museum** and **Wapusk General Store**.

Accommodation and Dining

Excellent hotels, lodges and bed and breakfasts are available in Churchill. Prices range from $70 to $120 for a hotel room, and from $25 to $75 for a B&B. Book well in advance for the busy months of June through October. There are dining rooms in the Tundra Inn (**Wong Kee Restaurant**), **Seaport Hotel**, **Churchill Hotel** and **Northern Nights Lodge**. Other restaurants in town include the **Trader's Table**, **Gypsy Bakery**, the **Launch Pad Café** and the **Lazy Bear Café**.

Events

The PTA Carnival is held in the Churchill Complex during the Queen Victoria holiday weekend in May. On July 1, the brave or foolish dive into the icy waters of Hudson Bay outside the complex for the Polar Bear Dip.

Services

Churchill's health and recreation complex houses a hospital, pharmacy and out-patient clinic, day care, library, swimming pool, ice arena, cinema, arcade, and a wonderful wall-hanging display.

DIRECTORY

Accommodation/ Outfitters/Tour Operators/Visitors Centre

Churchill Chamber of Commerce
For details on accommodations and tours.
Tel.: 1-888-389-2327 (toll-free in North America) or (204) 675-2022
Fax: (204) 675-2164
E-mail: cccomm@cancom.net
Web site: www.cancom.net/~cccomm

Parks Canada Visitor Reception Centre
Tel.: (204) 675-8863
Fax: (204) 675-2026

Restaurants

Churchill Hotel Restaurant
Tel.: (204) 675-8853

Gypsy Bakery
Tel.: (204) 675-2322

Launch Pad Café
Tel.: (204) 675-8845

Lazy Bear Café
Tel.: (204) 675-2969

Northern Nights Diner
Tel.: (204) 675-2403

Seaport Hotel Dining Room
Tel.: (204) 675-8807

Trader's Table
Tel.: (204) 675-2141

Wong Kee Restaurant
In the Tundra Inn.
Tel.: (204) 675-2827

Services

Airlines

Calm Air
Tel.: (204) 675-8858

Canadian Airlines
Tel.: 1-800-665-1177

Skyward Aviation
Tel.: (204) 675-2967

Churchill Northern Studies Centre
Tel.: (204) 675-2307
Fax: (204) 675-2139

Taxi

Churchill Taxi
Tel.: (204) 675-2345

Via Rail
Train station.
Tel.: 1-800-561-8630 (Canada),
1-800-561-3949 (USA), (204) 675-2149
or (204) 675-2629

Shopping

Arctic Trading Company
Tel.: (204) 675-8804
Fax: (204) 675-2164

Bear Country Inn
Tel.: (204) 675-8299
Fax: (204) 675-8803

Eskimo Museum
Call museum for hours.
Tel.: (204) 675-2030
Fax: (204) 675-2140

Great White Bear Tours Gift Shop
Tel.: (204) 675-2781
Fax: (204) 675-2930

Northern Images
Tel.: (204) 675-2681
Fax: (204) 675-2681

Polar Inn Gift Shop
Tel.: (204) 675-8878
Fax: (204) 675-2647

Tundra Buggy Gift Shop
Tel.: (204) 675-2121
Fax: (204) 675-2877

Wapusk General Store
Tel.: (204) 675-2887

Nunavut Communities: Facilities									
Community	Hotels*	Restaurant in Hotels	Restaurant Outside Hotels	Guest House/Bed & Breakfast*	Campground	Hiking Trails	Taxi	Arts/Crafts Workshop	Visitors Centre/Museum
Arctic Bay	●	●				●	●		
Arviat	●	●	●	●			●	●	●
Baker Lake	●	●	●		●	●	●	●	●
Bathurst Inlet	●	●				●			
Broughton Island	●	●			●	●		●	
Cambridge Bay	●	●	●			●	●	●	●
Cape Dorset	●	●	●	●		●	●	●	●
Chesterfield Inlet	●	●				●	●		
Clyde River	●	●		●			●	●	●
Coral Harbour	●	●					●		
Gjoa Haven	●	●	●			●		●	●
Grise Fiord	●	●							
Hall Beach	●	●	●				●		
Igloolik	●	●	●	●			●		
Iqaluit	●	●	●	●	●	●	●	●	●
Kimmirut	●	●		●		●			●
Kugluktuk	●	●	●		●	●	●		
Nanisivik									
Pangnirtung	●	●	●		●	●	●	●	●
Pelly Bay	●	●	●				●		
Pond Inlet	●	●	●		●	●		●	●
Rankin Inlet	●	●	●			●	●	●	●
Repulse Bay	●	●	●					●	
Resolute	●	●		●					
Sanikiluaq	●	●				●		●	
Taloyoak	●	●						●	
Umingmaktok				●					
Whale Cove	●	●					●		

*Licensed facilities only.

59. RANKIN INLET
by Jimi Onalik

Ask someone from Nunavut for their first impression of Rankin Inlet, and they may tell you about the wind.

Population:	2,058 (Inuit: 76%, non-Inuit: 24%) Source: 1996 Census of Canada
Telephone Area Code:	867
Time Zone:	Central Time
Postal Code:	X0C 0G0
How to Get There:	Possible routes:
	• Winnipeg-Rankin Inlet
	• Edmonton-Yellowknife-Rankin Inlet
	• Ottawa/Montreal-Iqaluit-Rankin Inlet
	• Kangerlussuaq (Greenland)-Iqaluit-Rankin Inlet
	Winnipeg to Rankin Inlet (1,470 kilometres north) is via Calm Air.
	First Air also serves Rankin Inlet
Banks:	The Royal Bank (which also has an automated banking machine) and the CIBC
Alcohol:	Controlled. Alcohol for personal consumption may be ordered from Yellowknife or brought in from Southern Canada under an import permit. In the community, it's available only to registered hotel guests
Taxis:	Yes

They probably formed that impression the moment they arrived. Located on the western shores of Hudson Bay, the community is well known for its severe winter storms, which can make the walk from the airplane to the air terminal seem like one of the coldest on Earth. But just as there's more to New York than crime, there's more to Rankin Inlet than the wind.

Today, Rankin Inlet, or *Kangiq&iniq* as it is known in Inuktitut (meaning "deep bay/inlet"), is a bustling community that serves as both a government town and a transportation hub for the Kivalliq Region. It is Nunavut's second-largest community and the self-described "business capital" of the territory. For the past 20 years, Rankin has been a regional centre for the government of the Northwest Territories, traditionally the largest employer here. Recent cutbacks and layoffs, however, have caused many people to rely less on government as a source of income. Instead, many Inuit have become entrepreneurs, and their stores, freight expediter services, electrical, plumbing and real estate companies are flourishing. Rankin Inlet has become a community of which its residents are immensely proud.

Originally, Rankin Inlet's roots were in mining, and the 1990s suggest the return of mining companies here. Rich mineral deposits in the region, including gold, have led to a bit of a boom in exploration. The existence of several major exploration camps nearby hints that an operating mine may someday return.

Rankin Inlet Street Map

To Airport,
Treasures,
Keewatin
Regional
Visitors
Centre,
Nunavut
Tourism

N

Key to Map Locations

1 Anglican Church
2 Coffee Delights
3 Community Hall
4 Department of Sustainable Development
   (or until April/99, RWED)
5 Glad Tidings Fellowship Church
6 Hamlet Office
7 Health Centre
8 Hunters and Trappers Organization
9 Inuit Cultural Institute
10 Ivalu
11 Kissarvik Co-op Store and CIBC
12 Kowmuk's
13 Leo Ussak Elementary School (includes
   Rankin Inlet Community Access Centre)
14 Maani Ulujuk Ilinniavik School
   (includes John Ayaruaq Library)
15 Matchbox Gallery
16 Nanuq Inn
17 Northern Store (includes Quick Stop
   fast food restaurant)
18 Nunavut Arctic College
19 Police (RCMP)
20 Post Office
21 Roman Catholic Church
22 Royal Bank
23 Sakku Drugs and Dental Clinic
24 Siniktarvik Hotel

Rankin Inlet, a gateway to the Kivalliq Region, also attracts tourists who visit to fish, hunt, canoe, or enjoy the land and wildlife. Each year, hundreds of travellers bound for other destinations spend some time in the community.

In 1993, with the signing of the Nunavut Land Claims Agreement, Rankin became a major political centre for budding land claims organizations. The head office of the Kivalliq Inuit Association, as well as regional offices for Nunavut Tunngavik Incorporated, are located here.

History

The history of Rankin Inlet is a story of a people who have triumphed over adversity. The vibrant nature of the community today attests to the determination of Inuit to overcome their hardships.

Although Inuit seldom used the actual town site of Rankin Inlet, they hunted and fished in the surrounding area for many years. Artifacts that reveal this use can be found throughout the region. In nearby Ijiraliq (Meliadine) River Territorial Historic Park, for example, generations of Inuit fished for arctic char during the spring and fall.

The Rankin Inlet area has also been an important meeting place for Inuit and outsiders. The mid-1800s saw the arrival of fleets of American and European whalers in Hudson Bay. To maximize their profits after long journeys to the whaling grounds, the whalers often spent a winter or two frozen into the ice. One of these overwintering locations was at Marble Island, about 70 kilometres from Rankin.

Archeological remains that may still be found on Marble Island paint a stark picture of the whalers' life here. Despite their best efforts, those men from warmer latitudes weren't fully able to deal with the arctic climate. Signs of their efforts to adapt — their cabins, storage shacks and even an amphitheatre where they performed plays for each other — are scattered across the island. If you're touring around Marble Island at low tide, you'll spot a ship underwater. On nearby Deadman's Island, whalers' graves are a silent reminder of those who could not adapt.

For Inuit, Marble Island also has legendary significance; even today, when they visit it, they crawl up to the tide level, out of respect for an old woman whose spirit is said to reside there. Legend has it that those who don't crawl will encounter bad luck on the anniversary of their visit.

The relationship between Inuit and whalers continued until the early years of the 20th century. By 1910, when whale stocks had severely declined, the whalers stopped coming to the Rankin Inlet area. During the first half of this century, Inuit contact with outsiders was limited to missionaries and Hudson's Bay Co. traders.

The 1940s and 1950s were grim times for the Inuit of the entire Kivalliq Region. A shift in the migration patterns of caribou led to wide-spread starvation among inland Caribou Inuit. To provide food and supplies to starving Inuit, the Canadian government established communities along the west coast of Hudson Bay. The communities of Arviat, Whale Cove and Baker Lake were created to serve the needs of the local people.

Rankin Inlet, however, was formed with a different goal in mind. The Canadian government of the 1950s believed that the subsistence economy was no longer viable and that modern technology would provide comfort to all. The Inuit must be brought into a wage-based economy. The discovery of large amounts of nickel at Rankin Inlet, and the high price of the mineral during the Korean War, convinced the government to do just that.

In 1955, North Rankin Nickel Mines began production. Many Inuit hunters and trappers moved with their families to Rankin Inlet and became miners, working for a wage underground and in the mill. Inuit were brought in from Repulse Bay, Coral Harbour, Chesterfield Inlet, and Arviat to take part in what was viewed as a bold new experiment. This experiment was to introduce Inuit to the necessary skills for hard-rock mining and to a lifestyle of shift work and paycheques.

North Rankin Nickel Mines produced high-quality ore and plenty of work for seven years. The Inuit employees were very hard-working and much appreciated by the mine owners. In fact, many Inuit who worked here went on to other mines in Southern Canada. Many residents of Rankin Inlet still have mementoes from friends and relatives who worked in towns such as Lynn Lake, Manitoba, and Sudbury, Ontario.

In 1962, the mine closed, bringing about another period of hardship that almost closed the hamlet. Families were now pressured to return to their home communities. Only after a period of negotiations with residents determined to keep their new home on the map did the government allow Rankin Inlet to stay open. By now, however, the several hundred people who remained were used to the wage economy; they needed to find a means to support their families. As a result, the mid-1960s were marked by a series of enterprising, sometimes bizarre, economic development schemes, not all as successful as the nickel mine.

In one venture, Rankin Inlet was briefly the site of one of the most northerly farms in Canada, producing chicken and pork for local use. After accounting for the costs of their accommodations, the chickens and eggs from this "farm" proved very expensive. Furthermore, the only affordable food available for the pigs was fish, leading, as you can imagine, to some pretty fishy-flavored pork.

In another case, a cannery was opened to preserve local foods. Apparently, though, the market for tinned seal meat and *maktaaq* in Southern Canada was limited, because this project didn't last very long.

A successful, albeit short-lived, experiment was the creation of a ceramics studio in 1964. The fine pieces produced by the hunters, trappers, miners and artists were collected by individuals and galleries around the world. Despite the project's artistic and commercial success, the newly formed GNWT never fully backed it; in the early 1970s, it died a slow death. Happily for art-lovers everywhere, this unique studio has been revived recently through the efforts of a local artist. Now a new generation of artists works here alongside their elders to produce exotic, eerily beautiful work.

By the early 1970s, the headquarters for the Kivalliq Region moved from Churchill, Manitoba, to Rankin Inlet. So Rankin was now a government town. The arrival of civil servants and their families revitalized the community. Elders who were born on the land and who became miners, farmers, and artists, could not make the transition into government jobs. Their children, however, did find work in the new bureaucracy. They, like

We know the territory

For 20 years, Nortext Multimedia has launched many successful marketing and communication strategies in the North. The next one could be yours.

Whether it's a simple brochure, an annual report, web site creation, or all the above, see why Nortext was recognized as the 1998 NWT Business of the Year for innovation and excellence in business practices.

Get our northern expertise working for you. Nortext Multimedia — our job is helping our clients succeed.

Nortext

strategic communications • marketing
publishing • web site design • internet marketing
promotion & displays • surveys & databases

Call us today, in Iqaluit at: (867) 979-4376.

On time. Every time.

Canadian *NORTH*
Canadi♦n

We'll get you there.

Whether you're travelling across the North, throughout Canada, or around the world, fly Canadian North, the airline whose Northern service, schedules and routes and connections are unmatched. We have the connections you want with the frequency you need — to get you wherever you need to go... all year round.

At Canadian North, our people, facilities and aircraft are dedicated to maintain a Northern service heritage spanning over seventy years.

We always strive to meet your business and leisure travel needs with value, quality and a friendly Northern attitude. Call your travel agent or Canadian North. We'll get you to where you want to be.

Canadi♦n *NORTH*
We'll get you there!

their parents, had experienced enormous change. Today they hold positions of power in Rankin Inlet.

Many believe that the resilience of Inuit, born out of the intense necessity to adapt to enormous change over the past 50 years, will help the people of Rankin Inlet as they face even greater changes with the creation of Nunavut.

Rankin Inlet: Its Land and Wildlife

The land around Rankin Inlet possesses a subtle beauty. It's often said that its splendor can best be appreciated by seeing it as if through a wide-angle lens, or by viewing it up close, as if under a microscope. The huge expanse of rolling hills and sky gives a haunting feeling of closeness to the land. Intricate rock formations, tiny flowers, and natural wind-sculpted snowdrifts reveal the triumph of art over a harsh climate.

All this beauty is easily accessible. The relative flatness of the land and the many all-terrain vehicles (ATVs) and walking trails nearby make it fairly easy to get out of town and enjoy the glories of the tundra. A five-minute hike from the edge of the hamlet will have you in a land that appears untouched by humans. You'll likely discover *siksiit*. In fact, summer and fall belong to these ground squirrels, which are everywhere, chattering incessantly from their perches on top of sandy bumps in the land. Overhead, majestic birds of prey, such as the peregrine and gyrfalcon, keep a watchful eye on the happenings below. Loons, geese, swans and sandhill cranes are other sights to keep your shutter-finger busy.

Farther out on the land, you may see small herds of caribou jaunting across the tundra in their endless search for lichen and other food. Curious foxes and an occasional wolf may also appear, usually in the distance. Sun-tanning seals dot the sea ice nearby, or you may see their small heads bobbing in waters close to shore. A complete description of all the animals in the area would take up an entire afternoon of sitting and drinking tea with local elders.

You may bump into some animals, however, that are best seen from afar. In the fall, it's not uncommon for polar bears to wander close to town; and in summer, wolverines and even grizzly bears sometimes appear. Unless you're willing to go down in local lore as the tourist who left town with fewer limbs than when you arrived, be sure that on your outings you're accompanied by someone who's familiar with local conditions.

The weather in Rankin? It can be damn cold here. Winter, which lasts from the end of October until mid to late March, has temperatures averaging in the –30° C to –35° C range, with some pretty ferocious Kivalliq winds of 15 to 25 kilometres an hour. The many blizzards wreak havoc with flight schedules. It gets warmer during blizzards and a lot colder on clear days. To stay warm, you'll have to wear clothing that's at least as sophisticated as that worn by lunar astronauts!

Thankfully, though, the climate isn't always this harsh. Many days in spring and summer are calm and sunny. The trick is to be prepared for a wide range of weather conditions.

Spring is one of the best times to visit Rankin. Temperatures warm up to the –10° C to –20° C range. As days grow longer, visitors may enjoy

naturalists who come to view polar bears, caribou and other wildlife, and to tour the tundra and archeological sites.

As the ease of travelling on the tundra may cause you to become complacent, it's always advisable to go out with an experienced, licensed guide. The weather can be very unpredictable and you can soon learn that during a storm, it's far better to be bored in a hotel room than to be panic-stricken on the land. Preparedness is essential.

Several licensed firms offer tours of the community and surrounding area, including **Kivalliq Tours** (ask for Caroline Anawak) and **Tumi Tours**, which has the best dogsled teams in town. For further information on licensed outfitters and tours, contact **Nunavut Tourism**, the Keewatin Regional Visitors Centre, the Rankin Inlet office of the **Department of Sustainable Development** (or until April 1999, **Resources, Wildlife and Economic Development**), or the **Aqiggiak Hunters and Trappers Organization**.

Shopping

Rankin Inlet has a thriving arts and crafts community. In recent years, ceramics has made a comeback here. This stunning pottery, as well as more traditional carvings and wall hangings, provide a wide variety of treasures to choose from. You'll find several places where you can view or purchase the work of local artists.

The **Matchbox Gallery**, owned by local artists Jim and Sue Shirley, carries drawings, paintings, watercolors and prints of Kivalliq images and impressions. The gallery also provides local artists with a place to produce spectacular pottery, and it exhibits their work.

Ivalu is Rankin's fashion centre. Local seamstresses have sewn beautiful inner and outerwear in contemporary Inuit designs. The store has a great selection of hats, jackets, vests, and the like.

The Siniktarvik Hotel has a modest assortment of carvings and other local handiwork in its gift shop. **Treasures** sells a wide variety of local art and southern gifts. It's also a great place to buy jewelry.

Ask around. Many local artists sell their work privately. Inquire at your hotel or at the Keewatin Regional Visitors Centre for information on how to contact them.

Events

Like residents of other Nunavut communities, the people of Rankin love square dancing. Holidays and community celebrations are basically an excuse to hold a square dance. The Kivalliq style of dancing slightly resembles the Scottish variety, with movements that are very fast and tricky. From the vantage point of a spectator seated along the walls of a community hall, the dances appear impossible to learn. Have courage, though. Newcomers will find that Rankin residents are always willing to indoctrinate a first-timer. Just remember to bounce up and down a lot and keep your elbows out; the other dancers will hurl you in the right direction!

All Christian holidays, such as Christmas and Easter, as well as Canada Day, are celebrated in grand style. For several days, everyone joins in square dances, games for adults and children, dogteam and snowmobile races, Inuit games and hockey games. If you haven't seen a snowmobile race where drivers tow someone sitting on a plastic jerry can, you haven't lived a full life!

Each May, the community celebrates Pakallak Time. This festival offers many of the same activities as other holidays, but with something extra. After a long winter, it's a joyous celebration of the warmth and sunlight of spring. Pakallak Time is a great way to meet people from Rankin, as well as those who come from other communities to join in the fun.

Rankin Inlet is also home to a healthy and competitive population of dogsled mushers. For a real Nunavut experience, take a trip from Rankin by dogteam in winter or spring. Some enterprising mushers have organized tours ranging from half an hour to a day or longer. Ask the staff at your hotel or contact the Aqiggiak Hunters and Trappers Organization for more information. Remember to ask as well about the many exciting dogteam races held in and around Rankin.

At the community hall, located in the Singiittuq Complex, flea markets, craft sales and games are occasionally held. For details, ask local residents, call the hamlet recreation co-ordinator, or watch the community announcement channel on Cable 15. Actually, watching this station is entertainment in itself, as the Kissarvik Co-op, which operates the channel, is always on the lookout for new and improved ways to misspell the English language.

Accommodation and Dining

Of the two hotels in Rankin, the 45-room **Siniktarvik Hotel** is *the* business facility in town. The hotel, which can accommodate 94, provides rooms and services similar to those found at medium-priced southern establishments, including conference facilities for 120 people, and catering services. All rooms have private washrooms, phones and TVs. During conferences, the hotel may be particularly busy; guests can also expect parties and dances at the hotel. Rooms are $165 per person per day for single occupancy and $100 per person for double. The restaurant features an à la carte menu and serves both hotel guests and the public. At 8 p.m., the restaurant closes, and a licensed bar area opens at 9 p.m. for hotel guests only.

The **Nanuq Inn** offers less luxurious, though comfortable, lodging. It has nine rooms, each with a private washroom and TV. Rooms are $125 per person per day for single occupancy and $95 per person for double. The restaurant has an extensive à la carte menu and a partitioned non-smoking area. It is licensed for hotel guests. The inn has conference and banquet facilities and holds community dances occasionally.

Visitors to Rankin Inlet can also snack at two other spots in town. The **Quick Stop**, located in the Northern store, sells Kentucky Fried Chicken, Subway, and Pizza Hut fast foods. **Coffee Delights**, a smoke-free venue, offers desserts plus a wide variety of gourmet coffees.

And on the subject of snacks: how about caribou processed into sausage or pastrami, or smoked char or char jerky? These and other delicacies, processed at the local Keewatin Meat and Fish plant, are available at the **Northern store** and the **Kissarvik Co-op**.

Services

Several airlines serve Rankin Inlet. Travellers on a budget should compare different access routes and their fares; the roundabout Toronto-Edmonton-Yellowknife-Rankin Inlet trip on Canadian or Air Canada/First Air can prove cheaper than the Toronto-Ottawa-Iqaluit-Rankin Inlet route via Air Canada/First Air.

The **John Ayaruaq Library**, open to the public, has a fairly good selection of books on the history of the region and of the North in general. Call for library hours.

Located next to the Nanuq Inn, the Youth and Elders Centre is a popular meeting place for the young and old in Rankin. Although the Centre's hours are sporadic, it's well worthwhile to check out the activities offered here.

If you need a regular fix of time on the Internet, the **Rankin Inlet Community Access Centre** is for you. Located in the **Leo Ussak Elementary School**, the facility provides free access to the Internet. As the Centre has limited hours, call ahead for information.

Rankin Inlet has a fairly good transportation system. The four taxi companies — **Airut Taxi**, **Ernie's Taxi**, **Jay's Taxi**, and **M & M Taxi** — charge $4 for trips in town and $5 for trips to or from the airport. Taxis usually take less than two minutes to appear at your door; sometimes before south-bound flights, however, the wait is a little longer. Be ready to hop in the van once you hang up the phone. But if you're headed for the **airport**, don't be surprised if it takes up to 10 minutes for the cab to arrive.

If you'd enjoy the freedom of your own vehicle while in town, you can rent a truck from **Y&C Enterprises**, or ask Nunavut Tourism about where to rent an ATV, snowmobile or sea-doo.

The Bombardier is another interesting form of transportation available in Rankin Inlet. This is an overgrown, enclosed snowmobile that runs on tracks and skis. In winter and spring, there are regularly scheduled trips from Rankin Inlet to Arviat and other communities. To experience this new form of travel, call **Kowmuk's**.

DIRECTORY

*Outfitters and tour operators licensed at time of writing.
After March 31/99, check for updated status.

Accommodation and Dining

Coffee Delights
Summer hours: noon–10 p.m.,
Monday to Saturday. Closed Sunday.
Fall: evenings only. Winter: closed.
Tel.: (867) 645-2582

Nanuq Inn
VISA, Diners Club/enRoute.
Tel.: (867) 645-2513
Fax: (867) 645-2393

Quick Stop
VISA, MasterCard, Interac.
10 a.m.–7 p.m., Monday to Wednesday;
10 a.m.–9 p.m., Thursday to Saturday;
1–5 p.m., Sunday.
Tel.: (867) 645-2055

Siniktarvik Hotel
VISA, MasterCard, American Express,
Diners Club/enRoute, Interac.
Tel.: (867) 645-2949
Fax: (867) 645-2999
E-mail: sinik@arctic.ca

*Outfitters/Tour Operators/Visitors Centre

Aqiggiak Hunters and Trappers Organization
Tel.: (867) 645-2350
Fax: (867) 645-2867

Kivalliq Tours
Tel.: (867) 645-2731
Fax: (867) 645-2362

Nunavut Tourism
Located at the airport. Operates the **Keewatin Regional Visitors Centre**.
Tel.: (867) 645-3838
Fax: (867) 645-3904
E-mail: silatour@arctic.ca

Sila Lodge
Frontiers North
173 Ragsdill Rd., Winnipeg MB,
R2G 4C6 Canada
Tel.: (204) 949-2050 or 1-800-663-9832
Fax: (204) 663-6375
E-mail: fn@silalodge.com

Tumi Tours — Dogsledding Adventures
Tel.: (867) 645-2650
Fax: (867) 645-2640
E-mail: sleddog@arctic.ca

Services

Airport
Tel.: (867) 645-3048 (Calm Air)
Tel.: (867) 645-3200 (Skyward Aviation)
Tel.: (867) 645-2961 (First Air)

Banks

CIBC
10 a.m.–3 p.m., Monday to Thursday;
10 a.m.–5 p.m., Friday. Closed weekends.
ATM open 8:30 a.m.–6 p.m., Monday to
Thursday; 8:30 a.m.–8:30 p.m., Friday;
10 a.m.–6 p.m., Saturday.
Tel.: (867) 645-2863
Fax: (867) 645-2573

Royal Bank
10 a.m.–4 p.m., Monday to Thursday;
10 a.m.–5 p.m., Friday. Closed weekends.
ATM always open.
Tel.: (867) 645-3260
Fax: (867) 645-3261

CBC Radio Station (FM 105.1)
Tel.: (867) 645-2244
Fax: (867) 645-2820

Churches

Catholic Church
Services: 11 a.m., Sunday (in Inuktitut
and English). 5:30 p.m. mass from
Monday to Saturday.
Tel.: (867) 645-2824

Glad Tidings Fellowship
Services: 11 a.m. and 7 p.m., Sunday;
7:30 p.m., Wednesday.
Tel.: (867) 645-2018

Holy Comforter Anglican Church
Services: 11 a.m. (in Inuktitut and
English) and 7 p.m. (in Inuktitut),
Sunday.
Tel.: (867) 645-2657
Fax: (867) 645-3240
E-mail: pwilliam@arctic.ca

Dental Clinic
Tel.: (867) 645-2776
Fax: (867) 645-2750

Department of Sustainable Development, Government of Nunavut
(or until April/99, GNWT's **Resources, Wildlife and Economic Development**)
Tel.: (867) 645-5037
Fax: (867) 645-2007

Hamlet Office
Tel.: (867) 645-2895
Fax: (867) 645-2146
E-mail: munri@arctic.ca

Health Centre
Tel.: (867) 645-2816
Fax: (867) 645-2688

Inuit Cultural Institute
Tel.: (867) 645-3010
Fax: (867) 645-3020

John Ayaruaq Library
Located in the Maani Ulujuk
Ilinniavik School.
Tel.: (867) 645-5034
Fax: (867) 645-2889

Police (RCMP)
Tel.: (867) 645-2822
Fax: (867) 645-2568

Post Office
Scheduled to move to new location across from mall housing Sakku Drugs in 1999.
10 a.m.–5 p.m., Monday to Friday.
Tel.: (867) 645-2680

Rankin Inlet Community Access Centre
Located in the Leo Ussak Elementary School.
Tel.: (867) 645-2814
Web site: www.arctic.ca/LUS/CAC.html

Schools
Leo Ussak Elementary School
Tel.: (867) 645-2814
Fax: (867) 645-2333
E-mail: ussak@arctic.ca
Web site: www.arctic.ca/LUS

Maani Ulujuk Ilinniavik School
Grades 5 and up. Grade 9–12 students will move to the new Simon Aliattuq Ford School when it opens in 1999.
Tel.: (867) 645-2761
Fax: (867) 645-2209

Nunavut Arctic College
Tel.: (867) 645-2529
Fax: (867) 645-2387

Taxis
Airut Taxi
Tel.: (867) 645-2411

Ernie's Taxi
Tel.: (867) 645-3668

Jay's Taxi
Tel.: (867) 645-2420
Fax: (867) 645-2644

Kowmuk's Taxi
Tel.: (867) 645-3034
Fax: (867) 645-2478

M & M Taxi
Tel.: (867) 645-2892

Weather Information
Tel.: (867) 645-2672
Fax: (867) 645-2859
Web site weather forecast:
www.tor.ec.gc.ca/forecasts/index.html
(check under Regional Weather Summaries) or www.infonorth.org

Y&C Enterprises
Tel.: (867) 645-3754

Shopping
Ivalu
9 a.m.–5 p.m., Monday to Friday.
Closed weekends.
VISA accepted.
Tel.: (867) 645-3400
Fax: (867) 645-2115
Web site: www.arctic-can.nt.ca/ivalu/
index.html

Kissarvik Co-op
9:30 a.m.–6 p.m., Monday to Thursday and Saturday. 9:30 a.m.–8 p.m., Friday. Closed Sunday.
VISA, MasterCard, Interac.
Tel.: (867) 645-2801

Matchbox Gallery
10 a.m.–12 p.m., 1–4 p.m., Monday to Saturday, or call for an appointment.
VISA, MasterCard.
Tel.: (867) 645-2674
Fax: (867) 645-2674

Northern Store
10 a.m.–6 p.m., Monday to Wednesday; 10 a.m.–7 p.m., Thursday; 10 a.m.–8 p.m., Friday; 10 a.m.–6 p.m., Saturday. Closed Sunday.
VISA, MasterCard, Interac.
Tel.: (867) 645-2823
Fax: (867) 645-2082

Sakku Drugs
10 a.m.–6 p.m., Monday to Saturday. Closed Sunday.
VISA, MasterCard, Interac.
Tel.: (867) 645-2811
Fax: (867) 645-2860

Treasures
At airport.
9 a.m.–6 p.m., Monday to Friday.
Closed weekends.
VISA, MasterCard, Interac.
Tel.: (867) 645-3373
Fax: (867) 645-3374

60. IJIRALIQ (MELIADINE) RIVER TERRITORIAL HISTORIC PARK

by Karen LeGresley Hamre

Just inland from the west coast of Hudson Bay, about 10 kilometres northwest of Rankin Inlet, lies the beautiful Ijiraliq (Meliadine) River Territorial Historic Park, straddling the Meliadine River in the Meliadine River Valley.

In summer, visitors and residents of Rankin Inlet come to enjoy the park's magnificent scenery, pristine waters, good fishing and abundant wildlife — including the endangered peregrine falcon. The park's most outstanding features, however, are its many excellent archeological sites.

The Land and Wildlife

The park's geology is noteworthy. On the south side of the Meliadine River stands a massive esker — a sand and gravel ridge that forms a spine along the park. The main road and trails run along the top of it, providing spectacular views of the Meliadine Valley and beyond. Because the tundra at the esker is covered by lichen-moss, which is highly sensitive to disturbance, visitors should walk on the roads and paths wherever possible. Most of the park is covered by a variety of glacial deposits. A bedrock outcrop that rises about 47 metres above sea level is the park's highest point.

At least 24 unusual species of plants may be found in the park, including the rare three-awned grass (*Trisetum triflorum*), which grows only in the rich soil at the Thule ruins. It is unknown elsewhere in the Kivalliq.

The best time to visit the park is during July and early August. Even then, the weather can be variable. Generally, summers here begin in June and last until September. Some years, however, the weather is cool and rather nasty throughout. So come prepared for sudden climate changes. When you walk through the lovely Meliadine Valley on a warm, sunny day, however, you may easily forget other dismal times.

What to See and Do

The main attractions and facilities here lie on the south side of the Meliadine River, along a one-kilometre-wide by five-kilometre-long strip. The road from Rankin Inlet branches off towards the river and leads to the park's major archeological site, Ijiraliq. A small path leads through the primary archeological features, some of which are marked by interpretive signs. The main road then winds its way up to a small, shallow lake called Sandy Lake, perched above the river. Most summers, the lake is warm enough to provide delightful swimming. Nearby, you can have a picnic and camp. Fishing is popular in the river. A bit further on, an elders' cabin can be reserved for community events. (Elders usually hold meetings out on the land.) The road ends at the cabin, but a trail, passable by all-terrain vehicle or on foot, continues upstream.

The history of land use by earlier inhabitants here spans some three millennia. The park has more than 45 archeological sites, some dating as far back as the Pre-Dorset period from 1000 BC to 500 BC. Although many features aren't yet dated, most appear to be of the Thule period, between 1300 and 1600. Archeological evidence indicates that ancient peoples used the lands for fishing and hunting caribou in summer and fall.

Of all the old sites, Ijiraliq, situated on a small esker off the main road, is the most striking. (Like other ruins in the park, Ijiraliq derives its name from an Inuit legend. *Ijiralik*, as the park's name is properly spelled in Inuktitut, one who turns into a caribou, or other spirit, that whistles.)

During Thule times, when sea levels rose as a result of glacial melting, the site lay closer to the shores of Hudson Bay than it does today. Referred to as simply "KfJm.3" by archeologists, Ijiraliq boasts many intriguing artifacts dating from the 1400s to modern times. In an area of about 100 metres by 150 metres, you'll find tent rings, caches, ingenious fox traps, graves, semi-subterranean houses, *inuksuit*, kayak stands and curious little structures believed to be puppy houses.

As the sites are precious historical records in stone and are protected under government legislation, visitors must not disturb them.

Planning a Trip

The hike to Ijiraliq (Meliadine) River Territorial Historic Park is a long, though not uncomfortable, trek of about 10 kilometres. To reach the elders' cabin, you'll have to go another four kilometres. Fortunately, though, the road along the top of the esker is well drained, allowing for easy walking. And the breeze at this height keeps the hordes of mosquitoes at bay.

Kivalliq Tours, and Caroline Anawak in particular, are the licensed guides to the park. Anawak knows the archeological sites and other attractions intimately. If you want to join Kivalliq Tours for a half-day or day-long tour, you'll need to travel in a group. Outfitters find that it's not worth the wear and tear on their vehicle from the bumpy road to take out only one or two visitors at a time. Check with Kivalliq Tours; they might put you in touch with other visitors wishing to tour the park.

You can also take a taxi to the park and around the sites, and arrange to be picked up later. But it will cost you a hefty $100 to get out to Meliadine. If you prefer to drive yourself, you may be able to rent a truck or four-wheel all-terrain vehicle. Check with **Nunavut Tourism** to see what companies have rentals. Please remember, though, that driving off-road here is not permitted. Although the hamlet continues to extend and improve the road down to the river valley, road conditions to and within the park can vary in their state of repair.

Crossing from the south to the north side of the Meliadine River is no easy feat. If you don't mind getting cold and wet, you can wade across in some locations, depending on water levels. To date, there are no plans to build a road or trails across the river. Most visitors prefer to leave the north side of the river to the plants and wildlife, and to enjoy the view from the south.

You need to be self-sufficient for camping here. In addition to your shelter, food and warm clothing, you'll need to bring everything necessary to ensure your health and hygiene. There are tent pads at Sandy Lake, with picnic tables and an outhouse. The pads are available on a "first come, first served" basis, and don't require a permit. It's best to bring a large water container. The river, the source of fresh water, is about 200 metres away, a bit far if you're walking at midnight!

You can get away from the bugs and wind temporarily at the elders' cabin, but it's not really intended for overnight use. You may camp at other locations, but not at archeological sites or in private cabins within the park boundaries. Even though permits aren't required, **the hamlet** likes to be informed if you plan to camp.

Remember that there are no emergency services or park wardens to check on you. Have plenty of bug juice on hand and come equipped with a bug jacket/hat. That way, when the wind dies, you'll be protected. Generally, the Kivalliq is notoriously windy. But the rare summer evenings when the wind is still can be exceedingly unpleasant, unless you've come to study biting insects. Be prepared for all sorts of weather: rain, sun and cool temperatures. Bring waterproof clothing, a warm hat and one to keep off the·sun, sturdy waterproof hiking boots, and sunglasses and sunscreen for those long hours of sunlight.

DIRECTORY

Hamlet of Rankin Inlet
Tel.: (867) 645-2895
Fax: (867) 645-2146
E-mail: munri@arctic.ca

Kivalliq Tours
Tel.: (867) 645-2731
Fax: (867) 645-2362

Nunavut Tourism
Rankin Inlet office:
Tel.: (867) 645-3838
Fax: (867) 645-3904
E-mail: silatour@arctic.ca

61. ARVIAT
by Shirley Tagalik

For centuries, Arviat (pronounced "arq-viat") has been a site that welcomed visitors to her sandy shores. Much of what makes Arviat an interesting place to visit today is rooted in this history.

Population:	1,559 (Inuit: 94%, non-Inuit: 6%) Source: 1996 Census of Canada
Telephone Area Code:	867
Time Zone:	Central Time
Postal Code:	X0C 0E0
How to Get There:	Possible routes:
	• Winnipeg-Arviat
	• Edmonton-Yellowknife-Rankin Inlet-Arviat
	• Ottawa/Montreal-Iqaluit-Rankin Inlet-Arviat
	• Kangerlussuaq (Greenland)-Iqaluit-Rankin Inlet-Arviat
	Winnipeg to Arviat (1,300 kilometres north) is via Calm Air.
	Rankin Inlet to Arviat (200 kilometres south) is via Calm Air or Skyward Aviation
Banks:	None. Cash and traveller's cheques are preferable. Credit cards are accepted by certain businesses
Alcohol:	Alcohol and alcoholic beverages are prohibited. If you plan to carry alcohol from Arviat to nearby destinations, contact the RCMP
Taxis:	Yes

The industrious *Paallirmiut* were the original residents of this coastal area of western Hudson Bay. A self-sufficient group of Inuit, they were able to sustain large camps. They were joined by the traditionally isolated *Ahiarmiut* — inland Inuit who knew only caribou — and by sophisticated ex-whalers from the Repulse Bay and Coral Harbour areas. The way these groups hunt, raise children, speak, build *igluit*, make tools and sew clothes, all differs. Each group has struggled to keep its own identity while uniting to build a community that can creatively address social problems: 80 per cent unemployment and a high birthrate that sees 60 children born yearly.

Today, the community is recognized as being particularly rich in traditional knowledge and values, where Inuktitut is spoken widely and valued highly, and where hunting traditions are maintained.

History
Still identified on many maps by its former name, Eskimo Point, Arviat comes from the Inuktitut name for bowhead whale, *arviq*.

Thule culture sites here date back to AD 1100. Many ancient *qajaq* stands found at traditional summer camp sites are evidence that hundreds of Inuit gathered in this area. Summer brought *Paallirmiut* families together to hunt whales, seals, and walrus for meat and oil. Two of these sites, Arvia'juaq (an island shaped like a big bowhead) and Qikiqtaarjuk (little island), were designated National Historic Sites in 1995.

When the Hudson's Bay Co. established a post here in 1921, camp sites were moved into the vicinity as trapping became increasingly profitable. Arctic fox were plentiful and the harsh Keewatin (now called Kivalliq) climate ensured thick, full coats. A visit to *Nuvuk*, the site of the old post, will introduce visitors to one of the last York boats to ply the waters of Hudson Bay. It carried supplies in trade for furs.

The early history of the Roman Catholic mission, established in 1924, can be viewed through exhibits at the **Mikilaaq Centre**, a diocese-operated community centre located in the original **Roman Catholic church**. The **Anglican mission**, founded in 1926, brought missionaries Donald and Winifred Marsh of England to the Arctic. Their books, including *Echoes from a Frozen Land* (Edmonton: Hurtig, 1987), paint a colorful picture of the area in the early days.

At the same time that caribou migration patterns changed, demand for furs dwindled, creating hardship for many groups of Inuit. Among the hardest hit were the *Ahiarmiut*, described in Canadian author Farley Mowat's books, *People of the Deer* and *The Desperate People*. Eventually, the Canadian government relocated them to Arviat. The community's Federal Day School opened in 1959, marking the beginning of permanent settlement.

Arviat: Its Land and Wildlife

Dotted with shallow lakes, this land, rich in flora and fauna, is glacial terrain consisting of sandy low marsh, muskeg, and long tidal flats. Between June and August, the area attracts thousands of nesting migratory birds. The McConnell River Migratory Bird Sanctuary, south of the community, is a good spot to view nesting pairs of geese, sandhill cranes, swans, ducks and loons. Nesting sites attract snowy owls, peregrine falcons and gyrfalcons. At the tidal flats, swarms of sandpipers, plovers, phalaropes, arctic terns, gulls and jaegers can also be found, fiercely protecting their nests. A short walk from town will introduce you to this rich feathered world. In August and September, snow geese are especially accommodating, when parents march their gaggles right into town, taking over any grassy spots left to nibble. Pods of belugas can be seen in the bays. Many Inuit hunt whales at this time and trips can always be arranged.

Trips up rivers near the community take you to great fishing grounds where you'll also see migrating caribou. Caribou hide is still widely used for winter clothing, and families camp at caribou grounds at this time of year.

Tours

Late October and early November are the months to view the polar bear migration. On a trip by dogteam or snowmobile, you'll see bears hunting seals along the edge of the newly forming ice. Like the geese, bears also tend to check out the dump for fast food. Sport hunts can be arranged through **Arviat Tundra Adventures**.

Lake trout, arctic grayling, white fish and cod are available throughout the year; the arctic char runs in June and September/October are special events. Outfitters such as **Arctic Skies Outpost Camps** can take you on a seven-day package tour to the best fishing grounds. Small planes and helicopters are available for charter in summer and fall by contacting **Helimax Nunavut**.

Nuyaituq Outpost Camp offers a five-day package that includes tours on land and sea. In spring 1999, it plans to open a fishing camp 64 kilometres north of Arviat. Tours with other outfitters can be arranged through the Arviat Tourism Office or Arviat Tundra Adventures.

The **Margaret Aniksak Visitors Centre** is open from mid-June to early September. Exhibits include an interesting interpretive display of traditional Inuit life and artifacts collected from the Arvia'juaq archeological site. Information on guided tours to national historical sites can also be obtained at the **Parks Canada** web site and by contacting the **Arviat Historical Society**.

Hiking trails and about 20 kilometres of gravel roads outside town allow you to explore the area on your own. A one-kilometre road leads to Eskimo Point; a two-kilometre road follows the coast heading south; a third heads north for 17 kilometres towards Maguse River. You'll find picnic tables along the roads and, at the end of them, many trails suitable for all-terrain vehicles.

The **Sivulinut Elders Society** sponsors cultural programs, drum dances and interpretive events, held in their own homes. Sometimes the elders set up "open house" in a caribou tent and dress in beaded *amautit* (women's parkas) and other traditional clothes. Here they teach string games and throat singing, and hold cookouts of caribou heads, hoofs, and other delicacies. The **Arviat Tourism Office** will arrange for you to attend an open house.

From February to March, elders organize the **Classroom in the *Iglu*** through the **Levi Angmak Iliniavialaaq Elementary School**. Through stories and traditional activities, they show what life was like in a traditional camp. Elders take turns staying in a multi-chambered *iglu* and visitors often ask to stay the night! A traditional fall camp was added to the September program. Contact principal Elisapee Karetak for details.

Shopping

Since contact with newcomers began in the 1920s, Arviat's artistic community has thrived. The missionary Winifred Marsh, a talented painter, captured the wonderful beaded *amautit* in her book, *People of the Willow*. Today, fashion designers and artists specializing in wall hangings use this intricate beadwork. Typically, Arviat wall hangings show caribou skin figures with faces carved from bone or antler. Dolls with soapstone or dried sealskin faces, made by artists Martina Anoee and Alice Akkamuk, are also treasured. (They sell work from their homes.) The Arviat Tourism Office will direct you to any artisan you'd like to meet. You'll also want to visit the **Kiluk Sewing Centre**, which produces a variety of machine-made articles.

The Arviat style of carving — often described as minimalist — was introduced to the world by Canadian author and academic George Swinton at the Osaka Expo in the 1960s. The show propelled carvers such as Elizabeth Nuturaluk, Tasseor Tuksweetuk, John Pungnark and Miki to world fame. Today, a new generation of carvers explores art in exciting, innovative ways, as you'll see if you visit the **Ulimaut Carving Shop** next door to the **Qitiqliq high school**. Here you can watch young carvers at work and inquire about other members of the carvers' society.

At **Nunavut Arctic College**, a fascinating trend in jewelry-making is taking root. Using metal, stone, ivory and bone, artisans are producing beautiful pins, pendants, earrings and bracelets.

Traditionally, people made clothing for hunting and arctic living. Today, some Arviat designers are adapting traditional styles to create modern fashions. Among them are Charlotte St. John (contact her through Eskimo Point Lumber Supply) and Jackie King (contact **Jackie's Sewing Centre**). Their clothes are sold privately and are usually custom-made. The Arviat Tourism Office can also direct you to clothing designers and artisans specializing in miniature artifacts, paintings, prints, weaving and pottery.

Some local artwork, dry goods, and produce are sold through the **Padlei Co-op** and the **Northern store**. Hardware, materials and groceries can be found at **Eskimo Point Lumber Supply**.

Accommodation and Dining

Padlei Inns North has 23 beds in 13 rooms, each with a private bathroom and TV. A lounge with a telephone adjoins the dining room, where full-course meals are served. Prices are $175 per person per night with meals or $125 per person per night without meals. Visitors not staying at the hotel can eat in the hotel's dining room or order take-out from the kitchen.

Ralph's Bed and Breakfast is a nine-bed, six-room "bed and breakfast/lunch/dinner" ($175 per person per night) or bed and breakfast ($125 per person per night). Group rates are available. This homey two-storey house has shared bathrooms on each floor, a TV in every room and a lounge. Like Padlei Inns North, it's lived-in but in good condition.

At the time of writing, another bed and breakfast, **Jeannie's Place**, was scheduled to open. Housed in an addition to **Jeannie's Bakery**, it would accommodate five people in four rooms at a rate of $150 per person per day with meals. The lounge has cable TV. Guests would eat in the bakery.

The **Arviat Meat and Fish Processing Plant** produces excellent "country food" such as smoked and dried fish products, caribou sausage and jerky. Tours of the plant can be arranged.

Sweets, baked goods and fast food are available from **Neevee's Coffee Shop**, Jeannie's Bakery, **Ralph's Arcade**, the Mikilaaq Centre and **Cecilia Karlak Confectionery** (temporarily closed but re-opening in the spring of 1999).

Events

Arviat has a strong musical tradition, boasting such renowned Inuit performers as Charlie Panigoniak and Susan Aglukark. Labor Day weekend combines the Inuumariit Music Festival, a weekend of wonderful music and dancing, with the Hamlet Day celebrations. The Nunavut Dogteam Derby is usually held in March. Exciting snowmobile races take place in early May, and the fishing derby drops anchor during the long weekend in May.

Services

Arviat's **Health Centre** has a walk-in clinic from 9 a.m. to 11:30 a.m. weekdays. From 1 to 5 p.m., the clinic's public health programs are by appointment only. A nurse is always on call for emergencies. The community has an **RCMP** detachment. The **Donald Suluk Library** has a selection of northern books and houses the Iyi Society Access Centre, where residents and visitors can access the Internet.

DIRECTORY

*Outfitters and tour operators licensed at time of writing.
After March 31/99, check for updated status.

Accommodation and Dining

Jeannie's Bakery
7 a.m.–7 p.m., Monday to Saturday;
8 a.m.–7 p.m., Sunday.
Tel.: (867) 857-2720 or (867) 857-2906
Fax: (867) 857-2901

Jeannie's Place
VISA, American Express, Interac.
Tel.: (867) 857-2906
Fax: (867) 857-2901

Neevee's Coffee Shop
Afternoons and evenings only.
Tel.: (867) 857-2999
Fax: (867) 857-2963

Padlei Inns North
VISA, Diners Club/enRoute, Interac.
Tel.: (867) 857-2919
Fax: (867) 857-2762

Ralph's Bed and Breakfast
These are also contact numbers for
Ralph's Arcade and **Jackie's Sewing Centre**. Cash, traveller's cheques, billing for later payment.
Tel.: (867) 857-2653
Fax: (867) 857-2623

*Outfitters/Tour Operators/Visitors Centre

Arctic Skies Outpost Camps
For sport fishing.
Contact Shawn Maley.
Box 588, Rankin Inlet NT,
X0C 0G0 Canada
Tel.: (867) 645-3789
E-mail: tidjii@arctic.ca

Arviat Cultural Tours
For visits with carvers, drum dances, etc.
Tel.: (867) 857-2941
Fax: (867) 857-2499

Arviat Meat and Fish Processing Plant
For tours of the plant.
9 a.m.–5 p.m., Monday to Friday.
Closed weekends.
Tel.: (867) 857-2381

Arviat Tourism Office
c/o Economic Development Office.
Tel.: (867) 857-2941
Fax: (867) 857-2499

Arviat Tundra Adventures
Contact Angeline Suluk.
Tel.: (867) 857-2636
Fax: (867) 857-2488

Classroom in the Iglu/Classroom at the Fall Camp
Ask for elementary school principal
Elisapee Karetak.
Tel.: (867) 857-2547
Fax: (867) 857-2656

Margaret Aniksak Visitors Centre
Call hamlet office.
Tel.: (867) 857-2841
Fax: (867) 857-2519

Nuyaituq Outpost Camp
Contact Airo Pameolik.
Tel.: (867) 857-2819

Services

Airport
Tel.: (867) 857-2997 (Calm Air)
Tel.: (867) 857-2424 (Skyward Aviation)

Angukkait Snowmobile Rentals
Contact Job Mukjungnik.
Tel.: (867) 857-2941
Fax: (867) 857-2499

Arviat Historical Society
Contact David Ukutak.
Tel.: (867) 857-2806
Fax: (867) 857-2806

Arviat Truck Rental and General Contracting
Tel.: (867) 857-2187
Fax: (867) 857-2446

Churches

Alliance Church
Services: 11 a.m. and 7 p.m., Sunday.
Tel.: (867) 857-2950
Fax: (867) 857-2608

Anglican Mission
Services: 11 a.m. and 7 p.m., Sunday;
7 p.m., Monday and Wednesday.
Tel.: (867) 857-2948
Fax: (867) 857-2252

Roman Catholic Church
Services: 11 a.m., Sunday; 7 p.m.,
Wednesday.
Tel.: (867) 857-2840

Department of Sustainable Development, Government of Nunavut
(or until April/99, GNWT's Resources,
Wildlife and Economic Development)
Tel.: (867) 857-2941
Fax: (867) 857-2499

Hamlet Office
Tel.: (867) 857-2841
Fax: (867) 857-2519

Health Centre
Tel.: (867) 857-2816
Fax: (867) 857-2980

Helimax Nunavut
Tel.: (867) 857-2374
Fax: (867) 857-2508

Hunters and Trappers Organization
Tel.: (867) 857-2636
Fax: (867) 857-2488

Library
Tel.: (867) 857-2579

Mikilaaq Centre
Tel.: (867) 857-2521
Fax: (867) 857-2531

Parks Canada
Web site: www.parkscanada.pch.gc.ca

Police (RCMP)
Tel.: (867) 857-2822
Fax: (867) 857-2691

Post Office
Located in the centre of Arviat.
8:30 a.m.–12 p.m., 1–5:30 p.m.
weekdays.
Tel.: (867) 857-2859

Radio Station (FM 105.1)
Tel.: (867) 857-2939 or (867) 857-2810

Schools

Levi Angmak Iliniavialaaq Elementary School
Tel.: (867) 857-2547
Fax: (867) 857-2656

Nunavut Arctic College
Tel.: (867) 857-2903
Fax: (867) 857-2928

Qitiqliq Secondary School
Tel.: (867) 857-2778
Fax: (867) 857-2669

Sivulinut Elders Society
Tel.: (867) 857-2941
Fax: (867) 857-2499

Taxis

Bill's Taxi
Tel.: (867) 857-2906

Paul's Taxi and Van Rentals
Tel.: (867) 857-2677

Ralph's Taxi
Tel.: (867) 857-2020

Weather Information
Tel.: (867) 857-2802
Web site weather forecast:
www.infonorth.org

Shopping

Eskimo Point Lumber Supply
VISA, Interac.
9 a.m.–5:30 p.m., Monday to Friday;
1–5 p.m., Saturday. Closed Sunday.
Tel.: (867) 857-2752
Fax: (867) 857-2883

Cecilia Karlak Confectionery
Re-opening in spring, 1999.
Tel.: (867) 857-2586

Kiluk Sewing Centre
8:30 a.m.–5 p.m., Monday to Friday.
VISA, cheques.
Tel.: (867) 857-2713
Fax: (867) 857-2714
E-mail: kiluk@net.com

Northern Store
10 a.m.–6 p.m., Monday to Thursday;
10 a.m.–8 p.m., Friday; 10 a.m.–6 p.m.,
Saturday. Closed Sunday.
VISA, MasterCard, Interac.
Tel.: (867) 857-2826
Fax: (867) 857-2925

Padlei Co-op
May 1 to Aug. 31: 9 a.m.–10 p.m.,
Monday to Saturday. Closed Sunday.

From Sept. 1 to April 30:
10 a.m.–10 p.m., Monday to
Saturday. Closed Sunday.
VISA, Diners Club/enRoute, Interac.
Tel.: (867) 857-2933
Fax: (867) 857-2762

Ulimaut Carving Shop
Tel.: (867) 857-2941
Fax: (867) 857-2499

62. WHALE COVE

by Ulrike Komaksiutiksak

I will always remember our arrival in Whale Cove in 1995. My daughter was four at the time and previously had lived with us in some larger communities in the Northwest Territories.

Population:	301 (Inuit: 93%, non-Inuit: 7%) Source: 1996 Census of Canada
Telephone Area Code:	867
Time Zone:	Central Time
Postal Code:	X0C 0J0
How to Get There:	Possible routes:
	• Winnipeg-Rankin Inlet-Whale Cove
	• Edmonton-Yellowknife-Rankin Inlet-Whale Cove
	• Ottawa/Montreal-Iqaluit-Rankin Inlet-Whale Cove
	• Kangerlussuaq (Greenland)-Iqaluit-Rankin Inlet-Whale Cove
	Rankin Inlet to Whale Cove (76 kilometres south) is via Calm Air or
	Skyward Aviation
Banks:	None, although there is a Royal Bank automated teller machine
	at the Co-op. Credit cards are accepted by certain businesses
Alcohol:	Alcohol and alcoholic beverages are prohibited
Taxis:	Yes

When we touched down, she looked around and saw only the landing strip, the small trailer that serves as airport terminal and some cabins in the distance. She glanced at me and asked, "Mom, are we going to live outside?"

Whale Cove's **airport** is a 15-minute drive out of town, unusually far for a small northern community. Visitors often ask why this is so. Some residents believe the rocky land was unsuitable for an airport to be built close to town. Others say it was a decision of the *kuujjangajuq* ("upside-down person"), the Inuktitut name for the settlement managers of the old days. In any case, the taxi ride into Whale Cove — or *Tikirarjuaq*, meaning "long point" — gives you an excellent view of the tundra surrounding the settlement.

The community is on the west coast of Hudson Bay, just south of Rankin Inlet. The land around Whale Cove is rugged, with rolling hills and many small, pristine lakes. During winter, nearby Wilson Bay is covered by sea ice; in summer, huge waves from the bay crash onto the rocky shoreline, creating beautiful spectacles. The town itself is nestled in a cove facing the waters of Hudson Bay.

History

In the 1600s, explorers Thomas Button and later, Luke Foxe, sailed along the coastline near Whale Cove in search of the Northwest Passage. In the 1700s, Hudson's Bay Co. men moved into the area to ply their trade with the Inuit. About an hour and a half by snowmobile from town lies the abandoned community of Tavani, a former Hudson's Bay Co. post.

Whale Cove was created during the Keewatin famine in the winter of 1957 to 1958, when many Inuit faced starvation as the caribou disappeared. Federal government officials chose this area to relocate survivors of the famine. They believed that the abundance of wildlife here would allow the Inuit to pursue their traditional lifestyle of hunting, fishing and trapping. The proximity of the site to Rankin Inlet would make it easy for government to administer the community. Both inland and coastal Inuit were brought from areas in and around Baker Lake, Arviat and Rankin Inlet.

Typical of government decision-making at that time, the site was chosen and the community planned without the input of Inuit. Little thought was given to kinship ties or the cultural skills of the Inuit. The settlement was formed of three distinctly different groups of people who spoke three different dialects. The inland Inuit had to adapt their hunting methods to coastal conditions. Later, other Inuit arrived when the nickel mine in Rankin Inlet closed in the early 1960s.

The economy of Whale Cove then was one of traditional subsistence, supplemented by some commercial resource harvesting. For a brief time, a cannery operated in the community, producing canned *maktaaq* and seal that was shipped to the South. In 1967, the Whale's Tail Monument, a project honoring Canada's centennial, was built on a hill overlooking the settlement. Still today, tourists enjoy the splendid view from here.

Whale Cove: Its Land and Wildlife

Whale Cove's people are closely connected with nature. This predominantly Inuit community still follows the rhythms of the seasons. In spring, at the end of May, it is rare for many people to remain in town. Most are off camping on the land, fishing for arctic char or lake trout at favorite spots nearby. Hunting geese and gathering eggs are other traditional springtime activities.

In late June or July, the ice in Hudson Bay breaks up, and the waters sparkle in shades of deep blue-green. Many Inuit take to their boats to catch seal and walrus. By late August, the harvest of the beluga whale begins. The *maktaaq* is a mainstay of the diet here. *Maktaaq* and arctic char may also be sold to the local fish plant. Arctic flowers bloom in profusion at this time of year, painting the tundra in vivid colors. Local residents who aren't out on the land can usually be found at Reagan's Lake or Old Water Lake, popular swimming holes just out of town.

Berry-picking is a favorite autumn activity, when *paurngait* (blackberries) and *aqpiit* (bakeapple) ripen to the delight of young and old. In October, polar bear hunting season begins, continuing until the community's quota is filled. This can be a dangerous time for the community; residents are kept on close alert in case a bear wanders through town. Fox-trapping and wolf-hunting begin now, too, continuing through the winter. Caribou is hunted year round.

Throughout the year, women sew for their families, again reflecting the community's close ties to the seasons. During autumn, they get busy sewing parkas and wind pants in preparation for winter. Throughout winter, they prepare for months of travelling in spring, making hats, *kamiit* and mittens for family members. *Amautit* are made to carry new babies, and traditional Inuit hunting clothes are sewn from hides and fur.

The variety of traditional foods reflects the abundance of wildlife here. Travellers may want to sample such delicacies as *igunaq* (in this case, aged *maktaaq*), *pipsi* (dried char), *innaluaq* (seal intestine), *nipku* (dried caribou), and *quaq* (frozen caribou).

Visitors strolling through town may notice caribou hides hanging out to dry and men working on their snowmobiles, all-terrain vehicles, or *qamutiit*. A carver or two may be busy at work. Fishermen come and go on the beaches of Kisarvik or Itivia. The Co-op is a meeting place for local people and for visitors who want to get to know residents and find out information. On the outskirts of the community you'll hear the sound of silence. Don't be surprised if a *siksik* (ground squirrel) pops up to greet you or an arctic hare darts across your path.

Tours

Although there are currently no licensed outfitters in town, both the local **Hunters and Trappers Organization** (HTO) and the Co-op are working to obtain that status. They are excellent contacts and sources of information for travellers who wish to take a tour, fish, or hunt outside the community. Visitors can enjoy day trips to good fishing spots at Long Lake, Solomon Lake, or Wilson River. All are located within an hour from the community by snowmobile. (Check with the HTO to find out the best spots for fishing, as this depends upon the season. Early fall, for example, is best for lake trout and char.) Those who want to camp for a few days may travel to Pistol Bay, White Rock, or Ferguson River. Before setting out, however, be sure to check with local people about weather conditions and the surrounding wildlife. Weather can change rapidly and without warning. And, of course, during summer, be prepared for lots of mosquitoes!

Events

Community gatherings include feasts, square dances and many indoor and outdoor games. Traditional arctic games, contests such as tea- and bannock-making, igloo-building, *inuksuk*-building, snowmobile racing and rabbit-hunting, are some of the activities visitors may enjoy. Watch for the annual fishing derby during Victoria Day weekend, plus Canada Day and Hamlet Day festivities in July. Christmas and New Year's celebrations and Easter festivities are joy-filled times, too. For more information, contact the **Hamlet of Whale Cove**'s recreation leader.

Shopping

The two places to shop in town aren't always well stocked. Travellers are wise to phone ahead to check what supplies are available in the community. The **Issatik Co-op** sells groceries, clothes, hardware, souvenirs, arts and crafts, and some sports, fishing and gaming gear. **AT&T Enterprises**, better known as "The Shop," is a convenience store carrying some groceries and dry goods. It also has video rentals.

Sewing is a source of pride and income for many residents of Whale Cove. Visitors may buy clothes and wall hangings from local seamstresses or from the Co-op.

Accommodation and Dining

The **Tavani Inns North** is operated by the Co-op. It has six rooms, with two beds per room. Each room has a TV and private bathroom. The price is $200 per night single occupancy, and $175 for double occupancy (rates include meals).

Non-guests can make arrangements for dining by contacting the Co-op manager. Check for meal prices. The hotel also has a public phone and laundry facilities.

Services

The Whale Cove **Health Centre** is open for walk-ins from 8:30 a.m. to noon, Monday to Friday. Emergencies are accepted at any time. The Centre has one nurse, who consults with doctors in Churchill or Rankin Inlet as needed.

The **post office**, located in the Issatik Co-op, is open from 1 to 5 p.m., Monday to Friday. There is no **RCMP** station in Whale Cove. Officers from Rankin Inlet are on call and visit the community monthly.

In winter, Bombardiers (large, enclosed snowmobiles) may be chartered from Rankin Inlet. **Kowmuk's Taxi** has scheduled rides to Whale Cove.

The Issatikpaluk Radio Society operates the local **radio station**. Programs with announcements and advertisements are broadcast in the morning, at noon, and in the evening.

DIRECTORY

Accommodation and Dining

Tavani Inns North
VISA, MasterCard, Diners Club/enRoute.
Tel.: (867) 896-9252
Fax: (867) 896-9087

Services

Airport
Tel.: (867) 896-9973
Fax: (867) 896-9973

Church

Whale Cove Roman Catholic Church
Services: 10:30 a.m., Sunday. Inuktitut only.
Tel.: (867) 896-9932

Department of Sustainable Development, Government of Nunavut
(or until April/99, GNWT's Resources, Wildlife and Economic Development)
Contact Rankin Inlet office.
Tel.: (867) 645-5037
Fax: (867) 645-2007

Hamlet Office
Tel.: (867) 896-9961
Fax: (867) 896-9109

Health Centre
Tel.: (867) 896-9916
Fax: (867) 896-9115

Hunters and Trappers Organization
Tel.: (867) 896-9944
Fax: (867) 896-9143

Police (RCMP)
Based in Rankin Inlet.
Tel.: (867) 645-2822
Fax: (867) 645-2568

Post Office
Located in the Issatik Co-op.
Tel.: (867) 896-9956

Radio Station (FM 106.2)
Tel.: (867) 896-9903 (off air) or
(867) 896-9930 (on air)

School

Inuglak School
Tel.: (867) 896-9300
Fax: (867) 896-9005

Taxis

Kowmuk's Taxi
Based in Rankin Inlet.
Tel.: (867) 645-3034
Fax: (867) 645-2478

Sigininq Taxi
Tel.: (867) 896-9089

Weather Information
Hamlet office.
Tel.: (867) 896-9961
Fax: (867) 896-9109
Web site weather forecast:
www.infonorth.org

Shopping

AT&T Enterprises
5:30–10 p.m., Monday to Thursday;
5:30–11 p.m., Friday; 1–11 p.m.,
Saturday; 1–6:30 p.m. and 8–11 p.m.,
Sunday. Cash only.
Tel.: (867) 896-9365
Fax: (867) 896-9358

Issatik Co-op
9 a.m.–5:30 p.m., Monday to Thursday;
9 a.m.–8 p.m., Friday. Closed on
weekends. VISA, MasterCard, Diners
Club/enRoute, Interac.
Tel.: (867) 896-9927 or (867) 896-9956
Fax: (867) 896-9087

63. CHESTERFIELD INLET
by Jennifer Bernius

About nine years ago, a huge polar bear wandered into town and ended up on the front porch of local resident Victor Sammurtok, a respected elder whose name was bestowed upon the local school.

Population:	337 (Inuit: 92%, non-Inuit: 8%)
Telephone Area Code:	867
Time Zone:	Central Time
Postal Code:	X0C 0B0
How to Get There:	Possible routes:
	• Winnipeg-Rankin Inlet-Chesterfield Inlet
	• Edmonton-Yellowknife-Rankin Inlet-Chesterfield Inlet
	• Ottawa/Montreal-Iqaluit-Rankin Inlet-Chesterfield Inlet
	• Kangerlussuaq (Greenland)-Iqaluit-Rankin Inlet-Chesterfield Inlet
	Rankin Inlet to Chesterfield Inlet (80 kilometres) is via Calm Air or Skyward Aviation
Banks:	None. Cash and traveller's cheques are preferable. Credit cards are accepted by certain businesses
Alcohol:	Alcohol may be brought into Chesterfield Inlet, governed only by the provisions of the *NWT Liquor Act*. However, there's no place to buy alcohol in the community
Taxis:	Yes

Sammurtok had only time to load his rifle and shoot the bear, right on his porch. It made for one of his shortest hunting trips ever.

Fortunately, polar bears in the community are a once in a blue moon occurrence. Chesterfield Inlet is known more for its glory days when it was a regional centre of power.

Some folks here like to remind visitors that their town is the oldest continuing community in the eastern Arctic. The old mission was built between 1911 and 1912, the first Roman Catholic building in the region. At the same time, the Hudson's Bay Co. established its first permanent post in the Arctic at Chesterfield Inlet. The venerable Hudson's Bay Co., chartered in 1670 with headquarters in London, England, is the English-speaking world's oldest incorporated joint-stock merchandising company, and is now headquartered in Winnipeg, Canada.

In 1914, the Northwest Mounted Police (now the RCMP) moved their base from Cape Fullerton to Chesterfield, setting up a station here.

Today, Chesterfield Inlet is a closely knit Inuit settlement of more than 300 people. Families are so intertwined, that just about everyone is related. There's a strong community spirit here and a comfortable blend of traditional and modern lifestyles.

You'll find many of the same modern structures in Chesterfield as in other northern settlements: houses, a nursing station, a school, a Co-op and a Northern store. But you'll also spot polar bear and caribou hides drying outside people's homes. Local women sew these into sleeping mats and make parkas from caribou calf skins that may also be drying outside. As for that pink fish drying over there — that's *pipsi* or dried arctic char. Some of the Inuit men may be working outside on snowmobiles and *qamutiit*. Out in the inlet in summer, you'll see men with nets fishing for char.

In winter, most people remain in the community. But in spring, they're off to the lakes nearby fishing for char and lake trout. In late June and July, they head to the floe edge about a half-hour away, to hunt ringed, bearded and harp seals. In October and November, they quickly fill their quota of the polar bears that roam the region — that sometimes make unwelcome appearances in the community! Throughout the year, caribou are only about an hour or so outside of town, making the men's hunting easier.

History

The Inuit name for Chesterfield Inlet is *Igluligaarjuk*, meaning "place with a few *igluit* (igloos)." For many years, the ancestors of modern Inuit, the Thule, inhabited the land around Chesterfield Inlet. These resourceful people travelled inland by dogteam in search of caribou, then returned to the inlet to hunt whales and other marine life from their skin boats. Over time, they established large settlements of sod houses in the region, one of which lies just outside Chesterfield Inlet.

In the 1700s, explorers in search of the Northwest Passage plied the waters of Chesterfield Inlet. Captains John Bean and William Christopher thought the inlet itself might be the route that would lead them to China. But though they didn't find their elusive Passage here, they did discover many whales in Hudson Bay.

From the mid-1800s to the beginning of this century, whalers visited the area regularly and often overwintered here. They counted on local Inuit to hunt caribou for them and to man their whaleboats. At Chesterfield Inlet, Inuit often gathered to trade and seek employment with the whalers.

Until the mid-1950s, the community was a major centre north of Churchill. It was the Hudson's Bay Co.'s main supply centre for other posts in the area. It was also the site of the largest RCMP barracks and the largest Roman Catholic mission in the eastern Arctic, as well as a medical and educational centre.

Yet people have predicted the death of Chesterfield Inlet. When the nickel mine opened in Rankin Inlet in 1955, many Inuit left their traditional lifestyle in Chesterfield for paid work underground. Some of those Inuit returned to the community when the mine closed in the early 1960s. Then in the early 1970s, when Rankin became prominent as a regional centre, people again feared the end of Chesterfield as residents left to seek work there. But Chesterfield Inlet lives on, a community of people committed to their settlement and to their traditions.

In 1953–1954, a residential school opened, operated on behalf of the Canadian government by the Roman Catholic Church. One purpose of the Turquetil Hall/Joseph Bernier Federal Day School was to instil in students the customs and values of the outsiders. Young children were taken from their camps and settlements by the RCMP and missionaries, and forced to attend the school, the first established in the Keewatin. Some 80 Inuit children from across the region came to spend 10 months a year at the hostel. Here they were forbidden to speak their language, Inuktitut; all their cultural and spiritual traditions were denied them. The school was taken over by the government in the mid-1960s, and remained in existence until the late 1980s, when a modern one was built.

In June 1995, an 18-month RCMP investigation concluded that there had been widespread physical and sexual abuse of students, suffered at the hands of school staff. Similar incidents were reported at other residential schools in Canada. In January 1998, the Canadian government issued a formal apology to victims of sexual and physical abuse in the residential school system, and committed $350 million to support community-based healing. A portion of those funds will permit former students of the Turquetil Hall/Joseph Bernier Federal Day School to begin the healing process, too.

Despite everything, many former students stress that the school produced the best and brightest of leaders in Nunavut. This, they say, was because there was commitment, endurance and discipline at the school.

Chesterfield Inlet: Its Land and Wildlife

Located at the mouth of Chesterfield Inlet is a picturesque setting overlooking Fish Bay, where you'll notice a few small fishing boats. (Chesterfield Inlet has a fish plant that processes arctic char for shipment to the South.) If you're in town in late August, you'll spot beluga whales cavorting right in the harbor. In the distance, you may even catch sight of an orca feeding on char in the waters of the inlet.

An easy ride by all-terrain vehicle will take you to several excellent fishing spots. For char and lake trout, local people travel to First, Second and Third lakes, all within 25 kilometres of the settlement. In the inlet near the community are islands — *Pikiulaaqtuuq*, *Nanujumaaq*, and *Qikiqtaarjuk* — where people go in June to gather eggs from geese, ducks, terns and seagulls. They also hunt geese in this area. Other notable birds found in the rugged land around the town include eider ducks, king eiders, snowy owls, gyrfalcons and, occasionally, peregrine falcons.

Tours

For a glimpse of the community's rich history, try the Chesterfield Inlet Historic Trail. This self-guided walking tour leads you through the early years of the settlement. It includes the original Hudson's Bay Co. trading post (now part of the Northern store), the oldest building in the town; the original **Roman Catholic mission**, completed in 1912; and the St. Theresa Hospital, built in 1931 by the **Grey Nuns**, who still run it as a 12-bed home for the severely handicapped. Although most of the tour is along gravel roads, sections cross rock and tundra, so be sure to wear sturdy boots. The tour takes two hours. Copies of the tour guidebook are available in the **hamlet office** in the community complex.

Just north of Chesterfield, within walking distance, lies a large Thule site believed to be about 300 years old. Here you'll see the remains of many ancient sod houses, fox traps and food caches. You'll need to go with a guide, though, as polar bears may prowl in the area. Find out more from the Hunters and Trappers Organization or hamlet office.

Another area worth visiting is the site of the first detachment of the Northwest Mounted Police, established at Cape Fullerton in 1903. The post was built to oversee the activities of American whalers. If you contact a local outfitter, they'll arrange a boat tour for you to the post — weather permitting! The boat trip takes four to six hours. Many visitors camp overnight at the area before returning to Chesterfield.

For information about these and other tours, contact Andre Tautu, **Northwind Outfitting** (for boat tours and fishing) and Peter Tautu, **Long Inlet Safari and Adventure** (for sightseeing and sport fishing). You may also contact the **Aqigiq Hunters and Trappers Organization** for information on tours. The HTO was to be licensed to offer caribou hunting tours by the autumn of 1998. Hunts would be conducted from a camp at Ranger Seal Bay, about 80 kilometres from the community.

Shopping

The **Northern store** and **Pitsiulak Co-op** sell groceries, clothes, hardware, souvenirs and crafts, as well as some sporting goods. You might want to check before you visit Chesterfield, however, to ensure that the items you need are in stock. The Co-op also sells locally crocheted hats and jewelry carved from caribou antler. **L & C Taxi** operates a confectionery store where you can buy some outdoor clothing, fabrics and snack foods.

If you'd like to take carvings home with you, the outfitters listed above can suggest local artists.

Accommodation and Dining

The **Tangmavik Hotel/Inns North**, owned by the Pitsiulak Co-op, is located in the former Joseph Bernier School building. It accommodates 20 in seven rooms; bathrooms are shared. The hotel has a TV, laundry facilities, informal dining room, small lounge, conference and banquet facilities. The price is $170 per person per night, meals included.

Services

Chesterfield Inlet's **health centre** is open for walk-ins from 8:30 to 11:45 a.m., Monday to Friday. A nurse is always on call for emergencies. An **RCMP** officer from Rankin Inlet visits Chesterfield Inlet occasionally.

DIRECTORY

*Outfitters and tour operators licensed at time of writing.
After March 31/99, check for updated status.

Accommodation and Dining

Tangmavik Hotel/Inns North
VISA, MasterCard, Diners Club/enRoute.
Tel.: (867) 898-9975 or (867) 898-9190
Fax: (867) 898-9056

* Outfitters/Tour Operators

Aqigiq Hunters and Trappers Organization
Tel.: (867) 898-9063
Fax: (867) 898-9079

Long Inlet Safari and Adventure
Tel.: (867) 898-9322
Fax: (867) 898-9153

Northwind Outfitting
Tel.: (867) 898-9931
Fax: (867) 898-9108

Services

Airport
Tel.: (867) 898-9940
Fax: (867) 898-9940

Church
Our Lady Roman Catholic Mission
Services: Sunday 10:30 a.m. (in Inuktitut);
7 p.m. when priest is in town (in English).
Tel.: (867) 898-9197 or (867) 898-9917
Fax: (867) 898-9127

Department of Sustainable Development, Government of Nunavut
(or until April/99, GNWT's Resources, Wildlife and Economic Development)
Ask for William Autut.
Tel.: (867) 898-9206
Fax: (867) 898-9108

Grey Nuns
Hospital for the handicapped.
Tel.: (867) 898-9917
Fax: (867) 898-9080

Hamlet Office
Tel.: (867) 898-9951
Fax: (867) 898-9108
Economic development officer (afternoons only).
Tel.: (867) 898-9206
Fax: (867) 898-9108

Health Centre
Tel.: (867) 898-9968
Fax: (867) 898-9122

Police (RCMP)
Occasional visits from Rankin Inlet.
Contact hamlet office for bylaw officer.
Tel.: (867) 898-9951 or (867) 898-9926

Post Office
In Co-op store.
10:30 a.m.–12 p.m. and 1–5 p.m., Monday, Wednesday, Friday; 1–5 p.m., Tuesday, Thursday.
Tel.: (867) 898-9975

Radio Station (FM 107.1)
Tel.: (867) 898-9934
Fax: (867) 898-9108

Schools
Nunavut Arctic College
Tel.: (867) 898-9048
Fax: (867) 898-9101

Victor Sammurtok School
Elementary and secondary.
Tel.: (867) 898-9913
Fax: (867) 898-9153

Taxi
L & C Taxi
Also rents vehicles.
Tel.: (867) 898-9966
Fax: (867) 898-9103

Weather Information
Tel.: (867) 898-9940
Fax: (867) 898-9940

Shopping

L & C Taxi and Store
9 a.m.–12 p.m., 1–5 p.m. and 6:30–10:30 p.m., Monday to Friday; 6:30–10:30 p.m., Saturday; and 7:30–10:30 p.m., Sunday.
Credit cards not accepted.
Tel.: (867) 898-9966
Fax: (867) 898-9103

Northern Store
10 a.m.–12 p.m. and 1–6 p.m., Monday to Friday. Closed Saturday and Sunday.
VISA, MasterCard, Interac.
Tel.: (867) 898-9920
Fax: (867) 898-9160

Pitsiulak Co-op
9:30 a.m.–12 p.m. and 1–6 p.m., Monday to Friday; 9:30 a.m.–12 p.m., Saturday.
VISA, MasterCard, Interac.
Tel.: (867) 898-9975 or (867) 898-9981
Fax: (867) 898-9056

64. BAKER LAKE

by Darren Keith

I'm on my way to Baker Lake. I know this because of my growing excitement, and because I am glued to the window of the plane searching for familiar landforms.

Population:	1,385 (Inuit: 91%, non-Inuit: 9%) Source: 1996 Census of Canada
Telephone Area Code:	867
Time Zone:	Central Time
Postal Code:	X0C 0A0
How to Get There:	Possible routes:
	• Winnipeg-Rankin Inlet-Baker Lake
	• Ottawa/Montreal-Iqaluit-Rankin Inlet-Baker Lake
	• Edmonton-Yellowknife-Rankin Inlet-Baker Lake
	• Kangerlussuaq (Greenland)-Iqaluit-Rankin Inlet-Baker Lake
	Rankin Inlet to Baker Lake (almost 300 kilometres northwest) is via Calm Air or Skyward Aviation
Banks:	None. Cash and traveller's cheques are preferable. Credit cards are accepted by certain businesses
Alcohol:	Alcohol is not restricted, governed only by the provisions of the *NWT Liquor Act*. However, alcohol cannot be purchased in Baker Lake, nor is it served at the hotels
Taxis:	Yes

The source of my excitement is the sheer vastness of the barren lands that surround me, and the opportunity to meet people who belong in that landscape. Warning. The power of this land can become a passion that will bring you back again and again.

Our flight path from Rankin Inlet has brought us over the great expanse of Baker Lake or *Qamani'tuaq*, meaning "a huge widening of a river." Out the window to the south, I can see the serpentine form of the Kazan River stretching from the horizon to its mouth at Baker Lake, where it ends its 850-kilometre journey through the heart of the barren lands. I wonder at the skill and knowledge of the Inuit whose lives have depended on the Kazan River for centuries. The abundant archeological sites along the river testify to the people's prosperity and hardship. In historic times, the river was used by explorers like Joseph Tyrrell, and the members of the Fifth Thule Expedition. Recently, the river has become one of the premier routes for experienced wilderness paddlers. The Kazan well deserves its designation as a Canadian heritage river.

As we descend into Baker Lake, I look to the northeast and see the area's other Canadian heritage river, the Thelon River, curving out of the

Half-Way hills in the distance. The Thelon River is also steeped in history. It was home to Inuit from its mouth up to the Beverly Lake area in what is now the Thelon Wildlife Sanctuary. Joseph Tyrrell also explored this river in 1893, followed by David Hanbury in 1899 and 1901 to 1902. Many other modern-day explorers paddle the river each year.

Out the other window, I can see the community of Baker Lake. The sight of the community perched on the edge of this huge lake, surrounded on all sides by hundreds of kilometres of tundra, reinforces how remote this village is at the geographical centre of Canada. Nowhere else can one have such a deep experience of the barren lands and its people. My travels on water, snow and ice with Inuit friends have given me a glimpse into their world. To them, these are not "barren" lands, but named and understood places, where they and their ancestors have struggled and flourished as an integral part of this unique landscape. Their claim to this place as their homeland has been hard-earned. Their profound sense of belonging here is evident in their faces and their easy movement through the landscape.

At the tiny Baker Lake airport, we walk from the plane into a crowd of smiling faces. A proud family has come out to greet a mother and her newborn child. An elder addresses the child as "my mother," due to its name. Although born in Southern Canada, this child's soul — in the Inuit belief system — has always lived here among them. Still bathed in the warmth of this scene, I meet an elderly friend and shake his hand. *"Tunngahugit,"* he says. Welcome to Baker Lake. I feel it, and you will, too.

History

When Captain William Christopher of the Hudson's Bay Co. sailed through Chesterfield Inlet in 1761 and gave *Qamani'tuaq* its English name, Baker Lake, the area had already been known to Inuit for centuries. In the channels of Chesterfield Inlet, today's visitor can see an abundance of *inuksuit*, tent rings and other archeological evidence of Inuit occupation.

The community of Baker Lake is very young. Until the mid-1950s, most Inuit still lived on the land in areas surrounding Baker Lake. The *Utkuhiksalingmiut* came from the Back River; the *Hanningajurmiut* from the Garry Lake area; the *Akilinirmiut* from the Thelon River area around Beverly Lake; the *Qairnirmiut* from the lower Thelon River, Baker Lake and Chesterfield Inlet; and the *Harvaqtuurmiut* from the Kazan River area. All these groups share a history of life lived almost exclusively inland. They all relied on the resources of the barren lands, mainly caribou and fish.

With the exception of the Back River, the area surrounding Baker Lake has only recently become known to European Canadians. In 1834, George Back descended the river that today bears his name. It was not until 1893 that the Thelon was descended by Joseph and James Tyrrell of the Geological Survey of Canada, via the Dubawnt River. The two brothers carried on through Baker Lake and Chesterfield Inlet and south along Hudson Bay to Churchill. James Tyrrell continued exploring the next year by descending the Kazan River to a short distance below Yathkyed Lake, and then east via the Ferguson River to Hudson Bay and Churchill.

In 1899, British explorer David Hanbury travelled by dogteam up the coast of Hudson Bay and through Chesterfield Inlet. From Chesterfield

Baker Lake Street Map

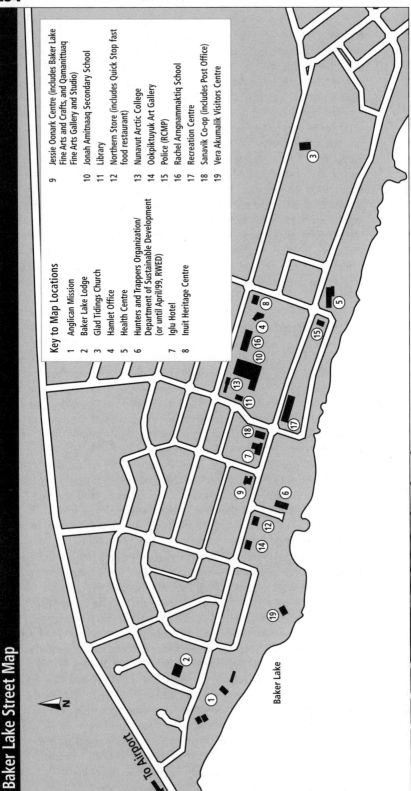

Key to Map Locations

1 Anglican Mission
2 Baker Lake Lodge
3 Glad Tidings Church
4 Hamlet Office
5 Health Centre
6 Hunters and Trappers Organization/ Department of Sustainable Development (or until April/99, RWED)
7 Iglu Hotel
8 Inuit Heritage Centre
9 Jessie Oonark Centre (includes Baker Lake Fine Arts and Crafts, and Qamanittuaq Fine Arts Gallery and Studio)
10 Jonah Amitnaaq Secondary School
11 Library
12 Northern Store (includes Quick Stop fast food restaurant)
13 Nunavut Arctic College
14 Ookpiktuyuk Art Gallery
15 Police (RCMP)
16 Rachel Arngnammaktiq School
17 Recreation Centre
18 Sanavik Co-op (includes Post Office)
19 Vera Akumalik Visitors Centre

N

To Airport

Baker Lake

Inlet, Hanbury travelled by boat through Baker Lake and up the Thelon River, gaining access to Great Slave Lake via the Hanbury River and Artillery Lake. Hanbury returned again between 1901 and 1902, spending much time in the area between Chesterfield Inlet and Beverly Lake on the Thelon River, where he befriended many Inuit.

In the spring of 1922, anthropologists Kaj Birket-Smith and Knud Rasmussen travelled up the Kazan River to Yathkyed Lake and met with *Harvaqtuurmiut* and *Paallirmiut*. Their report stands as the earliest and most descriptive study of historic Inuit life in the area.

European Canadians didn't establish a permanent presence at Baker Lake until the Hudson's Bay Co. post was built at *Uqpiktujuq*, or Big Hips Island, in 1916. Competition arrived in the form of the Revillion Frères in 1924, who set up a trading post at the mouth of the Thelon River. In 1926, the Hudson's Bay Co. also moved to the mouth of the Thelon near the present location of Baker Lake. Two men from Chesterfield Inlet, Naittuq and Singiittuq, played an important role in piloting supply ships through the narrows of Chesterfield Inlet and into Baker Lake using their knowledge of the depth changes in the inlet. After years of competition, the Hudson's Bay Co. bought out the Revillion Frères in 1936 and moved the operation into their building. The original building is now the **Vera Akumalik Visitors Centre**.

In the fall of 1927, both the Anglican and Roman Catholic missions arrived to begin the competition for the souls of the Inuit. The original **Anglican mission**, **St. Aiden's**, was built in 1930 and still stands today.

Government arrived in force during the 1950s and '60s. The nursing station (or health centre) was built in 1956 and the Federal School in 1957. Children were brought into town to go to school. This, in combination with some hard years of starvation, brought Inuit into the settlement to stay. In 1962, houses were built for Inuit by the Department of Northern Affairs and National Resources. Although some Inuit families were still on the land in the '60s, it was only a matter of time before everyone lived in town.

Baker Lake: Its Land and Wildlife

The barren lands surrounding Baker Lake offer many and varied landscapes to explore. Many of these areas have been recognized as Canadian treasures through assorted designations.

In the west, in the area of the upper Thelon River, is the Thelon Wildlife Sanctuary. The Thelon, and Baker Lake's other major river, the Kazan, are Canadian heritage rivers, recognized for their rich natural and cultural heritage. A section of the Kazan River between Thirty Mile Lake and Kazan Falls has also been designated a national historic site. The Fall Caribou Crossing National Historic Site commemorates the historic fall caribou hunt. From their *qajait* (kayaks), hunters lanced migrating caribou as they swam across the river. The success of this hunt determined the survival of Inuit over the long winter.

To the north of Baker Lake, the splendor of Wager Bay boasts populations of polar bears, seals, beluga whales, wolves, caribou and other wildlife. Negotiations are currently under way to turn the Wager Bay area into a national park.

Tours

Tourist information is available at the Vera Akumalik Visitors Centre, on the beach behind the Northern store. It's usually open June through Labor Day. Contact the hamlet's community economic development officer for details.

Opened on June 3, 1998, by the Governor General of Canada, Roméo LeBlanc, the **Inuit Heritage Centre** is the pride of Baker Lake. The Centre interprets the inland way of life of all Inuit groups now living in Baker Lake. Exhibits include a depiction of the Fall Caribou Crossing National Historic Site. Contact the Centre for details and a schedule of activities.

Outfitters in Baker Lake can take you on tours of the community and the surrounding area. In summer, you can travel by boat to hunt caribou, or fish for lake trout or arctic char. Many visitors also choose to explore this area by canoe. Some of the most challenging and remote barren-land rivers are located in the Baker Lake area: the Thelon, Kazan and Back rivers. At the same time, you can glimpse wildlife or visit historical and archeological sites.

Edwin Evo Outfitting and Naturalist Tours is a reputable outfitting firm that provides visitors with an entertaining and safe journey. Owner and operator Edwin Evo stresses safety, and is very knowledgeable about the area. He will take visitors out sport fishing or wildlife viewing, and may stop for a hike or to view archeological sites. Evo will also pick up customers at the end of their paddle down the Kazan, Thelon or Quoich rivers.

Sila Lodge is a well-established tourist lodge at Wager Bay that permits an organized and safe way to view arctic landscapes, wildlife, and Inuit and European historic sites. The Wager Bay area is well known for its polar bear population. These majestic animals, along with an abundance of other wildlife, such as ringed and bearded seals, beluga whales, caribou, wolves, and many species of birds, make the area a photographer's dream. Visitors can see it all while boating or hiking under the watchful eye of trained guides. The lodge has five three-bedroom guest cabins and a main lodge with dining room. By all reports the dining here is excellent. A one-week stay at Sila Lodge plus one night in Baker Lake (airfare from Baker Lake included) is about $4,000.

The Baker Lake **Hunters and Trappers Organization** is licensed to outfit sport hunts for caribou and muskoxen. Caribou hunts are held in August and September and hunters are transported by boat. Muskoxen hunts run in the second or third week of March. Due to the season and the long distances that have to be travelled by snowmobile, muskoxen hunts are only for the adventurous few with very good winter clothing. The HTO guides all have excellent land skills and, if you're interested, you may even learn something about Inuit culture. **Canada North Outfitting Inc.** works in tandem with the HTO to provide these hunts.

Exploring the wilderness around Baker Lake can be exciting, but also challenging. This area can be very windy and the weather may change quickly, so don't be surprised if you have to spend some time sitting out the weather on your tour. In addition, mosquitoes can be very bad in the Baker Lake area. Take precautions by bringing a head net and/or bug jacket. Speak with your outfitter or tour operator about what clothing and other gear you should bring, and what conditions to expect during the trip.

Shopping

Ookpiktuyuk Art Gallery, located next to the Northern store, is run by Henry and his son, David Ford. Henry's father, Harry Ford, operated the first Hudson's Bay Co. trading post at Baker Lake on Big Hips Island or *Uqpiktujuq* (*Ookpiktuyuk* is an old spelling of the word). The gallery specializes in the wholesale and distribution of carvings, wall hangings, tapestries and drawings to art galleries in Southern Canada and around the world. Visitors can drop in to view the latest offerings from local Inuit carvers. Whether you buy something or not, you'll undoubtedly come away a little richer having heard a story or two from Henry and David.

Baker Lake Fine Arts and Crafts is in the Jessie Oonark Centre (artist Jessie Oonark brought Baker Lake's art to the attention of the world). The store carries carvings, wall hangings, crafts, traditional tools and jewelry. Owner/operator Sally Qimminunaaq Webster works with many local artists and craftspeople to export genuine Baker Lake products.

The **Qamanittuaq Fine Arts Gallery and Studio** has recently opened in the Jessie Oonark Centre. Owned and operated by Frederick G. Ford and Kyra V. Fisher, the gallery sells a variety of artwork in paper, stone sculpture, fabric arts, wire drawings and objects made from local materials.

In the past year, the world-renowned Baker Lake print tradition has been revived. Elder artists such as Victoria Mamnguqsualuk, Janet Kigusiuq, Magdalene Ukpatiku, Janet Ikuutqaq, Nancy Sevoga, and Thomas and Philippa Irsiraq share techniques with younger artists to produce unique prints. Contact the artists through the Qamanittuaq Fine Arts Gallery and Studio.

The **Northern store** and **Sanavik Co-op** sell groceries, supplies, clothing, hardware — you name it. The Northern has a fast food restaurant in the front called the **Quick Stop**. It also has a professional butcher on staff.

Flea markets are held from time to time at either the **Jonah Amitnaaq school** or the Recreation Centre. This is a good place to find traditional clothing such as caribou mitts, *kamiit*, parkas and *amautit*.

Events

Hamlet Days, a spring celebration usually held in mid-May, is a time for games, dogteam races and a children's carnival. **The Hamlet of Baker Lake**'s recreation co-ordinator can supply more details.

Baker Lake is famous for its square dances. They happen often and seemingly without warning. When in town, ask anyone if they know when the next square dance is going to be held, or call the recreation co-ordinator. Dances are always at the Recreation Centre.

Accommodation and Dining

The **Iglu Hotel** accommodates up to 52 people in 21 rooms, each with private bathroom, TV, telephone and two or three single beds. There is a lounge with a TV and pool table, conference facilities, and a dining room that serves hearty meals. Rooms are $150 per night single occupancy; $125 per person per night double occupancy; or $100 per person per night triple occupancy (meals not included). Meals are $15 for breakfast, $25 for lunch, and $30 for dinner.

At **Baker Lake Lodge,** guests choose from five sleeping cabins, which have a central bath-house, or four rooms, each with a private bath and TV. Prices for cabins are $65 per person per cabin (each cabin sleeps three to four people). Prices for rooms are $100 per night single occupancy, or $165 per night double occupancy. Meals are not included in accommodation rates. The main lodge building has a lounge with a nice atmosphere and a dining room offering standard southern cuisine (breakfast is $10, lunch is $17, and dinner is $25). The lodge, located on the edge of town closest to the airport, is a short walk to the centre of Baker Lake and all attractions. Courtesy airport pickup is available.

On the road to the **airport** is a **campground** intended for canoeists. It has four tent pads, a bathroom and cook shelter. There's also a campground operated by the hamlet at the mouth of the Kazan River where canoeists can wait out the weather, or wait for a pickup from Baker Lake. It's free to the public.

The Quick Stop at the Northern store is one of Baker Lake's gathering places — a good place to get fast food or have a coffee and chat.

Services

In addition to scheduled flights, charter service is available from Calm Air, Skyward Aviation and others out of Rankin Inlet.

Visitors must make appointments for the Baker Lake **Health Centre**'s public sick clinic, held from 9 a.m. to noon, Monday through Friday. There is 24-hour emergency service. Baker Lake's **post office** is located at the Co-op.

DIRECTORY

*Outfitters and tour operators licensed at time of writing.
After March 31/99, check for updated status.

Accommodation and Dining

Baker Lake Lodge
VISA accepted.
Tel.: (867) 793-2905
Fax: (867) 793-2965

Campgrounds
Hamlet office.
Tel.: (867) 793-2874
Fax: (867) 793-2509

Iglu Hotel
VISA, Interac, Diners Club/enRoute.
Tel.: (867) 793-2801
Fax: (867) 793-2711

Quick Stop
In the Northern store.
10 a.m.–8 p.m., Monday to Wednesday;
10 a.m.–9 p.m., Thursday and Friday;
1–9 p.m., Saturday; 1–6 p.m., Sunday.
Tel.: (867) 793-2211

* Outfitters/Tour Operators/Visitors Centre

Canada North Outfitting Inc.
Tel.: (613) 256-4057
Fax: (613) 256-4512
E-mail: cnonorth@istar.ca

Edwin Evo Outfitting and Naturalist Tours
Tel.: (867) 793-2293
Fax: (867) 793-2045

Hunters and Trappers Organization
Tel.: (867) 793-2520
Fax: (867) 793-2034

Sila Lodge Ltd.
Tel.: 1-800-663-9832 or (204) 949-2050
Fax: (204) 663-6375
E-mail: fn@silalodge.com

Vera Akumalik Visitors Centre
Open seasonally, usually June until
Labor Day.
Tel.: (867) 793-2456
Fax: (867) 793-2509

Excite your senses

Nunavut Territorial Parks

Visit the territorial parks of Nunavut and feel your senses come alive. Hike amid a land that fills you with awe, experience the exhilaration of a dog sled adventure, traverse our pristine lakes and rivers. The territorial parks of Nunavut — so vast, so beautiful — they're *sense*-sational. Explore them today and discover the lure of the land.

For more information call Nunavut Tourism toll-free at 1-800-491-7910 or visit our web site at www.nunavutparks.com

Northwest Territories
Resources, Wildlife and Economic Development
Parks and Tourism Division

Nunavut

where the sky dances
to an ancient melody
only the polar bear
remembers

Northern

Your Everyday Value Store
in 22 Nunavut communitie

■ **IQALUIT** ■ ARCTIC BAY ■ ARVIAT ■ BAKER LAK
■ BROUGHTON ISLAND ■ CAMBRIDGE BAY ■ CAPE DORSE
■ CHESTERFIELD INLET ■ CLYDE RIVER ■ CORAL HARBOUR ■ GJOA HAVE
■ HALL BEACH ■ IGLOOLIK ■ KUGLUKTUK ■ KIMMIRUT ■ NANISIVIK ■ PANGNIRTUN
■ POND INLET ■ RANKIN INLET ■ REPULSE BAY ■ SANIKILUAQ ■ TALOYOA

Services

Airport
Tel.: (867) 793-2564
Fax: (867) 793-2572

Churches
Glad Tidings
Services: 11 a.m. and 7 p.m., Sunday;
7:30 p.m., Wednesday.
Tel.: (867) 793-2233
Fax: (867) 793-2205

St. Aiden's Anglican Mission
Services: 11 a.m. and 7 p.m., Sunday;
7 p.m., Thursday.
Tel.: (867) 793-2433

Dental Clinic
Tel.: (867) 793-2288 or (867) 793-2287
Fax: (867) 793-2289

Department of Sustainable Development, Government of Nunavut
(or until April/99, GNWT's Resources, Wildlife and Economic Development)
Tel.: (867) 793-2944
Fax: (867) 793-2514

Hamlet Office
Tel.: (867) 793-2874
Fax: (867) 793-2509

Health Centre
Tel.: (867) 793-2816
Fax: (867) 793-2812

Inuit Heritage Centre
Tel.: (867) 793-2598
Fax: (867) 793-2509

Library
Tel.: (867) 793-2909

Police (RCMP)
Tel.: (867) 793-2922

Post Office
Located at the Co-op.
10 a.m.–5:30 p.m., Monday to Friday.
Tel.: (867) 793-2912

Radio Station (FM 99.3)
Tel.: (867) 793-2962

Schools
Jonah Amitnaaq Secondary School
Tel.: (867) 793-2842
Fax: (867) 793-2029

Nunavut Arctic College
Tel.: (867) 793-2971
Fax: (867) 793-2181

Rachel Arngnammaktiq School
Elementary school.
Tel.: (867) 793-2513
Fax: (867) 793-2500

Taxi
D.C. Cabs Ltd.
Tel.: (867) 793-2558
Fax: (867) 793-2665

Weather Information
Tel.: (867) 793-2931
Fax: (867) 793-2440
Web site weather forecast:
www.tor.ec.gc.ca/forecasts/index.html
(check under Regional Weather Summaries) or www.infonorth.org

Shopping

Baker Lake Fine Arts and Crafts
1:30–5 p.m., Monday, Wednesday and Friday. VISA accepted.
Tel.: (867) 793-2865
Fax: (867) 793-2000

Northern Store
10 a.m.–6 p.m., Monday to Thursday;
10 a.m.–9 p.m., Friday; 1–6 p.m., Saturday. In winter, 10 a.m.–6 p.m., Saturday. VISA, MasterCard, Interac.
Tel.: (867) 793-2920
Fax: (867) 793-2565

Ookpiktuyuk Art Gallery
9 a.m.–12 p.m., 1–5 p.m., Monday to Friday; weekends by appointment.
Tel.: (867) 793-2534
Fax: (867) 793-2422

Qamanittuaq Fine Arts Gallery and Studio
10 a.m.–5 p.m., Monday to Friday;
1–5 p.m., Saturday.
Tel.: (867) 793-2662 or (867) 793-2366
Fax: (867) 793-2366
E-mail: fredryka@aol.com

Sanavik Co-op Association
10 a.m.–6 p.m., Monday to Thursday;
10 a.m.–9 p.m., Friday. Closed Sunday.
In summer: 1–6 p.m., Saturday.
VISA, Interac.
Tel.: (867) 793-2912
Fax: (867) 793-2594

65. THELON WILDLIFE SANCTUARY

by Darren Keith

The Thelon Wildlife Sanctuary, an expanse of 52,000 square kilometres, straddles the border between Nunavut and the western Northwest Territories about halfway between Baker Lake and Yellowknife.

The sanctuary was designed to conserve muskox populations that were shrinking from decades of over-hunting to feed a skin trade encouraged by whalers and the Hudson's Bay Co. The local muskox population has gone from an estimated 300 in 1936 to 1,100 in 1994, but its protected status, which prohibits hunting, has also been detrimental to the Inuit and Dene who depended on its resources for survival.

The Land and Wildlife

The Thelon Wildlife Sanctuary — centre, source, homeland. These words seem to approach the essence of the place. It's a centre because it's the meeting place of different worlds. Here the Kivalliq tundra meets the boreal forest of the West forming the tree line. The territories of ancient neighbors — Inuit and Dene — overlap, and many places have two names: one Inuktitut and one Chipewyan.

It's a source because the great rivers of the Arctic and Hudson Bay drainages, the Back and Thelon rivers, flow from the sanctuary. The eternal pull of the Thelon draws driftwood into the barrens to rest on the shores of Beverly Lake, or *Tipjalik* in Inuktitut (meaning "it has driftwood"), furnishing precious building materials to countless generations of Inuit. Most importantly today, as always, the sanctuary is a source for muskoxen and caribou that seem to spill over from within its boundaries, providing sustenance to Inuit and Dene alike. Last, the area of the sanctuary is a homeland because it has provided for people for thousands of years, most recently the *Akilinirmiut* whose members now reside in Baker Lake.

The People and Their History

Archeology documents the first arrival of people to the area 8,000 years ago, shortly after the retreat of the continental glacier. Paleoeskimo caribou hunters moved here around 1500 BC after climatic changes in the Arctic closed the ice leads on the Arctic Ocean, making seal hunting impossible. Ancestors of modern Dene peopled the Thelon valley around 2,500 years ago, and then around AD 1000, Thule Inuit whale hunters moved east across the Arctic islands from Alaska in pursuit of the bowhead whale. These people, too, were ultimately attracted by the caribou and muskoxen of the Thelon valley, and by the trees and driftwood they found there.

The modern Inuit descendants of the Thule continued to draw on the sanctuary's resources. The area around Beverly Lake and the middle Thelon River was home to the *Akilinirmiut*, so named because of the *Akiliniq* hills on the north side of Beverly Lake. Their historical life, based mainly on caribou hunting, is much in evidence here in the form of stone features such as tent rings, meat caches and *inuksuit*.

This part of the sanctuary has also drawn Inuit inland from such far-flung areas as Bathurst Inlet, the Back River/Chantrey Inlet, and the Kazan River. All sought the valuable driftwood brought to the shores of Beverly Lake by the Thelon and Dubawnt rivers. These trips were made by dogteam during winter, and likely involved many chance meetings of Inuit from distant and diverse areas of Nunavut. These occasions were opportunities to exchange material goods and information, and it has been recorded that *Akiliniq* was a trade centre for the central Arctic.

The land of the *Akilinirmiut* was not visited by Euro-Canadians until 1893, when brothers Joseph and James Tyrrell, in the employ of the Geological Survey of Canada, descended the Dubawnt River. A return trip in 1900 convinced James Tyrrell to lobby for the creation of a game sanctuary to protect the muskox population, whose numbers had been drastically reduced due to the trade in muskox hides. Tyrrell's idea was not acted upon until the Department of the Interior sent John Hornby and Captain J. C. Critchell-Bullock to assess the area's resources in 1924–25. These men added their voices to the call for a protective sanctuary.

Established as the Thelon Game Sanctuary in 1927, the boundary of the original 39,000 square kilometres was changed in 1956 to accommodate mining interests in the southwest portion, and the sanctuary grew to 56,000 square kilometres.

From the beginning, hunting was off limits. Billy Hoare, the sanctuary's first and last warden, journeyed inland with warden A. J. Knox of Wood Buffalo National Park to spend many arduous months hauling equipment and supplies from Great Slave Lake to the Thelon, although always availing themselves of the opportunity to inform the local Dene of the rules of the sanctuary. A warden outpost was established at what is now known as Warden's Grove near the Hanbury-Thelon junction in October 1928. Canoeists today can still view the log structures built by Hoare and Knox.

After Hoare's tenure as warden ended in 1932, the RCMP continued the task of informing native people that the sanctuary was off limits for hunting. These warnings were taken seriously by Inuit, and their self-restraint, in addition to a few arrests for hunting, caused much hardship and ill will.

Although the sanctuary was imposed on its aboriginal inhabitants, it did succeed in its purpose. A muskox population once limited to the area of the sanctuary has flourished and expanded beyond the Kazan River to the east. A process for determining the fate of the Thelon Wildlife Sanctuary with the full participation of Inuit was included in the Nunavut Final Agreement. It is a tribute to the foresight of the Inuit of Baker Lake that they continue to support the sanctuary as a protected area. The draft management plan proposes an expansion of the boundaries to more fully protect the calving grounds of the Beverly caribou herd, and to allow aboriginal subsistence hunting.

Planning a Visit

Due to the very remote nature of the Thelon Wildlife Sanctuary, it is still only accessible to those adventurous enough to travel the Thelon River by canoe. The attraction to canoeists is not the technical difficulty of the river, as there is relatively little challenging white water, but the abundant wildlife. Muskoxen are numerous. Caribou may be seen swimming across the river on their annual migration. Other wildlife such as moose, wolves, grizzly bears and waterfowl are also there in plenty.

Be very careful, however, when observing or photographing muskoxen. Their defensive strategy is not to outrun pursuers, but to form a circle and defend themselves with their horns. They will charge you! It is equally important to always be mindful of grizzly bears on the barrens. A sure sign that grizzlies are in the area is freshly turned soil from a bear digging for ground squirrels. If you encounter these signs, camp somewhere else, or be very wary. Firearms may be carried in the sanctuary for protection; however, there have been no incidents of defence kills of grizzly bears in recent years. Always keep a clean camp. See Chapter 36, "Land Mammals," for more details on wildlife concerns.

Access to the Thelon by bush plane can be had from Baker Lake, Fort Smith or Yellowknife, and is an expensive proposition, especially paddling only the sanctuary portion of the river. If your itinerary extends to Baker Lake, scheduled flights are available. Still, the many large lakes along the way can be dangerous due to commonly windy conditions on the barrens. Calculate a few extra days in your trip to allow for being wind-bound.

For more information about water, weather and camping conditions, contact the **Northern Frontier Regional Visitors Centre** in Yellowknife and request a copy of a trip report for the Thelon. There is no registration or permit requirement to travel in the sanctuary; however, you should inform the local RCMP of your travel plans (see Chapter 11, "Adventure Travel").

For those uncertain about their ability to pull off such a trip independently, there are licensed outfitters who will arrange everything, including guided trips.

DIRECTORY

Bathurst Arctic Services
P.O. Box 820, Yellowknife NT,
X1A 2N6 Canada
Tel.: (867) 873-2595
Fax: (867) 920-4263
E-mail: bathurst@internorth.com
Web site: www.virtualnorth.com/
    bathurst/

Canoe Arctic
P.O. Box 130, Fort Smith NT,
X0E 0P0 Canada
Tel.: (867) 872-2308
Web site: www.auroranet.nt.ca/canoe

Great Canadian Ecoventures
Box 2481, Yellowknife NT,
X1A 2P8 Canada
Tel.: 1-800-667-9453, (867) 920-7110,
or (403) 352-5414
Fax: (867) 920-7180 or (403) 352-5449
E-mail: tundra@thelon.com
Web site: www.thelon.com

**Northern Frontier Regional
Visitors Centre**
Tel.: (867) 873-4262
Fax: (867) 873-3654
E-mail: nfva@internorth.com
Web site: www.northernfrontier.com

66. CORAL HARBOUR
by Ken Beardsall

When I first visited Coral Harbour as a teenager on a school exchange trip 21 years ago, the community left a lasting impression on me.

Population:	669 (Inuit: 93%, non-Inuit: 7%) Source: 1996 Census of Canada
Telephone Area Code:	867
Time Zone:	Eastern Standard Time all year
	(Coral Harbour doesn't use Daylight Saving Time)
Postal Code:	X0C 0C0
How to Get There:	Possible routes:
	• Winnipeg-Rankin Inlet-Coral Harbour
	• Edmonton-Yellowknife-Rankin Inlet-Coral Harbour
	• Ottawa/Montreal-Iqaluit-Coral Harbour
	• Kangerlussuaq (Greenland)-Iqaluit-Coral Harbour
	Rankin Inlet to Coral Harbour (500 kilometres east) is via Calm Air.
	From Iqaluit (more than 700 kilometres west), it's via First Air
Banks:	None. Cash and traveller's cheques are preferable. Credit cards are
	accepted by certain businesses
Alcohol:	Alcohol and alcoholic beverages are prohibited
Taxis:	Yes

For the past 10 years, I've been living and teaching here, and Coral Harbour's appeal is as strong as ever. Is it the warmth of the local people that I value most? The wide-open rocky tundra around the settlement and offshore waters that abound with wildlife each spring? Or the intriguing history of the former inhabitants? These must be why I live in Coral Harbour — excellent reasons, too, for tourists to travel here.

In Inuktitut, Coral Harbour is called *Salliq*, meaning a large, flat island in front of the mainland. The English explorer Sir Thomas Button named the land Southampton Island, to honor his benefactor, the Earl of Southampton, who promoted his voyage in 1604 in search of the Northwest Passage. There's nothing southern, however, about this island in northern Hudson Bay, except the name of its only community, Coral Harbour.

Incredibly, in the icy waters near the settlement, you can find coral! I've discovered bits of it while picking mussels and jigging for arctic cod in the harbor. It's fossilized coral that once flourished when Northern Canada had a warmer climate. Today, of course, the local climate is not conducive to its growth.

Coral Harbour is a thriving community, where its largely young population blends the traditional with the modern. While walrus meat sits on the dock for everyone to share, for example, a front-end loader prepares a lot for construction nearby. You'll see people busily carving soapstone, ivory, whalebone or the marvelous limestone from nearby Bear Island.

History

Europeans and Americans brought previously unknown diseases to Nunavut. Southampton Island is the setting of a tragedy involving such a newly introduced disease. In the late 19th century, European and American whalers were exploiting the rich bowhead whale grounds off the coast of the island. At times they landed; on one of these occasions, they met an isolated and shy group of Inuit (the *Sallirmiut*) who were unfamiliar with iron and other Euro-American trade goods.

In 1899, the Scottish established a permanent whaling station on the southern tip of Southampton Island at Cape Low. Living at this station were Inuit from the west coast of Hudson Bay. They regarded the *Sallirmiut* not as Inuit but as *Tuniit* (a people who, according to oral history, inhabited Nunavut prior to the arrival of Inuit. Some archeologists think these might be the people of the Dorset culture). Although the *Sallirmiut* kept mostly to themselves, they did visit the whaling station. In the winter of 1902, the *Sallirmiut* contracted a virulent gastrointestinal disease introduced by the crew of the Scottish whaler *Active*. By the spring of 1903, almost all the *Sallirmiut* had died from this infection. Only one woman and four children survived to be adopted by Inuit families elsewhere.

You can visit a large *Sallirmiut* camp site at Native Point, about 64 kilometres southeast of Coral Harbour, by boat in summer or by snowmobile or dogteam in spring. (Tours to Native Point are available through **Kajjaarnaq Arctic Tours** and **Appa Tours**.) Here, on a high peninsula, you'll find the remains of 12 sod huts, many bones and animal parts, plus a curious feature: Avaalak's rock. Legend has it that Avaalak, a *Sallirmiut*, carried a boulder up a hill from the beach to display his superhuman strength. He's also said to have killed bowhead whales by himself from a kayak. His people were known for their remarkable strength, short stature, strange hairdos and their ancient language.

After the turn of the century, the whaling industry finally collapsed. The last whaler into Hudson Bay, the *A.T. Gifford*, burned and was lost with its crew off Coats Island, about 130 kilometres south of Coral Harbour, in 1915.

In 1924, Inuit began to settle in Coral Harbour after a local hunter, Audlanaq — whom whalers called John Ell — convinced the Hudson's Bay Co. to establish a trading post on Southampton Island. The Company set up the post after abandoning its operations on Coats Island. Inuit from Baffin Island, northern Quebec and the mainland Keewatin (now called the Kivalliq Region) began moving to Southampton Island to share its wealth.

Just outside Coral Harbour, Americans built a major military base to service thousands of aircraft ferried to Europe during the Second World War. Later, they used the airport as a depot during construction of DEW Line stations further north. After the War, when they abandoned the site, they left behind much of their equipment, including thousands of oil drums. Other long-buried items, such as tools and bottles, surface occasionally — reminders of Coral Harbour's role in the War. Today the base is protected under territorial legislation; artifacts are not to be removed.

In the 1950s and '60s, federal government presence in the region increased with the building of a school in 1950, a nursing station in 1963, and public housing. The government encouraged Inuit to move from their camps to the community to receive health care and social services. An Anglican mission was started in Coral Harbour by Luke Kidlapik, an Inuit catechist trained at Blacklead Island in Cumberland Sound. The **Roman Catholic mission** was established shortly thereafter.

Coral Harbour: Its Land and Wildlife

Today, visitors come to Coral Harbour to experience the wonderful diversity of wildlife here. Offshore waters are alive with walrus, beluga whales and seals.

A large population of polar bears dwells on the island; if you're travelling by boat, you may spot these magnificent animals lumbering along the coastline. As well, the island is home to a large herd of caribou. During the 1950s, caribou were hunted to extinction; in 1967, however, they were airlifted here from Coats Island. Since then, their numbers have grown so much that they're now hunted commercially by local people.

Birdwatchers will be delighted by multitudes of migratory species on the island. Two areas worth visiting are the East Bay Migratory Bird Sanctuary, about 70 kilometres east of Coral, and the Harry Gibbons Migratory Bird Sanctuary, about 140 kilometres southwest of the community. Here you'll spot snow geese by the thousands, as well as tundra swans, sandhill cranes and many other species.

Tours

Boating is an ideal way to view marine mammals at close range, and the harbor here attracts many crafts, including several fishing boats from Nova Scotia and Prince Edward Island. There are three-to-six-day guided tours to Coats, Bencas and Walrus islands that can also include a stopover at Native Point. Visitors travel by boat to see herds of walrus lounging on the rocks; they could also catch a glimpse of a polar bear or two. At the towering Akpa Cliffs, on Coats Island, flocks of thick-billed murres, glaucous gulls and black guillemots perch contentedly in their nests or wheel about majestically. Coats Island is a particularly good vantage point for watching birds, either by surveying them from a boat at the bottom of the cliffs or from perches at the top. The best time for birdwatching is mid-July to mid-August.

Visitors can also travel by snowmobile or all-terrain vehicle to beautiful Kirchoffer Falls, 24 kilometres from Coral Harbour. Here, gyrfalcons and peregrines soar to and from their nests on the cliffs beside the mighty Kirchoffer River. One might also see caribou, snowy owls and many other species of breeding birds.

Shopping

Coral Harbour boasts many fine artisans who carve in walrus ivory, soapstone, whalebone and a rare type of pure white limestone unique to Coral Harbour. Of particular note are intricately carved ivory pieces, including rings and other jewelry. The women of Coral Harbour are well known for working wonders with sealskin. Visitors can buy these treasures at the **Katudgevik Co-op** and Leonie's Place Hotel or directly from the artist. Groceries and dry goods are also available at the **Northern store** and the Co-op.

Accommodation and Dining

Leonie's Place is a small, comfortable, non-smoking hotel with six double-occupancy rooms, all with private washrooms and radios. There is a TV in the lounge. Rooms are $120 per person per day without meals and $180 with meals. Guests who stay longer than two weeks receive a discounted rate of $150 per day with meals. Meals, priced at $10 for breakfast, $20 for lunch, and $30 for supper, are served to hotel guests only.

The recently renovated **Esungarq Motel**, owned by the Co-op, has three rooms, each with a private washroom and TV. Rates are $135 per day without meals and $180 per day with meals. There is a pay phone at the motel; for local calls, guests can use the kitchen phone for free. If given at least an hour's notice, the motel can prepare meals for non-guests as well. Breakfast is $15, lunch is $20, and supper is $30.

Services

The **Health Centre**'s general clinic runs from 8:30 to 11:30 a.m. weekdays; public health programs take place from 1 to 5 p.m. weekdays. There is 24-hour emergency service. There is also an **RCMP** detachment in Coral Harbour.

DIRECTORY

*Outfitters and tour operators licensed at time of writing.
After March 31/99, check for updated status.

Accommodation and Dining

Esungarq Motel
VISA, Diners Club/enRoute.
Tel.: (867) 925-9926
Fax: (867) 925-8308

Leonie's Place Hotel
VISA, traveller's cheques.
Tel.: (867) 925-9751 or (867) 925-8810
Fax: (867) 925-8606

*Outfitters/Tour Operators

Appa Tours
Tel.: (867) 925-8861

Kajjaarnaq Arctic Tours
Tel.: (867) 925-8366
Fax: (867) 925-8593
E-mail: kajtours@arctic.ca

Services

Airport
Tel.: (867) 925-9711
Fax: (867) 925-8291

Aiviit Hunters and Trappers Organization
Tel.: (867) 925-8622
Fax: (867) 925-8300

Churches

Glad Tidings Church
Services: 11 a.m., Sunday.
Tel.: (867) 925-8875

St. Joseph's Roman Catholic Mission
Services: 11 a.m. and 7 p.m., Sunday.
Tel.: (867) 925-8277

St. Mark's Anglican Church
Services: Sunday, 9:30 a.m. (English);
11 a.m. and 7 p.m. (Inuktitut).
Tel.: (867) 925-8397
Fax: (867) 925-8233

Department of Sustainable Development, Government of Nunavut
(or until April/99, GNWT's Resources, Wildlife and Economic Development)
Tel.: (867) 925-8823
Fax: (867) 925-8460

Hamlet Office
Tel.: (867) 925-8867
Fax: (867) 925-8233

Health Centre
Tel.: (867) 925-9916
Fax: (867) 925-8380

Police (RCMP)
Tel.: (867) 925-9954
Fax: (867) 925-8483

Post Office
Located at the Katudgevik Co-op.
1–5 p.m. weekdays.
Tel.: (867) 925-9909

Radio Station (FM 103.9)
Tel.: (867) 925-9711
Fax: (867) 925-8291

Schools

Nunavut Arctic College
Tel.: (867) 925-9746
Fax: (867) 925-8410

Sakku School
Tel.: (867) 925-9923
Fax: (867) 925-8410

Taxis

Eleven Mile Trek
Tel.: (867) 925-9767

Veronica's Taxi
Tel.: (867) 925-8324

Weather and Flight Information
Tel.: (867) 925-9711
Fax: (867) 925-8291
Web site weather forecast:
www.infonorth.org

Shopping

Katudgevik Co-op
10 a.m.–9 p.m., Monday to Friday;
8 a.m.–6 p.m., Saturday. Closed
Sunday.
VISA, Interac.
Tel.: (867) 925-9969
Fax: (867) 925-8308

Leonie's Place Hotel Craft Shop
3–5 p.m., Monday and Wednesday;
3–6 p.m., Friday; 1–3 p.m., Saturday.
Closed Sunday.
VISA, traveller's cheques.
Tel.: (867) 925-8626
Fax: (867) 925-8606

Northern Store
10 a.m.–6 p.m., Monday to Wednesday;
10 a.m.–7 p.m., Thursday and Friday;
10 a.m.–4 p.m., Saturday. Closed
Sunday.
VISA, MasterCard, Interac.
Tel.: (867) 925-9920
Fax: (867) 925-8863

67. IGLOOLIK

by John MacDonald, with contributions from George Qulaut and Louis Tapardjuk

Situated on an island adjacent to the flat expanse of the Melville Peninsula's eastern coastal plain, the settlement of Igloolik has long been off the beaten track for tourists in the eastern Arctic.

Population:	1,174 (Inuit: 93%, non-Inuit: 7%) Source: 1996 Census of Canada
Telephone Area Code:	867
Time Zone:	Eastern Time
Postal Code:	X0A 0L0
How to Get There:	Possible routes:
	• Ottawa/Montreal-Iqaluit-Igloolik
	• Winnipeg-Rankin Inlet-Iqaluit-Igloolik
	• Edmonton-Yellowknife-Rankin Inlet-Iqaluit-Igloolik
	• Kangerlussuaq (Greenland)-Iqaluit-Igloolik
	Iqaluit to Igloolik (about 800 kilometres northwest) is via First Air
Banks:	None. Cash and traveller's cheques are preferable. Credit cards are accepted by certain businesses
Alcohol:	Alcohol and alcoholic beverages cannot be purchased in Igloolik. Visitors who want to bring alcohol into the community must first obtain a permit from the community's **Alcohol Education Committee**
Taxis:	Yes

Today, whether you come to see people, wildlife or a wilderness vastly different from Baffin Island's craggy peaks and fiords, you will find a region rich in its own treasures and well worth exploring.

A visit here takes you not only to the geographic centre of Nunavut but also to what is widely considered the cultural hub of Nunavut. Ancient ties to northern and southern Baffin Island, as well as the Kivalliq and eastern Kitikmeot regions, contribute to the distinct mix of Inuit cultural traditions practised in Igloolik today. The area has long been blessed with abundant natural resources central to Inuit culture and identity: walruses, seals, whales, polar bears, caribou, fish and waterfowl. These resources continue to provide the economic, spiritual and intellectual basis for cultural continuity within Igloolik. People here take immense pride in nurturing Inuit heritage and traditions while embracing the inevitable changes brought on by modernization. The challenge in maintaining this balance is the very essence of Igloolik's vibrancy.

History

The fertile seas around Igloolik have attracted and sustained arctic hunting peoples for millennia. Information about the area's earliest inhabitants comes mainly from the numerous archeological sites on the island, some dating back more than 4,000 years. The island's history also lives in timeless Inuit traditions about the legendary *Tuniit*, believed by archeologists to be the people of the Dorset culture who inhabited the region for almost 1,500 years.

Many Igloolik families are descended from members of the famed Qitdlarssuaq migration to Greenland in the mid-1800s. Then some 40 Inuit, including a number from the Igloolik area, embarked on an epic journey led by Qillaq, a renowned shaman who was said to be evading a blood feud. Qillaq and his companions eventually reached northwest Greenland, where they settled among Inuit already there. (Qillaq — spelled as Qitdlaq in Greenlandic form — later became known as Qitdlarssuaq, "the great Qitdlaq," after arriving in Greenland.)

First direct contact with Europeans occurred when British Navy ships *Fury* and *Hecla*, under the command of Captain William Edward Parry, wintered at Igloolik in 1822. Parry's expedition failed in its main goal — the discovery of a northwest passage. However, with the help of Inuit (in particular, Iligliuk and Ewerat, who drew accurate maps of the area for the expedition's officers), Parry added considerably to European knowledge of the people, lands and seas to the north of Hudson Bay. According to local accounts, Parry's ships were driven from Igloolik by a vengeful shaman who vowed that white men would never again return to the area by sea. Indeed, it was well over 100 years before another ship was seen in Igloolik waters.

The island was visited briefly in 1867 and 1868 by the American explorer Charles Francis Hall during his futile search for survivors of the lost Franklin Expedition. In 1913, Alfred Tremblay, a French-Canadian prospector with Captain Joseph Bernier's expedition to Pond Inlet, extended his mineral explorations overland to Igloolik, and in 1921, members of Knud Rasmussen's Fifth Thule Expedition visited the island. Published reports of that expedition provide a detailed picture of traditional Inuit life just before "modernization" began.

The first permanent presence of outsiders on Igloolik Island came with the establishment of a **Roman Catholic mission** in the 1930s. By the end of the decade, the Hudson's Bay Co. had also set up a post on the island. Over the next 20 years, most of the region's Inuit continued to live in traditional camps in the nearby coastal areas and islands of northern Foxe Basin.

During this time, two individuals, Ittuksaarjuat and his wife Ataguttaaluk, emerged as highly respected leaders, caring for their people in times of hardship, sharing resources and ensuring co-operation among the region's camps. Igloolik's school is named in memory of Ataguttaaluk.

The present community of Igloolik dates from the late 1950s, with the federal government's increasing administrative interest in the Arctic. By the mid-1960s, a school, nursing station and **RCMP** detachment were permanently established, as well as the **Anglican mission** (1959) and the Igloolik Co-operative (1963). As with other settlements in the eastern Arctic, Igloolik grew rapidly as Inuit families from surrounding camps moved into the community to avail themselves of services offered by government agencies.

Throughout the changes brought about by growth and modernization, Igloolik has never lost sight of its cultural roots, a fact reflected in the day-to-day life of the community and in the activities of a number of local organizations. An active elders group, the Inullariit Society, teaches land skills and traditional sewing to the community's youth and, in co-operation with the **Igloolik Research Centre**, sponsors a major oral history project aimed at documenting the elders' rich traditional knowledge. In mid-January of each year, the Society also organizes a festival to celebrate the return of the sun after winter's dark period. Igloolik is home to two video production organizations: Igloolik Isuma Productions Inc., an independent company specializing in Inuit cultural programming, and a local office of the Nunavut-wide Inuit Broadcasting Corporation. A number of Nunavut government departments have established regional offices in Igloolik, adding significantly to the community's infrastructure and population.

Igloolik: Its Land and Wildlife

In season, the island's flat, accessible terrain, in many parts blanketed with flowering tundra plants, makes birdwatching, hiking and camping especially rewarding. Numerous migratory birds visit the area in late spring and summer, many of them nesting locally, including loons, geese, eider ducks, terns, jaegers, plovers, snow buntings and snowy owls.

From late April until June, conditions are usually superb for dogteam trips through nearby valleys, lakes and bays, or out to the floe edge. Scattered herds of caribou, basking seals and even walruses can often be seen on these trips.

Breakup of the sea ice around Igloolik Island usually occurs in late July or early August. During the subsequent open-water season, which lasts until mid-October, boating excursions into Fury and Hecla Strait are frequently rewarded with the unforgettable sight of bowhead whales on their summer migration in northern Foxe Basin.

Tours

Igloolik offers a variety of activities based on the area's natural attractions and seasonal cycle. The best time to visit, however, is from mid-April to early September, when the sky barely darkens and temperatures creep ever higher.

There is a good view of Igloolik and the surrounding landscape from atop the limestone bluff two kilometres north of town. Most of the island can be seen from this point. The low shoreline of Melville Peninsula fills the horizon to the west and south. With good visibility you can see north across Fury and Hecla Strait to the distant mountains of Baffin Island.

There are numerous archeological sites on Igloolik Island. These sites are best visited during the snow-free season (mid-June to mid-September) when they are fully exposed. Fine examples of Dorset and Thule dwellings, some recently excavated, are found in the vicinity of Arnaqquaksat Point, five kilometres from town and a pleasant walk by road and pathway. The impressive ruins of an old Thule settlement can be seen at Ungalujat Point, 18 kilometres from town by dirt road. Here there are more than 30 significant structures, including the walls and stone benches of a circular ceremonial house once used for festivities following a successful whale hunt. A drive to the site by taxi can be arranged when the road is passable, usually from July to mid-September. You can also arrange with a local outfitter to get there by snowmobile, dogteam or boat, depending on the season.

On the way to Ungalujat Point there is the grave of an English sailor who died here in 1823 during Parry's expedition. The spot is marked by a finely engraved headstone carved from local limestone. Further along the coast to the east is Igloolik Point, site of the old Inuit village for which the island is named. The area around Igloolik Point is still a favorite spot of Inuit residents for summer camping and for the community's summer walrus hunt.

A short distance off Igloolik's northwest shore lie the islands of Avvajjaq, one of them the site of a former Inuit settlement and an abandoned Roman Catholic mission house dating from the 1930s. The rolling granite hills and winding valleys of the Avvajjaq area offer excellent cross-country skiing from mid-April through May. Its maze of sheltered islands and narrow passageways would delight sea-kayaking enthusiasts in summer.

There is no fishing to speak of on Igloolik Island itself. Mogg Bay (*Naluqqajarvik*), 24 kilometres southwest of Igloolik on the Melville Peninsula, is the nearest good fishing spot for arctic char. Lake trout and char can also be fished in adjoining lakes. August brings excellent open-water fishing along the shores and fiords of Baffin Island, but weather and ice conditions in Fury and Hecla Strait often make access to this area difficult.

Shopping

The **Igloolik Co-operative** and the **Northern store** are the community's main retail outlets, offering a wide variety of merchandise and groceries. Naphtha for camp stoves is sold only at the Co-op.

In season, frozen arctic char and caribou can be purchased from the local **Hunters and Trappers Organization** (HTO). Traditional skin clothing and hunting implements are occasionally sold there as well.

Igloolik is also a fine place to purchase Inuit art; artisans here most commonly produce sculptures. Carvings are sold mainly through the Co-op, though you may also buy them from individual artists. Wall hangings and paintings by local artists are frequently displayed for sale in the **Co-op restaurant**.

Accommodation and Dining

There are two hotels in Igloolik and several private homes offering bed and breakfast-type accommodation. A list of bed and breakfasts can be obtained from the local economic development officer.

The **Tujormivik Hotel** has eight rooms (one single occupancy, seven double occupancy). Bathroom facilities are shared. All rooms have cable TV. There's a pay phone in the hotel lounge. Generous meals served in the dining room often include local foods such as arctic char and caribou. Guests with particular dietary needs or preferences can, with sufficient notice, arrange to have special meals prepared at no additional cost. Daily rates are $190 per person (including meals), or $125 per person (excluding meals), single or double occupancy.

The Igloolik Inn, opened in 1998 and run by the Igloolik Co-op, has seven rooms (three single occupancy, four double occupancy). All rooms have private bath, phone and cable TV. Daily rates are $150 single occupancy, or $125 per person double occupancy.

The dining room is open at 8 a.m. for guests and 10 a.m. for non-guests. They serve solid meals at reasonable prices (breakfast $8, lunch $10, dinner $25). The Tujormivik Hotel also serves meals to non-guests (breakfast $20, lunch $20, dinner $35); give them a few hours' notice. Snacks or light meals can be obtained at the **Co-op's coffee shop**.

Services

A number of organizations around town welcome visitors. The **Igloolik Hamlet Office** provides up-to-date information about the town and its services. The **Ataguttaaluk Elementary School** — which also houses the community's excellent **public library** — has a permanent gallery depicting the town's history.

Tours are given by the Igloolik Research Centre, a territorial government facility that supports scientific research in the area. The Centre also runs a number of environmental monitoring programs, has a general reference library and houses a large collection of traditional knowledge and oral history materials contributed by members of the Inullariit Society.

Igloolik's **health centre** is staffed by four resident nurses. Walk-in clinics are 9 to 11:30 a.m., Monday to Friday. There are special clinics every weekday afternoon. A nurse is on call 24 hours a day. Physicians from Iqaluit visit the community regularly.

DIRECTORY

*Outfitters and tour operators licensed at time of writing.
After March 31/99, check for updated status.

Accommodation and Dining

Co-op Coffee Shop
9 a.m.–11 p.m., Monday through Saturday; 1–6 p.m. and 8–11 p.m., Sunday.
Tel.: (867) 934-8948

The Igloolik Inn
VISA accepted.
Tel.: (867) 934-8595
Fax: (867) 934-8740

Dining room:
10 a.m.–8 p.m., Monday to Wednesday;
10 a.m.–9 p.m., Thursday to Saturday;
12–7 p.m., Sunday.

Tujormivik Hotel
VISA accepted.
Tel.: (867) 934-8814
Fax: (867) 934-8816

*Outfitters/Tour Operators

Hunters and Trappers Organization
Tel.: (867) 934-8807
Fax: (867) 934-8067

Services

Airport
Tel.: (867) 934-8973
Fax: (867) 934-8955

Alcohol Education Committee
Tel.: (867) 934-8905

Churches

Anglican Church
Services: 11 a.m. and 7 p.m., Sunday;
7:30 p.m., Tuesday (Inuktitut only).
Tel.: (867) 934-8586
Fax: (867) 934-8586

Full Gospel Church
Phone number unavailable.

Roman Catholic Church
Services: 11 a.m. and 7 p.m., Sunday;
weekdays at 7 p.m. (Inuktitut only).
Tel.: (867) 934-8846
Fax: (867) 934-8757

Department of Sustainable Development, Government of Nunavut
(or until April/99, GNWT's Resources,
Wildlife and Economic Development)
Tel.: (867) 934-8999
Fax: (867) 934-8995

Hamlet Office
Tel.: (867) 934-8830
Fax: (867) 934-8757

Health Centre
Tel.: (867) 934-8837
Fax: (867) 934-8901

Igloolik Research Centre
Tel.: (867) 934-8836
Fax: (867) 934-8792
E-mail: igloonri@nunanet.com

Police (RCMP)
Tel.: (867) 934-8828
Fax: (867) 934-8723

Post Office
In Igloolik Co-operative.
Tel.: (867) 934-8727

Public Library
In Ataguttaaluk Elementary School.
Tel.: (867) 934-8812

Radio Station (FM 105.2)
Tel.: (867) 934-8824 (off air)
Tel.: (867) 934-8832 (on air)

Schools

Ataguttaaluk Elementary School
Tel.: (867) 934-8996

Nunavut Arctic College
Tel.: (867) 934-8876

Taxi

Qamaniq Taxi
Tel.: (867) 934-8942

Weather Information
Tel.: (867) 934-8947
Web site weather forecast:
www.infonorth.org

Shopping

Igloolik Co-operative
9 a.m.–6 p.m., Monday to Wednesday
and Saturday; 9 a.m.–9 p.m., Thursday
and Friday. Closed Sunday.
VISA, traveller's cheques, Interac.
Tel.: (867) 934-8938
Fax: (867) 934-8740

Northern Store
10 a.m.–6:30 p.m., Monday to
Wednesday and Saturday;
10 a.m.–9 p.m., Thursday and Friday.
Closed Sunday.
VISA, MasterCard.
Tel.: (867) 934-8822
Fax: (867) 934-8978

68. HALL BEACH
by Lyn Hancock

Hall Beach is the kind of community you don't find featured in many tourist brochures.

Population:	543 (Inuit: 92%, non-Inuit: 8%) Source: 1996 Census of Canada
Telephone Area Code:	867
Time Zone:	Eastern Time
Postal Code:	X0A 0K0
How to Get There:	Possible routes:
	• Ottawa or Montreal-Iqaluit-Hall Beach
	• Kangerlussuaq (Greenland)-Iqaluit-Hall Beach
	• Winnipeg-Rankin Inlet-Iqaluit-Hall Beach
	• Edmonton-Yellowknife-Rankin Inlet-Iqaluit-Hall Beach
	Iqaluit to Hall Beach (about 800 kilometres northwest) is via First Air
Banks:	None. Cash and traveller's cheques are preferable. Credit cards are accepted by certain businesses
Alcohol:	Alcohol and alcoholic beverages cannot be purchased in Hall Beach. Visitors who want to bring alcohol into the community must first obtain a permit from the **Alcohol Education Committee**
Taxis:	Yes

Spread along a series of exposed sand and gravel beaches on the shore of Foxe Basin, and backed by a soggy carpet of lakes and tundra ponds, the place can seem rather desolate.

Yet despite its bleak facade, Hall Beach can be a rich experience for tourists. My most treasured moments in Nunavut took place here: drifting through a maze of ice sculptures at the floe edge, watching walruses and polar bears; trooping down to the beach to greet hunters bringing in belugas; and warming my hands in the body of a whale.

History

While most communities in Nunavut grew around trading posts, whaling stations or seasonal hunting and fishing camps, Hall Beach was created instantly when a Distant Early Warning (DEW) Line site was built here in 1957 to help monitor Canadian air space in the Far North. Today, the community is home to a North Warning System radar site, a technologically advanced model of the DEW Line.

Modern artifacts such as these stand in stark contrast to the piles of stone and bone strewn over gravel beaches at both ends of town, evidence of Thule-culture Inuit and earlier Dorset peoples. Tent rings, food caches, grave sites, *qarmait* (sod houses) and semi-subterranean houses are found to the north of the community at places called *Qimmiqturvik* and *Nappaqut*.

Resting on raised beaches at the southern end of town are many Thule winter houses. Still visible are the flagstone floors, stone sleeping platforms and massive bowhead whale skulls that formed doors, rafters and walls. Blocks of sod that once covered roofs lie fallen on the ground.

Early contact between Inuit and outsiders was sporadic but intense. Explorers William Edward Parry and G. F. Lyon were the first Europeans to visit the area in 1822–1823, while wintering in their ships at Igloolik. In the 1860s, American explorer Charles Francis Hall came to this region briefly and travelled with Inuit; Hall Beach and Hall Lake bear his name. In 1912, Canadian Alfred Tremblay, a prospector with Captain Joseph Bernier's expedition to Pond Inlet, spent time in the area. In the 1920s, members of the Fifth Thule Expedition came to document the life of local Inuit.

In the 1950s and 1960s, Inuit moved from surrounding camps to work and settle around the DEW Line site. (*Sanirajak*, meaning "one that is along the coast" in Inuktitut, refers to the broad region encompassing Hall Beach.) Yet despite the rapid changes that have occurred since those years, Hall Beach remains one of the most traditional communities in Nunavut.

Hall Beach: Its Land and Wildlife

Opportunities for birdwatching in Hall Beach are endless. In late spring and summer, dozens of species of ducks, geese, swans and other waterfowl migrate north to nest on the many tundra ponds behind the community. Visitors will spot common eiders, long-tailed ducks (formerly known as oldsquaws), brant, tundra swans, phalaropes, Sabine's gulls, and in high lemming years, snowy owls. Peregrine falcons can be found in hilly areas on the far side of Hall Lake.

The tundra is also a paradise for botanists and photographers. Though sparse, the soil produces carpets of moss, lichen and ground-hugging flowers such as arctic cotton, arctic heather, mountain avens, moss campion, and lots of louseworts and saxifrages. Residents rave about the spectacular sunsets of early spring and late fall, which are accentuated by the flatness of the landscape.

Tours

A visit to Hall Beach is a visit to the heart of Inuit tradition and hospitality. While strolling along the shore, you'll find residents camped in tents during the sunny days and nights of an all-too-brief summer. Here they tend fishing nets, stew cauldrons of walrus meat, slice *maktaaq* (skin of the beluga whale) and hang crimson strips of arctic char to dry. With three months of endless daylight, people like to get out of their houses as much as possible.

Someone may be scraping blubber from the hide of a seal for a pair of *kamiit* (boots). Another may be chiselling soapstone into a walrus or polar bear. Show an interest in the people and their activities, and you may be invited for tea, bannock (a fried bread imported by Scottish whalers and traders that remains a staple of the Inuit diet), a pot of walrus stew spiced with coiled intestines, or even *igunaq* (aged meat, which in this case is aged walrus meat). Elders say *igunaq* tastes like cheese. Some members of the younger generation describe it differently.

Contact the **Hunters and Trappers Organization** (HTO) for information on fishing and hunting. Fishing is best from mid-July through late August. Charter trips to popular fishing spots such as Hall Lake or *Nursarnaarjuq* (also known as Fisherman's Lake) can be arranged. See Chapter 16, "Flying to Nunavut and Its Communities," for airlines offering charter service. You can also fish from the shore of the community.

Mid- to late August is the best time for caribou hunting. Prime polar bear hunting is late October and late April. Hall Beach is one of the few places in Canada where walruses are still numerous, and walrus hunting is a common activity between July and September. Ask staff at the HTO, Co-op, **Co-op Hotel**, or **hamlet office** to recommend someone to take you.

Other noteworthy sights are the remains of an old whale carcass on the edge of town (estimated to be between 350 and 800 years old and still of pungent odor); the wreckage of a World War II Lancaster bomber that crashed near Hall Lake in the mid-1950s while carrying supplies during construction of the DEW Line station; and five waterfalls in a steep river-canyon at Nunaparvik, about 70 kilometres south of town near Roche Bay.

Events

A good time to visit Hall Beach is Hamlet Day, April 1, when visitors can join a community feast, traditional games and square dancing. Hamlet Day celebrates the imminent return of continuous daylight from mid-April through mid-August.

Accommodation and Dining

The Hall Beach Co-op runs a small hotel that accommodates 15 people in five rooms. Be prepared to share your room, though. Rooms at the **Hall Beach Co-op Hotel** don't have TVs, phones or private washrooms. The hotel has a common area with a phone, two bathrooms with showers, washer/dryer, TV and VCR with free videos. Rooms are $170 per person per night, including meals. Seniors get a 15 per cent discount. The Co-op store also operates a small **canteen**.

Shopping

The two stores here are the **Northern store** and the new **Hall Beach Co-op**. Each sells general merchandise and groceries, including frozen meat and some fresh vegetables. You can also buy arctic char at the HTO.

Although no big-name artists live here, Philomene Nattuq and Leah Anguilianuk are well known in Hall Beach for their carvings and personalized jewelry. Isaki Angkotautok, who also runs an outfitting business, can produce a work of art from almost anything. The Co-op can tell you of other artists who welcome visitors into their homes to buy arts, crafts and sewing. Ask and you may be inundated, however. Many have things to sell; be sure they're what you want.

Services

Two resident nurses run the Hall Beach **Health Centre**, open 8:30 a.m. to 12 p.m. (general clinic), and 1 to 5 p.m. (public health programs) weekdays. For emergencies, call anytime. Hall Beach has also recently acquired an ice rink and its own **RCMP** office.

DIRECTORY

*Outfitters and tour operators licensed at time of writing.
After March 31/99, check for updated status.

Accommodation and Dining

Co-op Canteen
At the Hall Beach Co-op.
10 a.m.–10 p.m., Monday to Friday;
1–10 p.m., Saturday and Sunday.
Tel.: (867) 928-8876
Fax: (867) 928-8926

Hall Beach Co-op Hotel
VISA, MasterCard, American Express.
Tel.: (867) 928-8952 or (867) 928-8876
Fax: (867) 928-8926

* Outfitters/Tour Operators

Hunters and Trappers Organization
Tel.: (867) 928-8994
Fax: (867) 928-8765

Kungut Outfitting
Tel.: (867) 928-8994
Fax: (867) 928-8765

Services

Airport
Tel.: (867) 928-8919
Fax: (867) 928-8914

Alcohol Education Committee
Tel.: (867) 928-8880

Churches

St. Francis Roman Catholic Church
Priest comes to town every few
months.
Tel.: (867) 928-8872

St. Silas Anglican Church
No telephone.

Department of Sustainable Development, Government of Nunavut
(or until April/99, GNWT's Resources,
Wildlife and Economic Development)
With hamlet office.
Tel.: (867) 928-8276
Fax: (867) 928-8871

Frontec Logistics
Runs the North Warning System
radar site.
Tel.: (867) 928-8987

Hamlet Office
Tel.: (867) 928-8844
Fax: (867) 928-8355

Health Centre
Tel.: (867) 928-8827
Fax: (867) 928-8847

Police (RCMP)
Tel.: (867) 928-8930
Fax: (867) 928-8949

Post Office
Located at the Co-op.
3–6 p.m., weekdays.
Tel.: (867) 928-8821

Radio Station (FM 106.1)
Tel.: (867) 928-8829

Schools

Arnaqjuaq School
Elementary and high school.
Tel.: (867) 928-8855
Fax: (867) 928-8810

Nunavut Arctic College
Tel.: (867) 928-8803
Fax: (867) 928-8979

Taxi

Co-op Taxi
Tel.: (867) 928-8876

Weather Information
Tel.: (867) 928-8807
Web site weather forecast:
www.infonorth.org

Shopping

Hall Beach Co-op
10 a.m.–10 p.m., Monday to Friday;
1–10 p.m., Saturday; 1–10 p.m.,
Sunday (canteen only).
VISA accepted.
Tel.: (867) 928-8876
Fax: (867) 928-8926

Northern Store
10 a.m.–6:30 p.m., Monday to
Wednesday; 10 a.m.–8 p.m., Thursday
and Friday; 1–6:30 p.m., Saturday.
Closed Sunday.
VISA, MasterCard, Interac.
Tel.: (867) 928-8875
Fax: (867) 928-8874

69. REPULSE BAY

by Peter Ernerk

Would you like to see an Inuk elder teaching Inuit youth how to drum dance and sing traditional Inuit songs?

Population:	559 (Inuit: 95%, non-Inuit: 5%) Source: 1996 Census of Canada
Telephone Area Code:	867
Time Zone:	Central Time
Postal Code:	X0C 0H0
How to Get There:	Possible routes:
	• Winnipeg-Rankin Inlet-Repulse Bay
	• Edmonton-Yellowknife-Rankin Inlet-Repulse Bay
	• Ottawa/Montreal-Iqaluit-Rankin Inlet-Repulse Bay
	• Kangerlussuaq (Greenland)-Iqaluit-Rankin Inlet-Repulse Bay
	Rankin Inlet to Repulse Bay (about 500 kilometres north) is via Calm Air
Banks:	None. Cash and traveller's cheques are preferable. Credit cards are accepted by certain businesses
Alcohol:	Alcohol and alcoholic beverages are not sold in Repulse Bay. Alcohol can only be imported if prior permission is obtained from the **Alcohol Education Committee.** However, the Committee meets infrequently and has no contact phone number, so it is extremely difficult to bring alcohol into the community
Taxis:	No

You can when you reach the Arctic Circle and Repulse Bay, an Inuit community still steeped in tradition — and one of the last places in the Arctic to join the 20th century.

Repulse Bay thrives on hunting, fishing and trapping; many elders, like **Victor Tungilik**, have spent a lifetime doing so. This is a place where it's not unusual in the summer to see hunters returning home with fish, narwhals, belugas, seals and walruses.

Victor has almost always lived in *Naujaat* — the Inuktitut name for Repulse Bay. Born in 1924, this cultural performer is also the composer of several traditional songs, and is sometimes found at Repulse Bay's **Tusarvik School**, where he teaches youth to drum and sing. Daughter Elizabeth Mapsalak can arrange for visitors to hear Victor's teachings about Inuit culture firsthand. Or those new in town may want to drop by **Nunavut Arctic College**, where elder Abraham Tagornak often lectures.

Repulse Bay residents are proud of their community and of the beautiful surrounding landscape. The horizon is dotted with scenic inlets and hills of all shapes, some of which are snow-covered year round. When you land and enter the Repulse Bay air terminal, you'll be met by the smiles of local residents. If you're not sure how to find your way around, just ask anyone. Everyone in *Naujaat* is proud to share their history and culture with visitors.

In May 1964, I returned home after attending a high school in Yellowknife, and encountered a professor from Winnipeg, George Swinton of the University of Manitoba. He wanted to document Repulse Bay carvers for a book he was writing. I had learned to speak English a bit, and was now able to translate "pretty good" from English to Inuktitut. After George finished his work, he asked me what I wanted for helping. I liked, and got, the nice beige pants from the store.

Was there anything that my parents wanted? Some tea and tobacco. Before he departed, George came to take a picture of my family. My mother had an *ulu* (a woman's knife) that he liked very much and wanted to buy. My mother, always very generous with people, said because the professor had done so much already for us, he could have the *ulu* for free. That was how we showed our appreciation to this southern visitor and, you know, we were happy doing it. As for the *ulu*, we've learned it now resides at the Winnipeg Art Gallery.

History

Surrounding Repulse Bay are endless *inuksuk* landmarks. *Inuksuit* (the plural of *inuksuk*) are rocks piled on top of each other in the shape of a human, and they are referred to as stone cairns in English. Inuit built them countless years ago to show where they had travelled. These landmarks are built to be noticed.

Many years ago, the Inuit of Repulse Bay travelled back and forth by *qamutiit* and boat to the land of *Amitturmiut* — the people from *Iglulik* (Igloolik) and *Sanirajak* (Hall Beach). These travellers marked their way with *inuksuit*. For centuries there's been continuous contact with the people of *Arviligjuaq* (Pelly Bay), and many marriages have taken place between the Inuit of *Iglulik*, *Naujaat* and *Arviligjuaq*.

Whalers began making regular voyages to Repulse Bay in 1860, but by 1914, commercial whaling had all but stopped. The Hudson's Bay Co. opened a permanent trading post in 1919 (in 1987, the North West Company, which operates the Northern stores department chain, took over). In the 1940s and 1950s, the Inuit of *Naujaat* trapped mostly white foxes. Fur prices were considered very good then, and the price of goods affordable ($0.50 a gallon for kerosene for the primus stove). Many people traded their fox furs and sealskins with the Hudson's Bay Co., and then purchased whaling boats, canoes and outboard motors.

In the 1930s, missionaries came to this area and altered the course of Inuit life. The very name "missionaries" implies that we Inuit were to be saved. Not surprisingly, perhaps, religious affiliation matched tribal membership. The *Amitturmiut* converted to the Anglican religion, settling mostly near the Hudson's Bay Co. trading post on the west side of the community's small hill. Roman Catholics, consisting of *Nattilikmiut* (people who originally hailed from Pelly Bay) and *Aivilingmiun* (people whose ancestry can be traced to Repulse Bay), settled on the east side. On this unnamed hill is a traditional grave site. By the 1950s it was not uncommon to hear Inuit arguing among themselves as to whose religious faith was better. This was especially common among the children. This division, of course, was not an Inuit choice.

In the 1940s, people started carving in a big way, working largely in soapstone, ivory, and occasionally whalebone. This allowed Inuit to live well, providing them with additional income. It also freed them from their dependence on government support. The Inuit of *Naujaat* led the way in carving, as did the Inuit of *Kinngait* (Cape Dorset). Repulse Bay produced a good number of the best, including the late Marc Tungilik, who became very famous for his miniature ivory carvings, and Irene Katak (the author's mother).

Many of Repulse Bay's famous carvers have since passed away: Lucy Agalakti Mapsalak, Celina Putulik, Paul Akuarjuk, Christine Aalu Sivaniqtuq, Madeline Isiqqut Kringayak, Athanasi Ulikattaq, Bernadette Iguttaq Tungilik. But others, such as John Kaunak and Paul Maliki, still practise their craft in *Naujaat*, while others, like Mariano Aupilardjuk and Bernadette Saumik, live in Rankin Inlet. Many of these carvers' pieces can be viewed at art galleries and museums in Canada. A large collection of *Naujaat* carvings is on permanent display at the Eskimo Museum in Churchill, Manitoba.

The Canadian government introduced the Eskimo Rental Housing Program in 1968, and almost all of the area's Inuit settled in *Naujaat*. A new wage economy was helped along by the presence of government institutions that hired locally.

Repulse Bay: Its Land and Wildlife

About five kilometres north of the community is a cliff where seagulls nest every June. It is from this nesting place that *Naujaat* got its name: "fledgling," or baby seagull, in Inuktitut. The English name of Repulse Bay came in 1742 from a disgruntled Captain Christopher Middleton, sailing on behalf of the British Admiralty. Disappointed that he had journeyed so far north and not found the elusive Northwest Passage, Middleton named the body of water he had sailed into "Repulse Bay."

During May and June, *Naujaat* comes alive with the arrival of migratory birds. The small birds, among them snow buntings, arrive first, a real sign of spring. Numerous species of larger birds follow. Chanting in monotone late into the night, loons are particularly entertaining, especially when one is at an outpost and just beginning to fall asleep. Other notable birds are eider ducks, long-tailed (formerly known as oldsquaw) ducks, seagulls (*naujat*) and jaegers. The jaegers and seagulls often pick fights with one another, usually over a piece of meat. Visitors will also spot ptarmigan, tundra swans, peregrine falcons, gyrfalcons, rough-legged hawks and sandhill cranes. Geese, including the Canada, snow and greater species, are more abundant today than they were in the 1950s and 1960s, perhaps due to improved vegetation. Further out from the community, arctic terns and black guillemots can be seen.

In *Naujaat*, June is known for its *manniit* (eggs). Arctic terns have some of the best-tasting eggs in the Arctic, but when walking along the small ponds where these birds lay their eggs, it's best to avoid them. Arctic terns are very protective, and swoop down so low that they've been known to knock a person's head with their beak. Be careful!

In fall and winter, ravens and white snowy owls can be seen further out from the community.

Marine wildlife around Repulse Bay is plentiful, too: in addition to families of bearded, ringed, harp and harbor seals, the waters in this area are home to bowhead whales.

Tours

One can walk back in time and visit the historical ruins and sod houses just north of *Naujaat. Inuksuit* and old stone graves are all within walking distance.

In September 1991, Repulse Bay saw the return and reburial of 63 skeletal remains "stolen" from the community's traditional archeological site in 1922 by members of the Danish Fifth Thule Expedition, headed by crew member Therkel Mathiassen. Thousands of artifacts were taken to Denmark along with these skeletal remains, which were used first for medical training and later displayed at a local museum. The community of *Naujaat* is still working to bring home the 3,500 artifacts that lie scattered now in museums throughout Denmark, Germany, the United States and elsewhere. But because of the red tape involved, the task promises to be a daunting one.

If boating or viewing marine life is your pleasure, contact chairman Andreasi Siutinuar of the **Arviq Hunters and Trappers Organization** to arrange a boat outing. View seals, birds, walrus, and caribou, or head about 18 kilometres southwest to the *Qikiqtat* (Harbour Islands) and *Niaqunguut* (North Pole River) to see the old stone house of early explorer Dr. John Rae of the Hudson's Bay Co. This journey is accessible by boat in the summer. Take your camera to record your own history of *Naujaat*.

Shopping

At the **Naujat Co-op**, you can buy a carving or two for your friends. If you're not from Canada, though, check with the local wildlife officer to see what you can and can't take home. United States residents, for example, can't import whalebone or ivory carvings.

Groceries and other everyday goods are available from the Co-op and the **Northern store**.

The **Nuksutet Sewing Group** will custom tailor anything from *kamiit* (boots) and mitts to *amautit* (women's parkas) and other clothing. Phone manager Elizabeth Kidlapik to place an order.

Events

Many festivals are annual occurrences in *Naujaat*. Easter Games feature igloo-building, snowmobile and dogteam racing, and indoor and outdoor games. The Fishing Derby usually drops anchor in May, and Canada's birthday on July 1 sets the scene for Hamlet Day celebrations. For more information on recreational and sports activities, contact recreational director William Beveridge at the **hamlet office**.

Accommodation and Dining

Inns North, operated by the Naujat Co-op, has 13 rooms, 12 with two twin beds and one with a double. All have private washrooms and color TVs with cable. Rooms don't have phones, but there is a public phone near the lobby and a lounge with a TV for guests. There is also one suite with a living room area, hot plate and fridge. Altogether, the hotel accommodates 25 people.

Rooms are $125 per person per day (without meals) or $180 with meals. The suite is $145 per person per day without meals, and $200 including meals. Meals are priced as follows: breakfast $10, lunch $20, and supper $25, and are served at posted times. Visitors who aren't staying at Inns North can also make prior arrangements to eat there. Hotel guests can do their own laundry if they arrange it first with the hotel manager.

The recreation committee operates a year-round canteen at the Community Complex (during the winter, there's also one at the Community Arena).

Services

With flights from Rankin Inlet to *Naujaat* running a minimum of four times weekly, air transportation is good.

If you have a medical emergency while visiting the community, a nurse can be reached by phoning the **Health Centre**. There is 24-hour emergency service. Although there are no doctors in the community, nurses do consultations over the phone with an on-call doctor in Churchill. General clinics run from 8:30 a.m. to 5 p.m., Monday to Friday.

The community gymnasium (used for volleyball, basketball, soccer and public meetings), the **post office**, and local **radio station** are all located at the Hamlet Office Complex. Another gymnasium was recently added to the school.

DIRECTORY

*Outfitters and tour operators licensed at time of writing.
After March 31/99, check for updated status.

Accommodation and Dining

Inns North
VISA, MasterCard, Diners Club/enRoute, American Express, Interac.
Tel.: (867) 462-9943
Fax: (867) 462-4152

* Outfitters/Tour Operators

Arviq Hunters and Trappers Organization
9 a.m.–12 p.m. and
1–5 p.m., Monday to Friday.
Tel.: (867) 462-4334
Fax: (867) 462-4335

Services

Airport
6:45 a.m.–5:15 p.m., Monday to Friday;
8:45 a.m.–3:15 p.m., weekends.
Tel.: (867) 462-9973
Fax: (867) 462-4146

Alcohol Education Committee
No telephone. Contact hamlet for information.
Tel.: (867) 462-9952

Churches

Glad Tidings Church
No telephone.

Repulse Bay Anglican Church
No telephone.

Repulse Bay Roman Catholic Church
Services: 7 p.m., Monday to Sunday;
11 a.m., Sunday (Inuktitut only).
Tel.: (867) 462-9912

Department of Sustainable Development, Government of Nunavut
(or until April/99, GNWT's Resources, Wildlife and Economic Development)
Tel.: (867) 462-4002
Fax: (867) 462-4400
If office is closed, call Arviat office at (867) 857-2828.

Hamlet Office

Contact hamlet manager.
Tel.: (867) 462-9952
Fax: (867) 462-4144

Health Centre

Tel.: (867) 462-9916
Fax: (867) 462-4212

Police (RCMP)

Call detachment in Rankin Inlet.
Tel.: (867) 645-2822
Fax: (867) 645-2568

Post Office

Located in the Hamlet Office Complex.
1–5 p.m., Monday to Friday.
Tel.: (867) 462-4194

Radio Station (107.1 FM)

To place public information and
announcements, call Friday from
6–10:30 p.m.
Tel.: (867) 462-4061

Schools

Nunavut Arctic College

Tel.: (867) 462-4281 or (867) 462-4601
Fax: (867) 462-4293

Tusarvik Elementary and High School

Also provides library services.
Tel.: (867) 462-9920
Fax: (867) 462-4232

Victor Tungilik
(Cultural Performances)

Contact Elizabeth Mapsalak for
arrangements. A fee applies.
Tel.: (867) 462-4203

Weather Information

Tel.: (867) 462-9973
Fax: (867) 462-4146
Web site weather forecast:
www.infonorth.org

Shopping

Naujat Co-op

10 a.m.–7 p.m., Monday to Thursday;
10 a.m.–9 p.m., Friday; 1–5 p.m.,
Saturday.
VISA, MasterCard, Diners
Club/enRoute, American Express,
Interac.
Tel.: (867) 462-9943
Fax: (867) 462-4152

Northern Store

10 a.m.–6 p.m., Monday to Wednesday;
10 a.m.–7 p.m., Thursday and Friday;
10 a.m.–6 p.m., Saturday.
VISA, MasterCard, Interac.
Tel.: (867) 462-9923
Fax: (867) 462-4011

Nuksutet Sewing Group

1–5 p.m., Monday to Friday.
Tel.: (867) 462-4500 or (867) 462-4121

70. PELLY BAY

by Steven W. Metzger

In early April, the night sky is completely dark for only a few hours; by late May, the sun will be up for 24 hours.

Population:	496 (Inuit: 94%, non-Inuit: 6%) Source: 1996 Census of Canada
Telephone Area Code:	867
Time Zone:	Mountain Time
Postal Code:	X0E 1K0
How to Get There:	Possible route:
	• Edmonton-Yellowknife-Pelly Bay
	Yellowknife to Pelly Bay (about 1,300 kilometres northeast) is via First Air.
	All passengers coming from Central or Eastern Canada must stay
	overnight in Yellowknife or Edmonton. Pelly Bay can only be accessed by air
Banks:	None. Cash and traveller's cheques are preferable. Credit cards are
	accepted by certain businesses
Alcohol:	Alcohol and alcoholic beverages are prohibited in Pelly Bay
Taxis:	Yes

But the warmth of May is still a dream, and the *tuktuit* (caribou) are still far away. The men spend many hours fishing, waiting for warmer weather and the return of the caribou, enduring as they always have. They travel in the bitter cold to *Kuuk* (Kellet River) or to one of the many other bountiful lakes and rivers in the area, to tend their fish nets. Arctic char and whitefish are in good supply, and occasionally a seal is caught near *Qurvigjuaq* ("big urine pot"). Still, everyone longs for the caribou to return, to complete the group of animals — seal, caribou and fish — that are synonymous with life.

I moved here five years ago, and after countless journeys on the land, I'm still captivated by its stark beauty and isolation. I marvel at a culture that enabled Inuit to thrive for centuries in this challenging environment using only animal products, stone and snow. Elders welcome visitors to the community, and relish the chance to retell the old stories. As they talk, their warmth and joy fill my spirit. I sense their bond with the land, and I feel my growing respect for the *Arviligjuaqmiut* (those living in the area of *Arviligjuaq*, the "place with lots of bowhead whales"), which is the Inuit name for Pelly Bay. The English name came from early explorers who chose it to honor Sir John Pelly, a governor of the Hudson's Bay Co. The bowhead whales of the Inuktitut name ply these waters no more.

History

In 1968, the Canadian government transported 32 prefabricated houses into Pelly Bay. Until then, the *Arviligjuaqmiut* lived a semi-nomadic lifestyle. Small family groups, living in *igluit* (igloos) and skin tents, followed the wildlife that sustained them. Occasionally, groups would come together to hunt and fish. In 1937, when the Catholic mission was established here, groups would meet for Christmas celebrations at *Kugaarjuk* (the mouth of the Kugajuk River), then separate again to pursue their nomadic cycle.

The first Catholic missionary, Father Pierre Henry, arrived in 1935. He built a small stone chapel/house, but soon learned that stone wasn't a good insulator in this harsh climate. Instead, he adopted Inuit ways, living in an *iglu* and wearing traditional Inuit clothing during the cold months. He and Father Franz Van de Velde, who remained a powerful force in the community until 1965, built the stone church in 1941. Recently, the Hamlet of Pelly Bay received a government grant to restore the deteriorating church as a historic site.

Until 1955, when the DEW Line construction began, people here had almost no contact with the outside world. In 1829, English explorer John Ross camped nearby, but no whalers or Hudson's Bay Co. trading post ever came to Pelly Bay. Ice jams around the islands guarding the bay's mouth made access almost impossible.

The rapid arrival of the modern world has led to an interesting blend of cultures. It's not unusual when visiting a home to find family members watching the latest movie on a large-screen TV, while eating raw arctic char cut from a fish lying on a square of cardboard in the centre of the room.

Created by the Canadian government to help assert its sovereignty over the North, Pelly Bay is now a small settlement with a wage economy. Although traditional activities remain very important here, the community is in rapid transition: cable TV has arrived, and Internet access began in 1998. Only a few elders who have lived more than half their lives in the old ways on the land remain. And while efforts are being made to preserve Inuktitut, English is now the first language of many preschoolers.

Pelly Bay: Its Land and Wildlife

Between the bay to the west and the seemingly endless, flat tundra to the east, Pelly Bay is nestled in the coastal mountains at *Kugaarjuk*. The settlement's stone church, set off by a group of large *inuksuit*, and its cross, built by hand atop the mountain across the river using 45-gallon drums, are distinctive features of the scene you discover when you arrive by air.

July to September marks a time of rapid change. The sea ice melts and the tundra becomes a multi-colored carpet of wildflowers. Migrating birds arrive from the South, including falcons, rough-legged hawks, snowy owls, seagulls, ravens, terns, jaegers, ptarmigans, cranes, ducks, geese, and swans. Over the past few years, a small number of narwhal have visited the bay in August. By the end of September, the ice starts to form again. You can fish for arctic char and explore archeological sites. The wide-open tundra and mountain valleys provide unlimited hiking and camping opportunities. In early August, Inuit fish with *kakivait* (traditional spears) at an ancient *saputit* (stone weir) on the Kugajuk River. Insect repellent is a must during July.

Tours

For tours on the land, contact the **Hunters and Trappers Organization**. Pelly Bay's only licensed outfitter is **Kayak Tours**, a sea-kayaking enterprise. As for other outings, residents in the community are very friendly and willing to help you enjoy your visit. Although rental of all-terrain vehicles and snow machines is uncertain, you can arrange a trip on a *qamutik* pulled by dogs or snow machines.

Between October and November, visitors can camp with Inuit at the Kellet River for the fall arctic char run. Arrange an early-season dogsled or snow machine trip. Low light angles create a paradise for landscape photographers.

For those who want to experience an arctic winter, the time to do so is from December to February. Between early December and mid-January, the sun doesn't rise. While winter travel on the land is for seasoned adventure travellers, those who qualify may want to accompany Inuit on a traditional seal hunt. Enjoy the displays of northern lights.

Visitors can celebrate spring from March to June, but remember that sunglasses are a must. Mid-April to May is especially great for touring the land and viewing wildlife by dogsled and snow machine. You can also see baby seals basking on the sea ice, or do some ice fishing.

If you plan to visit Pelly Bay between November and March, it's essential to wear clothing for extremely cold weather. Although some caribou clothing is available for rent, you're best to come prepared.

Events

On Easter weekend, cheer on the athletes at the Spring Games, where you'll see such contests as harpoon throwing. Christmas games are held during the last week of December, and the annual fishing contest is on the weekend of Hamlet Day (second Monday in May). Come April 1, 1999, when Nunavut officially and legally becomes a territory, celebrations begin in earnest.

Shopping

The **Koomiut Co-op** is the only store in Pelly Bay. Prices are high, but basic food, clothing and personal items are available.

Pelly Bay carvers work with ivory, whalebone, antler and stone. Many women make excellent traditional clothing, and accept orders from visitors. Depending on the time of year and the materials needed for clothing, waiting periods may be lengthy.

Accommodation and Dining

The **Inukshuk Inn** is operated by the Koomiut Co-op. The hotel has eight rooms (two ensuite, six with shared facilities) to accommodate 16 guests. Each room has cable TV and a VCR. The daily rate is $135 per person, and includes complimentary **airport** pickup. Meals, served at scheduled times, are $10 for breakfast, $15 for lunch, and $25 for dinner.

Canteens are open in the gym (in the hamlet office building) and between October and April in the **Nattilik Ice Arena**.

Services

The Pelly Bay **Health Centre** is staffed by two nurses who handle routine and emergency medical needs. Hours are 8:30 a.m. to 5 p.m., Monday to Friday. One of the nurses is always on call, while a doctor in Yellowknife is always on call for telephone consultations.

The hamlet recreation department offers programs in the hamlet gym; from October to April, it operates the Nattilik Ice Arena.

A single-member **RCMP** unit provides 24-hour service.

DIRECTORY

*Outfitters and tour operators licensed at time of writing.
After March 31/99, check for updated status.

Accommodation and Dining

Inukshuk Inn
VISA, Diners Club/enRoute.
Tel.: (867) 769-7211

*Outfitters/Tour Operators

Kayak Tours
Tel.: (867) 769-6606
Fax: (867) 769-6098

Services

Airport
10 a.m.–12 p.m., 1–5 p.m., Monday,
Tuesday, Thursday and Friday;
1–5 p.m., Wednesday.
Tel.: (867) 769-7505
Fax: (867) 769-7302

Church

Roman Catholic Church
Services: 7 p.m., Monday to Sunday;
11 a.m., Sunday.
Tel.: (867) 769-6261
Fax: (867) 769-6261

Department of Sustainable Development, Government of Nunavut
(or until April/99, GNWT's Resources,
Wildlife and Economic Development)
Export permits, hunting/fishing licences.
8:30 a.m.–5 p.m., Monday to Friday.
Tel.: (867) 769-7011
Fax: (867) 769-7968

Executive Service Office
GNWT liaison office – permits,
licences, documents.
1–5 p.m., Monday to Friday.
Tel.: (867) 769-7411
Fax: (867) 769-7706

Hamlet Office
Tel.: (867) 769-6281
Fax: (867) 769-6069

Health Centre
Tel.: (867) 769-6441
Fax: (867) 769-6059

Hunters and Trappers Organization
1–5 p.m., Monday to Friday.
Tel.: (867) 769-6071
Fax: (867) 769-6713

Nattilik Arena
October to April; hours vary.
Tel.: (867) 769-7969

Police (RCMP)
Tel.: (867) 769-7221
Fax: (867) 769-6032

Post Office
In hamlet office.
10–11:30 a.m., 1–4 p.m., Monday to
Friday.
Tel.: (867) 769-6011

Radio Station (FM 107.1)
Can be used for public announcements.
Noon–1 p.m., 5:30–6:30 p.m., daily.
Tel.: (867) 769-6099 (off air)
Tel.: (867) 769-6221 (on air)

Schools

Kugaarjuk School
Tel.: (867) 769-6281
Fax: (867) 769-6116

Nunavut Arctic College
Call hamlet office for information.
Tel.: (867) 769-6281
Fax: (867) 769-6069

Taxi

Co-op Taxi
Tel.: (867) 769-6231

Weather Information
6 a.m.–5 p.m., Monday to Friday.
Tel.: (867) 769-6567
Web site weather forecast:
www.infonorth.org

Shopping

Koomiut Co-op
9 a.m.–5:30 p.m., Monday to Friday.
Between October and May, open on
Saturday from 12–3 p.m. Closed Sunday.
VISA, Interac.
Tel.: (867) 769-6231
Fax: (867) 769-6098

71. TALOYOAK

by George Bohlender

Sitting at the foot of a series of rocky hills on the shores of a small body of water known as Stanners Harbour, Taloyoak is the northernmost community on the Canadian mainland (69° 32' north latitude).

Population:	648 (Inuit: 92%, non-Inuit: 8%) Source: 1996 Census of Canada
Telephone Area Code:	867
Time Zone:	Mountain Time
Postal Code:	X0E 1B0
How to Get There:	Possible route:
	• Edmonton-Yellowknife-Taloyoak
	Yellowknife to Taloyoak (about 1,200 kilometres northeast) is via First Air.
	Passengers stay overnight in Edmonton or Yellowknife
Banks:	None. Traveller's cheques and cash are preferable. Credit cards are
	accepted by certain businesses
Alcohol:	Alcohol is not restricted, and is governed only by the provisions of the
	NWT Liquor Act. However, there's no place to buy alcohol
	in the community
Taxis:	No. Visitors should arrange for airport pickup when booking hotel rooms

The word *taloyoak* is a misspelling of the Inuktitut word *talurjuaq*, meaning "large blind." It refers to a stone caribou blind traditionally used by Inuit of the area to corral and harvest caribou.

History

The traditional inhabitants of the Taloyoak (pronounced "ta-low-ruaq") area were the *Nattilik* Inuit, the *Nattilingmiut*, a people largely sustained by the abundance of seals in the region, which provided their main source of food and clothing.

The search for the Northwest Passage has played an important role in the contemporary history of the Taloyoak region. The first significant European exploration here occurred between 1829 and 1833, when Sir John Ross and his crew combed the area after their ship became trapped in ice. Between 1848 and 1860, the area was visited extensively by British and American sailors searching for the lost Franklin Expedition.

The foundation of the modern community began in 1948, when poor ice conditions forced the Hudson's Bay Co. to close its trading post at Fort Ross on the south coast of Somerset Island, some 250 kilometres north of Taloyoak. The post was relocated to its present location at Stanners Harbour, and Taloyoak — then known as Spence Bay — was born.

Shortly after the establishment of the Hudson's Bay Co. post, the RCMP arrived. They were followed by Catholic and Anglican missionaries in the early 1950s. These entities formed the nucleus of the burgeoning community, which grew as the federal government encouraged Inuit to settle in Spence Bay. In Taloyoak today, traditional activities such as hunting and trapping remain a prominent part of everyday life. These activities are supplemented by carving, crafts production, and wage employment, which combine to provide a lifestyle balanced between old and new.

Taloyoak: Its Land and Wildlife

As with other Nunavut communities, plants burst to life every spring and summer on the tundra. Countless berries blanket surrounding hills; wild blueberries and bearberries are harvested by residents throughout the summer. Fields of arctic cotton are reminiscent of fluffy white dandelions, and fragrant, dried arctic heather is used as tinder for campfires in this treeless land.

Local bird life includes ravens, seagulls, jaegers, and ptarmigan. Gyrfalcons nest quite close to the community, and snowy owls have been seen from the roadside between Taloyoak and nearby Middle Lake. Huge flocks of ducks and Canada geese also fly over the community on their migrations.

Animals encountered in and near the community include ground squirrels (*siksiit*), lemmings, weasels, arctic hares, and arctic foxes. Wolves are not usually found near town, and hunters must also travel some distance for caribou. Muskoxen are present further north on the Boothia Peninsula and Somerset Island, and on the barren lands to the south.

The waters around Taloyoak are rich with ringed seals. Whales are generally scarce, but are occasionally spotted further north. Polar bears are found in coastal areas to the north and west.

There are many outstanding fishing spots within walking distance of town. Arctic char can be caught during their autumn run in local lakes and rivers. Ice fishing for lake trout and whitefish is common during late winter and spring. Middle Lake, which is linked to Taloyoak by a seven-kilometre road, is a popular year-round fishing destination. It is also a favorite camping spot in summer, and many families have cabins there.

Tours

Several buildings still stand at Thom Bay, which was a Roman Catholic mission during the 1940s. The site, 80 kilometres northeast of town, is easily reached by snowmobile in late winter and early spring.

The shores of Netsilik Lake offer fine examples of previous habitation. The remains of dozens of stone and sod houses can be seen here, about 25 kilometres southeast of town. The lake can be reached by both snowmobile (in winter and spring) and boat (in summer). At present there are no licensed outfitters in Taloyoak, but the **Spence Bay Hunters and Trappers Organization** is a good clearing house for information about weather conditions and the surrounding land.

The history of the area is well represented within the community itself. The stone caribou blind for which Taloyoak is named is located on the southeast side of the harbor, near the Northern store. The original Hudson's Bay Co. warehouses and the stone church built by Catholic missionaries in the 1950s are also still standing.

Monuments in the community formally identify its diverse history. One is to John Stanners, the town's first Bay manager. It is located across from the Northern store's staff house. Two plaques commemorate the exploits of European explorers Sir John Ross and Sir James Clark Ross. But the most interesting monument in town commemorates a local hero, David Kootook. Kootook was aboard a bush plane that crashed in the western Northwest Territories during a medical evacuation flight in 1973. Kootook helped the pilot, Martin Hartwell, survive, but perished before help arrived. The monument is located across from the **airport** terminal.

Shopping

Taluq Designs Ltd. produces the famous Spence Bay "packing dolls," arctic animals carrying their young in wool duffel parkas, in a modern facility across from the Co-op. Here you can also pick up other sewn crafts and garments, which are either created at the shop or imported from other Nunavut and western Northwest Territories communities.

Visitors interested in carvings will have no problem watching the artists in action, as most work outside their homes during the 24-hour sunlight of spring and summer. Carvers and craftspeople make regular visits to hotels to sell their latest works; a selection of carvings is also available at the Co-op.

Groceries and dry goods can be purchased at the **Northern store** and the **Paleajook Co-op**.

Accommodation and Dining

The **Boothia Inn** provides shared accommodation for up to 17 people in seven rooms. All have cable TV and three have private bathrooms. The daily rate is $170 per person, including meals, or $125 without meals.

The **Paleajook Co-op Hotel/Inns North** accommodates 18 people in nine rooms. Unlike the Boothia Inn, however, there are no private bathrooms. All rooms have cable TV. The cost is $160 per person per night, including meals, or $110 without meals.

There are no restaurants in Taloyoak. Both hotels can provide meals for non-guests and those with special dietary requirements, given sufficient notice. At the Paleajook, breakfast costs $10, lunch $15, and dinner is $25. Breakfast at the Boothia is $12.50, lunch $17.50, and dinner is $30.

Services

At Taloyoak's **health centre**, patients are seen between 9 a.m. and 11:30 a.m., Monday to Friday, and other times on an emergency basis.

RESPONSIBLE DEVELOPMENT STARTS HERE

AS A 100% INUIT OWNED COMPANY, KITIKMEOT CORPORATION

is working towards improving the economic status and self-reliance of the Kitikmeot Inuit. Hiring locally, joint venture opportunities, responsible development ventures – all are ways we're working hard to develop our region and help Inuit succeed.

For information contact: Business Development Officer
Tel: 1 867 983-2200 · Fax: 1 867 983-2995 · E-mail: kitcorp@polarnet.ca

DIRECTORY

Accommodation and Dining

Boothia Inn
VISA accepted.
Tel.: (867) 561-5300
Fax: (867) 561-5318

Paleajook Co-op Hotel/Inns North
VISA, MasterCard, Diners Club/enRoute.
Tel.: (867) 561-5803 or (867) 561-5221
Fax: (867) 561-5603

Services

Airport
First Air
Tel.: (867) 561-5400

Churches
Good Shepherd Anglican Church
Services: 11 a.m. and 6 p.m., Sunday.
Tel.: (867) 561-5710

Roman Catholic Church
Tel.: (867) 561-5161

Department of Sustainable Development, Government of Nunavut
(or until April/99, GNWT's Resources, Wildlife and Economic Development)
Tel.: (867) 561-6231
Fax: (867) 561-6810

Hamlet Office
Tel.: (867) 561-6341
Fax: (867) 561-5057

Health Centre
Tel.: (867) 561-5111
Fax: (867) 561-6906

Police (RCMP)
Tel.: (867) 561-5201
Fax: (867) 561-5094

Post Office
Located at Paleajook Co-op.
1:30–5 p.m., Monday to Friday.
Tel.: (867) 561-5221

Radio Station (105.1 FM)
Tel.: (867) 561-6808 (off air)
Tel.: (867) 561-6581 (on air)
Fax: (867) 561-5002

Schools

Netsilik School
Tel.: (867) 561-5181
Fax: (867) 561-5036

Nunavut Arctic College
Tel.: (867) 561-5371
Fax: (867) 561-5202

Spence Bay Hunters and Trappers Organization
Tel.: (867) 561-5066
Fax: (867) 561-5066

Weather Information
Tel.: (867) 561-6241
Fax: (867) 561-6241
Web site weather forecast:
www.infonorth.org

Shopping

Northern Store
10 a.m.–12:30 p.m. and 1:30–6 p.m., Monday to Thursday; 1–6 p.m. and 7–8:30 p.m., Friday; 12:30–4:30 p.m., Saturday. Closed Sunday.
VISA, MasterCard, Diners Club/enRoute, Interac.
Tel.: (867) 561-5121
Fax: (867) 561-5708

Paleajook Co-op
10 a.m.–12:30 p.m. and 1:30–6 p.m., Monday to Thursday; 10 a.m.–12:30 p.m. and 1:30–8 p.m., Friday; 1–5 p.m., Saturday. Closed Sunday.
VISA, MasterCard, Diners Club/enRoute, Interac.
Tel.: (867) 561-5221
Fax: (867) 561-5603

Taluq Designs Ltd.
9 a.m.–12 p.m. and 1–5 p.m., Monday to Friday (September to May). June to August by appointment only (call Mona Igutsaq at 561-6820).
VISA accepted.
Tel.: (867) 561-5280
Fax: (867) 561-6500
Web site: www.arctic-can.nt.ca/
taluq/index.html

72. GJOA HAVEN

by Michael P. Ellsworth

Gjoa Haven was dubbed "the finest little harbor in the world" by Norwegian explorer Roald Amundsen, and that probably explains why this inlet, nestled on the southeast coast of King William Island on the Northwest Passage, also became the namesake of the wooden ship that Amundsen sailed through the Northwest Passage between 1903 and 1906 — the *Gjoa.*

Population:	879 (Inuit: 94%, non-Inuit: 6%) Source: 1996 Census of Canada
Telephone Area Code:	867
Time Zone:	Mountain Time
Postal Code:	X0E 1J0
How to Get There:	Possible route:
	• Edmonton-Yellowknife-Gjoa Haven
	Yellowknife to Gjoa Haven (about 1,100 kilometres northeast) is via
	First Air. All passengers, including those coming from Central or Eastern
	Canada, must stay overnight in Yellowknife
Banks:	None. Cash and traveller's cheques are preferable. Credit cards are
	accepted by certain businesses
Alcohol:	Alcohol and alcoholic beverages are prohibited
Taxis:	No

To local residents, the community is called *Uqsuqtuuq*, the "place of plenty of fat," a reference to the fattened fish in the nearby waters.

On Aug. 28, 1903, Amundsen, with his crew of six, arrived here aboard the *Gjoa* in a quest to find the Passage and to gain information on the North Magnetic Pole. The deep narrow harbor offered a safe haven from treacherous pack ice so common in this area. Amundsen's successful navigation of the route may have been partly due to his willingness to adopt some of the traditional ways of the *Nattilik* people here, such as their methods of hunting, fishing and travelling. Amundsen and his crew also fathered a few children during their time here; many local people trace their ancestry to the Norwegians.

Today, Gjoa Haven (Gjoa is pronounced as "Joe") is one of the fastest-growing communities in the Kitikmeot, with a population creeping toward 1,000. (In 1961, only 100 people lived here.) In recent years, families from Back River (*Utkuhiksalingmiut*), Cambridge Bay, Parry River, and Spence Bay — now called Taloyoak — moved to the settlement for schooling, trading, health care, housing, and other services. Although the *Nattilik* seem to lead a modern lifestyle, they are very traditional people. Families spend a month or two out on the land each summer. Many still travel by dogteam. They hold drum dances often, enjoy throat singing, and frequently wear traditional caribou clothing.

History

Many elders in Gjoa Haven are living histories of the time *qallunaat* came in their tall ships. Over a cup of tea, they may eagerly tell you stories they heard from their grandparents of starving explorers such as Franklin's men, who are believed to have deserted their ice-locked ships in Terror Bay. That was in 1847, the year summer never came to the North. Those desperate men walked for miles pulling sleds filled not with supplies, but with books and fine china. You may even hear rumors that people here know the location of Franklin's grave. Out of respect for the dead, however, they refuse to tell outsiders.

Elders may also recall encounters with Amundsen and with Catholic and Anglican missionaries. They'll tell you about the early days of the Hudson's Bay Co. trading post. Back in 1927, the Hudson's Bay Co. took advantage of Gjoa Haven's excellent harbor by establishing a trading post here. White fox were abundant on the island then, and many *Nattilik* travelled far to trade. Although people forget the first manager's real name, some elders still think of him as *Putuguittuq* or No Big-Toe. The Hudson's Bay Co. here was one of the last to use round aluminum tokens in trading for furs. Store manager George Porter used tokens as late as the 1960s, because local people didn't yet trust Canadian currency.

Gjoa Haven: Its Land and Wildlife

Gjoa Haven is built on sand and boulders covering limestone bedrock. In spring and summer, the rolling tundra outside the settlement blooms with a variety of lichen, moss, and arctic willow that cover the island. You'll find many lakes and ponds with water so pure you can drink directly from them. In fact, the community's water supply comes from Water Lake, about two kilometres northwest of town.

Although you may spot a caribou, muskox, wolf, fox, or snowy owl on the tundra, local people often have to travel far to hunt wildlife to supplement their diet. Other wildlife found here are geese, swans, falcons, eider ducks and arctic hares. There is also arctic char, found in the bay in June and July, as well as seal, trout, and cod, used mainly as dog food. In spring, many families go to Back River for the whitefish that are plentiful there. When the char leave Gjoa Haven in early August, local people travel, as they have for generations, to *Iqalungmiut*, to fish in the Kakivakturvik River, a traditional weir 45 kilometres northeast of the settlement.

Tours

The Northwest Passage Territorial Historic Park, about 3.2 kilometres long, can be visited easily in an afternoon. (See Chapter 73, "Northwest Passage Territorial Historic Park.")

If you walk along the beach, you may notice many narwhal and beluga bones that have washed ashore. You can camp near others from town at Swan Lakes, about two kilometres north of Gjoa, or Koka Lake, about 15 kilometres southwest of the community. Keep an eye out for old Inuit camp sites, rock circles that were bases for sealskin tents. Or you may see caches, piles of rocks preserving fish or caribou. You might even stumble across the remains of early expeditions! As the ice in the bay lasts about nine months, you can also travel by snowmobile to Honeymoon Island and Hovguard Island, about 15 kilometres south of Gjoa Haven, where you'll see old camp sites, *inuksuit* and possibly a caribou or two.

For a tour of King William Island to view caribou, muskoxen, seal or polar bears, contact **Gjoa Haven Tours**. The **Hunters and Trappers Organization** (HTO) is a good source of information about the surrounding land and wildlife. The HTO also organizes polar bear and muskoxen hunts.

Around the bay and along the beaches within walking distance of the community, arctic char and arctic cod fishing is excellent, especially in July.

Shopping

Among Gjoa Haven's fine carvers are Nelson Takkiruq, Paul Aaluk, Joseph Suqslak, Uriash Pukiqnak and Wayne Pukiqnak; some, such as Judas Ullulaq, are world-renowned. You can buy their work at the local **Northern store**, the **Qikiqtaq Co-op**, or at their homes. A local women's group, **Qaqmaq's**, sells finely crafted wall hangings, and clothing such as *kamiit* (sealskin boots) and parkas.

Events

Each summer, an annual fishing derby is held at a lake near Gjoa Haven. In mid-August, golfers tee off in the challenging Sun Golf Classic at Canada's most northerly 18-hole golf course. In the spring of 1998, dogteams raced from Gjoa Haven to Taloyoak and back in what promises to become an annual event. For more information on recreation and sports, contact the hamlet's recreation department.

Accommodation and Dining

Built in 1995, the **Amundsen Hotel** accommodates up to 26 people in 13 rooms (two of which have suites), and it's building another six rooms. Each room has cable TV and a private washroom; some also have a fridge and stove. The hotel has complimentary airport pickup. Rooms are $210 a night (the suites are $250) and include breakfast, lunch and dinner ($150/night without meals). With advance notice, non-guests can also eat at the hotel's restaurant. Breakfast is $10, lunch is $20, and dinner is $30.

A canteen at the **arena** is open nightly during hockey and curling matches. An arcade, **Gjoa's Shop**, serves snacks nightly.

Services

The **Health Centre**, staffed by four nurses, is open from 8:30 a.m. to 12 p.m. daily. Special clinics, such as prenatal classes, are offered each afternoon until 5 p.m. A nurse is always on call for emergencies.

The hamlet's recreation department uses facilities in the local school for volleyball, wrestling, soccer, floor hockey and badminton. A new arena has a standard-sized skating rink and two curling rinks that are used from October to May. Sliders and brooms can be used without charge. You can skate for free most Saturdays and Sundays. Gjoa Haven also has a baseball diamond and, as of 1997, a new community **library**.

The **post office**, located in the Qikiqtaq Co-op, is open Monday to Friday from 10 a.m. to 5 p.m. The George Porter **hamlet office** has a canteen, community hall, **museum**, local **radio station**, and council boardroom, as well as offices for local government workers.

DIRECTORY
*Outfitters and tour operators licensed at time of writing.
After March 31/99, check for updated status.

Accommodation and Dining

Amundsen Hotel
VISA, Diners Club/enRoute.
Tel.: (867) 360-6176
Fax: (867) 360-6283

* Outfitters/Tour Operators

Gjoa Haven Tours
General Delivery, Gjoa Haven NT,
X0E 1J0 Canada
No telephone or fax numbers.

Hunters and Trappers Organization
Tel.: (867) 360-6028
Fax: (867) 360-6913

Services

Arctic Airport
Tel.: (867) 360-6321
Fax: (867) 360-6321

Arena
Tel.: (867) 360-6105

Churches

Anglican Mission
Services: 11 a.m. and 7 p.m., Sunday;
7 p.m., Wednesday.
Tel.: (867) 360-6511 (ask for Rosie
Kununak)

Roman Catholic Church
Tel.: (867) 360-6071

Dental Clinic
Located at Quqshuun Ilihakvik School.
Tel.: (867) 360-6041

Department of Sustainable Development, Government of Nunavut
(or until April/99, GNWT's Resources,
Wildlife and Economic Development)
Tel.: (867) 360-7605
Fax: (867) 360-7804

Hamlet Office
Tel.: (867) 360-7141
Fax: (867) 360-6309
Economic development officer:
Tel.: (867) 360-6008
Fax: (867) 360-6142
Recreation office:
Tel.: (867) 360-7151

Health Centre
Tel.: (867) 360-7441
Fax: (867) 360-6110

Library
In the school.
Tel.: (867) 360-7201
Fax: (867) 360-6204

Northwest Passage Historical Society
For information, call the economic
development officer.
Tel.: (867) 360-6008
Fax: (867) 360-6142

Northwest Passage Museum
Tel.: (867) 360-6008
Fax: (867) 360-6142

Police (RCMP)
Tel.: (867) 360-6201
Fax: (867) 360-6147

Post Office
Located in the Qikiqtaq Co-op.
Tel.: (867) 360-7271

Radio Station (AM 64)
Tel.: (867) 360-6075

Schools

Nunavut Arctic College
Tel.: (867) 360-7561
Fax: (867) 360-6049

Qiqirtaq Ilihakvik High School
Tel.: (867) 360-7201
Fax: (867) 360-7314

Quqshuun Ilihakvik School
Kindergarten to Grade 6.
Tel.: (867) 360-7201
Fax: (867) 360-6204

Weather Information
Tel.: (867) 360-6321
Fax: (867) 360-6321
Web site weather forecast:
www.infonorth.org

Shopping

Gjoa's Shop
6 p.m.–12:30 a.m., Monday to Friday;
7 p.m.–1:30 a.m., Saturday and Sunday.
Cash only.
No telephone.

Northern Store
10 a.m.–6 p.m., Monday to Friday;
1–4 p.m., Saturday. Closed Sunday.
VISA, MasterCard, Interac.
Tel.: (867) 360-7261
Fax: (867) 360-7905

Qaqmaq's
1–3 p.m. Operates irregularly throughout year. Does not accept credit cards.
Tel.: (867) 360-7514 (ask for Simona
Akkikungnak)

Qikiqtaq Co-op
VISA, MasterCard, Diners
Club/enRoute, Interac.
Tel.: (867) 360-7271
Fax: (867) 360-6018

73. NORTHWEST PASSAGE TERRITORIAL HISTORIC PARK

by Michael P. Ellsworth

Many explorers searched for a northern sea route that would take them from the Old World to the Orient.

You may know them from the lands and waters that bear their names: Martin Frobisher and John Davis, of the 16th century; Henry Hudson, of the 17th; Edward Parry, John Ross, John Franklin, Robert McClure and Richard Collinson of the 19th century. Despite terrible odds, these adventurers sailed into perilous waters, armed with the knowledge they'd gained from previous voyagers. Yet the successful navigation of the Northwest Passage occurred not only because of the contributions of these earlier expeditions, but because of the knowledge of the Inuit inhabitants of the North. Roald Amundsen was the first to adopt certain survival techniques of the *Nattilik* people on King William Island, such as hunting, fishing and toolmaking. He was also the first to traverse the Passage.

In Gjoa Haven on King William Island, you can learn about the extraordinary quest for the Passage by journeying along the Northwest Passage Territorial Historic Park walking trail. Here a historical route unveils more about the land that was home to Amundsen and his six crew-men from 1903 until 1906. At six locations around the community, you'll find signs describing the historical significance of the area.

The route begins at the George Porter Hamlet Centre, where you'll find a miniature replica (1:50) of Amundsen's ship, the *Gjoa*. Here you can examine traditional tools such as *uluit* (knives used by women) and *kakivait* (spears), as well as caribou clothing and water containers, a kayak, and photos taken by one of Amundsen's crew during his stay in Gjoa Haven. You can also learn the history of explorers such as Franklin and Amundsen, plus that of the *Nattilik* people.

Your first stop will be at the "magnet," a shelter Amundsen used in his observations of the North Magnetic Pole. In 1903, the Pole was about 90 kilometres north of Gjoa Haven. The magnets and other instruments that Amundsen used here are on display in a museum in Norway.

To help him in this work, the explorer and his men constructed the shelter from packing crates filled with sand and covered with sailcloth. In their construction, they had to take care not to use copper nails, as these would interfere with magnetic observations. The crates also offered a space where crewmen could pursue leisure activities during long, dark winter months. Two crewmen stayed in this shelter, while the others lived aboard the icebound *Gjoa*.

The second site is the "observatory" Amundsen built to house his scientific instruments. In this refuge made of sailcloth, he spent many hours documenting his findings on the Pole. Perhaps, too, he reflected on his teacher and mentor, George Von Neumayer, for before leaving Gjoa Haven, Amundsen erected a cairn here to honor him. Below the cairn was a marble slab that supported Amundsen's scientific instruments. Years later, the Hudson's Bay Co. rebuilt the cairn; the marble slab remains intact to this day. Close to the observatory, a third site shows where Amundsen's crew collected fresh water from a lake nearby. Recently, the lake was filled in because its location next to the local school was hazardous to children.

A key to Amundsen's discovery of the Passage may have been his finding what he called "the finest little harbor in the world" — Gjoa Haven. At the fourth site, you'll note the geography of this natural harbor. On Sept. 9, 1903, the *Gjoa* entered a haven in this deep, narrow inlet. It provided refuge from massive pack ice and stormy seas. Here, after their arduous journey, Amundsen and his crew found a peaceful place to pursue their scientific work and to learn about the land from the *Nattilik*.

The fifth site is a grim reminder of the challenges facing arctic expeditions. Here, high on a sandy plateau, it's believed the remains of some of Franklin's crew were brought to rest after they were discovered on the southwest coast of King William Island. Their grave site is one of many scattered across the North. You can also see the gravestone of William Harold, a Hudson's Bay Co. employee, who was found frozen to death on Oct. 22, 1905. The young man had apparently perished while on his way out to hunt seals. On the chilly day of his death, his body was found without a hat or mitts.

As you walk to the Hudson's Bay Co. complex, the final site along the trail, you'll see an old wooden ship docked along the sandy shoal nearby. No, it isn't the *Gjoa*! It's a supply ship, the *Qingalik*, hauled here by barge from Holman Island in 1993. Vessels like this were used to transport supplies to the Hudson's Bay Co. posts across the North. And the goods they brought, such as firearms, ammunition, southern food, clothing, tea and tobacco, transformed the nomadic lifestyle of the *Nattilik* forever. In 1927, both the Hudson's Bay Co. and Can Alaska trading companies moved to Gjoa Haven from a port near Douglas Bay, about 50 kilometres from Gjoa Haven. Their outbuildings were the first modern structures in Gjoa. Today they are used by the Northern store.

In April 1998, a plaque commemorating the 150th anniversary of the Franklin Expedition was placed at Victory Point on the upper northwest coast of King William Island. A museum devoted to the history of the Northwest Passage was slated to open in Gjoa Haven in early 1999. The public can view artifacts of expeditions, such as those of Franklin, Amundsen and Larson, from June through August.

DIRECTORY

Northwest Passage Museum
Contact the economic development officer.
Tel.: (867) 360-6008
Fax: (867) 360-6142

74. UMINGMAKTOK
by Joe Otokiak

On the map of Canada, the official spelling of this tiny outpost camp is "Umingmaktok."

Population:	51 (Inuit: 98%, non-Inuit: 2%) Source: 1996 Census of Canada
Telephone Area Code:	None. Regular telephone service does not exist yet. High frequency
	(HF) radio is the usual method of communication (channels 5046, 5031).
	There is one satellite-powered telephone for emergencies only.
	The HTO can be e-mailed
Time Zone:	Mountain Time
Postal Code:	Write to Umingmaktok, General Delivery, c/o Cambridge Bay NT,
	X0E 0C0 Canada
How to Get There:	Charter flights only
Banks:	None. Bring cash or traveller's cheques
Alcohol:	Alcohol is not restricted, and is governed only by the provisions of the *NWT*
	Liquor Act. However, alcohol cannot be purchased in Umingmaktok
Taxis:	No

In the language of Inuit, Umingmaktok means "he or she caught a muskox." But Inuit call this settlement Umingmak*tuuq* — "like a muskox." Located about 80 kilometres due north of the community of Bathurst Inlet on the eastern shore of its namesake inlet, the settlement was until recently called Bay Chimo. I believe the English name originated from the ship, the *Bay Chimo*, that sailed through the area many years ago. This chapter will refer to the community as Inuit refer to it — *Umingmaktuuq*.

Nestled in a little bay, *Umingmaktuuq* — pronounced "oo-ming-mak-took" — has a **Co-op store**, a couple of warehouses for store supplies, a one-classroom school, and a smattering of homes in three locations near bays, each a few kilometres from the other. In outpost camps, Inuit live as they have for thousands of years, hunting and fishing to feed and clothe themselves and their families. The tiny settlement's population has become even smaller since the last census; it was down to 39 in 1998.

Umingmaktuuq, which isn't even connected to the rest of the world yet by telephone, is one of the last hunting communities in Nunavut to be almost completely self-sustained. By southern standards, the homes here seem to be mere cabins, but for the Inuit, they're a little more comfortable than living in snowhouses, especially during winter.

The one-room school houses students from kindergarten to about Grade 8. Teacher Peter Kapolak is quite busy during school days. There's a generator that supplies electricity to the classroom and other buildings close by. All heating is done by diesel fuel stoves and heaters, which are very quiet, compared to furnaces. In *Umingmaktuuq*, one can even watch a little television — through videos on VCR machines.

Although aided by modern hunting tools such as snowmobiles, GPS receivers, boats, motors, guns and scopes, Inuit here continue to lead traditional lives. The head of each household still harvests food for the table, most of it from the land, and the wives tend to family needs in addition to their daily chores. Most days are busily spent hunting for food and gathering pelts for trade in order to purchase gas to operate new equipment.

Evenings are filled by carving life's experiences into soapstone, a commodity that is in abundance not far from the community.

Families still call each other over for a cup of tea or coffee, and a chat. You need a good set of lungs and a keen sense of hearing. It's polite to heed the call as soon as possible if you want to fit socially into this small community. Here, even in small ways, everyone contributes to the survival of all. Country food is shared with those who are less fortunate or unable to go hunting. In fact, as long as there's enough to go around, you can share anything, knowing that kindness will be rewarded later on.

History

Umingmaktuuq's roots go back to the 1960s. That's when the store arrived, making trade for cash goods possible. Since then, an airstrip has been constructed, and the local **HTO** has built wind turbines and solar generators to power the community's 10 food freezers.

Umingmaktuuq: Its Land and Wildlife

Within a radius of about 120 kilometres from *Umingmaktuuq*, there are many camp sites, mostly along the coastal areas. These include Parry Bay to the north, Brown Sound to the southwest, and Gordon Bay to the south. Some families occupy these areas for most of the year.

The winter months are busy, but not as busy as spring and summer, when the environment seems to come alive. Plants such as crowberries, blackberries and cranberries grow in and around the settlement. A variety of wildlife can be seen as birds migrate north to nest and animals birth their young. Arctic char and caribou are plentiful in this area. Before you come to *Umingmaktuuq*, remember to obtain a fishing licence from the Cambridge Bay office of the **Department of Sustainable Development** (or the GNWT's **Resources, Wildlife and Economic Development** until April 1999).

Tours and Events

The local HTO conducts guided tours of the area.

The Kalvik Frolics, one of the biggest events in the community, is held during Easter weekend. *Umingmaktuuq*'s population almost doubles with the influx of neighboring snowmobilers. The crowning touch is the search for a beautiful wolverine pelt.

More information on tourist attractions in the Kitikmeot Region is available from the **Arctic Coast Visitors Centre** in Cambridge Bay and Nunavut Tourism.

Shopping, Accommodation and Dining

The Co-op store also doubles as a hotel for three visitors. Be prepared to do a little cooking and tidying up, as chores are shared among guests. Since you can't phone to book reservations, write to store manager Gwen Tikhak at least a month in advance of your visit. Include your phone number. Tikhak will call back to confirm the reservation. Rates are $125 per person per night (meals not included). Although there's a fold-out bed and foam mattresses, you should bring a sleeping bag as well. Lodging can be paid for by cheque; you can buy store items with cash or traveller's cheques only. If you have special food requirements that include frozen food, let the manager know that in advance, too.

When the summer barge arrives with the winter's supply of goods, the little store is filled to overflowing. In May and June, shelves may be nearly bare, except for some food staples and a few dry goods. The store is open from 10 a.m. to 5 p.m., Monday to Saturday, but if you need something at another time, Tikhak will open it for you. With Inuit coming and going in the community, the hours of operation are flexible.

For information on camping spots in the area, e-mail the local Hunters and Trappers Organization.

Services

Should you need medical care or if an emergency occurs, a lay dispenser (a liaison person in the community) will contact medical personnel in Cambridge Bay for instructions. If you require special medication, bring the name of the drug with you so that information can be relayed to Cambridge Bay if necessary.

Recently, air charters from Cambridge Bay have increased, bringing people from government and various organizations who come to do business in the community. Telephone service is due to arrive in *Umingmaktuuq* once commercial power is installed, although when that will happen is still unknown. Meanwhile, every household has an HF radio that allows users to reach others in Cambridge Bay to the northeast, and Kugluktuk to the west. In *Umingmaktuuq*, HF radios are usually used from the time you get up, approximately 6 a.m. or earlier during spring, to about 10 or 11 p.m., or whenever reception deteriorates.

Visitors are always welcome in *Umingmaktuuq*, where you're sure to have many wonderful experiences. *Qakugulu* (kah-goo-goo-loo) — see you soon!

DIRECTORY

*Outfitters and tour operators licensed at time of writing.
After March 31/99, check for updated status.

Arctic Coast Visitors Centre
Tel.: (867) 983-2224
Fax: (867) 983-2302

Cambridge Bay Health Centre
Tel.: (867) 983-2531
Fax: (867) 983-2262

Co-op Store
To make reservations for lodging, write to manager Gwen Tikhak, Co-op store, General Delivery, c/o Cambridge Bay NT, X0E 0C0 Canada.
Credit cards not accepted. Bring cash, traveller's cheques, or for lodging, personal cheques.

Department of Sustainable Development, Government of Nunavut
(or until April/99, GNWT's **Resources, Wildlife and Economic Development**)
In Cambridge Bay.
Tel.: (867) 983-7219 or (867) 983-7222
Fax: (867) 983-2802

Police (RCMP)
RCMP detachment in Cambridge Bay.
Tel.: (867) 983-2111
Fax: (867) 983-2498

Umingmaktok Hunters and Trappers Organization
Contact Peter Kapolak, president.
E-mail: peterk@polarnet.ca

75. BATHURST INLET
by Lyn Hancock

If you can visit only one place in Nunavut, I recommend Bathurst Inlet, an oasis of culture and wildlife on the mid-Arctic coast where people live in a more traditional way than in many other areas of the territory.

Population:	18 (although the 1996 Census of Canada does not indicate population breakdown by ethnic group, all permanent residents are Inuit)
Telephone Area Code:	No regular phone service. The HTO operates a satellite phone
Time Zone:	Mountain Time
Postal Code:	No regular mail service. Mail sent to the Yellowknife office of Bathurst Inlet Lodge will be forwarded to the community
How to Get There:	Charter flights only
Banks:	None. Cash and traveller's cheques are preferable
Alcohol:	Alcohol may be brought into Bathurst Inlet, governed only by the provisions of the *NWT Liquor Act*
Taxis:	No

In its 1996 census, Statistics Canada pegged Bathurst Inlet's tiny population at 18, but it's really 27 when everyone's at home.

Elsewhere in Nunavut, when Inuit were abandoning their camps for the amenities of settlements, the people of Bathurst Inlet chose to remain on the land. Only recently have they begun to take jobs in the wage economy to help support their traditional lifestyle.

Residents of Bathurst Inlet — located at the southern end of the inlet that bears the same name — are known as the *Qingaunmiut* or people of "the hill that looks like a nose," a reference to a hill behind the community. The settlement is best known for the **Bathurst Inlet Lodge**, a naturalist facility that was once a Hudson's Bay Co. trading post and a Roman Catholic mission. In fact, the lodge still bears the distinctive red and white colors that adorned all Hudson's Bay Co. buildings in years past.

History

Excellent interpretation by local guides brings the inlet's rich history to life. Whether you travel by boat, plane or on foot, you'll see many archeological signs of Inuit heritage: stone traps and caches, tent rings, caribou-decoy *inuksuit*, and even the bleached bones and treasured possessions of the dead in open grave sites dotting the tundra.

Located on an island in the Burnside River, *Nadluq*, "caribou crossing place," is a site about 80 kilometres southwest of Bathurst Inlet. As long as 600 years ago, local Copper Inuit hunted caribou here, using the animals' antlers for the walls and roofs of their semi-subterranean homes. During their expedition of 1821, Sir John Franklin and his men travelled down Bathurst Inlet and the Hood River toward Fort Enterprise, until they were thwarted by the mighty 49-metre-high Wilberforce Falls and forced to continue their trek on foot. Of the 20 men who started the journey, only nine survived.

Outsiders began to settle in Bathurst Inlet in 1929, when a mining exploration camp was established here. A Hudson's Bay Co. trading post and an Oblate mission soon followed. In 1964, the Hudson's Bay Co. abandoned its Bathurst Inlet post and moved north to Umingmaktok, where seal-trading opportunities were more promising. In 1969, RCMP officer Glenn Warner and his wife, Trish, transformed the deserted buildings into Bathurst Inlet Lodge. Today, the Warners are partners in the lodge with the people of the community.

Bathurst Inlet: Its Land and Wildlife

Bathurst Inlet is truly splendor in the middle of the barren lands; a place of rolling tundra hills, snaking eskers, meandering rivers, and awesome gorges through which water spills dramatically over ancient, twisted rock. Not far from here, you'll find Wilberforce Falls, the highest arctic waterfall in the world, and the Quadyuk Islands, great pyramidal humps that run down the inlet like a dinosaur's backbone.

The mild climate at the southern end of the inlet encourages diverse and luxuriant vegetation, which provides prime wildlife habitat. More than 125 species of wildflowers flourish here, alongside some 80 varieties of nesting birds and 13 types of mammals. At the Bathurst Inlet Lodge, you'll find canoes, boats and planes to take you where you want to go, and reliable guides who make it easy for you to spot the wondrous creatures.

Bathurst Inlet has one of the largest and healthiest populations of peregrine falcons in the world. The inlet is also an important staging ground for migratory waterfowl such as Canada geese, snow geese, and white-fronted geese. East of the inlet is the Queen Maud Gulf Migratory Bird Sanctuary, the nesting ground of more than 95 per cent of the world's population of once-threatened Ross's geese. Flights to this six-million-plus-hectare migratory bird sanctuary — Canada's largest — can be arranged through the lodge. Independent travellers must first obtain a permit from the **Canadian Wildlife Service**, which monitors human activity in the sanctuary. Allow at least 45 days for a reply.

Muskoxen and barren-ground caribou also breed at Bathurst Inlet. With a population of nearly 500,000, the Bathurst caribou herd is one of the largest free-roaming mammal herds in the world. Each spring, these animals pass near the southern end of the inlet en route to calving grounds to the northeast. Other relatively abundant mammals include barren-ground grizzlies, wolves, foxes, and wolverines.

Although fishing isn't emphasized at the lodge, anglers will find plenty of land-locked arctic char, lake trout and grayling to keep them happy.

Tours

Long before ecotourism became trendy, Inuit of Bathurst Inlet shared their land and lifestyle with visitors. For three generations, the Warner family and the *Qingaunmiut* have lived and worked together. Their remarkably successful partnership is based on true cross-cultural co-operation. They have worked together in related companies such as Bathurst Arctic Services, Air Tindi, and Top of the World Travel. Bathurst Lodge began as a naturalist lodge, but now also serves geologists, prospectors and surveyors.

The lodge runs naturalist programs from the last week in June until mid-July. A week's stay, which includes return airfare from Yellowknife, accommodation, and day trips (excluding special charters), costs $3,180. Alternatively, throughout the summer you may camp at one of the lodge's more affordable outposts in the central barren lands. A week of fishing or caribou-viewing in a cabin at Esker Camp on Pellatt Lake, about 200 kilometres south, or at the newly opened Treeline Lake Lodge (formerly Salmita mining camp), costs $2,000 and includes transportation from Yellowknife.

Shopping/Accommodation and Dining/Services

There are no commercial facilities in the Bathurst Inlet settlement other than the lodge, which, with the Hunters and Trappers Organization, supplies power to local homes from its generator. Guests of the lodge receive three home-cooked meals and an afternoon tea daily. The lodge accommodates 25 guests and boasts a lounge, conference room, library, and the only self-serve bar in Nunavut. Guests help themselves, sign a log book, and pay when they leave. Community residents occasionally sell arts and crafts to visitors.

There's no scheduled air service to Bathurst Inlet. Air Tindi and First Air in Yellowknife, and Adlair Air and Aklak Air in Cambridge Bay provide charter services. It costs between $3,100 and $3,500 to charter a Twin Otter between Bathurst Inlet and Cambridge Bay, and from $2,000 to $5,000 to charter a plane between Yellowknife and Bathurst Inlet, depending on the type of aircraft.

Since there's only one satellite phone in Bathurst Inlet (it belongs to the HTO), most people communicate via HF radio, channel 5046. The Yellowknife office of Bathurst Inlet Lodge will take calls for people in the community.

You'll find no health facility or RCMP detachment here. The closest medical help is 100 kilometres away in Umingmaktok, where many people from Bathurst Inlet regularly shop.

DIRECTORY

Bathurst Inlet Lodge
P.O. Box 820, Yellowknife NT,
X1A 2N6 Canada
Tel.: (867) 873-2595 or (867) 920-4330
Fax: (867) 920-4263
E-mail: bathurst@internorth.com
Web site: virtualnorth.com/bathurst/

Canadian Wildlife Service
Tel.: (867) 669-4700
Fax: (867) 873-8185
E-mail: enviroinfo@cpgsv1am.doe.ca

76. KUGLUKTUK

by Millie Kuliktana

Set between the banks of the mighty Coppermine River and the shores of Coronation Gulf on the Arctic Ocean, the name Kugluktuk (formerly known as Coppermine) was intended to reflect the meaning "the place of moving water" in Inuinnaqtun.

Population:	1,201 (Inuit: 89%, non-Inuit: 11%) Source: 1996 Census of Canada
Telephone Area Code:	867
Time Zone:	Mountain Time
Postal Code:	X0E 0E0
How to Get There:	Possible route:
	• Edmonton-Yellowknife-Kugluktuk
	Yellowknife to Kugluktuk (about 600 kilometres north) is via First Air.
	Flight connections usually (not always) require an overnight stay in
	Yellowknife
Banks:	None. Cash and traveller's cheques are preferable. Credit cards are
	accepted by certain businesses
Alcohol:	Alcohol is not restricted, and is governed only by the provisions of the
	NWT Liquor Act. However, alcohol cannot be purchased in Kugluktuk
Taxis:	Yes

However, something was lost in the naming process and the proper spelling, *Qurluqtuq*, fell by the wayside. Kugluktuk actually means "two startled people"! The community's peaceful demeanor, though, is unlikely to startle newcomers.

The Inuit of this area are known as the Copper Inuit, a name born of the nearby Copper Mountains. Many hunters still use local copper to fashion tools, a valuable asset for a people that spend many months hunting and fishing. By spending so much time on the land, Inuit of Kugluktuk ensure their traditional skills are passed on to younger generations, whether it be sewing fur clothing, hunting wild game, carving soapstone, preparing traditional food, drum dancing, or enjoying good old-time fiddling.

History

Kugluktuk is not far from historic Bloody Falls, on the Coppermine River. In 1771, Bloody Falls was the site of a fierce battle between local Inuit families and a group of travelling Chipewyan.

The river is also the site of a well-known murder. In 1913, two hunters, Sinisiak and Uluksak, murdered two Oblate priests, Father Jean-Baptiste Rouvière and Father Guillaume LeRoux. The priests, en route to Dene Indian lands, were afraid they couldn't make it without these two Inuit men guiding them. The hunters, forced to lead the trip, feared for their lives and the welfare of their families back at home. Sinisiak and

Uluksak were taken to Edmonton in 1917 for trial. Although sentenced to life imprisonment at Fort Resolution, they were released in 1919.

The Hudson's Bay Co. built a trading post at Kugluktuk in 1927, and the following year the Anglican Church established a presence, too, joining the Catholic Church, which had already been there more than a decade. The RCMP arrived in 1932. The arrival of these organizations in Kugluktuk forced traditional medicine men and shamans to cease their practices, hunters to work for wages, children to become formally educated, and traditional methods of discipline to be halted.

Kugluktuk's more contemporary history is highlighted by a special ceremony on July 9, 1993, that marked the proclamation of the *Nunavut Land Claims Agreement Act* and the *Nunavut Act*, federal legislation creating, in the latter case, the new territory of Nunavut. Musicians, artists, Inuit leaders, dignitaries, adults, children and elders sang, laughed, cried and feasted together, celebrating this historic day under warm, sunny skies.

Kugluktuk: Its Land and Wildlife

In Kugluktuk, the activities of both people and wildlife are seasonal. With spring comes the return of geese and snow buntings, and the scurry of the squirrel. Residents spend more time outdoors in the ever-increasing sunlight; you'll see many making "dry meat" by hanging strips of meat in the midday sun.

In summer, the glimmering tundra and the waters around the community come to life. The tundra, close to the tree line here, is home to a wide variety of wildlife, including moose, wolverines, wolves, foxes, muskoxen, barren-ground grizzlies, and caribou. All species bring an abundance of food and fur to the hunters and trappers of the community. The **Coppermine Hunters and Trappers Organization**, working in conjunction with outfitter **Fred Webb**, can also arrange sport hunts and fishing trips for visitors. Hunts zero in on muskoxen, caribou, grizzly bears, and wolf trophy sport hunting.

The animals can be nuisances, too, especially grizzlies, which tend to wreck cabins and tent frames, shredding the canvas tarps used for roofs. An interesting Inuit belief is that a foggy morning in the spring is a sign of a grizzly that's bellowed a blast of warm air into the cool morning air after waking from its long winter hibernation.

The rare visit of beluga whales excites local hunters. They seek the *maktaaq* of the beluga, the chewy outer layer of skin and fat considered a delicacy by Inuit. The most common marine mammal in the area is the ringed seal, which is an important part of the summer and autumn diet. Fishing for arctic char also plays a large role at these times.

The cliffs that erupt from the ground to the east and west of the community are havens for the peregrine falcons and ravens that crowd the southern faces of the cliffs to bask in the heat of the sun. Summer also means time for Kugluktuk's gardeners to exercise their green thumbs. Some successfully grow a variety of vegetables, including potatoes.

Tours

Many tourists come to Kugluktuk via the Coppermine River, a favorite waterway for northern paddlers. Among the many who have ventured down the broad, swift river are former Canadian prime ministers Pierre Trudeau and John Turner, England's Prince Andrew, and Canadian singer Gordon Lightfoot.

Bloody Falls Territorial Historic Park is a great place for a walk through the history of our people. You can hike the 13-kilometre trail, drive an all-terrain vehicle, or ride in a boat with an experienced river navigator. While there you can stop for a picnic and some fishing.

A boat trip on the Arctic Ocean will take you north of Kugluktuk to Cape Krusenstern. Here you'll find the remains of an old trading post that once belonged to Slim Semmler, an early independent fur trader.

Despite its location north of the Arctic Circle, Kugluktuk is one of few communities in Nunavut where summer days get warm enough to let you wile away hours on the beach. In July and August, avid swimmers take advantage of the hamlet's Waterfront Beach Program where the Coppermine River empties into Coronation Gulf.

The warm temperatures also aid a longer boating season, which begins in late June and ends in early October. **Northwest Passage Expeditions Ltd.** provides outings in the Coronation Gulf area in its 30-foot cabin cruiser, checking out old trading posts, abandoned DEW Line sites and historic reminders of earlier explorers along the way.

A boat ride will get you to the **Coronation Golf Club**, an 18-hole course located on a sandbar between the community and the ocean. Summer is the best time to play there, since early autumn rain and high winds can flood the course.

The **MacDonalds Pool Hall** is an alcohol- and smoke-free centre for youth, located in the centre of Kugluktuk. There's pool, video games, movie rentals and fast food available.

Shopping

The **Kugluktuk Co-op**, here since 1960, sells groceries, dry goods, hardware and local arts and crafts. The **Northern store** also sells groceries and dry goods.

The local **Kugluktuk Anguniaqtiit Association** offers a variety of country foods, including arctic char, caribou, and muskox jerky.

The Kugluktuk Visitors Centre in the James Koighok Cultural Centre on Coronation Drive displays arts and crafts that are usually for sale. (The visitors centre is reopening as the **Kugluktuk Heritage Centre** in 1999 following extensive renovations.) Kugluktuk is the home of *iglu* carvings. These soapstone igloos have removable tops and display a traditional Inuit family scene inside. The women of Kugluktuk are also well known for their prowess in making dolls, which you may be able to buy here. Some dolls are made with soapstone faces; others are made of fur.

Events

The annual Nattiq Frolics brings families from surrounding communities to Kugluktuk every April to visit and compete in a variety of contests. These contests include traditional seal hunting, sealskinning, snowmobile races, and Inuit games. There's also traditional feasting and lots of square dancing.

Early autumn brings lots of great fishing and expensive fishing rods to the annual Ikalukpik Fishing Derby. Anglers of all ages try for the heaviest char and best fishing story.

Accommodation and Dining

The **Coppermine Inn** can accommodate 26 people in 14 rooms (all but two are double occupancy). Four rooms have private bathrooms; the rest have shared bathrooms. All have televisions, and there is a pay phone in the lobby. Rates are $200 per person per night (including meals), or $135 without meals. The restaurant is open to non-guests, who should make reservations with sufficient notice. Meals are $15 for breakfast, $20 for lunch and $30 for dinner.

The **Enokhok Inn** takes up to six people in three rooms (two of which have shared bathrooms). All rooms have televisions. There's also a TV in the lobby, plus a public phone. Rates are $170 per person per night (including meals), or $125 without meals. Meals are $10 for breakfast, $15 for lunch and $20 for supper. The restaurant is open to hotel guests only, but non-guests may make reservations as long as plenty of notice is given.

There's also a **coffee shop** in the Co-op store.

A campground located beside the beach is free to the public. It has an outdoor washroom and a few picnic tables.

DIRECTORY

*Outfitters and tour operators licensed at time of writing.
After March 31/99, check for updated status.

Accommodation and Dining

Co-op Coffee Shop
Noon–8 p.m., every day.
Tel.: (867) 982-4231

Coppermine Inn
VISA accepted.
Tel.: (867) 982-3333
Fax: (867) 982-3340

Enokhok Inn
VISA, Diners Club/enRoute.
Tel.: (867) 982-3197
Fax: (867) 982-4291

* Outfitters/Tour Operators/Visitors Centre

Coppermine HTA-Webb Ltd.
Sport hunting.
Tel.: (604) 463-2035
Fax: (604) 463-2026
E-mail: 73204.2734@compuserve.com
Web site: fordinfo.com/fredwebb

Coppermine Hunters and Trappers Organization
Tel.: (867) 982-4908
Fax: (867) 982-4047

Kugluktuk Heritage Centre
Known as Kugluktuk Visitors Centre before 1999 reopening.
Tel.: (867) 982-3232
Fax: (867) 982-3229

Northwest Passage Expeditions Ltd.
Tel.: (604) 463-2035
Fax: (604) 463-2026
E-mail: 73204.2734@compuserve.com
Web site: fordinfo.com/fredwebb

Services

Airport
First Air
Tel.: (867) 982-3208

Churches
Pentacostal Church
Services: 7 p.m., Sunday (English).
Tel.: (867) 982-4161

St. Andrew's Anglican Church
Services: 10 a.m. (English),
11 a.m. (Inuinnaqtun),
7 p.m. (English and Inuinnaqtun),
and 2 p.m. Sunday School (English
and Inuinnaqtun), Sunday;
7 p.m. service and Bible study
(English and Inuinnaqtun), Thursday.
Tel.: (867) 982-3073
Fax: (867) 982-3487

Coronation Golf Club
Tel.: (867) 982-3186
Fax: (867) 982-3060

Dental Clinic
Tel.: (867) 982-4511
Fax: (867) 982-4512

Department of Sustainable Development, Government of Nunavut
(or until April/99, GNWT's Resources,
Wildlife and Economic Development)
Tel.: (867) 982-7240
Fax: (867) 982-3701

Hamlet Office
Tel.: (867) 982-4471
Fax: (867) 982-3060

Health Centre
Tel.: (867) 982-4531
Fax: (867) 982-3115

Library
6–9 p.m., Monday, Tuesday, Thursday;
3–6 p.m., Wednesday; 1–4 p.m., Saturday.
Tel.: (867) 982-3098

MacDonalds Pool Hall
No telephone. Try CB Radio
channel No. 7.

Police (RCMP)
Tel.: (867) 982-4111
Fax: (867) 982-3390

Post Office
Centrally located in the community.
10 a.m.–5:30 p.m., Monday to Friday.
Tel.: (867) 982-5905

Radio Station (FM 105.1)
Tel.: (867) 982-7206

Schools

Jimmy Hikok Ilihakvik Elementary School
Tel.: (867) 982-5001
Fax: (867) 982-5706

Kugluktuk High School
Tel.: (867) 982-4406
Fax: (867) 982-3404

Nunavut Arctic College
Tel.: (867) 982-4491 or (867) 982-5151
Fax: (867) 982-4004 or (867) 982-5108

Taxi

Triple A Taxi
Tel.: (867) 982-3280

Weather Information
Tel.: (867) 982-4131
Fax: (867) 982-3248
Web site weather forecast:
www.infonorth.org

Shopping

Kugluktuk Anguniaqtiit Association
Affiliated with Coppermine HTO.
Tel.: (867) 982-5902
Fax: (867) 982-4047

Kugluktuk Co-op
10 a.m.–6:30 p.m., Monday to
Wednesday; 10 a.m.–8 p.m., Thursday
and Friday; 12:30–5:30 p.m., Saturday.
Closed Sunday.
VISA, Interac.
Tel.: (867) 982-4231
Fax: (867) 982-3070

Kugluktuk Heritage Centre
July–Aug.: 9 a.m.–9 p.m., Monday to
Saturday. Closed Sunday.
Sept.–June: 9 a.m.–5 p.m., Monday to
Friday. Closed weekends.
Cash only.
Tel.: (867) 982-3232
Fax: (867) 982-3229

Northern Store
10 a.m.–6:30 p.m., Monday to
Wednesday; 10 a.m.–8 p.m., Thursday
and Friday; 1–6:30 p.m., Saturday.
Closed Sunday.
VISA, MasterCard, Interac.
Tel.: (867) 982-4171
Fax: (867) 982-3607

77. CAMBRIDGE BAY
by Joe Otokiak

Along the shores of the Queen Maud Gulf on the southeast coast of Victoria Island lies the regional centre for the Kitikmeot Region, Cambridge Bay.

Population:	1,351 (Inuit: 75%, non-Inuit: 25%) Source: 1996 Census of Canada
Telephone Area Code:	867
Time Zone:	Mountain Time
Postal Code:	X0E 0C0
How to Get There:	Possible routes:
	• Edmonton-Yellowknife-Cambridge Bay
	• Ottawa/Montreal-Iqaluit-Resolute-Cambridge Bay
	• Winnipeg-Rankin Inlet-Cambridge Bay
	• Ottawa/Montreal-Iqaluit-Rankin Inlet-Cambridge Bay
	• Kangerlussuaq (Greenland)-Iqaluit-Rankin Inlet-Cambridge Bay
	Yellowknife to Cambridge Bay (almost 900 kilometres northeast) is via
	First Air or Canadian North (Canadian Airlines)
Banks:	Yes – Royal Bank of Canada
Alcohol:	Alcohol is not restricted, and is governed only by the provisions of
	the *NWT Liquor Act.* Supplies are ordered from Yellowknife or brought
	in under permit. If individuals are found to have misused liquor, their
	eligibility to place orders may be withdrawn
Taxis:	Yes

The traditional name for Cambridge Bay, *Iqaluktuuttiaq*, means "one with plenty of fish," for the excellent fishing to be found in lakes and rivers nearby.

As in other northern settlements, there's a strong sense of expectancy these days among the Inuit of Cambridge Bay. On April 1, 1999, the Nunavut government will be created, and people here are preparing for momentous change. Many Inuit are busily educating themselves so that, in a few short months, they will be ready to administer their own territory.

In the meantime, the GNWT continues to employ most Inuit here. Nunavut Tunngavik Incorporated, the organization implementing the Nunavut Land Claims Agreement, also employs many local people. Increasingly, too, an entrepreneurial spirit fills the air, as Inuit venture into business for themselves or work for others, such as the Inuit-owned Ikaluktutiak Co-operative. Mineral deposits near Cambridge Bay and throughout the Kitikmeot mean many Inuit are working for mining and exploration companies in the region.

Despite this activity, the people of Cambridge Bay still value their traditional lifestyle. Many elders depend on the abundant wildlife here for their food. Others, who are educated in southern ways and work in 9 to 5 jobs, leave town when they can to hunt and fish nearby. Even young people, who rely on the goods and services of outsiders, are becoming conscious of the importance of protecting their cultural heritage.

290

Cambridge Bay Street Map

Key to Map Locations

1 Anglican Church
2 Arctic Coast Visitors Centre
3 Arctic Islands Lodge
4 Bank and Post Office
5 Community Hall
6 Dental Clinic
7 Department of Sustainable Development (or until April/99, RWED)
8 Eniknigiit Katimayet Elders Centre
9 Glad Tidings Church
10 Hamlet Office
11 Health Centre
12 Hunters and Trappers Organization
13 Ikalukutiak Co-operative Store
14 Ikalukutiak Co-op/Inns North
15 Kitikmeot Foods
16 Kitikmeot Supplies
17 Kullik Ilihakvik Elementary School
18 Northern Store building (includes Nunavut Tunngavik Incorporated and Kitikmeot Inuit Association)
19a Nunavut Arctic College
19b Nunavut Arctic College
20 Police (RCMP)
21 Roman Catholic Church

To Airport

Cambridge Bay

History

In the early 1950s, the community of Cambridge Bay grew with the establishment of a DEW Line station and a military airstrip. The little bay here offered an excellent harbor where the Hudson's Bay Co. could set up a post nearby and offload supplies. Services typical of most northern towns were soon provided: an administrator's office, an RCMP station, federal day school, nursing station, Anglican and Roman Catholic churches, and a Ministry of Transport office. The Inuit came to the community from areas to the west, and many still have relatives and close ties in settlements as far away as Tuktoyaktuk in the western Arctic. Those who had formerly lived in makeshift shanties of wood scraps and discarded materials from work sites, now moved into tiny "matchboxes" — plywood one-room structures with a washroom. Life as the people had known it would never be the same.

Increasingly, those Inuit who still lived on the land were drawn to the community to trade their furs for hunting supplies. Gradually, as employment opportunities increased, especially at the DEW Line site, families began to settle down in permanent homes. But then the fur trade declined, and some who had come here expecting to find work, now became dependent on government handouts. At this time, as well, families had to move into town so their children could attend the local school. The men, who had counted on their wives' assistance while out on the land, now travelled alone to the hunting grounds or in the company of other men. Wives remained at home to raise their school-aged children. Other children, whose parents still lived on the land away from Cambridge Bay, were rounded up by plane and sent to boarding schools in Inuvik and Fort Simpson in the western Arctic.

For many years, a commercial char fishery, operated by the Ikaluktutiak Co-operative, provided seasonal employment and additional income for some hunters and trappers. Later, however, as aquaculture of salmon and trout reduced prices, the fishery was a less lucrative source of employment. At about the same time, the fur industry nearly collapsed when international animal rights activists protested the inhumane capture of animals — in particular, the hunting of seals in Eastern Canada and the trapping of other animals for their fur. The territorial government offered a few manual jobs to the Inuit until they could attain higher education or work experience and assume jobs in management.

Cambridge Bay: Its Land and Wildlife

Of the many interesting stories local elders like to tell, one in particular explains the existence of the high hills that lie to the north of the community. Mount Pelly (*Uvajuq*), the largest landmark in the area, is said to be a male giant; Baby Pelly (*Inuuhuktuq*), standing just behind it, is next; while furthest away is Lady Pelly (*Amaaqtuq*). The hills were believed to be a family that travelled through the area from sea to sea in search of food. Eventually, they perished of starvation. As they waded across the sea onto Victoria Island, the man was first to die, as he faced southeast. The young lad behind him, as indicated by the name, *Inuuhuktuq*, died next. Lastly came the mother, *Amaaqtuq*, who was carrying her baby. For miles around this rocky barren land of tiny ground-hugging plants and gently rolling hills, these landmarks can be seen.

On the outskirts of the community, the land is home to caribou, muskoxen, foxes, wolves, lemmings and weasels. Further afield, you'll find polar bears, wolves, wolverines, grizzly bears and ground squirrels. If you look into the harbor, you'll spot the gleaming heads of ringed seals bobbing about, while further offshore towards the mainland, you'll notice bearded seals.

Throughout the year, trout remain in the lakes, while char migrate to coastal areas in spring and summer, then return upstream to the lakes for the winter.

In spring and summer, the tundra bursts into life with the arrival of migratory birds. First on the scene are snow buntings and whistling swans. Soon they are joined by seagulls, Canada geese, Ross's geese, black Brants, snow geese, king and common eiders, pintails, long-tailed (oldsquaw) ducks, jaegers, peregrine falcons and many other species. Throughout the year, snowy owls, rock and willow ptarmigan and ravens can be seen.

One concern you may face when travelling by land or on water is foul weather and the possibility of getting lost in winter or swamped while boating. But you learn to be patient and to wait out bad weather. As the saying goes, "It'll calm down sometime 'cause it won't blow forever." It's like pursuing game: you have to be very patient if you're to survive in the North.

Tours

Within walking distance of the community, you'll discover many archeological sites near the river to the northeast and the Mount Pelly area. (The land here is being developed as a territorial park.) Historic sites have interpretive signs along the well-maintained roads that wind around the bay and up to Mount Pelly. At the end of the road, you can hike wherever your heart desires or fish for char or trout in lakes nearby. For information on tours to the sites, contact the **Arctic Coast Visitors Centre**. And while you're out on the land, be sure to bring warm clothing, good hiking boots, and insect repellent.

For tours of the community and points of interest nearby, you have several options available. Some tours are organized as part of big game sport hunting or fishing packages offered by **High Arctic Lodge** and other licensed outfitters. The **Ekaluktutiak Hunters and Trappers Organization** conducts sport hunts for polar bears, muskoxen and caribou. The HTO also sells camping equipment from their office.

Events

The highlight of the year's events is the Omingmak Frolics, a festival held in the third weekend of May that features a competitive seal hunt, talent show, snowmobile races, children's games, cooking and tea boiling, ice chiselling and fishing contests.

Another not-to-be-missed occasion is the music festival held in July as part of Nunavut Day festivities. Artists from across Nunavut perform music, old and new. Other activities include displays of traditional and modern northern fashion.

Shopping

The modern **Northern store** and the local **Co-op** usually stock everything from fresh produce to camping equipment. **Kitikmeot Supplies** sells hardware, lumber, office supplies, household goods, snowmobiles and petroleum products for trucks and other vehicles. At the **Eniknigiit Katimayet Elders Centre**, you can ask local women to sew you traditional garments. You may also find a few items for sale, such as parkas and footwear.

To purchase works of art by local carvers, ask around to see who has pieces available. The Co-op also sells carvings and prints by local artists and those from other communities.

Visitors with a taste for "country foods" won't want to miss the local meat and fish processing plant, **Kitikmeot Foods**, owned and operated by the territorial government and the HTO. Here you'll find caribou, muskox and a variety of fish products prepared and packaged in many ways.

Accommodation and Dining

Arctic Islands Lodge has 26 luxurious rooms, of which 17 are single occupancy, eight are double occupancy, and one is a suite. Some are non-smoking rooms. All have a private washroom, telephone, and cable TV. Prices of rooms at peak season are $175 for a single-occupancy room and $195 for a double-occupancy room; prices could well be lower at other times of the year. The suite is usually booked in advance, says lodge management, and so it declines to reveal the suite rate. The lodge has a restaurant and coffee shop with designated non-smoking areas, which are open during regular working hours. Laundry facilities, fax, and photocopying are also available to guests. In spring and summer, nature and wildlife tours are conducted, weather permitting. A conference room accommodates up to 125 people. There are also tour package rates; contact the lodge or check their web site for details.

The **Ikaluktutiak Co-op Hotel/Inns North** accommodates 45 guests in 21 double-occupancy rooms, and three single-occupancy rooms (one of which is an apartment). The hotel has a non-smoking restaurant and dining room that are also open to local residents. Rooms have a TV and radio. Bathrooms are shared. Other facilities include laundry services, phones in some rooms, a fax machine, and a conference room that hosts up to 100 people. Daily room rates, excluding meals, are $160 for doubles and $130 for singles, except for the apartment, which is $160 for one person, or $170 for two. The apartment includes a kitchen, living and dining room, and private bathroom. Cost of meals is as follows: breakfast $10.50; lunch $13.99; and dinner $25.

On Victoria Island, almost 140 kilometres northwest of Cambridge Bay, is the High Arctic Lodge. Operating from early July to the end of August, this hunting and fishing lodge accommodates 12 guests in five cabins. A gift shop is located in the main lodge. Week-long adventures start at $3,295. This includes the flight from Cambridge Bay, meals, guides and overnight fly-out to an outpost camp near Hadley Bay at Victoria Island's north end. The lodge also organizes naturalist, canoeing and muskox hunting packages, and outings to archeological sites of ancient Inuit camps. Call the lodge for prices and dates.

The Northern store sells fast food such as pizza and Kentucky Fried Chicken at its **Quick Stop** snack bar. You may also rent videos here. At the **Olapkivik** arcade, you can play pool or pinball and stock up on snack food.

Services

Cambridge Bay provides residents and visitors with a **health centre** that is open from 8:30 a.m. to 5 p.m. weekdays, as well as a dental clinic open weekdays from 9 a.m. to 12 p.m. and 1 to 6 p.m. The dental clinic travels to other communities, so call ahead. Cambridge Bay also has a **post office, RCMP** detachment, weather information and visitors centre, recreational activities such as hockey and curling, as well as a fitness centre. In 1998, a fire destroyed the local high school and the valuable library that resided there.

The Co-op offers **taxi** service for airport arrivals and departures from 9 a.m. to 7 p.m. during weekdays and after hours. You'll need to order a taxi in advance. Local schools teach students from kindergarten to Grade 12, and **Nunavut Arctic College** offers training to adults in many areas.

Canadian and First Air provide scheduled flights into Cambridge Bay, while Adlair Aviation Ltd. and Aklak Air offer charter service to the community. Northern Transportation Ltd. (NTCL) provides shipping to the region in summer.

Local residents increasingly turn to telecommunications, including computers, fax machines and the Internet, via local Internet service provider Polarnet. Radio broadcasting is provided by CBC Radio and a local **radio station**.

DIRECTORY

*Outfitters and tour operators licensed at time of writing.
After March 31/99, check for updated status.

Accommodation and Dining

Arctic Islands Lodge
VISA, MasterCard, American Express, Diners Club/enRoute, Interac.
Tel.: (867) 983-2345
Fax: (867) 983-2480
E-mail: ailfr@polarnet.ca
Web site: www.worldsites.net/
    arcticislandslodge

Ikaluktutiak Co-op/Inns North
VISA, MasterCard, American Express, Diners Club/enRoute, Interac.
Tel.: (867) 983-2215
Fax: (867) 983-2023

Quick Stop
11 a.m.–6:30 p.m., Monday to Friday; 12–5 p.m., Saturday; 1–5 p.m., Sunday.
VISA, MasterCard, Interac.
Tel.: (867) 983-2566

* Outfitters/Tour Operators/Visitors Centre

Arctic Coast Visitors Centre
Tel.: (867) 983-2224
Fax: (867) 983-2302

Central Arctic Tours and Outfitters
Tours out on the land.
Tel.: (867) 983-2024
Fax: (867) 983-2821

Ekaluktutiak Hunters and Trappers Organization
Tel.: (867) 983-2426
Fax: (867) 983-2427

High Arctic Lodge
Cash, traveller's cheques, personal cheques.
Tel.: 1-800-661-3880 or (250) 493-3300
Fax: (250) 493-3900
E-mail: higharctic@vip.net

Ice Dancer Boat Tours
Tel.: (867) 983-2268
Fax: (867) 983-2258
E-mail: wilfw@polarnet.ca

Services

Airport
Tel.: (867) 983-2501

CBC Radio Station (FM 101.9)
Tel.: (867) 983-2077
Fax: (867) 983-2872

Churches

Glad Tidings Church
Services: 11 a.m., 7:30 p.m., Sunday;
7:30 p.m., Wednesday; 7:30 p.m., Friday
(English and Inuktitut).
Tel.: (867) 983-2387

Roman Catholic Diocesan Centre
Tel.: (867) 983-2521

St. George's Anglican Church
Services: 9:30 a.m. (English) and
11 a.m. (Inuktitut), Sunday.
Tel.: (867) 983-2440

Dental Clinic
Tel.: (867) 983-2285
Fax: (867) 983-2168

Department of Sustainable Development, Government of Nunavut
(or until April/99, GNWT's Resources,
Wildlife and Economic Development)
Tel.: (867) 983-7222 or (867) 983-7219
Fax: (867) 983-2802

Eniknigiit Katimayet Elders Centre
Tel.: (867) 983-2912

Hamlet Office
Tel.: (867) 983-2337
Fax: (867) 983-2193

Health Centre
Tel.: (867) 983-2531
Fax: (867) 983-2262

Police (RCMP)
Tel.: (867) 983-2111
Fax: (867) 983-2498

Post Office
Across from firehall.
8:30–11:30 a.m., 12:30–5 p.m.,
Monday to Friday.
Tel.: (867) 983-2243

Radio Station (FM 105.1)
Tel.: (867) 983-2077
Fax: (867) 983-2872

Royal Bank of Canada
10 a.m.–4 p.m., Monday to Thursday;
10 a.m.–5 p.m., Friday. Closed Saturday.
Tel.: (867) 983-2007
Fax: (867) 983-2754

Schools

Kullik Ilihakvik Elementary School
Tel.: (867) 983-2510
Fax: (867) 983-2515

Nunavut Arctic College
Tel.: (867) 983-7234
Fax: (867) 983-2404

Taxi

Ikaluktutiak Co-op Taxi
Tel.: (867) 983-2201

Weather Information
Tel.: (867) 983-2254 or (867) 983-2501
Fax: (867) 983-2512
Web site weather forecast:
www.infonorth.org

Shopping

Ikaluktutiak Co-operative Ltd.
10 a.m.–7 p.m., Monday to Friday;
10 a.m.–5 p.m., Saturday. Closed Sunday.
VISA, MasterCard, Diners Club/enRoute,
Interac.
Tel.: (867) 983-2201
Fax: (867) 983-2085

Kitikmeot Foods
8:30 a.m.–12 p.m., 1–5 p.m., Monday to
Friday. Open seasonally on Saturday.
Closed Sunday.
VISA accepted.
Tel.: (867) 983-2881
Fax: (867) 983-2801

Kitikmeot Supplies Ltd.
7 a.m.–5:30 p.m., Monday to Friday;
8 a.m.–5 p.m., Saturday. Closed Sunday.
VISA, Interac.
Tel.: (867) 983-2227
Fax: (867) 983-2220

Northern Store
10 a.m.–6:30 p.m., Monday to Friday;
10 a.m.–5 p.m., Saturday. Closed Sunday.
VISA, MasterCard, Interac.
Tel.: (867) 983-2571
Fax: (867) 983-2452

Olapkivik
Arcade and convenience store.
7–11 p.m., Monday to Thursday;
7 p.m.–12 a.m., Friday to Sunday.
Cash only.
Tel.: (867) 983-2379

78. BLOODY FALLS
TERRITORIAL HISTORIC PARK

by John Laird

Bloody Falls Territorial Historic Park in the central Arctic is one of Nunavut's few parks with a shared history between the Inuit and the North's other primary aboriginal group, the Dene Indians.

Unfortunately, this history hasn't always been amiable. In fact, the falls got their English name in 1771, when European explorer Samuel Hearne witnessed the massacre of unsuspecting Inuit by the Chipewyan warriors with whom he was travelling. (Chipewyan was an earlier name for Dene.) Today, Bloody Falls is recognized as a national historic site. The Inuit enjoy sharing their heritage with visitors, but ask that you respect the land of their ancestors.

Despite its gory contemporary moniker, northern peoples have gathered at this special place on the Coppermine River for thousands of years. Here, age-old volcanic rock forces the broad, swift-flowing river into a narrow channel of boiling rapids and twisting eddies. The roar of Bloody Falls calls out as you approach across the broad, silent tundra. Inuit refer to the camp site below the falls as *Unnuagarhiurvik*, the place where you "stay all night," a name that recalls a time when fishing was an integral part of their nomadic lives. Even today Inuit camp here to fish, and some have cabins along the Coppermine River.

This region has been inhabited by the Copper Inuit, a people known for making tools from copper found in the Copper Mountains, about 80 kilometres south of the park. Many explorers, including an early expedition of doomed arctic explorer Sir John Franklin, have travelled through the area.

The Land and Wildlife

The golden eagles that soar above Coppermine River throughout the summer nest along the steep cliffs at the falls, and at other locations along the river. Also watch for rough-legged hawks, peregrine falcons and gyrfalcons. Other avian cliff dwellers include countless swallows, which nest under rock ledges at the falls.

Watch for animal tracks as you walk along the muddy shore above and below the falls. Barren-ground caribou migrate nearby in spring and autumn. Caribou may also occasionally appear within the park or along the trail from Kugluktuk in summer.

The barren lands, or tundra, are also home to barren-ground grizzly bears. Although your chances of encountering one are rare, you should still take precautions. When camping, store food well away from your tent, pack out all garbage when you leave the park, and keep fire pits clean and free of food. For more information on bears, contact Kugluktuk's **Department of Sustainable Development** (or until April/99, **Resources, Wildlife and Economic Development**).

Wildflowers jump into bloom in late June, dotting the tundra with bright colors for three to four weeks. One of the more interesting plants found at Bloody Falls is the black-tipped groundsel, which was described here in 1821 by John Richardson, a surgeon-naturalist on the Franklin Expedition. The plant's black tips inspired Richardson to name it *senecio lugens*, from the Latin word *lugeo* ("to mourn"), a name that recalls the slaughter that once occurred at the site. By late August, the bright greens of summer give way to golden yellow, the tundra's last hurrah before winter begins.

What to See and Do

Located on the west side of the river, Bloody Falls Territorial Historic Park covers a 7.5-square-kilometre tract of land centred on the falls. The park landscape is typical of the area, with rolling tundra occasionally interrupted by escarpments and rocky outcrops. Closer to the river, steep cliffs and sandy hills descend in plateaus to the valley below. From the park's highest hill, you can barely make out the community of Kugluktuk and the Arctic Ocean, about 13 kilometres to the north.

The ancestors of both the Inuit and Dene fished and hunted at Bloody Falls. At the falls you'll find stone remnants of winter houses used more than 500 years ago by people of the Thule culture. Other archeological evidence indicates earlier inhabitants, the Pre-Dorset, camped at the falls more than 3,500 years ago.

The remains of early caribou-hunting camps dating back some 1,500 years have also been found in the park and are linked with the Taltheilei, a prehistoric Dene people. These camps are scattered on sand plateaus along the west bank, downstream from the falls, but may be difficult to spot since they've been obscured by blowing sand.

Bloody Falls is a great fishing spot, popular with local people and visitors alike. In spring, arctic char migrate down the Coppermine River to the Arctic Ocean; some people say they taste best at this time of year. In late August, when the char begin to travel upstream again, the nearby community of Kugluktuk holds its annual fishing derby, an event enjoyed by many visitors.

Both Kugluktuk residents and Coppermine River travellers camp at Bloody Falls. The area isn't heavily used, however, so you may have the park to yourself. There is a wonderful camp site near the falls that's somewhat sheltered by waist-high willows. There are a few picnic tables and an outhouse at the camp site, but no other services. Drinking water can be obtained from the river and nearby lakes.

Planning a Trip

A rough, 13-kilometre trail stretches across the tundra from Kugluktuk to Bloody Falls. You can hike to the park in four or five hours, but be prepared for wet, spongy ground and a few stream crossings. Despite these minor obstacles, it's a beautiful hike, taking you past many little lakes. Keep an eye out for grizzly bears! You can also rent an all-terrain vehicle (ATV) in Kugluktuk and drive to the park in two hours. ATV rentals cost about $75 to $100 per day; contact the economic development officer for the Hamlet of Kugluktuk or the **Kugluktuk Heritage Centre** for more information.

Licensed outfitters will also take you on a 45-minute trip to the park by motorboat. Trips cost around $70 per person, slightly less per person for groups of up to four people. Bring a picnic lunch if your guide isn't supplying one. Note that the river is sometimes shallow, especially in August and September, so you may have to hike the last one or two kilometres to Bloody Falls. Contact the Kugluktuk Heritage Centre for more information on licensed outfitters in the community. Canoes can be rented for $50 per day. And for those interested in boat or guided walking tours, the cost is $250 per person per day.

Many outfitters offer rafting and canoeing trips down the Coppermine River. These companies fly groups from Yellowknife to points along the river for one- to two-week adventures that usually terminate at Kugluktuk. If you take one of these trips, Bloody Falls should be a scheduled stop along the way, but check with your trip leader. For more information on companies offering such trips, contact **Nunavut Tourism**.

You can also visit the park in winter, although it's highly recommended you do so with an outfitter who's familiar with the area, since blowing snow can obliterate landmarks in a frighteningly short time. The falls and river will be frozen, although water continues to run below the ice.

DIRECTORY

Department of Sustainable Development, Government of Nunavut
(or until April/99, GNWT's **Resources, Wildlife and Economic Development**)
Economic development officer, located in Kugluktuk.
Tel.: (867) 982-7206
Fax: (867) 982-3119

Kugluktuk Heritage Centre
Tel.: (867) 982-3232
Fax: (867) 982-3229

Nunavut Tourism
Cambridge Bay office.
Tel.: (867) 983-2842
Fax: (867) 983-2302
E-mail: arcticst@polarnet.ca
Web site: www.nunatour.nt.ca

79. ULTIMA THULE, AND THE NORTH POLE

by Renee Wissink

From Sir James Lancaster's namesake sound at 74 N to Ward Hunt Island at 83 N latitude, the High Arctic (or Queen Elizabeth Islands, as they appear on maps) is the world's most northerly region.

For those who inhabit gentler climates, the High Arctic is the ultimate conquest — a landscape of inspiration, a land of extremes, of abused superlatives, reserved in imagination as an untouched place.

The Quest for Adventure

In 330 BC the Greek explorer Pytheas sailed north from the Mediterranean and became the first recorded voyager to cross the Arctic Circle. He had learned of a mysterious archipelago called Thule (pronounced "too-lee"), somewhere to the north. Thule became an irresistible attraction to the human imagination, but also an elusive goal. As the frontiers of arctic exploration moved north, so did Thule, until it took on mythical proportions, becoming in poetry "Ultima Thule" — the land farthest north.

The affliction was not just ascribed to non-aboriginal peoples. The renowned Inuit shaman Qillaq (who later became known as "Qitdlarssuaq," meaning the great Qitdlaq) also thirsted for the undiscovered. He led the last great Inuit migration from the Lancaster Sound district to northwest Greenland, home of the Polar Inuit. The world's most northerly populated region has since been named Thule. It appears that Qillaq's motives were no more pragmatic than others, as he is quoted around 1858 as having said: "Do you know the desire to see new land? Do you know the desire to see new people?"

For centuries the quest for Ultima Thule became the pursuit of the geographic North Pole, the most coveted of all polar prizes. The geographic North Pole, situated permanently in the Arctic Ocean, is the rotational axis of the Earth in the Northern Hemisphere. It should not be confused with the much more southerly North Magnetic Pole on southwest Ellef Ringnes Island — the point from which the Earth's magnetic field radiates. The North Magnetic Pole is in constant lateral motion, having moved several hundred kilometres from the point where it was originally located in 1831. For technical reasons, a magnetic compass won't work within several hundred kilometres of the North Magnetic Pole, but it can still be used for treks to the geographic North Pole as long as you calculate the magnetic declination to get a true reading on direction (for more details, see Chapter 11, "Adventure Travel").

The dream of reaching Ultima Thule became reality when Robert E. Peary reached the area near the North Pole on April 6, 1909. Completing one of the most arduous chapters in polar history, he exclaimed: "The Pole at last! The prize of three centuries, my dream and ambition for 23 years, mine at last."

Still, the dream did not die for other explorers. Just as mountain climbers did not stop attempting to conquer Mount Everest after Edmund Hillary and Tenzing Norgay stood on the summit, so too have many attempted to follow in Robert Peary's footsteps. All who have stood at the North Pole have realized that the goal was not the slab of ice upon which they stood — indeed, the area of the Pole is indistinguishable from all the rest of the ice in the nearly six-million-square-kilometre expanse of the Arctic Ocean.

Rather, the goal was within themselves, their personal Ultima Thule, their quest for adventure.

The Easy Way

Several tour operators organize North Pole trips from Resolute on Cornwallis Island. Most itineraries are for a week to 10 days. This provides a "weather window" for the polar flight and allows visitors to see other High Arctic sites, such as the Polaris mine on Little Cornwallis Island, the North Magnetic Pole, the fossil forest on Axel Heiberg Island, the community of Grise Fiord, and the Fort Conger Historic Site in Ellesmere Island National Park. Only two airlines fly to the Pole — Kenn Borek Air and First Air, each using Twin Otters on skis. Both airlines depart from Resolute and use the Environment Canada weather station at Eureka as their staging point.

Once at Eureka, you await your weather window. Weather reports are checked and double checked and when all looks good, you're off on your assault of the Pole. Like a major mountain expedition using supply camps at different elevations, your next stop is at a fuel cache in the vicinity of 86 N latitude, some 120 nautical miles north of the most northerly land in the world. A homing beacon placed with the cache allows your pilot to find this most northern of fuel stations out on the moving polar pack ice. After refuelling, you begin the final leg. Below is a seemingly endless scene of white with only the plane's global positioning system (GPS) navigating you to that point that Robert Peary christened "the Big Nail."

Once over the Pole, your pilots will search for a suitable stretch of ice to land on, a procedure not without risk — at least one Twin Otter lies at the bottom of the Polar Basin. As you circle, the latitude readings on the plane's GPS change wildly and with each loop you circle all the world's time zones. Your stop at the Pole will be approximately one hour, just enough time to feel the magic, take a few photos, and toast your success. You will have reached your Ultima Thule: as you stand at the North Pole, north itself is no more and south lies in every direction.

If you are contemplating an arctic adventure, start by contacting **Nunavut Tourism**, **Parks Canada**, the government of Nunavut's **Department of Sustainable Development** (or until April 1999, the GNWT's Department of **Resources, Wildlife and Economic Development**), and local licensed outfitters. Some packages fly you within a few kilometres of the North Pole, where you can dogsled or ski the last leg in.

First Air and Kenn Borek Air, as well as Nunavut Tourism, can tell you which tour operators offer North Pole tours. Expect to part with between $8,500 and $14,000, depending on the package.

The Hard Way

The North Pole remains the ultimate polar challenge. For this "horizontal Everest," Ward Hunt Island just off the north coast of Ellesmere Island is the base camp, as each year a new crop of "pole vaulters" sets out from this small island on the gruelling 772-kilometre journey to the Pole. Sadly, like Everest base camp, Ward Hunt Island is strewn with piles of equipment and garbage abandoned by expeditions from many countries. A walk through the flotsam and jetsam on Ward Hunt — now administered by Parks Canada as part of Ellesmere Island National Park — is a walk through a field of dreams, shattered and realized. Each new expedition establishes its own particular challenge: the first by ski, the first by ultralight aircraft, by hot-air balloon, helicopter, motorcycle, and the list continues to grow.

Northerners have serious concerns about polar trekkers, and some involve search and rescue. While the Baffin Region has a search and rescue program administered by the RCMP Emergency Measures Organization in Iqaluit and supplemented by National Parks Public Safety Plans, the cost for search and rescue could become burdensome to the taxpayer. For example, the cost of a search for one overdue North Pole trekker topped the $250,000 mark. Full cost recovery and mandatory expedition insurance are two avenues being explored by territorial and federal governments to offset these costs.

Protection of wildlife is also a concern. Arctic wolves and polar bears have been killed by expeditions. Northerners want to ensure that expedition members are properly instructed on how to avoid and deter aggressive polar bears. While such encounters are dangerous, not all need end in the death of a bear. There is also concern about how expeditions cache fuel and food, and how they dispose of their waste.

DIRECTORY

Department of Sustainable Development, Government of Nunavut
(or until April/99, GNWT's **Resources, Wildlife and Economic Development**)
Tel.: (867) 979-5070
Fax: (867) 979-6026

Nunavut Tourism
P.O. Box 1450, Iqaluit NT,
X0A 0H0 Canada
Tel.: 1-800-491-7910 (for Canada and the United States)
Tel.: (867) 979-6551
Fax: (867) 979-1261
E-mail: nunatour@nunanet.com
Web site: www.nunatour.nt.ca

Parks Canada
Tel.: (867) 473-8828
Fax: (867) 473-8612
E-mail: nunavut_info@pch.gc.ca

80. ELLESMERE ISLAND NATIONAL PARK

by Renee Wissink

Encompassing Canada's northernmost lands, Ellesmere Island National Park is an enclave of sedimentary mountain ranges, ice caps, glaciers, fiords and fertile arctic oases.

At 37,775 square kilometres, it is Canada's second-largest national park, and six and a half times the size of Canada's smallest province, Prince Edward Island. It covers half of that portion of Ellesmere Island north of Greely Fiord, and a third of the island's northern coastline. Seven major fiords indent its coast, and ice shelves along its northern coast feature predominantly, abutting the Arctic Ocean. The scale of the land is immense and, at the same time, intimate. Patterns of rock, frost-cracked ground, willows and wildflowers form intricate networks that extend to vistas of mountains and glaciers which, in the clear, dry air, seem near enough to touch.

Like Auyuittuq National Park on Baffin Island, Ellesmere Island was originally named a national park reserve. "Reserve" indicates that certain lands were subject to a land claims process. Although the park area was modified by the *Nunavut Land Claims Agreement Act*, it was still to be called a park reserve until an Inuit Impact and Benefits Agreement had been successfully completed. These negotiations were slated to wind up by the autumn of 1998, as this book was going to press. If negotiations were delayed, though, Ellesmere would remain a park reserve for the purposes of park management.

The Land and Wildlife

Much of Ellesmere Island National Park, including the Hazen Plateau, is a polar desert, with some areas receiving less annual precipitation — about 2.5 centimetres — than the Sahara. Still, there is enough water from snow and glacial melt to support a broad network of vegetated areas, including highly productive grass-sedge meadows, and some of the most productive wildlife habitats in the High Arctic. The park's thermal oases — including the Lake Hazen basin and the Tanquary Fiord region — spring to life each summer and are home to herds of muskoxen and small roaming bands of endangered Peary caribou. About 30 species of birds, including several Old World migrants, like the Red Knot, can be found here. Arctic wolves roam over huge territories and den at sites they've been reusing for up to three millennia. Arctic hares are ubiquitous and have been seen in herds numbering in the thousands — heaps of hares! Other species include arctic fox, ermine, collared lemming, ringed seals, walrus, and occasionally whales and polar bears in coastal areas.

Due to their inexperience with humans, animals in the park often appear innocent around people, in a Galapagos-like manner. This condition is referred to as "ecological naïveté," and should not be confused with tameness. Avoid the temptation to touch or feed wolves or foxes that approach closely. It is against the law, and wolves and foxes on Ellesmere Island have been

Iqaluit, the capital of Nunavut. Inset: The iglu-shaped St. Jude's Cathedral in downtown Iqaluit was designed and built by members of the congregation

Katannilik Territorial Park Reserve follows the course of the Soper River; the lush Soper River Valley harbors a thermal oasis and abundant vegetation

As in many of Nunavut's smaller communities, Repulse Bay residents generally earn their living the traditional way: hunting, fishing, and trapping

Catholic missionaries to Pelly Bay found snowhouses (igluit) *warmer than stone dwellings, but in 1941 they built a stone church to provide a more permanent place of worship*

Picturesque Pangnirtung, home to a thriving tapestry weaving industry, also provides easy access to Auyuittuq National Park and Kekerten Territorial Historic Park

An interpretive trail through Kekerten Territorial Historic Park reveals more about the 19th-century station that was once the hub of whaling activity in Cumberland Sound

Kugluktuk's annual Nattiq Frolics showcase traditional harvesting skills, including sealskinning. Here, a deftly wielded ulu *(woman's knife) helps simplify the job*

Like many students in Nunavut, these Gjoa Haven children are computer-savvy. Community by community, the new territory is linking up to the rest of the world via the Internet

With my hands...
Aggamnut...
ᐊᒡᒐᒪᓄᑦ...

I make what is in my thoughts.
I touch the healing spirit within.

Nunavut Arts & Crafts
CED *Division*

Northwest Territories Resources, Wildlife and Economic Development

Photo of Gideon Qaujuaq, Taloyoak. Hat crochet pattern courtesy of Uqqurmiut Centre for Arts & Crafts, Pangnirtung.

known to carry rabies. **Parks Canada** recommends, in fact, that visitors to Ellesmere Island National Park obtain precautionary vaccinations against rabies and tetanus before coming to the park.

Ellesmere Island National Park contains most of the major ice shelves within North America. Ice shelves are ancient deposits of very thick freshwater ice (up to 60 metres in depth), tightly frozen to the land and extending several kilometres seaward as a rigid cover over the Arctic Ocean. In summer, the surface of these shelves is covered with a series of low, white ice ridges and shallow blue water troughs running parallel to the coast for many miles. Sometimes huge pieces of these shelves, many square kilometres in extent, break away and float free for years, propelled by ocean currents — particularly the Polar Gyre. During their travels they have been used by scientists as bases for floating research stations, complete with aircraft landing strips.

The park's northern coast, only 720 kilometres from the North Pole, is rugged with medium-sized sedimentary mountains and deeply incised glacial valleys and fiords. Glaciers spill down the sides of some valleys (Piper Pass, for example), spreading out on the valley floors like giant pancakes.

To the south lie the vast Grant Land Mountains and Ice Cap, comprised of two nearly parallel ranges (the British Empire Range and the United States Range). Mount Barbeau, at 2,616 metres, is the highest mountain east of the Rockies in North America. Most of the mountains are partially "submerged" *nunatat* ("pieces of land"), their peaks sticking through a vast ice cap up to 900 metres thick. From the air, the austere beauty of this landscape resembles a mini-Antarctica. This enormous reservoir of ice covers about a third of the park, and its glaciers flow north toward the Arctic Ocean, and south toward the Hazen Plateau.

CFS Alert

Situated in an enclave in the northwest corner of the park is Canadian Forces Station (CFS) Alert. The station is physically closer to Moscow than to Ottawa, so is ideally suited for its primary role as a listening post. With the end of the Cold War and the advent of new technologies allowing for remote interpretation of data, the base has been reduced to a quarter of its original overwintering population of 200. Although the station has the best airstrip on the island, access is restricted to military personnel.

What to See and Do

The Henrietta Nesmith Glacier overlooks a broad basin called the Hazen Plateau to the south and ends only a short distance from Lake Hazen, the core of the park. Because of the slope of the land in the Lake Hazen basin and its orientation toward the sun, this thermal oasis provides an ecosystem during the warmest years with a frost-free season rivalling Schefferville, Quebec — 3,200 kilometres southeast.

The Lake Hazen warden station, located on the site of the old Defence Research Board camp (established in 1957), is on the north shore of Lake Hazen. A small cluster of modest buildings located on a flattened knoll house the warden station and a tent site for visitors. Many interesting side trips are accessible from the Hazen camp, including a number of short hikes into the Garfield Range. As at the Tanquary Fiord warden station, visitors to Hazen camp must register with park staff upon arrival — providing information on their travel routes, equipment, supplies, southern contacts and expected departure date. They must also close their registration when leaving to confirm departure.

Lake Hazen (500-square-kilometre-plus surface area) is one of the largest freshwater lakes in the circumpolar world. The only fish here are arctic char, joined by sparse populations of zooplankton and phytoplankton. Although there is limited sport fishing, a park-wide ban is being considered to protect this northernmost char population.

To the southeast is Lady Franklin Bay, where visitors can find Fort Conger, a historic site of global significance. The remaining buildings have the same protective status as the Parliament Buildings in Ottawa. Fort Conger played a pivotal role in the early voyages of explorers and scientists to the area, and was a base for those seeking the North Pole. Visitors to this relic-strewn site are asked to follow the special precautions outlined in the park's Fort Conger information brochure, available at registration.

The southwestern boundary of the park encloses the upper end of the exquisite Tanquary Fiord. An airstrip, visitor shelter, camp site and staff buildings are located near the head of the fiord, and many scenic features can be seen within a day's hike.

The terrain is relatively easy, and the local flora and fauna are a good cross-section of High Arctic species.

A small scenic kettle lake lies in a depression a short distance from the Tanquary warden station. Its margins are well vegetated with many species of flowering plants. Nearby are the stone ruins of an early Inuit occupation, including two kinds of stone foxtraps and a muskox ambush structure. Park staff is on hand during the summer to discuss local attractions, travel plans, safety measures and conservation tips.

Visitors hiking the Tanquary-to-Lake Hazen corridor should start their trek at the Lake Hazen warden station. This is because the length and condition of the Lake Hazen airstrip limits aircraft takeoff weight. All aircraft landings, particularly those other than at the Tanquary Fiord and Lake Hazen warden stations, require a permit from the park. Make arrangements as far in advance as possible.

As in all arctic parks, visitors must arrive fully equipped and self-reliant. There is no local source of equipment or supplies, and search and rescue capability in the region is very limited. In the event of a personal emergency, it will take considerable time and expense to perform an air evacuation. There are no standby rescue aircraft in the area and the only civil airbase in the High Arctic is at Resolute, about 960 kilometres from the park.

The park has several emergency caches at locations other than Tanquary Fiord and Lake Hazen, but the supplies — food, tent, fuel, radio, personal locator beacon and other goods — are to be used only in true emergencies. Any use of emergency cache supplies must be reported to park staff as soon as possible.

Planning a Trip

Entry to the High Arctic is through Resolute, served several times a week by scheduled airlines with connections to Edmonton, Montreal and Ottawa. Prudent visitors will have previously made plans for travel to and from the park and accommodation in Resolute. Last-minute shopping and return travel arrangements must be completed before leaving Resolute, because civilization will lie behind you once you depart for the park.

Air travel, by far the most popular way of getting to the park, is by Twin Otter, a rugged and reliable Canadian-built turboprop aircraft that has made a name for itself as the workhorse of the Canadian Arctic. The charter cost from Resolute to the park and back is high — between $17,000 and $18,000 (includes pickup trip). The plane carries about 10 to 12 people and their gear.

There are two ways to substantially reduce the cost of the trip. The first is to travel with a pre-arranged group (this could drop your cost to under $4,000 if at least six people are making the trip). The second is to split your charter with another group. If the airline can fly another group out after dropping you off, the plane doesn't fly an empty leg, thus cutting costs in half. You may wish to make a side trip to the tiny picturesque hamlet of Grise Fiord.

The *Visitor Handbook,* available at registration, has sections on polar bears, trail etiquette, species lists, a sport fishing guide, and information on Fort Conger. Tour operators are well prepared to handle problems, and visitors planning a trip to the High Arctic should use the services of a licensed tour operator or outfitter with experience in the area. Make arrangements well in advance, and check with **Nunavut Tourism**, as well as the Parks Canada office in Pangnirtung, for up-to-date information on outfitters and other services such as HF radio rental. There is also an entry fee to Ellesmere Island National Park ($15 per person for one day, $40 per person for up to three nights, and $100 per person for more than three days).

You'll need four map sheets at a scale of 1:250,000 to cover the entire park:

• Clements Markham Inlet 120F and 120G-67
• McClintock Inlet 340D-67
• Tanquary Fiord 340D-67
• Lady Franklin Bay 120 C and D-67

Sections of the park are currently being mapped at 1:50,000. Groups entering the park can get a 1:64,000 air photo mosaic of the Tanquary-to-Lake Hazen corridor with some recommended travel routes. Obtain one beforehand by contacting the Parks Canada office in Pangnirtung, or upon registration.

DIRECTORY

Federal Maps

Tel.: 1-888-545-8111 or (613) 723-6366
Fax: (613) 723-6995
E-mail: fedmaps@istar.ca
Web site: www.fedmaps.com/

Nunavut Tourism

Tel.: 1-800-491-7910 (for Canada and the United States)
Tel.: (867) 979-6551
Fax: (867) 979-1261
E-mail: nunatour@nunanet.com
Web site: www.nunatour.nt.ca

Parks Canada, Pangnirtung

(c/o Senior Warden, Ellesmere Island National Park)
For a copy of the *Visitor Handbook* or the park's information brochure, *Canada at the Top of the World.*
Tel.: (867) 473-8828
Fax: (867) 473-8612
E-mail: nunavut_info@pch.gc.ca

81. RESOLUTE

by Terry Jesudason

A popular T-shirt in Resolute once boasted: "Resolute is not the end of the world, but you can see it from here."

Population:	198 (Inuit: 81%, non-Inuit: 19%) Source: 1996 Census of Canada
Telephone Area Code:	867
Time Zone:	Central Time
Postal Code:	X0A 0V0
How to Get There:	Possible routes:
	• Ottawa/Montreal-Iqaluit-Resolute
	• Winnipeg-Rankin Inlet-Iqaluit-Resolute
	• Calgary/Edmonton-Yellowknife-Cambridge Bay-Resolute
	• Kangerlussuaq (Greenland)-Iqaluit-Resolute
	Iqaluit to Resolute (about 1,500 kilometres north) is via First Air.
	Passengers must stay overnight in Iqaluit. Cambridge Bay to Resolute
	(about 700 kilometres northeast) is via Canadian North
Banks:	None. Cash and traveller's cheques are preferable. Credit cards are
	accepted by certain businesses
Alcohol:	Alcohol and alcoholic beverages cannot be purchased in Resolute.
	Visitors who want to bring alcohol into the community must first obtain
	a permit from the **Alcohol and Drug Education Committee**
Taxis:	No. Drivers will usually offer a ride to anyone walking the
	seven kilometres between the airport and town

Indeed. Located on the south coast of Cornwallis Island at almost 75 N latitude, Resolute is the gateway to the High Arctic.

In this, Canada's second most northerly community, looks can often be deceiving. First-time visitors may see only an endless sea of grey shale rocks, but between those rocks grow the small, colorful arctic flowers that burst to life for a short period each summer. Winter travellers are greeted with countless miles of snow and ice, but across that white expanse you can go forever.

Excellent jet service from Eastern and Western Canada, as well as two local charter airline companies, make Nunavut's northernmost reaches easily accessible from here. Whether you're planning a trek to the geographic or North Magnetic poles, a hiking excursion in Ellesmere Island National Park, Canada's most northerly national park, a season of scientific research or a simple visit to the land of the midnight sun, Resolute is often the first chapter in an adventure.

History

Though Inuit have travelled and camped on the shores of Resolute for many hundreds of years, the area is steeped in a European history matched by few other Nunavut communities. Resolute is known as *Qausuittuq* in Inuktitut; there are several translations for the name, but the most popular is "place with no dawn." The site was a critical juncture along the Northwest Passage, the famed route to Asia sought so desperately by European explorers in the 18th and 19th centuries. The community bears the name of the *HMS Resolute*, one of the vessels that came in search of the lost British expedition under Sir John Franklin.

After the Second World War, when many parts of the Arctic were becoming strategically important, a weather station was established at Resolute. Two years later an airstrip was opened and the community became a focal point for arctic transportation. In 1953 the first Inuit families to live in the modern community of Resolute arrived when they were moved here by the federal government from Pond Inlet and the northern Quebec community of Inukjuak.

A contentious and highly emotional point in Nunavut's history, the reasons for the move have been interpreted differently by the federal government and the 17 families who were moved to either Resolute or Grise Fiord. The Canadian government says Inuit from Inukjuak were going hungry because caribou and other resources were scarce, and so the Inuit families voluntarily agreed to move to an area where game was more plentiful.

Members of the Inuit families, however, felt they were forced to abandon their homes for a harsh and alien land, and were used by the Canadian government to help assert sovereignty in the High Arctic. The debate resulted in hearings by the Royal Commission on Aboriginal Peoples, and in the spring of 1996, the survivors of the federal government's High Arctic Relocation Project were awarded $10 million in compensation from the federal government. The government did not admit any wrongdoing, however, and did not extend an apology as survivors had requested.

Since the 1950s, Resolute has also been a centre for scientific research in the High Arctic, with a logistics support base provided by the federal government at the **Polar Continental Shelf Project**. A federal school was opened and a major housing program initiated in the 1960s. In 1975, the community was relocated to the present townsite.

Resolute: Its Land and Wildlife

Resolute springs to life for a brief but fertile period every summer. In June, thousands of birds — including ivory gulls, arctic terns, snow buntings, jaegers and red-throated loons — nest on nearby islands. Arctic wildflowers begin to bloom near the end of the month, peaking by late July. Arctic poppies, purple saxifrages, mountain avens, chickweeds and buttercups are among the more visible species.

Travellers who venture out on the sea ice with local guides in April and May have a very good chance of seeing seals, and perhaps polar bears, in their natural habitat. In the summer you can go beluga watching and char fishing on Somerset Island. Air charters are organized through First Air or Kenn Borek Air Ltd. Fishing is best done in late June and early July.

Tours

The waters of Resolute Bay are frozen most of the year, so visitors can walk on the famous Northwest Passage, which passes directly in front of the village. Hiking is good in summer; the area is an old seabed, rich with fossils dating back 400 million years. Near the village, the Mecham River forms small rock pools of clear, cold meltwater where children swim the long days of summer away.

If not already booked with sport hunting trips, local guides with dogteams can also be hired for short trips. **Inuktitut Outfitting and Guide** organizes day trips by snowmobile and sledge (sled) in spring, or by boat in summer. **Nanuk Outfitting Ltd.** provides guides for polar bear and muskox sport hunting trips from March to May.

Archeology buffs can visit the sites of Thule tent rings about five kilometres from the airstrip. Two sites have been reconstructed with stones and whalebone to illustrate living conditions more than 500 years ago.

From Resolute there is air charter access to many nearby attractions. Beechey Island, the wintering site of Sir John Franklin's ill-fated 1845 expedition, is about 100 kilometres from town. You can also access Ellesmere Island National Park, or the limestone cliffs of Prince Leopold Island Migratory Bird Sanctuary, where hundreds of thousands of thick-billed murres, northern fulmars, black-legged kittiwakes and black guillemots nest.

Another attraction that can be reached by air charter is Polar Bear Pass National Wildlife Area, 120 kilometres northwest of Resolute on Bathurst Island. Polar Bear Pass is an unusually productive habitat in the midst of a polar desert. Some 54 species of birds have been identified here, but mammals are the most significant feature of the area. In addition to the many polar bears that travel through the pass, Polar Bear Pass also has the largest concentration of muskoxen on Bathurst Island. Endangered Peary caribou can also be found here, although their numbers are diminishing.

A new park is currently proposed for the northern part of Bathurst Island. If approved, the park — which will shelter a major calving area for Peary caribou — will cover about one-quarter of the island.

The North Magnetic Pole is approximately 500 kilometres from Resolute; the geographic North Pole is 1,700 kilometres away. Both are accessible by air charter in spring by ski-equipped aircraft. Several companies offer tour flights to both poles in April.

Visitors can see the base station of the Polar Continental Shelf Project by contacting the camp manager.

Shopping

Groceries, dry goods and hardware can be purchased at the **Tudjaat Co-op**. Souvenirs and handicrafts are available at the **Co-op Gift Shop** in the airport terminal building. These items are sometimes available directly from local carvers, who work mainly in soapstone, ivory and whalebone.

Accommodation and Dining

The **Narwhal Inn**, near the airport, accommodates 36 people in 30 rooms with single and double occupancy. Cafeteria-style meals are served in a spacious dining room. Bathrooms and a TV room are shared. The rate is $235.40 per person per night and includes all meals, airport transportation and GST. Accommodation without meals is $155.15 (including GST) per person per night.

Newly opened, the **South Camp Inn**, located in an apartment building, accommodates 18 people in nine rooms. Each room has a TV, phone and modem for fax hook-up. Two rooms have private washrooms; the rest have shared facilities. Prices are $185 per person per day (meals included), or $155 without meals. Non-guests may also eat at the hotel's dining room.

Qausuittuq Inns North, operated by Resolute's Tudjaat Co-op, is located in the hamlet and accommodates 24 people in 12 rooms. Laundry facilities, freezer space, and local sightseeing trips are also available. The homestyle meals include northern foods like muskox stew and arctic char. Qausuittuq (pronounced "cow-sweet-took") is expanding to include a new facility opening in the spring of 1999. In the new facility, each double-occupancy room will have a private bath, TV, telephone and computer hook-up. The rate is $144.45 per person per night, which includes **airport** transportation and GST. Meals are extra.

Some Inuit families are willing to board visitors. Arrangements vary and meals may not be included, although guests are allowed use of the kitchen. Personnel at the **hamlet office** will be able to point you in the right direction.

There are several good places to camp, all of which are close to sources of fresh drinking water. One is near Resolute Lake, about one kilometre from the airport. Another good area is near the Mecham River, not far from the village. Keep in mind that camping areas are exposed and Resolute weather is often fickle, so bring a sturdy tent and stake it well. Campers are expected to respect the land and remove their garbage.

Non-guests can dine at the Narwhal Inn (breakfast $15, lunch $25, dinner $35) or at the Qausuittuq Inns North restaurant (the menu is à la carte).

Services

In addition to jet service from both Eastern and Western Canada, Resolute is serviced regularly by Kenn Borek Air Ltd., with twice-weekly flights to Grise Fiord, and weekly flights to Pond Inlet and Arctic Bay.

The **Health Centre**'s walk-in clinic is Monday to Friday from 9 a.m. to 12 p.m. Public health clinics take place in the afternoon, from 1 to 5 p.m. Resident nurses are also on call for emergencies. There is an **RCMP** detachment in town; trekkers and expeditions would be well advised to fill out a Wilderness Travel Registration Form here before setting out.

Vehicles can be rented from **Narwhal Arctic Services**, **South Camp Enterprises** or **Diane Guy**.

DIRECTORY

*Outfitters and tour operators licensed at time of writing.
After March 31/99, check for updated status.

Accommodation and Dining

Narwhal Inn
VISA, MasterCard, Diners Club/enRoute.
Tel.: (867) 252-3968
Fax: (867) 252-3960

Qausuittuq Inns North
VISA, MasterCard, Diners Club/enRoute, Interac.
Tel.: 1-888-866-6784 (in North America)
Tel.: (867) 252-3900 or (867) 252-3901
Fax: (867) 252-3766

South Camp Inn
Cash, traveller's cheques.
Tel.: (867) 252-3737
Fax: (867) 252-3838

*Outfitters/Tour Operators

High Arctic International Explorer Services Ltd.
Tel.: (867) 252-3875
Fax: (867) 252-3766

Inuktitut Outfitting and Guide
Tel.: (867) 252-3174
Fax: (867) 252-3929

Jessco Logistics Ltd.
Tel.: (403) 282-2268
Fax: (403) 282-2195

Nanuk Outfitting Ltd.
Tel.: (867) 252-3694
Fax: (867) 252-3119
E-mail: nkalluk@aol.com

Polar Ice Expeditions Ltd.
Tel.: (867) 252-3747
Fax: (867) 252-3747

Services

Airport
Tel.: (867) 252-3923
Fax: (867) 252-3684

Alcohol and Drug Education Committee
Tel.: (867) 252-3660
Fax: (867) 252-3201

Church

St. Barnabas Anglican Church
No telephone.

Department of Sustainable Development, Government of Nunavut
(or until April/99, GNWT's Resources, Wildlife and Economic Development)
Tel.: (867) 252-3879
Fax: (867) 252-3752

Diane Guy
Vehicle rentals.
Tel.: (867) 252-3747
Fax: (867) 252-3747

Hamlet Office
Tel.: (867) 252-3616
Fax: (867) 252-3749

Health Centre
Tel.: (867) 252-3844
Fax: (867) 252-3601

Hunters and Trappers Organization
Tel.: (867) 252-3170
Fax: (867) 252-3800

Narwhal Arctic Services
Tel.: (867) 252-3925
Fax: (867) 252-3649

Polar Continental Shelf Project
Tel.: (867) 252-3872
Fax: (867) 252-3605

Police (RCMP)
Tel.: (867) 252-3817
Fax: (867) 252-3775

Post Office
At the Tudjaat Co-op.
Tel.: (867) 252-3959

Radio Station (FM 105.1)
Tel.: (867) 252-3683

Schools

Nunavut Arctic College
Tel.: (867) 252-3782
Fax: (867) 252-3778

Qarmartalik School
Tel.: (867) 252-3888
Fax: (867) 252-3690

South Camp Enterprises
Tel.: (867) 252-3701
Fax: (867) 252-3663

Weather Office
Tel.: (867) 252-3883 (office) or
(867) 252-3876 (weather forecast)
Web site weather forecast:
www.tor.ec.gc.ca/forecasts/index.html
(check under Regional Weather
Summaries) or www.infonorth.org
(check under Resolute)

Shopping

Co-op Gift Shop
Open at flight time, and from 1–5 p.m.
in the summer.
VISA, MasterCard, Diners
Club/enRoute, Interac.
Tel.: (867) 252-3718

Tudjaat Co-op
10 a.m.–12 p.m. and 1–5:30 p.m.,
Monday to Friday; 1–5 p.m., Saturday.
Closed Sunday.
VISA, MasterCard, Diners
Club/enRoute, Interac.
Tel.: (867) 252-3854
Fax: (867) 252-3618

82. BEECHEY ISLAND
by Kenn Harper

This is the island of lost souls. A rocky parcel of land off the southwest coast of Devon Island, Beechey is steeped in the lore of the lost Franklin Expedition, which sailed into Lancaster Sound in 1845 and disappeared forever.

After sailing up Wellington Channel in his quest to find a northern route to the riches of the Orient, British explorer Sir John Franklin and his crew of 129 men were stopped by ice and returned to spend the winter of 1845–1846 at Beechey. His ships, the *Erebus* and *Terror*, moored safely to the east of the island in the excellent harbor that now bears their name.

The following spring, Franklin and his men continued to the southwest on their fatal quest. They most likely sailed along the ice-choked waters of Peel Sound and the strait that now bears Franklin's name. In September 1846, the two ships were beset by ice to the north of King William Island. There they remained until April 1848, when the vessels were finally abandoned. The remaining men trekked south along King William Island toward the mainland. Not one lived to tell the tale.

Traces of Franklin's winter on Beechey were found by other explorers in 1850: the remains of three storehouses, workshops, a wash house, large numbers of empty meat tins, and three graves. No written records were found. Nonetheless, Beechey became an important depot and meeting place for Franklin searchers for a few years in the 1850s.

In 1852–1853, Commander W.J.S. Pullen of the Belcher Expedition built Northumberland House on Beechey. Constructed from the masts and spars of a wrecked whaling ship, Northumberland House was intended as a supply depot for members of the Franklin Expedition, should they return to Beechey. They never did. In the late 19th and early 20th centuries, Northumberland House was used by Canadian and British sailors as a winter refuge and site for securing messages and stores.

In recent years, Joseph MacInnis and Owen Beattie have brought the island renewed prominence. In 1980, MacInnis located the *Breadalbane*, a British vessel sent out in 1853 to resupply Franklin search ships in the area. On Aug. 21 of that year, the *Breadalbane* was nipped in the ice off Beechey Island and sank in 15 minutes. All 21 crew members were saved. MacInnis described the image of the *Breadalbane* that he saw on a side-scan sonar from an icebreaker as "a pale ghost beneath the ice."

In the spring of 1999, Jessco Logistics Ltd. of Calgary, with Deep Expeditions of Brampton, Ontario, plan to run submarine tours under eight feet of ice, onto the wreck of the *Breadalbane*. Contact **Deep Sea Voyages**, a division of Zegrahm Expeditions of Seattle, Washington, for an update on plans.

Forensic anthropologist Beattie conducted a well-publicized exhumation of three seamen buried in 1845–1846 by Franklin at Beechey: John Torrington, John Hartness and William Braine. Beattie's 1987 best-seller, *Frozen in Time*, attracted particular attention to the island; few who have seen the book will easily forget the garish photo of Torrington's frozen and wizened face on the cover. Beattie, along with co-author John Geiger, concluded that the men probably died from poisoning caused by the lead used to seal meat tins at the time. In the last two decades, a few eccentric history buffs have chosen to be buried on Beechey, near the remains of Franklin's unlucky shipmates.

Beechey is only an island at high tide. At low tide it is joined to Devon Island by a sandbar. It has never been permanently inhabited, nor have Inuit traditionally camped there.

Relatively inaccessible, Beechey Island can be reached most easily from Resolute, 75 kilometres to the west, by chartered Twin Otter aircraft. However, the island has no tourist facilities. For more information, contact First Air or Kenn Borek Air in Resolute.

DIRECTORY

Deep Sea Voyages (a division of Zegrahm Expeditions)
Tel.: 1-888-772-2366 or (206) 285-3743
Fax: (206) 285-7390
E-mail: zdv@deepseavoyages.com
Web site: www.deepseavoyages.com

83. GRISE FIORD

by Larry and Laisa Audlaluk

On the southern coast of Ellesmere Island, in a landscape of stunning grandeur, lies Canada's most northerly community, Grise Fiord.

Population:	148 (Inuit: 95%, non-Inuit: 5%) Source: 1996 Census of Canada
Telephone Area Code:	867
Time Zone:	Eastern Time
Postal Code:	X0A 0J0
How to Get There:	Possible routes:
	• Ottawa/Montreal-Iqaluit-Resolute-Grise Fiord
	• Kangerlussuaq (Greenland)-Iqaluit-Resolute-Grise Fiord
	• Edmonton-Yellowknife-Resolute-Grise Fiord
	Iqaluit to Grise Fiord (almost 2,000 kilometres north) is via First Air as far as Resolute. Passengers either stay one night in Resolute or change planes immediately to proceed aboard Kenn Borek Air to Grise Fiord. Yellowknife to Grise Fiord (about 1,900 kilometres northeast) is via Canadian North as far as Resolute, where passengers disembark for a three-night stay before heading to Grise Fiord on Kenn Borek Air
Banks:	None. Cash and traveller's cheques are preferable. Credit cards are accepted by certain businesses
Alcohol:	Except for a period of prohibition during the month of December and first week of January, alcohol is not restricted in Grise Fiord, and is governed only by the provisions of the *NWT Liquor Act*. However, there's no place to buy alcohol in the community
Taxis:	No

Visitors to this tiny hamlet in the High Arctic are often awestruck by the vista of magnificent mountains, icebergs and glaciers they discover here.

There is good reason for its Inuktitut name, *Aujuittuq* — "the place that never thaws out."

Grise Fiord owes its English name to the Norwegian explorer Otto Sverdrup, who charted the south and east coasts of Ellesmere Island from 1899 to 1903. Among the many names he gave to fiords in the area, he called this particular one Grise Fiord, which means "pig fiord" in Norwegian. It seems that the sounds made by the many walrus here reminded him of the grunting of pigs!

History

Ellesmere Island is rich in prehistoric Inuit sites. In historic times, however, no Inuit lived here except those who passed through as part of the great migration of Baffin Inuit from the Igloolik/Pond Inlet area to northern Greenland, led by Qillaq (later called Qitdlarssuaq) in the mid-1800s.

In 1922, the RCMP established a post at Craig Harbour, 55 kilometres west of Grise Fiord. Between 1926 and 1940, the post closed and reopened several times. Then in 1951, the post opened once again, after a detachment at Dundas Harbour on Devon Island was closed.

In 1953, the federal government resettled eight Inuit families from Inukjuak (formerly known as Port Harrison) in northern Quebec, and Pond Inlet, to Craig Harbour.

As in Resolute, the move of the High Arctic exiles remains a controversial one. (See Chapter 81, "Resolute," for more details.)

In 1956, the RCMP post moved from Craig Harbour to Grise Fiord. At the same time, some relocated Inuit who had been living at Lindstrom Peninsula eight kilometres across from Grise Fiord started trading here at the government store. In 1962, once a federal school was built and a housing program begun in Grise Fiord, the families from Lindstrom Peninsula moved to the community.

Grise Fiord: Its Land and Wildlife

Many visitors find that the land surrounding Grise Fiord is among the most strikingly beautiful in the North. And with endless daylight from May to late August, there's lots of time to explore it! The South Cape Fiord, 40 kilometres west of the community, is an ideal spot for viewing and photographing towering icebergs. If you want to see walrus, beluga whales, guillemots, murres, seals and even polar bears, you can arrange a trip to the floe edge where the sea ice meets open water, about 50 kilometres east of the community. To do so, you're best to make travel arrangements before you arrive in Grise Fiord.

By late May, many birds return from the South to nest in the area of Grise Fiord. Along the fiords eight kilometres north of the community, you'll find seagulls by the thousands at this time. In June, snow geese, king eiders, and eider ducks, among others, arrive on the scene; by late June, most of the snow geese are nesting. From April right through the summer, you'll spot snow buntings and rock ptarmigan throughout southern Ellesmere Island.

About 100 kilometres southeast of Grise Fiord is Nirjutiqavvik National Wildlife Area, encompassing Coburg Island and the surrounding waters. This area is considered one of the most important nesting spots for seabirds in the Canadian Arctic.

Tours

You'll find archeological sites as close as two kilometres from the airport; others further away from town you can visit by boat or snowmobile. A 30-minute ride across the fiord will take you to a polar bear trap of the Thule culture. Another area to visit is the site of three Inuit camps from the time of the 1953 relocation, at Lindstrom Peninsula, 11 kilometres from Grise Fiord. This is a popular picnic spot for local people. About 45 kilometres west of the community, at Harbour Fiord, you'll see a cross erected to the memory of a sailor, one of Otto Sverdrup's men, who died here.

You might also take an excursion to Goose Fiord, roughly 70 kilometres west of Grise Fiord. That's the location where Sverdrup was forced by ice to stay an extra year in the narrows of the fiord that didn't break up one summer. If you head over to Fram Fiord, about 50 kilometres east of the community, you may encounter muskoxen grazing on the tundra. This is the fiord where Sverdrup, in his ship, the *Fram*, sought shelter during a storm.

For 10 months of the year, the sea around Grise Fiord is frozen; breakup usually isn't complete until mid-August. By mid-May, the sun shines for 24 hours a day in the High Arctic, so expect to see people on the move at all hours of the day and "night." In mid-August, the sun is lower on the horizon and evenings are chilly.

Qutsittumiut Outfitting is the only licensed outfitter in Grise Fiord, and can be contacted through the local **Hunters and Trappers Organization**. In addition, local people will arrange snowmobile trips for you to archeological sites or to view the wildlife, to be part of a dogteam ride or to stay overnight in an igloo you've helped to build.

Shopping

Grise Fiord is noted for miniature ivory carvings, traditional clothing, and other arts and crafts such as the arctic tuque. Raw narwhal tusks are sometimes available, but you must also have an export permit to remove them from the area. You can buy arts and crafts from the **Grise Fiord Inuit Co-op Ltd.**, which also sells groceries and assorted dry goods.

Accommodation and Dining

The **Grise Fiord Lodge**, operated by the Grise Fiord Inuit Co-op Ltd., is a nine-room facility accommodating up to 24 guests. The daily rate is $195 per person, meals included. Each room has a television, but bathrooms are shared. There's a pay telephone, plus a TV and VCR in the lounge. Transportation to and from the airport is courtesy of the Co-op.

Several nearby camp sites are close to running creeks and are open, at no charge, from spring through summer.

Grise Fiord has no restaurants. Visitors can buy a meal at the Grise Fiord Lodge by prior arrangement with the Co-op.

Services

Grise Fiord's **health centre** is open from 9 a.m. to 11:30 a.m. on weekdays for walk-in traffic. Public health sessions run from 1 to 5 p.m. A nurse is on call for emergencies at all times. There is an **RCMP** detachment here, too.

As well, an airport terminal was to have been built at the airstrip in the autumn of 1998.

DIRECTORY

*Outfitters and tour operators licensed at time of writing.
After March 31/99, check for updated status.

Accommodation and Dining

Grise Fiord Lodge
VISA, Diners Club/enRoute, Interac.
Tel.: (867) 980-9913 or (867) 980-9135
Fax: (867) 980-9954

* Outfitters/Tour Operators

Qutsittumiut Outfitting
Contact Seeglook Akeeagok.
Tel.: (867) 980-4164

Services

Air Travel
Kenn Borek Air
Resolute office.
Tel.: (867) 252-3845
Fax: (867) 252-3777

Church
Anglican Church
Tel.: (867) 980-9929

Department of Sustainable Development, Government of Nunavut
(or until April/99, GNWT's Resources, Wildlife and Economic Development)
Tel.: (867) 980-4164
Fax: (867) 980-9145

Hamlet Office
Tel.: (867) 980-9959
Fax: (867) 980-9052

Health Centre
Tel.: (867) 980-9923
Fax: (867) 980-9067

Hunters and Trappers Organization
Tel.: (867) 980-9063
Fax: (867) 980-4311

Police (RCMP)
Tel.: (867) 980-9912
Fax: (867) 980-9095

Post Office
Located in the Co-op store.
11 a.m.–12 p.m., 1–5 p.m.,
weekdays only.
Tel.: (867) 980-9913

Radio Station (FM 107.1)
Broadcasts: 10–11 a.m., 5–6 p.m.,
10–11:30 p.m.
Tel.: (867) 980-9951

Schools
Nunavut Arctic College
Tel.: (867) 980-9081
Fax: (867) 980-9128

Ummimak School
Tel.: (867) 980-9921
Fax: (867) 980-9043

Weather Information
Tel.: (867) 980-9946
Fax: (867) 980-4253
Web site weather forecast:
www.infonorth.org

Shopping

Grise Fiord Inuit Co-op Ltd.
11 a.m.–12 p.m., 1–5 p.m., Monday
to Friday; 3–4 p.m., Saturday.
Closed Sunday.
VISA, Diners Club/enRoute, Interac.
Tel.: (867) 980-9913
Fax: (867) 980-9954

84. ARCTIC BAY
by Kenn Harper

Arctic Bay is called *Ikpiarjuk* — "the pocket" — because of the high hills that surround the almost landlocked bay from which the community gets its name.

Population:	639 (Inuit: 92%, non-Inuit: 8%) Source: 1996 Census of Canada
Telephone Area Code:	867
Time Zone:	Eastern Time
Postal Code:	X0A 0A0
How to Get There:	Possible routes:
	• Ottawa or Montreal-Iqaluit-Nanisivik, continuing to Arctic Bay by road
	• Kangerlussuaq (Greenland)-Iqaluit-Nanisivik, continuing to Arctic Bay by road
	• Edmonton-Yellowknife-Resolute-Nanisivik, continuing to Arctic Bay by road
	Flights to Nanisivik are via First Air from Ottawa or Montreal, or from Edmonton via Yellowknife and Resolute. Visitors already in Resolute can fly to Arctic Bay via Kenn Borek Air, on a once-a-week flight
Banks:	None. Cash and traveller's cheques are preferable. Credit cards are accepted by certain businesses
Alcohol:	Alcohol and alcoholic beverages cannot be purchased in Arctic Bay. Visitors who want to bring alcohol into the community must first obtain a permit from the hamlet's **Alcohol Education Committee**
Taxis:	Yes

As you look southward from the community toward Adams Sound, Uluksan Point is on your right, while Holy Cross Point is at the end of the long peninsula to your left. Arctic Bay is connected by a 21-kilometre road to Nanisivik, a mining town developed in the mid-1970s.

History

Captain William Adams was the first non-Inuk to see Arctic Bay; he entered the bay in 1872 with his whaling ship, the *Arctic*. Another *Arctic*, an official Canadian government steamship under the command of explorer Joseph E. Bernier, wintered in the bay in 1910–1911. A Hudson's Bay Co. post was established here in 1926 but closed the following year. The post was re-established in 1936, when Inuit originally from Pangnirtung and Cape Dorset were relocated here from the unsuccessful Hudson's Bay post at Dundas Harbour.

The Anglican Church built a mission at Moffet Inlet, south of Arctic Bay, in 1937. It closed 10 years later, after the accidental shooting and subsequent death of Canon John Turner. A Roman Catholic mission operated in Arctic Bay for a short time in the 1930s. As with most other

Baffin Island communities, the present town developed as a result of government housing initiatives in the 1960s.

Arctic Bay: Its Land and Wildlife

Arctic Bay is on Borden Peninsula, an uneven, undulating plateau dissected by numerous river valleys. In the northern part of the peninsula, where the community is located, mountains reach as high as 1,300 metres. Flat-topped King George V Mountain dominates the view to the southeast from the community.

Terrestrial wildlife around Arctic Bay is minimal. In the last few years, caribou have come close to the community, but sightings are more common farther south near Admiralty Inlet. Polar bears also frequent the area.

Every summer, Admiralty Inlet plays host to a variety of marine mammals. Narwhals frequent the waters and occasionally come into Arctic Bay itself. Narwhals are hunted for their ivory tusk and *maktaaq*. Killer whales are often present along the west coast of Admiralty Inlet. Bowhead sightings, like the whales themselves, are rare. Walrus are often seen in western Admiralty Inlet. Ringed seals are ubiquitous.

Tours

Near the old airstrip on the western end of town stands the original Department of Transport house, which served as a weather station between 1942 and 1952 and is still used as a dwelling. Also located in this area is the residence of the Northern store manager and some 50-year-old outbuildings. The store and its large warehouse were built more recently. Locals recall the legend of Jimmy Bell, a former Hudson's Bay Co. manager whose ghost was said to have haunted the residence until the death of his former best friend, Amagoalik. The Taqqut Co-op building, in the centre of town, originally came from Blacklead Island with the Hudson's Bay Co. in the 1920s.

At Uluksan Point, a low promontory with surprisingly lush summer vegetation, there are the remains of many stone houses, some at the very edge of the water and some that were occupied in recent times. Uluksan is a pleasant walk from the community and a favorite picnic site in late spring and summer. The cairn that dominates Holy Cross Point was erected by Bernier on his 1910–1911 wintering.

A summer road stretches northwest from Arctic Bay over the hill and then along the shores of a lake known locally as Dead Dog Lake. The road continues on to Victor Bay, where many Inuit pitch tents in summer, both for holidays and hunting. This road is also an excellent hiking route.

King George V Mountain is a challenge for hikers and climbers alike. Allow a day to reach the top and return to the community. A spectacular view awaits those who attain the summit.

Niglasuk Company, owned by the local HTO, provides outfitting and guide services. Dogteam or snowmobile trips are available in spring, and boat trips can be taken during summer and early autumn. In summer you may be lucky enough to observe a narwhal hunt. The company's main offerings are a floe edge trip in June and a week-long caribou hunt in late August. They also offer polar bear hunts in late winter, but these must be booked a number of years in advance. Local people may also be interested in taking visitors out on trips by snowmobile and *qamutik*, dogteam or boat. Arrangements can be made after your arrival in the community, but it is advisable to make them beforehand.

Shopping

Arctic Bay is noted for miniature ivory carvings, traditional clothing and other arts and crafts. Stone used here is grey argillite, similar to that used in Sanikiluaq far to the south, but with brownish blotches and streaks. Carvings made from this stone are often very small, and pieces are sometimes made so that the brown markings stunningly enhance their features. Unfortunately, the carving of this stone has declined in recent years. The **Taqqut Co-op** offers a selection of locally made soapstone carvings, and both the Co-op and the **Northern store** sell northern souvenirs. Narwhal tusks are often available in summer and autumn.

Groceries and hard goods are sold at both the Northern and Co-op.

Events

The most important tourist event of the year in both Arctic Bay and neighboring Nanisivik is a gruelling set of runs of various lengths between the two communities, the Midnight Sun Marathon. Often billed as one of the world's toughest foot races, it takes place on the weekend closest to Canada Day, July 1. The race, which attracts experienced marathoners the world over, starts in front of Taqqut Co-op in Arctic Bay.

Recent changes in ownership and management at **Nanisivik Mines** have caused concern among some participants, as a former mine manager was always the driving force behind the marathon. But, so far, new management continues to support this event. Interested participants should contact Nanisivik Mines for details.

Accommodation and Dining

Enokseot Hotel is the only hotel in Arctic Bay. It sleeps 16 guests in eight rooms. Bathrooms are shared. Single rooms cannot generally be reserved, especially during the busy summer months. Cafeteria-style meals are served in a small but comfortable dining room. There is also a very small common lounge with a television, and a public telephone in the lobby. Hotel rooms do not have phones or TVs. The room rate is $140 per person per night; meals are an additional $70 per day.

There is no formal campground in Arctic Bay, although good camping sites abound. Inquire at the **hamlet office** before you set up your camp.

There is no restaurant in Arctic Bay. With sufficient notice, however, Enokseot Hotel can provide meals for non-guests.

Services

The **Health Centre** is staffed by resident nurses. Walk-in clinics are from 8:30 a.m. to 12 p.m., and health clinics are from 1 to 5 p.m., Monday to Friday. Nurses are also on call after hours for emergencies.

DIRECTORY

*Outfitters and tour operators licensed at time of writing.
After March 31/99, check for updated status.

Accommodation and Dining

Enokseot Hotel
VISA accepted.
Tel.: (867) 439-8811
Fax: (867) 439-8242

* Outfitters/Tour Operators

Niglasuk Company
Tel.: (867) 439-9949
Fax: (867) 439-8341

Services

Airport
In Nanisivik.
Tel.: (867) 436-7554
Fax: (867) 436-7273

Alcohol Education Committee
Tel.: (867) 439-8476
Fax: (867) 439-8767

Churches

All Saints Anglican Church
Services: 11 a.m. (Inuktitut), 7 p.m.
(Inuktitut and English), Sunday; 7 p.m.
(Inuktitut), Thursday.
Tel.: (867) 439-8869
Fax: (867) 439-8054

Full Gospel Church
Services: 11 a.m., 7 p.m., Sunday.
Tel.: (867) 439-8227

Department of Sustainable Development, Government of Nunavut
(or until April/99, GNWT's Resources, Wildlife and Economic Development)
Tel.: (867) 439-9945
Fax: (867) 439-8480

Hamlet Office
Tel.: (867) 439-9917
Fax: (867) 439-8767

Health Centre
Tel.: (867) 439-8816
Fax: (867) 439-8315

Hunters and Trappers Organization
Tel.: (867) 439-9949
Fax: (867) 439-8341

Nanisivik Mines Ltd.
Tel.: (867) 436-7502 or (867) 436-7426
(for information about the Midnight Sun Marathon)
Fax: (867) 436-7435

Police (RCMP)
Tel.: (867) 439-9966 or (867) 436-7474
Fax: (867) 436-7557

Post Office
Located near the Hunters and Trappers Organization.
Tel.: (867) 439-8494

Radio Station (FM 107.1)
Tel.: (867) 439-9922 (off air)
Tel.: (867) 439-8709 (on air)

Schools

Inuujaq School
Tel.: (867) 439-8843
Fax: (867) 439-8766

Nunavut Arctic College
Tel.: (867) 439-9913
Fax: (867) 439-8393

Taxi

Arqvartuuq Services
Tel.: (867) 439-8227

Weather Information
Tel.: (867) 436-7554
Fax: (867) 436-7273
Web site weather forecast:
www.infonorth.org

Shopping

Northern Store
10 a.m.–12:30 p.m. and 2–6:30 p.m.,
Monday to Thursday;
10 a.m.–12:30 p.m. and 2–8 p.m.,
Friday; 10 a.m.–12:30 p.m. and
2–6 p.m., Saturday; Closed Sunday.
VISA, MasterCard, traveller's cheques, Interac.
Tel.: (867) 439-9914
Fax: (867) 439-8725

Taqqut Co-op
10 a.m.–10 p.m., Monday to Friday;
2–10 p.m., Saturday. Closed Sunday.
VISA, traveller's cheques, Interac.
Tel.: (867) 439-9934
Fax: (867) 439-8765

85. NANISIVIK
by Kenn Harper

The Nanisivik townsite was developed as part of the infrastructure of the Nanisivik lead/zinc mine, which opened in 1974.

Population:	287 (Inuit: 16%, non-Inuit: 84%) Source: 1996 Census of Canada
Telephone Area Code:	867
Time Zone:	Eastern Time
Postal Code:	X0A 0X0
How to Get There:	Possible routes:
	• Ottawa or Montreal-Iqaluit-Nanisivik
	• Kangerlussuaq (Greenland)-Iqaluit-Nanisivik
	• Edmonton-Yellowknife-Nanisivik
	Iqaluit to Nanisivik is 1,200 kilometres north. Flights from Ottawa, Montreal and Edmonton to Nanisivik are all via First Air. Kenn Borek Air flies to Nanisivik from Resolute or Pond Inlet
Banks:	None. The Northern store accepts credit cards
Alcohol:	Alcohol may be brought into Nanisivik, governed only by the provisions of the *NWT Liquor Act*
Taxis:	No. However, **Arqvartuuq Services** in neighboring Arctic Bay provides taxi service between the communities and to the **Nanisivik Airport**

Nanisivik is an Inuktitut word that means, appropriately, "the place where one finds things." The ore body was first discovered in 1910–1911 by Arthur English, a prospector on Captain Joseph Bernier's second Canadian government expedition to the High Arctic.

The architecture in Nanisivik is quite different from that of other northern settlements. Many residences have curved exterior walls to fend off the incredible winds that howl through the community. The settlement is dominated by a large white dome that serves as a cafeteria for the mining company. Surrounding it on two sides is a large metal-clad complex known as the Town Centre. This building houses the Northern store, a recreation complex (including one of only two swimming pools in Nunavut), **school**, day-care centre, **post office**, fire hall, **RCMP** detachment, **health centre** and government offices. **St. Piren's**, a brightly painted church in Nanisivik, is Nunavut's only multi-denominational place of worship, serving both Anglicans and Catholics.

Tours
This is a mining town. Other than the Midnight Sun Marathon and its midwinter counterpart, the Brain Dead Marathon, there are no activities for visitors here: no hotel, no outfitters and no organized tours. The town is best visited on day trips from Arctic Bay, although there is not much to do other than hike. No mine tours are offered, except by special arrangement with **Nanisivik Mines**.

If you go, heed the signs identifying West Twin Lake, a pristine-looking body of water to the south of the community off the airport road. Despite its attractive appearance, West Twin Lake is the tailings pond for the mine and as such receives the waste products of ore processing. East Twin Lake is the source of the community's fresh water.

Behind the community is a mountain known locally to non-Inuit as Mount Fuji; Inuit call it *Nasallugannguaq* because of its hat-like appearance. Locals ski or snowboard here.

Down the hill from the townsite, the mountainside is pocked with holes, the result of more than 20 years of underground mining. Ore is stockpiled in a large storage shed on the beach, where it awaits summer shipment to Europe. Nanisivik has the only deep-water harbor on Baffin Island.

Events

Each year, on the weekend closest to July 1 (Canada's national holiday), Nanisivik hosts the Midnight Sun Marathon, an internationally known 42-kilometre run from Arctic Bay to Nanisivik. Transportation to the event is by chartered or scheduled aircraft. Those interested in participating should contact Nanisivik Mines for details.

In recent years, a group of diehard local runners has organized the Brain Dead Marathon, a parody of the summer marathon. The Brain Dead Marathon sees participants run across the snow and ice of Strathcona Sound and back to Nanisivik in the depths of mid-December's cold and darkness.

Accommodation and Dining

There is no hotel or camp site in Nanisivik. Transients may be accommodated in a bunkhouse operated by Nanisivik Mines, although the company's staff takes priority. Except during the Midnight Sun Marathon, visitors are encouraged to stay in nearby Arctic Bay.

There is no restaurant in Nanisivik. Cafeteria-style meals are available in the large dome building operated by the mining company for its employees. Meal hours are limited. Groceries can be purchased from the **Northern store**.

DIRECTORY

Services

Airport
Tel.: (867) 436-7554
Fax: (867) 436-7273

Church

St. Piren's Anglican Church
Service: 11 a.m., Sunday (Inuktitut). The church is also used by visiting Roman Catholic priests. Call minister in Arctic Bay.
Tel.: (867) 439-8869
Fax: (867) 439-8054

Department of Sustainable Development, Government of Nunavut
(or until April/99, GNWT's Resources, Wildlife and Economic Development) Contact Arctic Bay office.
Tel.: (867) 439-9945
Fax: (867) 439-8480

Health Centre
Tel.: (867) 436-7482
Fax: (867) 436-7495

Nanisivik Mines Ltd.
Tel.: (867) 436-7502
For information about the marathon:
Tel.: (867) 436-7426
Fax: (867) 436-7435

Police (RCMP)
Tel.: (867) 436-7474
Fax: (867) 436-7557

Post Office
10 a.m.–6 p.m., Monday to Friday.
Tel.: (867) 436-7371

School

Allurut School
Tel.: (867) 436-7350

Taxi

Arqvartuuq Services
In Arctic Bay.
Tel.: (867) 439-8227

Weather Information
Tel.: (867) 436-7554
Fax: (867) 436-7273
Web site weather forecast:
www.infonorth.org

Shopping

Northern Store
10 a.m.–12:30 p.m. and 1:30–6:30 p.m.,
Monday to Wednesday; 10 a.m.–noon
and 1:30–7 p.m., Thursday; 12–6 p.m.,
Friday and Saturday. Closed Sunday.
VISA, MasterCard, Interac.
Tel.: (867) 436-7322
Fax: (867) 436-7477

86. POND INLET
by Marian and Mike Ferguson

Traditional Inuit culture thrives in the modern community of Pond Inlet, a bewitching array of past and present at the northern tip of Baffin Island.

Population:	1,154 (Inuit: 95%, non-Inuit: 5%) Source: 1996 Census of Canada
Telephone Area Code:	867
Time Zone:	Eastern Time
Postal Code:	X0A 0S0
How to Get There:	Possible routes:
	• Ottawa/Montreal-Iqaluit-Pond Inlet
	• Edmonton-Yellowknife-Resolute-Pond Inlet
	• Edmonton-Yellowknife-Rankin Inlet-Iqaluit-Pond Inlet
	• Kangerlussuaq (Greenland)-Iqaluit-Pond Inlet
	• Winnipeg-Rankin Inlet-Iqaluit-Pond Inlet
	Iqaluit to Pond Inlet (1,066 kilometres north) is via First Air. Almost all flights require passengers to stay overnight in Iqaluit. However, one flight weekly flies from Ottawa to Pond Inlet in a day. Once a week, Kenn Borek Air flies from Resolute to Pond Inlet return
Banks:	None. Cash and traveller's cheques are preferable. Credit cards are accepted by certain businesses
Alcohol:	Alcohol and alcoholic beverages cannot be purchased in Pond Inlet. Visitors who want to bring alcohol into the community must first obtain a permit from the **Alcohol Review Board**
Taxis:	No. Hotel guests are transported to and from the airport by the hotel van

Near a satellite dish that brings southern culture into the community you'll find caribou and sealskins drying for winter clothing, while dogteams howl in the distance.

Inuit and other arctic inhabitants have occupied this area for thousands of years. The people of Pond Inlet and the surrounding area are the *Tununirmiut*, the people of *Tununiq*, "the land that faces away from the sun." This is the area around Pond Inlet and Eclipse Sound where rivers flow north to the sea. Pond Inlet is called *Mittimatalik*, the place where Mittima is buried, or literally translated, "where there is Mittima." Exactly who Mittima was, however, remains a mystery.

History

Explorer John Ross gave the body of water between Bylot Island and Baffin Island its English name in 1818 when he dubbed it "Pond's Bay" after a British astronomer. Whalers had arrived a year earlier, in search of the valuable bowhead whale. It would be almost 100 years before the area's first whaling station was established in 1903, but by then the industry had all but collapsed. By 1912, only one whaling ship attempted a bowhead hunt in the area, with no success. A nearby national historic site commemorates the whaling industry in the eastern Arctic.

In the mid-1800s, a shaman (*angakkuq*) and powerful leader, Qillaq, led some 60 Inuit on a migration from *Tununiq* to Greenland. Qillaq was apparently fleeing from Inuit who were enemies of his family. The migration by Qitdlarssuaq (Qillaq's Greenlandic name) had a profound effect on the lives of the Polar Inuit, who had been isolated in northern Greenland for more than 100 years. The newcomers reintroduced important Inuit technology such as the *qayaq* (kayak), bow and arrow, and *kakivak* (fish spear) to their Greenlandic brethren. To this day the Polar Inuit and *Tununirmiut* are closely related.

In 1912, three expeditions arrived in Pond Inlet looking for gold. Although none was found, the expeditions opened small trading posts, and Pond Inlet became a trading centre. The Hudson's Bay Co. arrived in 1921, when they bought out the Arctic Gold Exploration Syndicate.

Pond Inlet became the site of arctic intrigue in 1920, when Robert Janes, an independent trader from the Pond Inlet area, was murdered en route to Igloolik. Apparently, Inuit greatly distrusted Janes and decided his activities could no longer be tolerated. News of the killing travelled out of the North and the RCMP arrived in 1921 to investigate. In 1923, three Inuit were tried on a ship near Pond Inlet; two were convicted, and one was taken to a penitentiary in Southern Canada.

The Anglican and Catholic missions were established by 1929, and served to partially divide some Inuit for years. Elders still recall being told not to visit the other mission, despite their curiosity. The original Roman Catholic mission was recently renovated after a tragic 1994 fire destroyed the previous chapel. The fire took the life of Father Guy Mary-Rousselière, a priest and world-renowned archeologist who had lived in Pond Inlet for 37 years.

A federal school was built in the 1960s, along with residences for some children whose parents lived on the land. Eventually, most Inuit moved into town as the government provided more housing. Today, four families continue to live on the land in what are called "outpost camps."

Pond Inlet: Its Land and Wildlife

Wildlife abounds among the mountains and in the waters around Pond Inlet. You can frequently see caribou in March and April, when they may be within sight of town or on Bylot Island. In May, they migrate into the picturesque fiords southwest of Pond Inlet where wolves may also be seen. Large bulls graze in the fiords during summer, and in August and September, females return from the South with young calves. More than 30 species of birds nest and raise their young from May to September.

The fiords and floe edge are favored camping and fishing areas for local families in spring and summer. You may encounter polar bears near the floe edge in spring and almost anywhere during the open-water season. The local renewable resources officer with the government of Nunavut's **Department of Sustainable Development** (or until April 1999, the GNWT's Department of **Resources, Wildlife and Economic Development**) can provide information on avoiding dangerous encounters. The **Mittimatalik Hunters and Trappers Organization** (HTO) can arrange polar bear or caribou hunts.

Seals are seen basking on the sea ice in May and June. With an experienced guide, photographers can approach seals very closely on the ice. Caribou may cross the ice as they migrate south from Bylot Island in May and early June. Seals, seabirds, polar bears and narwhals — and even walrus, bowhead, belugas or killer whales — may appear at the floe edge from mid-May through June. Narwhals and seabirds can be readily photographed here. Marine mammals are seen in many places once the ice breaks up.

Tours

A good place to begin your exploration of Pond Inlet is at the **Nattinnak Centre**, where the natural and cultural heritage of the area is featured in an interpretive display of local artifacts. The **Rebecca P. Idlout Library**, located in the same building, has an extensive collection of historical books, references and photographs about the area's natural and human history.

Through a tour operator or outfitter, you could also arrange to visit a local carver, enjoy a drum dance or take a guided nature walk.

In addition to several outstanding archeological sites, visitors will find magnificent scenery, intriguing geological formations, abundant wildlife and colorful plants near Pond Inlet. Cross-country skiing, dogsledding, snowmobiling, hiking, kayaking, boating, fishing, hunting and exploring are some activities that visitors enjoy. April and May are the best months for cross-country skiing to a nearby iceberg, to the old coal mine about 45 minutes by snowmobile from Pond Inlet, or to the hills near *Qilalukkat* (Salmon Creek) — all popular meeting places for picnics and sliding. *Qilalukkat* is two kilometres west of Pond Inlet.

Whatever your mode of transportation, long distances can be travelled with continual daylight from May through August. Overnight dogsled and snowmobile trips are available from April to June through outfitters and tour operators, and can be booked in advance. If guides are available when you arrive, shorter trips may also be arranged.

Hiking opportunities abound in Pond Inlet. Experienced backpackers can trek to the glaciers and mountains southeast of Pond Inlet in two to five days. If you are careful wading across Janes Creek (it is often impassable in July), you can hike 15 kilometres east of town to climb a trail up Mount Herodier. The view from its 765-metre peak is breathtaking. You can also pitch a tent at the base of Mount Herodier, near where many local families camp during summer.

For a shorter trek, hike to *Qilalukkat* to see the remains of a Thule village. A local tour operator offers guided interpretive walks to the area. En route you will see colorful wildflowers and examples of land patterned by permafrost along the coastal escarpment. In July and August, you can fish for arctic char along the coast towards Salmon River, two kilometres west of *Qilalukkat*.

Pond Inlet is becoming a popular destination for experienced arctic kayakers. Outfitters can take you to the floe edge in May and June, but always exercise caution in your kayak. Whales can appear unexpectedly from under the ice, and drifting floes can move quickly with changes in wind direction. Ice conditions are unfavorable during July, making progress very slow. August is the best month for kayaking. Even so, severe winds — although infrequent — can keep you pinned in a safe harbor for a day or so.

Char fishing is best done through frozen lakes in April or May, or along the coast in August. Fishing trips can take one or more days, or fishing can be mixed with other activities. Fishing licences must be obtained from the renewable resources officer.

Polar Sea Adventures, **Tagak Outfitting Services**, **Toonoonik Sahoonik Outfitters**, and **Tununiq Travel and Adventure** offer a variety of guided tours. Most outfitters prefer groups of four to eight persons, with most trips lasting five to nine days. They will customize trips to meet customers' needs, however. Book trips directly with an outfitter, or through Tununiq Travel and Adventure, a local tour operator working with outfitters to design packages for individuals or groups.

Visitors planning to travel on the land, ice or water occasionally encounter delays of hours, and perhaps a couple of days. Guides know the dangers that a seemingly innocuous wind or snowfall may foretell. You should remain patient, and trust your guide's judgment as he attempts to take you to your destination without risking your life.

Shopping

Several Inuit produce fine sculptures of soapstone, ivory, whalebone and marble. Both green and red soapstone come from local sources. Beautiful wall hangings, pencil drawings and caribou-hair tuftings are also produced by local artists. **Toonoonik Sahoonik Co-op** has display cases filled with excellent examples of these products and other souvenirs.

The Toonoonik Sahoonik Co-op and the **Northern store** both sell a wide variety of hard goods, groceries and country foods. Both stores get fresh produce, dairy products, bread and meats from Southern Canada once a week. For those interested in sampling local country food, the **Mittima Butcher Shop** at the HTO has various cuts of caribou and char for sale, as well as *maktaaq* (narwhal skin) and occasionally walrus meat. You need a permit to take certain country foods out of the Northwest Territories, so check with the renewable resources officer.

JM Sportswear has a selection of sporting goods, souvenirs, and novelties. Also in the Co-op Mall is **B&E Entertainment**, with novelty items and video rentals. The Co-op Mall is up the hill, between the airport and the hotel.

Events

Country foods, like caribou, arctic char, seal and *maktaaq* are still the staples of the Inuit diet. On special occasions, these foods are offered at community feasts, which are open to visitors.

Accommodation and Dining

Operated by Toonoonik Sahoonik Co-op, the **Sauniq Hotel** has 17 guest rooms with double occupancy, each with cable television and private bath. The price is $155 per person per night, not including meals. With meal plan, the price is $230. Guests can chat or play cribbage in the sitting room. Laundry facilities are available.

From May through September, some visitors camp on the tundra north of the **airport** or along the beach west of the hamlet. There is a territorial camping area with picnic tables and tent platforms at *Qilalukkat*.

There is a bed and breakfast operating in Pond Inlet, but at the time of writing, it was not licensed.

The **Arctic Research Establishment** has accommodations and other facilities for researchers holding scientific research licences and permits. The Nunavut Research Institute in Iqaluit provides advice on obtaining research permits.

The Sauniq Hotel's dining room serves three hearty meals daily at set hours, but reservations are required if you are not a hotel guest. Subject to change, breakfast costs $20, lunch $25, and dinner $30. The Toonoonik Sahoonik Co-op operates a restaurant that is open during its store hours, and on Sunday from 3 to 7 p.m.

Services

At the **Health Centre**, near **Ulaajuk School**, nurses provide out-patient services by appointment between 9 and 11:30 a.m., Monday through Friday. For emergencies, you can call the Centre at any time. For non-medical emergencies, call the local **RCMP** detachment.

DIRECTORY

*Outfitters and tour operators licensed at time of writing.
After March 31/99, check for updated status.

Accommodation and Dining

Arctic Research Establishment
For researchers only.
Tel.: (867) 899-8737
Fax: (867) 899-8737

Sauniq Hotel
VISA, MasterCard, American Express.
Tel.: (867) 899-8928
Fax: (867) 899-8364

Toonoonik Sahoonik Restaurant
10 a.m.–8 p.m., Monday to Friday;
1–8 p.m., Saturday; 3–7 p.m., Sunday.
VISA, MasterCard.
Tel.: (867) 899-8912
Fax: (867) 899-8770

*Outfitters/Tour Operators/Visitors Centre

Mittimatalik Hunters and Trappers Organization
Tel.: (867) 899-8856
Fax: (867) 899-8095

Nattinnak Centre
Hours change seasonally; open daily with extended hours during tourist seasons. Check posted hours at library, stores and hotel.
Tel.: (867) 899-8225
Fax: (867) 899-8246

Polar Sea Adventures
Tel.: (867) 899-8870
Fax: (867) 899-8817

Tagak Outfitting Services
Tel.: (867) 899-8932
Fax: (867) 899-8616

Toonoonik Sahoonik Outfitters
Tel.: (867) 899-8366
Fax: (867) 899-8364
Web site: www.pondtour.com

Tununiq Travel and Adventure
Tel.: (867) 899-8194
Fax: (867) 899-8194
E-mail: Marian@tununiq.com or
visit@tununiq.com
Web site: www.tununiq.com

Services

Airport

First Air:
Tel.: (867) 899-8882

Alcohol Review Board
Tel.: (867) 899-8934
Fax: (867) 899-8940

Churches

Roman Catholic Mission
Tel.: (867) 899-8083

Saint Timothy's Anglican Church
Tel.: (867) 899-8534

Department of Sustainable Development, Government of Nunavut
(or until April/99, GNWT's **Resources, Wildlife and Economic Development**)
Renewable resources officer:
Tel.: (867) 899-8819
Fax: (867) 899-8711
Regional wildlife biologist:
Tel.: (867) 899-8876
Fax: (867) 899-8711
E-mail: Michael_Ferguson@gov.nt.ca

Hamlet Office
Tel.: (867) 899-8935
Fax: (867) 899-8940

Health Centre
Tel.: (867) 899-8840
Fax: (867) 899-8997

Police (RCMP)
Tel.: (867) 899-8822
Fax: (867) 899-8832

Post Office
Located in the former hamlet office.
10:30 a.m.–12 p.m. and 1–4 p.m., Monday to Friday.
Tel.: (867) 899-8343

Radio Station (FM 105.1)
Tel.: (867) 899-8884

Rebecca P. Idlout Library
Hours change seasonally.
Check posted hours at library, stores and hotel.
Tel.: (867) 899-8972

Schools

Nunavut Arctic College
Tel.: (867) 899-8837
Fax: (867) 899-8960

Takijualuk School
High school. A new high school is due to open in 1999.
Tel: (867) 899-8864
Fax: (867) 899-8875

Ulaajuk School
Elementary school.
Tel.: (867) 899-8964
Fax: (867) 899-8780

Weather Information
Tel.: (867) 899-8976
Web site weather forecast:
www.infonorth.org

Shopping

B&E Entertainment
3–8 p.m., Monday to Saturday.
Tel.: (867) 899-8133

JM Sportswear
1–8 p.m., Monday to Friday; 3–8 p.m., Saturday. Closed Sunday.
Cash, personal cheques.
Tel.: (867) 899-8390

Mittima Butcher Shop
Located at the Mittimatalik HTO's office.
10 a.m.–6 p.m., Monday to Friday.
Closed weekends.
Cash only.
Tel.: (867) 899-8856 or (867) 899-8322
Fax: (867) 899-8095

Northern Store
10 a.m.–8 p.m., Monday to Friday.
1–6 p.m., Saturday. Closed Sunday.
VISA, MasterCard, Interac.
Tel.: (867) 899-8848
Fax: (867) 899-8854

Toonoonik Sahoonik Co-op
10 a.m.–8 p.m., Monday to Friday.
1–8 p.m., Saturday. Closed Sunday.
VISA, MasterCard, American Express, Diners Club/enRoute, Interac.
Tel.: (867) 899-8912
Fax: (867) 899-8770

87. SIRMILIK NATIONAL PARK

by Marian and Mike Ferguson

L ying 700 kilometres north of the Arctic Circle and 600 kilometres west of Greenland in the High Arctic, Sirmilik ("glacier") National Park is one of the richest wildlife areas in all of Nunavut.

A diversity of migratory birds, and land and marine mammals is framed by rugged mountains, deep fiords and inlets, intricate glaciers, precipitous cliffs and productive lowlands.

In the late 1970s, Inuit proposed a national park in the North Baffin/Lancaster Sound area in response to plans by the petroleum industry to explore for oil in Lancaster Sound. The 1993 Nunavut Land Claims Agreement made provision for the park and, in 1998, Inuit and the federal government completed necessary negotiations. Sirmilik National Park officially opens in 1999 and will protect about 22,000 square kilometres in three separate areas: the mountains and uplands surrounding Oliver Sound, the rugged plateau of eastern Borden Peninsula, and the mountains and lowlands of Bylot Island. Bylot Island will also retain the status it has held since 1965 as a national migratory bird sanctuary. Park headquarters will be set up in Pond Inlet at some point in 1999 but, until then, information on Sirmilik National Park is available from the regional Parks Canada office in Pangnirtung. Excellent guiding, outfitting and other services are available from businesses in Pond Inlet and Arctic Bay.

The Land and Its Wildlife

With mountains rising 2,000 metres out of Baffin Bay, Sirmilik National Park marks the terminus of a Precambrian mountain range that forms the spine of Baffin Island. Ice fields are pierced by peaks and ridges, and cut by deep fiords and valleys, producing numerous glaciers flowing to the sea. Many of the mountains drop into the water off sheer 300-metre-high cliffs, broken occasionally by steep-walled valleys that act as solar collectors. Although there are more than 360 plant species in the park, vegetation is sparse on moraines of retreating glaciers and in eroded sandstone valleys.

Distinctive hoodoos are formed by the erosion of sandstone around a harder "cap" rock. Eventually, erosion produces tall, 10-to-15-metre pillars of sandstone below the cap rock. A mixture of sedimentary, metamorphic and igneous rocks in the park contain fossilized dinosaur bones and coal seams, as well as minerals such as pyrite, serpentine and garnet. The waters of Baffin Bay off Bylot Island cover one of the most active earthquake zones in eastern North America.

In the park's uplands you'll find low-lying shrubs, flowering herbs and lichens. Carpets of colorful wildflowers proliferate from June to August on soils that have escaped continental glaciation for perhaps 80,000 years. Besides arctic foxes, snowy owls, weasels, arctic hares, gyrfalcons and lemmings, you may also see caribou. In the early 1990s, caribou left over-grazed wintering areas southwest of Oliver Sound to graze near Pond Inlet after an absence of more than 40 years. As predicted by Inuit elders, the caribou have devastated the upland lichens that they need during winter. After only about five winters, the caribou have moved on to Bylot Island and eastern Borden Peninsula to search for winter forage.

The southwest corner of Bylot Island is a 1,300-square-kilometre rolling plain of lush wetlands covered by cotton-grass, willow and moss. These wetlands form the nesting grounds of the world's largest colony of greater snow geese (*kanguq*), one of 30 species of breeding birds found here. In 1993, the colony numbered 75,000 adult geese, after growing by 300 per cent over the previous decade. Seeing signs that the geese may be over-abundant, biologists are studying their habitat to assess the impact of their increase.

The lands within Sirmilik National Park are dissected by waters teeming with life. A large polynya — year-round open water — occurs in Baffin Bay, producing floe edges along the land-fast ice where marine animals congregate to feed during spring. Floe edges occur east of Bylot Island in Baffin Bay and north of Borden Peninsula in Lancaster Sound. The northeastern coast of Bylot Island is an extensive winter denning area for polar bears, and bears are common near the floe edges in spring. In summer, these majestic carnivores are most common along the Baffin Bay and Lancaster Sound coasts, although they can be seen almost anywhere in the park.

Along the floe edge in spring and in the fiords in summer, visitors may encounter up to five species of seals, walrus, narwhal, bowheads, beluga and killer whales. The cliffs of Bylot Island are summer home to 320,000 thick-billed murres (*akpa*) and 80,000 black-legged kittiwakes (*nauluktuapik*). You can watch these curious birds feeding at the floe edge and nesting on cliffs near the southeast and northwest corners of the island.

The People and Their History

The abundant wildlife has drawn people to this area for 4,000 years. The numerous archeological sites in the park, which are protected by law, are evidence of the prehistoric lives of Inuit and earlier inhabitants.

In 1616, Robert Bylot and William Baffin were the first Europeans to see this area. In the 1800s, whalers hunted the bowhead in these waters until the industry collapsed in the early 1900s. Traders arrived in 1912, and missionaries followed 17 years later. After schools were built in Pond Inlet and Arctic Bay for Inuit children in the early 1960s, Inuit families gradually moved from their traditional camps and settled in government-sponsored housing in the late 1960s and early 1970s.

Some areas initially proposed as part of the park were excluded as a result of land claims negotiations. These are Inuit-owned lands. For information on public access to these areas, contact Parks Canada, or the **Qikiqtani Inuit Association**, which will direct queries to the community lands and resources committees in Pond Inlet and Arctic Bay. The land claims agreement guarantees Inuit the right to harvest wildlife, establish outpost camps and remove stone for carving from all national parks in Nunavut. The park and surrounding area is a "back yard" for residents of Pond Inlet and Arctic Bay, who continue to hunt, fish and trap here for sources of food and income.

Planning a Visit

Sirmilik National Park is accessible from Pond Inlet and Arctic Bay year-round, except during ice breakup in July and freezeup in October and November. From March to June, you can travel throughout the park by dogsledding, snowmobiling or cross-country skiing. Be careful during June because there will be open water in many areas. In August and September, guides can take you by boat or kayak while keeping a close eye on the weather. In any season, weather in different parts of the park can vary greatly and change abruptly from that in Pond Inlet and Arctic Bay. For example, on a clear, calm day, your guide may refuse to set out from Pond Inlet if fog obscures the bottom of Bylot's mountains or if other subtle signs suggest dangers that should not be tested. Knowledgeable local guides are highly advised here and elsewhere in the High Arctic, as some unfortunate accidents remind us.

Sirmilik National Park has no facilities or equipment at the moment, and Parks Canada staff have not yet decided what type of facilities might be built. To arrange a trip to the park, contact a licensed tour operator or outfitter with extensive knowledge and experience in this area. Make arrangements well in advance to plan and book your travel, and to reserve any equipment you may need to rent. Operators will help you to obtain entry permits. Independent travellers can contact Parks Canada for more information on permits and fees.

DIRECTORY

Nattinnak Centre
In Pond Inlet.
For information on the park.
Tel.: (867) 899-8225
Fax: (867) 899-8246

Niglasuk Co. Ltd.
In Arctic Bay.
Tel.: (867) 439-9949
Fax: (867) 439-8341

Polar Sea Adventures
In Pond Inlet.
Tel.: (867) 899-8870
Fax: (867) 899-8817

Qikiqtani Inuit Association
Tel.: (867) 979-5391
Fax: (867) 979-3238
Web site: www.qikiqtani.nu.ca

Sirmilik National Park
P.O. Box 353, Pangnirtung NT,
X0A 0R0 Canada
Tel.: (867) 473-8828
Fax: (867) 473-8612
E-mail: nunavut_info@pch.gc.ca
Web site: Was go on line in late 1998.
Contact Parks Canada for the address.

Tagak Outfitting Services
In Pond Inlet.
Tel.: (867) 899-8932
Fax: (867) 899-8616

Toonoonik Sahoonik Outfitters
In Pond Inlet.
Tel.: (867) 899-8366
Fax: (867) 899-8364
Web site: www.pondtour.com

Tununiq Travel and Adventure
In Pond Inlet.
Tel.: (867) 899-8194
Fax: (867) 899-8194
E-mail: visit@tununiq.com
Web site: www.tununiq.com

88. CLYDE RIVER
by Beverly Illauq

Sometimes called the "Gateway to the Great Fiords," Clyde River is on Baffin Island's east coast in the shelter of Patricia Bay, off Clyde Inlet — a fiord that stretches west almost to the tip of the Barnes Ice Cap.

Population:	708 (Inuit: 95%, non-Inuit: 5%) Source: 1996 Census of Canada
Telephone Area Code:	867
Time Zone:	Eastern Time
Postal Code:	X0A 0E0
How to Get There:	Possible routes:
	• Winnipeg-Rankin Inlet-Iqaluit-Clyde River
	• Edmonton-Yellowknife-Iqaluit-Clyde River
	• Ottawa/Montreal-Iqaluit-Clyde River
	• Kangerlussuaq (Greenland)-Iqaluit-Clyde River
	Iqaluit to Clyde River (about 750 kilometres north) is via First Air
Banks:	None. Cash and traveller's cheques are preferable. Credit cards are accepted by certain businesses
Alcohol:	Alcohol and alcoholic beverages cannot be purchased in Clyde River. Visitors who want to bring alcohol into the community must first obtain a permit from the hamlet office
Taxis:	Yes

In fact, *Kangiqtugaapik*, the Inuktitut name for Clyde River, means "nice little inlet."

Perched on a flood plain, Clyde River is the contact point for travel into Sam Ford Fiord and other deep fiords of central Baffin that have become internationally renowned for their soaring walls and spectacular scenery. Glaciers and icebergs abound in the region, and there are 10 fiords within a 100-kilometre radius of the hamlet.

For most Clyde River families, hunting and camping in spring and summer remain major activities. Skin clothing is still made and worn, and many people depend on the animals harvested throughout the year for food. In early June when school finishes, families leave the community en masse and travel by snowmobile and *qamutiit* over cracks in the sea ice to traditional camp sites on the shores of fiords. Many of these locations are ancient, and a visitor with a keen eye for history can find three or more styles of dwellings and landmarks, some dating back at least 2,000 years.

Since the decline of the sealskin and fur markets, government jobs and handicrafts have become the most important sources of income. Still, subsistence hunting holds a special place in people's lives. Tourism is seen by many as a way to show others the vibrancy of traditional culture, and is key to the economic life of the community.

Most residents over 40 and children nine years old and under speak very little English. Young people communicate quite easily in English, and at least one person in Clyde River speaks French.

With the coming of Nunavut, the community has become very politically active. Another important issue is the development of the Igaliqtuuq (Isabella Bay) Biosphere Reserve and National Wildlife Area, an area world-renowned for the eastern Arctic bowhead whale population that summers and breeds in the vicinity. Since travel here is along an exposed coastline and access is difficult, tourism in this area is restricted.

History

Vikings may have arrived here 1,000 years ago. Norwegian explorer and author Helge Ingstad considers Cape Aston to be the *Helluland*, or Flat-Stone Land of Norse sagas. Six centuries later, in 1616, British explorers Robert Bylot and William Baffin mapped the area.

For generations, Inuit families have migrated through this area, travelling from as far away as Repulse Bay and the Iqaluit region to seek spouses and visit relatives. Groups of Inuit scoured the fiords' headlands in winter and spring, searching for marine mammals. In summer they walked miles inland, following caribou and living in lightweight skin tents that the dogs carried on their backs.

In 1818, Clyde River was given its English moniker by British explorer John Ross during his visit here. Beginning in 1820, whalers — particularly Scots — regularly crossed from Greenland to Baffin Island via Melville Bay and searched south along the Baffin coast for bowhead whales. There were few Inuit on this part of the coast, and many left to trade with whalers at more popular shore points to the north and south.

As whaling declined early this century, trading increased. In 1924, a Hudson's Bay Co. post was established at Clyde River. Inuit began to make visits — at Christmas, in the late spring and when the ice first formed — to trade furs for supplies and exchange news. During the Second World War, a U.S. Coast Guard weather station was erected at Cape Christian near Clyde River. A small federal school was built in 1960. Between 1967 and 1970, the community was moved to a new site across Patricia Bay to take advantage of a better water supply and a good airstrip location.

Clyde River: Its Land and Wildlife

At times, high winds prevent water travel during summer and fall. In winter and early spring, there may be whiteout conditions with blowing snow. Blizzards usually last between 24 and 48 hours. From the end of May through June, water on top of the ice can be a problem. Travellers should bring a good, warm pair of waterproof boots. Due to the mountainous terrain, weather conditions may vary dramatically within five kilometres of land or water.

Clyde River's "dark season" begins about Nov. 22 when the sun sets, and ends when it rises again about Jan. 20. During this period, peak light occurs at 11:15 a.m., with varying degrees of twilight between 9 a.m., and 2 p.m. By April, Clyde River is flooded with sunshine, and from May 13 until Aug. 9, there is 24-hour-a-day sunlight.

Seals (ringed, harp, bearded and hooded) live here and the polar bears that prey on them can be seen year-round. Narwhals can be spotted right in Patricia Bay, but are more often seen in Clyde Inlet. Bowhead whales have been seen in Patricia Bay as well, but you'll have a much better chance of spying them around Cape Christian or along the coast on a trip to their breeding grounds in Isabella Bay.

Caribou may be glimpsed in nearby fiords. Hares, arctic foxes and lemmings are also common. Nearby are nesting grounds for arctic terns, greater snow geese, Brant's geese, king eiders, gyrfalcons, snowy owls and a variety of gulls, waterfowl and shorebirds. Ravens and ptarmigans are the only birds that winter here. Arctic char populate lakes and rivers as well as fiords and bays. Arctic cod and sculpin are fished by children throughout the summer, and there is a small turbot fishery. Greenland sharks and killer whales inhabit area waters.

Although there are no hiking trails, several good hikes can be plotted using topographical maps. You may need to travel by boat to the end of a fiord to access an interesting trail. Drinking water can be in short supply in July and August after the snow has melted. Sawtooth Mountain, a hike of about 15 kilometres, is a fine vantage point for the breathtaking scenery. If birding is a passion, see the waterfowl nesting sites north of the community in August. Hiking along the Clyde River is beautiful from June to September. But keep in mind that hiking on the tundra can be very difficult during wet summers if the ground is soggy.

Adventure travellers, or anyone intending to be alone outside Clyde River without a licensed outfitter, should register with the local **RCMP** and fill out a Wilderness Travel Registration Form. (See Chapter 11, "Adventure Travel," for more important travel advice, including information on HF radios, personal locator beacons, and global positioning system receivers.) The local search and rescue team requests that all expeditions carry a battery-powered HF radio. Rental is about $100 per week.

HF radio channels 5210 and 5031 are monitored constantly by Inuit hunters and outpost camp residents. Although many of these people don't speak English and fewer still speak French or other European languages, they can contact people in any community who can speak with visitors by HF radio, should it be required. Don't hesitate to break into the Inuktitut chatter of 5031. Channel 5210 is supposed to be for emergencies, although it's used casually. Personal locator beacons and global positioning system receivers work well in this area, but the mountainous terrain interferes with the reception of MSAT radios.

Fishing for arctic char is particularly good from mid-July to mid-August. Some rivers may be good fly-fishing sites, but few people have been successful.

Local residents hunt seal, caribou and small game year-round; some hunters are willing to take visitors out hunting with them. Methods of hunting seal and caribou vary according to the season. An outfitter or the **Department of Sustainable Development** officer can tell you what's in season. (This department is known as **Resources, Wildlife and Economic Development** until April 1999.)

Seal dens can be viewed in late April and May; young seals are on top of the ice in June.

Between August and October, hungry polar bears frequent the community and camp sites along the fiords. They're waiting for the sea ice to form so they can hunt seals once again. In April, you'll see bears hunting seal pups, and throughout the spring, bears can be seen hunting seals on the ice.

Polar bear hunting begins in March for local hunters and at the beginning of April for sport hunters. Seven bears are reserved for out-of-town sport hunters. Arrangements must be made well in advance through **Canada North Outfitting Inc.** Polar bear skins can sometimes be purchased from individual hunters.

Tours

Visitors can take Inuit cultural tours, or view wildlife and the dramatic scenery of the eastern fiords from November through May by dogteam travel with an outfitter. Camping at traditional camp sites is also popular. Skin clothing for winter travel is highly recommended. It can be rented or purchased custom-made if at least one month's notice is given to the HTO or an outfitter. Prices run about $75 for mitts, $200 for *kamiit* (sealskin boots), and $800 for caribou-skin suits.

Depending on ice conditions, people can travel by boat from the beginning of August through to mid-September to view scenery and wildlife, and hunker down at traditional camp sites in the fiords. All licensed guides and outfitters must supply visitors with floater suits. Life-jackets are inadequate for the Arctic. Clyde River's many fiords and inlets provide challenging sea kayaking, and big-wall climbing and mountaineering in Sam Ford Fiord have recently attracted lots of international interest.

Prehistoric Thule and Dorset period tent rings, stone houses, fox traps and storage bins can be viewed at Cape Hewitt, about 32 kilometres from the settlement. Some artifacts left by European whalers and early Inuit inhabitants distinguish other camp sites. Another interesting day trip is to the abandoned Cape Christian U.S. air navigation base, about 16 kilometres by snowmobile or all-terrain vehicle. Take a rifle as protection from the bears that frequent this site (see Chapter 2, "Entering Canada," for information about Canada's firearms regulations), or hire a guide who's trained to use a rifle. He will act as a bear monitor for you.

There are three active outpost camps within about 32 kilometres of the settlement. You can arrange to visit them through an outfitter.

Newcomers are welcome to visit **Quluaq School**, the **hamlet office** and the Department of Sustainable Development office. The school has some artifacts on display, including three historic kayaks.

The **Apitak Development Corporation** employs four local guides who give community tours in English. Cost is $30 an hour.

Qullikkut Guides Ltd. employs seven Inuit hunters who show visitors their land, wildlife and the Inuit lifestyle. Custom or package tours are offered by dogteam, snowmobile or boat. Support services are given to climbers, hikers and other adventurers.

Shopping

Clyde River carvers work in whalebone, soapstone, granite, antler and ivory. The **Northern store** sells high-quality, pricey carvings, souvenirs and

Baffin Wildlife & Fisheries

Committed to Conservation and Sustainable Development

As Nunavut's environmental stewards, we're helping to preserve the beauty and intrinsic value of our land's natural resources for the enjoyment of everyone, today, and in the future.

Look to us to answer your questions on hunting, fishing or resource development involving:
- Territorial Parks & Tourism
- Environmental Protection
- Wildlife & Fisheries

For information, contact your local Wildlife & Fisheries Officer or the Baffin Regional Office at: (867) 979-5011.

Northwest Territories
Resources, Wildlife and Economic Development
Wildlife and Fisheries Division
Parks and Tourism Division

Explore the beauty of Pangnirtung with us

Let **Auyuittuq Lodge**

be your home away from home in Pangnirtung –
where hiking, boating, wildlife photography, history
and exceptional Inuit arts and crafts
are all at your doorstep.

Auyuittuq Lodge is also your point of entry
to beautiful Auyuittuq National Park, the ultimate in
mountaineering and wilderness hiking. Come visit us and
experience the warmth of Inuit hospitality.

AUYUITTUQ LODGE

For more information, please contact:
Auyuittuq Lodge, Pangnirtung, NT X0A 0R0 CANADA
Tel: (867) 473-8955 • Fax: (867) 473-8611

the largest selection in town of dry goods, clothing and food. An outfitter can direct you to carvers, artisans and traditional sewers so you can watch them make stone and ivory carvings, traditional tools and skin clothing. To purchase arts and crafts, contact a community tour guide through Apitak Development Corporation or an outfitter who will help you visit carvers to view their work. Some will work to order; several like to show how they work.

Igutaq, a small arts and crafts workshop near the Northern store, showcases articles sewn by hand by local seamstresses.

Accommodation and Dining

The **Qammaq Hotel** has 12 beds in double-occupancy rooms at $126.50 per night (meals not included), with bathroom, shower and laundry facilities. Meals are available for hotel guests only. Breakfast is $16.50, lunch is $22, and dinner is $27.50.

The **Visitors Centre** is a two-bedroom house accommodating up to six people. Guests cook their own meals in a well-equipped kitchen. Laundry facilities are available. Cost is $80 per person per night. The house, located in a residential section of town, has a beautiful view.

An outfitter can set you up in a tent or igloo, in the settlement or at a traditional camp site. Four cabins located at remote camp sites are on a first come, first served basis. Campers should contact an outfitter before arriving in the community.

The Northern store sells groceries and will microwave snacks on request. Staple items may be scarce during spring and summer before the sealift. If you depend on the Northern for food, check with a local outfitter to make sure that the items you require are in stock.

Kaukittuq, located next to the Department of Sustainable Development office, sells "country food," including frozen arctic char, *maktaaq*, smoked and dried fish, and dried caribou meat. Make an appointment with the HTO to purchase food here.

Services

First Air has four passenger flights in and out of Clyde River weekly. Chartered flights into Clyde River can be arranged through First Air or Air Nunavut.

Some visitors travel to Clyde River via dogteam, snowmobile, boat or kayak. Before you arrive, contact a local outfitter, the secretary/manager at the hamlet office, the RCMP, or the Department of Sustainable Development to ensure that someone will meet you and help make arrangements during your stay.

A nurse is always on call for emergencies at Clyde River's **health centre**. For regular medical attention, make an appointment between 8:30 and 11:30 a.m. weekdays. Public health programs are held from 1 to 4:30 p.m. weekdays.

You'll find fax services at the Northern store, Qullikkut Guides' office, and the hamlet office. A modem at Qullikkut Guides' office makes access to e-mail accounts available, for a small fee.

CBC Northern Service broadcasts on the **radio** in Inuktitut and English. Every day from 12 to 12:30 p.m., 5 to 6:30 p.m., and 9:30 to 11:30 p.m., the local radio society broadcasts, too. Calls for a tour, for clothing to be made, or other requests can be phoned in to the station and announced on air.

Avingaq Taxi runs a van between the airport and the community. Fares are $5 per person one way. The van is also used to transport mail and perishables from the airstrip. Since these are offloaded first, passengers aren't taken into town until the second or third run. Patience is required! Reservations for trips to the airport should be made the night before your flight.

DIRECTORY

*Outfitters and tour operators licensed at time of writing.
After March 31/99, check for updated status.

Accommodation and Dining

Qammaq Hotel
VISA, Interac.
Tel.: (867) 924-6201 or (867) 924-6222
Fax: (867) 924-6140

* Outfitters/Tour Operators/Visitors Centre

Apitak Development Corporation
Tel.: (867) 924-6033
Fax: (867) 924-6362

Canada North Outfitting Inc.
Box 3100, Almonte ON,
K0A 1A0 Canada
Tel.: (613) 256-4057
Fax: (613) 256-4512
E-mail: cnonorth@istar.ca

Clyde River Visitors Centre
Also provides accommodation to visitors.
VISA accepted.
Tel.: (867) 924-6033 or (867) 924-6034
Fax: (867) 924-6362

Department of Sustainable Development, Government of Nunavut
(or until April/99, GNWT's **Resources, Wildlife and Economic Development**)
For fishing licences/export permits for skins, etc. Visit during regular office hours.
Tel.: (867) 924-6235
Fax: (867) 924-6356

Hunters and Trappers Organization
9 a.m.–5 p.m., Monday to Friday.
Tel.: (867) 924-6202 or (867) 924-6191
After hours, call Apiusie Apak at (867) 924-6351 or Patrick Palluq at (867) 924-6415.
Fax: (867) 924-6197

Qullikkut Guides Ltd.
Also sells maps, guidebooks, souvenirs, postcards. Open 9 a.m.–5 p.m. or by appointment.
VISA accepted.
Tel.: (867) 924-6268
Fax: (867) 924-6362
E-mail: qullikkut@arctic.ca

Services

Airport
First Air:
Tel.: (867) 924-6365
Fax: (867) 924-6397

Church
Anglican Church of the Redeemer
Services: 11 a.m., 2 p.m. (for children and teenagers), 7 p.m., Sunday; 7 p.m., Wednesday. Services in Inuktitut, with translation into English when required.
Call Abraham Tigullaraq.
Tel.: (867) 924-6345

Hamlet Office
Tel.: (867) 924-6220
Fax: (867) 924-6293

Health Centre
Tel.: (867) 924-6377
Fax: (867) 924-6244

Library

Located in the Ilisaqsivik building.
3–6 p.m. daily.
Tel.: (867) 924-6266

Police (RCMP)

Tel.: (867) 924-6200
Fax: (867) 924-6276

Post Office

Located inside the Northern store.
10 a.m.–6 p.m.
Tel.: (867) 924-6465

Radio Station (FM 107.1)

Tel.: (867) 924-6265 (off air)
Tel.: (867) 924-6264 (on air)

Schools

Nunavut Arctic College

Tel.: (867) 924-6371
Fax: (867) 924-6248

Quluaq School

Tel.: (867) 924-6309

Taxi

Avingaq Taxi

Tel.: (867) 924-6033

Weather Information

Tel.: (867) 924-6344
Fax: (867) 924-6363
Web site weather forecast:
www.infonorth.org

Shopping

Kangiqtugaapik Qayait Rentals

Kayak rentals.
Cash, traveller's cheques.
Tel.: (867) 924-6278

Kaukittuq

At the community freezer beside
the Department of Sustainable
Development office.
9 a.m.–5 p.m., Monday to Friday.
Cash only.
Tel.: (867) 924-6202

Nangmautuq

Sells hunting equipment and ammunition. Operated by the HTO, it's located
beside the community freezer.
9 a.m.–5 p.m., Monday to Friday.
Cash only.
Tel.: (867) 924-6202
Fax: (867) 924-6197

Northern Store

VISA, certified cheques, Interac.
10 a.m.–12:30 p.m., 2–6 p.m., Monday,
Tuesday, Wednesday and Friday;
10:30 a.m.–12:30 p.m., 2–8 p.m.,
Thursday; 1–5 p.m., Saturday.
Tel.: (867) 924-6260 or (867) 924-6262
Fax: (867) 924-6386

89. AUYUITTUQ NATIONAL PARK

by Bruce Rigby

Set aside in 1972 by the government of Canada, Auyuittuq National Park, or "the land that never melts," was the first national park north of the Arctic Circle.

The area was given "reserve" status to denote that the identified lands were subject to a land claims process. Although the park area was modified by the *Nunavut Land Claims Agreement Act*, it was still to be termed a park reserve until an Inuit Impact and Benefits Agreement had been successfully completed. These negotiations were to have been finalized by the autumn of 1998. If delayed, though, Auyuittuq would remain a park reserve for the purposes of park management.

Located on Baffin Island's breathtaking Cumberland Peninsula, Auyuittuq (pronounced "ow-you-ee-tuk") covers 19,500 square kilometres of deep mountain valleys, dramatic fiords, ancient glaciers, and spiny peaks. Most visitors travel in Akshayuk Pass (formerly Pangnirtung Pass), although the remote northern section of the park holds its own mysteries as well.

Akshayuk Pass is a valley system bordered by mountains and cliffs that runs between North and South Pangnirtung Fiords. The pass, which splits the line of mountains along Cumberland Peninsula, is a popular year-round transportation route through the park. Skiers and hikers traverse its 97 kilometres in spring and summer while residents of Broughton Island and Pangnirtung use it for snowmobile travel between their communities in winter. The part of Akshayuk Pass most frequented is the section between Overlord Mountain and Summit Lake.

In stark comparison to Akshayuk Pass lies the north side of Auyuittuq, a remote mosaic of brittle glaciers and deeply incised fiords. This region contains areas of historical interest and provides excellent opportunities for viewing marine life. More difficult to access in summer, the north end of the park is best seen during spring. Fewer visitors venture into this distant part of the park.

A large part of Auyuittuq's north side is the rarely accessed Penny Ice Cap. This vestige of the last Ice Age occupies approximately 5,100 square kilometres and reaches some 2,100 metres in elevation. With ice as thick as 300 metres in places, the ice cap provides an excellent record of past climates and has been the base for several major scientific studies into climatic change and global warming. The ice cap also has an uncanny effect on local weather conditions: winds passing over the glaciers become cooler and increase in velocity as they descend through nearby mountain passes.

The Land and Wildlife

With its excellent examples of past and current glacial activity, Auyuittuq is a geologist's dream. Icy tendrils of glaciers hang ominously overhead; loud explosions rattle through Akshayuk Pass as house-sized chunks of Precambrian granite crash to the valley floor. Glacial debris litter the pass, and erratics (large boulders) can be found balanced or perched in interesting and unusual positions. The work of water and wind is also evident, creating large deposits of sand and glacial moraines, and carving sinuous patterns in the landscape.

The horns, cirques and polished pinnacles of Auyuittuq offer more evidence of glacial activity. The scoured surface of Mount Thor is one of the tallest uninterrupted cliff faces on the planet, attracting climbers from around the world. The truncated twin peaks of Mount Asgard can be seen from the Summit Lake area. Visitors may recognize Asgard from the James Bond film *The Spy Who Loved Me*.

Glacial processes are still very active in the park. This can be seen in Auyuittuq's mountain streams, which are best crossed in the early morning before melting glacial ice increases their flow dramatically. Wind erosion is also present, and gales carrying sand particles have been known to strip paint from buildings and machinery and pit the heavy windows of cabins. For these reasons, care should be taken at all times. There are many examples of active rock and glacier slides, and flash flooding can occur in periods of heavy rain. On one occasion, a park warden was obliged to dump his pack and run to avoid being overtaken by a landslide. Avoid camping in areas bare of vegetation or lichen, or which look cleaner than others around them, as they may still be an active slope or subject to active erosion.

Because of the extremely slow growth and recovery rate of arctic vegetation, the most frequently visited parts of the park lack the showy displays of vegetation found in other areas of Nunavut. Plants grow low to the ground and are predominately made up of lichens, mosses, sedges, dwarf willows or smaller patches of flowering plants. Cotton grasses can be found in lower lying areas, and the eastern version of fireweed — the broad-leafed willow herb — can be found in sandy areas along stream beds.

The timing of your visit, the length of your stay and your location within the park will all affect the types of wildlife you see in Auyuittuq. Wildlife tend to avoid the more well-travelled areas at times when higher concentrations of visitors are present. Those travelling in off-seasons and in smaller groups should see more wildlife. The following birds have all been seen in the park: snow buntings, peregrine falcons, redpolls, ptarmigan, ravens, red-throated loons, glaucous gulls and Canada geese. Land mammals that visitors are most likely to see include lemmings, ermine (weasels), foxes and arctic hares. Caribou have also been viewed in the park, but in areas not usually seen by most visitors. Unlike other parts of Nunavut, there are relatively few caribou in the park.

What to See and Do

The southern part of Auyuittuq comprises the land between Overlord Mountain and Summit Lake; Akshayuk Pass is the most common route between the two. This part of the park is usually travelled in spring and summer. The season begins in March, as groups of mountain climbers tackle some of the most challenging terrain in the world. Other spring visitors plan on skiing Akshayuk Pass, only to find that the brutal winds of winter have peppered the snow with sand and gravel. Those willing to hike with skis on their backs will find many pockets of snow in protected valleys, however.

Most visitors enter Auyuittuq through the park's southern entrance at Overlord, a 25-kilometre trip from the community of Pangnirtung. Local outfitters will take you there either by snowmobile or boat, depending on the season. The $75 per person fee for travel to the park (minimum two people) is set by the **Pangnirtung Outfitters' Association**. This fee is subject to change. It may seem steep, but the fee represents the costs of maintaining and operating vehicles in a remote environment.

Note that from roughly mid-June to mid-July, ice conditions in South Pangnirtung Fiord are unsafe for snowmobiles and preclude the use of boats. Visitors must therefore enter the park by foot, about a two-day walk from Pangnirtung. The same holds true for autumn, although travellers rarely visit Auyuittuq this late in the season.

The rudimentary camp sites at Overlord are grouped among the boulders around the warden cabin and shelter. The site has an outhouse; fresh water can be obtained from a nearby stream. Remember that the water contains high levels of glacial sediment, so let it settle before drinking. Also remember that the estuary of the Weasel River is affected by tides. What appears as an expansive mud plain when the tide is out can quickly turn your tent into an impromptu waterbed. Stay well back from the shore. From Overlord a well-marked trail enters the park, continuing into Akshayuk Pass.

The trail loops to Summit Lake and back, a total distance of about 66 kilometres. Few groups hike the entire pass in this direction, mainly because summer ice conditions between North Pangnirtung Fiord and Broughton Island are erratic and make trip planning difficult. There have been instances where hikers have arrived at North Pangnirtung Fiord only to find it impossible to be picked up. The subsequent 97-kilometre trek back to Overlord is a long one. Plan your trip well.

The trail typically followed is from Overlord to Windy Lake, on the east side of the Weasel River, and from Windy Lake to Summit Lake on the west side of the river. A suspension bridge straddles Weasel River at a set of rapids north of the Windy Lake warden cabin. Most hikers follow this route, since the trail is well marked and passes by the Mount Thor emergency shelter.

Hikers could also stay on the east side of the Weasel River until they come to a cable crossing near Summit Lake. This route is much more demanding. There are quite a few streams that you'll have to ford.

The northern half of Akshayuk Pass can be accessed through North Pangnirtung Fiord from Qikiqtarjuaq (formerly known as Broughton Island) by foot, skis, snowmobile or boat, a distance of approximately 80 kilometres. Since Qikiqtarjuaq is indeed an island, this end of the pass is not accessible by foot during breakup and freezeup. The fiord usually becomes ice-free in August, although local wind conditions may occasionally push ice back into the fiord, causing unexpected delays in drop-offs and pickups.

The rest of northern Auyuittuq is best seen during spring and in the company of outfitters from Qikiqtarjuaq. Dogsled or snowmobile trips can be arranged, and opportunities for wildlife viewing abound. Remote fiords create a splendid backdrop for viewing seabird colonies and marine mammals such as polar bears, seals and whales. Exploring northern Auyuittuq on foot is only for seasoned backcountry travellers who are experienced in arctic travel.

Unlike Pangnirtung, outfitters in Qikiqtarjuaq negotiate their own fees. Be prepared to pay somewhere around $200 per person to get into the park. Contact the park office to obtain a listing of licensed outfitters and their current rates.

A word of warning: The north end of the park is frequented by polar bears at various times throughout the year, so special precautions should be taken. Park officials may find it necessary to close parts of the park when the number of bears is high and the risk of a "negative encounter" great. If you wish to plan a trip into the north part of the park, contact park officials for information about which areas to consider avoiding, and things to remember when travelling in polar bear country. And consider using a guide.

Planning a Trip

The majority of Auyuittuq's visitors come in July and August, and spend most of their time in the southern part of the park. While Auyuittuq has much to offer, anyone looking for a wilderness experience with extensive solitude may wish to reconsider visiting the park during this time, or make arrangements to visit a less heavily travelled region. Park staff and outfitters will both be happy to assist in planning your visit.

As with other Canadian national parks, Parks Canada now charges an entry fee to Auyuittuq. The fee is $15 per person for a single day, $40 per person for up to three nights, and $100 per person for more than three days. The $100 fee is good for one year, and valid in Nunavut's national parks, Nahanni National Park Reserve, and in Aulavik National Park.

DIRECTORY

Auyuittuq National Park
P.O. Box 353, Pangnirtung NT,
X0A 0R0 Canada
Tel.: (867) 473-8828
Fax: (867) 473-8612
E-mail: nunavut_info@pch.gc.ca

Pangnirtung Outfitters' Association
Contact the outfitters directly or call the Angmarlik Interpretive Centre in Pangnirtung.
Tel.: (867) 473-8737
Fax: (867) 473-8685

90. KEKERTEN TERRITORIAL HISTORIC PARK

by Mike Vlessides

Like many other historical sites in Nunavut, the legacy of Kekerten Island is born of the often checkered relationship between Inuit and the British and American whalers that pillaged arctic waters in the 18th, 19th and 20th centuries.

Located on the north shore of Cumberland Sound some 50 kilometres from Pangnirtung, Kekerten (properly spelled as *Qikiqtan* in Inuktitut) was once the hub of whaling activity in the sound.

Today, Kekerten Territorial Historic Park is a fascinating destination for visitors to Pangnirtung wishing to make a day trip into this turbulent world. Here you'll find the remnants of a bygone era described by signage along an interpretive trail. Among the many features of the site are the foundations of three storehouses built in 1857 by Scottish whalers, large cast-iron pots once used for rendering whale oil, blubber-hauling pins and the remains of a whaleboat slip.

The People and Their History

Commercial whaling did not enter Canadian Arctic waters until 1820, when British whalers ventured north from their traditional territory off southeast Greenland into the area around Pond Inlet and Lancaster Sound. They were not disappointed. These untested waters were rich with their principal quarry, the bowhead whale, and for the next two decades became the primary destination of the British whaling fleet. Indeed, the new-found region proved so fecund that between 1820 and 1840, more than 13,000 whales were slaughtered here.

But for all its profitability, bowhead whaling was an uncertain undertaking. During these two decades, the ravages of arctic weather took a heavy toll on the whalers, resulting in hundreds of deaths and dozens of lost ships. In 1830 alone, 19 ships were lost and myriad others damaged.

As a result of these dangerous conditions — as well as a rapidly decreasing bowhead population in the immediate area — the whalers were forced to consider alternative methods of performing their livelihood. The prevailing sentiment was that a permanent whaling settlement in more southerly waters would provide the refuge so badly needed by both men and ships.

The answer came by way of a rumor. For years, whalers had heard tales of a large southerly bay that not only abounded with bowheads, but was also free of ice until well into January. In the spring of 1840, Scottish whaler William Penny decided to find the legendary body of water. He elicited the aid of a young Inuk named Eenoolooapik, who directed the whaler into the mouth of what is now known as Cumberland Sound. British whaling was resuscitated. Within a few years, both British and American whaling ships were visiting the sound with increasing regularity.

In 1852, a group of American whalers aboard the vessel *McLellan* became the first group to spend the winter in Cumberland Sound, setting a precedent that was soon to become standard practice for most whalers in the region. Five years later, Penny established a permanent station in the sound when he erected a station house at Kekerten for the Arctic Aberdeen Company. The Americans soon followed suit. The establishment of these wintering stations created a permanent foundation for contact and trade between Inuit and non-Inuit; neither group would ever be the same.

Attracted by a culture rich with material items of which they were enamored, Inuit flocked to the whaling stations to perform services that would get them the items they so desired. Among other things, Inuit transported blubber between the floe edge and the harbor, rendered whale oil, and worked as whaleboat crews. They also supplied the whalers with fresh meat and fur clothing. In exchange, the whalers gave Inuit a host of manufactured items, including rifles, telescopes, knives, needles and kettles. Inuit also got dry goods such as biscuits and tobacco.

And while much good came of the relationship that was forged between the two cultures, Inuit suffered desperately for their newly found ties with the whalers. Inuit were highly susceptible to the alien diseases of the Europeans and Americans, and viruses ravaged native settlements. By 1857, some 17 years after their initial contact with the whalers, the 1,000-strong Inuit of Cumberland Sound had seen their population reduced to less than 350. To exacerbate the problem, working with whalers drastically altered traditional Inuit subsistence patterns, and many failed to cache adequate food stores for times of shortage, often resulting in needless starvation.

The late 1850s and early 1860s were the golden years for bowhead whaling in Cumberland Sound. As many as 30 ships visited the area each autumn; about a dozen regularly spent the winter in the vicinity of Kekerten, or Penny's Harbour as it was known to the whalers. By 1860, stations at Blacklead Island (on the south shore of the sound) and Cape Haven (near the mouth of the sound) joined Kekerten as permanent whaling posts.

It was in this same year, however, that American whaling ships first ventured into Hudson Bay and discovered it to be a fertile whaling area. Most of the American fleet would concentrate on the area for a number of years, spending summers there and wintering in Cumberland Sound. It would only take five years for bowhead stocks in these new waters to shrink precipitously, so ships began returning to the sound.

They were met with a similar situation. Cumberland Sound was yielding fewer whales each year, the result of two decades of intense exploitation. The Arctic Aberdeen Company sold its stations, effectively ending William Penny's participation in the whale fishery. After 1864, the "discoverer" of Cumberland Sound never set foot in the Arctic again.

By 1870, the number of ships visiting the sound had declined to only half that of a decade earlier. But despite the relative dearth of whales, Cumberland Sound was still the location of choice for a dwindling industry. A few ships from each nation overwintered there until the late 1870s. By 1882, American involvement in eastern Arctic whaling was practically nil. The only permanent station still operating was at Kekerten.

As bowhead populations shrank, whaling companies looked to other mammals to fill the void in their pocketbooks. As early as 1872, an American company was netting beluga whales at the head of the sound. More attention was paid to seals, however, which boasted enormous populations in the sound. The 1870s saw increasing trade for sealskins and seal blubber.

As a result of this novel demand for seal products, Inuit returned to preferred sealing grounds across the sound, where they would await the arrival of whaling companies and the products for which they traded. Within 20 years, the seal population had been thoroughly decimated, leaving local Inuit with little food sources to see them through the winter. This probably caused many Inuit to move back to the stations in large numbers in the late 1800s. By the waning months of the 19th century, both Blacklead and Kekerten were home to a few hundred Inuit and a handful of non-Inuit whalers.

When the price of whalebone dropped 17¢ per kilogram in 1912, the fate of the bowhead fishery was sealed. After 1913, no whaling ships left for the Arctic. Nonetheless, Inuit at Blacklead and Kekerten continued to hunt whales there for five more years; by this time the whale fishery had become an important part of their culture. Both Kekerten and Blacklead served intermittently as trading posts, but were abandoned in the mid-1920s and late 1930s, respectively.

Today, whaling is largely a memory in the minds of a few Pangnirtung elders. In July 1998, however, that memory was briefly reignited when a historic bowhead whale hunt, negotiated as part of the Nunavut Land Claims Agreement, saw several elders successfully harvest a single bowhead a short distance from the Kekerten whaling station.

Planning a Trip

Trips to Kekerten are best arranged in Pangnirtung through the Angmarlik Interpretive Centre, the local visitors centre and museum. Inquire about the different outfitters and services offered. Outfitters recommended by the Angmarlik Centre stay with visitors while at the park and provide interpretive tours. They also supply meals.

In late spring — early May to mid-June — most people reach Kekerten by snowmobile, although those with ample time and energy can ski. Regardless of your mode of transportation, always prepare for unexpectedly cold temperatures and winds that eat through several layers of clothing. Note that during the latter weeks of June and early July, travelling on the ice is an uncertain proposition and best left to Inuit who are well versed in pre-breakup travel.

Summer travel to Kekerten is usually by Lake Winnipeg boat or freighter canoe. Don't plan a seaward trip for earlier than July 15, since ice often lingers this late in the year. Once the ice clears, boat trips to the park are possible until late September, when the waters slowly begin to congeal once again. Dress warmly, even on the balmiest days. It's also worth carrying waterproof clothing, including rubber boots. Your licensed guide or outfitter will provide a survival suit for boat travel. If travelling without an outfitter, rent a survival suit somewhere in town. Pangnirtung Fiord is subject to tremendous tides and will dictate your departure and arrival times.

Aside from ski excursions, a round trip to Kekerten — with time out to enjoy the park — takes about 12 hours. You can't camp in the park proper, but camping is permitted on the rest of the island. A cabin at the park provides shelter in case of emergency; ask your guide if he or she carries survival gear before you embark. If you plan to ski there, then plan on camping for the night somewhere outside the park.

91. PANGNIRTUNG

by Kenn Harper

Pangnirtung — "the place of the bull caribou" — is located on a narrow coastal plain against a spectacular backdrop of high mountains and a winding river valley.

Population:	1,243 (Inuit: 93%, non-Inuit: 7%) Source: 1996 Census of Canada
Telephone Area Code:	867
Time Zone:	Eastern Time
Postal Code:	X0A 0R0
How to Get There:	Possible routes:
	• Ottawa/Montreal-Iqaluit-Pangnirtung
	• Kangerlussuaq (Greenland)-Iqaluit-Pangnirtung
	• Winnipeg-Rankin Inlet-Iqaluit-Pangnirtung
	• Edmonton-Yellowknife-Rankin Inlet-Iqaluit-Pangnirtung
	Iqaluit to Pangnirtung (297 kilometres northeast) is via First Air
	or Kenn Borek Air
Banks:	None. Cash and traveller's cheques are preferable. Credit cards are accepted by certain businesses
Alcohol:	Alcohol and alcoholic beverages are prohibited
Taxis:	Yes

Legend says a hunter named Atagooyuk gave the place its name well over 100 years ago when caribou had not yet changed their patterns as a result of the incursions of man.

History

Cumberland Sound, the large body of water Pangnirtung Fiord opens into, has been a traditional home of Inuit for more than 1,000 years. Here, they and their predecessors of the Thule and Dorset cultures lived in small hunting camps along the shore. Their survival depended on the seals, walruses and beluga whales that populated the waters of Cumberland Sound, and on the magnificent bowhead whale that also frequented these waters.

Englishman John Davis was the first non-Inuk known to have entered Cumberland Sound, although it is probable that Norse from Greenland occasionally visited the area as well. Davis, an explorer in search of a northwest passage to the presumed riches of the Orient, navigated the sound in 1585 and again in 1587. The sound was not re-entered by Europeans until 1840.

In 1839, a Scottish whaler named William Penny took a young Inuk man, Eenoolooapik, to Scotland to spend the winter. The following spring Eenoolooapik guided Penny into the mouth of Cumberland Sound. What ensued was 80 years of exploitation by whalers and free traders. The effect of bowhead whaling on the Inuit was cataclysmic. Traditional settlement

Pangnirtung Street Map

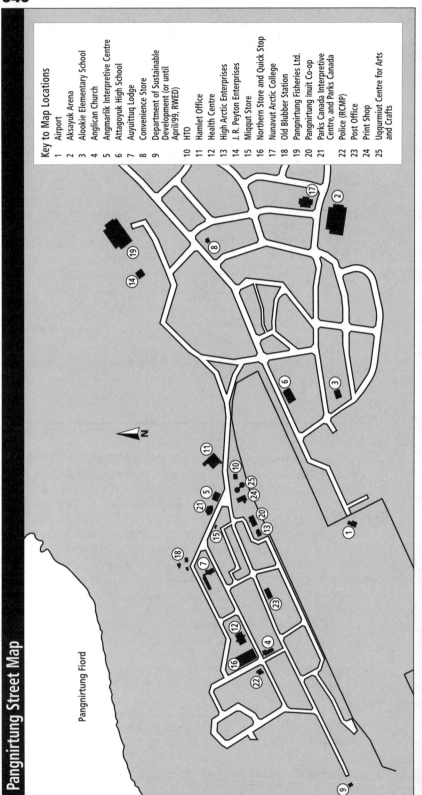

Pangnirtung Fiord

Key to Map Locations

1 Airport
2 Aksayuk Arena
3 Alookie Elementary School
4 Anglican Church
5 Angmarlik Interpretive Centre
6 Attagoyuk High School
7 Auyuittuq Lodge
8 Convenience Store
9 Department of Sustainable
  Development (or until
  April/99, RWED)
10 HTO
11 Hamlet Office
12 Health Centre
13 High Arctic Enterprises
14 J. R. Peyton Enterprises
15 Miqqut Store
16 Northern Store and Quick Stop
17 Nunavut Arctic College
18 Old Blubber Station
19 Pangnirtung Fisheries Ltd.
20 Pangnirtung Inuit Co-op
21 Parks Canada Interpretive
   Centre, and Parks Canada
22 Police (RCMP)
23 Post Office
24 Print Shop
25 Uqqurmiut Centre for Arts
   and Crafts

N

patterns changed as many abandoned their hunting camps to congregate at two main whaling stations: Blacklead Island off the south coast of the sound, and Kekerten off its north coast. Although whaling brought access to guns, ammunition and wooden boats, many Inuit succumbed to diseases to which they had no immunity.

In 1894, in the declining years of the whaling industry, an event of paramount importance to the people of Baffin Island occurred: The Church Missionary Society of London, England, established a mission station at Blacklead Island under the pioneering leadership of Reverend Edmund James Peck, a veteran of almost two decades of mission work in northern Quebec. Peck brought with him the gift of a written language, for he promoted the use of the syllabic writing system — adapted from the Cree system — for the Inuit language. Inuit learned the syllabic system quickly, and passed knowledge of it up the coast to camps that had never seen a missionary. Peck produced biblical material in syllabics; this material also spread quickly throughout the region. After the last missionary left Blacklead Island in the early 1900s, Inuit catechists kept both religion and literacy alive.

When whaling declined, Inuit returned to life in camps scattered throughout Cumberland Sound. The establishment of a trading post by the Hudson's Bay Co. in 1921 was followed two years later by a detachment of the RCMP. In 1929, St. Luke's Mission Hospital was established under Dr. Lesley Livingstone. Until the 1960s, most Inuit continued to live in traditional camps, although a few opted for Pangnirtung and employment. Jim Kilabuk, who worked for the Hudson's Bay Co. for 45 years, was a competent traveller and guide — the mentor of many young traders who came and went during his tenure. Nookiguak was the special constable who assisted the RCMP by guiding their patrols of the sound and the east Baffin coast; after his death in 1949, he was replaced by Joanasie Dialla, who held the position for more than 20 years. Etuangat, who died in his mid-90s in late 1995, was the last of the Inuit whalemen. He also spent many years guiding doctors stationed in Pangnirtung to camps throughout the region. These are the unsung heroes of the three establishments — the Hudson's Bay Co., the RCMP, and the mission hospital — that formed the foundation for the modern town of Pangnirtung (pronounced in Inuktitut as "Pangniqtuuq").

The history of Pangnirtung would not be complete without mention of William Duval, after whom the mountain to the east of the community and the river that flows between it and the town are named. Sivutiksaq, as he was known to Inuit, was a German-born American whaler who came to Cumberland Sound as a young man in the 1870s and spent his life in the Arctic. He is the grandfather or great-grandfather of any Pangnirtung resident with the surname Akpalialuk. Duval died at Usualuk camp in Cumberland Sound in 1931.

In 1956, the federal government sent its first teacher to Pangnirtung, and in 1962 it established an administrative office. That same year, a disastrous distemper epidemic killed most of the dogs in Cumberland Sound, threatening Inuit livelihood. A number of families moved into the community of Pangnirtung from the land. The resulting change in lifestyle was an abrupt one.

The last few decades, though filled with promise, have also been fraught with difficulties for the people of Pangnirtung. This was a seal-hunting community, and when sealskin prices declined precipitously in the 1970s and 1980s, hunting became uneconomical. At the same time, improved health care dramatically increased life expectancy. These t vo factors, combined with a high birthrate, made for a rapidly increasing population with high unemployment; the social problems that accompany such a situation soon followed. With substantial government assistance, the community currently operates a turbot fishery. The government has also encouraged development of arts and crafts, including Pangnirtung's unique weaving industry.

Pangnirtung: Its Land and Wildlife

The beauty of Pangnirtung is largely born of its backdrop, the lofty mountains of Cumberland Peninsula, where some peaks reach 2,200 metres. The peninsula is bisected by both Akshayuk and Kingnait passes, providing an overland route from Cumberland Sound to Davis Strait. The central part of the peninsula is dominated by the massive Penny Ice Cap, from which many glaciers flow to the sea. Most of the better-known peaks in Cumberland Peninsula were named during a 1953 expedition of the Arctic Institute of North America.

Marine life has been important in the history of Cumberland Sound. Large numbers of beluga whales may be seen at their calving grounds in Millet Bay near the head of the sound; they sometimes wander into Pangnirtung Fiord. Walruses can be seen in the sound; occasionally, so can bowhead whales. Polar bears, which frequent the sea ice near the mouth of the sound, are rarely spotted close to Pangnirtung. Ringed seals are found throughout the sound and the fiord.

Caribou are typically found a considerable distance from Pangnirtung, in the hills past the head of Clearwater Fiord or inland from the south coast of Cumberland Sound, toward Nettilling Lake.

The Pangnirtung area has always been well known for its arctic char fishing. One camp currently operates at Kingnait Fiord. This is a hard business and the season is short, so many camps do not survive. It is best to contact the **Angmarlik Interpretive Centre**, the local visitors centre, before booking a fishing trip.

Tours

"Downtown" Pangnirtung is a living testimony to the community's history. The Angmarlik Interpretive Centre functions as a community museum, library and elders' centre. Displays represent traditional Inuit and whaling life in Cumberland Sound. Elders are often present during the afternoon, either playing cards, knitting or just reminiscing with each other. You may have an opportunity to chat with some of them, if the staff are free to act as interpreters.

Next door is the **interpretive centre operated by Parks Canada**, which houses displays and exhibits to help interpret the varied nature of nearby Auyuittuq National Park. **Parks Canada** has its office in the same building.

To the other side of the Angmarlik Centre is a small, old building painted bright yellow. Although originally on a different site, this was the home of the community's first doctor.

In the middle of downtown Pangnirtung stands the former St. Luke's Mission Hospital and associated church buildings, most of them clad in the drab grey shingles typical of Anglican buildings in the Arctic. The old hospital now houses the Arthur Turner Training School, where Inuit catechists from throughout the Diocese of the Arctic are trained.

Behind the **church** stands the shortest two-storey house imaginable. This is where Jim Kilabuk lived and raised his family. A cluster of buildings behind the Northern store were the former Hudson's Bay Co. buildings. The remains of a small rail track can be seen near the beach in this area; on it supplies were hauled up from the beach at shiptime (in those days, the supply ship only arrived once a year). On a high rock near the shore is a small black cannon that was only fired at shiptime. On the beach near Auyuittuq Lodge are the buildings of the old whaling station, operated by the Hudson's Bay Co. until 1964. They have been refurbished in recent years; a traditional whaleboat complements the scene.

For those not ready for the challenge of hiking in Auyuittuq National Park, there are a few good hiking trails that start just outside Pangnirtung. The Ukuma Trail skirts the Duval River and heads toward Kingnait Fiord, which parallels Pangnirtung Fiord over the mountains behind the community. You can also spend a day climbing Mount Duval, but exercise caution, especially when snow covers the ground. A few years ago, a doctor ventured too close to the sheer face of this mountain and plunged to his death. In the 1950s a clerk from the Hudson's Bay Co. fell from the top, and slid, bounced and scraped his way to the bottom. Inuit found him unconscious, but he had miraculously suffered no broken bones and lived to tell the tale.

Hikers needing gasoline and naphtha should contact **J. R. Peyton Enterprises**, the local fuel distributor. Their depot is in a small building beside the tank farm on the beach. Hours are limited.

There is an ever-changing number of outfitters in Pangnirtung. Over the years, the most reliable has been **Alivaktuk Outfitting Services**, operated by Joavee Alivaktuk. Others may be contacted through the Angmarlik Interpretive Centre. Summer visitors can arrange for boat tours to Auyuittuq National Park or Kekerten Territorial Historic Park. Snowmobile tours may be arranged in spring. As of this writing, nobody offers tours by dogteam, but this could change.

Tour operators also bring groups of tourists to Pangnirtung for activities both in the community and the wilderness beyond. In 1996, Arctic Odysseys of Seattle, Washington, pioneered Twin Otter-based skiing in the mountains of the park and Cumberland Peninsula; participants reported world-class descents of more than 1,200 metres per run. They have not returned, but nonetheless this activity shows promise for the future.

Shopping

The **Uqqurmiut Centre for Arts and Crafts** is a locally owned business that is primarily a tapestry studio, print shop and craft gallery. The unique design of this building, reminiscent of a cluster of tents at a traditional camp site, makes it a warm and friendly place for artists to work in, and is equally inviting to visitors. A small shop sells tapestries and prints, as well as crocheted hats, soapstone and whalebone carvings, brooches, and pins by many local artists. The weaving shop also produces blankets, scarves and sweaters.

Weaving was introduced to Pangnirtung almost 30 years ago as Inuit searched for ways to create an economic lifestyle after the wholesale move from traditional camps to Pangnirtung. Don Stuart, an artist from Southern Canada, moved to the community and taught local women his craft. Each tapestry bears the name of both the artist who created the scene and the weaver. At the front desk you will be able to arrange a tour. The shop's friendly weavers are mostly monolingual Inuktitut speakers, so unless you speak Inuktitut, conversation will be limited. Those wishing to take pictures are encouraged to leave a donation.

Pangnirtung is also well known for its prints. A new collection is produced each year, to be marketed in Southern Canada. Artists typically focus on legends, whaling and traditional activities. The interactions of whalers and traders with Inuit are often the subjects of these colorful productions.

Carving is also important to Pangnirtung. A small but dedicated group of local carvers produces objects in stone imported from Cape Dorset and Kimmirut. Whalebone carvings are still made, although the ready supply of whalebone at traditional sites in Cumberland Sound has been largely exhausted. It is important to note that the whalebone used in carvings is not the same 'whalebone' of whaling literature. Whalers referred to the long and valuable strips of baleen from the mouth of the bowhead as whalebone; the whalebone used by artists is actual bone, usually of the bowhead's vertebrae or skull, cream-colored and very porous. Carvings can be purchased in the Uqqurmiut Centre. Many artists also visit the hotel during mealtimes to sell their wares; this is a time for barter or shrewd bargaining.

Three stores sell groceries in Pangnirtung: the **Northern store**, **Pangnirtung Inuit Co-op**, and **High Arctic Enterprises**. Basic foodstuffs are always available, but the vagaries of plane schedules determine whether fresh, imported items like milk, eggs, bread, fruit and vegetables are in stock. The Northern also runs a small **convenience store** in the east section of the community.

Accommodation and Dining

There is only one hotel in town. **Auyuittuq Lodge** is in the downtown area of Pangnirtung, a stone's throw from the fiord. Its lounge provides a spectacular view of surrounding peaks, the tidal flats and the comings and goings of local hunters and fishermen. The lodge has 44 beds in 22 double rooms. Count on sharing your room with another guest in the peak summer season. None of the rooms have private baths, but there are central washrooms on each floor. The rate is $135 per person per night without meals. With the meal plan, the cost per night is $200. Meals are $15 for breakfast, $20 for lunch, and $30 for supper. Call and ask about tourist discounts.

The menu is fixed. If you have any food prohibitions or allergies, advise the manager well in advance of mealtime. Mealtimes are well posted. If you plan on skipping a meal, advise the manager in advance or you will be charged for it. With advance notice, the staff can prepare box lunches for hikers. If you are not a guest in the lodge, make a reservation if you wish to dine there.

At Auyuittuq Lodge you will rub shoulders with construction workers, prospectors, accountants, engineers, people on meetings and courses, and many others — a random sampling of those who make the northern economy tick. The lodge is almost entirely Inuit staffed. Auyuittuq Lodge is one of few hotels in Nunavut offering separate lounges for smokers and non-smokers. The lodge offers group rates.

Campers can stay in the Pisuktinu Tungavik Territorial Campground on a raised area just above the beach past the Duval River. There is a daily $5 per tent fee to use the campground, which is open from June until September. Services are minimal. There is no shower, and many trekkers use the washroom facilities at Auyuittuq Lodge for a small fee. High winds can rise spontaneously in Pangnirtung at any time of the year, so campers should have very strong tents. Be careful not to leave any valuables unattended at the camp site, or even outside your tent while you sleep at night. Like many northern communities, Pangnirtung has a great deal of petty theft and vandalism, a result of the high unemployment and unrealizable expectations of today's youth.

Fast food has recently come to Pangnirtung. The Northern store's **Quick Stop** offers selected items from Pizza Hut and Kentucky Fried Chicken as well as other snacks, but no burgers or sandwiches.

Services

The Pangnirtung **Health Centre**, next to the Northern, operates a medical clinic from 9 a.m. to 12 p.m. weekdays. Public health sessions run from 1 to 5 p.m. Emergencies are handled as necessary. There is also a **dental clinic** in town, as well as an **RCMP** detachment.

Pangnirtung is currently served by two airlines. First Air has served the community the longest and with the most reliability. Kenn Borek Air also provides passenger and freight service. They are both based in Iqaluit. Depending on the day of the week, their schedules may allow connections from Pangnirtung and Qikiqtarjuaq (formerly known as Broughton Island).

DIRECTORY

*Outfitters and tour operators licensed at time of writing.
After March 31/99, check for updated status.

Accommodation and Dining

Auyuittuq Lodge
VISA, MasterCard, Diners Club/enRoute.
Tel.: (867) 473-8955
Fax: (867) 473-8611

Quick Stop
10 a.m.–7 p.m., Monday to Wednesday;
10 a.m.–9 p.m., Thursday to Saturday.
Closed Sunday.
VISA, MasterCard, Interac.
Tel.: (867) 473-8026
Fax: (867) 473-8610

* Outfitters/Tour Operators/Visitors Centre

Adventure Canada
Tel.: (905) 271-4243
Fax: (905) 271-5595
E-mail: info@adventurecanada.com
Web site: www.adventurecanada.com

Alivaktuk Outfitting Services
Tel.: (867) 473-8721
Fax: (867) 473-8721

Angmarlik Interpretive Centre
For outfitter information.
From June to mid-September:
9 a.m.–9 p.m., Monday to Saturday.
1–9 p.m., Sunday. Other times of
year: 8:30 a.m.–5 p.m., Monday to Friday.
Tel.: (867) 473-8737
Fax: (867) 473-8685

Services

Airport
Tel.: (867) 473-8907 or (867) 473-8746

Church

St. Luke's Anglican Church
Services: 9:30 a.m. (English), 11 a.m.
(Inuktitut), 6:30 p.m. (Inuktitut),
Sunday.
Tel.: (867) 473-8014
Fax: (867) 473-8383

**Department of Sustainable
Development, Government
of Nunavut**
(or until April/99, GNWT's Resources,
Wildlife and Economic Development)
Tel.: (867) 473-8937
Fax: (867) 473-8326

Hamlet Office
Tel.: (867) 473-8953 or (867) 473-8931
Fax: (867) 473-8832

Health Centre (and Dental Clinic)
Tel.: (867) 473-8977
Fax: (867) 473-8519

Hunters and Trappers Organization
Tel.: (867) 473-8751
Fax: (867) 473-8741

**Parks Canada Interpretive Centre,
and Parks Canada**
Tel.: (867) 473-8828
Fax: (867) 473-8612
E-mail: nunavut_info@pch.gc.ca

Police (RCMP)
Tel.: (867) 473-8833
Fax: (867) 473-8915

Post Office
In former hamlet office.
Tel.: (867) 473-8940

Radio Station (FM 105)
Tel.: (867) 473-8975

Schools

Alookie Elementary School
Tel.: (867) 473-8803
Fax: (867) 473-8718

Attagoyuk High School
Tel.: (867) 473-8815
Fax: (867) 473-8858

Nunavut Arctic College
Tel.: (867) 473-8923
Fax: (867) 473-8664

Taxi

Tiriaq Taxi
Tel.: (867) 473-8050
Fax: (867) 473-8305

Weather Information
Tel.: (867) 473-8907
Web site weather forecast:
www.infonorth.org

Shopping

Convenience Store
11 a.m.–9 p.m., Monday to Friday;
1–9 p.m., Saturday and Sunday.
Tel.: (867) 473-8306

High Arctic Enterprises
10 a.m.–12:30 p.m., 2–6 p.m.,
7–10 p.m., Monday to Friday; 2–6 p.m.,
7–10 p.m., Saturday. Closed Sunday.
VISA, MasterCard, Interac.
Tel.: (867) 473-8648
Fax: (867) 473-8993

J. R. Peyton Enterprises
10 a.m.–12 p.m., Monday to Thursday;
1–6 p.m. and 7–9 p.m., Friday. Closed
Saturday and Sunday.
VISA, Interac.
Tel.: (867) 473-8896
Fax: (867) 473-8924

Northern Store
10 a.m.–6 p.m., Monday to Thursday
and Saturday; 10 a.m.–8 p.m., Friday.
Closed Sunday.
VISA, MasterCard, Interac.
Tel.: (867) 473-8935
Fax: (867) 473-8610

Pangnirtung Inuit Co-op
9 a.m.–10 p.m., Monday to Friday;
10 a.m.–10 p.m., Saturday.
Closed Sunday.
VISA accepted.
Tel.: (867) 473-8936
Fax: (867) 473-8657

Uqqurmiut Centre for Arts and Crafts
9 a.m.–5 p.m., Monday to Friday;
Saturday by appointment.
VISA, MasterCard, Interac.
Tel.: (867) 473-8870
Fax: (867) 473-8634
E-mail: inuitart@nunanet.com
Web site: www.uqqurmiut.com

92. QIKIQTARJUAQ (BROUGHTON ISLAND)

by Don Pickle

Frequently called "the iceberg capital of the North," Qikiqtarjuaq sits off the coast of Baffin Island some 96 kilometres north of the Arctic Circle.

Population:	488 (Inuit: 95%, non-Inuit: 5%) Source: 1996 Census of Canada
Telephone Area Code:	867
Time Zone:	Eastern Time
Postal Code:	X0A 0B0
How to Get There:	Possible routes:
	• Ottawa/Montreal-Iqaluit-Qikiqtarjuaq
	• Winnipeg-Rankin Inlet-Iqaluit-Qikiqtarjuaq
	• Edmonton-Yellowknife-Rankin Inlet-Iqaluit-Qikiqtarjuaq
	• Kangerlussuaq (Greenland)-Iqaluit-Qikiqtarjuaq
	Iqaluit to Qikiqtarjuaq (470 kilometres northeast) is via First Air
Banks:	None. Cash and traveller's cheques are preferable. Credit cards are accepted by certain businesses
Alcohol:	Alcohol and alcoholic beverages cannot be purchased in Qikiqtarjuaq. Visitors who want to bring alcohol into Qikiqtarjuaq must first obtain a permit from the **Alcohol and Drug Education Committee**
Taxis:	No

Qikiqtarjuaq (which just changed its name from Broughton Island in late 1998), means "big island" in Inuktitut, even though the island that the community calls home is only about 16 kilometres long and 12 kilometres wide.

Hunting and fishing are still important parts of daily life here, and families often spend much of their time on the land during spring and summer. Inuktitut is the language of choice in Qikiqtarjuaq, although an increasing number of people speak English. Children are taught in Inuktitut until Grade 4, when some English instruction begins.

History

The area around Qikiqtarjuaq may have been inhabited as many as 4,000 years ago. Approximately 1,000 years ago, people of the Thule culture entered the region. Today's Inuit — including those in Qikiqtarjuaq — are direct descendants of the Thule. Evidence of this culture around Qikiqtarjuaq dates back almost 800 years and can be seen at a Thule camp site approximately 90 minutes from town by boat.

John Davis was the first European to explore the area; he named nearby Cumberland Peninsula in 1585. Kivitoo, about 60 kilometres northwest of Qikiqtarjuaq, and Padloping Island, roughly 90 kilometres to the south, soon became important stops for bowhead whalers. Kivitoo was abandoned in the mid-1920s, although the iron vats used for rendering whale blubber were left behind. These relics, as well as a small graveyard, can still be seen today.

In 1955, construction began on a DEW Line site at Qikiqtarjuaq, attracting Inuit from Clyde River, Pangnirtung, Kivitoo and Padloping Island, who came to Qikiqtarjuaq to find employment. The site became fully operational in 1957; a Hudson's Bay Co. store was established three years later. By 1968, the federal Department of Indian Affairs and Northern Development had relocated residents from Kivitoo and Padloping Island to Qikiqtarjuaq. On Aug. 31, 1979, Qikiqtarjuaq obtained hamlet status.

Qikiqtarjuaq: Its Land and Wildlife

Scores of oddly shaped icebergs can usually be found in the waters around Qikiqtarjuaq, hence the community's nickname. Outfitters will take visitors on snowmobile and boat trips to see icebergs. If travelling by boat, exercise extreme caution around these behemoths, as they're always shifting and breaking apart. Don't ask your guide to get dangerously close to an iceberg, since they can unexpectedly flip, smashing your boat to splinters.

The island and surrounding area are also home to spectacular landforms and wildlife. Nearby lies the massive Penny Ice Cap, the largest ice cap on Baffin Island, and the many glaciers it has sired. Waters abound with walruses, polar bears, seals, narwhals, belugas and even occasional bowhead whales. This district is also the largest fulmar nesting area in the eastern Arctic.

Tours

There are a number of good hiking trails on this island. Information can be obtained from the economic development officer with the **Department of Sustainable Development** (GNWT's Department of **Resources, Wildlife and Economic Development** until April/99) or the manager of the Tulugak Co-op Hotel. Be sure to file your intended route and expected return time with someone in the community, preferably the RCMP, before heading out on the land. You should also check with the wildlife officer about the proximity of polar bears, which frequent the area in summer and autumn.

The primary tourist seasons are spring and summer. Guided trips by boat, dogteam, or snowmobile can take you along the Baffin Island coast. Snowmobile and dogteam trips are possible from January through June; boat travel starts in August and continues through November. Visitors may also ski or backpack in **Auyuittuq National Park**.

Shopping

Traditionally, whalebone carving was most common in this area, but contemporary carvers use primarily stone and ivory. Although carving isn't as prevalent as it once was, there are still noted artists in Qikiqtarjuaq. Local crafts and carvings are available from the **Siijamiut store** or, when in operation, the **Minnguq Sewing Group**. The sewing group is renowned for excellent traditional sealskin and caribou-skin clothing. Artisans specialize in sealskin boots (*kamiit*), pants and parkas. The sewing group, which had been in limbo for more than a year, was expected at the time of writing to resume operations soon. You can also ask the economic development officer to assist you in contacting local artists.

Groceries are available from the **Northern** and Siijamiut stores, but selection is seasonal and availability depends on flight service.

Accommodation and Dining

The **Tulugak Co-op Hotel** has nine rooms with double occupancy, each with private bath and cable TV. The cafeteria-style restaurant has a set menu, although requests for traditional foods and special diets are accommodated, with sufficient notice. The cost is $185 per person per night, including meals, or $120 per person per night without meals. Guests staying a month or two pay $150 per person per day, including meals. Visitors not staying at the hotel can dine there, but must give ample notice.

The **Siku Hotel**, with eight beds in four rooms, is adjacent to the river on Qikiqtarjuaq, which lends the atmosphere of a babbling brook in spring. You can cook your own meals in the kitchen or eat at the Tulugak Co-op Hotel. The cost is $120 per person per night; if you choose to prepare three meals daily in their kitchen, it's $150.

There is also a campground outside town, overlooking the community. Here you'll find tent platforms, an outhouse, drinking water and little else. The campground is free, but rapid weather changes and polar bears sometimes make you wish you'd paid to stay elsewhere.

Qikiqtarjuaq has a hostel, but it is not licensed.

Services

Qikiqtarjuaq's **health centre** is staffed by two registered nurses. Walk-in service is available Monday to Friday from 8:30 to 11:30 a.m. Between 1 and 4:30 p.m., visitors must first make an appointment. Emergency service is always available. There is also a local **RCMP** detachment.

DIRECTORY

*Outfitters and tour operators licensed at time of writing.
After March 31/99, check for updated status.

Accommodation and Dining

Quick Stop
Snack bar in the front of the Northern store.
4–8 p.m., Monday to Saturday.
Tel.: (867) 927-8917

Siku Hotel
Traveller's cheques accepted.
Tel.: (867) 927-8111

Tulugak Co-op Hotel
VISA, Diners Club/enRoute.
Tel.: (867) 927-8874 or (867) 927-8833
Fax: (867) 927-8124

* Outfitters/Tour Operators

Auyuittuq National Park
Summer season only. Otherwise, the park's Pangnirtung contact information applies.
Tel.: (867) 927-8834
Fax: (867) 927-8454

Iceberg Outfitting
Ask for Stevie Audlakiak.
Tel.: (867) 927-8459
Fax: (867) 927-8296

Nauyak Outfitting
Ask for Allan Kooneeliusie.
Tel.: (867) 927-8427
Fax: (867) 927-8120

Pikaluyak Outfitting
Ask for Pauloosie or Tia Kooneeliusie.
Tel.: (867) 927-8390
Fax: (867) 927-8404
E-mail: icebound@nunanet.com
Web site: www.arctic-travel.com/
    PIKALUYAK

Services

Airport

First Air
Tel.: (867) 927-8873

Kenn Borek
Tel.: (867) 927-8179

**Alcohol and Drug
Education Committee**
Tel.: (867) 927-8428

Churches

Katisivik Full Gospel Church
Services: 11 a.m. and 7 p.m., Sunday;
7:30 p.m., Wednesday.
Tel.: (867) 927-8852
Fax: (867) 927-8344

**St. Michaels and All Saints
Anglican Church**
Services: 11 a.m. and 6:30 p.m.,
Sunday.
No telephone.

**Department of Sustainable
Development, Government
of Nunavut**
(**Resources, Wildlife and Economic
Development**, GNWT until April/99)
Ask for the economic development
officer or the renewable resources officer.
Tel.: (867) 927-8966
Fax: (867) 927-8450

Hamlet Office
Tel.: (867) 927-8832
Fax: (867) 927-8120

Health Centre
Tel.: (867) 927-8916
Fax: (867) 927-8217

Hunters and Trappers Organization
Tel.: (867) 927-8836
Fax: (867) 927-8525

Police (RCMP)
Tel.: (867) 927-8967
Fax: (867) 927-8309

Post Office
In hamlet building.
1:30–5:30 p.m., Monday to Saturday.
No telephone.

Radio Station (FM 107.1)
Tel.: (867) 927-8971 or (867) 927-8852

Schools

Inuksuit School
Tel.: (867) 927-8938
Fax: (867) 927-8067

Nunavut Arctic College
Tel.: (867) 927-8847
Fax: (867) 927-8219

Weather Information
Tel.: (867) 927-8792
Fax: (867) 927-8032
Web site weather forecast:
www.infonorth.org

Shopping

Minnguq Sewing Group
Call hamlet office for information.
Tel.: (867) 927-8832 or (867) 927-8879
Fax: (867) 927-8102

Northern Store
10 a.m.–12 p.m., 1:30–6 p.m., Monday
to Friday; 2:30–6 p.m., Saturday.
Closed Sunday.
VISA, Interac
Tel.: (867) 927-8917
Fax: (867) 927-8070

Siijamiut Store
8–10 p.m., Monday to Friday; 4–6 p.m.
and 8–10 p.m., Saturday and Sunday.
Cash only.
Tel.: (867) 927-8102
Fax: (867) 927-8019
E-mail: icebound@nunanet.com

Tulugak Co-op Hotel Gift Shop
9:30 a.m.–12 p.m. and 1–5:30 p.m.,
Monday to Saturday. Closed Sunday.
VISA accepted.
Tel.: (867) 927-8874 or (867) 927-8833
Fax: (867) 927-8124

93. IQALUIT
by Alootook Ipellie and Carol Rigby

If Mexico City is the largest metropolis on Earth, then Iqaluit easily gets the same designation within the new territory of Nunavut.

Population:	4,220 (Inuit: 61%, non-Inuit: 39%) Source: 1996 Census of Canada
Telephone Area Code:	867
Time Zone:	Eastern Time
Postal Code:	X0A 0H0 (General Delivery and P.O. Box 1–1949)
	X0A 1H0 (P.O. Box 5001–5090)
How to Get There:	Possible routes:
	• Ottawa/Montreal-Iqaluit
	• Winnipeg-Rankin Inlet-Iqaluit
	• Edmonton-Yellowknife-Rankin Inlet-Iqaluit
	• Kangerlussuaq (Greenland)-Iqaluit
	Ottawa to Iqaluit and Montreal to Iqaluit (both about 2,100 kilometres north) are via First Air, which also serves the Greenland route.
	Rankin Inlet to Iqaluit (about 1,200 kilometres east) is via
	Canadian Airlines or First Air
Banks:	Yes — the Royal Bank of Canada and the Bank of Montreal
Alcohol:	Alcohol and alcoholic beverages cannot be purchased in Iqaluit, although licensed restaurants, bars and private clubs serve alcohol. Visitors who want to bring alcohol into the community must first obtain a permit from the **NWT Liquor Commission** in Iqaluit
Taxis:	Yes

When you arrive at the bustling Iqaluit **Airport**, you might feel as though you've entered a frontier town. In several ways, you have. Iqaluit is the transportation hub to other Baffin Island communities, as well as to Greenland. And in December 1995, it was selected in a Nunavut-wide plebiscite to be the capital of the new central and eastern Arctic territory. That historic day arrives on April 1, 1999, and signs that Iqaluit is readying itself have been apparent for some time, most visibly in construction of the new legislative assembly building near the Parnaivik Building.

The main portion of Iqaluit (pronounced "ee-ka-loo-eet") overlooks Koojesse Inlet, which has some of the country's longest stretches of exposed area at low tide. At one time, these beaches were dotted with clusters of Inuit huts. Later, as modern houses, shops and public buildings were constructed, this little village grew to reflect its increasing population and impending importance as a government town. A decentralized government that will add jobs to almost half of all Nunavut communities is expected to bring hundreds of jobs to Iqaluit alone, and private enterprises built around this public sector growth are burgeoning as well. An unrelated but interesting side industry is the southern movie business; actors and directors have

Iqaluit Street Map

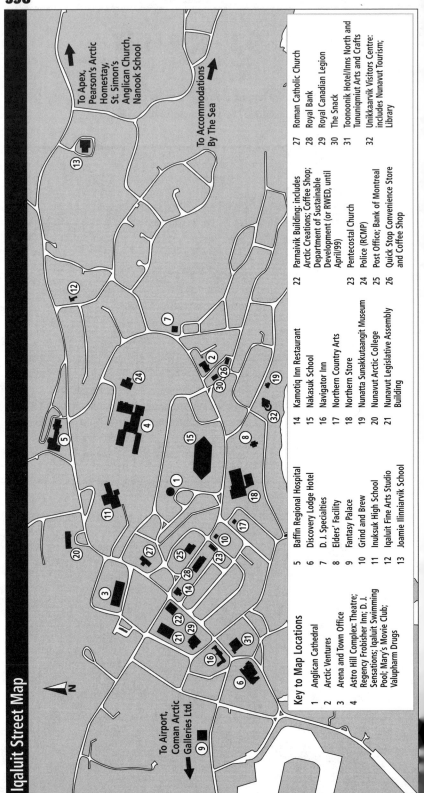

To Apex,
Pearson's Arctic
Homestay,
St. Simon's
Anglican Church,
Nanook School

To Accommodations
By The Sea

N

To Airport,
Coman Arctic
Galleries Ltd.

Key to Map Locations

1 Anglican Cathedral
2 Arctic Ventures
3 D.J. Specialties
4 Arena and Town Office
   Astro Hill Complex: Theatre;
   Regency Frobisher Inn; D.J.
   Sensations; Iqaluit Swimming
   Pool; Mary's Movie Club;
   Valupharm Drugs
5 Baffin Regional Hospital
6 Discovery Lodge Hotel
7 D.J. Specialties
8 Elders' Facility
9 Fantasy Palace
10 Grind and Brew
11 Inuksuk High School
12 Iqaluit Fine Arts Studio
13 Joamie Ilinniarvik School

14 Kamotiq Inn Restaurant
15 Nakasuk School
16 Navigator Inn
17 Northern Country Arts
18 Northern Store
19 Nunatta Sunakkutaangit Museum
20 Nunavut Arctic College
21 Nunavut Legislative Assembly
   Building

22 Parnaivik Building: includes
   Arctic Creations; Coffee Shop;
   Department of Sustainable
   Development (or RWED, until
   April/99)
23 Pentecostal Church
24 Police (RCMP)
25 Post Office; Bank of Montreal
26 Quick Stop Convenience Store
   and Coffee Shop

27 Roman Catholic Church
28 Royal Bank
29 Royal Canadian Legion
30 The Snack
31 Toonoonik Hotel/Inns North and
   Tununiqmiut Arts and Crafts
32 Unikkaarvik Visitors Centre:
   includes Nunavut Tourism;
   Library

dropped in to town from time to time to film authentic Arctic location shots. Iqaluit's population too is a mix: a mix of cultures (less than two-thirds of residents here are Inuit, compared to other communities that are more than 90 per cent Inuit) and languages. Iqaluit, due north of the province of Quebec, is also home to about 400 francophones and a French-language radio station.

The United States (U.S.) airbase to the north of town used to be separate from the main village, with a road linking the two sites. What was once wide open country is now one large urban development. About eight kilometres to the south lies the small suburb of *Niaqunngut*, or Apex as it's officially called. Built by the Canadian government as a model community in 1955, it used to be the main centre of activity, with a public school, nursing station, community centre and fire hall. The Hudson's Bay Co. store and warehouses were also built nearby.

History

Thousands of years ago, when Iqaluit, like the rest of the Arctic, was still uncharted wilderness, the ancient explorers of the Dorset and Thule cultures hunted and camped on this pure and silent land. The lands and waters here were prime hunting and fishing grounds; local vegetation provided edible plants and berries in season. These nomadic hunters would remain as long as there was game, then move on to other areas where animals were more plentiful.

In 1942, during the Second World War, the U.S. Air Force, with the blessing of the Canadian government, selected Iqaluit as an ideal site to build an airstrip. It was to be long enough to handle large aircraft transporting war materials from the United States to its European allies. During this time, many Inuit from surrounding hunting camps were recruited to help construct the airstrip, aircraft hangars and related buildings.

These hunters and their families had no choice but to begin building year-round huts on the beaches of Koojesse Inlet, using wood discarded from the airbase and the local dump. The Inuit referred to the little village that grew here as Iqaluit, meaning "fish" (plural). Fish, especially arctic char, abound here in spring and summer, after their swim down the Sylvia Grinnell River, two kilometres west of the village. They reappear in droves in autumn, when it's time for them to swim back up to Sylvia Grinnell Lake for the winter.

Before long, the village, together with the airbase and Apex Hill (its previous name), appeared on official government maps as Frobisher Bay. And this is how it came to be known to the outside world. The name was in honor of Martin Frobisher, the English sailor who "discovered" the bay in 1576 while searching with his crew for the Northwest Passage to the Orient. Frobisher made three voyages to the bay, mainly to mine black ore from Kodlunarn Island at the mouth of the bay. Frobisher believed the island contained gold. Several skirmishes with local Inuit ensued; in one incident, Inuit took five of Frobisher's men hostage. They were never heard from again. In other instances, Frobisher captured four Inuit whom he took back with him to England, presumably to display to the Royal Family and to the curious English public. The Inuit did not live long in that strange land.

In another clash with Inuit, Frobisher was stabbed in the buttocks by an arrow, earning him the dubious distinction of being the first Englishman known to have been wounded by an Inuk. As for the precious ore he and his men carried to England, it turned out to be fool's gold! Thus ended Frobisher's quest for polar gold and his explorations of the lands and waters beyond the bay that later bore his name.

In the 18th and 19th centuries, other explorers and whalers from Europe and later, North America, embarked on similar northern expeditions. The impact of western culture intensified in south Baffin Island when missionaries arrived, spreading the Christian religion that would replace centuries-old Inuit shamanistic rituals and beliefs.

Like other Inuit communities throughout the North, Iqaluit couldn't escape westernization of its traditional culture and heritage. The Hudson's Bay Co. trading post, for example, moved to Iqaluit in 1950 from Ward Inlet, almost 50 kilometres south on the north coast of Frobisher Bay. In 1955, activity further escalated when supplies and workers arrived in Iqaluit as construction of the eastern section of the DEW Line began. By 1957, Iqaluit had a population of approximately 1,200, of whom 489 were Inuit.

The United States turned over its airbase to the Royal Canadian Air Force after the Second World War. By 1963, the Americans had gone, and Iqaluit was to become the Canadian government administration, communications and transportation centre for the eastern Arctic. This coincided with Canada's efforts, during these Cold War years, to claim sovereignty in the Canadian North.

Since its early days as a village, Iqaluit has been home to many strong Inuit leaders. Simonie Michael is one who comes to mind. A carpenter by trade, Simonie became chairman of the Sisi Housing Co-op in Apex Hill. In that position, he was one of the first community leaders to make decisions affecting both Inuit and Euro-Canadians. By the mid-1960s, he became president of Inook Ltd., the first Inuit-owned company in Iqaluit and in Canada. Simonie was also president of the Frobisher Community Council and a member of the St. Simon's Anglican Church Council.

Abraham "Abe" Okpik, a MacKenzie Delta Inuk who became chairman of the Apex Hill Community Association in 1963, was the first Inuk to be appointed to the Northwest Territories Territorial Council, the Ottawa-based forerunner to the Northwest Territories legislative assembly. He also served, from 1968 to 1970, as the head of Project Surname, a plan that required all Inuit families to select a surname to replace the disk-numbers previously assigned to them as identification by the federal government. Shortly after, the Canadian government awarded Okpik the country's highest honor, the Order of Canada.

Another able leader was Simonie Alainga, an inspirational hunting and traditional games instructor to many young Inuit. Simonie was the thread connecting many Inuit community dwellers to the land and to their hunting traditions. In the early 1960s, he was among the first to encourage those having difficulty with community life to return to the land if they chose. His memory has endured as a comfort to Inuit caught in the clash between western and traditional values.

Anakudluk was another traditionalist who became a lay reader in the Anglican ministry. He was always a source of great spiritual strength to a community in transition. Arnaitok Ipeelie, too, became a lay reader and was among the first Inuit to teach youngsters to read and write Inuktitut syllabics. He was a respected orator and a powerful singer, as well.

Inutsiaq was one of the first of Iqaluit's leaders to organize Inuit games during festive seasons. A deeply spiritual man, he was a wonderful storyteller who often told his tales over the radio. He was also famous for his childbirth carvings, sought by collectors from across Canada and abroad.

Then there are Iqaluit's eccentric Euro-Canadians! Scotsman Bill MacKenzie, a long-time resident who came here as a Hudson's Bay Co. clerk, will always be remembered as the first, and perhaps last, farmer in the eastern Arctic. Former mayor and GNWT legislative assembly member Bryan Pearson, whom Inuit know as "Salluq," the skinny one, could be pretender to Frobisher's fame in these parts. If you want to hear a good yarn about Iqaluit in the early days, "Salluq" is your man!

Another respected resident is Gordon Rennie, the smiling, long-time former manager of the Northern store, who's fluent in Inuktitut. The late Fred Coman, as an art dealer and businessman, contributed much to the community through his entrepreneurship and volunteer work over many years.

Iqaluit: Its Land and Wildlife

Iqaluit sits in the gentle hills surrounding Koojesse Inlet. Although the local hills are perhaps less spectacular than, say, Pangnirtung's mountains, they are blessed with a wide variety of arctic wildflowers, which start appearing in late June and bloom through early August. Even the disturbed areas by the sides of the roads are bright in July with the hot pink of broad-leaved willow herb — the colorful roof of the Nunatta Campus building of **Nunavut Arctic College** is meant to echo this beautiful, showy flower.

The trickster of the North, the raven, is the one bird you will easily encounter all year round. The antics of this extremely intelligent (and large!) bird are always fascinating to watch, from soaring in the updrafts around Iqaluit's highrises to teasing dogs away from their food dishes. However, in the summer you may also spot snow buntings, ptarmigan, seagulls, the odd phalarope, and if you're particularly lucky, peregrine falcons. Winter expeditions to the outskirts of town often result in glimpses of large groups of caribou, as their migration patterns have brought them close to town in the last few years. In the summer, you might spot the very shy arctic hare and an occasional lemming. You are not likely to encounter any dangerous wildlife in the immediate environs of Iqaluit, except perhaps the odd arctic fox, which should be avoided in case of rabies. Seals can frequently be spotted in Koojesse Inlet when the ice is gone, but it's rare for the larger marine mammals to come in that far.

Iqaluit's Unikkaarvik Visitors Centre, located on the beach between the Pairijait Tigumivik Elders' Facility and the Nunatta Sunakkutaangit Museum, provides brochures describing day hikes in the vicinity of town. Recent building development in some areas, however, has caused a few trails to disappear, such as the one along the shoreline to Apex. On your walks, you may discover an *inuksuk* or two — those legendary stone markers that Inuit traditionally built as landmarks on many parts of the tundra. Some *inuksuit* were built to resemble humans, to help hunters lead caribou into lakes where they could be more easily killed from a *qajaq* (kayak).

Another popular local destination is Sylvia Grinnell Territorial Park on the banks of the Sylvia Grinnell River. A government-operated camp site here provides picnic tables, enclosed outdoor toilets, a foul-weather shelter and garbage receptacles. This is the best place to come if you wish to camp, unless you have connections in town who can provide you with other camp sites. It's even possible to get to the camp site by taxi, if you don't feel like lugging all your camping gear, although the fare is a little higher than the one normally charged for a ride in town. You can also arrange a visit with a licensed local outfitter to nearby Qaummaarviit Territorial Historic Park. Licensed outfitters in Iqaluit include: **Eetuk Outfitting**, **NorthWinds Arctic Adventures**, **Purlaavik Outfitting**, **Kimuk Adventure Tours**, and **Qairrulik Outfitting Ltd.** Yet another way to see the tundra is by helicopter, although you'll want to charter a group for this to divvy up the expense. **Canadian Helicopters** makes its small or large helicopters available for tours for $1,000 to $5,000 an hour. Their large Sikorski seats up to 15. Book in advance.

Tours

Essential early stops for any visitor to Iqaluit or to the Baffin Region should be at the visitors centre and the museum, conveniently located side by side on Iqaluit's beachfront.

The **Nunatta Sunakkutaangit Museum**, housed in a renovated Hudson's Bay Co. trading post building, is a compact but excellent museum whose permanent collection of artifacts relates to the history of south Baffin Island. It also maintains temporary displays of artwork.

Next door is the **Unikkaarvik Visitors Centre** and the offices of **Nunavut Tourism**, as well as the town's library. The visitors centre displays spectacular artwork, including a life-size marble carving of a drum dancer crafted by Inuit carvers under the tutelage of renowned Canadian sculptor George Pratt.

At the **Iqaluit Centennial Library**, visitors will discover the Thomas Manning collection of polar books, the personal collection of respected biologist Thomas Manning. The local collection is also strong in books on arctic flora, fauna, and history, and carries a high proportion of all materials published in Inuktitut.

Located on the beachfront, the **Pairijait Tigumivik Elders' Facility** was designed to convey the feeling of a traditional *qammaq*, or sod hut. As it's really for elders, whose enjoyment may be spoiled by too many visitors, call first to arrange an appropriate time to visit. When you go, take an interpreter with you, as most elders speak little or no English.

To see a real *qammaq*, visit Apex. Here you'll find a traditional sod hut used by local women for social gatherings, traditional sewing, and other activities. Alicee Joamie is the contact at this **Elders' Facility**. As she speaks Inuktitut only, you're best to call the **Town of Iqaluit's recreation department** to arrange a visit.

The "downtown" core of Iqaluit is undergoing considerable change, as the 'Four Corners' section is developed to accommodate the offices and legislative space needed for Nunavut's new capital. The existing Parnaivik Building will be accompanied by a legislative building and office complex. Construction in general is likely to be ongoing for the next few years, as there is a shortage of space available for the offices and residences needed to accommodate a new government.

Shopping

Iqaluit, like many of Nunavut's communities, is paradise for lovers of art and fine crafts. Among the stone carvings by local Inuit artists, you'll see depictions of arctic animals, some in dancing postures, as well as human and legendary heads and figures. The sculpture is generally realistic, and always well finished. The stone, an even-textured grey-green stone and a brighter green stone that has the look of marble, is the same as that used by artists in Kimmirut and Cape Dorset. Miniature carvings in antler and walrus ivory are also available.

In addition to the arts and crafts displayed in the museum, you'll find several commercial art outlets that sell graphics, paintings and other crafts. The following dealers have reputations for carrying quality artwork: **Arctic Ventures**, **Coman Arctic Galleries Ltd.**, **Iqaluit Fine Arts Studio**, **Northern Country Arts**, and **Tununiqmiut Arts and Crafts**. Try to shop around to compare prices. Some stores, like Arctic Ventures and **D.J. Sensations**, sell jewelry made from traditional materials, silver and other metals, plus small carvings. Here you may also find hand-sewn, knitted, and crocheted crafts such as duffel socks and tuques (knitted hats), and seal- or caribou-skin mitts and boots. In the Parnaivik Building at the core of the new downtown development area, **Arctic Creations** at first glance appears to be a fabric store (much appreciated by all the local seamstresses!). However, the proprietor, Monica Ell, also carries beautiful handmade parkas, sweaters, and other garments, in addition to some other craft items. The **Arts and Crafts Centre**, located in Nunavut Arctic College, displays artwork from the Baffin Region; although it doesn't sell to the public, it will refer you to local galleries that do. Of the non-Inuit artists who work in Iqaluit, some have gallery or display space in their homes. Contact the Unikkaarvik Visitors Centre for further information.

Events

Since 1964, Iqaluit residents have celebrated the coming of spring with their annual Toonik Tyme festival, held for a week sometime in the last two weeks of April. The festival attracts tourists from around the world who come to enjoy Inuit traditional games, snowmobile and dogteam races, entertainment and community feasts. Since it's organized each year by a volunteer committee, it's wise to confirm in advance the dates of festivities.

The festival is named after the *Tuniit*, those people whom legend claims were living in the land that's now Greenland and the eastern Canadian Arctic when ancestors of today's Inuit arrived from the West about 1,000 years ago. Many archeologists think the *Tuniit* were people of the so-called Dorset culture. Inuit stories describe their almost superhuman strength and stamina. Legends also say the *Tuniit* slept with their feet above their heads to make them better runners! Around Iqaluit, some elders believe that ghosts of the *Tuniit* can still be seen, dressed in caribou skins, moving across the hills near the community in spring.

Traditional Inuit games are one of the festival's biggest attractions. Local residents look forward to the fishing and hunting contests, while tourists gather to watch igloo-building, bannock-making and harpoon-throwing competitions. The snowmobile, which has largely replaced the dogsled, is featured in the annual heart-stopping hill climb and in the long-distance race to the community of Kimmirut and back, run every few years. In 1990, Johnny Mikijuk set a new record for the 156.9-kilometre round trip, completing it in four hours and 17 minutes. Iqaluit's mayor, Jimmy "Flash" Kilabuk, won his nickname from his record-breaking time in that race a few years earlier. Evenings at the festival feature indoor entertainment — dances, talent shows and concerts.

Temperatures during Toonik Tyme generally range from –20° C to –10° C. Daylight in late April is beginning to stretch into the evening and the sky is usually sunny and bright. It's still parka and boot weather, though, and visitors are advised to bring warm clothing. Sunglasses, sunscreen and lotion for dry skin are also recommended. Unusually warm weather or spring blizzards can wreak havoc with scheduled events; they may cause festivities to be cancelled! If possible, events are usually rescheduled. Everything in the North depends on the weather, so try to be flexible.

Accommodation

Iqaluit offers visitors more choice in accommodation than anywhere else in Nunavut. Depending on your preference and budget, you can choose from full-service hotels, bed and breakfasts (known as "tourist homes" in Nunavut), or the local campground. Unlike other communities in Nunavut, it's almost unheard-of in Iqaluit to share hotel rooms with strangers.

Book ahead, as rooms may be hard to find during busy summer months. Many lodges and hotels cater primarily to summer construction crews, so tourist accommodation isn't always a high priority. With the current boom in construction for the Nunavut capital, space is going to be at a premium. To help ease the crunch with the expected influx of visitors on April 1, 1999, the Town of Iqaluit is offering limited billeting arrangements. For more information, phone the town office.

The **Discovery Lodge Hotel** is a 52-room facility that accommodates 75 people. Single, double and executive-suite occupancy are available. All rooms have double beds, private bath, cable TV, radio and direct-dial telephone. Fax, photocopier, secretarial and telephone message services are available, as are conference facilities for up to 110 people. Guests can also avail themselves of laundry service and complimentary airport shuttle service. The hotel has a restaurant, but meals aren't included in the room rate ($140 per night single, $156 per night double, or for executive-suite rooms, $230 per night for single or $245 for double occupancy). The hotel is centrally located.

The **Regency Frobisher Inn**, located in the Astro Hill Complex, is a 50-room hotel offering single and double occupancy. It accommodates 80 people. Rooms have private bath, telephone and cable TV. Suites are available, as are laundry and room service. They'll also freeze fish caught by anglers staying at the hotel. There is a licensed dining room, banquet room and cocktail lounge, as well as conference facilities for up to 130 people. The room price doesn't include meals. Airport pickup is available on request. Daily room rates are: regular — $160 to $170; corporate, government and tours — $140 to $150.

The **Navigator Inn**, next door to the Discovery Lodge Hotel, accommodates 51 people in 35 rooms. Rooms are equipped with private bath, cable TV, radio and modem-ready telephone. The hotel has conference and translation facilities for up to 125 people, and provides a fax machine, photocopier, and access to e-mail and the Internet. It also has a banquet hall, licensed lounge and dining room, a coffee shop and food take-out service. Rates per night are $139 for single, and $154 for double rooms. The room price doesn't include meals.

The **Toonoonik Hotel/Inns North** is an 18-room, full-service hotel that accommodates up to 35 people. It's recently undergone renovations to its licensed dining room. All rooms have private baths, cable TV and telephone; laundry facilities are also available. Single rooms are $107.95, doubles are $134.95. Meals are not included. The hotel is located between the tip of Koojesse Inlet and the airport.

Pearson's Arctic Homestay, located on the road to Apex, is owned and operated by Iqaluit's former mayor, Bryan Pearson. Arctic Homestay can accommodate up to six people. Rates are $100 per person per night, including breakfast. Special rates are offered for families, and cots are available for children. A shuttle service is available.

Accommodations By The Sea is a six-bedroom facility located in the new Tundra Valley subdivision in Iqaluit. The bathroom facilities are shared. There is phone and cable TV service. Use of kitchen and laundry facilities can be arranged, as can an optional meal service and special long-term and group rates. Rates per night (including breakfast) are $95 for single, and $110 for double rooms. Arrangements can also be made to use the facilities for conferences or banquets. A shuttle service to and from the airport is available.

Restaurants

Because of its size, Iqaluit also offers more choice in dining than do other communities. Several Iqaluit establishments offer full-course meals, some including "country food" such as arctic char, caribou, muskox or *maktaaq*. Meals are expensive. A family of four having hamburger platters and drinks — two drinks for the parents — may easily pay $80. Meals at all major hotels and restaurants are of reasonable quality. The cooking can even be excellent, although quality varies according to the staff of the moment. Ask around to find out where the food is best at the time of your visit.

The following dining establishments are also licensed to serve alcoholic beverages.

The well-appointed **Granite Room** in the Discovery Lodge Hotel serves breakfast, lunch and dinner. Menus feature international cuisine, with some arctic foods available. Daily specials and Sunday brunch are also offered. Banquets, weddings and special events can be held here. This is one of the more expensive places to eat in town, but the quality is usually very good. You're advised to make reservations.

The dining room at the Regency Frobisher Inn specializes in arctic foods on both its lunch and dinner menus. Northern offerings include arctic char (smoked, poached or grilled), scallops, Greenland shrimp and caribou. Standard North American fare is also available, as is an all-you-can-eat Sunday brunch (11 a.m. to 2 p.m.), and a Monday-to-Friday buffet (11 a.m. to 1:30 p.m.).

The dining room at the Navigator Inn is a favorite with local residents for its pizza on Friday nights and its all-you-can-eat pizza buffet on Saturday nights. There is also a smorgasbord on Sunday (5 to 9 p.m.). Book ahead on those days. There are separate menus for breakfast and lunch, although the dining room is closed for breakfast and lunch on Sunday. The dinner menu has a wide range, from standard North American fare to arctic specialties like char and caribou. Daily hot and cold specials are offered. Reservations are recommended.

The igloo-shaped **Kamotiq Inn Restaurant**, complete with fireplace, has daily luncheon buffets as well as all-you-can-eat brunch on Sundays. The Kamotiq offers steaks, seafood, arctic cuisine, ribs, and some Mexican dishes.

The recently renovated dining room at the Toonoonik Hotel/Inns North, open from 7 a.m. to 9 p.m., offers lunch and dinner specials, with an emphasis on "country food."

The **Royal Canadian Legion** offers everything from snacks to full-course hot lunches, and has a cocktail lounge. You must be a member of the Legion or come as the guest of a member.

Several places in town sell snacks and fast food, but like the restaurants, they are expensive compared with their southern counterparts. At Arctic Ventures you can pick up sandwiches, drinks or the makings for a picnic. Arctic Ventures also operates a combined snack bar/gift and convenience store at the Iqaluit Airport. **Kanguk** is a convenience store in the Astro Hill Complex. The **Northern store** has a stand-up coffee shop and snack bar just off its lobby that sells sandwiches, snacks, hamburgers, and the like. The Navigator Inn, in addition to its dining room, has a sit-down coffee shop called **The Galley**, where you can buy quick snacks to eat there or take out. Open daily, the shop's menu includes breakfast and lunch items.

The Snack offers a large eat-in or take-out menu, including several kinds of pizza, burgers, submarine sandwiches, fried chicken and French-Canadian specialties such as *poutine* — french fries smothered with melted cheese and gravy. The Snack offers a 24-hour free delivery service. The **Quick Stop Convenience** store is Iqaluit's licensed outlet for Pizza Hut and Kentucky Fried Chicken, but with prices that make visitors blanch! They also offer other convenience foods.

The **cafeteria at Nunavut Arctic College** is open during college hours.

The **Grind and Brew** offers freshly brewed specialty coffees, desserts and chocolate, with smoking and non-smoking sections. There's also a **coffee shop in the Parnaivik Building**. A new and popular stop for coffee and dessert is the **Fantasy Palace**, on the road out to the airport.

Campers can pick up groceries at the Northern and Arctic Ventures stores.

Entertainment and Recreation

Iqaluit is the only community in the Baffin with a bit of a "night life." Your night on the town may be limited, though, to a meal in a restaurant, a visit to a hotel lounge, a movie, or dancing at the Royal Canadian Legion — if you have visiting privileges or know a member who can sign you in. The **Astro Hill Theatre**, located in the Astro Hill Complex, offers two first-run movies each week. If you're in the mood for a video and have access to a video cassette recorder (VCR), you can choose from video rental outlets: **Mary's Movie Club**, Quick Stop Convenience, and **Video Shack**, upstairs in the Arctic Ventures main store.

Other sources of entertainment are Friday-night bingos, held at varying times and locations to raise funds for service groups, and the occasional concert or dance. Notices for these events are usually posted on bulletin boards in places like the **post office** (located in the same building as the Bank of Montreal), the visitors centre, and banks; they're also announced on local radio shows. Although Iqaluit's entertainment may appeal to local

Canada's 14th capital – Iqaluit – IS A MAJOR CENTRE FOR BUSINESS AND TOURISM IN THE NEW TERRITORY OF NUNAVUT. STRATEGICALLY LOCATED, WE'RE THE GATEWAY TO THE BAFFIN REGION AND A CENTRAL HUB FOR TRANSPORTATION AND COMMUNICATION THROUGHOUT NUNAVUT.

IQALUIT'S BUSINESS COMMUNITY IS WELL-DEVELOPED, HIGHLY COMPETITIVE, AND INCLUDES THE LARGEST SKILLED WORKFORCE IN NUNAVUT. WHETHER YOU ARE VISITING NUNAVUT OR SEEKING A PERMANENT BASE FOR BUSINESS DEVELOPMENT, MAKE IQALUIT YOUR FIRST DESTINATION.

Iqaluit

A capital destination

For more information, please contact:
The Municipality of Iqaluit
Box 460, Iqaluit NT X0A 0H0
Tel: (867) 979-5600 • Fax: (867) 979-5922
E-mail: iqaluit@nunanet.com

Discovery Lodge Hotel

Iqaluit, Nunavut

★ Executive Suite

★ Renowned Licensed Dining

★ Conference Facilities

★ Telephone and Fax

★ Cable TV

★ Complimentary Shuttle Bus

Whether Iqaluit is your final destination or the gateway to your own Arctic adventure, discover for yourself why DISCOVERY LODGE HOTEL is the first choice of experienced northern travellers.

The DISCOVERY LODGE HOTEL is renowned for its excellence in service, comfort and hospitality. Attention to detail by our friendly and attentive staff is what sets us apart.

We offer courtesy vehicles that meet you at the airport, fine cuisine, comfortable rooms with full amenities, an Executive Suite and bright, spacious conference facilities. Laundry, facsimile, copier, secretarial and telephone message service(s) are also available. We are devoted to excellence.

For more information or reservations contact:
Discovery Lodge Hotel
PO Box 387, Iqaluit, NT X0A 0H0
Tel: (867) 979-4433 Fax: (867) 979-6591
www.arctic-travel.com/DIS/covery.html

citizens more than to visitors, you'll find occasional performances by local artists interesting. Community residents get most excited when southern musical groups such as the Barenaked Ladies come to town!

Recreation facilities in town include a **skating arena**, which offers skate rentals, and a **curling rink**, used in the winter. The local **swimming pool** may be closed during summer for repairs, so call ahead if you wish to swim. (Campers will also find showers here.) Several school gymnasiums are often booked by local groups for activities such as badminton, karate, fencing, and indoor soccer. The Town of Iqaluit's department of recreation offers programs at these facilities as well; call for more information. Several clubs and groups also provide a variety of activities such as karate or aquafitness that usually run from September to June. Visitors are welcome to participate, though occasionally a small fee will be charged. Again, contact the town's recreation department for details. The **Frobisher Racquet Club** has squash and racquetball courts, a fitness centre, pool tables, darts, shuffleboard, curling facilities, and a licensed bar and restaurant. To use these facilities, you must be signed in by a member.

Services

The **Baffin Regional Hospital** in Iqaluit handles most local health-care needs. For emergency medical attention, patients should get themselves to the hospital if they can. If an ambulance is required, call the emergency phone number and one will be sent. The municipality provides **ambulance service** 24 hours a day. If possible, call ahead and talk to the nurse-in-charge on emergency duty. For non-emergency medical care, contact the outpatient clinic at the hospital to make an appointment.

Although there's no resident eye doctor in Iqaluit, an ophthalmologist visits every three or four months. Inquire at the hospital. You can purchase eyeglasses at **Baffin Optical**, although you'll need to be in town for a week or two as glasses are made up in Yellowknife. The outlet can also make minor repairs for missing screws, bent arms, etc. If staff are dispensing glasses in other Baffin communities, Baffin Optical can be closed on any given week. A notice to this effect is usually posted. The **Iqaluit Dental Clinic** is located in Iqaluit House. The only drugstore on Baffin Island, **Valupharm Drugs**, is located in the Astro Hill Complex.

St. Jude's Anglican Cathedral, next door to the Nakasuk Elementary School, is an architectural gem. Shaped like an igloo with a spire on top, the church was designed and built by members of the congregation. Inside you'll see beautiful wall hangings behind the altar, depicting Inuit traditional life and church activity. Other unique furnishings include altar rails made from *qamutiit* (sleds) turned on their sides, a *qamutiik* pulpit, sealskin kneeling pads, an altar cross made of narwhal tusks, and a soapstone font dedicated by Queen Elizabeth II, who turned the sod for the building. The church is usually open during the day, but if it's closed, inquire at the Anglican mission house. Although there's no charge to see the church, donations are gratefully accepted. St. Jude's holds separate Sunday services in English and Inuktitut.

Services are also offered in Inuktitut at **St. Simon's Church** in Apex. Established more than 30 years ago, it was the first Anglican church in the area, and is typical of churches in the small communities. Services at **Our Lady of the Assumption** Roman Catholic Church are delivered in a combination of English, French and Inuktitut. Iqaluit also has a **Pentecostal Church** and a **Bahá'i House**. Consult the community calendar section of the local weekly newspaper, *Nunatsiaq News*, for up-to-date listings of church schedules and activities.

Among Iqaluit's service groups are the **Elks**, the **Rotary Club** (which holds lunches Wednesdays at noon in the Frobisher Inn), and the Royal Canadian Legion. **L'Association des francophones du Nunavut** (The Association of Nunavut Francophones) offers programs to promote the cultural and social life of Nunavut's French-speaking residents. It also runs a community **radio station**, CFRT (FM 107.3), which offers 20-plus hours of programming a week, mostly in French but with some Inuktitut and English programming. The Scouting movement is active here, as are several other community service groups that vary from year to year. Contact the Town of Iqaluit's recreation department for details.

DIRECTORY

*Outfitters and tour operators licensed at time of writing.
After March 31/99, check for updated status.

Accommodation

Accommodations By The Sea
Traveller's cheques accepted.
Tel.: (867) 979-6074, (867) 979-3344 or
(867) 979-0219 (leave a message)
Fax: (867) 979-1830
E-mail: BytheSea@VEmail.net

Discovery Lodge Hotel
VISA, MasterCard, American Express,
Diners Club/enRoute, Interac.
Tel.: (867) 979-4433
Fax: (867) 979-6591
E-mail: disclodg@nunanet.com

Navigator Inn
VISA, MasterCard, American Express,
Diners Club/enRoute, Interac.
Tel.: (867) 979-6201
Fax: (867) 979-4296
E-mail: navinn@nunanet.com

Pearson's Arctic Homestay
VISA, traveller's cheques.
Tel.: (867) 979-6408
Fax: (867) 979-6408

Regency Frobisher Inn
VISA, MasterCard, American Express,
Diners Club/enRoute, Interac.
Tel.: (867) 979-2222
Fax: (867) 979-0427
E-mail: frobinn@nunanet.com

Toonoonik Hotel/Inns North
VISA, MasterCard, American Express.
Tel.: (867) 979-6733
Fax: (867) 979-4210
E-mail: mmason@nunanet.com
Web site: www.nunanet.com/
~mmason/toonoo.html

Associations and Service Clubs

L'Association des francophones du Nunavut
The Association of Nunavut Francophones.
Tel.: (867) 979-4606
Fax: (867) 979-0800
E-mail: afi@nunanet.com
Web site: natsiq.nunanet.com/~afi

Elks
Tel.: (867) 979-5791

Rotary Club
No telephone number. Luncheons held Wednesday at Regency Frobisher Inn.

Royal Canadian Legion
Tel.: (867) 979-6215
Fax: (867) 979-4687

Churches

Bahá'í House
Iqaluit Bahá'í Centre.
Services: Call for time and location of upcoming prayer meetings, fireside feasts or gatherings. Bahá'ís visiting Iqaluit can call ahead to arrange temporary accommodation at the Iqaluit Bahá'í Centre, pending availability of room.
Tel.: (867) 979-6580
E-mail: wamphyri@nunanet.com
Web site: www.bahai.org

Our Lady of the Assumption
Roman Catholic Church.
Services: 10 a.m., Sunday mass.
Tel.: (867) 979-5805

Pentecostal Church
Services: 11 a.m., 7 p.m., Sunday;
7:30 p.m., Tuesday (in Inuktitut);
7:30 p.m. Bible study, Wednesday;
8 p.m. prayer service, Saturday.
Tel.: (867) 979-5779
E-mail: wmoore@nunanet.com
Web site: www.nunanet.com/~wmoore

St. Jude's Anglican Cathedral
Services: 10 a.m. (in English), 11 a.m., 7 p.m. (both in Inuktitut), Sunday.
Tel.: (867) 979-5595
E-mail: rbriggs@nunanet.com

St. Simon's Anglican Church
In Apex.
No telephone number.

Entertainment and Recreation

Astro Hill Theatre
Tel.: (867) 979-3500

Frobisher Racquet Club
Tel.: (867) 979-0020
Fax: (867) 979-0051
E-mail: themains@nunanet.com

Iqaluit Arena
Tel.: (867) 979-5621

Iqaluit Curling Rink
Tel.: (867) 979-5622

Iqaluit Department of Recreation
Tel.: (867) 979-5600
Fax: (867) 979-5922

Iqaluit Swimming Pool
Tel.: (867) 979-5624

Mary's Movie Club
1–11 p.m. daily.
Tel.: (867) 979-5722
Fax: (867) 979-5757

Video Shack
In Arctic Ventures store, upstairs.
2–10 p.m., Monday to Friday;
1–10 p.m., Saturday and Sunday.
Tel.: (867) 979-1351

Medical Services

Baffin Optical
10 a.m.–6 p.m., Monday to Friday.
Tel.: (867) 979-4300

Baffin Regional Hospital
General inquiries – Tel.: (867) 979-7300
Emergencies – Tel.: (867) 979-7350
For appointments – Tel.: (867) 979-7352

Iqaluit Dental Clinic
8:30 a.m.–5 p.m., Monday to Friday.
Tel.: (867) 979-4437
Fax: (867) 979-1365

Iqaluit Emergency Services (Ambulance and Fire)
Tel.: (867) 979-4422
Web site: www.nunanet.com/~jatagak

* Outfitters/Tour Operators/Visitors Centre

Eetuk Outfitting
Tel.: (867) 979-1984
Fax: (867) 979-1994

Kimuk Adventure Tours
Tel.: (867) 979-2777
Fax: (867) 979-1554
E-mail: kimuk@nunanet.com

NorthWinds Arctic Adventures
Tel.: (867) 979-0551
Fax: (867) 979-0573
E-mail: plandry@nunanet.com
Web site: www.northwinds-arctic.com

Nunavut Tourism
P.O. Box 1450, Iqaluit NT,
X0A 0H0 Canada
Tel.: 1-800-491-7910 (for Canada and the United States)
Tel.: (867) 979-6551
Fax: (867) 979-1261
E-mail: nunatour@nunanet.com
Web site: www.nunatour.nt.ca

Purlaavik Outfitting
Tel.: (867) 979-6094
Fax: (867) 979-4070

Qairrulik Outfitting Ltd.
Tel.: (867) 979-6280
Fax: (867) 979-1950

Unikkaarvik Visitors Centre
Tel.: (867) 979-4636
Fax: (867) 979-1261
E-mail: nunatour@nunanet.com

Restaurants/Snack Bars/Fast Food

Arctic Ventures
Tel.: (867) 979-5992

Cafeteria, Nunavut Arctic College
Call in the morning.
Tel.: (867) 979-1260

Fantasy Palace
Tel.: (867) 979-3963

The Galley
Tel.: (867) 979-6201

Granite Room
In Discovery Lodge Hotel.
Tel.: (867) 979-4433
Fax: (867) 979-6591

Grind and Brew
Tel.: (867) 979-0606
Fax: (867) 979-7081

Kamotiq Inn Restaurant
VISA, MasterCard, American Express,
Diners Club/enRoute.
Tel.: (867) 979-5937
Fax: (867) 979-6098

Kanguk Convenience and Coffee Shop
Tel.: (867) 979-4781

Navigator Inn
Tel.: (867) 979-6201
Fax: (867) 979-4296

Parnaivik Coffee Shop
Tel.: (867) 979-2860

Quick Stop Convenience and Coffee Shop
Tel.: (867) 979-0657 or (867) 979-2961

Regency Frobisher Inn
Tel.: (867) 979-2222
Fax: (867) 979-0427

Royal Canadian Legion
Tel.: (867) 979-6215
Fax: (867) 979-4687

The Snack
Tel.: (867) 979-6767

Toonoonik Hotel/Inns North
Tel.: (867) 979-6733
Fax: (867) 979-4210

Services

Airport
Tel.: (867) 979-5224 or (867) 979-5225

Baffin Regional Chamber of Commerce
Tel.: (867) 979-4653
Fax: (867) 979-2929
E-mail: brcc@nunanet.com
Web site: nunanet.com/~brcc

CBC Radio Station (AM 1230)
Tel.: (867) 979-6100
Fax: (867) 979-6147

Canadian Helicopters
Tel.: (709) 686-2095
Fax: (709) 686-2800
E-mail: gpenney@stjohns.chc.ca

Department of Sustainable Development, Government of Nunavut
(or until April/99, GNWT's Resources, Wildlife and Economic Development)
Tel.: (867) 979-7800
Fax: (867) 979-8809

Hunters and Trappers Organization
Tel.: (867) 979-6848
Fax: (867) 979-3390

Iqaluit Centennial Library
Tel.: (867) 979-5400
Fax: (867) 979-1373

Iqaluit Chamber of Commerce
Tel.: (867) 979-4095
Fax: (867) 979-2929

Iqaluit Town Office
Tel.: (867) 979-5600
For billeting arrangements on
April 1, 1999:
Tel.: (867) 979-5617
Fax: (867) 979-5922

Iqaluit Trade and Promotion Office
Tel.: (867) 979-3156
Fax: (867) 979-2929

NWT Liquor Commission/Iqaluit Liquor Warehouse
Tel.: (867) 979-5918
Fax: (867) 979-5386

Nunatsiaq News
Tel.: (867) 979-5357
Fax: (867) 979-4763
E-mail: nunat@nunanet.com
Web site: www.nunatsiaq.com

Police (RCMP)
Tel.: (867) 979-5211
Fax: (867) 979-1842

Post Office
In Iqaluit House.
Tel.: (867) 979-5864

Radio Iqaluit (CFRT – FM 107.3)
Tel.: (867) 979-4606
Web site: natsiq.nunanet.com/~afi/
 CFRT/index.html

Schools

Baffin Divisional Education Council
Tel.: (867) 979-5236

Inuksuk High School
Tel.: (867) 979-5281
Fax: (867) 979-4380

Joamie Ilinniarvik School
Tel.: (867) 979-6206
Fax: (867) 979-0686
Web site: www.nunanet.com/~joamie

Nakasuk School
Tel.: (867) 979-5335
Fax: (867) 979-5994
Web site: www.nunanet.com/~nakasuk/

Nanook School
Tel.: (867) 979-6597
Fax: (867) 979-0440

Nunavut Arctic College
Tel.: (867) 979-4100
Fax: (867) 979-4119
Web site: www.nunanet.com/~nachq

Taxis

Iqaluit Transport (Apex Auto)
Tel.: (867) 979-4235

Kilabuk and Parry Taxi Service
Tel.: (867) 979-8858

Nanook Polar Taxi Co.
Tel.: (867) 979-5333

Pai-Pa Taxi Ltd.
Tel.: (867) 979-5222

Weather Information
Tel.: (867) 979-6448
Web site weather forecast:
www.tor.ec.gc.ca/forecasts/index.html
(check under Regional Weather
Summaries) or www.infonorth.org

Shopping

Arctic Creations
Tel.: (867) 979-1841
Fax: (867) 979-0270
E-mail: mell@nunanet.com

Arctic Ventures
Main store:
10 a.m.–10 p.m., Monday to Saturday;
1–10 p.m., Sunday.
VISA, MasterCard, Interac.
Tel.: (867) 979-5992
Fax: (867) 979-4207
E-mail: ventures@nunanet.com

Airport outlet:
7:30 a.m.–6 p.m., Monday;
7:30 a.m.–3:30 p.m., Tuesday;
7:30 a.m.–5 p.m., Wednesday;
7:30 a.m.–7:30 p.m., Thursday;
7:30 a.m.–5 p.m., Friday;
9:30 a.m.–3:30 p.m., Saturday;
12–3 p.m., Sunday.
VISA, MasterCard, Interac.
Tel.: (867) 979-0043

Arts and Crafts Centre
Part of Nunavut Arctic College.
Tel.: (867) 979-7265

Coman Arctic Galleries Ltd.
10 a.m.–4 p.m., Monday to Friday.
Phone first for other times; will open
upon request.
VISA, MasterCard.
Tel.: (867) 979-2373
Fax: (867) 979-6854
E-mail: raisins@nunanet.com

D.J. Sensations
10 a.m.–5:30 p.m., Monday to Saturday.
Closed Sunday.
VISA, MasterCard, Interac.
Tel.: 1-888-979-0650 or (867) 979-0650
Fax: (867) 979-0045
E-mail: dj@nunanet.com

D.J. Specialties
Sells mainly groceries.
10 a.m.–10 p.m., Monday to Saturday;
noon–10 p.m., Sunday.
VISA, MasterCard, Interac.
Tel.: (867) 979-4351

Iqaluit Fine Arts Studio
8 a.m.–6 p.m., Monday to Saturday.
By appointment Sunday evening.
VISA, MasterCard, American Express,
Interac.
Tel.: (867) 979-5748
Fax: (867) 979-6092
E-mail: webster@nunanet.com

Kanguk Convenience Store
9 a.m.–8 p.m., Monday to Friday;
12–6 p.m., Saturday and Sunday.
Closed holidays.
VISA, MasterCard, Interac.
Tel.: (867) 979-4781
Fax: (867) 979-4869

Mary's Movie Club
1–11 p.m. every day except Christmas
and New Year's Day.
Tel.: (867) 979-5722
Fax: (867) 979-5757

Northern Country Arts
10 a.m.–6 p.m., Monday to Friday;
1–6 p.m., Saturday and Sunday.
VISA, Interac.
Tel.: (867) 979-0067
Fax: (867) 979-3330
E-mail: northart@nunanet.com
Web site: www.nunanet.com/~northart

Northern Store
10 a.m.–8 p.m., Monday
to Friday; 10 a.m.–6 p.m., Saturday.
VISA, MasterCard, Interac.
Tel.: (867) 979-5277
Fax: (867) 979-6635

Tununiqmiut Arts and Crafts
Located in the Toonoonik Hotel/
Inns North.
9 a.m.–9 p.m. every day.
Will open on request.
VISA, MasterCard, American Express,
Discovery, Interac.
Tel.: (867) 979-3511
Fax: (867) 979-4210

Valupharm Drugs
10 a.m.–1 p.m. and 2–6:30 p.m.,
Monday to Friday; 1–5 p.m., Saturday.
Closed Sunday.
VISA, MasterCard, Interac.
Tel.: (867) 979-0655 or (867) 979-3055
Fax: (867) 979-0654

Tours

Elders' Facilities
Contact recreation and community
services (Town of Iqaluit) to arrange
a visit to either the **Pairijait Tigumivik
Elders' Facility** or the **Qammaq** in Apex.
Tel.: (867) 979-5617
Fax: (867) 979-3712

Nunatta Sunakkutaangit Museum
1–5 p.m., Tuesday to Sunday.
Tel.: (867) 979-5537
Fax: (867) 979-4533
E-mail: museum@nunanet.com

94. QAUMMAARVIIT TERRITORIAL HISTORIC PARK
by Bruce Rigby

Qaummaarviit (pronounced "cow-mar-veet") is one of three territorial parks around Iqaluit, but the only one dedicated to preserving a cultural site of historic importance.

Called "places that have rays of light" in Inuktitut, the site has long been of interest to residents and visitors alike; well over 750 years of intermittent occupancy are evident here. Qaummaarviit was made a historic park by the GNWT in 1985.

The People and Their History
The narrow island on which Qaummaarviit sits is part of a small group of islands adjacent to Peterhead Inlet at the north end of Frobisher Bay. The island is only one-quarter square kilometre in total area. Archeologists generally agree that no more than 25 people lived here at any one time.

The site preserves a record of the Thule people, who originated in Alaska some 1,000 years ago and slowly spread across the Canadian Arctic to Greenland. Scientists aren't sure what precipitated this migration, although many feel the Thule were taking advantage of improved weather conditions to expand their harvesting area and travel to regions they were previously unable to reach.

Thule culture is distinguished from others that resided in Nunavut by its reputation for inventiveness and adaptability. In addition to using traditional modes of transportation such as the dogsled and *qajaq* (kayak), the Thule are also credited with developing the *umiaq*, or "women's boat." The *umiaq* was a large skin boat capable of holding entire families and their belongings. The *umiaq* was generally paddled by women, as men travelled in the faster and more mobile *qajaq*. The Thule were adept at hunting all forms of land and sea mammals, including the mammoth bowhead whale.

Upon their arrival here, the Thule discovered they were not alone. Already resident were the Dorset Inuit, or *Tuniit*, who had occupied the eastern Arctic for approximately 1,500 years. The *Tuniit* are still a popular folklore topic among Inuit. Elders tell stories of the giant-like people who produced intricate artwork, only to disappear after the arrival of the Thule. Some archeologists feel the demise of the *Tuniit* was precipitated by their inability to adapt to changes in wildlife and climate. Although there is no evidence that the *Tuniit* occupied Qaummaarviit itself, tools and implements have been found that show they used the area.

Although the Thule are generally understood to be a marine culture, the location of Qaummaarviit presents many questions to researchers, as it is located on one of the innermost inlets of Frobisher Bay and more than 100 kilometres from the normal winter location of the floe edge. However, the great variety of animal bones found at the site indicates it was likely chosen because of its proximity to abundant land species, which were used for both clothing and food.

Evidence shows that Qaummaarviit was occupied until approximately the end of the 18th century, when it was abandoned as a permanent site. Scientists have suggested that just as the expansion of the Thule into this region may have corresponded with a warming climatic period, the departure from the site roughly corresponds with a period termed the "little ice age," a period of global cooling that began around AD 1400.

What to See and Do

Qaummaarviit is comprised of a variety of features. In the summer, luxuriant patches of vegetation scattered throughout the park seem out of character with the rocky landscape around them. This is caused by the decay of buried organic materials that collected at the site over many years. Known by archeologists as "middens," these areas are usually rich with materials and artifacts for analysis. Thousands of tools have been recovered, as well as the remains of animals such as ringed and harp seals, caribou, walruses, bowhead whales, beluga whales, foxes, wolves, dogs and birds.

Central to the site are the remains of 11 semi-buried sod houses. These houses are more permanent versions of the snow *iglu* still occasionally used across Nunavut. And although sod houses used whalebone, sod and stone as their building materials, they exhibited many characteristics similar to the traditional snowhouse. As with the snow *iglu*, a sod house's entryway was constructed lower than the main living area to trap cold air and prevent it from entering the dwelling. Sod houses, like *igluit* (three or more igloos; two are *igluuk*), also used a "sleeping platform" from which daily activities were directed. Visitors will notice, too, that care was taken to align the dwellings in a southeasterly direction to maximize light and heat received from the sun. Several tent rings indicate Qaummaarviit was used in summer as well.

As part of the excavation and development of the site, two house foundations have been left open for viewing. A $3 guidebook available from the **Unikkaarvik Visitors Centre** in Iqaluit provides good background information and describes some of the sights along the island's well-marked trail. The trail winds its way from a small cove on the south end of the island and terminates at a series of grave sites, tent rings and meat caches. Interpretive signs explain features of interest at length.

Planning a Trip

Qaummaarviit is accessible by ski, dogsled or snowmobile in the winter months, and by boat during the open-water season. However, since the park is approximately 12 kilometres from Iqaluit, it is recommended that visitors take advantage of local outfitting services, many of which provide on-site interpretation and a snack. Arrangements can be made through the Unikkaarvik Visitors Centre.

If you hire an outfitter, try to go by dogteam, one of the most enjoyable ways to get to the park during the lengthening days of spring. Such trips can take place well into June, as the sea ice remains several metres thick and safe for travelling, despite a rather unsettling layer of surface water. If travelling this late in the season, don't be alarmed to find your excursion scheduled well into the evening hours to take advantage of the cooler temperatures that make sled-pulling easier for dogs. You may also find that your outfitter has dressed his or her dogs with colorful booties; these protect the animals' feet from the sharp edges of granular snow and sea ice. As the season progresses, cracks of open water will widen, eventually making it unsafe to travel to the island until breakup is complete.

If dogsled is your chosen mode of transportation, allow yourself the better part of a day to travel to and explore Qaummaarviit. Travel by snow-mobile and *qamutiik* is much quicker, and will significantly decrease the length of your trip. Skiing to the park takes a good day, depending on your experience and ability. Also, remember that Frobisher Bay is subject to tides of up to 15 metres, which can affect travel in any season. Earlier in the season this simply means there is a greater expanse of rough ice to climb to get to the island. Later in the season, tides affect both the amount of surface water on the ice and the amount and location of open water near the shore.

Whether travelling in winter or summer, visitors should dress warmly. New, high-tech gear has a lot to offer, but you'll find many locals opt for heavy parkas when on the bay. The air temperature here is generally cooler than on land, and the lack of any high topography or vegetation will ensure that even the lightest breeze will have a significant cooling effect. A general adage used by residents is "dress for the worst, enjoy the best," so make sure you have foul-weather gear, warm mitts or gloves and a woolen tuque. Good quality sunglasses are also a must to prevent snow blindness in spring and reduce the reflection of sunlight off the water in summer.

Breakup in the north end of Frobisher Bay usually takes place around mid-July. Remember that in the early open-water season there is often ice still floating in the bay. Strong onshore winds can trap even the most experienced boaters. Most local outfitters use 22- or 24-foot freighter canoes or Lake Winnipeg boats. These boats are designed to transport heavy loads over long distances and are powered by outboard motors. Boat travel to Qaummaarviit takes from 30 to 45 minutes, depending on tidal conditions and wind. Camping is not permitted.

DIRECTORY

Unikkaarvik Visitors Centre
In Iqaluit.
For assistance in planning a trip to the park.
Tel.: (867) 979-4636
Fax: (867) 979-1261
E-mail: nunatour@nunanet.com

95. SYLVIA GRINNELL TERRITORIAL PARK

by Colleen Dupuis

Set on the outskirts of Iqaluit, Sylvia Grinnell Territorial Park is 148 hectares of natural beauty bound to make an impression on any visitor. Bring your camera; photo opportunities abound!

As its name suggests, the park's most popular features are the gentle falls and crystal waters of the Sylvia Grinnell River, named for the daughter of one of the financiers of American explorer Charles Francis Hall. The lower part of the river — from the falls to nearby Koojesse Inlet — is part of the tidal system of the inlet and only navigable at high tide. During extremely high tides these gentle falls all but disappear, becoming an extensive series of rapids.

What to See and Do

Sylvia Grinnell Territorial Park is a favorite picnic site as well as a popular fishing spot. In the past, the river had an abundance of large arctic char. It is still a great place to catch smaller, pan-sized char. Remember to get a fishing licence before you drop your line.

Camping at the park is also quite common, although there are no tent platforms or running water. Small plateaus on the riverbank provide some shelter for campers. Future plans call for a short-term camping area about one kilometre upriver of the falls/viewing platform, just above the tidal flats at the foot of the bank. Other development is planned for the park on the west side of the river, around Peterhead Inlet and down to Qaummaarviit Territorial Historic Park.

The park is an ideal spot to spend a day exploring. Flora and fauna are varied and abundant. Several species of rare plants have been identified here, including the woodsia fern, one of the rarest plants in the country. In the summer, the tundra floor becomes a carpet of mountain avens, arctic heather, saxifrages, arctic poppies — the proposed official flower of Nunavut — and other wildflowers. The subtle colors and delicate foliage are a photographer's delight.

Wildlife sightings are not uncommon, either. Caribou frequent the area in winter and spring; a few remain throughout summer. Arctic fox dens are also located within the park, so keep your eyes peeled for mother foxes returning to feed their young.

Southern Baffin Island is an area of major bird activity in summer, and the park is no exception. As many as 40 species can be found here during the balmy days of June and July. This area is the most southerly breeding ground of the elusive common ringed plover. Other commonly sighted species include the Lapland longspur and the snow bunting. Avid birders should also be on the lookout for the Northern wheatear. Rarely seen in North America south of the Labrador coast, this bird nests in the park before its winter migration to Africa and India.

Once you've descended the steep riverbank, walking is relatively easy at Sylvia Grinnell. Nonetheless, the rocky tundra terrain is not the place for tennis shoes, so wear sturdy hiking boots. No formal trails exist in the park, but an old military road runs near the river. It traverses prime birding and wildlife-viewing areas before doubling back around the north end of the airport, an approximate 10-kilometre hike. The scenery is spectacular. Don't forget your binoculars, lunch and sunscreen.

The entire area around the park was gouged by massive glaciers; deposits are plentiful in the Sylvia Grinnell Valley. A recently constructed viewing platform, perched some 55 metres above the falls, offers a commanding view of the work of these ice-age behemoths. Here you can easily trace the path of the receding glaciers and the deposits they left behind. It's also a great place to watch the sun set.

If you are interested in archeological sites, there are also a few stone cairns and Thule ruins in the park. One of the best is just south of the falls on the east side of the river. Even in the absence of defined trails, navigation is easy: the river is to your right as you head south and to your left as you head north. Future development plans call for a footbridge across the river. Until the bridge is constructed, however, don't attempt to cross on your own. Sylvia Grinnell River may look relatively benign, but fording it is difficult and dangerous at the best of times. You may be able to make arrangements with local licensed outfitters to take you to the far side by boat during high tides. Outfitters are not always available, however.

Planning a Trip

From the centre of Iqaluit, it's an easy 30-minute walk to the park; new signage will help visitors find their way. From the three-way stop by the gas station, proceed north to the Aeroplex Building, number 1084. Turn left and continue past the yield sign, until you see the sign for Sylvia Grinnell Territorial Park. Turn right and follow the signs. This route will take you past some interesting local attractions, including an area near a stream where a local dogteam is kept for the summer. Feel free to take pictures, but be careful not to get too close to the dogs. If you don't want to walk, the short cab ride to the park is $5 per person. There are no phones in the park, so don't forget to make arrangements to be picked up later.

Facilities in the park include a parking area with two nearby outhouses, barbecue pits and the new viewing platform. There is no fee for either day use or camping. Vehicle use in the park is not encouraged, although you may encounter the odd all-terrain vehicle.

Enjoy your visit to the park, but always keep in mind that although just outside Iqaluit, going for a hike here means going out on the tundra. Use caution not to disturb flora any more than necessary; signs of your passing will remain long after you're gone. Carry out your garbage, too. And remember to let someone know your plans, and when you expect to be back.

96. KIMMIRUT

by Robert Jaffray

Take a stroll through this seaside community and you'll quickly notice how differently things are done here.

Population:	397 (Inuit: 91%, non-Inuit: 9%) Source: 1996 Census of Canada
Telephone Area Code:	867
Time Zone:	Eastern Time
Postal Code:	X0A 0N0
How to Get There:	Possible routes:
	• Ottawa/Montreal-Iqaluit-Kimmirut
	• Kangerlussuaq (Greenland)-Iqaluit-Kimmirut
	• Winnipeg-Rankin Inlet-Iqaluit-Kimmirut
	• Edmonton-Yellowknife-Rankin Inlet-Iqaluit-Kimmirut
	Iqaluit to Kimmirut (121 kilometres south) is via First Air
Banks:	None. Cash and traveller's cheques are preferable. Credit cards are accepted by certain businesses
Alcohol:	Alcohol and alcoholic beverages are prohibited
Taxis:	No, although the Co-op, which owns the Kimik Hotel, will meet planes and ferry guests around in their trucks

Houses usually face the water instead of the street so residents can keep an eye on the comings and goings of hunters and fishermen. Children play "Inuit baseball," where the runner runs the opposite direction from southern-style baseball and can be tagged out by a thrown ball. Young girls attend to baby siblings by carrying them in an *amauti*, a hooded woman's parka.

Most Kimmirut residents are carvers, and you can often watch them make their living with grinder and file outside their homes. But economic realities also require them to work in the wage economy for one of the local retail stores, the hamlet, or the territorial government. In addition, virtually everyone participates in the traditional economy of hunting and fishing, a vital link between old and new.

History

There is a long history of human presence in the area around Kimmirut (pronounced "kim-mi-root"). Archeological remains indicate people have occupied the region for some 4,000 years; evidence of Thule, Dorset and Pre-Dorset cultures is scattered throughout the area.

First contact with Europeans came in the 17th century when Hudson's Bay Co. supply ships travelling through Hudson Strait began trading with Inuit. Contact intensified in 1860 with the arrival of American and Scottish whalers. When Robert Kinnes of the Scottish-owned Tay Whale Fishing Company established a mica mine nearby, it drew Inuit to the area. In 1900, the Anglican Church established its second mission on Baffin Island, building a mission house across the bay from today's community. Hoping to capitalize on the abundant white fox population and the growing dependence of Inuit on non-traditional goods, the Hudson's Bay Co. erected Baffin Island's first trading post here in 1911. An RCMP post was established on the east side of Glasgow Inlet in 1927.

Until a U.S. army base arrived in Frobisher Bay in 1945, Kimmirut (known until recently as Lake Harbour) was the administrative centre for the south Baffin. RCMP officers from the Lake Harbour post patrolled as far north as Pangnirtung, west beyond Cape Dorset, and all the camps around the Hudson's Bay Co. post of Frobisher Bay. After the jet runway was built at Frobisher Bay (now called Iqaluit), focus began to shift away from Lake Harbour and toward Nunavut's future capital, Iqaluit.

The community continued to grow, however. A federal school was established in the 1950s, and a government-administered nursing station soon followed.

Kimmirut: Its Land and Wildlife

Kimmirut is situated beside the ocean at the northern extremity of Glasgow Inlet, part of a larger body of water known as North Bay. About 60 metres across the water lies the landmark for which the community is named — a *kimmirut* (heel), a rocky outcrop that resembles a human heel.

Visitors to Kimmirut will get a crash course in tidal action if they are here for more than a few hours. Tides, which are sometimes greater than 11 metres, are strikingly apparent as the water level rises and falls along the sheer rock face of the heel. In winter, very low tides sometimes pull the ice down far enough to reveal a dazzling ice wall more than 10 metres high.

The bulk of the town stretches along the narrow strip of land that runs north/south along the ocean. Recent housing additions dot surrounding hills. Most of the community's commercial ventures are in the older section of town. Here you'll find the hamlet administration, **school**, retail stores, and visitor services. A few home-run businesses are located 'uptown,' as are the **airport** and municipal services garages.

It is not uncommon to walk within minutes of the community and see a caribou lope across your path. Equally common are tiny lemmings that dart from rock to rock. Seagulls frequent the area; ravens talk to you from their perches overhead. On a calm summer day, a seal may pop its inquisitive head out of the water or a beluga whale may find its way into a nearby bay. Further afield you may see a fox, arctic hare, or even a wolf, at a distance. On rare occasions, polar bears have come into the community.

Throughout the community and the surrounding hillsides you'll find abundant and varied flora. Dwarf fireweed, white heather and arctic poppies add a delightful touch of color throughout summer. You may even see dandelions in some areas, their growth fostered by a climate warmer than any other on Baffin Island.

Tours

The best place to start exploring is **The Katannilik Park Centre**, located at the crossroads of the community in the white and green building with the large caribou logo on the outside. Just recently completed, the Centre has displays on the park, local geology, community history, traditional lifestyles and climatic anomalies, among others. The Centre also boasts a resource centre, video theatre, and working waterfall.

The Centre is also the place to pick up a community brochure, containing a detailed map of Kimmirut, local sites of interest, and a short history of the surrounding area. Added touches like a syllabics chart (Inuktitut, the language of Inuit, is often written in syllabics) and a concise list of useful phone numbers make it a good reference document.

You may want to hike to the top of the hill behind the runway for a great view of town and the surrounding area. To the south lies Hudson Strait. On clear days you can sometimes see *Qikiqtarjuaq* ("Big Island") to the southwest, the largest island on the south coast of Baffin Island.

Head due west of Kimmirut to get to the reversing falls, where Soper Lake drains into the ocean. You can hike overland, or take the new road. Try to time your hike with the high tide of a full or new moon and watch the ocean reverse this drainage and flood Soper Lake with sea water. You can also walk east from the town around the end of Glasgow Inlet and visit historic sites such as the original RCMP post and the site of the Anglican mission house. Here you can also climb onto the *kimmirut*. Longer treks can be made into Katannilik Territorial Park Reserve, which is a minimum six-hour round trip.

Two outfitters are currently registered in Kimmirut. The **Mayukalik Hunters and Trappers Organization** arranges ocean day trips to view wildlife, icebergs, waterfalls and sea mammals — usually ringed and harp seals, but occasionally walrus and beluga whales. They can also arrange community tours for individuals and groups ($30 per person), and offer shuttle service to and from Soper Lake for travellers arriving by canoe from Katannilik Territorial Park Reserve. **Qayaq Nunavut** also handles ocean trips, and arranges canoeing and hiking trips in the Soper Valley.

Shopping

Kimmirut's two largest retail stores are both located in the older section of town. The **Kimik Co-op** carries a good variety of groceries, as well as dry goods and hardware. It is also the only place in town that sells naphtha. The **Northern store** offers a similar selection of goods, but features more clothing and devotes less space to groceries. Both stores have a selection of souvenirs.

Events

Special events are sometimes held in the community centre, called the **Akavak Centre**. Contact the hamlet recreation co-ordinator for more details. When no events are scheduled, the Centre hosts a variety of sports activities.

Accommodation and Dining

The **Kimik Hotel** is located above the Co-op store. Sixteen people can stay in eight rooms, each with its own washroom, for $185 per person per night, including meals, or $125 per person without meals. Summers can be especially busy for the hotel, so it is necessary to phone ahead to make arrangements. Ask for a room facing the water; they offer great views of Glasgow Inlet and the area across the harbor. Sometimes seals and even whales can be seen from this vantage point. If your room doesn't face the water, you can still enjoy the view from the hotel's restaurant and coffee shop.

If you would prefer to stay with a local family for a few nights, you can contact the Hunters and Trappers Organization to participate in the community's unique Home Stay Program, in which a local family will host you for the night. The cost is $120 per person per night and includes both breakfast and a large traditional daytime or evening meal. Most home stay families can only accommodate two people, so larger groups will be divided throughout the community. These parties can still arrange to have their evening meal together, however.

Although there is no campground in Kimmirut, plans are in the works to designate one. Check at The Katannilik Park Centre for the best locations to pitch your tent or latest developments in a designated campground.

The hotel restaurant is open to the public, but serving hotel guests is their first priority. You can stop by any morning or afternoon for coffee; a muffin or piece of pie may also be available. If you're looking for a full meal, inquire with the cook or hotel manager. They will often allow you to dine with hotel guests, or even provide a second sitting, but give them a few hours' notice. Breakfast is $10, lunch is $20, and supper is $30. Local families also prepare meals for visitors and serve traditional foods such as caribou stew, char chowder, bannock (a traditional fried bread), berries and tea. Arrangements can be made through the Hunters and Trappers Organization, given at least a day's notice. The cost is currently $24 per person.

Services

Kimmirut's **Health Centre** is located beside the Northern store. Drop-in clinics run from 9 to 11:30 a.m. weekdays. Two resident nurses handle all medical situations, most of them on site.

DIRECTORY

*Outfitters and tour operators licensed at time of writing.
After March 31/99, check for updated status.

Accommodation and Dining

Kimik Hotel
VISA, MasterCard, American Express,
Diners Club/enRoute, Interac.
Tel.: (867) 939-2093
Fax: (867) 939-2005

* Outfitters/Tour Operators/Visitors Centre

The Katannilik Park Centre
Usually open 9 a.m.–12 p.m. and
1–5 p.m., Monday to Friday. May
have some evening and weekend
hours, which will likely be posted.
Tel.: (867) 939-2084
Fax: (867) 939-2406
E-mail: rjaffray@nunanet.com

Mayukalik Hunters and Trappers Organization
Inquire about Kimmirut's home stay
accommodation program here.
Tel.: (867) 939-2355
Fax: (867) 939-2112

Qayaq Nunavut
Tel.: (867) 939-2031 or (867) 939-2221
Fax: (867) 939-2334

Services

Airport
First Air
Tel.: (867) 939-2250
Fax: (867) 939-2158

Akavak Centre
Community centre.
Tel.: (867) 939-2113

Church
St. Paul's Anglican Church
No phone.

Department of Sustainable Development, Government of Nunavut
(or until April/99, Resources, Wildlife
and Economic Development, GNWT)
Tel.: (867) 939-2416
Fax: (867) 939-2406
E-mail: rjaffray@nunanet.com
Renewable resources officer:
Tel.: (867) 939-2004
Fax: (867) 939-2112

Hamlet Office
Tel.: (867) 939-2247
Fax: (867) 939-2045
Web site: www.arctic-travel.com/
kimmirut/index.html

Health Centre
Tel.: (867) 939-2217
Fax: (867) 939-2068

Police (RCMP)
Tel.: (867) 939-2333
Fax: (867) 939-2146

Post Office
Located on first floor of Kimmirut
Hamlet Office building.
10 a.m.–12 p.m., Monday to Friday.
Afternoon hours depend on plane
schedule and, hence, delivery of mail.
No phone.

Radio Station (FM 107.1)
Tel.: (867) 939-2126 or (867) 939-2380

Schools
Nunavut Arctic College
Tel.: (867) 939-2414
Fax: (867) 939-2299

Qaqqalik School
Tel.: (867) 939-2221
Fax: (867) 939-2334

Weather Information
Tel.: (867) 939-2254
Fax: (867) 939-2045
Web site weather forecast:
www.infonorth.org

Shopping

Kimik Co-op
9 a.m.–noon, 1–6 p.m., Monday and
Tuesday; 9 a.m.–noon, 1–8 p.m.,
Wednesday; 9 a.m.–noon, 1–9 p.m.,
Thursday and Friday; 9 a.m.–2 p.m.,
Saturday. Closed Sunday.
VISA, MasterCard, American Express,
Diners Club/enRoute, Interac.
Tel.: (867) 939-2322
Fax: (867) 939-2005

Northern Store
10 a.m.–noon, 1:30–6 p.m., Monday
to Wednesday; 10 a.m.–noon,
1:30–8 p.m., Thursday and Friday;
1–5 p.m., Saturday. Closed Saturdays
in summer, and every Sunday.
VISA, MasterCard, Interac.
Tel.: (867) 939-2242
Fax: (867) 939-2353

97. KATANNILIK TERRITORIAL PARK RESERVE
by Robert Jaffray

Spanning the Meta Incognita Peninsula in southern Baffin Island, Katannilik Territorial Park Reserve — "the place of waterfalls" — is a surprisingly fertile arctic oasis tucked in the middle of an ancient and unforgiving landscape.

Central to the park is the Soper River Valley, some 110 kilometres of meandering wilderness punctuated by countless cascades. Along the river itself, on its many tributaries, and in the streams and rivulets flowing down the sides of the valley, these waterfalls echo the recurring theme of the park.

Katannilik stretches northward from the top of Pleasant Inlet along the coast of Hudson Strait (just outside the community of Kimmirut) toward the south shore of Frobisher Bay, following the Soper Valley and a traditional overland trail called the *Itijjagiaq*. The park extends east and west beyond the valley, encompassing some of the rivers, lakes and hills that make up the low relief of the lower plateau. Known locally as *Kuujjuaq* — "big river" — the Soper was designated a Canadian heritage river in 1992 for its cultural significance in the lives of Inuit, its natural beauty and its countless opportunities for recreation.

The Land and Wildlife

A complex series of folds, plunges and shears dating from the formation of the Earth make Katannilik rich with a variety of rock formations and exposed geological domains. The park is comprised of three distinct landscapes.

The first starts at the south shore of Frobisher Bay, where the Itijjagiaq Trail begins. Rising 670 metres from sea level to the plateau of the Meta Incognita Peninsula, the landscape is a playground of deep gorges and sloping valleys. Increasing elevation means shelter becomes scarce as the topography flattens out. It also means a corresponding decrease in vegetation, as temperatures drop.

The plateau of the Meta Incognita Peninsula has changed little since the last glaciers receded. Glacial scars are readily discernible, and the shallow, rolling topography is testament to the force of these frozen behemoths. Rocks and boulders scattered across the smooth surface of the plateau look like they've fallen from the sky in a rock shower, adding to the already unearthly appearance.

The third region of the park is the Soper Valley, a product of receding glaciers, water erosion and the existing thermal oasis. Over the millennia, the water level of the river has fluctuated, leaving terraces throughout the valley floor. These terraces range from three to 30 metres above the current height of the river. The river valley is most impressive at its northern end. To the south, the valley broadens and the walls start to diminish as the topography descends gently toward Hudson Strait.

Plant life in Katannilik varies from virtually nil in some areas to astoundingly abundant in others. Where conditions are inhospitable, such as the plateau, you can still often find plant life within millimetres of the ground. You won't need to look so diligently in the abundant Soper Valley, however, where summer temperatures average some 5° C higher than nearby Kimmirut, itself the warmest community on Baffin Island.

In 1930, naturalist Joseph Dewey Soper, after whom the river was named, explored the area while working for the Canadian government. Soper catalogued much of the valley's plant life, including willow trees as high as 3.6 metres, the tallest in the region. Uncommonly large willows still grow in a few well-protected areas of the valley.

Four communities of vegetation have been identified in the valley, each composed of plants with common nutritive needs. The dwarf shrub/heath tundra community is primarily made up of willow, dwarf birch, Lapland rosebay, Labrador tea, and arctic heather. This community, which needs more warmth than others, is found in moist areas below 210 metres in elevation.

The grassland tundra group, with its characteristic tussocks of moss surrounded by shallow water, is the one you want to avoid hiking across. This group includes sedges, arctic cotton, sphagnum moss, bistorts and willows, and is usually found along bodies of water in the river valley.

The bedrock/hill summit community is in exposed areas that are neither wet nor warm. Generally lacking good soil, this community is characterized by large amounts of lichen, but also comprises purple saxifrage, arctic poppy, mountain avens, broad-leafed willow herb, and chickweed, all of which tend to grow close to the ground and form a mat of color as they bloom.

The snowpatch community is aptly named for its penchant for late-thawing areas where drifting has slowed the seasonal development of plants. As the snow melts, it permits arctic heather to grow first, followed by dwarf willows, mountain sorrel, and finally, mosses. This regimented pattern results in rings of vegetation that distinguish the community.

July and August is the best time to see Katannilik's vivid arctic bloom, starting with purple saxifrage, and followed by bluebells and dwarf fireweed. In late summer and early autumn, berries carpet the park. Inuit from Kimmirut flock to the valley to harvest blueberries, crowberries, mountain cranberries and bearberries as they have done for millennia.

Where there is vegetation you'll find wildlife. With a terrain as rich as any in the Baffin Region, the Soper Valley is no exception. With any luck you should be able to spot caribou, lemmings, hares, foxes and wolves. And while polar bears could enter the valley at any time, their preference for seals keeps them in coastal areas to the north and south.

The most common animal in the park is the caribou. These caribou do not undertake the long overland migrations of the mainland variety, but circulate throughout south Baffin Island, and the Meta Incognita Peninsula in particular. In summer and autumn, caribou prefer the lush vegetation of the valley. Winter and spring sees them moving to the uplands, where wind blows the ground free of snow and exposes lichens.

Wolves and foxes are also abundant throughout the park. Observant summer visitors may find fox dens in well-drained, rolling terrain throughout the valley; evidence of these winsome creatures is easier to spot in winter, as their tracks zigzag across the valley. Katannilik is home to both arctic and red foxes. The number of wolves in the park fluctuates with the availability of prey, though they are not as numerous as foxes.

Lemmings and hares are a favorite food of many larger predators and tend to make themselves scarce when creatures of the two-legged sort are in the vicinity. With some careful observation, however, you may be rewarded with a glimpse of one or both. Hares favor the protection of rocky hillsides. Lemmings can sometimes be seen darting from one tunnel to another.

Peregrine falcons and gyrfalcons are both present in Katannilik. Peregrines are found closer inland while gyrfalcons favor the coast. They are joined in the valley by two other predatory birds: the snowy owl, easily recognizable by its white plumage and unmistakable eyes, and the rough-legged hawk, one of the most common birds of prey in the Arctic.

The most common birds in Katannilik are the rock ptarmigan and snow bunting. The ptarmigan, which resides here throughout the year, is never easy to spot. In summer their mottled brown plumage blends in perfectly with the surroundings; in winter they are pure white. The snow bunting, a member of the finch family, spends all but winter in the area. Black and white males are more easily spotted than brownish females.

Migratory birds such as Canada geese and red-breasted mergansers frequent marshy areas of the river valley, while snow geese can be seen as they migrate in the spring and fall. All three species of loons are often present closer to the coast at the southern end of the park, as are other shorebirds such as murres, terns and black guillemots.

Although there are generally no char in the Soper River, they can sometimes be found at either Soper Falls or at the reversing falls, where Soper Lake drains into the ocean. Landlocked char can be found in the lakes on either side of the Soper Valley.

Three varieties of cod can be found in Soper Lake: Arctic, Greenland and Atlantic. Inuit catch these in summer and throughout the winter. They are easy to catch, and though they are eaten, the activity is considered mostly a form of recreation.

Geology

Minerals in Katannilik are as plentiful as they are varied. Exposed bedrock reveals diopside, marble, low-quality garnet and various other semi-precious gems. Apatite can be found in blue, green and rose hues. Bands of crystalline limestone transect the valley and the river.

Mining has been attempted sporadically in the Soper Valley since 1900, when a Scottish company extracted mica from a number of locales in and around the river. Graphite was also mined in the early 20th century. Outcrops of both are still easy to find.

A deposit of lapis lazuli, a brilliant blue gemstone found in only a few locations in the world, is also located in the valley. Though the stones here are of poor quality, their color and rarity make them worth seeking. Lapis lazuli too was mined, but abandoned in the early 1970s. The mica and lapis lazuli deposits are located on a parcel of Inuit-owned land within the park boundaries and require special permission to access.

What to See and Do

With careful planning, anyone can have a safe and enjoyable visit to this arctic oasis.

The mainstay of summer activity in Katannilik is hiking, centred around rafting or canoeing, and options are virtually limitless. You can enjoy a casual discovery walk along the river terraces or perhaps tackle the entire trip from Kimmirut to Frobisher Bay, a 10- to 12-day trek across the Meta Incognita Peninsula.

Complementing Katannilik's hiking opportunities is the accessibility of much of the park by water. You could combine the two modes of transportation and spend a week hiking along the Soper River while a guide transports your gear by boat and prepares your meals. Another option is to raft down the Soper for a few hours each day, leaving you ample opportunity to explore the surrounding hills.

The Itijjagiaq Trail is part of a route travelled for centuries by Inuit venturing north to the Nettilling Lake area to hunt caribou and meet with relatives from as far away as Pangnirtung. Although it is part of the park, Itijjagiaq is nonetheless a wilderness trail and should not be undertaken without careful consideration. The route is not marked, so hikers contemplating it should be experienced in backcountry travel, first aid and map reading. The trailhead on the south shore of Frobisher Bay can be reached by boat from Iqaluit. The **Unikkaarvik Visitors Centre** there has a list of licensed outfitters that provide this service.

Seven emergency shelters are located along the 120-kilometre trail. A heated cabin in the Soper Valley will accommodate larger parties. It has a table, counters, sleeping platforms, and washrooms. The park master plan includes building some park maintenance facilities, a second group facility, and installation of signs along hiking trails.

Hikers planning on tackling the trail should look into buying the *Itijjagiaq Trail Guide*. The guide provides a detailed description of the trail, including contour maps, emergency shelters, and points of interest. Park protocol and regulations are also included. It can be purchased for $15 from **The Katannilik Park Centre** in Kimmirut or the Unikkaarvik Visitors Centre in Iqaluit.

From Kimmirut, the cooling effects of the Arctic Ocean quickly fade as you hike inland into the park. As you approach the south end of the Soper Valley, where the river flows into the lake at Soper Falls, you'll find the first of several camping areas. Facilities here are limited to washrooms and tent platforms with windbreaks. Terraces further along the valley also provide good spots to set up camp. Day-hike possibilities from these areas abound.

As its name suggests, Katannilik is full of waterfalls. The largest is Soper Falls, where the emerald green Soper River flows into Soper Lake through a white marble chasm. Farther upstream, just before the Livingstone River flows into the Soper River, is Livingstone Falls; slightly further north, an easy day-hike up the Cascade River brings you to Cascade Falls, the highest waterfall in the park.

The *Soper River Guidebook* is a good resource for anyone travelling on the river. It provides detailed descriptions of points of interest along the river, the location and class of various rapids, and recommends a course through some of the trickier sections, all of which is referenced on accompanying maps. Available from the same sources that carry the *Itijjagiaq Trail Guide*, the *Soper River Guidebook* also includes useful park protocol and interpretive information.

In winter and spring, Katannilik is used by recreational snowmobilers, cross-country skiers, and dogsledding enthusiasts. Guided dogsled trips between Iqaluit and Kimmirut take about four days; on snowmobile it only takes some six hours. Dogsled trips are currently offered by NorthWinds Arctic Adventures in Iqaluit. Snowmobile rentals are available from Eetuk Outfitting Equipment Rentals, also in Iqaluit. Both outfitters rent clothing and other equipment for winter and summer excursions.

Planning a Trip

If you're planning a trip to Katannilik Territorial Park Reserve, start by contacting **Nunavut Tourism** staff at the Unikkaarvik Visitors Centre in Iqaluit or The Katannilik Park Centre in Kimmirut.

Katannilik is one of the most accessible parks in Nunavut. There are three ways to get there from Iqaluit. The simplest is to take a scheduled flight with First Air to Kimmirut, which flies five days per week much of the year. Those travelling in large groups may want to consider chartering a plane to Kimmirut.

The boundary of the park is only minutes from Kimmirut, although it will take you a good three hours to hike into the Soper Valley. For those more eager to get into the valley, boats can be hired in Kimmirut to take you across Soper Lake to Soper Falls at the south end of the valley. These services are offered by the **Mayukalik Hunters and Trappers Organization** and **Qayaq Nunavut**.

You can also get into the park by chartering an airplane to Mount Joy or the Livingstone River confluence, the two designated landing strips in the Soper Valley. This is the most popular method of getting into Katannilik. The strip at the Livingstone is on the west side of the river, though, and should only be used if you plan on taking some form of boat in with you. Both First Air and Kenn Borek have Twin Otters that can land on these strips. The cost varies from year to year but should be around $1,200.

Some Iqaluit outfitters, such as **Eetuk Outfitting** and **NorthWinds Arctic Adventures**, offer package tours of Katannilik Territorial Park Reserve that fly visitors in or transport them by dogsled in winter. As part of the service, visitors are taken across Frobisher Bay to the Itijjagiaq trailhead, where they can hike southwest to the Soper Valley and eventually Kimmirut. Book in advance. It's often not possible to book outfitters by the day.

DIRECTORY

Department of Sustainable Development, Government of Nunavut
(or until April/99, Resources, Wildlife and Economic Development, GNWT) Includes the Katannilik Territorial Park Reserve office.
Tel.: (867) 939-2416
Fax: (867) 939-2406
E-mail: rjaffray@nunanet.com

Eetuk Outfitting
In Iqaluit.
Tel.: (867) 979-1984
Fax: (867) 979-1994

The Katannilik Park Centre
Tel.: (867) 939-2084
Fax: (867) 939-2406
E-mail: rjaffray@nunanet.com

Mayukalik Hunters and Trappers Organization
In Kimmirut.
Tel.: (867) 939-2355
Fax: (867) 939-2112

NorthWinds Arctic Adventures
In Iqaluit.
Tel.: (867) 979-0551
Fax: (867) 979-0573
E-mail: plandry@nunanet.com
Web site: www.northwinds-arctic.com

Nunavut Tourism
P.O. Box 1450, Iqaluit NT,
X0A 0H0 Canada
Tel.: 1-800-491-7910 (for Canada and
the United States)
Tel.: (867) 979-6551
Fax: (867) 979-1261
E-mail: nunatour@nunanet.com
Web site: www.nunatour.nt.ca

Qayaq Nunavut
In Kimmirut.
Tel.: (867) 939-2031 or (867) 939-2221
Fax: (867) 939-2334

Unikkaarvik Visitors Centre
In Iqaluit.
Tel.: (867) 979-4636
Fax: (867) 979-1261
E-mail: nunatour@nunanet.com

98. CAPE DORSET
by John Laird

Along the northwest shore of Dorset Island, surrounded on one side by rocky hills and on the other, by Hudson Strait, lies Cape Dorset — a community that, since the 1950s, has come to be known as the Inuit art capital of the world.

Population:	1,118 (Inuit: 90%, non-Inuit: 10%) Source: 1996 Census of Canada
Telephone Area Code:	867
Time Zone:	Eastern Time
Postal Code:	X0A 0C0
How to Get There:	Possible routes:
	• Ottawa/Montreal-Iqaluit-Cape Dorset
	• Kangerlussuaq (Greenland)-Iqaluit-Cape Dorset
	• Winnipeg-Rankin Inlet-Iqaluit-Cape Dorset
	• Edmonton-Yellowknife-Rankin Inlet-Iqaluit-Cape Dorset
	Iqaluit to Cape Dorset (395 kilometres west) is via First Air or Kenn Borek
Banks:	None. Cash and traveller's cheques are preferable. Credit cards are accepted by certain businesses
Alcohol:	Alcohol and alcoholic beverages cannot be purchased in Cape Dorset. Visitors who want to bring alcohol into the community must first obtain a permit from the **Alcohol Education Committee**
Taxis:	Yes

In the distance are the jagged outlines of islands, and the inlets of Baffin Island's southern coast. Like most other settlements in Nunavut, Cape Dorset is a modern community, with winding gravel roads, small wooden

Cape Dorset Street Map

Key to Map Locations

1 Anglican Church
2 Community Hall
3 HTO and Department of Sustainable Development (or until April/99, RWED)
4 Hamlet Office
5 Health Centre
6 Huit Huit Tours
7 Kingnait Inn
8 Mallikjuaq Visitors Centre
9 Natsiq Sewing Centre
10 Northern Store (includes Post Office)
11 Nunavut Arctic College and Peter Pitseolak School
12 Pentecostal Church
13 Polar Lodge
14 Polar Supply Store
15 Police (RCMP)
16 Sam Pudlat School
17 Sikusilak Store
18 Uksivik Coffee Shop
19 West Baffin Eskimo Co-operative Print Shop
20 West Baffin Eskimo Co-operative Store

Tellik Inlet
(Arctic Ocean)

To Airport

houses, schools, stores, hotels, a nursing station, government offices and churches. But it is Cape Dorset's outstanding artists and their printmaking and stone-carving shop that have earned the town renown.

Each year, art lovers and naturalists flock to Cape Dorset to enjoy the treasures of the West Baffin Eskimo Co-operative and to chat with the acclaimed artists who work here. In 1995, then German Chancellor Helmut Kohl made the visit with Canadian Prime Minister Jean Chrétien. Visitors come, as well, to absorb the rich heritage of local Inuit, and to tour the breathtaking arctic landscape with its abundance of wildlife. The Mallikjuaq Visitors Centre, due to be completed in 1999, displays artifacts portraying the history of Dorset and Mallikjuaq islands.

History

"Since long ago," Cape Dorset elder Qupapik Ragee once said of his community, "our ancestors called it *Kinngait.*" *Kinngait* is the Inuktitut word for "mountains," describing the steep, rocky hills that overlook the town. The Inuit here are direct descendants of the Thule, who inhabited this region in small groups almost 1,000 years ago. You can explore remnants of their culture — such as stone foundations of their houses — at several sites on Dorset and Baffin islands. In 1925, Diamond Jenness became the first archeologist to identify the remains of an even earlier civilization, the Dorset, who lived here from about 800 BC to AD 1300. Other researchers have since discovered artifacts dating back 3,500 years to the Pre-Dorset, and even earlier, cultures.

European explorers, who arrived on these shores in the 17th century, were relatively recent visitors. They named the Foxe Peninsula after the English explorer, Luke Foxe. (Dorset Island lies off the south coast of this peninsula.) And they named Dorset Island to honor his benefactor, the Earl of Dorset. From 1850 to the early 1900s, whalers and missionaries visited the area. In 1913, the Hudson's Bay Co. set up a trading post here. Between 1938 and 1953, two churches, a school and a few houses were constructed. By the mid-1950s, Inuit began to build permanent homes in the area. This marked a major change in their lives, as now they increasingly felt the influence of government.

In 1947, the *Nascopie*, the supply ship that brought goods to the region from the South, ran aground off the coast of Dorset Island. Before she sank, the resourceful Inuit salvaged supplies, fuel, and even wood from the ship. They used this wood to construct their homes in Cape Dorset and along the coast of Dorset Island.

Today, most local Inuit are engaged in the same activities you might find in any small community in Canada: running businesses, working in offices, and attending school. If you walk the 1.2 kilometres from one end of town to the other, you'll see a blend of modern and traditional Inuit culture — snowmobiles and all-terrain vehicles parked outside homes; caribou and polar bear hides hanging from railings; arctic char fillets drying on racks; and perhaps a frozen seal or two resting on a doorstep. Children laugh and play in the streets, chattering in a steady stream of Inuktitut.

Cape Dorset: Its Land and Wildlife

Information and maps for day trips on Dorset and Mallikjuaq islands are included in the *Mallikjuaq Historic Park* trail guide, available from the **hamlet's**

community development department and Nunavut Tourism. The Mallikjuaq Visitors Centre, located next to the Kingnait Inn, contains displays and interpretive information on the archeology and trails on both Dorset and Mallikjuaq islands. (See Chapter 99, "Mallikjuaq Territorial Historic Park.") You can take a boat to Mallikjuaq Island or hike there at low tide. Check with the community development office for information on tides, and referrals to licensed tour operators providing boat rides. Costs for outfitters vary. Day trips by boat are $75 to $150 per person.

Other guided activities include winter dogsledding excursions, ranging in cost from $150 to $200 per person per day; or custom-designed trips for three to seven days from $200 to $300 per person per day and up. A guided snow machine outing ranges from $120 to $200 per person. **Aiviq Hunters and Trappers Organization** also provides licensed guides for sport hunting, fishing and ecotours. Examples of prices are: $5,000 to $10,000 per person for a polar bear hunt, complete with guides and dogteam; $3,500 for two people for a caribou hunt; and $100 per person per day for a cultural tour.

On Dorset Island, you'll find several interesting hikes. The waterfall route takes you from the south edge of town, past a little waterfall to the beach. The pipeline route goes to "T" Lake, the source of Cape Dorset's drinking water, then winds up into the hills to a lookout whose view spans the south end of Dorset Island, other distant islands, and Hudson Strait. Another hike takes you east past the tank farm, where fuel shipped to Cape Dorset is stored in house-sized tanks, and over the tundra and gravel, to the beach at Apalooktook Point. If you're walking with a guide, he or she will point out archeological sites on the island, such as Thule houses, caches and burial sites. Although there are no camping or picnic facilities on the island, staff at the community development office will tell you of suitable locations for camping. Be sure to bring your camp stove; there's no firewood.

While there are many hills and rocky areas on Dorset Island, you'll find accessible routes to most areas. Hiking will require stamina — no problem for those who exercise regularly. Wear sturdy, waterproof boots for trekking over the spongy, sometimes wet, tundra. As weather may be variable, wear clothing suitable for rain and cold. In summer, be sure to bring your insect repellent.

From March to May, daily hours of sunlight increase, although temperatures remain moderate. Because light reflected from the snow is intense, you're wise to wear sunscreen and sunglasses. Between late May and early August, hours of daylight continue to increase, reaching a maximum of 20 hours of light in June and July. Summer temperatures, however, are generally cool, with an average high of 7.2° C, dropping to a few degrees below zero at night. Between October and February, hours of daylight decrease, with a maximum of five hours of light on the shortest days in December. Winter temperatures drop to between –25° C and –35° C, and even colder. From December to late June, the ocean is frozen around the community, and people travel over the ice with snowmobiles or dogteams. Land travel to other regions is impossible in October and November, when the ocean is freezing, and again in June and sometimes in early July, during breakup.

In many areas of Dorset Island, you'll discover caribou, walrus, seals and a variety of arctic shore and migratory birds. In spring and fall, you might see migrating beluga whales and the odd bowhead whale pass near the community. Find out the best season for viewing wildlife. Remember that in spring and fall, polar bears may roam around the island; they're dangerous, so take a licensed guide to act as a bear monitor on your outings. For information on wildlife, and hunting and fishing licences, contact the **Department of Sustainable Development** (or until April/99, GNWT's Department of **Resources, Wildlife and Economic Development**) or Aiviq Hunters and Trappers Organization.

Tours

Huit Huit Tours has tailored different tours to different palates. A community tour stops in at the West Baffin Eskimo Co-operative where stonecut prints are made. A cultural evening in town features storytelling by elders, throat singers, and tea with artists.

Huit Huit also has on-the-land tours that introduce you to traditional seasonal activities of local Inuit, such as seal hunting or jigging for fish on the lake ice. There are also custom-designed outings: camping in an igloo or tent, for example, or fishing and hunting, as well as trips to the floe edge, to archeological sites, and to the hosts' cabin. Prices vary according to the activity and number of people involved. Costs may be shared by a group.

Siku Outfitting provides summer boat trips along the coast of Baffin Island. Visitors camp, eat "country food" and see archeological sites, wildlife, and icebergs. In Cape Dorset, visits are arranged to meet local artists and to tour the West Baffin Eskimo Co-operative. Jimmy Manning, the Siku tour operator, will happily provide more information about boat trips.

When cruise ships arrive in July and August, the Municipality of Cape Dorset organizes tours of the town, the West Baffin Eskimo Co-operative and archeological sites on Mallikjuaq Island. Elders dress in traditional clothing and demonstrate the hunting lifestyle that has served them and their families for generations. Tea and bannock (fried bread) are served, and translation is provided. For more information, contact the community development department.

Shopping

The **West Baffin Eskimo Co-operative** is a centre for stonecut printing, lithographic printmaking, etching, and Inuit sculpture. Many artists who work here are known by name in the global art community, and have exhibited their work in public and private galleries throughout Canada and abroad. Traditionally, Inuit carved small sculptures from ivory, bone and wood. The era of modern Inuit art began in 1948, after art school graduate James Houston returned from a trip to the Arctic and convinced the Canadian government that the small sculptures being produced by talented Inuit artists were marketable. Later, Houston, working as a government employee in Cape Dorset, helped bring about a local printmaking industry after Osuitok, an Inuk artist, asserted Inuit could create such artwork. By 1961, the Co-operative was incorporated, housing studios and marketing artwork for the benefit of the entire community.

The Co-operative sales outlet is located in the stonecut studio and is open year round. Visitors can purchase soapstone, bone and marble carvings, etchings, lithographic prints and postcards. Printmakers work in the studios from September to June, taking time off in summer. The Co-op will package and ship the art for you. For tours, contact the Co-op or the guides listed in this chapter.

You'll also find carvers at work outside their homes or in a small shed nearby. Although they appreciate your interest in their work, you'd be courteous to ask permission before taking their photographs. As some Inuit speak only Inuktitut, hire a guide who can interpret for you.

The **Natsiq Sewing Centre** offers courses in traditional activities such as sewing skin clothing. Here, traditional items such as sealskin boots or caribou and polar bear hide clothing can also be custom-made for you.

The **Polar Supply Store** sells Inuit carvings, snacks and a few groceries. They'll also repair and rent equipment, snow machines and trucks.

The **West Baffin Eskimo Co-operative Store** sells groceries and also includes the services of a mechanic, Yamaha and Home Hardware dealerships, and a gas station. Inuit prints and carvings are sold in the print shop across the road.

The **Northern store**, according to the manager, supplies everything from toothpicks to snow machines. That includes groceries, dry goods and hardware.

Finally, the **Sikusilak Store** is a convenience store selling snack foods and some groceries and clothing.

Accommodation and Dining

Renovated in 1995, the **Kingnait Inn** has 17 rooms, each with two single beds, TV, toilet and washbasin. Eight of these rooms also have showers; in remaining rooms, showers are shared. Although single accommodation is available, when the hotel is booked, you'll have to share a room. Laundry facilities are available for guests after 5 p.m. There is a pay phone in the hall. Rates are $200 per person per night with meals, or $150 without meals. The dining room is open from 7 a.m. to 8 p.m. seven days a week; guests eat at specific times, and meals are à la carte. Box lunches are available for $12 to $15; notify the cook the night before you require them. Guests are met at the **airport**.

The eight rooms in the **Polar Lodge** have two single beds per room, as well as a telephone and TV. Washrooms and showers are separate from rooms. On request, guests will be picked up at the airport. For cultural and sports activities, the lodge will direct you to local guides. Rates are $175 per person per night with meals, or $150 without meals. The dining room is open from 7 a.m. to 7 p.m. daily; meals are à la carte.

Huit Huit Tours offers home-style accommodation. Individuals or groups of up to eight can book the beach house or guest house. Each house is fully furnished and includes kitchen equipment, linens and towels. The houses have a kitchen, living and dining room, bedrooms, bathrooms, TV, telephone and laundry. Guests prepare their own meals. Both houses are centrally located with a view of the bay. Rates are $135 per person per night. Complimentary airport pickup is offered.

The **Uksivik Coffee Shop** provides coffee and light meals for lunch and supper.

Services

The **health centre** is open from 8:30 a.m. to 5 p.m., Monday to Friday. It is closed on holidays and weekends except for emergencies.

DIRECTORY

*Outfitters and tour operators licensed at time of writing.
After March 31/99, check for updated status.

Accommodation and Dining

Huit Huit Tours
Cash, traveller's cheques.
Tel.: (867) 897-8806
Fax: (867) 897-8434

Kingnait Inn
Traveller's cheques accepted.
Tel.: (867) 897-8863
Fax: (867) 897-8907

Polar Lodge
VISA, MasterCard, Interac.
Tel.: (867) 897-8335
Fax: (867) 897-8055

Uksivik Coffee Shop
11 a.m.–7 p.m., Monday to Friday
and Sunday. Closed Saturday.
Cash only.
Tel.: (867) 897-8548

* Outfitters/Tour Operators/Visitors Centre

Aiviq Hunters and Trappers Organization
Tel.: (867) 897-8978
Fax: (867) 897-8214

Hamlet of Cape Dorset
Tel.: (867) 897-8943
Fax: (867) 897-8475

Huit Huit Tours
Tel.: (867) 897-8806
Fax: (867) 897-8434

Mallikjuaq Visitors Centre
Tel.: (867) 897-8996
Fax: (867) 897-8475

Siku Outfitting
Tel.: (867) 897-8198
Fax: (867) 897-8186

Services

Airport

First Air
Tel.: (867) 897-8938
Fax: (867) 897-8180

Alcohol Education Committee
Tel.: (867) 897-8826
Fax: (867) 897-8495

Churches

Bahá'í
For information on meeting times,
contact Thelma Perry.
Tel.: (867) 897-8851

Pentecostal Church
Services: 11 a.m. and 7 p.m., Sunday;
7 p.m., Wednesday (all in Inuktitut and
occasionally Inuktitut and English).
Tel.: (867) 897-8966

St. John's Anglican Church
Services: 11 a.m. and 7 p.m., Sunday;
7 p.m., Wednesday (all in Inuktitut and
occasionally Inuktitut and English).
Tel.: (867) 897-8312
Fax: (867) 897-8495

Department of Sustainable Development, Government of Nunavut
(or until April/99, **Resources, Wildlife
and Economic Development**, GNWT)
Tel.: (867) 897-8932
Fax: (867) 897-8475

Hamlet Office
Tel.: (867) 897-8419 or (867) 897-8943
Fax: (867) 897-8030

Health Centre
Tel.: (867) 897-8820
Fax: (867) 897-8194

Police (RCMP)
Tel.: (867) 897-8855
Fax: (867) 897-8324

Post Office
Located in the Northern store.
10:30 a.m.–1 p.m. and 2:15–5:30 p.m.,
Monday to Friday.
Tel.: (867) 897-8811

Radio Station (FM 105.1)
Tel.: (867) 897-8875

Schools

Nunavut Arctic College
Tel.: (867) 897-8825
Fax: (867) 897-8244

Peter Pitseolak School
Secondary school.
Tel.: (867) 897-8826
Fax: (867) 897-8919

Sam Pudlat School
Elementary school.
Tel.: (867) 897-8332
Fax: (867) 897-8405

Taxi

Takukuluk Taxi
Tel.: (867) 897-8280

Weather Information
9 a.m.–6 p.m., Monday; 12–7 p.m.,
Tuesday; 9 a.m.–6 p.m., Wednesday;
8 a.m.–1 p.m., Thursday; 8 a.m.–6 p.m.,
Friday. Closed weekends.
Tel.: (867) 897-8330
Web site weather forecast:
www.infonorth.org

Shopping

Natsiq Sewing Centre
Usually open 1:30–5 p.m., Monday to
Friday. Closed for summer.
Tel.: (867) 897-8212

Northern Store
10 a.m.–6 p.m., Monday to Saturday.
Closed Sunday.
VISA, MasterCard, Interac.
Tel.: (867) 897-8811
Fax: (867) 897-8832

Polar Supply Store
1 p.m.–12 a.m. daily
(1–10 p.m. in winter).
VISA, MasterCard, Interac.
Tel.: (867) 897-8969
Fax: (867) 897-8055

Sikusilak Store
5–10 p.m., Monday to Thursday;
2 p.m.–12 a.m., Friday and Saturday;
2–10 p.m., Sunday.
Cash only.
Tel.: (867) 897-8009
Fax: (867) 897-8907

**West Baffin Eskimo
Co-operative Print Shop**
9 a.m.–5 p.m., Monday to Friday.
VISA, traveller's cheques, Interac.
Tel.: (867) 897-8944
Fax: (867) 897-8000

**West Baffin Eskimo
Co-operative Store**
9 a.m.–6 p.m., Monday to Wednesday;
9 a.m.–7 p.m., Thursday and Friday;
10 a.m.–5 p.m., Saturday. Closed
Sunday.
VISA, Interac.
Tel.: (867) 897-8997
Fax: (867) 897-8000

99. MALLIKJUAQ TERRITORIAL HISTORIC PARK
by John Laird

Mallikjuaq means "big wave" in Inuktitut, an appropriate name for an island where rounded rock hills and low tundra valleys resemble giant rolling waves.

But while Mallikjuaq Territorial Historic Park derives its name from its topography, it gets its spirit from its human history. A 45-minute walk from the community of Cape Dorset, you'll find excellent archeological sites and stone structures here dating back some three millennia.

The People and Their History

About 1,000 years ago, the people of the Thule culture lived on Mallikjuaq in low, stone houses framed with whalebone ribs and covered with hides and sod. The east arm of the island boasts the remains of nine winter houses with stone foundations still in place. Scattered throughout the area are the bones of whales, seals and walruses, a vital resource for the Thule. Archeological evidence indicates that people from the Dorset culture — predecessor of the Thule — also inhabited the island. The point of access to these winter houses is the southeast shore of Mallikjuaq Island. From the beach, walk on to the tundra toward a large pond where the houses are.

The northwest coast of Mallikjuaq Island boasts a number of more contemporary, though no less interesting, stone features. Tent rings, fireplaces and meat caches here date back between 50 and 200 years. The ingenuity of arctic inhabitants is illustrated by the many self-supporting stone structures they created, such as *qajaq* (kayak) stands and *inuksuit*. Other stone piles here represent fox traps and burial sites. Local Inuit elders ask visitors to respect their heritage by not disturbing the sites, which are protected by government legislation.

What to See and Do

Mallikjuaq's archeological sites are easy to reach and can be thoroughly toured in about two hours. The gentle slopes of the island's east end offer superb views of the undulating landscape as well as Hudson Strait. The steep rock hills in the southwest corner of the island are less easily scaled. Sandy beaches can be found among the island's more common offering of gravel and rocky shorelines; these make excellent places to camp. You can also kayak around nearby coves and islands.

Wildlife is plentiful in summer, and you may see caribou, arctic hares, peregrine falcons, snowy owls, ptarmigans and ducks. Polar bears roam the coast in spring and fall, an exciting yet potentially dangerous visitor. To avoid any unexpected encounters, travel with an experienced, licensed guide who can act as a bear monitor for you. Seals may appear at any time; beluga whales migrate through nearby waters in October and April. If you are very lucky you may even spot a massive bowhead whale, although they are infrequent visitors. Fishing for arctic char is popular in nearby bays.

The best time of year to visit Mallikjuaq is in July and August, when warm temperatures and abundant sunshine bring tundra wildflowers briefly to life. Large patches of tundra are covered with these colorful, ground-hugging plants. Autumn starts in late August, when patches of tundra turn a vibrant red and yellow.

The *Mallikjuaq Historic Park* trail guide offers clear directions to the island and interprets the park's many features. You can obtain a copy from the **Mallikjuaq Visitors Centre** or **Nunavut Tourism**.

Planning a Trip

In summer, local outfitters will take groups of up to three people on the 10-minute boat ride across the inlet for about $75. For an additional $75 or so, your guide will throw in a tour of the island's historic sites, wildlife and plants, as well as tea and bannock. If you ask, your guide may also supply local foods such as caribou, char or seal. Make arrangements well in advance of your arrival in Cape Dorset. Finding a guide on short notice is sometimes difficult. Your ideal guide is one who not only has a good understanding of the history of the island, but who also likes to tell stories about Inuit culture.

You can also hike to Mallikjuaq, a 45-minute trek from Cape Dorset to the northwest tip of Dorset Island and across the tidal flats of Tellik Inlet. This hike, which is only possible at low tide, is recommended for agile walkers prepared for slippery, algae-covered rocks and innumerable puddles. If foot is your chosen mode of transport, make sure you check tide times before heading out, or you may find yourself spending an evening on the island, alone and without food and shelter. The manager of the Mallikjuaq Visitors Centre has information about tides and walking trips to Mallikjuaq. If you hike without a guide, inform someone of your travel plans, such as the local RCMP detachment or the hotel, if you are a guest. Guides offer walking tours for $75 to $100; information is available from the hamlet and the **Aiviq Hunters and Trappers Organization**.

In winter, the landscape of Mallikjuaq takes on a completely different appearance as snow creates a variety of patterns on the rock hills. Archeological sites and vegetation will be covered by snow, although you may be lucky enough to see a caribou or arctic hare. Cape Dorset residents occasionally build igloos on the island.

At this time of year you can walk directly across the ice to Mallikjuaq, or for $120 to $200 hire a guide with a snowmobile. A great way to travel is by dogteam, bundled in caribou skins on a *qamutiik* and listening to the quiet crunch of the snow as you glide over it. A day trip by dogteam costs $150 to $200 per person. It is not possible to cross to Tellik Inlet during breakup and freezeup, which occur in June and October. A late breakup may delay crossing until early July.

Even though the area enjoys almost 20 hours of sunlight each day in summer, the temperature averages a high of just 7.2° C and can drop below zero any time. Winter temperatures can plummet below –40° C between December and March. The shortest days of December yield about five hours of sunshine.

Regardless of the season in which you travel, always be prepared for the unexpected, as weather conditions can vary throughout the day. Even in summer, you'll need warm and waterproof clothing, a hat, and mitts. Rubber boots are best for getting to shore from a boat; sturdy, waterproof hiking boots work best on the spongy and sometimes soggy tundra. Insect repellent is a worthy companion, as bugs can be voracious, especially on calm days. In winter, insulated clothing such as parkas, snow pants, mitts and boots are essential. Bring sunglasses and sunscreen in any season. In summer, they'll protect you from long hours of sunlight. In winter and spring, they'll guard against the bright sun reflecting off the snow.

Though Mallikjuaq is a territorial park, it remains untouched. There are no services or facilities on the island. Local people will drink water from the island's many streams and ponds, although it is recommended that you bring your own drinking water or boil water collected on the island. To preserve the park, carry out your garbage and leave the island as you found it. Groceries and some camping supplies can be purchased in Cape Dorset at the Co-op and the Northern store. The Kingnait Inn will provide a boxed lunch for about $15.

DIRECTORY

Aiviq Hunters and Trappers Organization
For information on local outfitters and guides.
Tel.: (867) 897-8978
Fax: (867) 897-8214

Mallikjuaq Visitors Centre
Tel.: (867) 897-8996
Fax: (867) 897-8475

Nunavut Tourism
Tel.: 1-800-491-7910 (for Canada and the United States)
Tel.: (867) 979-6551
Fax: (867) 979-1261
E-mail: nunatour@nunanet.com
Web site: www.nunatour.nt.ca

100. SANIKILUAQ
by Miriam Fleming

Nunavut's southernmost community, Sanikiluaq, is located on the Belcher Islands in southeastern Hudson Bay, about 150 kilometres off the coast of Quebec.

Population:	631 (Inuit: 94%, non-Inuit: 6%) Source: 1996 Census of Canada
Telephone Area Code:	867
Time Zone:	Eastern Time
Postal Code:	X0A 0W0
How to Get There:	Possible route:
	• Montreal-Kuujjuarapik-Umiujaq-Sanikiluaq
	Montreal to Sanikiluaq (almost 1,500 kilometres north) is via Air Inuit
Banks:	None. Visitors should bring traveller's cheques, cash or money orders.
	Credit cards are accepted by certain businesses
Alcohol:	Alcohol and alcoholic beverages are prohibited
Taxis:	Amaulik/Inns North will pick up and deliver hotel guests from the airport

Although more than 1,100 kilometres south of the Arctic Circle, the islands are distinctly arctic. No trees grow here and, except in valleys, only a thin layer of soil covers the ground. The islands' peak is 155 metres above sea level; some cliffs rise from 50 to 70 metres.

Fly on a clear day into Sanikiluaq via Umiujaq, Quebec, and you'll see the immensity of the Belcher Islands. Spread out over almost 3,000 square kilometres, they consist of about 1,500 islands — many of which are very small — and form the largest group of islands in Hudson Bay. The main group of the archipelago forms an S-shaped pattern whose long, narrow peninsulas are separated by clearly defined channels.

Although Sanikiluaq (pronounced "san-ee-kil-u-wak") is the only permanent settlement in the Belcher Islands, many Inuit live and camp throughout the archipelago during spring and summer. Sanikiluaq, named after an Inuk man who lived in the Belcher Islands, lies on the main group of islands, on a narrow piece of land near the north end of Flaherty Island, bounded by Eskimo Harbour to the north and by Sanikiluaq Lake to the south.

In a world that's being resculpted by industrial developments, Sanikiluaq residents have worked hard to ensure that traditional knowledge has a place in modern environmental management.

A recent community-conducted study has amassed traditional knowledge from 28 Inuit and Cree communities around Hudson Bay, James Bay and Hudson Strait, so that in the face of northern Quebec's Great Whale hydro-electric project, the traditional knowledge of aboriginal peoples would be used in the region's environmental assessment. The research has resulted in a book, *Voices from the Bay: Traditional Ecological Knowledge of Inuit and Cree in the Hudson Bay Bioregion* (Ottawa: Canadian Arctic Resources Committee

and the Environmental Committee of Sanikiluaq), as well as a 1995 award from the Friends of the United Nations, citing Sanikiluaq as one of 50 exemplary communities worldwide committed to building a sense of common unity. The study's headquarters are in the **Hudson Bay Office** in Sanikiluaq.

History

The Inuit have inhabited the Belcher Islands for centuries. While some ancestors of present-day inhabitants migrated here from northern Quebec, others came when the Thule culture was declining between AD 1200 and 1400. Earlier occupation is evidenced in the archeological sites of the Dorset culture from 500 BC to AD 1000.

The islands first came to the attention of outsiders after Henry Hudson spotted them in 1610. More than 230 years later, Thomas Wiegand, a servant of the Hudson's Bay Co., led an exploration party from Fort George (Chisasibi, Quebec) to the Belcher Islands. It was another 60 years before Robert Flaherty and his crew became the first *qallunaat* (white people) to winter here. In 1915, he and his crew survived the winter by using the wood from their ship for fuel.

The Inuit survived in the Belcher Islands through their ingenuity. In the late 1800s when caribou disappeared from the islands (due to icy conditions that made foraging impossible), women began sewing winter parkas from eider duck skins. The men were renowned for their knowledge of ice fields, and their dogs were popular trade items during annual trips to mainland posts. The men were respected as well for their kayaking skills and the two-person kayaks that they navigated adeptly around the islands and the bay.

A Hudson's Bay Co. trading post, first opened in 1928, operated sporadically until the 1950s. It was relocated from Tukarak Island to Eskimo Harbour in 1961. That same year, the federal government built a school in the southern part of Flaherty Island. During the 1960s, two communities existed in the islands: North Camp, where the trading post was located, and South Camp, where the school was built.

The community of Sanikiluaq wasn't established until 1971, when the federal government centralized its services and moved the buildings and inhabitants of South Camp to North Camp. Today, Sanikiluaq is a growing, modern settlement whose economy is based on subsistence hunting, fishing, tourism and soapstone carving.

Sanikiluaq: Its Land and Wildlife

Most of the small islands in the archipelago provide breeding grounds for several species of ducks and geese. Rock crevices, lakes and ponds are summer home to many other migrating birds. Most of the species that nest in the Belcher Islands or visit here are waterbirds, including common eider (which stay year round), red-throated loon, common loon, arctic loon, Canada goose, Brant, merganser, black guillemot, arctic tern and gulls. There are also a few land birds such as rock ptarmigan, rough-legged hawk, peregrine falcon, snowy owl, horned lark, Lapland longspur and snow bunting.

Arctic char are found in the rivers, lakes, and offshore waters, while whitefish swim in the lakes. Coastal waters are a source of cod, capelin, lump fish, and sculpin. They're also home to ringed seal, bearded seal, harbor seal, beluga whale, walrus and polar bear. On the tundra, fox, reindeer, arctic hare, and lemming may be seen. Reindeer were introduced in 1978 about 100 years after the caribou disappeared.

Sanikiluaq, anchored in Hudson Bay, has weather that can be blustery and unpredictable. The islands are surrounded by open sea, and high winds and storms can arise suddenly. Information on daily temperatures and wind conditions can be obtained from the observer/communicator at the local **airport**.

Tours

In the Sanikiluaq area, you'll find many trails that are great for both walking and driving all-terrain vehicles (ATVs). One trail that's visible from the Mitiq Co-op — one of Sanikiluaq's two major stores — is an easy walk to a small bay about three kilometres from the community.

The trail continues about two kilometres, then crosses a river. Once across, you can hike up a gentle valley slope to a point overlooking *Kattak* (Entrance). In July and August, this is a lovely spot for a picnic. The tundra here is carpeted with arctic flowers, and the panorama of Eskimo Harbour, Tukarak Island and the Baker's Dozen Islands is superb.

Eight kilometres from the settlement, you'll find Dorset and Thule archeological sites near *Kingaaluk* (Big Mountain) and *Katapik* (Small Entrance) on the west side of Eskimo Harbour.

Katapik is another good spot for a picnic, and can be easily reached by ATV, boat, or snowmobile. It's also Sanikiluaq's favored destination for gathering mussels, sea urchins, and sea cucumbers. On weekends, when the weather is fine, community picnics are often held here.

The best camp site in Sanikiluaq is the gravel beach just north of the harbor and east of the old boats. The view from the beach is pleasant, but remember that winds here can be strong. You should have a sturdy tent that can be secured to large rocks. To rent camping gear, snowmobiles and ATVs, call the **Qikiqtait Tour and Outfitting Company** or the **Hunters and Trappers Organization** in advance of your visit.

Tourists are still new to Sanikiluaq, and people here worry when they see visitors venture out on the land or water without a guide. For everyone's peace of mind — and your safety — please inform the **RCMP** of your destination. (You can also obtain emergency locator beacons from the **hamlet office**.)

Qikiqtait Tour and Outfitting Company, the only licensed outfitter in Sanikiluaq, offers seasonal group tours and will organize trips with Inuit guides, including boat trips to Wiegand Island (*Tungasitik*) and tours to the soapstone mines on Tukarak Island, 40 kilometres away.

To hunt and fish in the islands, you'll need a licence, and you can obtain information about that from the Sanikiluaq Hunters and Trappers Organization. Access restrictions exist on Inuit-owned land as a result of the Nunavut Land Claims Agreement, so if your hunting and fishing plans lead you to such private property, contact the Inuit Land Administration Office (Baffin Region) in advance of your trip for permission to cross onto the land. (See Chapter 11, "Adventure Travel," for more information.) To obtain a territorial wildlife export permit, contact the municipal liaison office located in the hamlet office.

Sanikiluaq Lake, on the south side of the community, is the settlement's main source of drinking water. All activities, including fishing or kayaking, are discouraged on this lake.

Shopping

The soapstone carvings of Sanikiluaq, found in offices and homes around the world, are usually realistic portrayals of the animals and birds that reside in the Belcher Islands. A selection of carvings may be available at the **Mitiq Co-operative**. The Co-op also sells groceries, hardware and dry goods.

Two other stores in Sanikiluaq are **Sanniit Co-operative Ltd.** and the **Northern store**. Sanniit sells eiderdown outerwear and duvets, ideal for arctic camping. The Northern store sells a range of goods, including groceries, clothing and hardware.

Accommodation and Dining

A new hotel that opened in the spring of 1998 has replaced the old Amaulik Hotel. Called **Amaulik/Inns North**, it is owned and operated by the Mitiq Co-operative Association, and accommodates 16 people in eight rooms. Each room has cable TV and a private washroom. Amaulik/Inns North also has a meeting room that seats up to 16 people. The hotel's restaurant serves the public as well as guests, and the chef prepares bagged lunches if given advance notice. Prices for rooms are $150 plus GST per person per night (without meals). Approximate prices for meals are: $10 for breakfast, $15 for lunch, and $25 for supper.

Services

The **health centre**, open weekdays from 8 a.m. to 12 p.m. and from 1 to 4:30 p.m., has two registered nurses and a community health representative who treat routine medical problems. Nurses are on call for emergencies, and can be reached by calling the health centre.

Sanikiluaq isn't yet hooked up to the Internet, but faxes can be sent through the Mitiq Co-op or the Amaulik/Inns North hotel. A small fee applies.

To help orient you while in Sanikiluaq, a community map can be obtained from the hamlet office.

Nuiyak School welcomes visitors to attend classes in history and cultural studies. Call the school principal for an invitation.

If you'd like to do some reading while in town, browse through the Hudson Bay Office. You'll find works on the Hudson Bay, James Bay and Hudson Strait marine, coastal and riverine areas.

Finally, if you would like to volunteer your services while you're in town, contact the community economic development officer at the hamlet office before you arrive to discuss possible opportunities. The experience may provide you with travel stories few can equal.

DIRECTORY

*Outfitters and tour operators licensed at time of writing.
After March 31/99, check for updated status.

Accommodation and Dining

Amaulik/Inns North
Restaurant open Monday to Saturday
from 7 a.m. to 6 p.m. Open only to
hotel guests on Sunday.
VISA, MasterCard, American Express,
Diners Club/enRoute, traveller's
cheques, Interac.
Tel.: (867) 266-8821 or (867) 266-8909
Fax: (867) 266-8844 or (867) 266-8727

*Outfitters/Tour Operators

Qikiqtait Tour and Outfitting Company
Contact Bill Fraser.
Tel.: (867) 266-8623
Fax: (867) 266-8844

Services

Airport
8 a.m.–6 p.m., Monday to Friday.
Tel.: (867) 266-8824

Church

St. Philip's Anglican Church
Services: 10 a.m. and 7 p.m., Sunday
(in Inuktitut); 7 p.m., Wednesday
(also in Inuktitut).
No telephone.

Department of Sustainable Development, Government of Nunavut
(or until April/99, GNWT's **Resources,
Wildlife and Economic Development**)
Contact the hamlet office
(municipal liaison officer).
Tel.: (867) 266-8874

Hamlet Office
Ask for the community economic
development officer or municipal
liaison officer.
Tel.: (867) 266-8874
Fax: (867) 266-8903

Health Centre
Tel.: (867) 266-8965
Fax: (867) 266-8802

Hudson Bay Office
No telephone.
Fax: (867) 266-8837

Hunters and Trappers Organization
Tel.: (867) 266-8709
Fax: (867) 266-8131

Police (RCMP)
Tel.: (867) 266-8812
Fax: (867) 266-8952

Post Office
Located in the Northern store.
10 a.m.–12 p.m., 1:30–5:30 p.m.,
Monday to Friday.
Tel.: (867) 266-8945

Radio Station (FM 106.1)
Tel.: (867) 266-8893 or (867) 266-8833

Schools

Nuiyak School
Tel.: (867) 266-8816 or (867) 266-8817
Fax: (867) 266-8843

Nunavut Arctic College
Tel.: (867) 266-8885

Weather Information
Tel.: (867) 266-8824
Fax: (867) 266-8947
Web site weather forecast:
www.infonorth.org

Shopping

Mitiq Co-op
9 a.m.–6 p.m., Monday to Saturday.
Closed Sunday.
VISA, MasterCard, American Express,
Diners Club/enRoute, traveller's
cheques, Interac.
Tel.: (867) 266-8909 or (867) 266-8821
Fax: (867) 266-8844 or (867) 266-8727

Northern Store
9:30 a.m.–6 p.m., Monday to Thursday;
9:30 a.m.–7 p.m., Friday; 9:30 a.m.–
6 p.m., Saturday. Closed Sunday.
VISA, MasterCard, traveller's cheques,
Interac.
Tel.: (867) 266-8836
Fax: (867) 266-8840

Sanniit Co-operative Ltd.
By appointment.
Traveller's cheques accepted.
Tel.: (867) 266-8866 or (867) 266-8920
Fax: (867) 266-8920

CONTRIBUTORS

John Amagoalik of Iqaluit is chief commissioner of the Nunavut Implementation Commission, the public institution that helped design Nunavut's government.

Randy Ames has investigated and written about social, economic, political, environmental, and aboriginal issues in many parts of Arctic Canada for more than 24 years. Among other northern organizations, he has worked with the Nunavut Implementation Commission, Tungavik Federation of Nunavut, the Nunavut Constitutional Forum, and Inuit Tapirisat of Canada. Ames, most recently a resident of Ottawa, is currently travelling abroad.

Former Grise Fiord resident **Laisa Audlaluk** now lives in Pangnirtung, working for Parks Canada as a heritage and client services officer. She is involved in the Baffin Regional Youth Council.

Larry Audlaluk of Grise Fiord is acting president of the Qikiqtani Inuit Association, a board member of Nunavut Tunngavik Incorporated, and president of the Grise Fiord Inuit Co-op Ltd. Audlaluk says he enjoys his work with the implementation of the Nunavut land claim, and is very interested in Nunavut's political development and excited about the creation of the new territory in 1999. Audlaluk was among those who were moved from Inukjuak, Quebec, to Grise Fiord in 1953; he has been involved in the High Arctic relocation issue as a result.

Ken Beardsall of Coral Harbour is a teacher and outfitter. He and his wife Emily, who is also from Coral Harbour, are kept busy raising their four boys. Beardsall also chairs the Southampton Island Historical Society, which is currently building a museum.

Mike Beedell is an internationally published photographer, adventurer, and guide who suffers from a chronic case of arctic fever. He is the author of *The Magnetic North* and his work is regularly featured in fine magazines throughout the world. Beedell's company, O!Canada Expeditions, runs adventure tours to many outstanding areas north of 60, and provides support to documentary film crews.

Jennifer Bernius is a writer and editor who lives in Ottawa. During the 1970s, she worked with Inuit Tapirisat of Canada, writing and editing stories for ITC's magazine, *Inuit Today*.

George Bohlender moved to the Northwest Territories from Toronto in 1985, working in retail management and consulting in Iqaluit and Pangnirtung, and as an economic development officer for the GNWT in Arctic Bay. He now lives in Taloyoak with wife Madelaine, daughter Gina, and son Erik. Employed by the Kitikmeot Economic Development Commission since

July 1995, Bohlender is the community economic development officer for Taloyoak and Pelly Bay in the Kitikmeot Region.

Iqaluit's **James Demcheson (*Tunngaaluk*)** works as a motor vehicles officer with the GNWT's Department of Transportation. An accomplished track and field athlete, Demcheson competed in sprint and relay events at territorial, provincial and national levels between 1989 and 1993, and plans to return to the sport in 1999 as a competitor and coach. Of Inuit, Scottish and Ukrainian descent, Demcheson believes in the philosophical statement, "Let your vision be world embracing." He studies languages in his spare time, and anticipates travelling to different parts of the world throughout his life.

Colleen Dupuis is a consultant whose involvement with community groups and a wide range of clients has provided her with a solid understanding of the Nunavut economy and related issues. Dupuis, who has lived in Iqaluit for five years, is active with the Baffin Regional Chamber of Commerce, and on the Nunavut political scene.

Michael P. Ellsworth teaches at Qiqirtaq Ilihakvik High School in Gjoa Haven. Although hired to teach, he willingly acknowledges the fact that it is he who continues to do much of the learning. He moved to Gjoa Haven in August 1996, along with his wife Jan, a fellow teacher. Ellsworth is originally from Prince Edward Island and enjoys his stay on another of Canada's great islands, King William Island.

Former Rankin Inlet resident **Peter Ernerk** is the deputy minister of the new government of Nunavut's Department of Culture, Language, Elders and Youth. Ernerk, now living in Iqaluit, is a longtime cultural activist who has worked as a freelance writer specializing in Inuit culture and northern political developments. He also served as minister of Social Development, Economic Development and Natural and Cultural Affairs with the government of the Northwest Territories between 1975 and 1979, and is a former director of Tungavik Federation of Nunavut.

Judy Farrow has lived in the Northwest Territories since 1971 and for 15 years made Iqaluit her home. In 1980, she received a Canada Council Grant to research Inuktitut names and traditional uses of arctic plants. Farrow currently lives in Yellowknife, working for the Métis Nation.

After living in Iqaluit for seven years, **Marian Ferguson** has resided in Pond Inlet since 1988. She is a freelance writer and travel consultant who designs adventures for Arctic travellers.

Mike Ferguson, a wildlife biologist, has travelled in most remote parts of Baffin Island over the past 16 years and has authored several scientific publications on Baffin caribou.

Miriam Fleming moved to Sanikiluaq in 1986 with her husband Brian, and works for the municipality of Sanikiluaq. She has a special interest in the importance and value of Inuit ecological knowledge.

Freelance writer **Lyn Hancock**, who has lived nine years full-time and 20 years part-time in the Northwest Territories, has travelled to almost every community in Nunavut and written extensively about her experiences in magazines and newspapers. The author of several books about the Canadian North, including *There's a Seal in My Sleeping Bag*, Hancock's newest book is *Winging It In the North*.

Iqaluit's **Kenn Harper** is a historian, linguist and businessman who has lived 30 years in the Arctic. He is the author of *Give Me My Father's Body: The Life of Minik, the New York Eskimo*.

Yellowknife's **Brad Heath**, former editor of the *Yellowknifer* newspaper, currently toils as a freelance writer and photographer.

Beverly Illauq arrived in Clyde River in 1983 to teach school for one year, married a local hunter, and is now deeply involved in education, community development and managing Qullikkut Guides and Outfitters.

Formerly from Iqaluit, **Alootook Ipellie** is a freelance writer and illustrator now living in Ottawa.

Robert Jaffray and his wife Jodi have been in the North since 1989, living first in Pangnirtung, and then Cape Dorset, before settling in Kimmirut. The Jaffrays, who were expecting their first child when they moved north, now have five children — three natural and two adopted. Jaffray wishes he could spend more time on the land camping with his family.

Terry Jesudason operates High Arctic International Explorer Services Ltd. and manages Qausuittuq Inns North in Resolute. She has more than 25 years experience in the High Arctic in the tourism industry, operating the guest home and providing support for polar expeditions.

Robin Johnstone of Edmonton is a wildlife biologist, ecotourism guide, and freelance photojournalist. He came to Canada from his native New Zealand to study peregrine falcons at Rankin Inlet for his PhD.

Darren Keith is a Yellowknife resident who takes his holidays on the tundra. Since graduating from the Native Studies Program at the University of Alberta, his passion for the North and its people has resulted in many journeys by boat and snowmobile in the Kivalliq Region of Nunavut. Keith is a writer/researcher, currently working on a masters degree at McGill University.

A biologist and author of 14 books on hunting and fishing, **Jerome Knap** of Almonte, Ontario, has worked since the late 1970s with the Ojibwa of Northern Ontario and the Inuit of the Northwest Territories to help develop and market hunting and fishing tourism endeavors.

Ulrike Komaksiutiksak came north 11 years ago to work for the NWT Aboveground Swimming Pool Program, spending a summer in Norman Wells and the following two summers in Rankin Inlet, this time under the auspices of Municipal and Community Affairs. Here, she says, she met her "arctic souvenir" — husband Jerry. Since marrying, they have lived in Yellowknife, Fort Smith, Iqaluit, Whale Cove and Rankin Inlet, and together are raising their four children.

Millie Kuliktana of Kugluktuk is an educator and consultant with the Kitikmeot Board of Education, focusing on culture and language preservation. She is also a wife and a mother of four children, and a community volunteer at large.

Simeonie Kunnuk is an Inuk from Igloolik who has resided in Ottawa since the 1980s. Most of his upbringing was in the North where he had direct experience with arctic games as a youth. He is now completing a course in computer applications and administration at Willis College of Business and Technology in Kanata. He periodically participates in cultural events in Ottawa, particularly in Inuit games demonstrations.

John Laird is principal for Laird & Associates, a firm with offices in Iqaluit and Yellowknife that is dedicated to planning, design and environmental compliance. Over the last nine years he has worked on various projects in Nunavut and the Northwest Territories.

Karen LeGresley Hamre is a landscape architect who has been based in Yellowknife since 1983. She has done designs for numerous parks, trails and interpretive sites across the North, including the Ijiraliq (Meliadine) River Territorial Historic Park, Sylvia Grinnell Territorial Park and Mount Pelly.

Olav Loken studied physical geography in Norway and Canada. Over a span of 25 years he held several federal government positions, always with a "northern connection." He is now a consultant in Ottawa, specializing in Antarctic issues.

John MacDonald makes his home in Igloolik where he is co-ordinator of the Nunavut Research Institute's Igloolik Research Centre. Periodically over the past 40 years he has lived and worked in various Inuit communities in Nunavut and Nunavik (Arctic Quebec). He is author of *The Arctic Sky*, a popular study of Inuit astronomy, star lore and legends.

A journalism graduate from Nunavut Arctic College, freelance writer **Ann Meekitjuk Hanson** of Iqaluit grew up "on the land" in the traditional Inuit lifestyle. She later attended school in Toronto, and subsequently worked as a broadcaster for the Canadian Broadcasting Corporation, airing cultural programming, current affairs, histories, and lifestyles programming in Inuktitut.

Former teacher **Steven W. Metzger** of Pelly Bay specializes in research and writing. Interested in developmental, educational and cultural issues, Metzger also has a universal love of land and landscapes. His motto, he says, is "to work hard, but never hurry."

Jimi Onalik grew up in Rankin Inlet and still considers it 'home' despite his current Iqaluit address. Onalik is a Nuna-crat, small business owner, and occasional writer who has both travelled extensively and worked within the tourism industry.

Freelance interpreter/translator — and now writer — **Joe Otokiak** of Cambridge Bay has lived in the Kitikmeot Region of Nunavut most of his life, and is married with five children and one grandchild. He says he just enjoys life and tries to be active as much as possible, traditionally and otherwise.

Photojournalist **Terry Pearce** of Iqaluit is a longtime backcountry skier who has travelled extensively in all seasons throughout Nunavut.

Qikiqtarjuaq's **Don Pickle** has lived in the North since 1994, working in both the Kitikmeot and the Baffin regions as a senior administrative officer for the hamlets of Taloyoak and Qikiqtarjuaq (formerly known as Broughton Island). He enjoys spending time on the land. Despite his capacity to get lost, Pickle says he has always made it home, thanks to the strong abilities of the Canadian Rangers.

George Qulaut, a hunter from Igloolik, worked for many years with the Igloolik Research Centre where he was instrumental in starting the Igloolik Oral History Project, a major, ongoing project which records and documents traditional knowledge of the *Iglulingmiut*. Between 1993 and 1998 he served as a commissioner with the Nunavut Implementation Commission, and is currently assistant deputy minister of Nunavut's Department of Culture, Language, Elders and Youth.

Bruce Rigby of Iqaluit came north in 1978 as part of a geologic mapping party with the Geological Survey of Canada. Since then he has been actively involved in the Baffin tourism industry as a guide, outfitter and tourism instructor, as chairman of the Environmental Technology Program of Nunavut Arctic College, and district superintendent for Parks Canada. He is currently chair of the scientific screening committee for the Polar Continental Shelf Project, a member of the Northern Science and Training Grants Program Awards Committee, and executive director of the Nunavut Research Institute.

Carol Rigby moved north in 1986, in husband Bruce's wake, with toddler and infant in tow. Since then she has taught business communications at Nunavut Arctic College, worked as an editor and writer with Nortext Multimedia Inc., and as a freelance writer, producing visitor guides to Iqaluit and the Baffin, including major contributions to *The Baffin Handbook*. A library technician at the Baffin Regional Library from '92 to '97, she is temporarily in Ottawa continuing her education and looks forward to returning home to Iqaluit in 1999.

Sue Rowley of Pittsburgh, Pennsylvania, is an archeologist and ethnohistorian, as well as a research associate of the Nunavut Research Institute.

Terry Rudden of Ottawa is a partner in the consulting firm Consilium. The former Iqaluit resident is also a writer, and lead guitar player for the group Paddies on the Tundra.

Iqaluit's **David Serkoak** graduated from the Teacher Education Program in Fort Smith, Northwest Territories, in 1978, moving to Arviat to teach there until 1989. A curator at the Museum of Mankind in London, England, for the "Living Arctic" exhibit prior to coming to Iqaluit, Serkoak has since taught at Nunavut Arctic College, Inuksuk High School, and now at Joamie School. He is married to Lesley and has three daughters. Serkoak, who makes Inuit drums as a hobby, drum dances with his youngest daughter, Karla.

Marion Soublière of Ottawa first became a devotee of northern issues through work with the Beverly and Qamanirjuaq Caribou Management Board, Nunavut Tunngavik Incorporated and other northern groups. The highlight of her time as managing editor of *The Nunavut Handbook* has been really getting to know the people of Canada's North.

For 25 years, **Dave Sutherland** of Yellowknife worked in the field of Inuit art with the government of the Northwest Territories, rising to the head of the art and crafts section. He has been a private consultant since 1986.

Shirley Tagalik has lived in Arviat since 1976. She works as an educator, and enjoys hunting, fishing and taking pleasure from the community's rich diversity with her husband and three daughters.

Louis Tapardjuk is from Igloolik, where he works closely with community elders and is actively involved in programs promoting Inuit traditional skills and values. In 1996, he was appointed executive director of the Nunavut Social Development Council.

Hunter **Andrew Taqtu** of Arctic Bay was born near Pond Inlet. He has worked at different jobs, and has been an outfitter for 13 years, taking out all kinds of people who do different things. "If they are divers I go diving with them," he says. Taqtu has taken tourist guide courses to level III.

After spending most of the past six years in the Arctic, outdoorsman, naturalist, and writer/editor **Mike Vlessides** is now quietly hunkered down in the Rocky Mountain town of Canmore, Alberta. Although known to visit the New York urban jungle in which he was raised, Vlessides makes more frequent peregrinations northward.

Tracy Wallace has lived in Chesterfield Inlet, Rankin Inlet, Winnipeg and the surrounding area, Scotland, and Ottawa. She considers each one to be home just as much as the other. Now a proud mother of two, she lives in Rankin Inlet, where she works in the field of commercial development for the GNWT Department of Transportation.

Renee Wissink, presently stationed at Terra Nova National Park on the east coast of Newfoundland, lived in Nunavut for 15 years and worked as a teacher, consultant and national park warden. He also headed the 1986 Qitdlarssuaq Expedition, retracing the 19th century Inuit migration from Baffin Island to Greenland led by the shaman Qillaq — who later became known as "Qitdlarssuaq" or the great Qitdlaq.

GLOSSARY

ATVs   all-terrain vehicles

amauti   ("a-mau-tee"); a woman's parka in which a baby is carried in the hood. An *amauti* is often pristine white and colorfully trimmed

Baffin Region   includes Sanikiluaq, Iqaluit, Kimmirut, Cape Dorset, Qikiqtarjuaq (Broughton Island), Pangnirtung, Nanisivik, Clyde River, Pond Inlet, Arctic Bay, Grise Fiord, Resolute, Igloolik, and Hall Beach. Total population (including 270 people who live in small outpost camps): 13,218 (1996 Census of Canada)

cache   meat that is stored outdoors on the land for future use

DEW Line   the Canadian government, pressed by the United States and urged as well by the Royal Canadian Air Force to install an arctic early-warning chain in the midst of the Cold War, began construction of a 22-station Distant Early Warning Line in 1953. It stretched along the Arctic coast from Alaska to Baffin Island

Dorset   the Dorset culture appeared around 2,700 years ago when the Nunavut climate cooled and the Paleoeskimo lifestyle underwent a period of rapid transition. The Dorset people had a rich artistic tradition, carving miniature masterpieces from ivory and antler for ceremonial and decorative use

Eskimo   a Cree Indian word that means "eaters of raw meat," Eskimo is considered a derogatory term that is no longer used to describe the Inuit of Nunavut

floe edge   the place where open water joins land-fast ice; where still waters meet waters propelled by currents

GNWT   government of the Northwest Territories

GPS   Global Positioning System. This handheld receiver uses satellite information to identify your current location

GST   the Goods and Services Tax is a seven per cent federal tax that consumers must pay. Non-residents of Canada are entitled to a refund on goods and accommodation, provided they stay less than one month at that accommodation. Visitors can also claim half of tax paid on tour packages

HF radio high frequency radio is used to communicate in emergencies and other situations, especially by hunters and people travelling or living on the land. The most common version is the Spillsbury SBX-11

HTO Hunters and Trappers Organization. HTOs, based in almost every community in Nunavut, serve the interests of local hunters and trappers. They are an invaluable source of information about wildlife in the area, and the lay of the land

hoodoos columns of strangely shaped rocks formed by the erosion of sandstone around a harder "cap" rock that eventually produces 10- to 15-metre pillars of sandstone. Found on Bylot Island off north Baffin Island

ice pans year-round sea ice that occasionally occurs. Ice pans floating in and out on the tides are common in summer

iglu igloo

Inuk ("ee-nook"); a person of Inuit descent. Two such people are *Inuuk*; three or more are *Inuit* ("ee-neu-eet"). Note that the plural is never used with an "s" (i.e. the Inuits)

inuksuit ("ee-nook-soo-eet"); rock cairns often shaped in the form of a human, these landmarks established where Inuit had travelled. The singular of the word is *inuksuk* ("like a human"). The anglicized version of the plural, *inuksuks*, is often heard

Inuktitut ("ee-nook-tee-tut"); the language of Inuit

kamiit ("cam-eet"); sealskin boots. The anglicized version of the plural, *kamiks*, is often heard

Keewatin the previous name for the Kivalliq Region. Since this name change has only recently taken place, many people still refer to the "Keewatin"

Kitikmeot Region includes Pelly Bay, Bathurst Inlet, Taloyoak, Kugluktuk, Gjoa Haven, Cambridge Bay and Umingmaktok. Total population: 4,644 (1996 Census of Canada). While the nearby community of Holman is currently part of the Kitikmeot, it has opted not to become part of Nunavut when the new territory forms in 1999

Kivalliq Region includes Repulse Bay, Arviat, Coral Harbour, Whale Cove, Rankin Inlet, Baker Lake, and Chesterfield Inlet. Total population: 6,868 (1996 Census of Canada)

leads   patches of open water found during spring breakup of sea ice

maktaaq   ("muk-tuk"); whale skin, considered a delicacy by Inuit

NWT   the Northwest Territories, which until April 1, 1999, comprises the central and eastern Arctic area that will become Nunavut, plus the western Arctic, which has yet to be renamed

nanuq   ("na-nook"); polar bear

Nunavut   ("noo-na-voot"); our land

Nunavut Settlement Area   the area defined in Section 3.1.1 of the Nunavut Land Claims Agreement

outpost camp   isolated camps where families of Inuit hunt, trap and fish to feed and clothe themselves and their families according to their traditional subsistence lifestyle

polynyas   places where there is regularly no, or very thin, sea ice; these conditions may be caused by a combination of winds and upwelling ocean currents. Polynyas are important for wildlife

qajaq   kayak

qallunaat   ("ka-bloo-na"); white people

qamutik/ qamutiik   ("ka-moo-tik"); a long, slatted wooden sled pulled by dogteam or snow machine. The plural is *qamutiit* ("ka-moo-teet"); the anglicized version, *qamutiks*, is frequently used, though

qulliq   ("coo-lik"); a soapstone oil lamp in the shape of a half-moon, its carved-out hollow contains the fat and wick

RCMP   the Royal Canadian Mounted Police is Canada's national police force

snow machine   a snowmobile

taima   ("tie-ma"); that is all

Thule   about 1,000 years ago, a new group of people emigrated from northern Alaska into what is now Nunavut. Archeologists believe the Thule ("too-lee") to be the first of two Neoeskimo subgroups

Temperature Conversions

Fahrenheit	Celsius
104°	40°
86°	30°
68°	20°
50°	10°
32°	0°
14°	-10°
-4°	-20°
-22°	-30°
-40°	-40°
-58°	-50°
-76°	-60°

Common Conversions

Metric to Imperial	
1 centimetre	.39 inch
1 metre	39.4 inches
1 kilometre	.62 mile
1 hectare	2.47 acres
1 gram	.04 ounce
1 kilogram	2.2 pounds
1 litre	.88 quart
1 litre	.22 gallon

Imperial to Metric	
1 inch	2.54 centimetres
1 foot	.30 metre
1 mile	1.61 kilometres
1 acre	.4 hectare
1 fluid ounce	28.41 millilitres
1 quart	1.14 litres
1 gallon	4.55 litres
1 pound	453.59 grams

Tuniit   the *Tuniit* ("too-neet") occupied Nunavut before the
               ancestors of Inuit arrived. Although there were intermarriages
               between the two groups, there were also fights, and the *Tuniit*
               removed themselves from areas occupied by the Thule.
               Eventually the *Tuniit* disappeared

weathered a local expression meaning bad weather has set in and thrown
out   a wrench into plans